The maps of this atlas explain the richly varied geography which lies behind the beauty of the images . . .

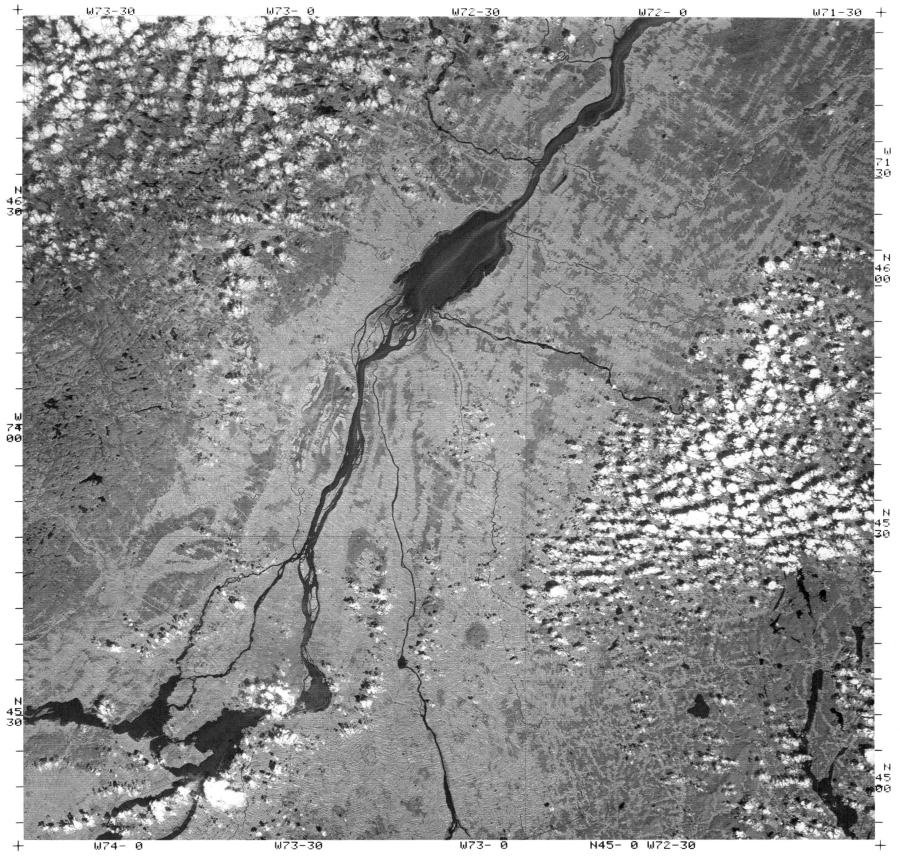

MONTRÉAL AREA — QUÉBEC

E – 1421 – 15103

September 17, 1973

The city of Montréal and part of the St. Lawrence Valley can be seen in this image. After its confluence with the Ottawa River, the St. Lawrence flows past Île de Montréal and about thirty-five miles downstream enters Lake St. Peter through a delta. Sediment carried by the current can be detected both in the river and in the lake.

Many features of the cultural landscape are visible. Greater Montréal dominates the image while other centres of urbanization can be seen at Trois-Rivières, Shawinigan, Drummondville, and St-Hyacinthe. In the rural areas the unique pattern of long narrow fields resulting from the seigneurial system of land division is of particular interest.

The region is bordered in the north-west by the rocky surfaces of the Laurentians, part of the Canadian Shield, and in the south-east by the Eastern Quebec Uplands. Both of these areas are partially obscured by cloud.

THE
NATIONAL
ATLAS OF
CANADA

THE
NATIONAL
ATLAS OF
CANADA

FOURTH EDITION
(Revised)

Published by
The Macmillan Company of Canada Limited,
Toronto, Ontario, in association with the
Department of Energy, Mines and Resources
and Information Canada

Ottawa, Canada
1974

© Crown Copyright
Information Canada
Ottawa 1974

Catalogue No. M61-1/1974
ISBN 0-660-00000-8

Published November 1974 by
The Macmillan Company of Canada
ISBN 0-7705-1198-8

Limited Collector's Edition
ISBN 0-7705-1243-7

The National Atlas of Canada
est aussi publié en français sous le titre
L'Atlas National du Canada.
ISBN 0-7705-1208-9

PREVIOUS EDITIONS
1st Edition 1906
Atlas of Canada, Department of the Interior
2nd Edition 1915
Atlas of Canada, Department of the Interior
3rd Edition 1957
Atlas of Canada and *Atlas du Canada*,
Department of Mines and Technical Surveys
4th Edition 1973
The National Atlas of Canada and *L'Atlas National du Canada*,
Department of Energy, Mines and Resources

DEDICATION

This National Atlas of Canada provides a window on the pageant of Canada's progress, not only for Canadians but for all the peoples of the world.

The Atlas gives a view of the extent of the national domain, the variety of its natural resources and climatic conditions. It affords also a clear vision of the significance of Canada's development, an achievement made possible, above all, by the unified effort of Canadians acting in the spirit of national purpose.

As a comprehensive study of the interaction between the people of this country and our physical environment, this graphic portrayal should serve to enrich and illuminate understanding and knowledge of Canada and of Canadians.

Pierre Elliott Trudeau
Prime Minister of Canada

FOREWORD

Just as man has gradually developed his vision of an ideal society from the concept of neighbourhood, so has the art of mapping progressed from depiction of localities to a broadening view of the nation as a whole and of its place in the world.

Maps are graphic means of portraying not only the geographical facts of topography and position but also the economic and cultural geography of a people. Such, indeed, are some of the basic functions that this atlas serves to perform. It seeks to communicate to users an awareness of Canada's diversity of climatic conditions, the variety and richness of its natural environment and resources, its history, and national development and to convey as well an image of the fundamental unity which exists among its citizens. In this regard an atlas can be more eloquent than any oration on the subject of nationhood in conveying a sense of the dynamic promise of our country.

But geography is not static. The human and physical systems which comprise the geography of a country and also our knowledge of those systems, are in constant transition and their depiction calls for periodic revision. Thus the publication of an atlas can never be a fully completed task. Surprising as it may seem, even a geological map may need frequent revision, not because the rocks are changing but because knowledge of them has increased. Conversely, a population map may require alterations periodically, not necessarily because knowledge of the population has increased but because the population itself has changed. Accordingly a single edition of a national atlas can give only a presentation that is limited, to some extent, in time, scope and significance. But an atlas published in successive editions issued at regular intervals, encompasses elements of transition and, taken in its entirety, more truly reflects the story of national development.

Recognizing the importance of the National Atlas to Canadians, the Government of Canada has established a continuing program in which a new edition will be issued within each census decade. With the implementation of this program, not only will serial publication be attained, but the atlas can be expected to undergo a progressive evolution by means of which its full potentiality as a national reference document will be realized.

Donald S. Macdonald

*Minister of Energy, Mines and Resources,
Canada*

PREFACE

At the Sixth International Geographical Congress held in London in 1895 the Geographical Society of Finland displayed a collection of maps and graphs intended to give an analytical picture of Finland's geography and culture. The success of the display convinced the government of Finland to give financial support towards organizing the material into book form, thereby making the maps easy to consult and distribute, and easy to compare one to another for possible relationships between subjects. In brief, the *Atlas of Finland,* published in 1899, introduced a technique of displaying a component-by-component model of the environment which, given the visual intelligibility of maps and the ease of comparing one to another, is understandable to a wide range of readers at different educational levels. Since 1899 about fifty countries have produced one or more editions of atlases that follow the principles of the original Finnish example. These have come to be known as "national atlases", a term that has been formally accepted by the International Geographical Union which in 1960 published a study on the subject entitled *Atlas Nationaux*[1], an English translation[2] of which was published in 1972.

Canada's first national atlas, second in the world after Finland's, was published in 1906 by the Department of the Interior. A second edition, enlarged and updated, was issued in 1915, but thereafter the program lapsed until 1948 when a new program was established. The new atlas, dated 1957, was published in English in 1958 followed two years later by a French version. The first three editions were entitled *Atlas of Canada*[3]. This phrase has occurred increasingly within the titles of various other publications, and it has therefore seemed advisable to adopt the title *The National Atlas of Canada* for the present and future editions in order to differentiate the national atlas from other types of atlas that refer to Canada.

There are, by and large, two poles of opinion as to the purposes of a national atlas. In one opinion the atlas is seen as a system of objective information whose compilation is justified by its direct contribution to utilitarian decision-making as for example in national and local planning. In the other opinion the atlas is seen as refining and extending the reader's perception of the nation, in which case the atlas contributes to national self-awareness and cultural evolution. The argument for the latter opinion would require lengthy elaboration, but its general outlines may be indicated by the following questions. How are the attitudes and behaviour of an individual affected by his mental image of the land in which he lives? Is the mental image brought to a more effective level of consciousness by the addition to it of visual images of the spatial dimensions of the contents of the country? Is there any more effective method of adding spatial dimensions to the mental image than through the agency of well designed maps? The two opinions are not necessarily mutually exclusive, and in a sense coincide in formal education where the atlas becomes a utilitarian instrument for instruction that influences attitudes and behaviour and therefore culture.

Whereas all national atlases follow essentially the same principles of organization and treatment of subjects, the degree to which a particular atlas serves one or the other purpose discussed above depends crucially on map scale, and this in turn is determined by the area and shape of the country and the practicality of a given page size. These controlling factors are recognized by the authors of *Atlas Nationaux* in their recommendation of different map scales for six size-categories of countries, ranging from 1:500,000 for the smallest to 1:10,000,000 for the largest. An atlas that can exploit the full cartographical possibilities of large scales will obviously be more useful in utilitarian decision-making than one that is confined to small scales. The atlas' influence on culture, on the other hand, is much less dependent on large map scale, since in the cultural function synopsis of the whole country is an important factor, and this can always be attained except where scale makes the map of the whole country larger than page size.

The foregoing leads to the conclusion that the national atlas of a country as large as Canada more aptly serves the purposes of cultural development than of utilitarian decision-making, although this is not to say that the data of the atlas are irrelevant to decision-making or to scientific uses. Were an atlas strongly biased towards the utilitarian purposes of decision-making, intensive use of it by relatively few specialists would presumably produce benefits that would diffuse to society, and the creation of these benefits would not depend upon wide distribution of the atlas itself. If, however, the atlas is biased towards cultural purposes, the opposite argument applies, that is, to produce optimum benefits the atlas requires wide distribution. To attain this distribution the atlas should be of a size and weight to facilitate marketing and to convenience the reader in his home and the student at his desk.

PREFACE (continued)

In the initial planning of the present edition the judgments outlined above led to a decision to make the new atlas of a more manageable size than its 1957 predecessor which had cover dimensions of 16.5 by 21 inches and a weight of 17.5 pounds (42 by 53 centimetres, and 8 kilograms). Through extensive use of insets, complex page layouts, sectioning of the country at scales larger than page-size scale, and a variety of cartographical refinements, the present atlas, with a page-size scale of 1:15,000,000 as against 1:10,000,000 for its predecessor, has sacrificed little of the detail and legibility of the 1957 atlas. It should be added, however, that for reasons of expediency unrelated to the reduction in physical size, some subjects legitimately included in the 1957 atlas have been omitted in the present edition. The atlas does not contain a gazetteer or reference maps of populated places; however, this subject is covered in the *Atlas and Gazetteer of Canada*[4] which was designed as a companion to the national atlas, and is in the same format.

In judging the advisability of reducing the physical size of the atlas, consideration was given to making it bilingual, but bilingualism would have greatly constrained the format possibilities and increased the page size. Additional difficulties would have been created by the necessity of double entry on the maps of the names of some places and features. In consultation with bilingual scholars a judgment was made that the more effective communication attainable with unilingualism in regard both to graphic design and marketing outweighed the desirability of bilingualism. The first two editions of Canada's national atlas were in English only. The French version of the third edition was published two years after the English. Simultaneous publication in French and English has been attained with the present edition.

All place names and feature names are officially approved by the Canadian Permanent Committee on Geographical Names. The names that appear on the base-maps are official as of September 1969. Authorization of names applicable to the substantive data of the maps is in some cases of more recent date. For textual matter French orthographic practice for capitalization, punctuation, etc. is followed in the French atlas with the exception of the punctuation of numerals. In this case the English practice is followed, i.e. periods for decimal points, and commas for the internal dividing of numbers.

The first printing of the fourth edition, completed in February 1974, was in a small press run of loose sheets which were made available for sale in a specially designed box. The bound volume supersedes the boxed sheets which will nevertheless be available from the Surveys and Mapping Branch until the supply is exhausted. It is planned to maintain a stock of individual loose sheets for sale to the public.

Gerald Fremlin

[1] La commission des Atlas Nationaux de l'Union Géographique Internationale. 1960. *Atlas Nationaux.* Rédigé par K.A. Salichtchev. Edition de l'Academie des Sciences de l'URSS.

[2] La Commission des Atlas Nationaux de l'Union Géographique Internationale. 1972. *National Atlases.* Translated by the Translation Bureau, Secretary of State Department, Ottawa. Translation edited by G. Fremlin and L.M. Sebert. In *Cartographica.* Monograph no. 4. Toronto: B.V. Gutsell, Department of Geography, York University.

[3] Department of the Interior. 1906. *Atlas of Canada.* James White, editor. Ottawa.

Department of the Interior. 1915. *Atlas of Canada.* J.E. Chalifour, editor. Ottawa.

Department of Mines and Technical Surveys. 1958. *Atlas of Canada.* N.L. Nicholson, editor. Ottawa.

Department of Mines and Technical Surveys. 1960. *Atlas du Canada.* N.L. Nicholson, editor. Ottawa.

[4] Department of Energy, Mines and Resources. 1969. *Atlas and Gazetteer of Canada,* The Queen's Printer, Ottawa.

Ministère de l'Énergie, des Mines et des Ressources. 1969. *Atlas et toponymie du Canada,* L'Imprimeur de la Reine, Ottawa.

ACKNOWLEDGEMENTS

The present edition of *The National Atlas of Canada* was started as a revision of the 1957 *Atlas of Canada,* and although numerous departures and innovations have been introduced, the older atlas must be acknowledged as having provided fundamental guidance for the new.

For the present edition there was no official editorial board or other formal advisory body. It is therefore important to acknowledge a series of extensive discussions on contents and methodology carried out individually with the late Dr. A.C. Gerlach of the *National Atlas of the United States,* Mr. T.W. Plumb of the *Atlas of Australian Resources* and Dr. B. Brouillette, professeur émérite de l'École des Hautes Études Commerciales, and jointly with Dr. A.H. Clark and Dr. J. L. Robinson of the University of Wisconsin and the University of British Columbia respectively. Dr. Brouillette warrants particular mention not only for his advice on methodology, contribution of substantive work and assistance in the translation to French, but also for a report he made to the Canadian Social Science Research Council in 1945 that had a major influence in reestablishing the national atlas program after its lapse in 1915.

The sources of data for the atlas are listed at the end of the book but a listing of sources gives little indication of the personal assistance in obtaining data given by a large number of people in federal and provincial government agencies, private organizations, and universities. The cooperation of these people, at the expense of interrupting their regular work, has been a vital factor in the production of the atlas. Particular acknowledgement is made to the Geological Survey of Canada, the Department of Agriculture, and Statistics Canada for provision of complex compilations especially processed for publication in the atlas, and also to The Macmillan Company of Canada for permission to publish material taken directly from *Economic Geography of Canada.* Individuals not on the atlas staff who made direct contributions of personal research are acknowledged by name in the Sources.

Reproduction material in the form of reverse-reading positive films was produced by the Map Production Division of the Surveys and Mapping Branch, Ottawa. The atlas was printed by Ashton-Potter Limited, Toronto, and bound by The Hunter Rose Company, Toronto.

The planning, research, translation to French, editing, and cartography for the atlas were carried out by the following personnel of the Geography Division, Surveys and Mapping Branch. The names of former members who contributed substantially are bracketed.

Geographers: B. Berghout, B. Cornwall - *Editor*, (J. Eyles), D. Fairbairn, G. Falconer - *Editor*, G. Fremlin, (H. Gagnon), (M. Horsdal), (P. Hubert), I. Jost, (C.R. Lloyd), (K. Lochhead), (H. McAllister), J.M.O. Morawiecki, (R. Page), M. Murty - *French Editor*, C.-P. Ravel, (D. Sherstone), M.A. Ward.

Cartographical Designer: H.E. Mindak.

Layout Planner: J.-C. Allen, (R. Trevor).

Compilers: C.L. Bohm, (R. Bonner), (B. Draper), R. Harvey, (D. Hewitt), E.F. Joly, R.B. Mathie, R.J. Medaglia, (R. Mitchell), J.M. St. Amand.

Draftsmen: P.T. Baldock, (K. Button), (E. Goodson), C.D. Proctor, K. Smith, G.E.J. Stuart, S.G. Swettenham, R. Valenzuela, T.L. Williams, of the Geography Division; P. Bazinet, J. Blais, B. Brown, P. Cooney, F. Evraire, A. Holding, R. Leduc, W.W. MacLarty, F. Plcuffe, R. Savard, J.Y. St-Martin, D. Trinque, G.Vadneau, of the Cartography Division.

Secretary: M. Botten.

Gerald Fremlin, *Editor in chief,*
March, 1974.

THE NATIONAL ATLAS OF CANADA
IS PRINTED BY ASHTON-POTTER LIMITED
ON ROLLAND OPAQUE, NATURAL WHITE, PAPER.
THE HUNTER ROSE COMPANY
BOUND THE BOOKS IN MAPLE LEAF BUCKRAM
MANUFACTURED BY COLUMBIA FINISHING MILLS
IN CORNWALL.

TABLE OF CONTENTS

TABLE OF CONTENTS (continued)

TABLE OF CONTENTS (continued)

TABLE OF CONTENTS (continued)

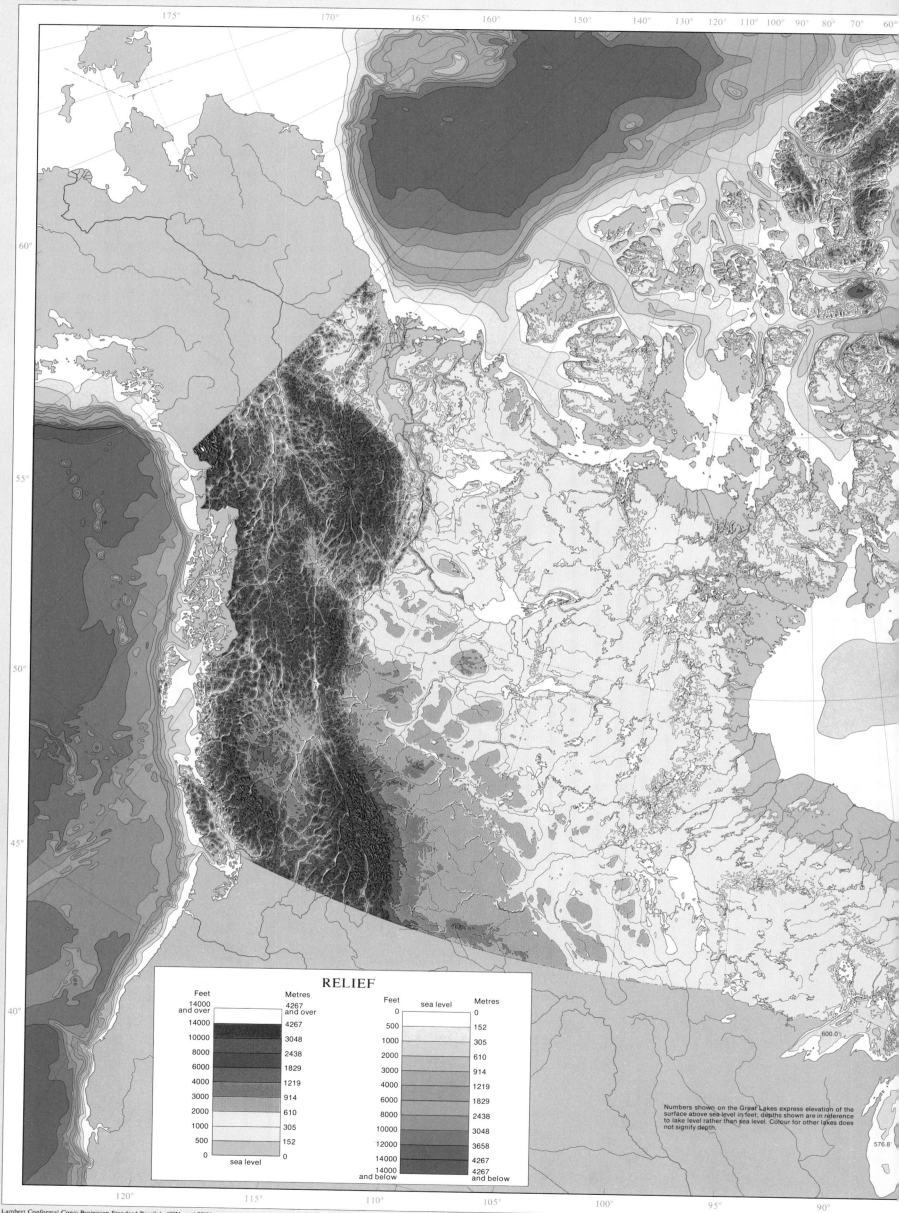

RELIEF

Feet		Metres
14000 and over		4267 and over
14000		4267
10000		3048
8000		2438
6000		1829
4000		1219
3000		914
2000		610
1000		305
500		152
0	sea level	0

Feet	sea level	Metres
0		0
500		152
1000		305
2000		610
3000		914
4000		1219
6000		1829
8000		2438
10000		3048
12000		3658
14000		4267
14000 and below		4267 and below

Numbers shown on the Great Lakes express elevation of the surface above sea level in feet; depths shown are in reference to lake level rather than sea level. Colour for other lakes does not signify depth.

600.0

576.8

Lambert Conformal Conic Projection Standard Parallels 49°N. and 77°N.

THE NATIONAL ATLAS OF CANADA

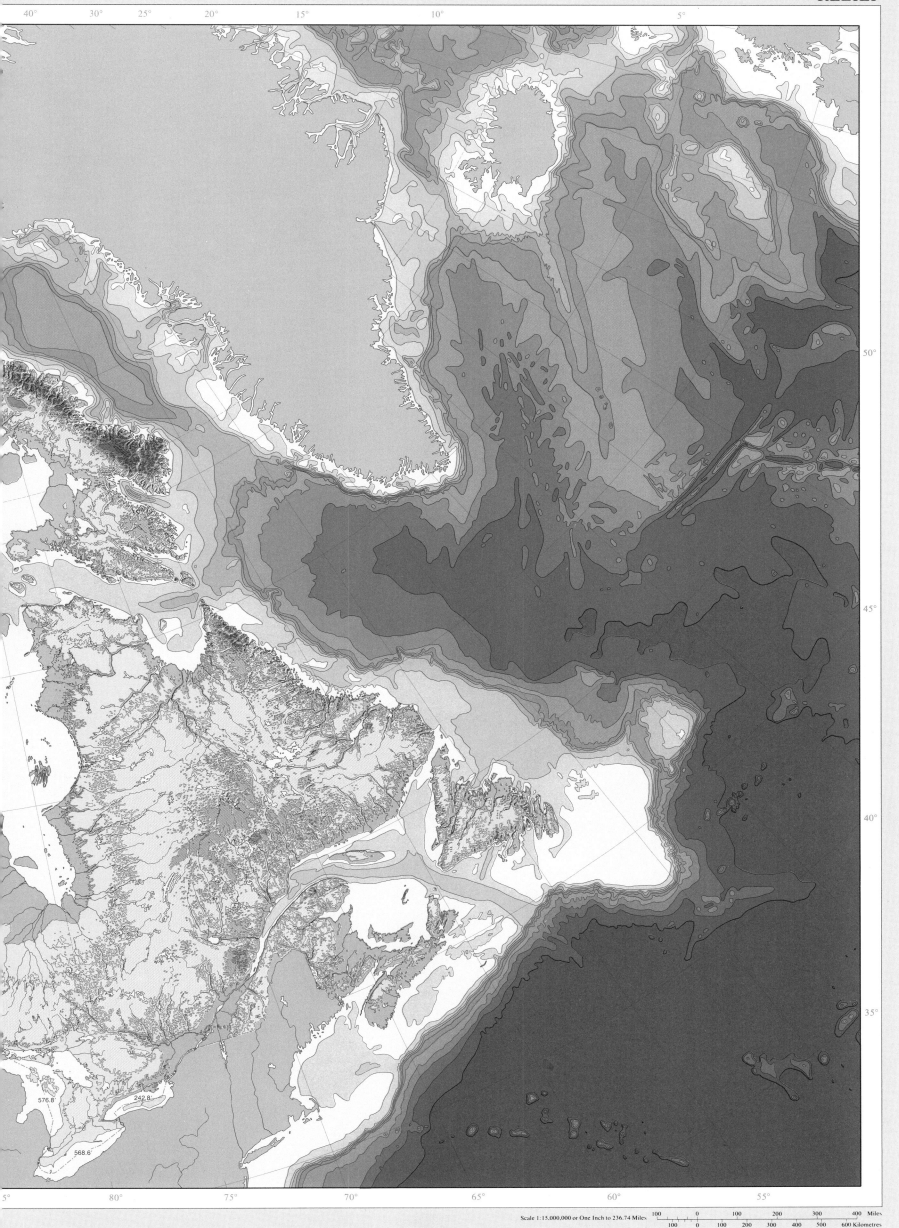

RELIEF PROFILES

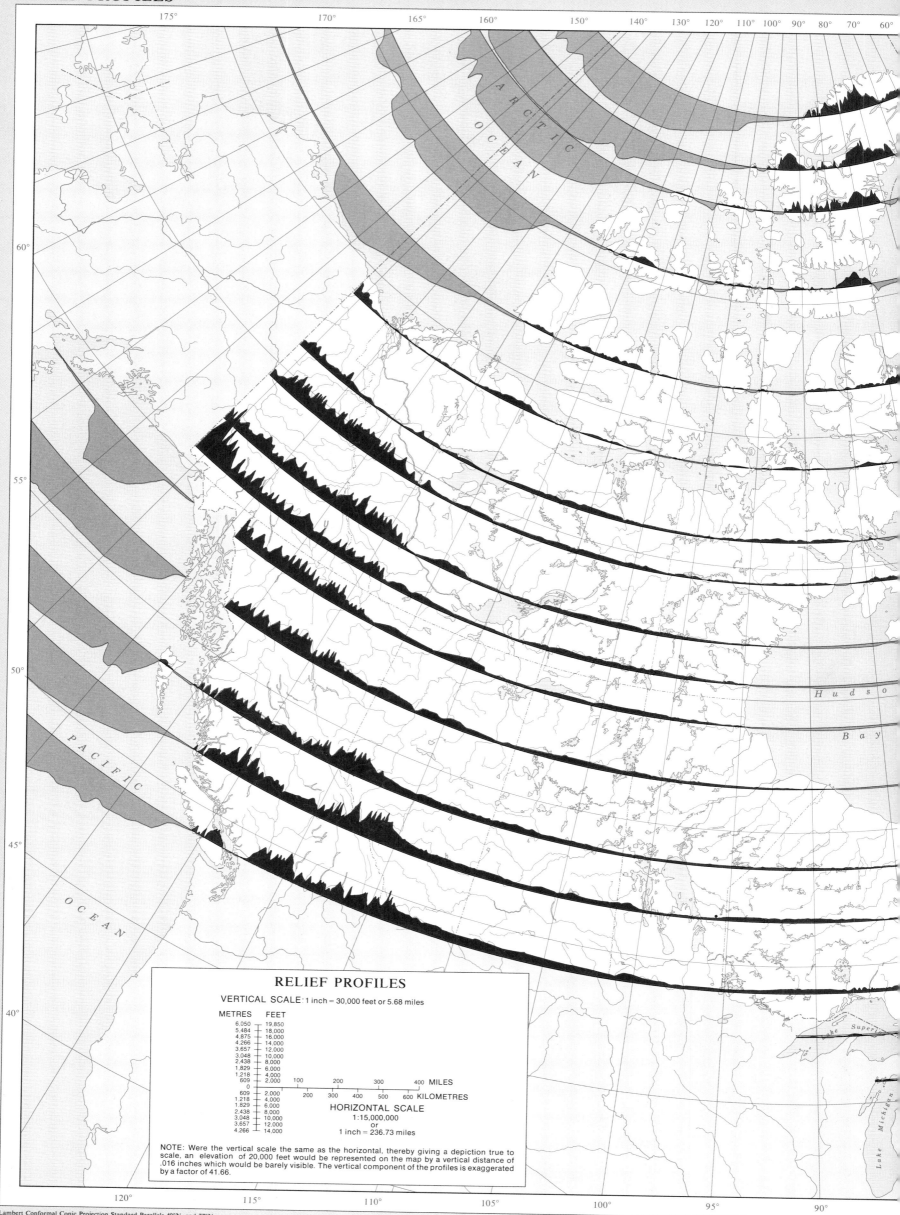

RELIEF PROFILES

VERTICAL SCALE: 1 inch = 30,000 feet or 5.68 miles

METRES	FEET
6,050	19,850
5,484	18,000
4,875	16,000
4,266	14,000
3,657	12,000
3,048	10,000
2,438	8,000
1,829	6,000
1,218	4,000
609	2,000
0	
609	2,000
1,218	4,000
1,829	6,000
2,438	8,000
3,048	10,000
3,657	12,000
4,266	14,000

100   200   300   400 MILES
200   300   400   500   600 KILOMETRES

HORIZONTAL SCALE
1:15,000,000
or
1 inch = 236.73 miles

NOTE: Were the vertical scale the same as the horizontal, thereby giving a depiction true to scale, an elevation of 20,000 feet would be represented on the map by a vertical distance of .016 inches which would be barely visible. The vertical component of the profiles is exaggerated by a factor of 41.66.

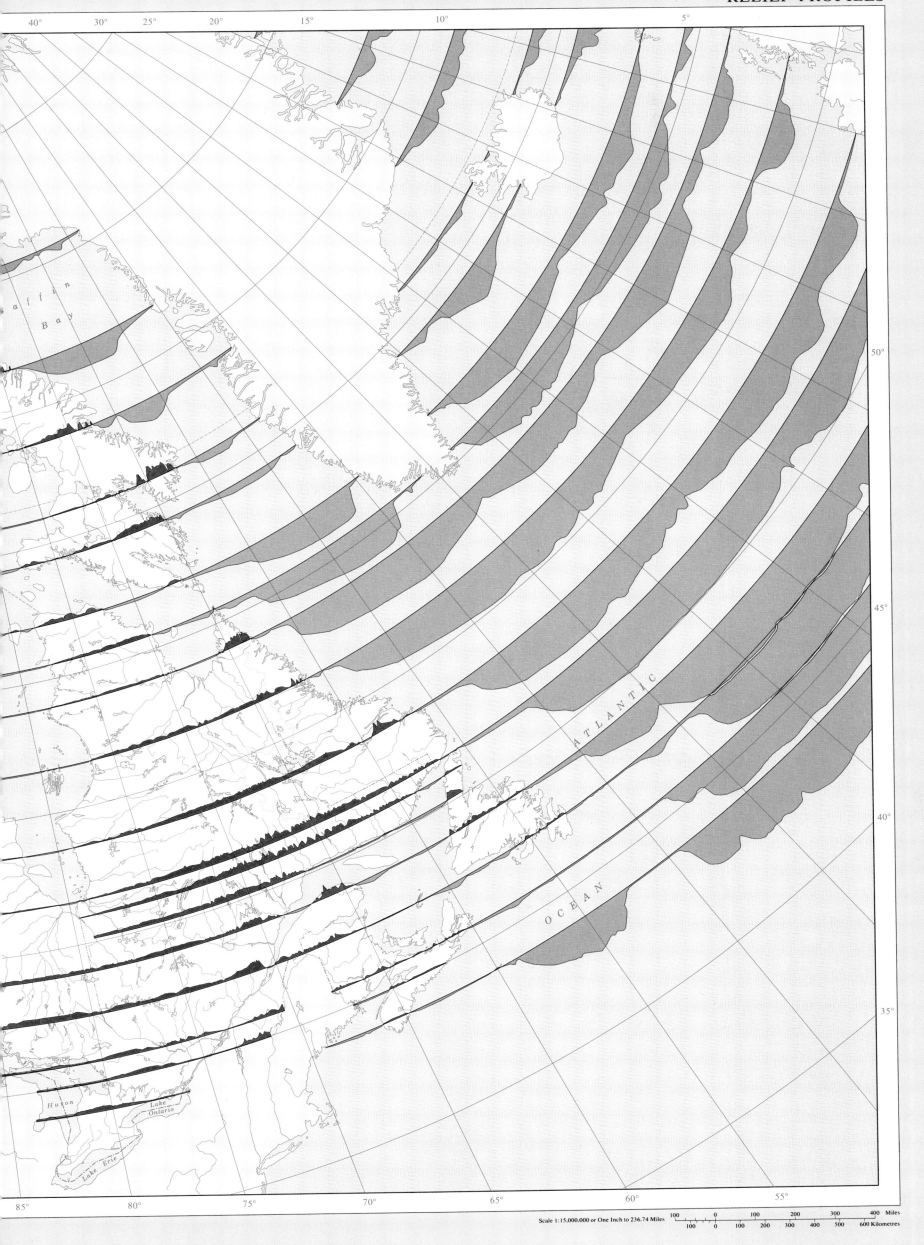

Scale 1:15,000,000 or One Inch to 236.74 Miles

PHYSIOGRAPHIC REGIONS

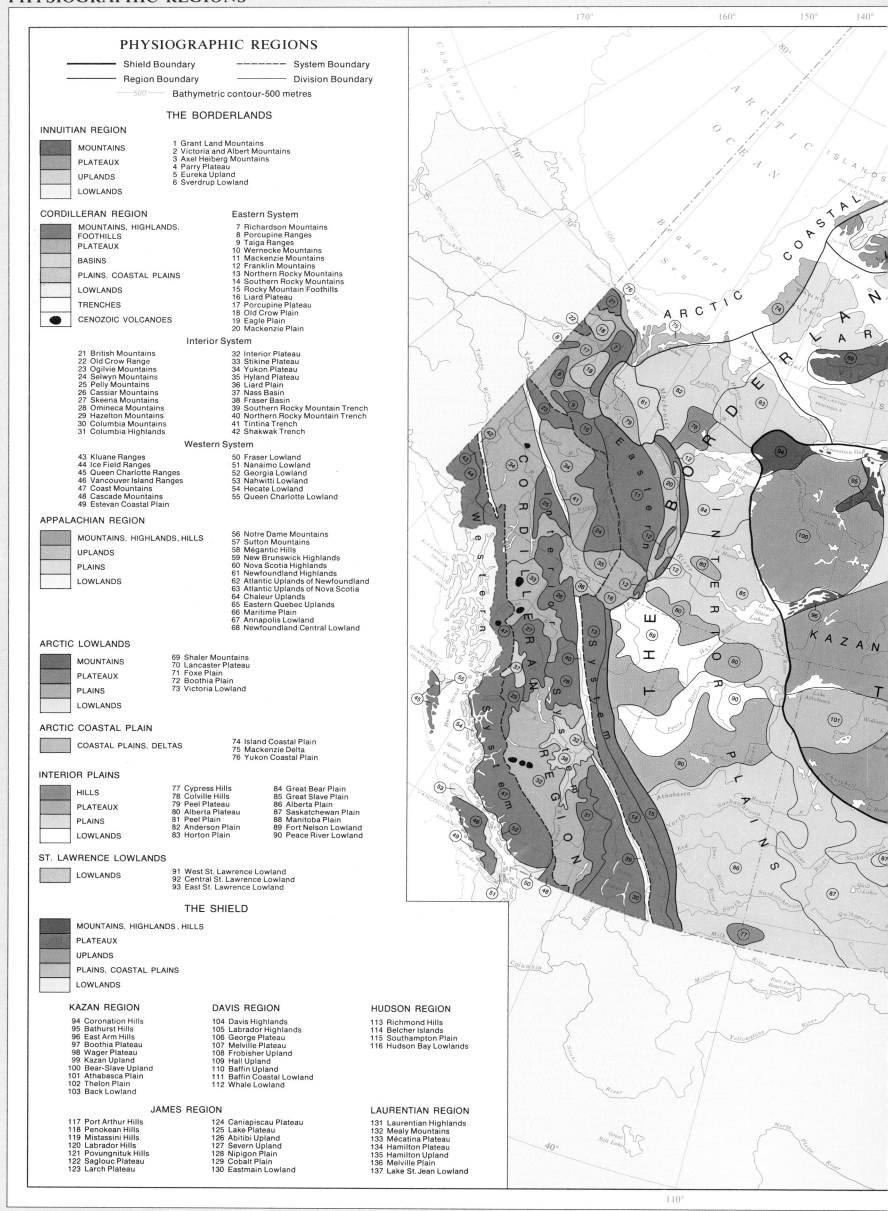

PHYSIOGRAPHIC REGIONS

	Shield Boundary		System Boundary
	Region Boundary		Division Boundary

— 500 — Bathymetric contour-500 metres

THE BORDERLANDS

INNUITIAN REGION

MOUNTAINS
PLATEAUX
UPLANDS
LOWLANDS

1 Grant Land Mountains
2 Victoria and Albert Mountains
3 Axel Heiberg Mountains
4 Parry Plateau
5 Eureka Upland
6 Sverdrup Lowland

CORDILLERAN REGION

MOUNTAINS, HIGHLANDS, FOOTHILLS
PLATEAUX
BASINS
PLAINS, COASTAL PLAINS
LOWLANDS
TRENCHES
CENOZOIC VOLCANOES

Eastern System

7 Richardson Mountains
8 Porcupine Ranges
9 Taiga Ranges
10 Wernecke Mountains
11 Mackenzie Mountains
12 Franklin Mountains
13 Northern Rocky Mountains
14 Southern Rocky Mountains
15 Rocky Mountain Foothills
16 Liard Plateau
17 Porcupine Plateau
18 Old Crow Plain
19 Eagle Plain
20 Mackenzie Plain

21 British Mountains
22 Old Crow Range
23 Ogilvie Mountains
24 Selwyn Mountains
25 Pelly Mountains
26 Cassiar Mountains
27 Skeena Mountains
28 Omineca Mountains
29 Hazelton Mountains
30 Columbia Mountains
31 Columbia Highlands

Interior System

32 Interior Plateau
33 Stikine Plateau
34 Yukon Plateau
35 Hyland Plateau
36 Liard Plain
37 Nass Basin
38 Fraser Basin
39 Southern Rocky Mountain Trench
40 Northern Rocky Mountain Trench
41 Tintina Trench
42 Shakwak Trench

43 Kluane Ranges
44 Ice Field Ranges
45 Queen Charlotte Ranges
46 Vancouver Island Ranges
47 Coast Mountains
48 Cascade Mountains
49 Estevan Coastal Plain

Western System

50 Fraser Lowland
51 Nanaimo Lowland
52 Georgia Lowland
53 Nahwitti Lowland
54 Hecate Lowland
55 Queen Charlotte Lowland

APPALACHIAN REGION

MOUNTAINS, HIGHLANDS, HILLS
UPLANDS
PLAINS
LOWLANDS

56 Notre Dame Mountains
57 Sutton Mountains
58 Mégantic Hills
59 New Brunswick Highlands
60 Nova Scotia Highlands
61 Newfoundland Highlands
62 Atlantic Uplands of Newfoundland
63 Atlantic Uplands of Nova Scotia
64 Chaleur Uplands
65 Eastern Quebec Uplands
66 Maritime Plain
67 Annapolis Lowland
68 Newfoundland Central Lowland

ARCTIC LOWLANDS

MOUNTAINS
PLATEAUX
PLAINS
LOWLANDS

69 Shaler Mountains
70 Lancaster Plateau
71 Foxe Plain
72 Boothia Plain
73 Victoria Lowland

ARCTIC COASTAL PLAIN

COASTAL PLAINS, DELTAS

74 Island Coastal Plain
75 Mackenzie Delta
76 Yukon Coastal Plain

INTERIOR PLAINS

HILLS
PLATEAUX
PLAINS
LOWLANDS

77 Cypress Hills
78 Colville Hills
79 Peel Plateau
80 Alberta Plateau
81 Peel Plain
82 Anderson Plain
83 Horton Plain

84 Great Bear Plain
85 Great Slave Plain
86 Alberta Plain
87 Saskatchewan Plain
88 Manitoba Plain
89 Fort Nelson Lowland
90 Peace River Lowland

ST. LAWRENCE LOWLANDS

LOWLANDS

91 West St. Lawrence Lowland
92 Central St. Lawrence Lowland
93 East St. Lawrence Lowland

THE SHIELD

MOUNTAINS, HIGHLANDS, HILLS
PLATEAUX
UPLANDS
PLAINS, COASTAL PLAINS
LOWLANDS

KAZAN REGION

94 Coronation Hills
95 Bathurst Hills
96 East Arm Hills
97 Boothia Plateau
98 Wager Plateau
99 Kazan Upland
100 Bear-Slave Upland
101 Athabasca Plain
102 Thelon Plain
103 Back Lowland

DAVIS REGION

104 Davis Highlands
105 Labrador Highlands
106 George Plateau
107 Melville Plateau
108 Frobisher Upland
109 Hall Upland
110 Baffin Upland
111 Baffin Coastal Lowland
112 Whale Lowland

HUDSON REGION

113 Richmond Hills
114 Belcher Islands
115 Southampton Plain
116 Hudson Bay Lowlands

JAMES REGION

117 Port Arthur Hills
118 Penokean Hills
119 Mistassini Hills
120 Labrador Hills
121 Povungnituk Hills
122 Saglouc Plateau
123 Larch Plateau

124 Caniapiscau Plateau
125 Lake Plateau
126 Abitibi Upland
127 Severn Upland
128 Nipigon Plain
129 Cobalt Plain
130 Eastmain Lowland

LAURENTIAN REGION

131 Laurentian Highlands
132 Mealy Mountains
133 Mécatina Plateau
134 Hamilton Plateau
135 Hamilton Upland
136 Melville Plain
137 Lake St. Jean Lowland

Lambert Conformal Conic Projection Standard Parallels 49°N. and 77°N.

THE NATIONAL ATLAS OF CANADA

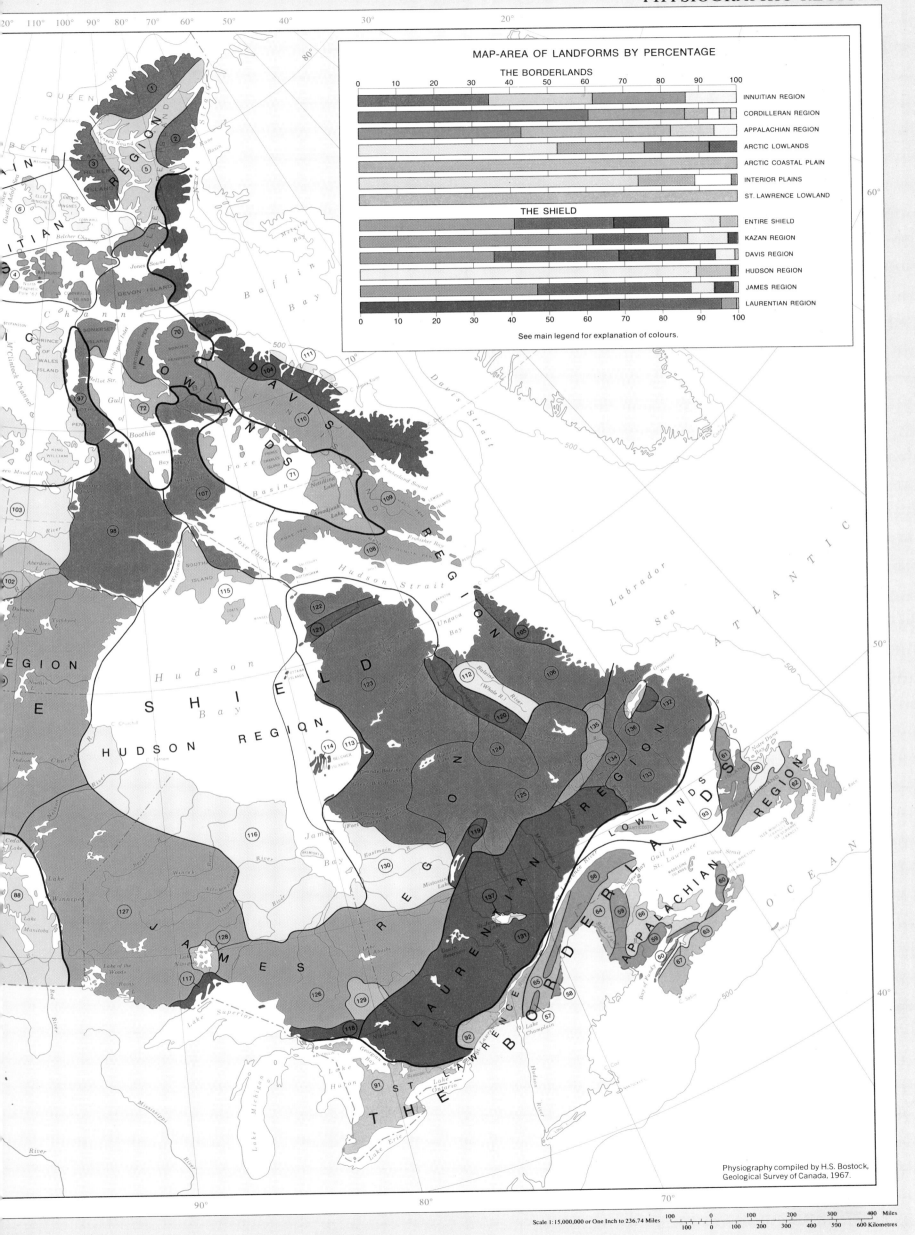

MAP-AREA OF LANDFORMS BY PERCENTAGE

THE BORDERLANDS

0 10 20 30 40 50 60 70 80 90 100

INNUITIAN REGION
CORDILLERAN REGION
APPALACHIAN REGION
ARCTIC LOWLANDS
ARCTIC COASTAL PLAIN
INTERIOR PLAINS
ST. LAWRENCE LOWLAND

THE SHIELD

ENTIRE SHIELD
KAZAN REGION
DAVIS REGION
HUDSON REGION
JAMES REGION
LAURENTIAN REGION

0 10 20 30 40 50 60 70 80 90 100

See main legend for explanation of colours.

Physiography compiled by H.S. Bostock,
Geological Survey of Canada, 1967.

Scale 1:15,000,000 or One Inch to 236.74 Miles

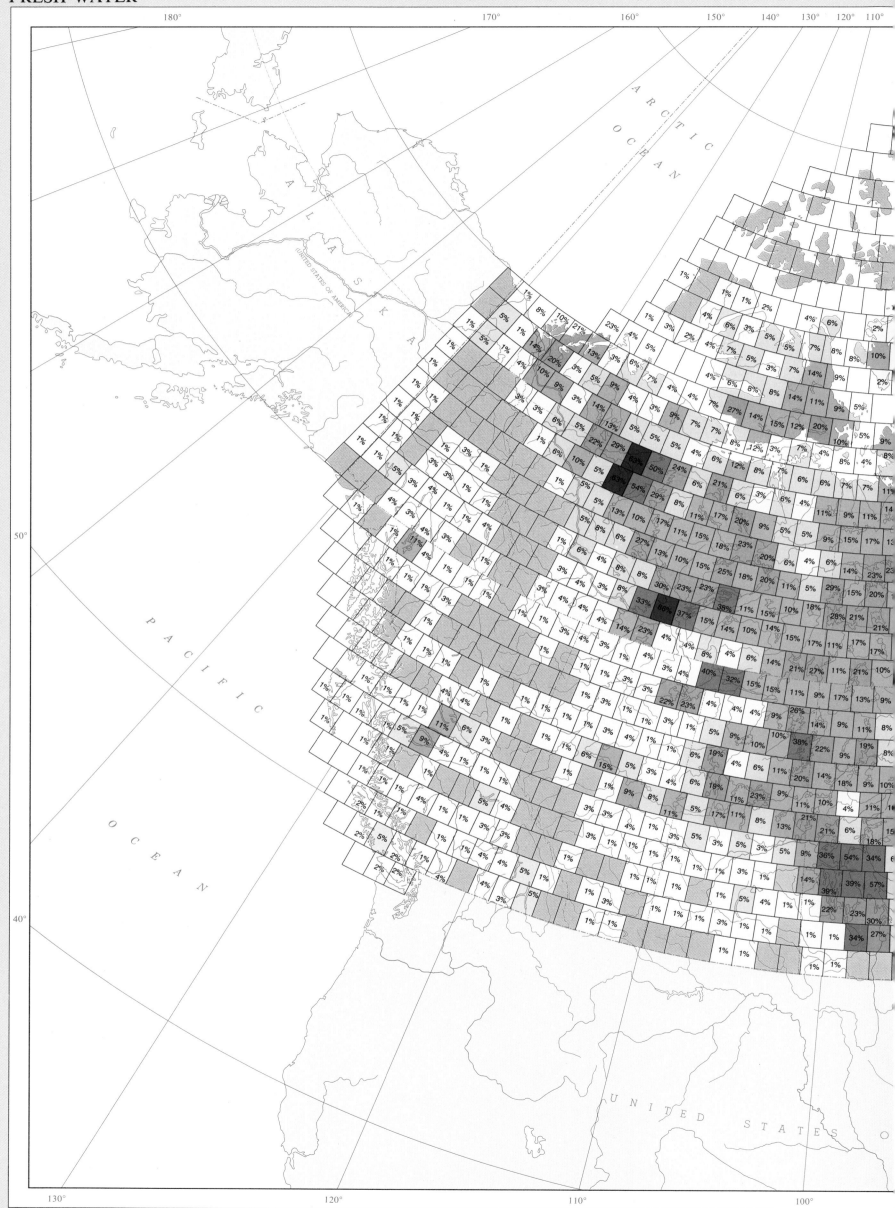

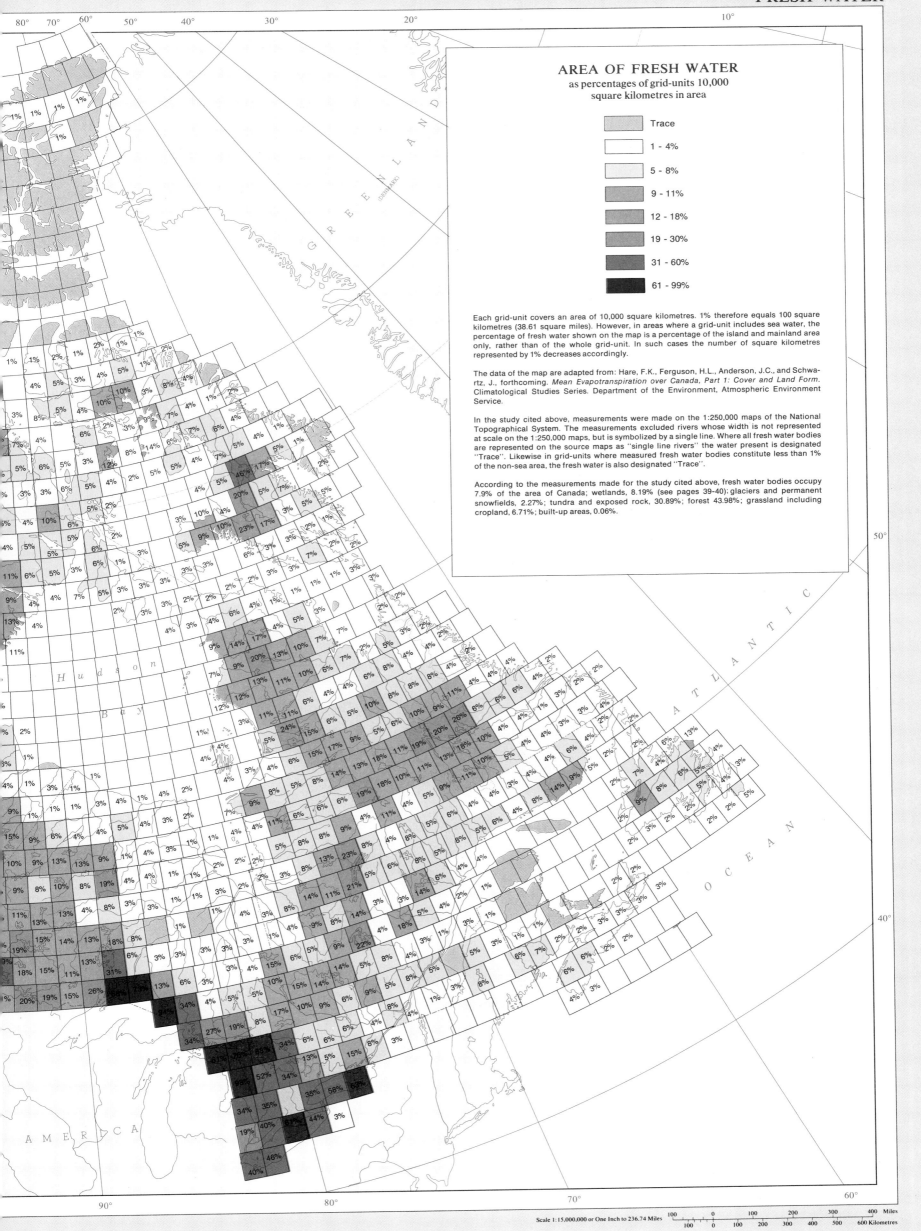

AREA OF FRESH WATER
as percentages of grid-units 10,000
square kilometres in area

	Trace
	1 - 4%
	5 - 8%
	9 - 11%
	12 - 18%
	19 - 30%
	31 - 60%
	61 - 99%

Each grid-unit covers an area of 10,000 square kilometres. 1% therefore equals 100 square kilometres (38.61 square miles). However, in areas where a grid-unit includes sea water, the percentage of fresh water shown on the map is a percentage of the island and mainland area only, rather than of the whole grid-unit. In such cases the number of square kilometres represented by 1% decreases accordingly.

The data of the map are adapted from: Hare, F.K., Ferguson, H.L., Anderson, J.C., and Schwartz, J., forthcoming. *Mean Evapotranspiration over Canada, Part 1: Cover and Land Form.* Climatological Studies Series. Department of the Environment, Atmospheric Environment Service.

In the study cited above, measurements were made on the 1:250,000 maps of the National Topographical System. The measurements excluded rivers whose width is not represented at scale on the 1:250,000 maps, but is symbolized by a single line. Where all fresh water bodies are represented on the source maps as "single line rivers" the water present is designated "Trace". Likewise in grid-units where measured fresh water bodies constitute less than 1% of the non-sea area, the fresh water is also designated "Trace".

According to the measurements made for the study cited above, fresh water bodies occupy 7.9% of the area of Canada; wetlands, 8.19% (see pages 39-40); glaciers and permanent snowfields, 2.27%; tundra and exposed rock, 30.89%; forest 43.98%; grassland including cropland, 6.71%; built-up areas, 0.06%.

LAKES, RIVERS AND GLACIERS

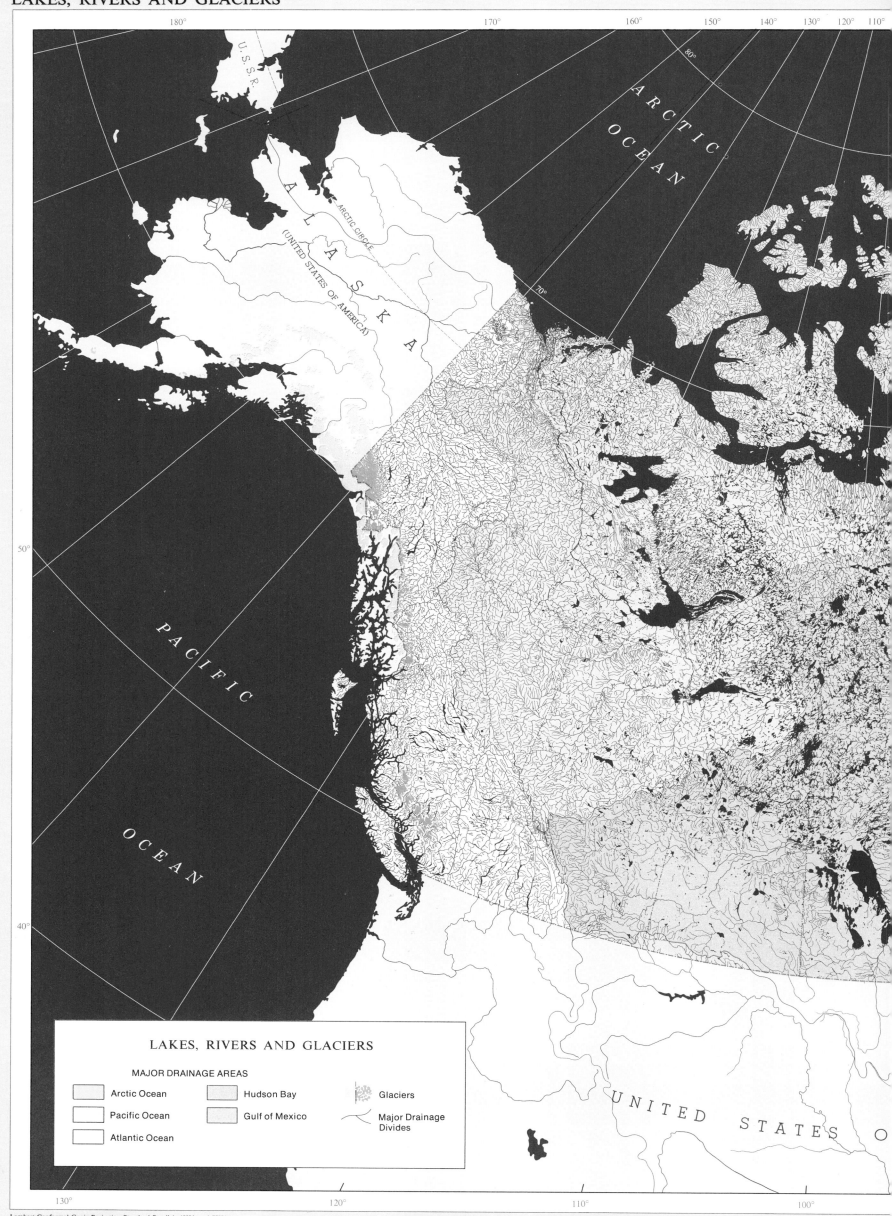

180° 170° 160° 150° 140° 130° 120° 110°

U.S.S.R.

80°

A R C T I C

O C E A N

ARCTIC CIRCLE

A L A S K A

(UNITED STATES OF AMERICA)

70°

50°

P A C I F I C

O C E A N

40°

LAKES, RIVERS AND GLACIERS

MAJOR DRAINAGE AREAS

Arctic Ocean   Hudson Bay   Glaciers

Pacific Ocean   Gulf of Mexico   Major Drainage Divides

Atlantic Ocean

U N I T E D   S T A T E S   O

130° 120° 110° 100°

Lambert Conformal Conic Projection Standard Parallels 49°N. and 77°N.

NATIONAL ATLAS OF CANADA

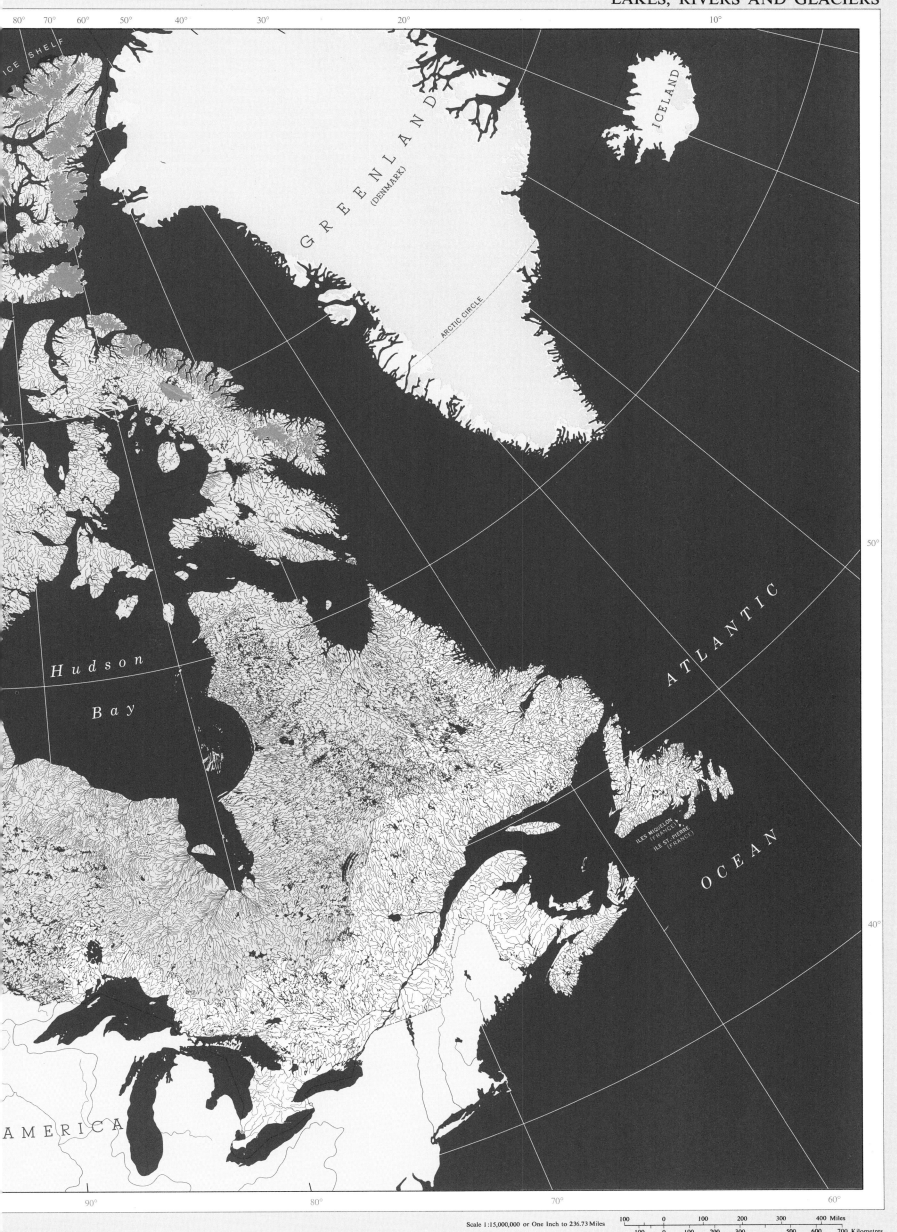

ICE SHELF

G R E E N L A N D
(DENMARK)

ICELAND

ARCTIC CIRCLE

50°

A T L A N T I C

Hudson

Bay

ILES MIQUELON
(FRANCE)
ILE ST. PIERRE
(FRANCE)

O C E A N

40°

A M E R I C A

90° 80° 70° 60°

Scale 1:15,000,000 or One Inch to 236.73 Miles

100 0 100 200 300 400 Miles

100 0 100 200 300 500 600 700 Kilometres

Permafrost

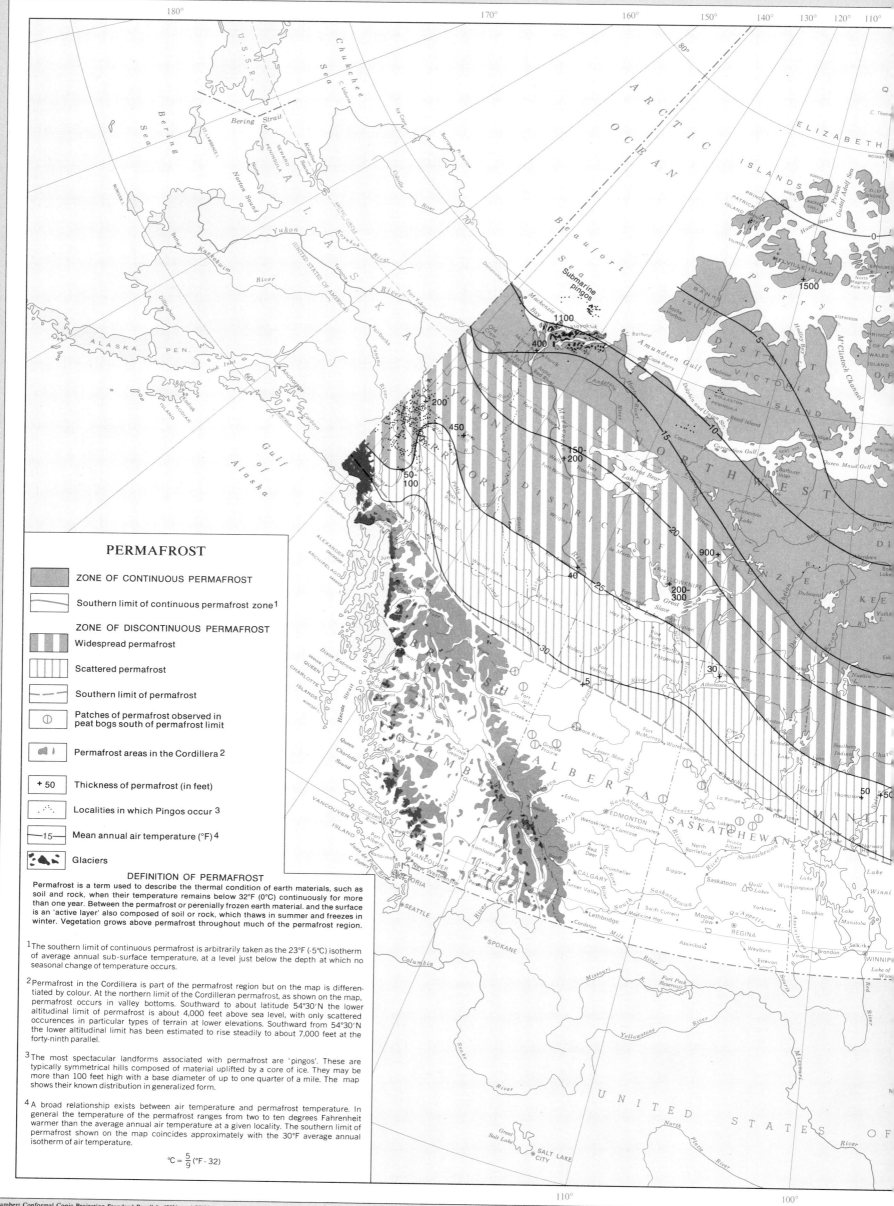

PERMAFROST

ZONE OF CONTINUOUS PERMAFROST

Southern limit of continuous permafrost zone[1]

ZONE OF DISCONTINUOUS PERMAFROST

Widespread permafrost

Scattered permafrost

Southern limit of permafrost

Patches of permafrost observed in peat bogs south of permafrost limit

Permafrost areas in the Cordillera[2]

+50 Thickness of permafrost (in feet)

Localities in which Pingos occur[3]

—15— Mean annual air temperature (°F)[4]

Glaciers

DEFINITION OF PERMAFROST

Permafrost is a term used to describe the thermal condition of earth materials, such as soil and rock, when their temperature remains below 32°F (0°C) continuously for more than one year. Between the permafrost or perenially frozen earth material. and the surface is an 'active layer' also composed of soil or rock, which thaws in summer and freezes in winter. Vegetation grows above permafrost throughout much of the permafrost region.

[1] The southern limit of continuous permafrost is arbitrarily taken as the 23°F (-5°C) isotherm of average annual sub-surface temperature, at a level just below the depth at which no seasonal change of temperature occurs.

[2] Permafrost in the Cordillera is part of the permafrost region but on the map is differentiated by colour. At the northern limit of the Cordilleran permafrost, as shown on the map, permafrost occurs in valley bottoms. Southward to about latitude 54°30'N the lower altitudinal limit of permafrost is about 4,000 feet above sea level, with only scattered occurences in particular types of terrain at lower elevations. Southward from 54°30'N the lower altitudinal limit has been estimated to rise steadily to about 7,000 feet at the forty-ninth parallel.

[3] The most spectacular landforms associated with permafrost are 'pingos'. These are typically symmetrical hills composed of material uplifted by a core of ice. They may be more than 100 feet high with a base diameter of up to one quarter of a mile. The map shows their known distribution in generalized form.

[4] A broad relationship exists between air temperature and permafrost temperature. In general the temperature of the permafrost ranges from two to ten degrees Fahrenheit warmer than the average annual air temperature at a given locality. The southern limit of permafrost shown on the map coincides approximately with the 30°F average annual isotherm of air temperature.

$$°C = \frac{5}{9}(°F - 32)$$

Modified from 'Permafrost in Canada' (Map 1246A, Geological Survey of Canada, 1967) prepared by R.J.E. Brown, National Research Council of Canada.

Scale 1:15,000,000 or One Inch to 236.74 Miles

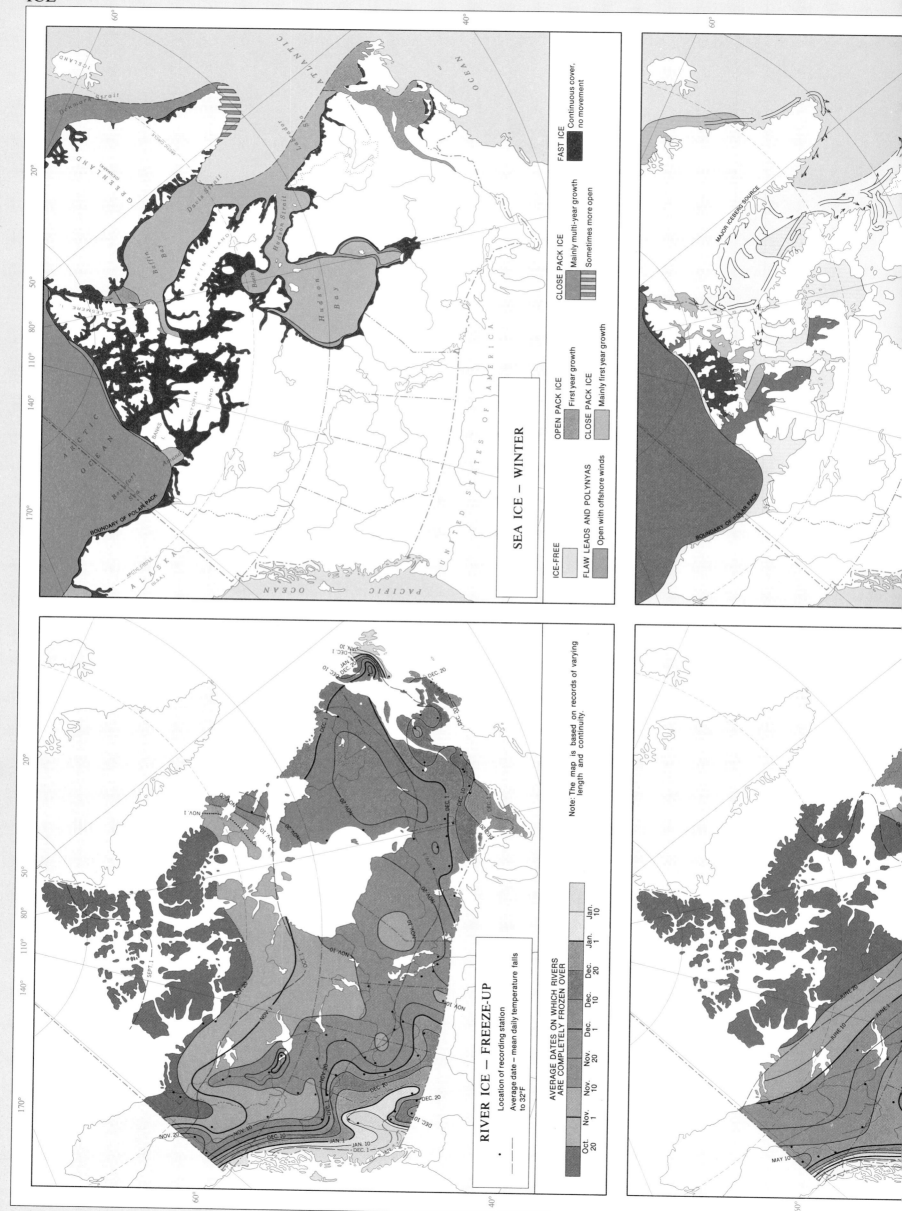

SEA ICE — WINTER

ICE-FREE

FLAW LEADS AND POLYNYAS
Open with offshore winds

OPEN PACK ICE
First year growth

CLOSE PACK ICE
Mainly first year growth

CLOSE PACK ICE
Mainly multi-year growth
Sometimes more open

FAST ICE
Continuous cover,
no movement

RIVER ICE — FREEZE-UP

• Location of recording station

— — — Average date – mean daily temperature falls
to 32°F

AVERAGE DATES ON WHICH RIVERS
ARE COMPLETELY FROZEN OVER

Oct. | Nov. | Nov. | Nov. | Dec. | Dec. | Jan. | Jan.
20 | 1 | 10 | 20 | 1 | 10 | 20 | 1 | 10

Note: The map is based on records of varying
length and continuity.

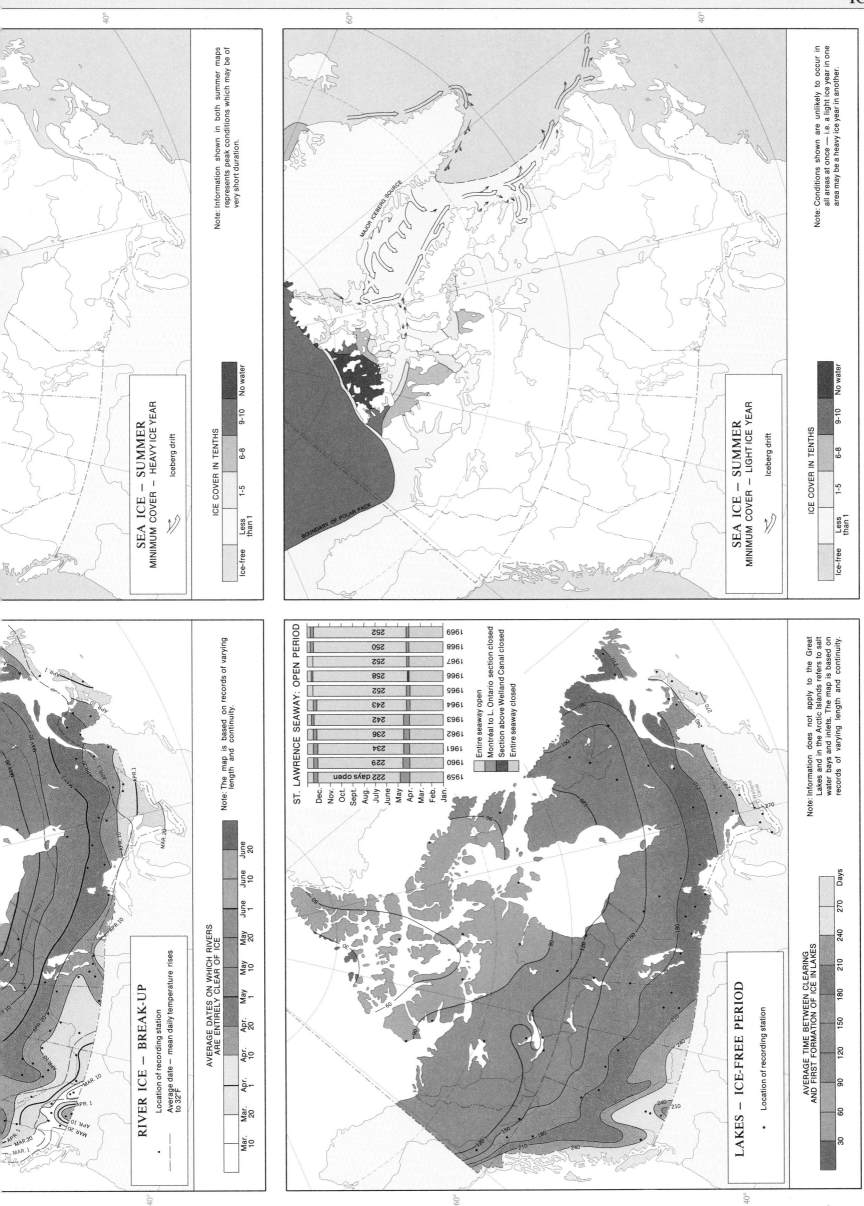

SEA ICE — SUMMER
MINIMUM COVER — HEAVY ICE YEAR

Iceberg drift

ICE COVER IN TENTHS

| Ice-free | Less than 1 | 1-5 | 6-8 | 9-10 | No water |

Note: Information shown in both summer maps represents peak conditions which may be of very short duration.

SEA ICE — SUMMER
MINIMUM COVER — LIGHT ICE YEAR

Iceberg drift

ICE COVER IN TENTHS

| Ice-free | Less than 1 | 1-5 | 6-8 | 9-10 | No water |

Note: Conditions shown are unlikely to occur in all areas at once — i.e. a light ice year in one area may be a heavy ice year in another.

Scale 1:35,000,000 or One Inch to 552.40 Miles

RIVER ICE — BREAK-UP

• Location of recording station

-- Average date — mean daily temperature rises to 32°F

AVERAGE DATES ON WHICH RIVERS ARE ENTIRELY CLEAR OF ICE

| Mar. 10 | Mar. 20 | Apr. 1 | Apr. 10 | Apr. 20 | May 1 | May 10 | May 20 | June 1 | June 10 | June 20 |

Note: The map is based on records of varying length and continuity.

ST. LAWRENCE SEAWAY: OPEN PERIOD

	1959	1960	1961	1962	1963	1964	1965	1966	1967	1968	1969
Dec.											
Nov.											
Oct.											
Sept.											
Aug.											
July											
June											
May											
Apr.											
Mar.											
Feb.											
Jan.											
	222 days open	229	234	236	242	243	252	258	252	250	252

Entire seaway open
Montréal to L. Ontario section closed
Section above Welland Canal closed
Entire seaway closed

LAKES — ICE-FREE PERIOD

• Location of recording station

AVERAGE TIME BETWEEN CLEARING AND FIRST FORMATION OF ICE IN LAKES

| 30 | 60 | 90 | 120 | 150 | 180 | 210 | 240 | 270 | Days |

Note: Information does not apply to the Great Lakes and in the Arctic Islands refers to salt water bays and inlets. The map is based on records of varying length and continuity.

Lambert Conformal Conic Projection Standard Parallels 49°N, and 77°N.

THE NATIONAL ATLAS OF CANADA

DRAINAGE BASINS

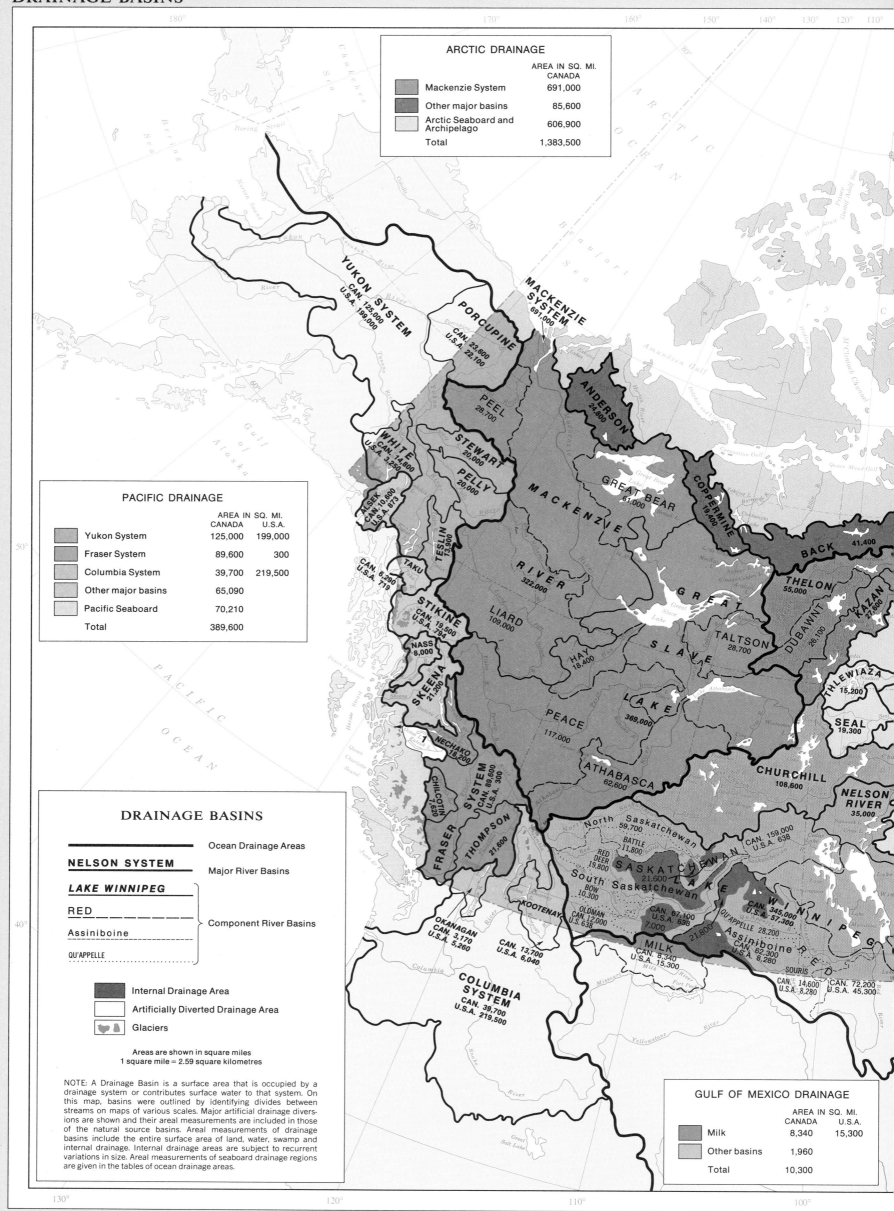

ARCTIC DRAINAGE

	AREA IN SQ. MI. CANADA
Mackenzie System	691,000
Other major basins	85,600
Arctic Seaboard and Archipelago	606,900
Total	1,383,500

PACIFIC DRAINAGE

	AREA IN SQ. MI. CANADA	U.S.A.
Yukon System	125,000	199,000
Fraser System	89,600	300
Columbia System	39,700	219,500
Other major basins	65,090	
Pacific Seaboard	70,210	
Total	389,600	

DRAINAGE BASINS

————	Ocean Drainage Areas
NELSON SYSTEM	Major River Basins
LAKE WINNIPEG	
RED —————————	Component River Basins
Assiniboine ············	
QU'APPELLE	

Internal Drainage Area

Artificially Diverted Drainage Area

Glaciers

Areas are shown in square miles
1 square mile = 2.59 square kilometres

NOTE: A Drainage Basin is a surface area that is occupied by a drainage system or contributes surface water to that system. On this map, basins were outlined by identifying divides between streams on maps of various scales. Major artificial drainage diversions are shown and their areal measurements are included in those of the natural source basins. Areal measurements of drainage basins include the entire surface area of land, water, swamp and internal drainage. Internal drainage areas are subject to recurrent variations in size. Areal measurements of seaboard drainage regions are given in the tables of ocean drainage areas.

GULF OF MEXICO DRAINAGE

	AREA IN SQ. MI. CANADA	U.S.A.
Milk	8,340	15,300
Other basins	1,960	
Total	10,300	

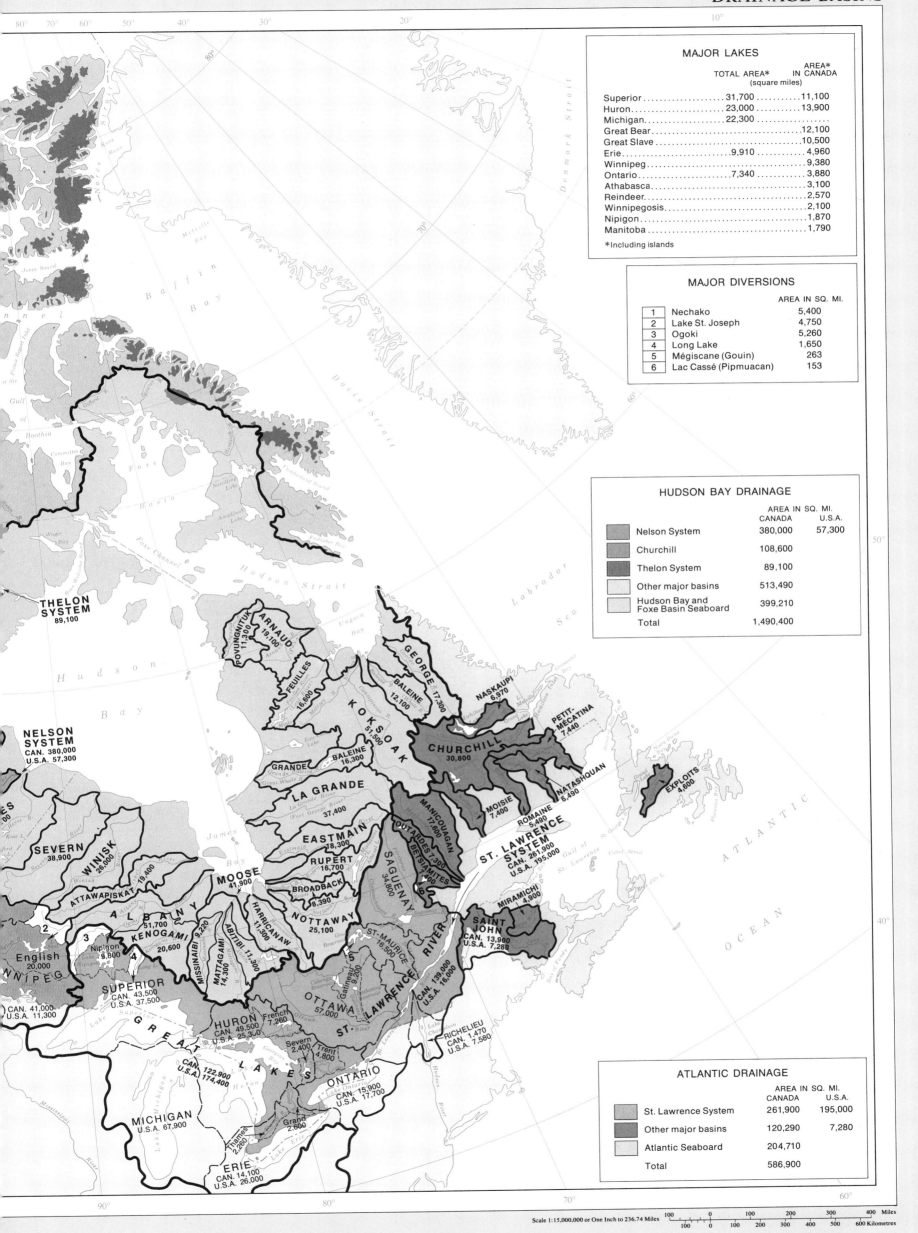

MAJOR LAKES

	TOTAL AREA* (square miles)	AREA* IN CANADA
Superior	31,700	11,100
Huron	23,000	13,900
Michigan	22,300	
Great Bear		12,100
Great Slave		10,500
Erie	9,910	4,960
Winnipeg		9,380
Ontario	7,340	3,880
Athabasca		3,100
Reindeer		2,570
Winnipegosis		2,100
Nipigon		1,870
Manitoba		1,790

*Including islands

MAJOR DIVERSIONS

		AREA IN SQ. MI.
1	Nechako	5,400
2	Lake St. Joseph	4,750
3	Ogoki	5,260
4	Long Lake	1,650
5	Mégiscane (Gouin)	263
6	Lac Cassé (Pipmuacan)	153

HUDSON BAY DRAINAGE

		AREA IN SQ. MI. CANADA	U.S.A.
	Nelson System	380,000	57,300
	Churchill	108,600	
	Thelon System	89,100	
	Other major basins	513,490	
	Hudson Bay and Foxe Basin Seaboard	399,210	
	Total	1,490,400	

ATLANTIC DRAINAGE

		AREA IN SQ. MI. CANADA	U.S.A.
	St. Lawrence System	261,900	195,000
	Other major basins	120,290	7,280
	Atlantic Seaboard	204,710	
	Total	586,900	

Scale 1:15,000,000 or One Inch to 236.74 Miles

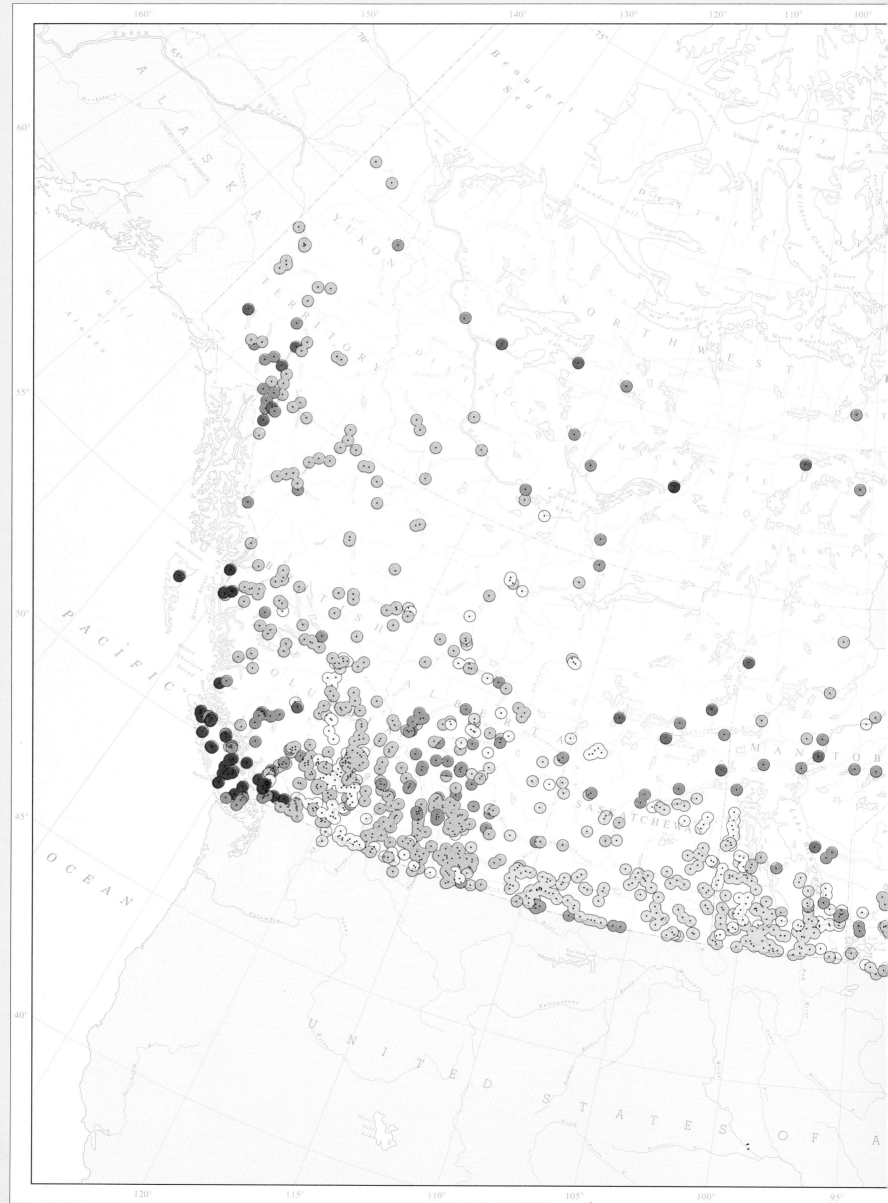

Lambert Conformal Conic Projection Standard Parallels 49°N. and 77°N.
THE NATIONAL ATLAS OF CANADA

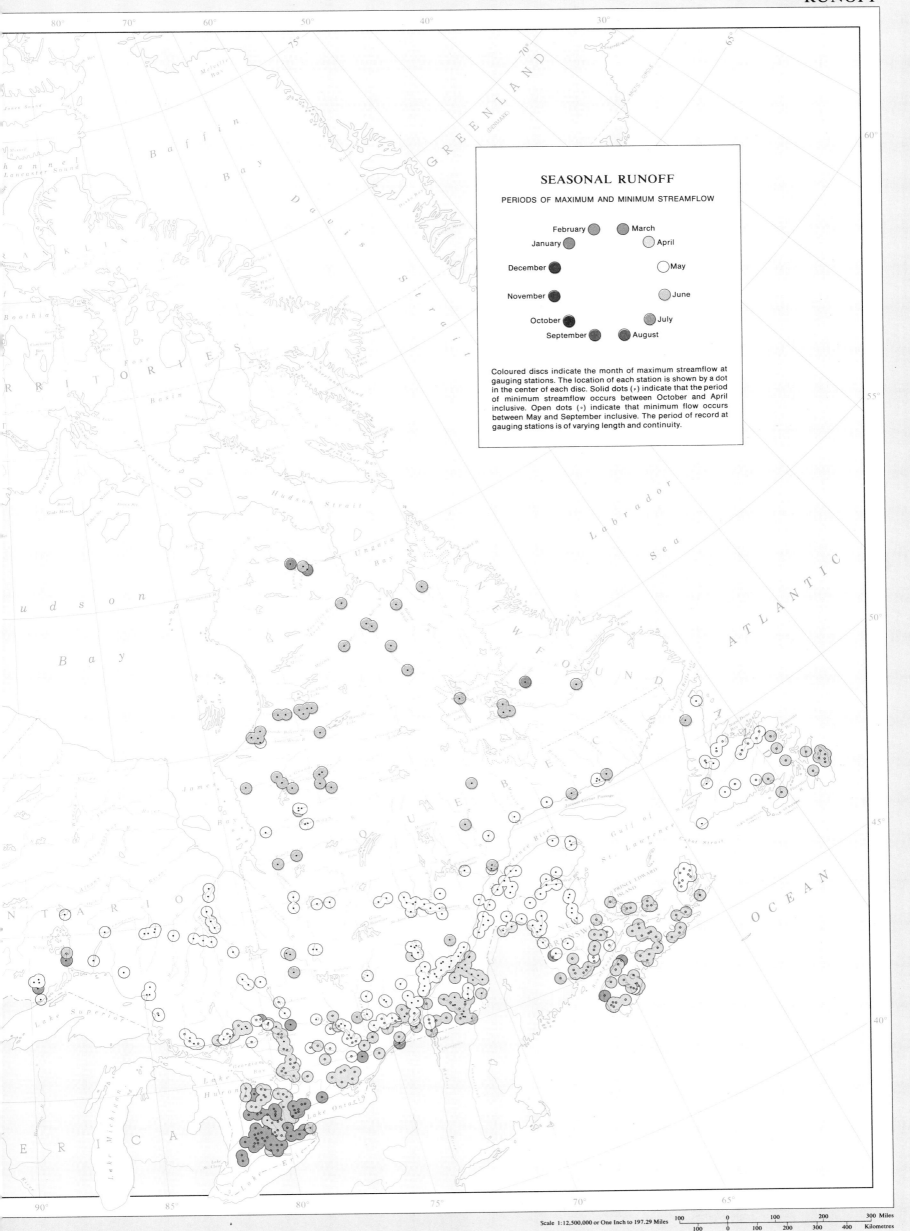

SEASONAL RUNOFF

PERIODS OF MAXIMUM AND MINIMUM STREAMFLOW

February   March
January   April
December   May
November   June
October   July
September   August

Coloured discs indicate the month of maximum streamflow at
gauging stations. The location of each station is shown by a dot
in the center of each disc. Solid dots (·) indicate that the period
of minimum streamflow occurs between October and April
inclusive. Open dots (○) indicate that minimum flow occurs
between May and September inclusive. The period of record at
gauging stations is of varying length and continuity.

Scale 1:12,500,000 or One Inch to 197.29 Miles

100   0   100   200   300 Miles

100   0   100   200   300   400   Kilometres

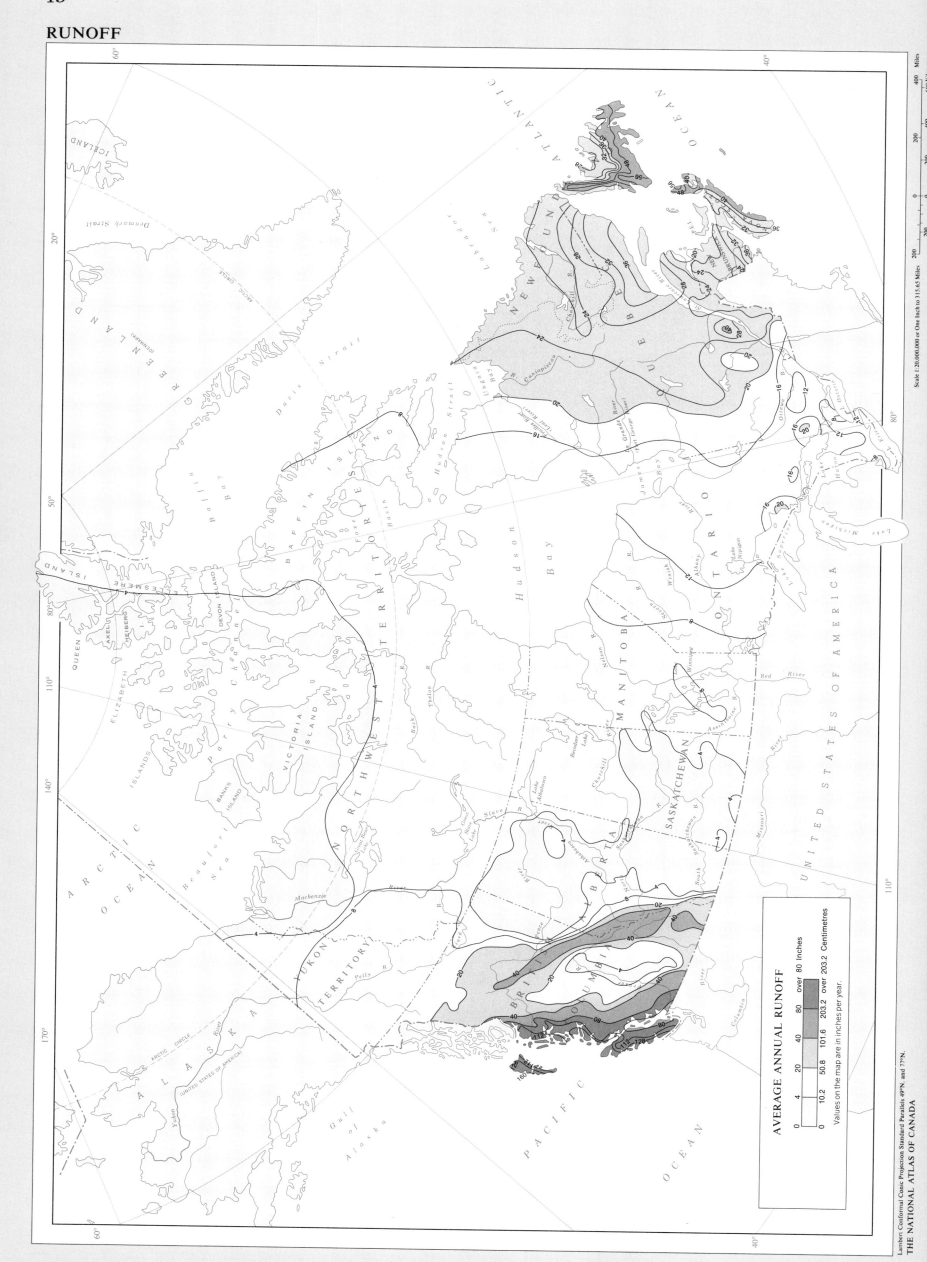

AVERAGE ANNUAL RUNOFF

		over 80 Inches
	80	203.2 over 203.2 Centimetres
	40	101.6
	20	50.8
	4	10.2
0		0

Values on the map are in inches per year.

Lambert Conformal Conic Projection Standard Parallels 49°N. and 77°N.

THE NATIONAL ATLAS OF CANADA

Scale 1:20,000,000 or One Inch to 315.65 Miles

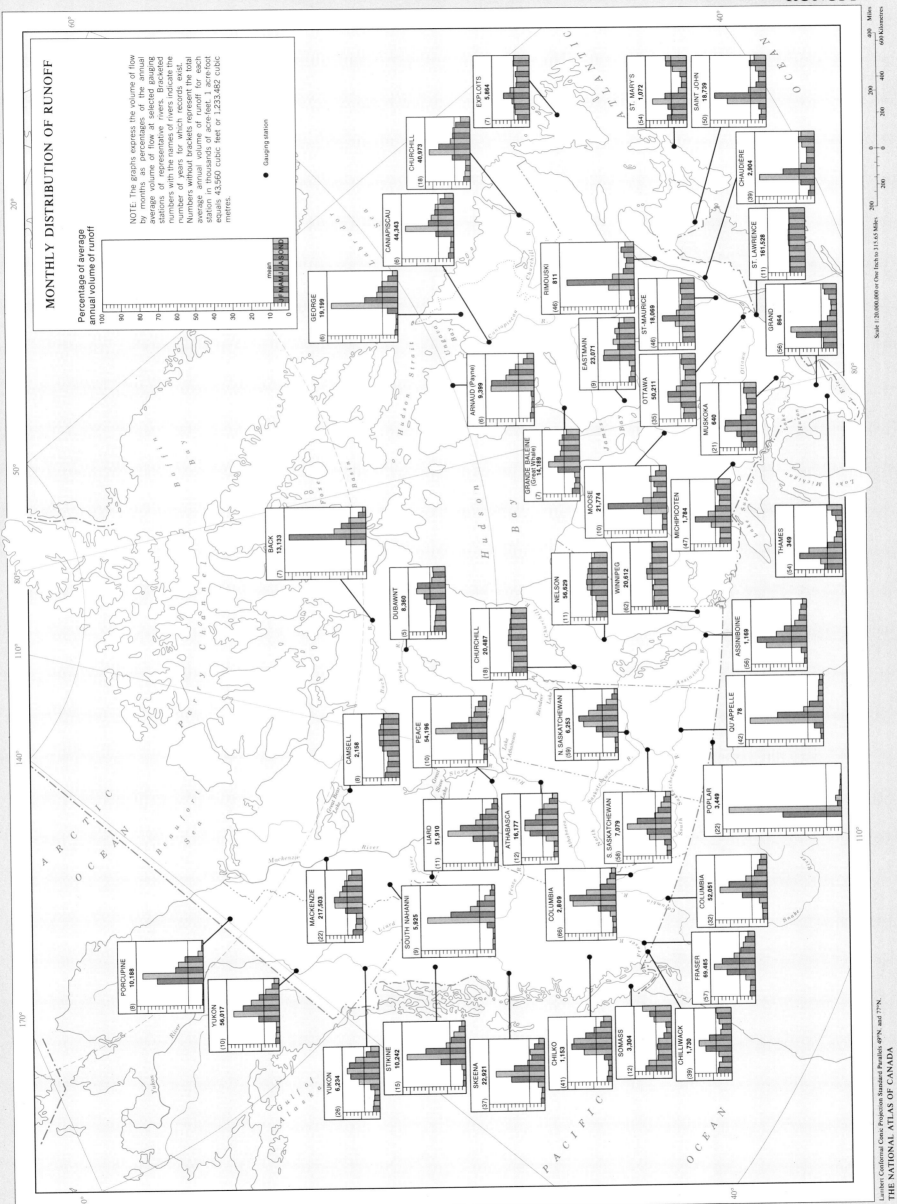

MONTHLY DISTRIBUTION OF RUNOFF

NOTE: The graphs express the volume of flow by months as percentages of the annual average volume of flow at selected gauging stations of representative rivers. Bracketed numbers with the names of rivers indicate the number of years for which records exist. Numbers without brackets represent the total average annual volume of runoff for each station in thousands of acre-feet. 1 acre-foot equals 43,560 cubic feet or 1,233.482 cubic metres.

● Gauging station

Percentage of average annual volume of runoff

mean

J F M A M J J A S O N D

Scale 1:20,000,000 or One Inch to 315.65 Miles

Lambert Conformal Conic Projection Standard Parallels 49°N. and 77°N.

THE NATIONAL ATLAS OF CANADA

RIVER DISCHARGE

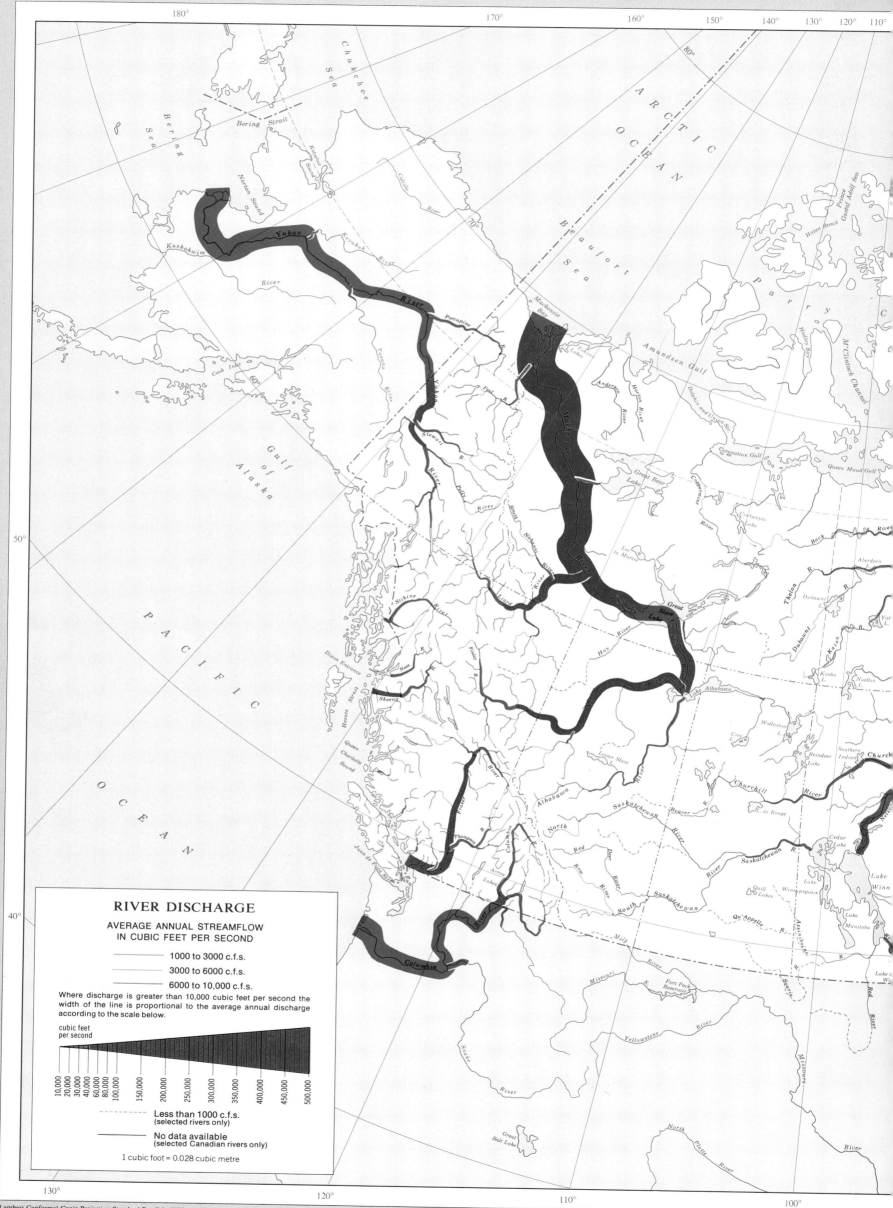

RIVER DISCHARGE

AVERAGE ANNUAL STREAMFLOW IN CUBIC FEET PER SECOND

— 1000 to 3000 c.f.s.
— 3000 to 6000 c.f.s.
— 6000 to 10,000 c.f.s.

Where discharge is greater than 10,000 cubic feet per second the width of the line is proportional to the average annual discharge according to the scale below.

cubic feet per second

10,000 20,000 30,000 40,000 60,000 80,000 100,000 150,000 200,000 250,000 300,000 350,000 400,000 450,000 500,000

---- Less than 1000 c.f.s.
(selected rivers only)

—— No data available
(selected Canadian rivers only)

1 cubic foot = 0.028 cubic metre

RELIABILITY OF
RIVER DISCHARGE DATA

Good

Fair to Poor

No Data

The map of River Discharge is based on
data which vary in accuracy. This inset
map shows in generalized form the
reliability of the data used.

Scale 1:40,000,000

Scale 1:15,000,000 or One Inch to 236.73 Miles

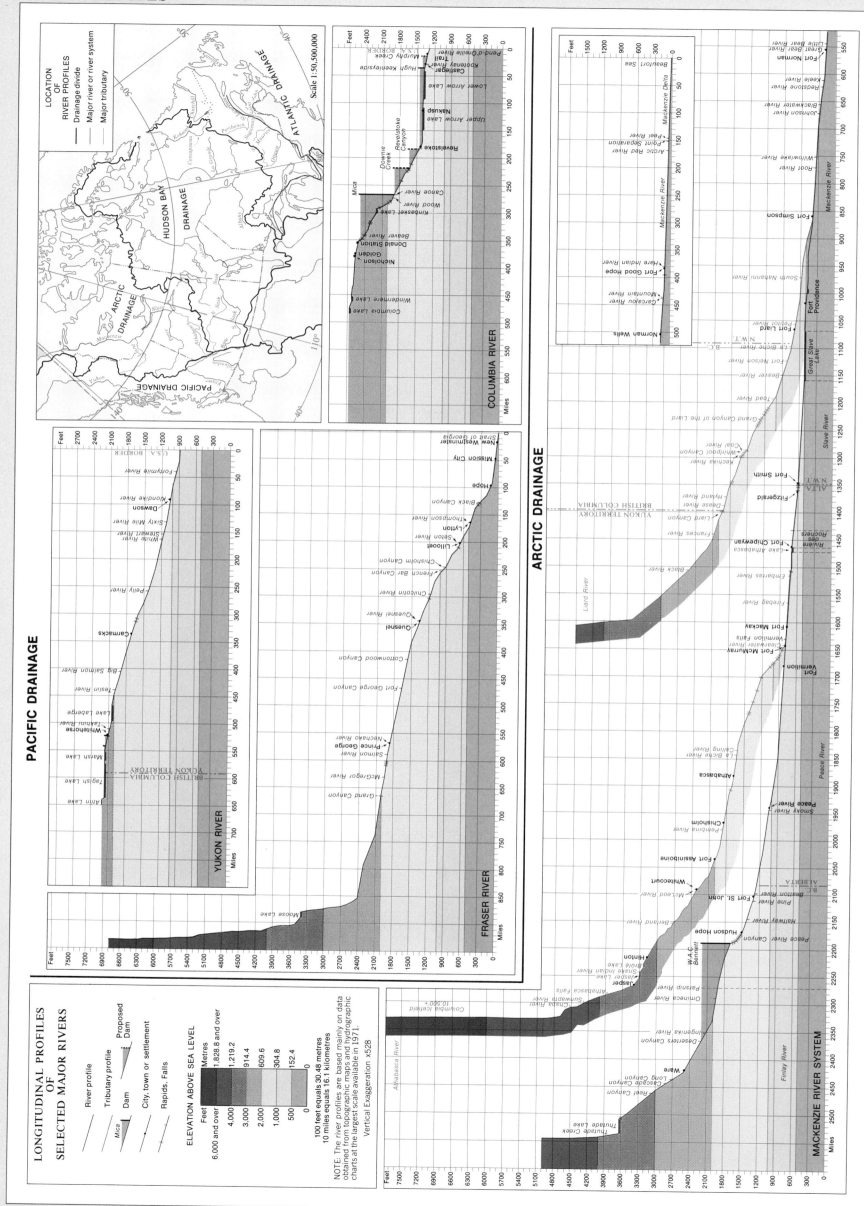

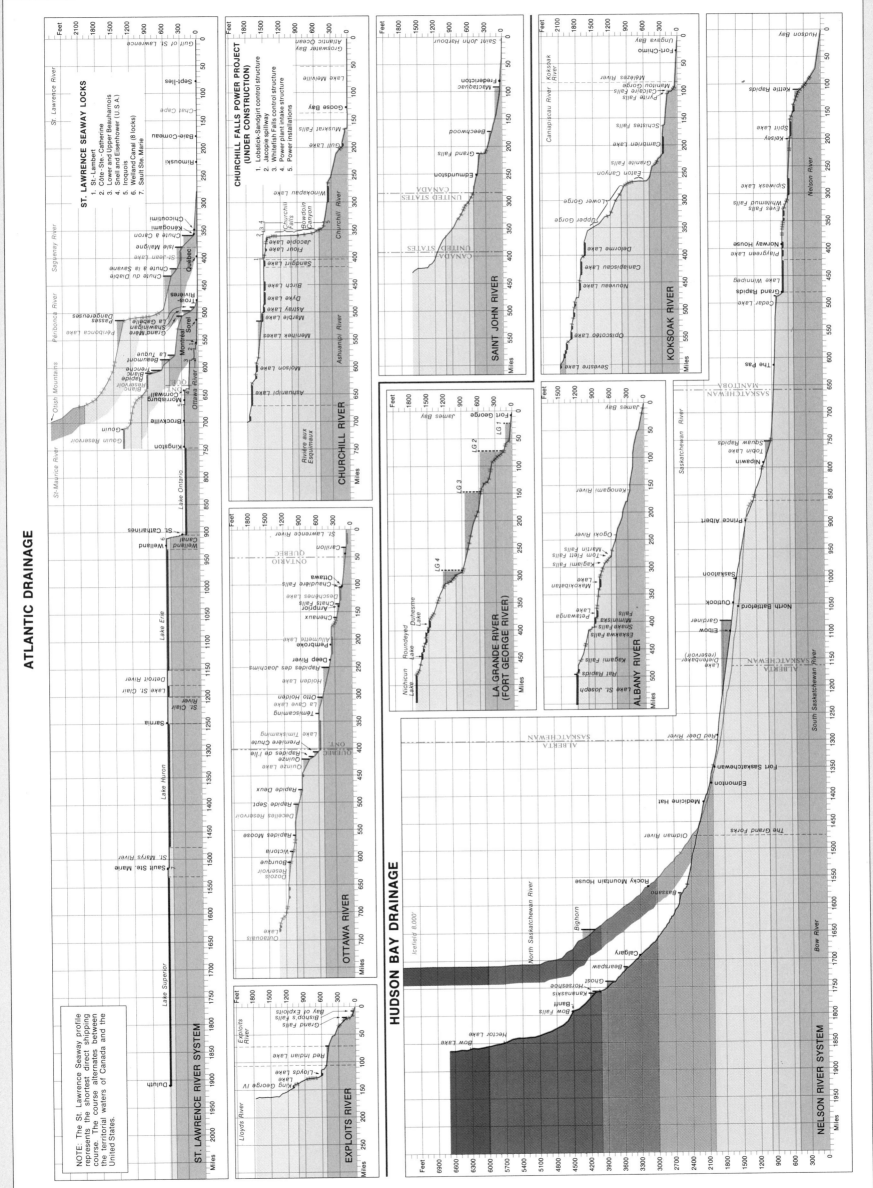

ATLANTIC DRAINAGE

NOTE: The St. Lawrence Seaway profile represents the shortest direct shipping course. The course alternates between the territorial waters of Canada and the United States.

ST. LAWRENCE SEAWAY LOCKS
1. St-Lambert
2. Côte-Ste-Catherine
3. Lower and Upper Beauharnois
4. Snell and Eisenhower (U.S.A.)
5. Iroquois
6. Welland Canal (8 locks)
7. Sault Ste. Marie

CHURCHILL FALLS POWER PROJECT (UNDER CONSTRUCTION)
1. Lobstick-Sandgirt control structure
2. Jacopie spillway
3. Whitefish Falls control structure
4. Power plant intake structure
5. Power installations

ST. LAWRENCE RIVER SYSTEM

CHURCHILL RIVER

SAINT JOHN RIVER

KOKSOAK RIVER

OTTAWA RIVER

EXPLOITS RIVER

LA GRANDE RIVER (FORT GEORGE RIVER)

ALBANY RIVER

NELSON RIVER SYSTEM

HUDSON BAY DRAINAGE

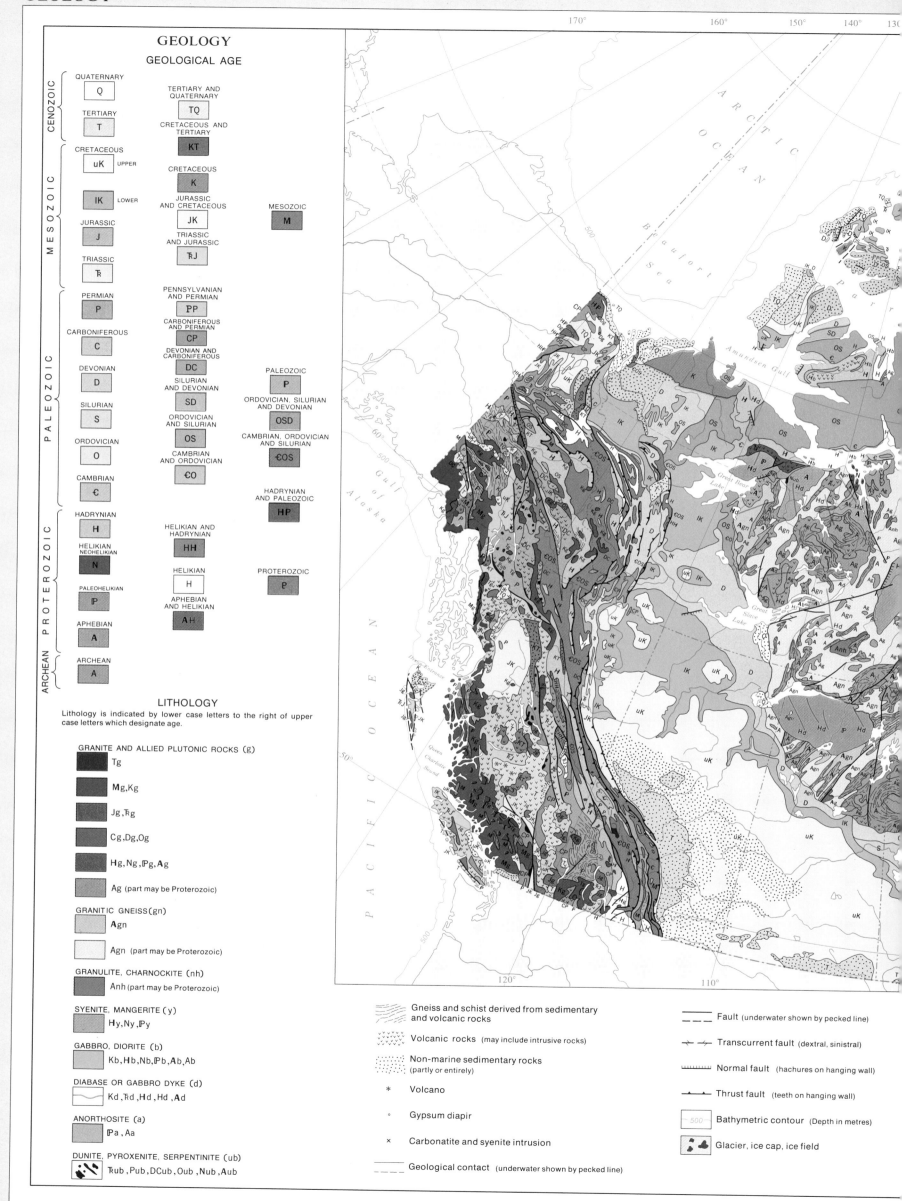

GEOLOGY
GEOLOGICAL AGE

CENOZOIC

QUATERNARY — Q

TERTIARY — T

TERTIARY AND QUATERNARY — TQ

CRETACEOUS AND TERTIARY — KT

MESOZOIC

CRETACEOUS — uK UPPER

— lK LOWER

CRETACEOUS — K

JURASSIC — J

JURASSIC AND CRETACEOUS — JK

TRIASSIC — Tr

TRIASSIC AND JURASSIC — TrJ

MESOZOIC — M

PALEOZOIC

PERMIAN — P

CARBONIFEROUS — C

DEVONIAN — D

SILURIAN — S

ORDOVICIAN — O

CAMBRIAN — C

PENNSYLVANIAN AND PERMIAN — PP

CARBONIFEROUS AND PERMIAN — CP

DEVONIAN AND CARBONIFEROUS — DC

SILURIAN AND DEVONIAN — SD

ORDOVICIAN AND SILURIAN — OS

CAMBRIAN AND ORDOVICIAN — CO

PALEOZOIC — P

ORDOVICIAN, SILURIAN AND DEVONIAN — OSD

CAMBRIAN, ORDOVICIAN AND SILURIAN — COS

PROTEROZOIC — ARCHEAN

HADRYNIAN — H

HELIKIAN NEOHELIKIAN — N

PALEOHELIKIAN — lP

APHEBIAN — A

ARCHEAN — A

HELIKIAN AND HADRYNIAN — HH

HELIKIAN — H

APHEBIAN AND HELIKIAN — AH

HADRYNIAN AND PALEOZOIC — HP

PROTEROZOIC — P

LITHOLOGY

Lithology is indicated by lower case letters to the right of upper case letters which designate age.

GRANITE AND ALLIED PLUTONIC ROCKS (g)

- Tg
- Mg, Kg
- Jg, Trg
- Cg, Dg, Og
- Hg, Ng, lPg, Ag
- Ag (part may be Proterozoic)

GRANITIC GNEISS (gn)

- Agn
- Agn (part may be Proterozoic)

GRANULITE, CHARNOCKITE (nh)

- Anh (part may be Proterozoic)

SYENITE, MANGERITE (y)

- Hy, Ny, lPy

GABBRO, DIORITE (b)

- Kb, Hb, Nb, lPb, Ab, Ab

DIABASE OR GABBRO DYKE (d)

- Kd, Trd, Hd, Hd, Ad

ANORTHOSITE (a)

- lPa, Aa

DUNITE, PYROXENITE, SERPENTINITE (ub)

- Trub, Pub, DCub, Oub, Nub, Aub

Gneiss and schist derived from sedimentary and volcanic rocks

Volcanic rocks (may include intrusive rocks)

Non-marine sedimentary rocks (partly or entirely)

* Volcano

∘ Gypsum diapir

✕ Carbonatite and syenite intrusion

Geological contact (underwater shown by pecked line)

Fault (underwater shown by pecked line)

Transcurrent fault (dextral, sinistral)

Normal fault (hachures on hanging wall)

Thrust fault (teeth on hanging wall)

500 Bathymetric contour (Depth in metres)

Glacier, ice cap, ice field

GEOLOGICAL PROVINCES
Scale 1:50,500,000

Geology compiled by R.J.W. Douglas,
Geological Survey of Canada, 1969.

Scale 1:15,000,000 or One Inch to 236.73 Miles

100   0   100   200   300   400 Miles

100   0   100   200   300   400   500   600   700 Kilometres

GEOLOGICAL PROVINCES

GEOLOGICAL PROVINCES

ATLANTIC CONTINENTAL SHELF

Scotian Shelf
Newfoundland Shelf
Labrador Shelf
Davis Shelf
Baffin Shelf
Atlantic Continental Slope

PACIFIC CONTINENTAL SHELF

PCP - Pacific Coastal Plain
Pacific Continental Slope

ARCTIC CONTINENTAL SHELF

Arctic Coastal Plain
Arctic Continental Slope
PPU - Prince Patrick Uplift
EG - Eglington Graben
BE - Banks Embayment
MD - Mackenzie Delta
AE - Anderson Embayment

GRENVILLE PROVINCE

NaFB - Naskaupi Fold Belt
GF - Grenville Front
NoFB - Normanville Fold Belt
Baie Comeau Belt
Central Granulite Terrane
Quebec Gneiss Belt
Ontario Gneiss Belt
MH - Mistassini Homocline
OH - Otish Homocline
LMG - Lake Melville Graben
MC - Manicouagan Caldera

SOUTHERN PROVINCE

PFB - Penokean Fold Belt
PAH - Port Arthur Homocline
LSB - Lake Superior Basin
NE - Nipigon Embayment
CE - Cobalt Embayment

BEAR PROVINCE

WOPMAY OROGEN

EFB - Epworth Fold Belt
HMB - Hepburn Metamorphic Belt
GBB - Great Bear Batholith
COPPERMINE HOMOCLINE

CHURCHILL PROVINCE

Labrador Fold Belt
MH - Menihek Homocline
Laporte Gneiss Belt
Nain Subprovince
EPB - Elsonian Plutonic Belt
MFB - Makkovik Fold Belt
CSFB - Cape Smith Fold Belt
Belcher Fold Belt
NH - Nastapoka Homocline
RE - Richmond Embayment
EAH - East Arm Homocline
Foxe Fold Belt
BE - Borden Embayment
EAFB - East Arm Fold Belt
MF - McDonald Fault
TF - Thelon Front
Thelon Basin
DG - Dubawnt Graben
Athabasca Basin
Tazin Belt
Ennadai Fold Belt
Kaminak Subprovince
Wollaston Lake Fold Belt
Lynn Lake Belt
FFB - Flin Flon Belt
TB - Thompson Belt
NF - Nelson Front
FRB - Fox River Belt
Committee Fold Belt
Dorset Fold Belt

NUTAK PROVINCE

SLAVE PROVINCE

BE - Bathurst Embayment
BF - Bathurst Fault

SUPERIOR PROVINCE

PB - Pikwitonei Belt
Sachigo Volcanic Belt
Berens Plutonic Belt
Uchi Volcanic Belt
English River Gneiss Belt
Wabigoon Volcanic Belt
Quetico Gneiss Belt
Wawa Belt
KF - Kapuskasing Fault Zone
Abitibi Volcanic Belt
PDF - Porcupine-Destor Fault
CB - Cadillac Break
PB - Pontiac Belt
Opatica Belt
CC - Clearwater Caldera
Ungava Belt

HUDSON PLATFORM

Moose River Basin
CHMA - Cape Henrietta Maria Arch
SI - Sutton Inliers
Hudson Bay Basin
Bell Arch
Hudson Strait Graben
Akpatok Basin

ST. LAWRENCE PLATFORM

Anticosti Basin
GNI - Great Northern Inlier
QB - Quebec Basin
OE - Ottawa Embayment
FA - Frontenac Arch
Algonquin Arch
Michigan Basin
Allegheny Trough

INTERIOR PLATFORM

RME - Rocky Mountain
Exogeosyncline
Peel Basin
BI - Brock Inlier
CA - Coppermine Arch
CFB - Colville Fold Belt
TA - Tathlina Arch
EPB - Elk Point Basin
PRA - Peace River Arch
AA - Alberta Arch
WB - Williston Basin
LE - Lloydminster Embayment

ARCTIC PLATFORM

Amundsen Basin
Minto Arch
WA - Wellington Arch
Melville Basin
Victoria Strait Basin
Boothia Uplift
CFB - Cornwallis Fold Belt
Jones-Lancaster Basin
Foxe Basin

APPALACHIAN OROGEN

*TACONIAN
AND ACADIAN OROGENS*

LL - Logan's Line
Quebec Anticlinorium
Gaspé Synclinorium
BMA - Boundary Mountain
Anticlinorium
MaA - Matapédia Anticlinorium
CS - Chaleurs Synclinorium
MiA - Miramichi Anticlinorium
FS - Fredericton Synclinorium
MFB - Meguma Fold Belt
HAK - Humber Arm Klippe
HBK - Hare Bay Klippe
BA - Burlington Anticlinorium
NDB - Notre Dame Belt
BB - Botwood Belt
GB - Gander Belt
HF - Hermitage Flexure
Avalon Fold Belt

FUNDY SUCCESSOR BASIN

MaFB - Maritime Fold Belt
CF - Cabot Fault
ChF - Chedabucto Fault
CSB - Cape Split Basin

CORDILLERAN OROGEN

EASTERN OROGENIC BELT

Northern Yukon Fold Complex
Mackenzie Fold Belt
Selwyn Fold Belt
Rocky Mountain Thrust Belt
RMT - Rocky Mountain Trench
TT - Tintina Trench
Cassiar Belt
Omineca Crystalline Belt
KA - Kootenay Arc
PA - Purcell Anticlinorium

WESTERN OROGENIC BELT

Columbia Intermontane Belt
Atlin Belt
Bowser Basin
SB - Sustut Basin
PF - Pinchi Fault
FF - Fraser Fault
YF - Yalakom Fault
CFB - Cascade Fold Belt
Coast Plutonic Complex
Yukon Crystalline Platform
ST - Shakwak Trench
St. Elias Fold Belt
IFB - Insular Fold Belt

INNUITIAN OROGEN

ELLESMERIAN OROGEN

NEFB - Northern Ellesmere Fold Belt
CEFB - Central Ellesmere Fold Belt
PIFB - Parry Islands Fold Belt

SVERDRUP BASIN

Eureka Sound Fold Belt
MFB - Melville Fold Belt

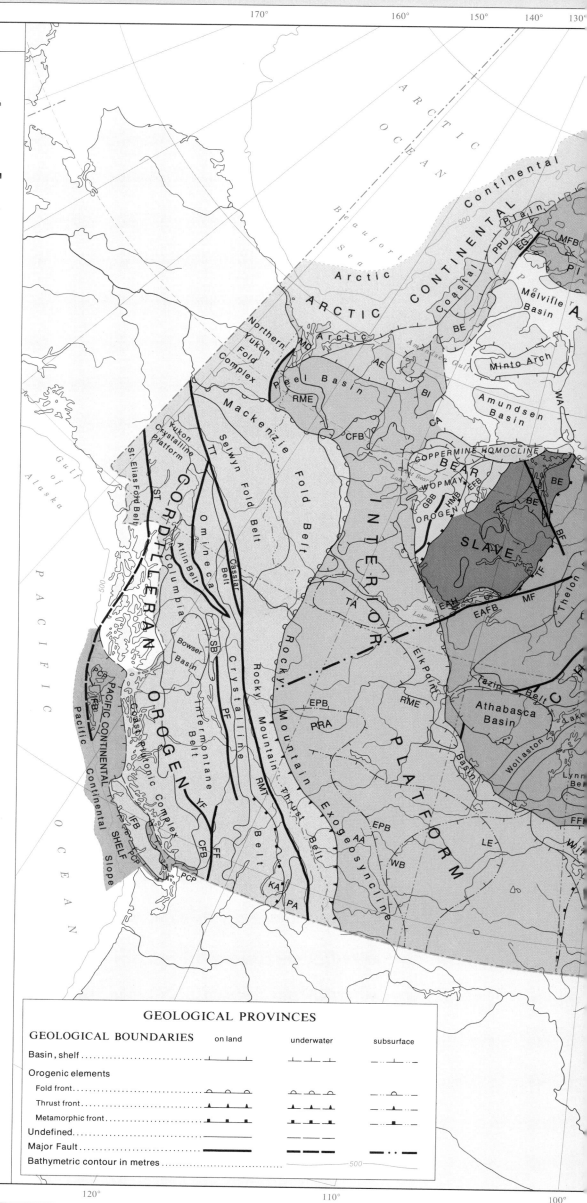

GEOLOGICAL PROVINCES

GEOLOGICAL BOUNDARIES	on land	underwater	subsurface
Basin, shelf			
Orogenic elements			
Fold front			
Thrust front			
Metamorphic front			
Undefined			
Major Fault			
Bathymetric contour in metres		500	

GEOLOGICAL PROVINCES

Canada is composed of some seventeen geological provinces, which may be grouped into four major categories - continental shelf, platform, orogen and shield. The geologically youngest provinces, the Atlantic, Pacific and Arctic Continental Shelves, are formed of little deformed sediments and volcanics, mainly of Mesozoic and Cenozoic age, that have accumulated and are still accumulating along the margins of the present continental mass. The St. Lawrence, Interior, Arctic and Hudson Platforms are formed of thick flat-lying Phanerozoic strata which cover large parts of the Canadian Shield. The Appalachian, Cordilleran and Innuitian Orogens are mountain belts of deformed and metamorphosed sedimentary and volcanic rocks mainly of Phanerozoic and Proterozoic age, intruded by granitic plutons. They were produced during the various Phanerozoic orogenies 50 to 500 million years ago. Of the seven provinces comprising the Precambrian Canadian Shield, the Grenville, Churchill, Southern and Bear embrace the orogenic belts that were produced during the Proterozoic orogenies, 900 to 1800 million years ago. The remaining three, the Superior, Slave and Nutak Provinces, were deformed during the Archean Eon, and include the oldest continental crust known in Canada, 2,500 to 3,000 million years old. The Precambrian orogenic belts have many features in common with those of Phanerozoic age but are so deeply eroded that the montainous parts are reduced to plains or lowlands and in many places the basement crystalline rocks upon which the sediments and volcanics initially accumulated are now exposed.

Shown on this map are the names given to the geological provinces and some of their principal subdivisions, these being parts of the provinces that are unified by having experienced similar orogenic events or that reflect similar tectonic environments during the time of accumulation of the rocks. On the geological map (Pages 25-26) some aspects of the geology are shown, namely the geological age of the rocks and their general lithology. On the tectonic map (Pages 29-30), the tectonic environment of the place of accumulation of various assemblages of rocks is indicated, and for the rocks of the orogenic belts, some aspects of their deformation and the time of the orogeny or orogenies to which they have been subjected are also shown.

Prepared by R.J.W. Douglas,
Geological Survey of Canada, 1973

Scale 1:15,000,000 or One Inch to 236.74 Miles

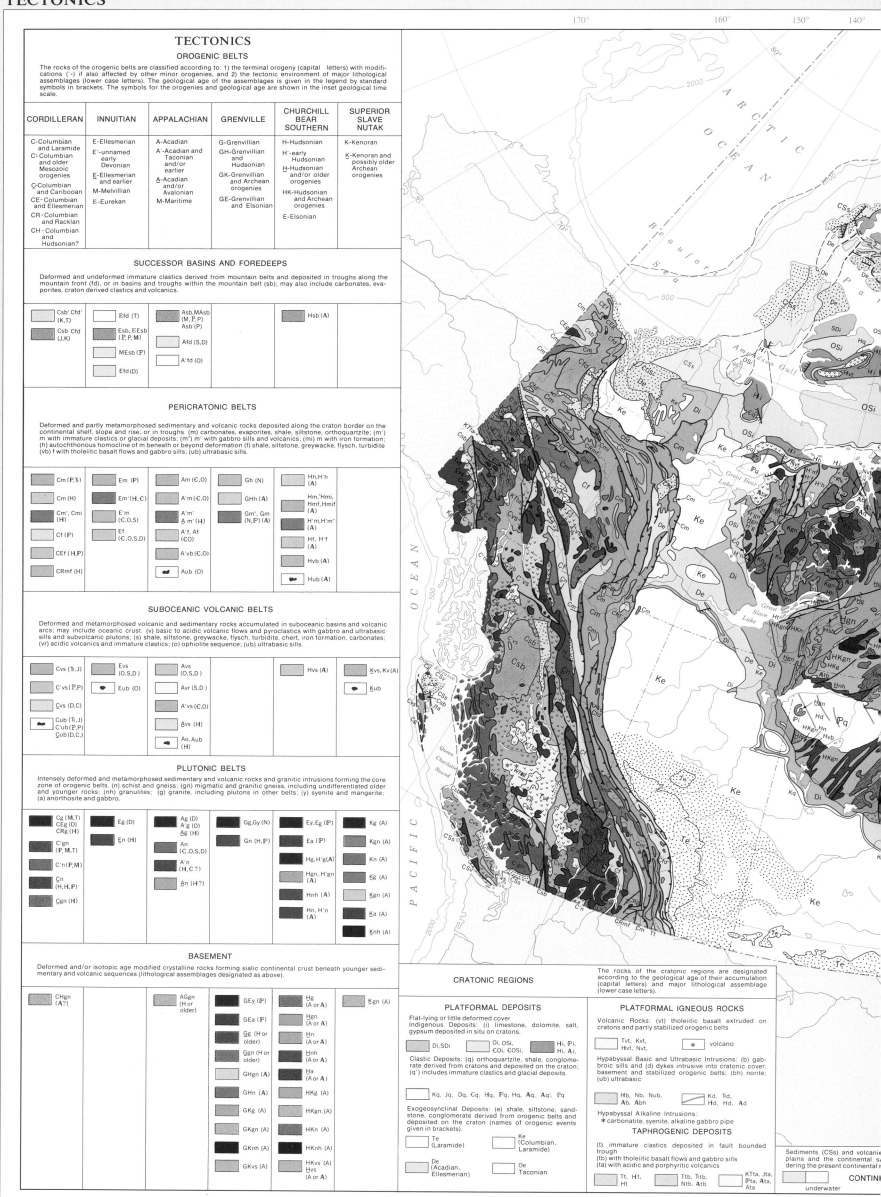

TECTONICS
OROGENIC BELTS

The rocks of the orogenic belts are classified according to: 1) the terminal orogeny (capital letters) with modifications (') if also affected by other minor orogenies, and 2) the tectonic environment of major lithological assemblages (lower case letters). The geological age of the assemblages is given in the legend by standard symbols in brackets. The symbols for the orogenies and geological age are shown in the inset geological time scale.

CORDILLERAN	INNUITIAN	APPALACHIAN	GRENVILLE	CHURCHILL BEAR SOUTHERN	SUPERIOR SLAVE NUTAK
C-Columbian and Laramide	E-Ellesmerian	A-Acadian	G-Grenvillian	H-Hudsonian	K-Kenoran
C'-Columbian and older Mesozoic orogenies	E'-unnamed early Devonian	A'-Acadian and Taconian and/or earlier	GH-Grenvillian and Hudsonian	H'-early Hudsonian	K'-Kenoran and possibly older Archean orogenies
C-Columbian and Caribooan	E-Ellesmerian and earlier	A-Acadian and/or Avalonian	GK-Grenvillian and Archean orogenies	H-Hudsonian and/or older orogenies	
CE-Columbian and Ellesmerian	M-Melvillian	M-Maritime	GE-Grenvillian and Elsonian	HK-Hudsonian and Archean orogenies	
CR-Columbian and Racklan	E-Eurekan		E-Elsonian		
CH-Columbian and Hudsonian?					

SUCCESSOR BASINS AND FOREDEEPS

Deformed and undeformed immature clastics derived from mountain belts and deposited in troughs along the mountain front (fd), or in basins and troughs within the mountain belt (sb); may also include carbonates, evaporites, craton derived clastics and volcanics.

Csb' Cfd' (K,T)	Efd (T)	Asb,MAsb (M,P,P)	Hsb (A)
Csb Cfd (J,K)	Esb, EEsb (P,P,M)	Asb' (P)	
	MEsb (P)	Afd (S,D)	
	Efd (D)	A'fd (O)	

PERICRATONIC BELTS

Deformed and partly metamorphosed sedimentary and volcanic rocks deposited along the craton border on the continental shelf, slope and rise, or in troughs. (m) carbonates, evaporites, shale, siltstone, orthoquartzite; (m') m with immature clastics or glacial deposits; (m") m with gabbro sills and volcanics; (mi) m with iron formation; (h) autochthonous homocline of m beneath or beyond deformation (f) shale, siltstone, greywacke, flysch, turbidite, (vb) f with tholeiitic basalt flows and gabbro sills; (ub) ultrabasic sills.

Cm (P,T)	Em (P)	Am (C,O)	Gh (N)	Hh,H'h (A)
Cm (H)	Em' (H,C)	A'm (C,O)	GHh (A)	Hm,'Hmi, Hmf,Hmif (A)
Cm', Cmi (H)	E'm (C,O,S)	A'm' (H)	Gm", Gm (N,P) (A)	H'm,H'm" (A)
Cf (P)	Ef (C,O,S,D)	A'f, Af (CO)		Hf, H'f (A)
CEf (H,P)		A'vb (C,O)		Hvb (A)
CRmf (H)		Aub (O)		Hub (A)

SUBOCEANIC VOLCANIC BELTS

Deformed and metamorphosed volcanic and sedimentary rocks accumulated in suboceanic basins and volcanic arcs; may include oceanic crust. (v) basic to acidic volcanic flows and pyroclastics with gabbro and ultrabasic sills and subvolcanic plutons; (s) shale, siltstone, greywacke, flysch, turbidite, chert, iron formation, carbonates; (vr) acidic volcanics and immature clastics; (o) ophiolite sequence; (ub) ultrabasic sills.

Cvs (T,J)	Evs (O,S,D)	Avs (O,S,D)	Hvs (A)	Kvs, Kv (A)
C'vs (P,P)	Eub (O)	Avr (S,D)		Kub
Cvs (D,C)		A'vs (C,O)		
Cub (T,J) C'ub (P,P)		Avs (H)		
Cub (D,C,)		Ao, Aub (H)		

PLUTONIC BELTS

Intensely deformed and metamorphosed sedimentary and volcanic rocks and granitic intrusions forming the core zone of orogenic belts. (n) schist and gneiss; (gn) migmatic and granitic gneiss, including undifferentiated older and younger rocks; (nh) granulites; (g) granite, including plutons in other belts; (y) syenite and mangerite; (a) anorthosite and gabbro.

Cg (M,T) CEg (D) CRg (H)	Eg (D)	Ag (D) A'g (O) Ag (H)	Gg,Gy (N)	Ey,Eg (P)	Kg (A)
C'gn (P, M,T)	En (H)	An (C,O,S,D)	Gn (H,P)	Ea (P)	Kgn (A)
C'n (P,M)		A'n (H,C?)		Hg,H'g(A)	Kn (A)
Cn (H,H,P)		An (H?)		Hgn, H'gn (A)	Kg (A)
Cgn (H)				Hnh (A)	Kgn (A)
				Hn, H'n (A)	Ka (A)
					Knh (A)

BASEMENT

Deformed and/or isotopic age modified crystalline rocks forming sialic continental crust beneath younger sedimentary and volcanic sequences (lithological assemblages designated as above).

CHgn (A?)		AGgn (H or older)	GEy (P)	Hg (A or A)	Kgn (A)
			GEa (P)	Hgn (A or A)	
			Gg (H or older)	Hn (A or A)	
			Ggn (H or older)	Hnh (A or A)	
			GHgn (A)	Ha (A or A)	
			GHn (A)	HKg (A)	
			GKg (A)	HKgn, (A)	
			GKgn (A)	HKn (A)	
			GKnh (A)	HKnh (A)	
			GKvs (A)	HKvs (A) Hvs (A or A)	

CRATONIC REGIONS

The rocks of the cratonic regions are designated according to the geological age of their accumulation (capital letters) and major lithological assemblage (lower case letters).

PLATFORMAL DEPOSITS

Flat-lying or little deformed cover
Indigenous Deposits: (i) limestone, dolomite, salt, gypsum deposited in situ on cratons

Di,SDi	Oi, OSi, COi, COSi,	Hi, IPi, Hi, Ai,

Clastic Deposits: (q) orthoquartzite, shale, conglomerate derived from cratons and deposited on the craton; (q') includes immature clastics and glacial deposits.

Kq, Jq, Dq, Cq, Hq, IPq, Hq, Aq, Aq', Pq

Exogeosynclinal Deposits: (e) shale, siltstone, sandstone, conglomerate derived from orogenic belts and deposited on the craton (names of orogenic events given in brackets).

Te (Laramide)	Ke (Columbian, Laramide)
De (Acadian, Ellesmerian)	Oe (Taconian)

PLATFORMAL IGNEOUS ROCKS

Volcanic Rocks: (vt) tholeiitic basalt extruded on cratons and partly stabilized orogenic belts

Tvt, Kvt, Hvt, Nvt,	* volcano

Hypabyssal Basic and Ultrabasic Intrusions: (b) gabbroic sills and (d) dykes intrusive into cratonic cover, basement and stabilized orogenic belts; (bh) norite; (ub) ultrabasic

Hb, Nb, Nub, Ab, Abh	Kd, Td, Hd, Hd, Ad

Hypabyssal Alkaline Intrusions:
* carbonatite, syenite, alkaline gabbro pipe

TAPHROGENIC DEPOSITS

(t) immature clastics deposited in fault bounded trough
(tb) with tholeiitic basalt flows and gabbro sills
(ta) with acidic and porphyritic volcanics

Tt, Ht, Ht	Ttb, Tttb, Ntb. Atb	KTta, Jta, IPta, Ata, Ata

Sediments (CSs) and volcanic... plains and the continental se... dering the present continental... underwater CONTIN...

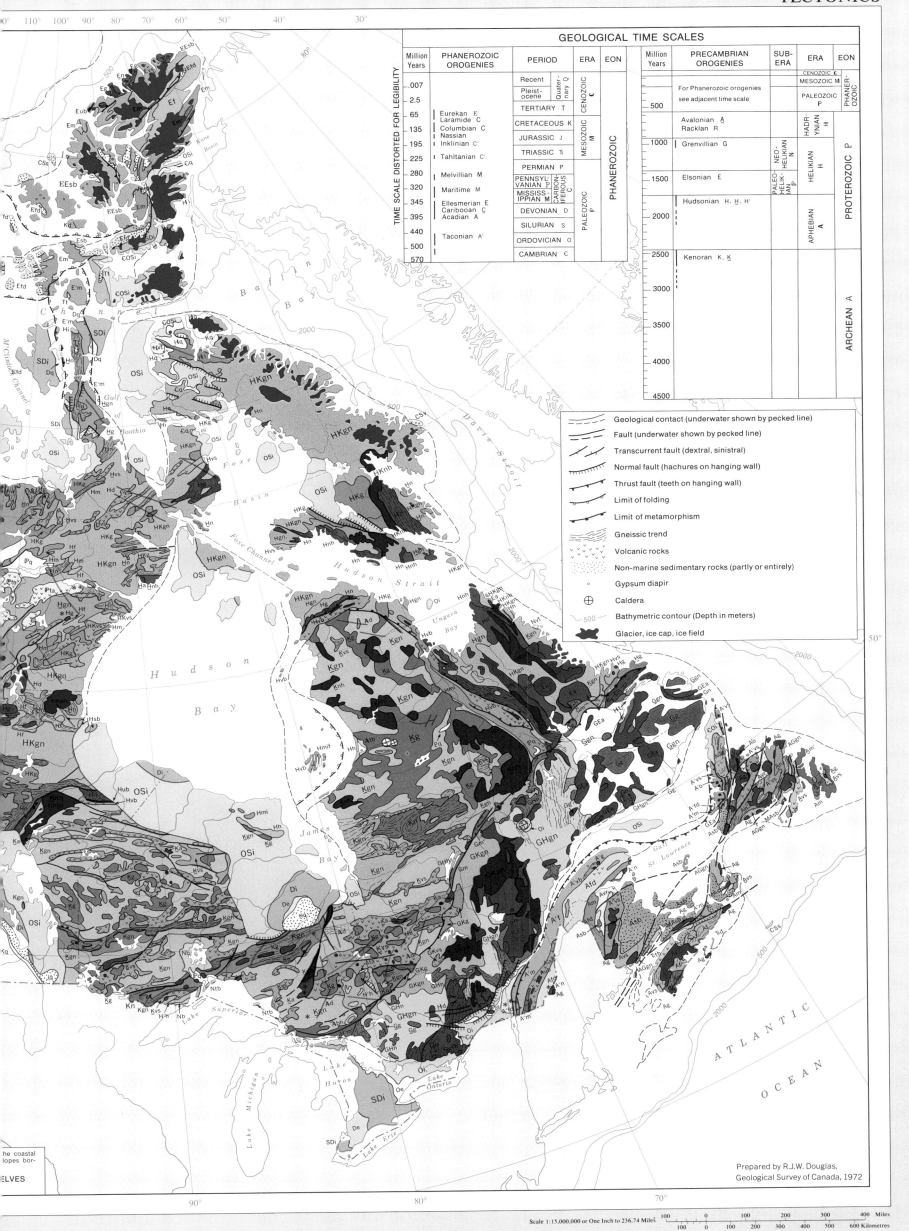

GEOLOGICAL TIME SCALES

Million Years	PHANEROZOIC OROGENIES	PERIOD	ERA	EON
.007		Recent		
2.5		Pleistocene	Quaternary Q	CENOZOIC C
65	Eurekan E	TERTIARY T		
135	Laramide C	CRETACEOUS K		
195	Columbian C / Nassian	JURASSIC J	MESOZOIC M	
225	Inklinian C'	TRIASSIC Tr		PHANEROZOIC
280	Tahltanian C'	PERMIAN P		
320	Melvillian M	PENNSYLVANIAN P	CARBONIFEROUS C	
345	Maritime M	MISSISSIPPIAN M		
395	Ellesmerian E / Caribooan C	DEVONIAN D	PALEOZOIC P	
440	Acadian A	SILURIAN S		
500	Taconian A'	ORDOVICIAN O		
570		CAMBRIAN C		

TIME SCALE DISTORTED FOR LEGIBILITY

Million Years	PRECAMBRIAN OROGENIES	SUB-ERA	ERA	EON
	For Phanerozoic orogenies see adjacent time scale		CENOZOIC C	PHANEROZOIC P
500			MESOZOIC M	
	Avalonian A / Racklan R		PALEOZOIC P	
1000	Grenvillian G	NEO-HELIKIAN N	HADRYNIAN H	
1500	Elsonian E	PALEO-HELIKIAN P	HELIKIAN H	PROTEROZOIC P
2000	Hudsonian H, H', H'		APHEBIAN A	
2500	Kenoran K, K'			
3000				
3500			ARCHEAN A	
4000				
4500				

Geological contact (underwater shown by pecked line)
Fault (underwater shown by pecked line)
Transcurrent fault (dextral, sinistral)
Normal fault (hachures on hanging wall)
Thrust fault (teeth on hanging wall)
Limit of folding
Limit of metamorphism
Gneissic trend
Volcanic rocks
Non-marine sedimentary rocks (partly or entirely)
○ Gypsum diapir
⊕ Caldera
500 Bathymetric contour (Depth in meters)
Glacier, ice cap, ice field

Prepared by R.J.W. Douglas,
Geological Survey of Canada, 1972

Scale 1:15,000,000 or One Inch to 236.74 Miles

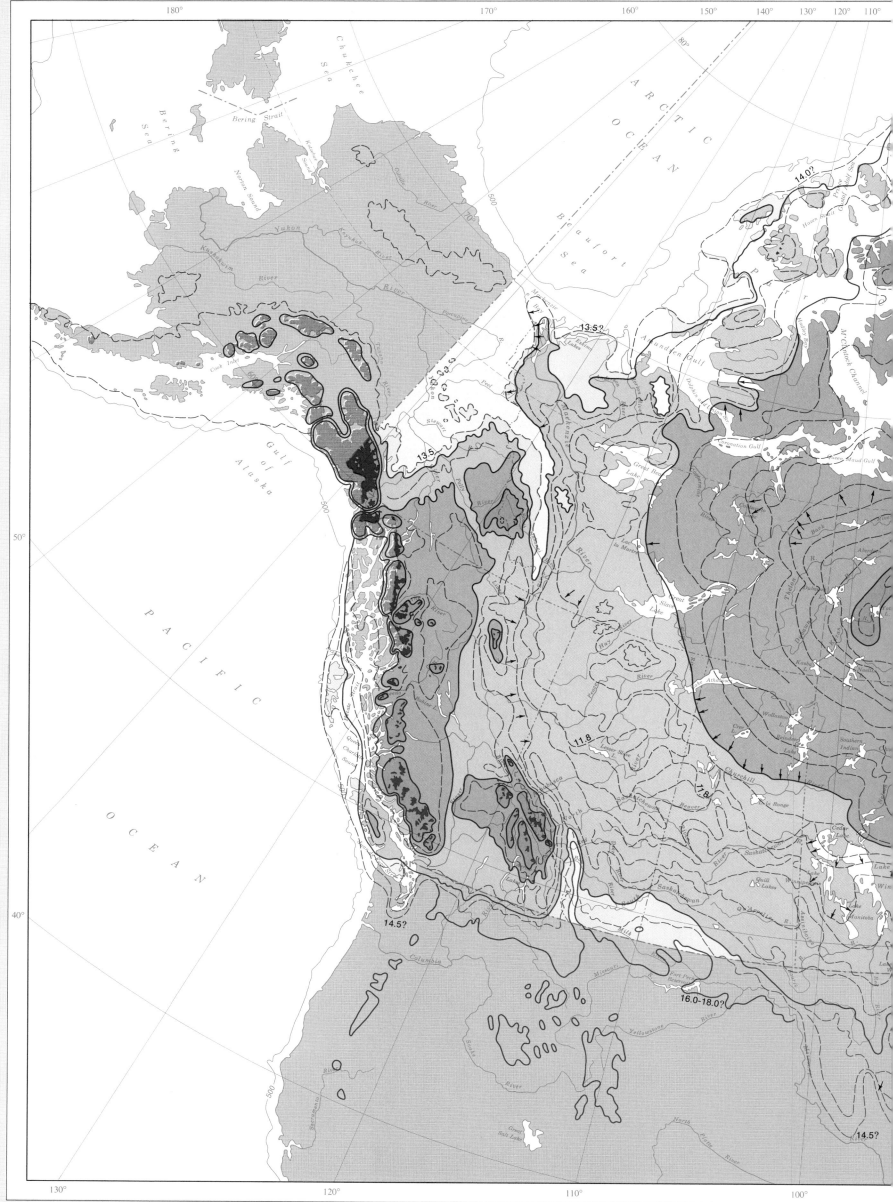

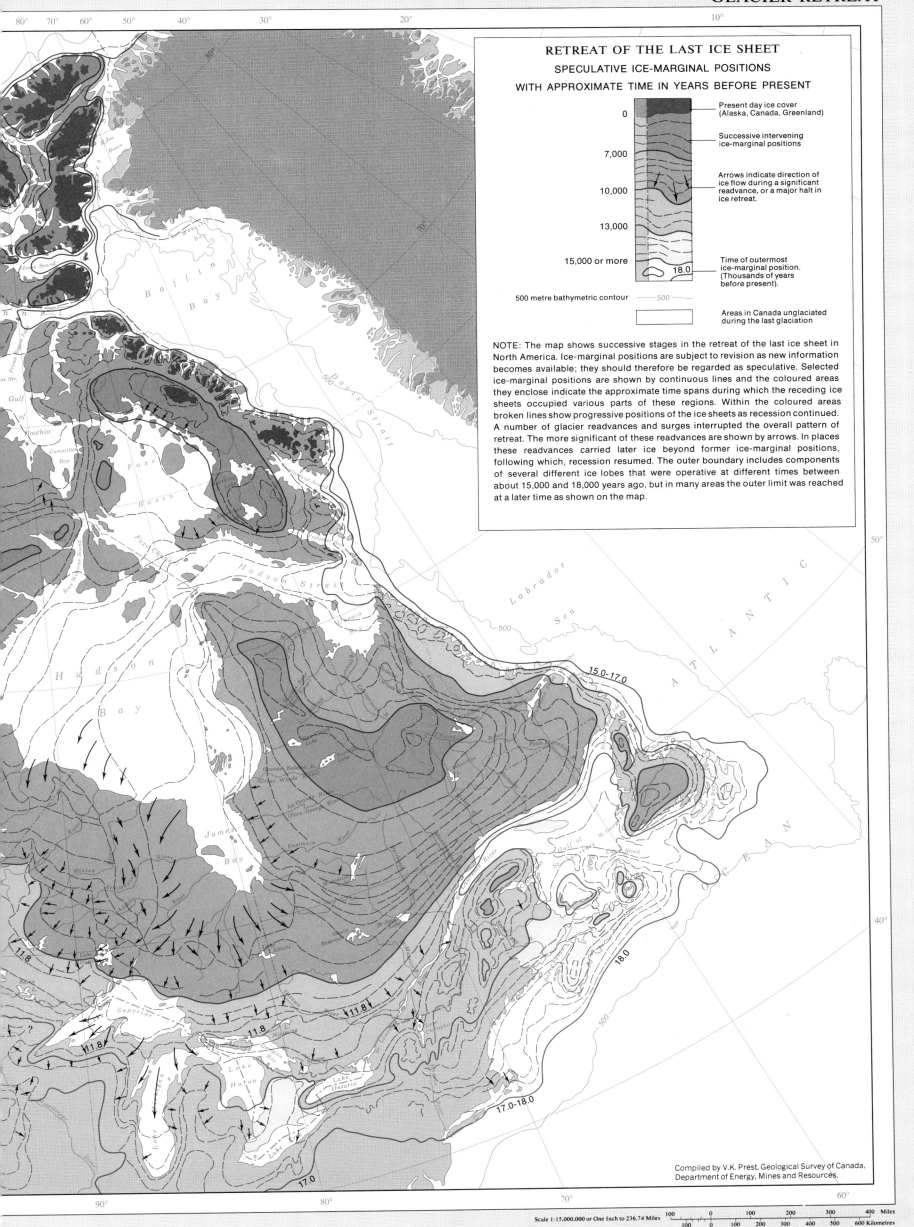

RETREAT OF THE LAST ICE SHEET
SPECULATIVE ICE-MARGINAL POSITIONS
WITH APPROXIMATE TIME IN YEARS BEFORE PRESENT

0 — Present day ice cover
(Alaska, Canada, Greenland)

— Successive intervening
ice-marginal positions

7,000

Arrows indicate direction of
ice flow during a significant
readvance, or a major halt in
ice retreat.

10,000

13,000

15,000 or more

18.0 — Time of outermost
ice-marginal position.
(Thousands of years
before present).

500 metre bathymetric contour ——— 500

Areas in Canada unglaciated
during the last glaciation

NOTE: The map shows successive stages in the retreat of the last ice sheet in
North America. Ice-marginal positions are subject to revision as new information
becomes available; they should therefore be regarded as speculative. Selected
ice-marginal positions are shown by continuous lines and the coloured areas
they enclose indicate the approximate time spans during which the receding ice
sheets occupied various parts of these regions. Within the coloured areas
broken lines show progressive positions of the ice sheets as recession continued.
A number of glacier readvances and surges interrupted the overall pattern of
retreat. The more significant of these readvances are shown by arrows. In places
these readvances carried later ice beyond former ice-marginal positions,
following which, recession resumed. The outer boundary includes components
of several different ice lobes that were operative at different times between
about 15,000 and 18,000 years ago, but in many areas the outer limit was reached
at a later time as shown on the map.

Compiled by V.K. Prest, Geological Survey of Canada,
Department of Energy, Mines and Resources.

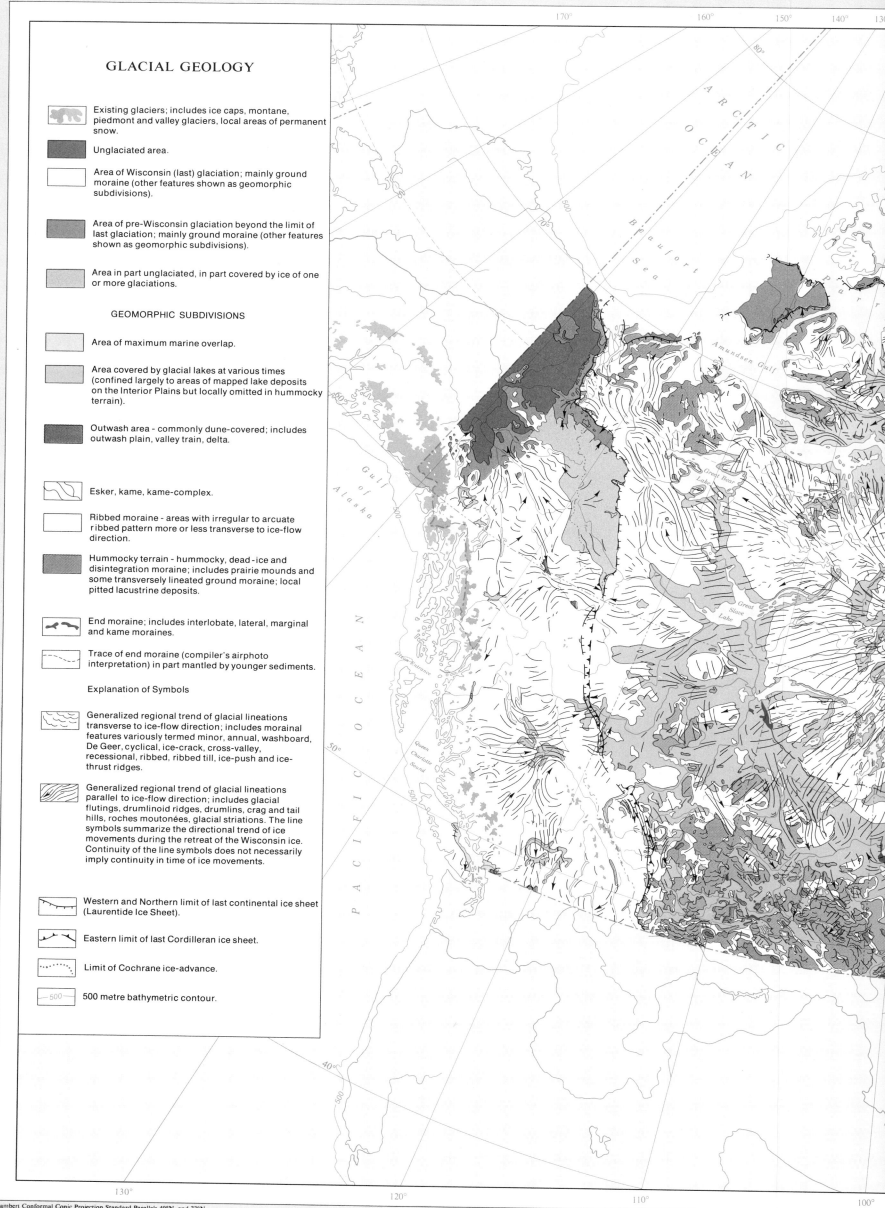

GLACIAL GEOLOGY

Existing glaciers; includes ice caps, montane, piedmont and valley glaciers, local areas of permanent snow.

Unglaciated area.

Area of Wisconsin (last) glaciation; mainly ground moraine (other features shown as geomorphic subdivisions).

Area of pre-Wisconsin glaciation beyond the limit of last glaciation; mainly ground moraine (other features shown as geomorphic subdivisions).

Area in part unglaciated, in part covered by ice of one or more glaciations.

GEOMORPHIC SUBDIVISIONS

Area of maximum marine overlap.

Area covered by glacial lakes at various times (confined largely to areas of mapped lake deposits on the Interior Plains but locally omitted in hummocky terrain).

Outwash area - commonly dune-covered; includes outwash plain, valley train, delta.

Esker, kame, kame-complex.

Ribbed moraine - areas with irregular to arcuate ribbed pattern more or less transverse to ice-flow direction.

Hummocky terrain - hummocky, dead-ice and disintegration moraine; includes prairie mounds and some transversely lineated ground moraine; local pitted lacustrine deposits.

End moraine; includes interlobate, lateral, marginal and kame moraines.

Trace of end moraine (compiler's airphoto interpretation) in part mantled by younger sediments.

Explanation of Symbols

Generalized regional trend of glacial lineations transverse to ice-flow direction; includes morainal features variously termed minor, annual, washboard, De Geer, cyclical, ice-crack, cross-valley, recessional, ribbed, ribbed till, ice-push and ice-thrust ridges.

Generalized regional trend of glacial lineations parallel to ice-flow direction; includes glacial flutings, drumlinoid ridges, drumlins, crag and tail hills, roches moutonées, glacial striations. The line symbols summarize the directional trend of ice movements during the retreat of the Wisconsin ice. Continuity of the line symbols does not necessarily imply continuity in time of ice movements.

Western and Northern limit of last continental ice sheet (Laurentide Ice Sheet).

Eastern limit of last Cordilleran ice sheet.

Limit of Cochrane ice-advance.

500 — 500 metre bathymetric contour.

Modified from 'Glacial Map of Canada' (1253A, 1968) compiled
1964-66 by V.K. Prest, D.R. Grant, and V.N. Rampton, Geological
Survey of Canada.

Scale 1:15,000,000 or One Inch to 236.74 Miles

POST-GLACIAL REBOUND

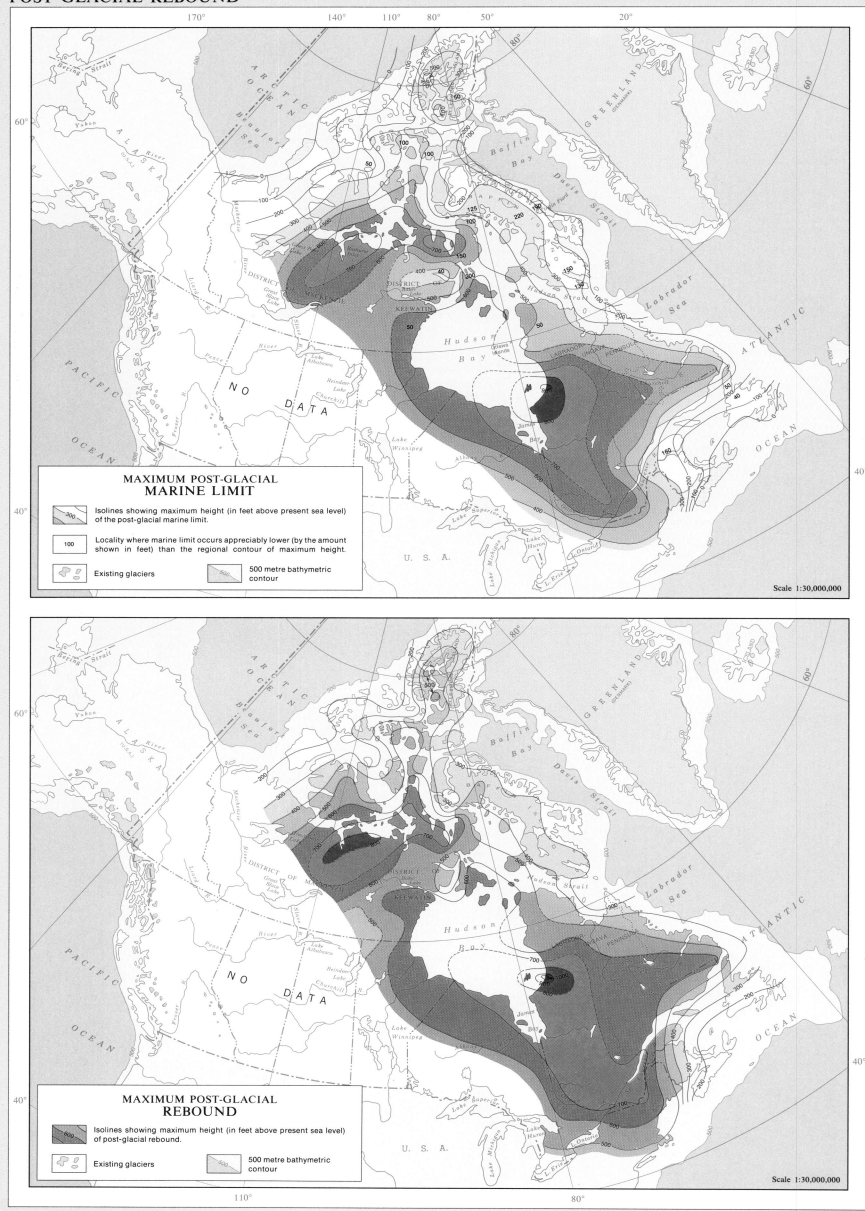

MAXIMUM POST-GLACIAL MARINE LIMIT

Isolines showing maximum height (in feet above present sea level) of the post-glacial marine limit.

100 — Locality where marine limit occurs appreciably lower (by the amount shown in feet) than the regional contour of maximum height.

Existing glaciers

500 metre bathymetric contour

Scale 1:30,000,000

MAXIMUM POST-GLACIAL REBOUND

Isolines showing maximum height (in feet above present sea level) of post-glacial rebound.

Existing glaciers

500 metre bathymetric contour

Scale 1:30,000,000

Lambert Conformal Conic Projection Standard Parallels 49°N. and 77°N.

THE NATIONAL ATLAS OF CANADA

POST-GLACIAL REBOUND

It may be difficult to think of the earth's crust being sufficiently flexible that it can be depressed by a heavy load. However, there is conclusive evidence that the earth's crust does respond in this way and moreover, as the load is removed the crust rebounds. Striking results of this response are seen in coastal areas of Canada where marine shells and ancient sea beaches can be found at various heights up to 930 feet above the present sea-level. What is the cause of this movement? It is accepted that during the last glaciation a considerable area of Canada and the northern United States was covered by a large ice cap. Thus, approximately 18,000 years ago, Canada could be compared with Antarctica or Greenland today. The growth of huge ice sheets required a considerable volume of water to be removed from the oceans. It has been estimated that at the maximum of the last glaciation, world sea level was 360 feet lower than today. By comparing the size of the oceans and volume of water removed it has also been estimated that the ice sheet over Canada had an average thickness of about 8,200 feet. At the centre of the ice cap the ice may have attained a depth of 15,000 feet.

The transfer and addition of this mass was enough to cause the earth's crust to sink. Opinions vary as to the amount of depression and estimates range from one quarter to one third of the overlying ice thickness, implying that the maximum depression due to the ice load ranged between 3,750 and 5,000 feet. However, as soon as the ice cap began to thin and retreat, the earth's crust started to rebound towards a new equilibrium. Thus part of the glacially controlled rebound (or glacio-isostatic rebound) occurred while the ice still covered the coastal areas. But in some places ice retreat exposed the coasts and the sea impinged on the depressed land surface. This upper level of marine action is called the "Marine Limit". It was formed at different times at different sites, varying from 13,000 years ago to less than 5,000 years ago in parts of Arctic Canada. Between the time that each marine limit was formed and today, rebound has occurred so that the marine limit is some height above present sea-level.

The marine limit elevation reflects only part of the post-glacial uplift or rebound. During the period of glacier melting and retreat, water was transferred back to the oceans and sea-level gradually rose. Ten thousand years ago sea-level is estimated to have been 100 feet lower than today. Suppose the sea cut a marine limit 10,000 years ago and that today this feature is 200 feet above sea-level. In this time sea-level has risen 100 feet, therefore the total post-glacial rebound would be 200 plus 100 or 300 feet.

At one time it was thought that the altitude of the marine limit gradually increased towards a centre near James Bay. However, research in the last decade indicates that the elevation of the marine limit can vary greatly in a few miles. This pattern is caused by differences in the rate of glacier retreat. Where the ice has been slow to retreat, thus preventing incursion by the sea, marine limits are relatively low compared to neighbouring areas.

There are now many hundreds of observations on the elevations of the marine limit throughout Canada and the maps presented here provide a generalized depiction of the varying height of this feature. In order to produce the map of the marine limit a grid was laid over a base map on which were plotted the known heights and locations of marine limit observations. A template was placed on 125 grid intersections. Approximately 33 percent of the country was sampled in this way. At each grid intersection the maximum marine limit elevation in the area covered by the template was plotted (the template covered 94 x 94 miles). The resulting network of points was then contoured.

Data is available only for coastal sites, hence the contours over parts of the Labrador-Ungava peninsula and the Districts of Keewatin and Mackenzie are interpretations. A note was made of sites where the marine limit is appreciably lower than the maximum value (see map), thus indicating the location of late lying ice masses. The resulting surface shows the *maximum post-glacial marine limit* for part of Canada. At each of the 125 grid intersections an addition was made for the estimated amount of eustatic sea-level rise since the time of marine limit formation, and a map of *maximum post-glacial rebound* was constructed. In both cases the maps show the *highest* possible marine limit or rebound. Some areas lying along a particular contour might for various reasons lie below a regional contour value. As the peripheral areas of the ice cap were freed from ice first, they have the largest sea-level correction; therefore, the main difference in the two contoured surfaces is that the post-glacial rebound surface has a lower gradient and is higher.

The maps show three centres of post-glacial rebound. The first is located north of James Bay; the second occurs over Bathurst Inlet and the third is centred over western Ellesmere Island. Two small, low cells are located over northwest Baffin Island and in the vicinity of Baker Lake. Elsewhere, the contours on both surfaces indicate an increase in post-glacial rebound and in the elevation of the marine limit towards the two main high zones.

The maps support the concept that the crustal rebound is related to glacial loading. The amount of post-glacial rebound is least on the margins of the former ice cap and increases towards the centre where the ice thickness was greatest. After the formation of a marine limit, emergence was at first very rapid and then became progressively slower as illustrated in the graphs below.

The curve on the left is from central Hudson Bay, that on the right is from east Baffin Island. Note that in the last 7,000 years Hudson Bay has emerged approximately 425 feet whereas east Baffin Island has emerged 130 feet. Curves such as the ones below are obtained by radio-carbon dating marine shells, whalebone, peats and driftwood found at various elevations below the marine limit.

J.T. Andrews.

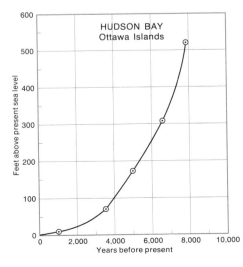

POST-GLACIAL LAND EMERGENCE
The graphs show land emergence in two areas during the last 9,000 years. The age of ancient organic material, collected from raised beaches at various heights, is plotted against the elevation (above present sea level) at which it is now found, thus indicating the form of land emergence.

⊙   Radio-carbon dated material

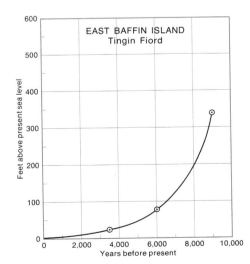

SURFACE MATERIALS

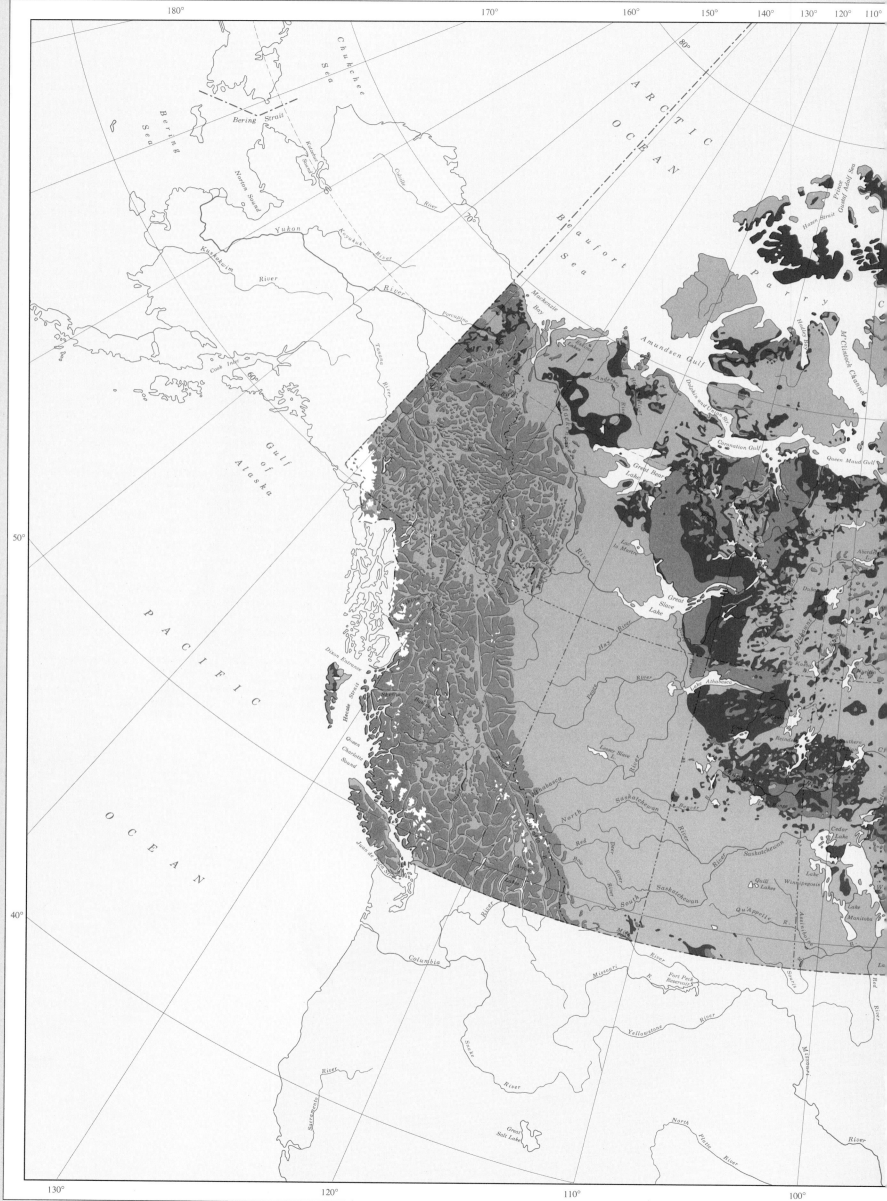

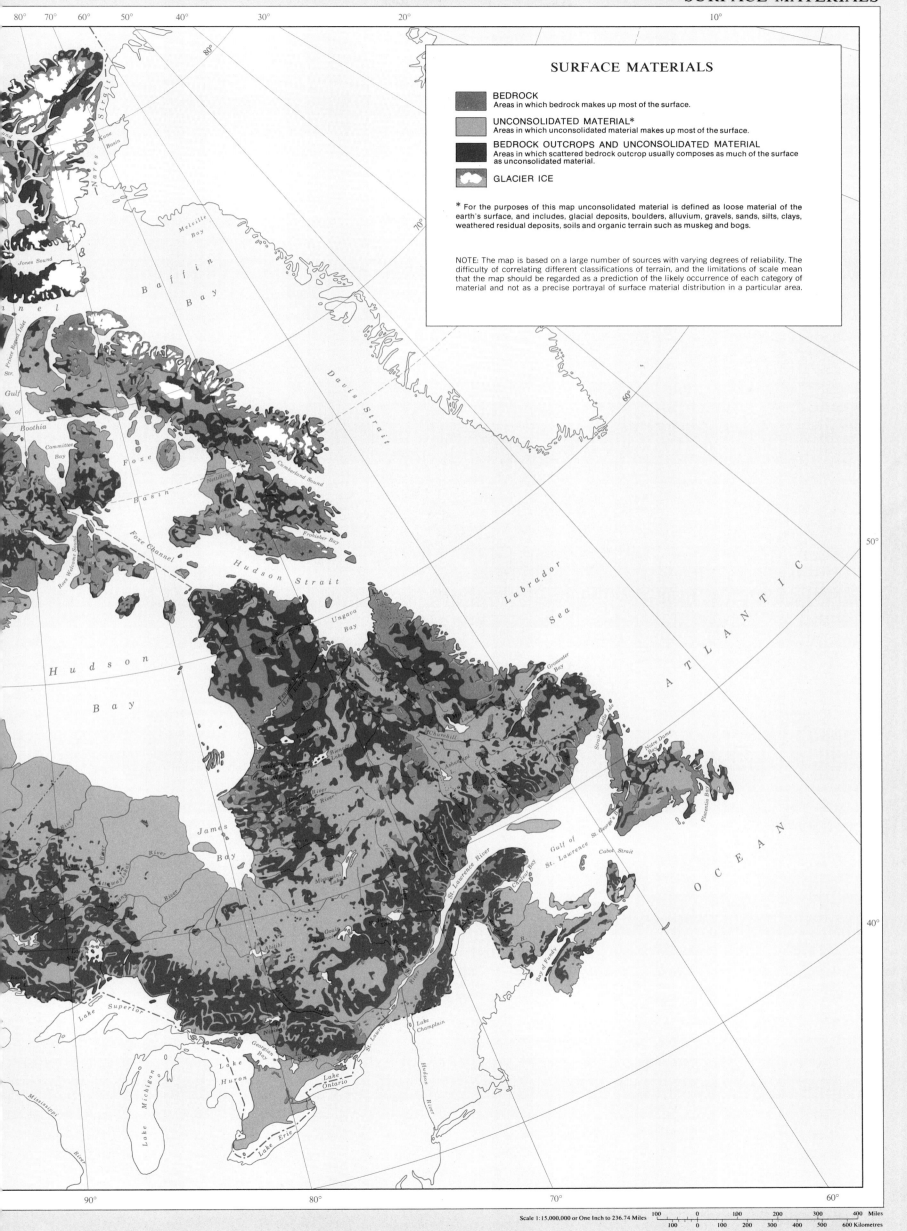

SURFACE MATERIALS

BEDROCK
Areas in which bedrock makes up most of the surface.

UNCONSOLIDATED MATERIAL*
Areas in which unconsolidated material makes up most of the surface.

BEDROCK OUTCROPS AND UNCONSOLIDATED MATERIAL
Areas in which scattered bedrock outcrop usually composes as much of the surface as unconsolidated material.

GLACIER ICE

* For the purposes of this map unconsolidated material is defined as loose material of the earth's surface, and includes, glacial deposits, boulders, alluvium, gravels, sands, silts, clays, weathered residual deposits, soils and organic terrain such as muskeg and bogs.

NOTE: The map is based on a large number of sources with varying degrees of reliability. The difficulty of correlating different classifications of terrain, and the limitations of scale mean that the map should be regarded as a prediction of the likely occurrence of each category of material and not as a precise portrayal of surface material distribution in a particular area.

Scale 1:15,000,000 or One Inch to 236.74 Miles

100   0   100   200   300   400 Miles

100 0   100   200   300   400   500   600 Kilometres

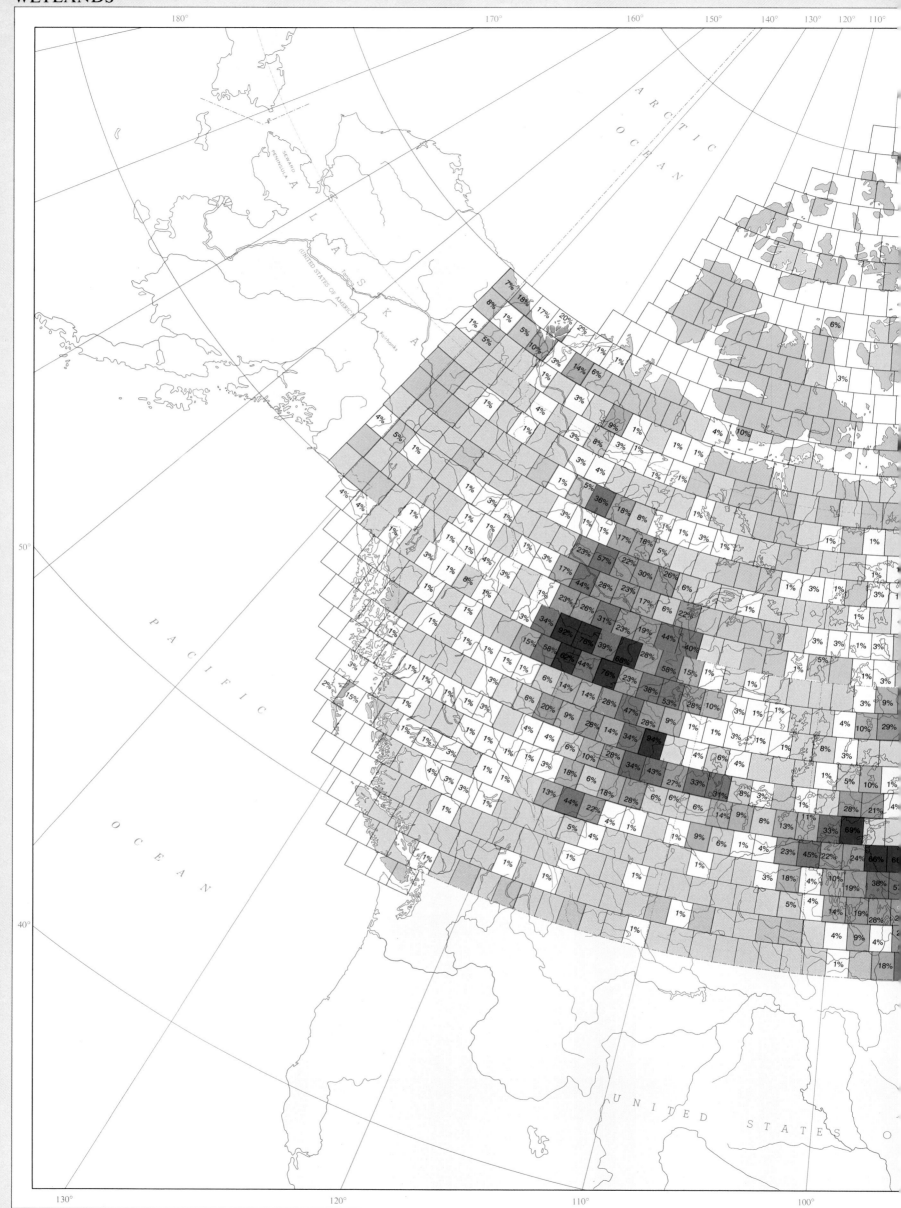

Lambert Conformal Conic Projection Standard Parallels 49°N. and 77°N.

THE NATIONAL ATLAS OF CANADA

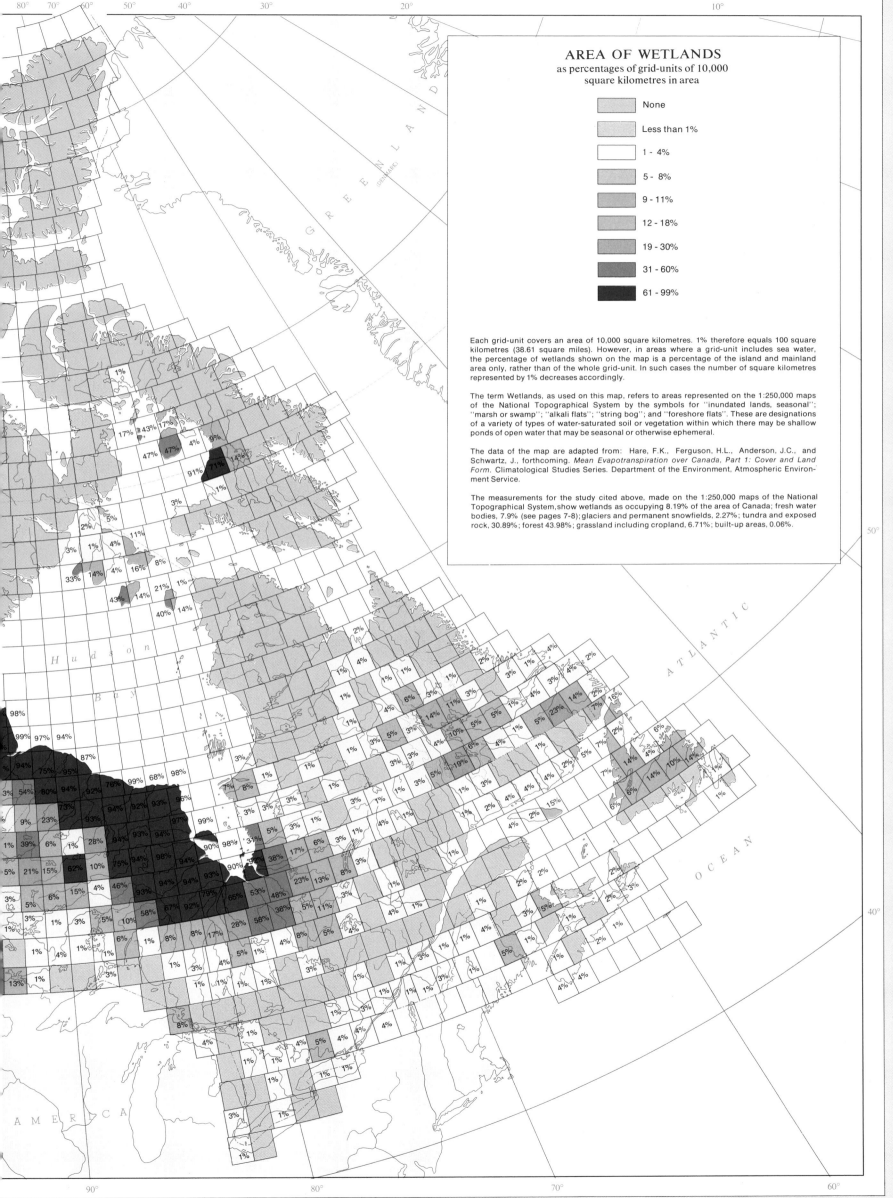

AREA OF WETLANDS
as percentages of grid-units of 10,000
square kilometres in area

	None
	Less than 1%
	1 - 4%
	5 - 8%
	9 - 11%
	12 - 18%
	19 - 30%
	31 - 60%
	61 - 99%

Each grid-unit covers an area of 10,000 square kilometres. 1% therefore equals 100 square kilometres (38.61 square miles). However, in areas where a grid-unit includes sea water, the percentage of wetlands shown on the map is a percentage of the island and mainland area only, rather than of the whole grid-unit. In such cases the number of square kilometres represented by 1% decreases accordingly.

The term Wetlands, as used on this map, refers to areas represented on the 1:250,000 maps of the National Topographical System by the symbols for ''inundated lands, seasonal''; ''marsh or swamp''; ''alkali flats''; ''string bog''; and ''foreshore flats''. These are designations of a variety of types of water-saturated soil or vegetation within which there may be shallow ponds of open water that may be seasonal or otherwise ephemeral.

The data of the map are adapted from: Hare, F.K., Ferguson, H.L., Anderson, J.C., and Schwartz, J., forthcoming. *Mean Evapotranspiration over Canada, Part 1: Cover and Land Form*. Climatological Studies Series. Department of the Environment, Atmospheric Environment Service.

The measurements for the study cited above, made on the 1:250,000 maps of the National Topographical System, show wetlands as occupying 8.19% of the area of Canada; fresh water bodies, 7.9% (see pages 7-8); glaciers and permanent snowfields, 2.27%; tundra and exposed rock, 30.89%; forest 43.98%; grassland including cropland, 6.71%; built-up areas, 0.06%.

SOIL PROFILES

A particular soil is recognized by identifying the various soil layers that make up its vertical cross-section or profile. These layers, known as 'horizons', occur approximately parallel to the land surface and each soil horizon differs from adjacent genetically related layers in properties such as, colour, structure, texture, consistency and chemical, biological and mineralogical composition.

The diagrams of soil profiles shown here depict the general horizon characteristics of the soils shown on the map.

Key to code letters used in the soil profile diagrams

ORGANIC LAYERS

L	Of
F	Om
H	Oh

L-F-H - well drained decomposing plant litter
  L - slightly decomposed, F - moderately decomposed,
  H - well decomposed
O - poorly drained decomposing peat and moss layers
  Of - *fibric* - slightly decomposed, Om - *mesic* - moderately decomposed, Oh - *humic* - well decomposed
A - organic-mineral horizons at or near the surface.

A HORIZONS

Ah
Ae   Ap

  Ah - dark-coloured, humus-rich horizon
  Ae - light-coloured, bleached and eluviated by removal of clay, iron, alumina or organic matter.
  Ap - horizons markedly disturbed by cultivation or pasture

AB   BA   AB,BA - horizons transitional to A and B
B - a mineral horizon differing from A and C by the following characteristics:

B HORIZONS

Bm
Bt
Bn
Bf
Bh
Bg

  m - colour or structure
  t - a significant accumulation of clay
  n - a columnar structure, hard consistence and significantly high exchangeable sodium.
  f - a significant accumulation of iron
  h - a significant accumulation of illuvial organic matter.
  g - a significant expression of gleying[1] with dull colours and mottles

BC   BC - a horizon transitional to B and C

C HORIZONS

Cca
Csa
Cg
Cs
Ck
C

C - a horizon comparatively unaffected by soil-forming processes, except for:
  ca - an accumulation of lime carbonate.
  sa - an accumulation of soluble salts.
  g - a significant expression of gleying[1] with dull colours and mottles
  s - the presence of salts.
  k - the presence of lime carbonate.

[1] "Gleying" or gleysation refers to a soil-forming process operating under poor drainage conditions which results in the reduction of iron and other elements and in gray colours, and mottles.

Note: The lower case code letters shown above in the B and C horizons are sometimes combined in the diagrams to express combinations of characteristics.

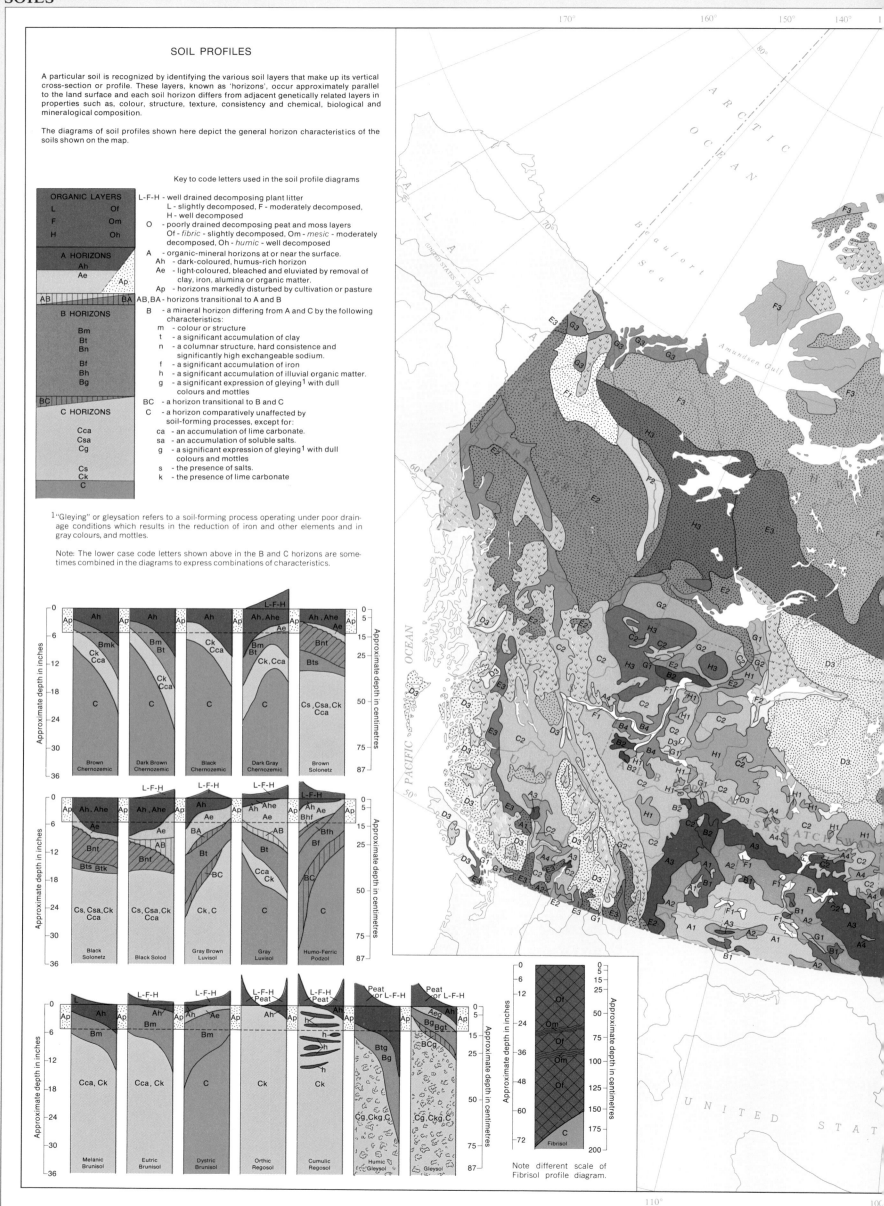

Note different scale of Fibrisol profile diagram.

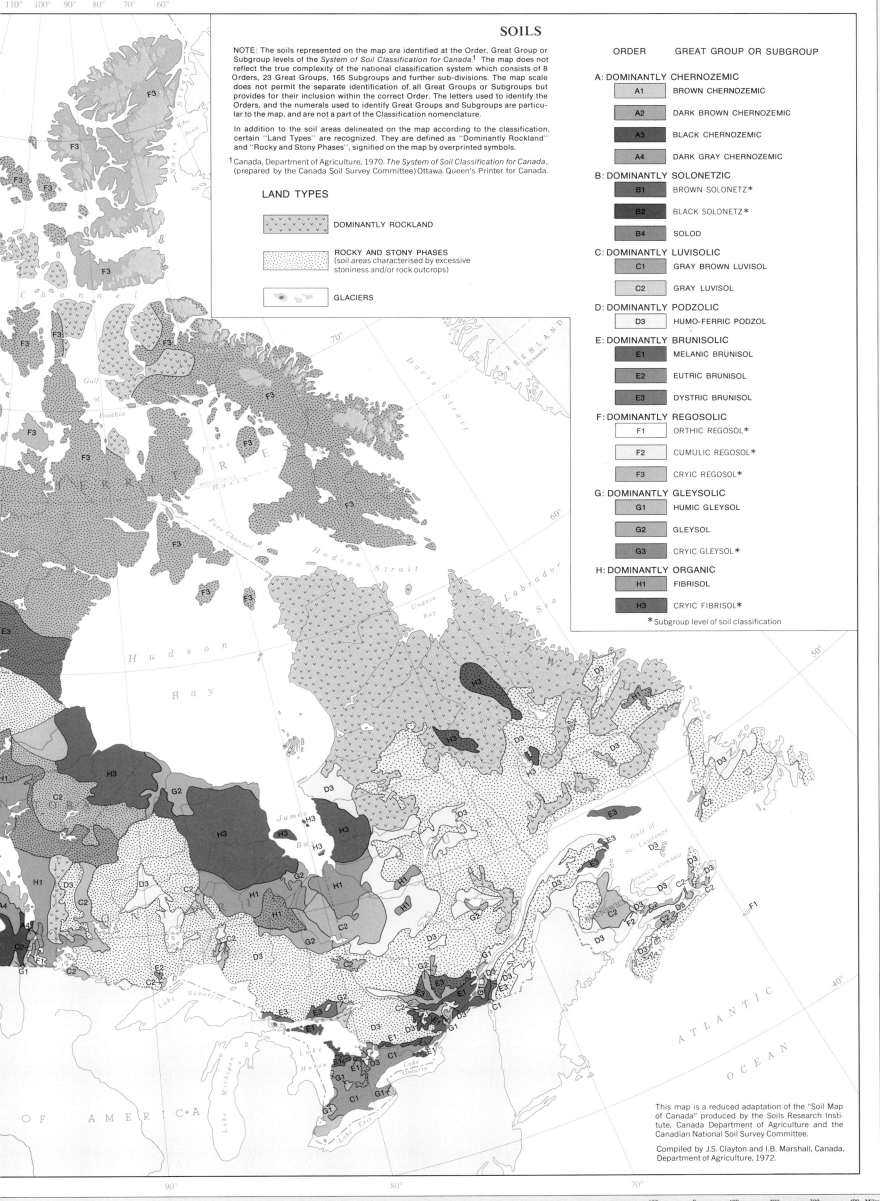

SOILS

NOTE: The soils represented on the map are identified at the Order, Great Group or Subgroup levels of the *System of Soil Classification for Canada*.[1] The map does not reflect the true complexity of the national classification system which consists of 8 Orders, 23 Great Groups, 165 Subgroups and further sub-divisions. The map scale does not permit the separate identification of all Great Groups or Subgroups but provides for their inclusion within the correct Order. The letters used to identify the Orders, and the numerals used to identify Great Groups and Subgroups are particular to the map, and are not a part of the Classification nomenclature.

In addition to the soil areas delineated on the map according to the classification, certain "Land Types" are recognized. They are defined as "Dominantly Rockland" and "Rocky and Stony Phases", signified on the map by overprinted symbols.

[1] Canada, Department of Agriculture, 1970. *The System of Soil Classification for Canada*, (prepared by the Canada Soil Survey Committee) Ottawa. Queen's Printer for Canada.

LAND TYPES

DOMINANTLY ROCKLAND

ROCKY AND STONY PHASES
(soil areas characterised by excessive stoniness and/or rock outcrops)

GLACIERS

ORDER	GREAT GROUP OR SUBGROUP
A: DOMINANTLY CHERNOZEMIC	
A1	BROWN CHERNOZEMIC
A2	DARK BROWN CHERNOZEMIC
A3	BLACK CHERNOZEMIC
A4	DARK GRAY CHERNOZEMIC
B: DOMINANTLY SOLONETZIC	
B1	BROWN SOLONETZ*
B2	BLACK SOLONETZ*
B4	SOLOD
C: DOMINANTLY LUVISOLIC	
C1	GRAY BROWN LUVISOL
C2	GRAY LUVISOL
D: DOMINANTLY PODZOLIC	
D3	HUMO-FERRIC PODZOL
E: DOMINANTLY BRUNISOLIC	
E1	MELANIC BRUNISOL
E2	EUTRIC BRUNISOL
E3	DYSTRIC BRUNISOL
F: DOMINANTLY REGOSOLIC	
F1	ORTHIC REGOSOL*
F2	CUMULIC REGOSOL*
F3	CRYIC REGOSOL*
G: DOMINANTLY GLEYSOLIC	
G1	HUMIC GLEYSOL
G2	GLEYSOL
G3	CRYIC GLEYSOL*
H: DOMINANTLY ORGANIC	
H1	FIBRISOL
H3	CRYIC FIBRISOL*

* Subgroup level of soil classification

This map is a reduced adaptation of the "Soil Map of Canada" produced by the Soils Research Institute, Canada Department of Agriculture and the Canadian National Soil Survey Committee.

Compiled by J.S. Clayton and I.B. Marshall, Canada, Department of Agriculture, 1972.

Scale 1:15,000,000 or One Inch to 236.74 Miles

100   0   100   200   300   400 Miles

100   0   100   200   300   400   500   600 Kilometres

SOIL CLIMATE

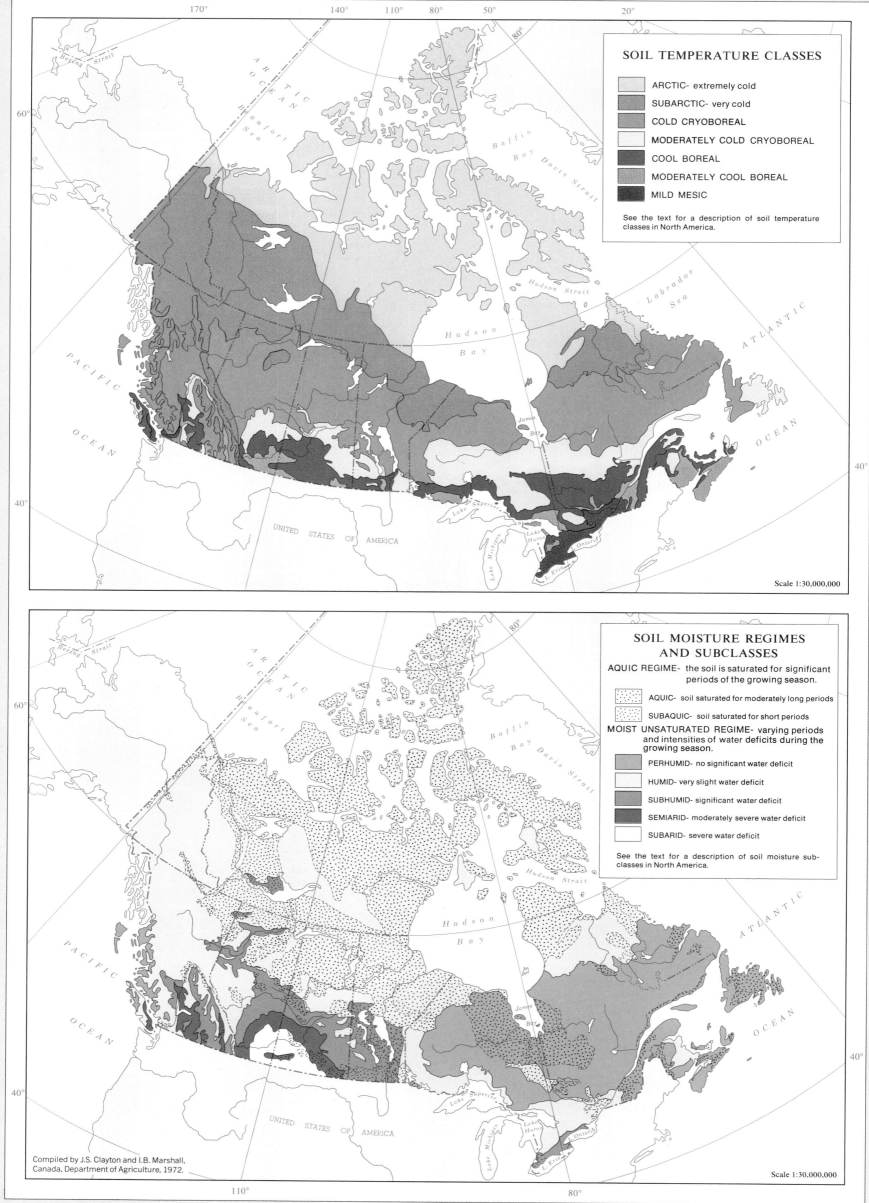

SOIL TEMPERATURE CLASSES

ARCTIC- extremely cold
SUBARCTIC- very cold
COLD CRYOBOREAL
MODERATELY COLD CRYOBOREAL
COOL BOREAL
MODERATELY COOL BOREAL
MILD MESIC

See the text for a description of soil temperature classes in North America.

Scale 1:30,000,000

SOIL MOISTURE REGIMES AND SUBCLASSES

AQUIC REGIME- the soil is saturated for significant periods of the growing season.

AQUIC- soil saturated for moderately long periods
SUBAQUIC- soil saturated for short periods

MOIST UNSATURATED REGIME- varying periods and intensities of water deficits during the growing season.

PERHUMID- no significant water deficit
HUMID- very slight water deficit
SUBHUMID- significant water deficit
SEMIARID- moderately severe water deficit
SUBARID- severe water deficit

See the text for a description of soil moisture subclasses in North America.

Compiled by J.S. Clayton and I.B. Marshall,
Canada, Department of Agriculture, 1972.

Scale 1:30,000,000

Lambert Conformal Conic Projection Standard Parallels 49°N. and 77°N.

THE NATIONAL ATLAS OF CANADA

THE SOIL CLIMATES OF CANADA

Many classification systems of climate emphasize the aerial biosphere and are based on direct interpretation of air temperatures and precipitation distributions together with probabilities of variable weather conditions. These factors do not account for the climate of the total plant environment, in which interaction takes place between the aerial climate associated with surface plant growth, and the soil climate relating to subaerial growth, root development, soil structure and the environment of the soil microflora and fauna. Soil climate responds to changes in aerial climate but these responses are affected in time and degree by the water content, depth, surface cover, landscape position, and man's manipulation of the soil.

The two maps on this sheet, one dealing with soil temperature, the other with soil moisture, together provide information for the delineation and designation of soil climates in Canada. The soil climates indicated for Canada are included within an overall classification for Canada and the United States, that is, the classification is continental in scope. It is based on the recognition of temperature and moisture conditions in the soil. The overall classification is outlined below. Five major temperatures classes, Arctic, Subarctic, Cryoboreal, Boreal and Mesic are recognized in Canada. Moisture subclasses are recognized on the basis of stated periods of saturation for the Aquic Regime and on calculations of increasing intensity and degree of moisture deficits during the growing season for the Moist Unsaturated Regime.

SOIL TEMPERATURE CLASSES

1 ARCTIC
EXTREMELY COLD. Mean annual soil temperature less than 20°F. Cold to very cool summer. Mean summer soil temperature less than 41°F. Regions in this class have continuous permafrost usually within a depth of 3 feet (1 metre).
**No significant growing season. Less than 15 days over 41°F. No warm thermal period over 59°F.*

2 SUBARCTIC
VERY COLD. Mean annual soil temperature 20° to 36°F. Moderately cool summer. Mean summer soil temperature 41° to 47°F. Regions in this class have sporadic permafrost. Some profiles do not have permafrost within a depth of 3 feet. Alpine soils are included in this class.
**Short growing season. Less than 120 days over 41°F. Less than 1000 degree days over 41°F. No warm thermal period over 59°F.*

3 CRYOBOREAL[1]
COLD TO MODERATELY COLD. Mean annual soil temperature 36° - 47°F. Mild summer. Mean summer soil temperature 47° to 59°F. Regions in this class have no permafrost but the soil is frozen annually.
**Moderately short to moderately long growing season. 120-220 days over 41°F. 1000 - 2250 degree days over 41°F. An insignificant or very short warm thermal period. 0-60 days over 59°F. Less than 60 degree days over 59°F.*

3.1 COLD CRYOBOREAL[1]
No (or insignificant) warm thermal period over 59°F.
**Moderately short growing season. 1000 to 2000 degree days over 41°F.*

3.2 MODERATELY COLD CRYOBOREAL[1]
Usually an insignificant warm thermal period over 59°F.
**Moderately short to moderately long growing season. 2000 - 2250 degree days over 41°F.*

4 BOREAL[2]
COOL TO MODERATELY COOL. Mean annual soil temperature 41° to 47°F. Mild to moderately warm summer. Mean summer soil temperature 59° to 65°F.
**Moderately short to moderately long growing season. 170-220 days over 41°F. 2250-3100 degree days over 41°F. Significant very short to short warm thermal period. More than 60 days over 59°F. 60 - 400 degree days over 59°F.*

4.1 COOL BOREAL[2]
Very short to short warm thermal period over 59°F.
**Moderately short to moderately long growing season. 2250 - 2500 degree days over 41°F.*

4.2 MODERATELY COOL BOREAL[2]
Short warm thermal period over 59°F.
**Moderately long growing season. 2500 - 3100 degree days over 41°F.*

5 MESIC[3]
MILD TO MODERATELY WARM. Mean annual soil temperature 47° - 59°F. Moderately warm to warm summer. Mean summer soil temperature 59° - 72°F.
**Moderately long to nearly continuous growing season. 200-365 days over 41°F. 3100 - 5000 degree days over 41°F. Short to moderately short warm thermal period. Less than 180 days over 59°F. 300-1200 degree days over 59°F.*

5.1 MILD MESIC[3]
Short warm thermal period over 59°F.
**Moderately long growing season. 3100 - 4000 degree days over 41°F.*

5.2 MODERATELY WARM MESIC[3]
Moderately short warm thermal period over 59°F.
**Moderately long to continuous growing season. 4000 to 5000 degree days over 41°F.*

6 THERMIC (Does not occur in Canada)
MODERATELY WARM TO WARM. Mean annual soil temperature 59° - 72°F.

7 HYPERTHERMIC (Does not occur in Canada)
VERY WARM TO HOT. Mean annual soil temperature over 72°F.

[1] In Canada the CRYOBOREAL class is separated into COLD CRYOBOREAL (3.1) and MODERATELY COLD CRYOBOREAL (3.2).

[2] In Canada the BOREAL class is separated into COOL BOREAL (4.1) and MODERATELY COOL BOREAL (4.2).

[3] In Canada the MESIC class is separated into MILD MESIC (5.1) and MODERATELY WARM MESIC (5.2). Because of scale limitation the two classes are combined as MILD MESIC on the map.

SOIL MOISTURE REGIMES AND SUBCLASSES

AQUIC REGIME
Soil is saturated for significant periods of the growing season.
Peraquic
Soil saturated for very long periods of the year (Greater than 300 days). Ground water level at or within capillary reach of the surface. (Because of scale limitation Peraquic is included with Aquic on the map).
Aquic
Soil saturated for moderately long periods of the year (120-300 days).
Subaquic
Soil saturated for short periods of the year (less than 120 days).
MOIST UNSATURATED REGIME
Varying periods and intensities of water deficits during the growing season.
Perhumid
Soil moist all year, seldom dry.
**No significant water deficit in the growing season. Water deficits 0 to 1". Climatic Moisture Index over 84.*
Humid
Soil not dry in any part as long as 90 consecutive days in most years.
**Very slight water deficit in the growing season. Water deficits 1 to 2.5". Climatic Moisture Index 74 to 84.*
Subhumid
Soil is dry in some parts when soil temperature is greater than 41°F in some years.
**Significant water deficit in the growing season. Water deficits 2.5 to 5.0". Climatic Moisture Index 59 to 73.*

Semiarid
Soil dry in some parts when soil temperature is greater than 41°F in most years.
**Moderately severe water deficit in the growing season. Water deficit 5.0 to 7.5". Climatic Moisture Index 46 to 58.*
Subarid
Soil dry in some or all parts most of the time when the soil temperature is greater than 41°F. Some periods as long as 90 consecutive days when the soil is moist.
**Severe water deficit in the growing season. Water deficit 7.5 to 15" in Boreal and Cryoboreal classes. 7.5 to 20" in Mesic or warmer classes. Climatic Moisture Index 25 to 45.*
Arid[1]
Soil dry in some or all parts most of the time when the soil temperature is greater than 41°F. No period as long as 90 consecutive days when soil is moist.
**Very severe water deficit in the growing season. Water deficits more than 15" in Boreal classes and more than 20" in Mesic or warmer classes. Climatic Moisture Index less than 25.*
Xeric[1]
Soil dry in all parts 45 consecutive days or more within the four month period (July to October) following the summer solstice, in more than 6 years out of 10.
**Soil moist in all parts for 45 consecutive days or more within the four month period (January to April) following the winter solstice, in more than 6 years out of 10.*

[1] These regimes are not believed to occur extensively in Canada but may be found in local areas of microclimate.

*Primary Classifier
**Secondary Classifier
For each Soil Temperature Class and each Soil Moisture Subclass there are primary classifiers in accordance with criteria established for the FAO/UNESCO Soil Climate Map of North America. The secondary classifiers are in accordance with criteria established for the Soil Climate Map of Canada (Canada Department of Agriculture, 1973).

DEFINITIONS

MEAN ANNUAL SOIL TEMPERATURE
- mean average temperature of the soil recorded for the 12 months of the year at a depth of 50 cm (19 11/16").
MEAN SUMMER SOIL TEMPERATURE
- mean average temperature of the soil recorded for the months of June, July and August at a depth of 50 cm (19 11/16").
PERMAFROST
- thermal condition of earth materials such as soil and rock when their temperature remains below 32°F continuously for a number of years.
GROWING SEASON
- period with soil temperatures over 41°F at a depth of 50 cm.
WATER DEFICIT
- the additional amount of water required by a crop during the growing season to meet consumptive need for water not readily available from the soil.

CLIMATIC MOISTURE INDEX
- expresses the growing season precipitation as a percentage of the potential water used by annual crops, when water is readily available from the soil.

$$CMI = \frac{P}{P + SM + IR} \times 100$$

P = observed growing season precipitation.
SM = water stored in the soil at the beginning of of the growing season, readily available to crops.
IR = irrigation requirement or water deficit for growing season.
CMI = Climatic Moisture Index.
DEGREE DAYS
- the difference between the mean daily temperature and a selected standard temperature, accumulated daily over a period of time, such as the growing season.

TEMPERATURE CONVERSION SCALE

Fahrenheit -40 -30 -20 -10 0 10 20 30 40 50 60 70 80 90 100   Degrees (°F)

Celsius -40   -30   -20   -10   0   10   20   30   40   Degrees (°C)

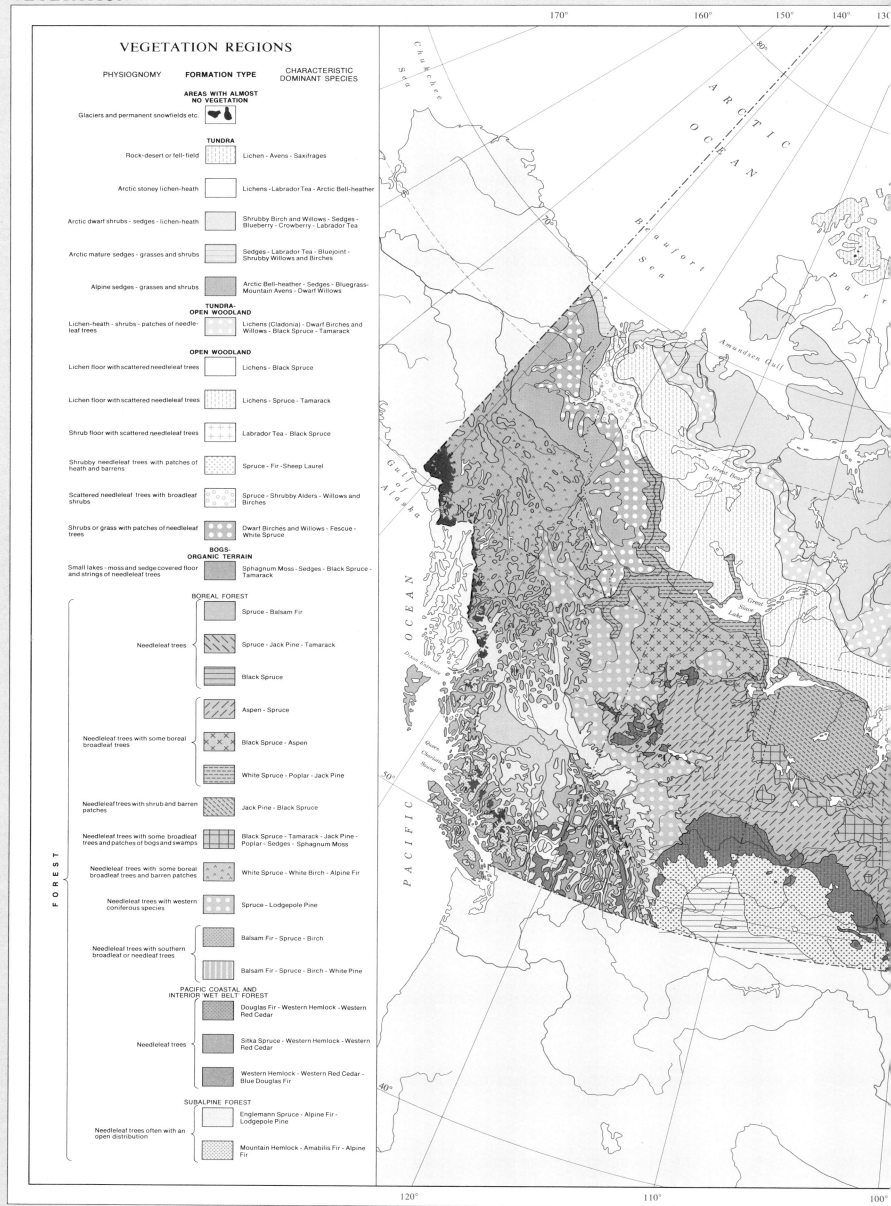

VEGETATION REGIONS

PHYSIOGNOMY	FORMATION TYPE	CHARACTERISTIC DOMINANT SPECIES
	AREAS WITH ALMOST NO VEGETATION	
Glaciers and permanent snowfields etc.		
	TUNDRA	
Rock-desert or fell-field		Lichen - Avens - Saxifrages
Arctic stoney lichen-heath		Lichens - Labrador Tea - Arctic Bell-heather
Arctic dwarf shrubs - sedges - lichen-heath		Shrubby Birch and Willows - Sedges - Blueberry - Crowberry - Labrador Tea
Arctic mature sedges - grasses and shrubs		Sedges - Labrador Tea - Bluejoint - Shrubby Willows and Birches
Alpine sedges - grasses and shrubs		Arctic Bell-heather - Sedges - Bluegrass- Mountain Avens - Dwarf Willows
	TUNDRA- OPEN WOODLAND	
Lichen-heath - shrubs - patches of needle- leaf trees		Lichens (Cladonia) - Dwarf Birches and Willows - Black Spruce - Tamarack
	OPEN WOODLAND	
Lichen floor with scattered needleleaf trees		Lichens - Black Spruce
Lichen floor with scattered needleleaf trees		Lichens - Spruce - Tamarack
Shrub floor with scattered needleleaf trees		Labrador Tea - Black Spruce
Shrubby needleleaf trees with patches of heath and barrens		Spruce - Fir -Sheep Laurel
Scattered needleleaf trees with broadleaf shrubs		Spruce - Shrubby Alders - Willows and Birches
Shrubs or grass with patches of needleleaf trees		Dwarf Birches and Willows - Fescue - White Spruce
	BOGS- ORGANIC TERRAIN	
Small lakes - moss and sedge covered floor and strings of needleleaf trees		Sphagnum Moss - Sedges - Black Spruce - Tamarack
	BOREAL FOREST	
		Spruce - Balsam Fir
Needleleaf trees		Spruce - Jack Pine - Tamarack
		Black Spruce
		Aspen - Spruce
Needleleaf trees with some boreal broadleaf trees		Black Spruce - Aspen
		White Spruce - Poplar - Jack Pine
Needleleaf trees with shrub and barren patches		Jack Pine - Black Spruce
Needleleaf trees with some broadleaf trees and patches of bogs and swamps		Black Spruce - Tamarack - Jack Pine - Poplar - Sedges - Sphagnum Moss
Needleleaf trees with some boreal broadleaf trees and barren patches		White Spruce - White Birch - Alpine Fir
Needleleaf trees with western coniferous species		Spruce - Lodgepole Pine
Needleleaf trees with southern broadleaf or needleleaf trees		Balsam Fir - Spruce - Birch
		Balsam Fir - Spruce - Birch - White Pine
	PACIFIC COASTAL AND INTERIOR WET BELT FOREST	
		Douglas Fir - Western Hemlock -Western Red Cedar
Needleleaf trees		Sitka Spruce - Western Hemlock - Western Red Cedar
		Western Hemlock - Western Red Cedar - Blue Douglas Fir
	SUBALPINE FOREST	
Needleleaf trees often with an open distribution		Englemann Spruce - Alpine Fir - Lodgepole Pine
		Mountain Hemlock - Amabilis Fir - Alpine Fir

FOREST

Lambert Conformal Conic Projection Standard Parallels 49°N. and 77°N.

THE NATIONAL ATLAS OF CANADA

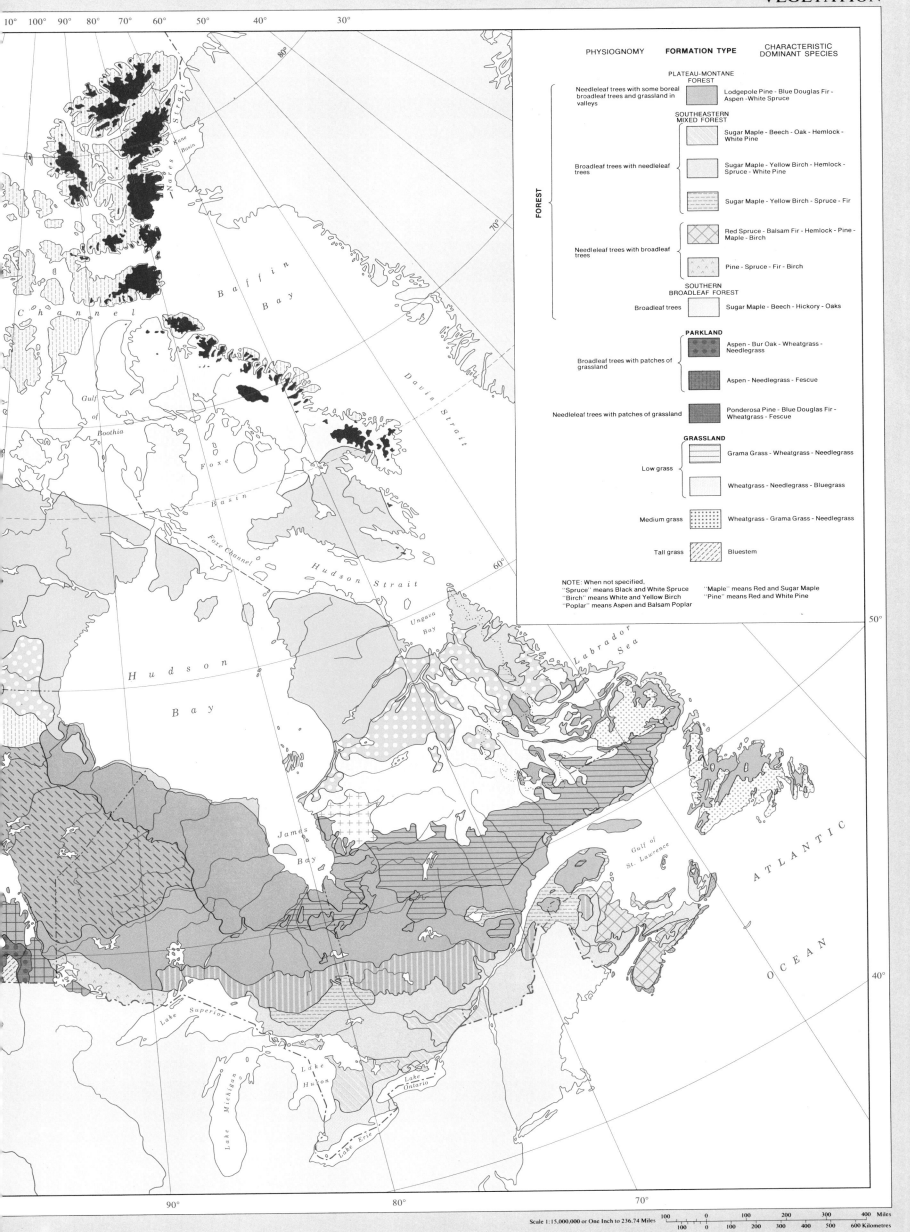

PHYSIOGNOMY	FORMATION TYPE	CHARACTERISTIC DOMINANT SPECIES
	PLATEAU-MONTANE FOREST	
Needleleaf trees with some boreal broadleaf trees and grassland in valleys		Lodgepole Pine - Blue Douglas Fir - Aspen - White Spruce
	SOUTHEASTERN MIXED FOREST	
Broadleaf trees with needleleaf trees		Sugar Maple - Beech - Oak - Hemlock - White Pine
		Sugar Maple - Yellow Birch - Hemlock - Spruce - White Pine
		Sugar Maple - Yellow Birch - Spruce - Fir
Needleleaf trees with broadleaf trees		Red Spruce - Balsam Fir - Hemlock - Pine - Maple - Birch
		Pine - Spruce - Fir - Birch
	SOUTHERN BROADLEAF FOREST	
Broadleaf trees		Sugar Maple - Beech - Hickory - Oaks
	PARKLAND	
Broadleaf trees with patches of grassland		Aspen - Bur Oak - Wheatgrass - Needlegrass
		Aspen - Needlegrass - Fescue
Needleleaf trees with patches of grassland		Ponderosa Pine - Blue Douglas Fir - Wheatgrass - Fescue
	GRASSLAND	
Low grass		Grama Grass - Wheatgrass - Needlegrass
		Wheatgrass - Needlegrass - Bluegrass
Medium grass		Wheatgrass - Grama Grass - Needlegrass
Tall grass		Bluestem

FOREST

NOTE: When not specified,
"Spruce" means Black and White Spruce   "Maple" means Red and Sugar Maple
"Birch" means White and Yellow Birch   "Pine" means Red and White Pine
"Poplar" means Aspen and Balsam Poplar

Scale 1:15,000,000 or One Inch to 236.74 Miles

100   0   100   200   300   400 Miles
100   0   100 200 300 400 500 600 Kilometres

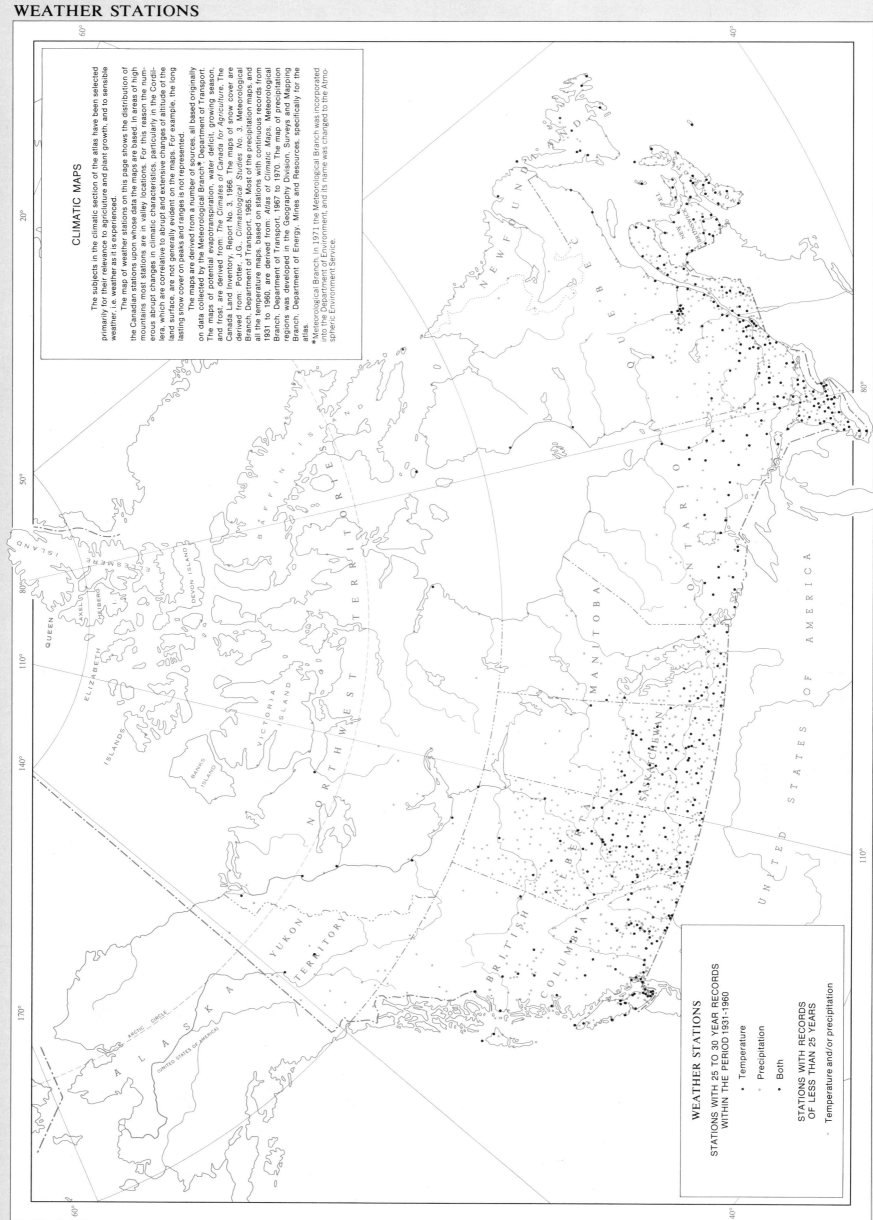

CLIMATIC MAPS

The subjects in the climatic section of the atlas have been selected primarily for their relevance to agriculture and plant growth, and to sensible weather, i.e. weather as it is experienced.

The map of weather stations on this page shows the distribution of the Canadian stations upon whose data the maps are based. In areas of high mountains most stations are in valley locations. For this reason the numerous abrupt changes in climatic characteristics, particularly in the Cordillera, which are correlative to abrupt and extensive changes of altitude of the land surface, are not generally evident on the maps. For example, the long lasting snow cover on peaks and ranges is not represented.

The maps are derived from a number of sources, all based originally on data collected by the Meteorological Branch,* Department of Transport. The maps of potential evapotranspiration, water deficit, growing season, and frost, are derived from: The Climates of Canada for Agriculture, The Canada Land Inventory, Report No. 3, 1966. The maps of snow cover are derived from: Potter, J.G., Climatological Studies No. 3. Meteorological Branch, Department of Transport, 1965. Most of the precipitation maps, and all the temperature maps, based on stations with continuous records from 1931 to 1960, are derived from: Atlas of Climatic Maps, Meteorological Branch, Department of Transport, 1967 to 1970. The map of precipitation regions was developed in the Geography Division, Surveys and Mapping Branch, Department of Energy, Mines and Resources, specifically for the atlas.

*Meteorological Branch. In 1971 the Meteorological Branch was incorporated into the Department of Environment, and its name was changed to the Atmospheric Environment Service.

WEATHER STATIONS

STATIONS WITH 25 TO 30 YEAR RECORDS
WITHIN THE PERIOD 1931-1960

· Temperature

· Precipitation

· Both

STATIONS WITH RECORDS
OF LESS THAN 25 YEARS

· Temperature and/or precipitation

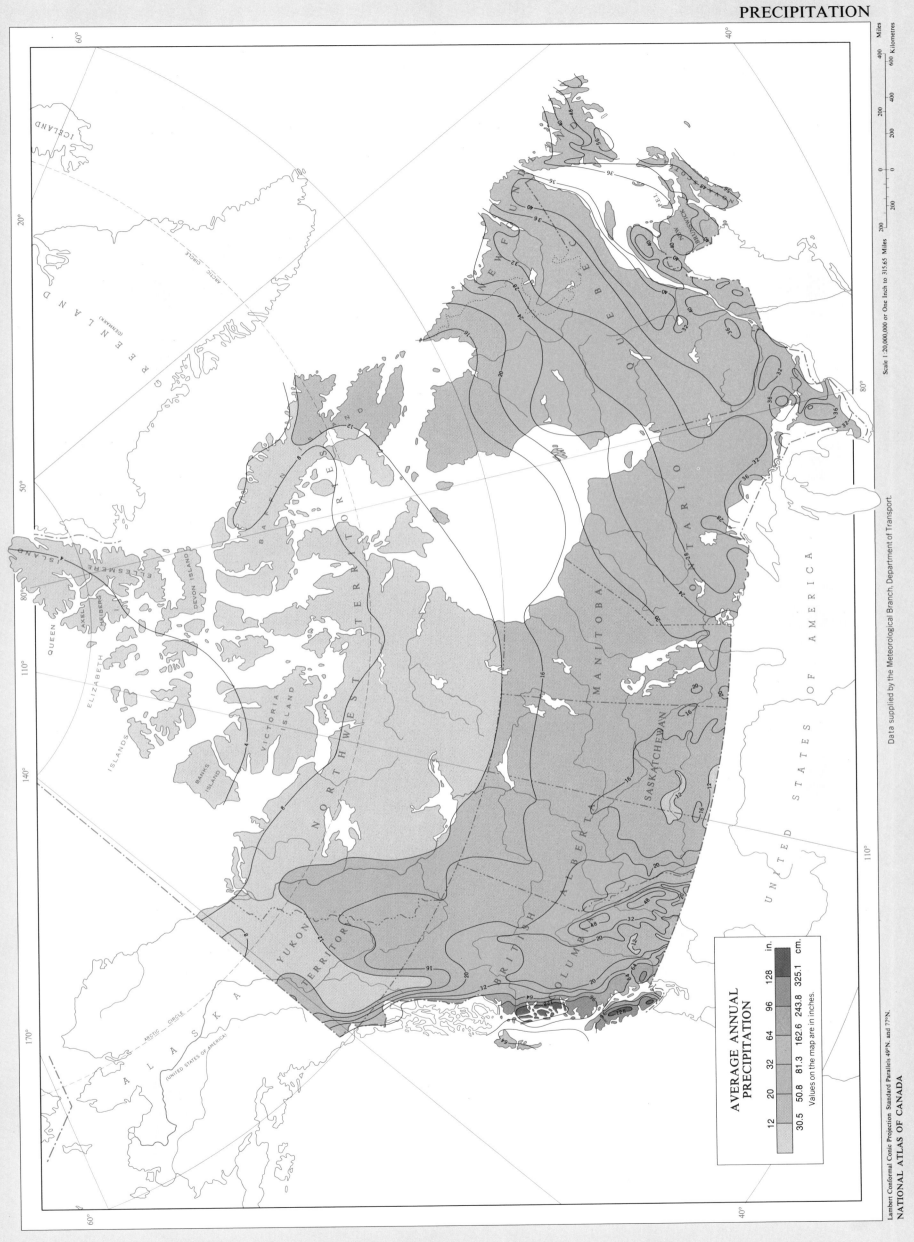

AVERAGE ANNUAL
PRECIPITATION

	12	20	32	64	96	128	in.
	30.5	50.8	81.3	162.6	243.8	325.1	cm.

Values on the map are in inches.

Lambert Conformal Conic Projection Standard Parallels 49°N. and 77°N.

NATIONAL ATLAS OF CANADA

Scale 1:20,000,000 or One Inch to 315.65 Miles

Data supplied by the Meteorological Branch, Department of Transport.

AVERAGE ANNUAL POTENTIAL EVAPOTRANSPIRATION

inches		centimetres
16	20	24
40.6	50.8	61.0

Potential Evapotranspiration: The potential water loss by evaporation and transpiration from ground and plant surfaces where there is a continuous vegetation cover and sufficient soil moisture for plant use.

Values on the map are in inches.

AVERAGE ANNUAL WATER DEFICIT

No Deficit 0			inches		
0	4	8	12		
0.0	10.2	20.3	30.5	centimetres

Water Deficit: The amount by which precipitation and soil moisture, during parts of the growing season, fail to supply sufficient water for theoretically full plant growth. Occurences of deficits in Canada indicate areas in which there are degrees of seasonal aridity.

Values on the map are in inches.

Lambert Conformal Conic Projection Standard Parallels 49°N. and 77°N.

Scale 1:20,000,000 or One Inch to 315.65 Miles

NATIONAL ATLAS OF CANADA

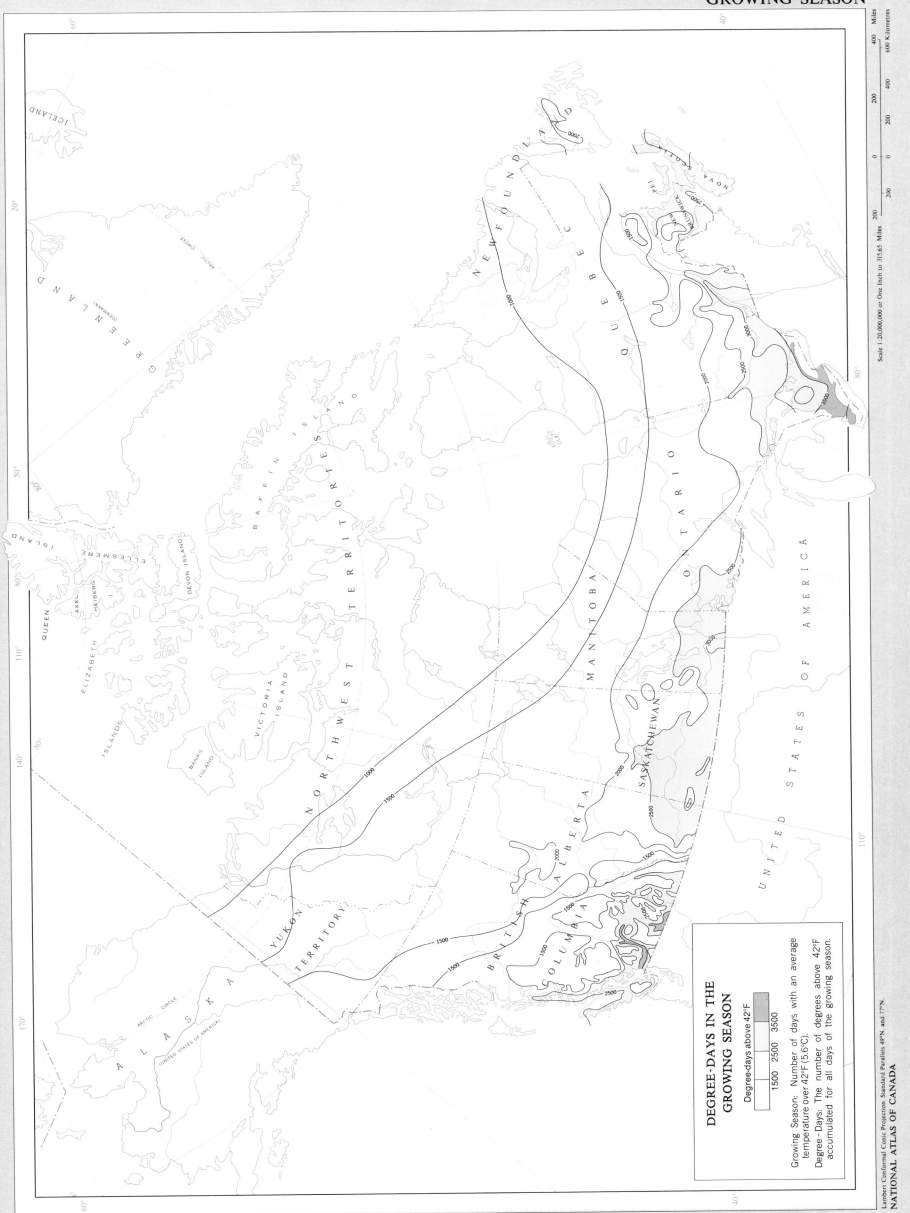

DEGREE-DAYS IN THE
GROWING SEASON

Degree-days above 42°F

1500   2500   3500

Growing Season: Number of days with an average
temperature over 42°F (5.6°C).

Degree-Days: The number of degrees above 42°F
accumulated for all days of the growing season.

Lambert Conformal Conic Projection Standard Parallels 49°N. and 77°N.
NATIONAL ATLAS OF CANADA

Scale 1:20,000,000 or One Inch to 315.65 Miles

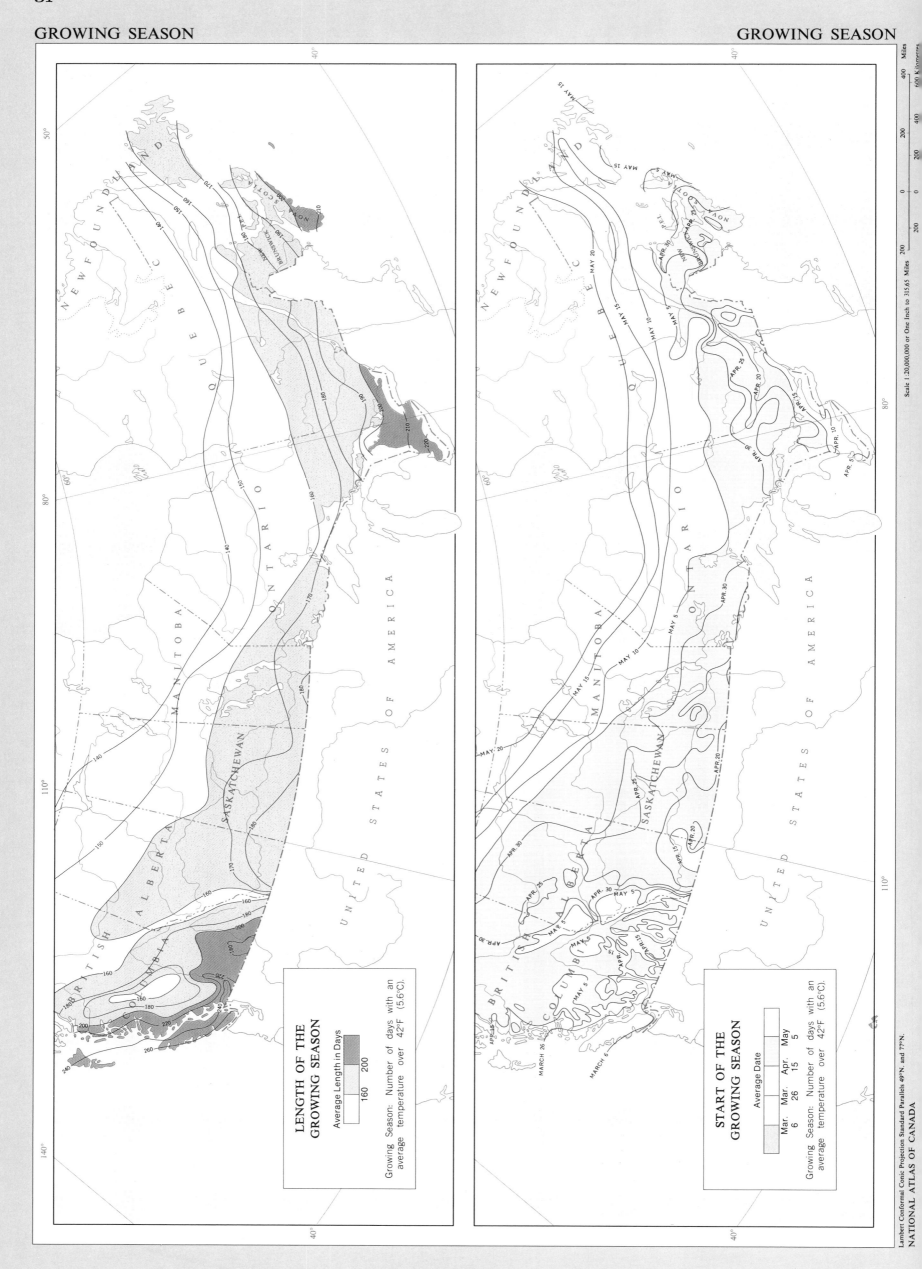

LENGTH OF THE
GROWING SEASON

Average Length in Days

160   200

Growing Season: Number of days with an
average temperature over 42°F (5.6°C).

START OF THE
GROWING SEASON

Average Date

Mar.   Mar.   Apr.   May
6   26   15   5

Growing Season: Number of days with an
average temperature over 42°F (5.6°C).

Lambert Conformal Conic Projection Standard Parallels 49°N. and 77°N.
NATIONAL ATLAS OF CANADA

Scale 1:20,000,000 or One Inch to 315.65 Miles

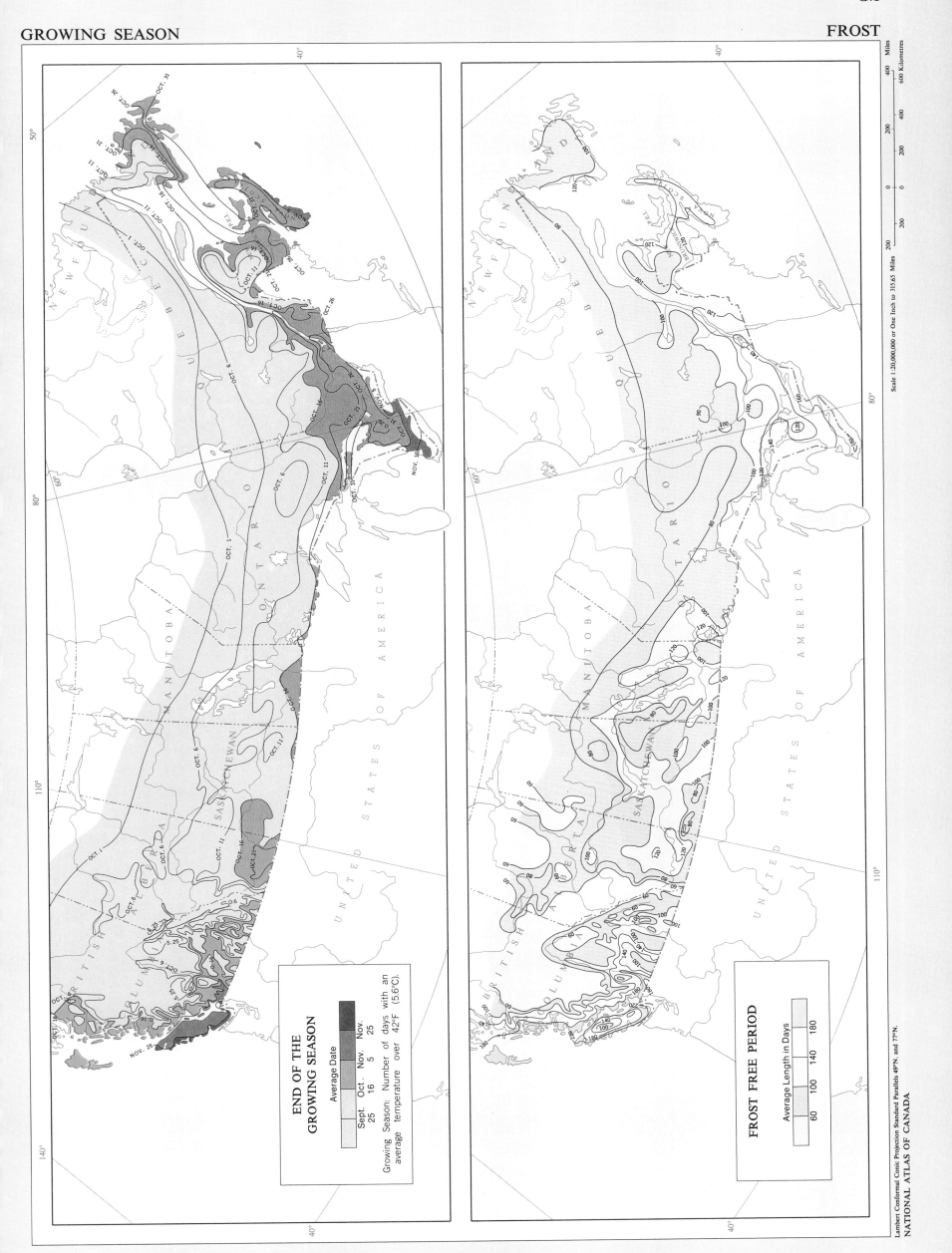

**END OF THE
GROWING SEASON**

Average Date

Sept.
25

Oct.
16

Nov.
5

Nov.
25

Growing Season: Number of days with an
average temperature over 42°F (5.6°C).

FROST FREE PERIOD

Average Length in Days

60   100   140   180

FROST

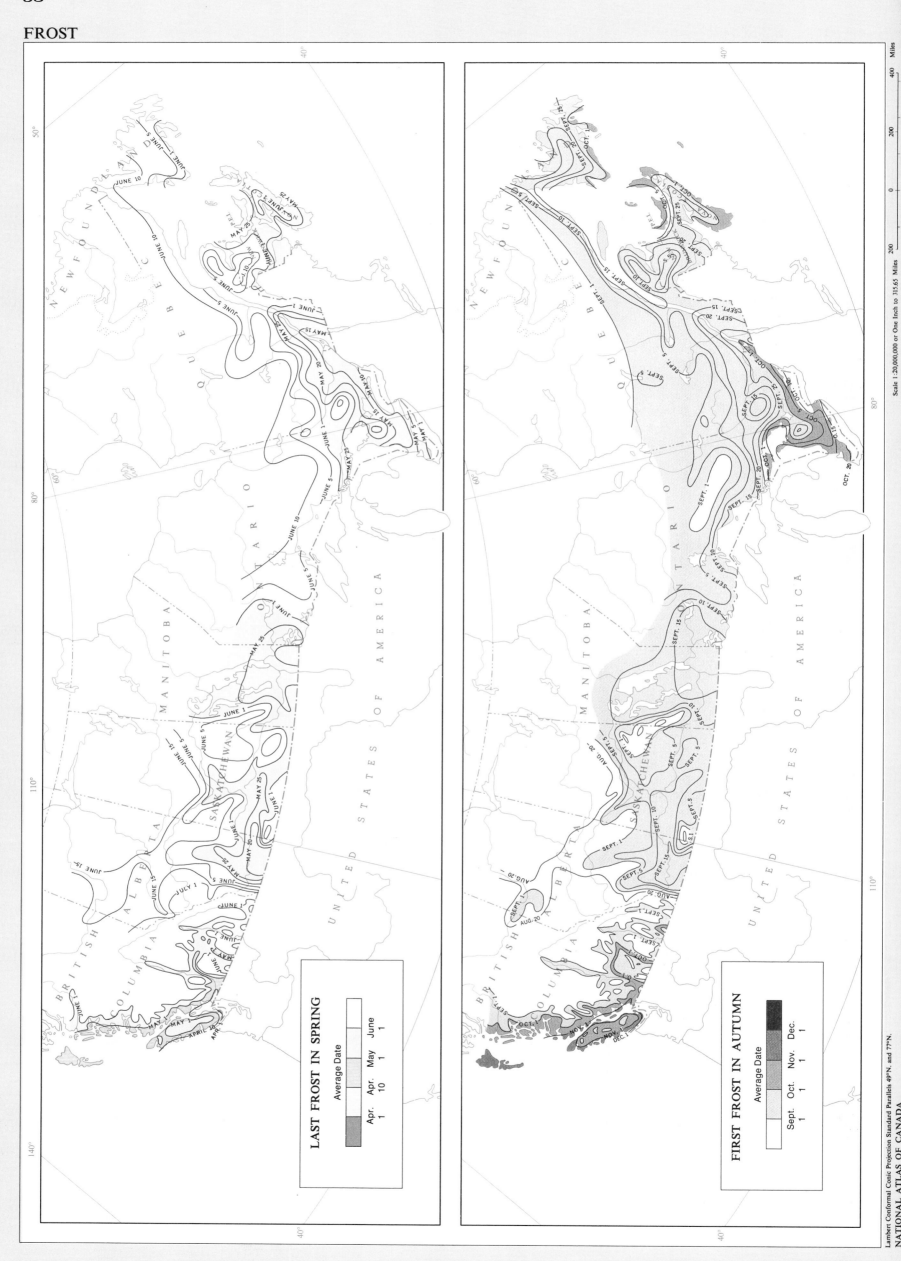

LAST FROST IN SPRING

Average Date

Apr. | Apr. | May | June
1 | 10 | 1 | 1

FIRST FROST IN AUTUMN

Average Date

Sept. | Oct. | Nov. | Dec.
1 | 1 | 1 | 1

Lambert Conformal Conic Projection Standard Parallels 49°N. and 77°N.

Scale 1:20,000,000 or One Inch to 315.65 Miles

NATIONAL ATLAS OF CANADA

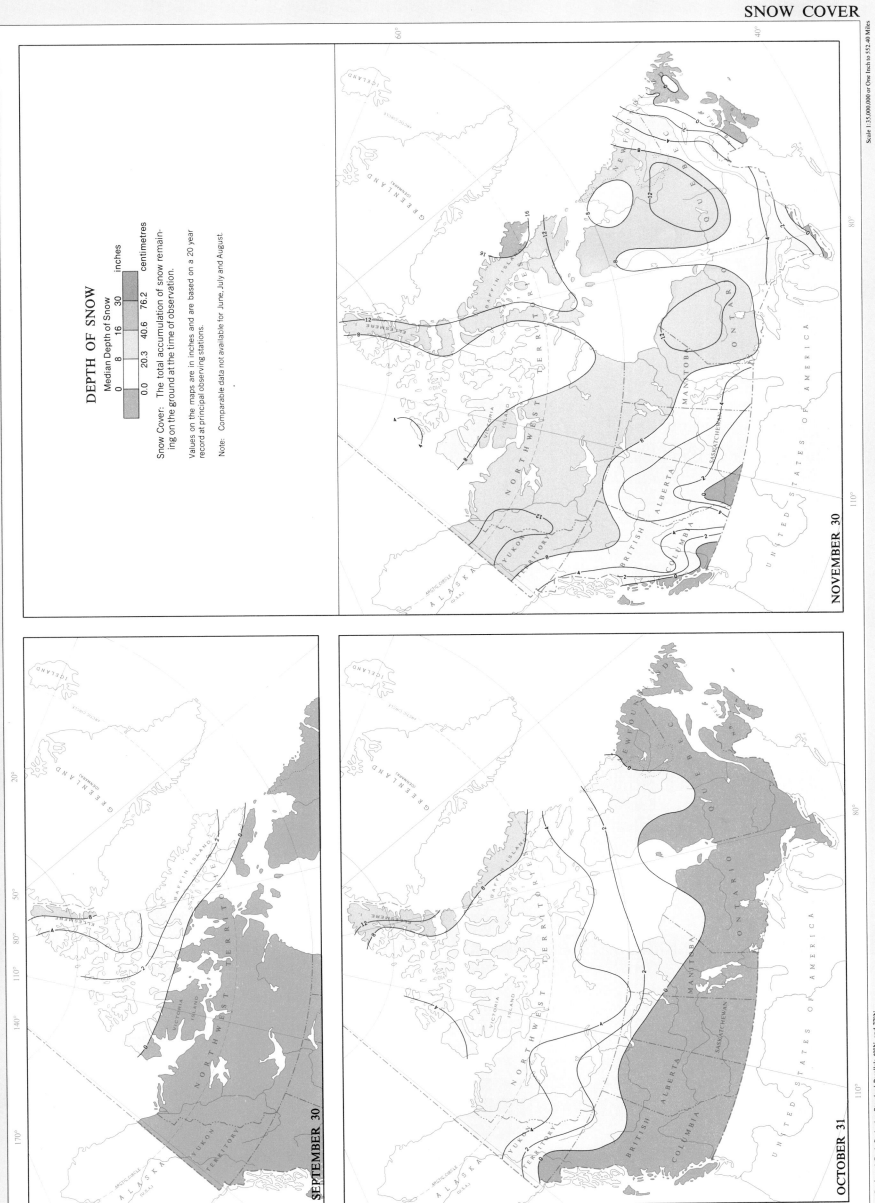

DEPTH OF SNOW

Median Depth of Snow

inches	0	8	16	30
centimetres	0.0	20.3	40.6	76.2

Snow Cover: The total accumulation of snow remaining on the ground at the time of observation.

Values on the maps are in inches and are based on a 20 year record at principal observing stations.

Note: Comparable data not available for June, July and August.

SEPTEMBER 30

OCTOBER 31

NOVEMBER 30

Scale 1:35,000,000 or One Inch to 552.40 Miles

Lambert Conformal Conic Projection Standard Parallels 49°N. and 77°N.

NATIONAL ATLAS OF CANADA

SNOW COVER

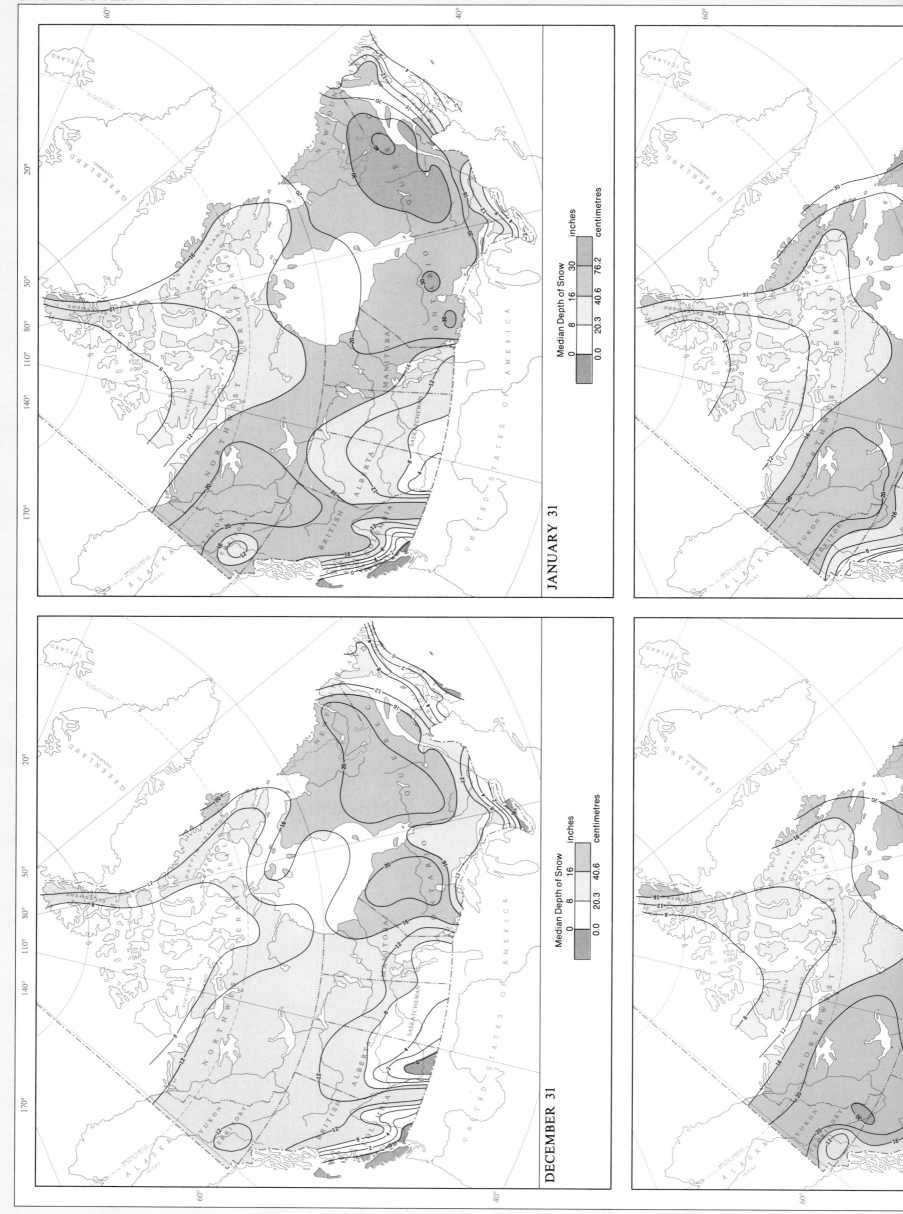

JANUARY 31

DECEMBER 31

Median Depth of Snow

inches
centimetres

0   8   16   30
0.0   20.3   40.6   76.2

Median Depth of Snow

inches
centimetres

0   8   16
0.0   20.3   40.6

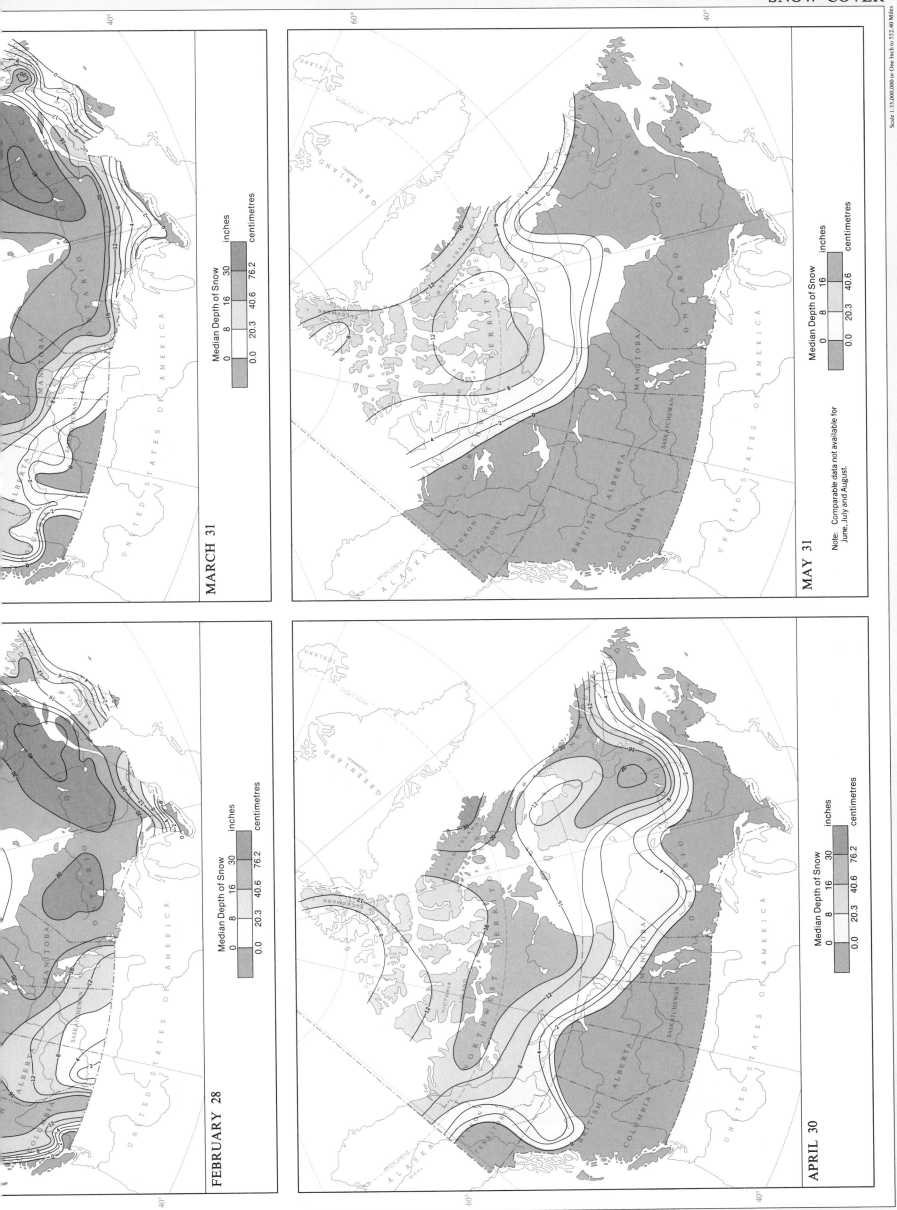

MARCH 31

Median Depth of Snow

inches
0   8   16   30
0.0   20.3   40.6   76.2
centimetres

MAY 31

Median Depth of Snow

inches
0   8   16
0.0   20.3   40.6
centimetres

Note: Comparable data not available for
        June, July and August.

FEBRUARY 28

Median Depth of Snow

inches
0   8   16   30
0.0   20.3   40.6   76.2
centimetres

APRIL 30

Median Depth of Snow

inches
0   8   16   30
0.0   20.3   40.6   76.2
centimetres

Scale 1:35,000,000 or One Inch to 552.40 Miles

Lambert Conformal Conic Projection Standard Parallels 49°N. and 77°N.
NATIONAL ATLAS OF CANADA

PRECIPITATION

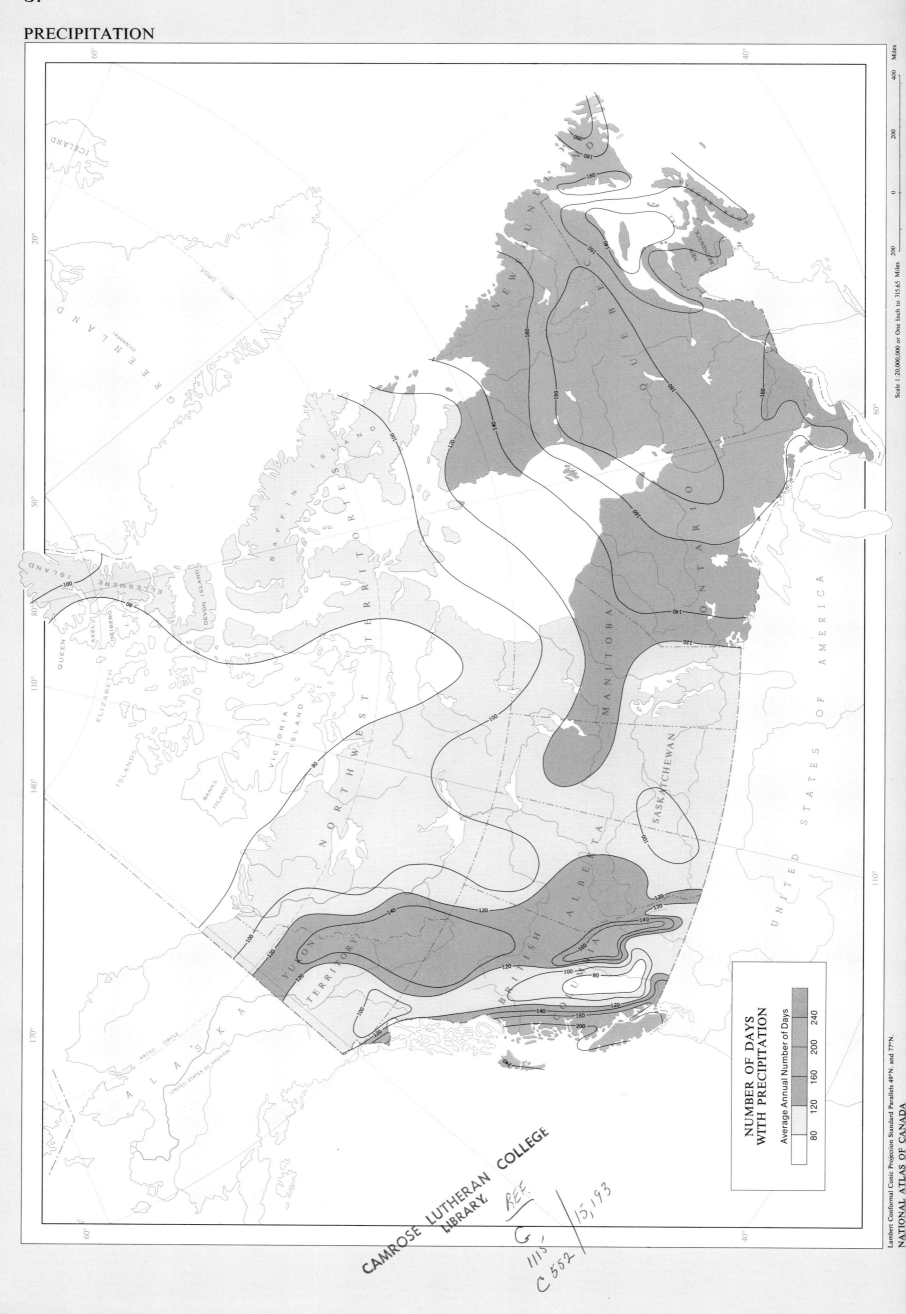

NUMBER OF DAYS
WITH PRECIPITATION

Average Annual Number of Days

80	120	160	200	240

Lambert Conformal Conic Projection Standard Parallels 49°N. and 77°N.

Scale 1:20,000,000 or One Inch to 315.65 Miles

NATIONAL ATLAS OF CANADA

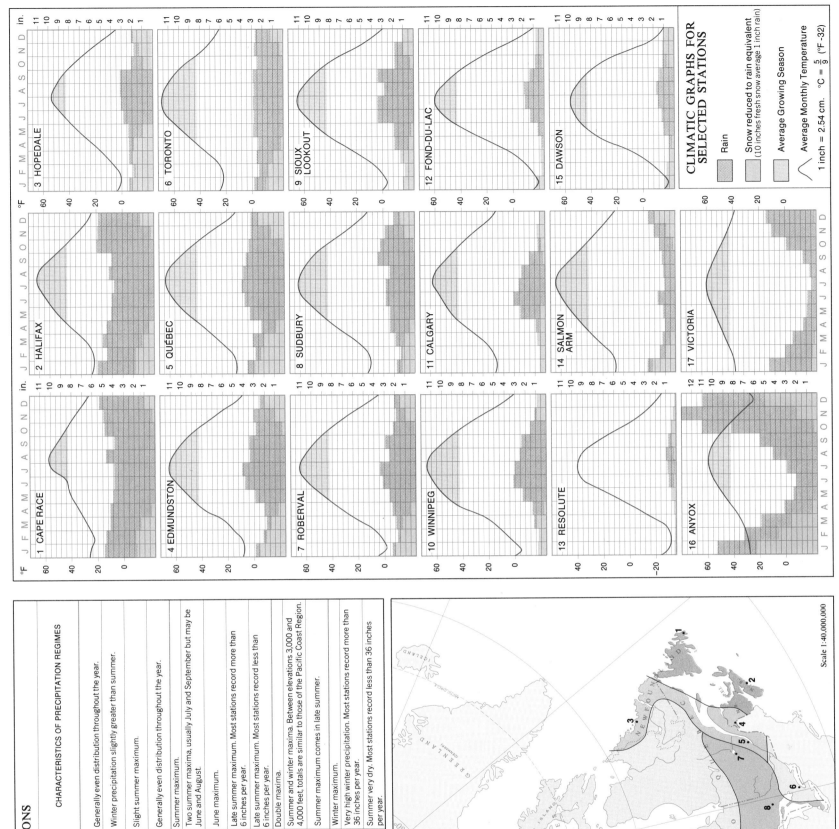

CLIMATIC GRAPHS FOR SELECTED STATIONS

- Rain
- Snow reduced to rain equivalent (10 inches fresh snow average 1 inch rain)
- Average Growing Season
- Average Monthly Temperature

1 inch = 2.54 cm. $°C = \frac{5}{9} (°F -32)$

PRECIPITATION REGIONS

REGIONS AND SUB-REGIONS WITH SIMILAR PRECIPITATION REGIMES	CLIMATIC GRAPH NUMBER	LOWEST AVERAGE ANNUAL PRECIPITATION in. (cm.)	HIGHEST AVERAGE ANNUAL PRECIPITATION in. (cm.)	CHARACTERISTICS OF PRECIPITATION REGIMES
EASTERN				
Atlantic	1, 2	30 (76.2)	60 (152.4)	Generally even distribution throughout the year.
St. Lawrence—Labrador	3, 4, 5	28 (71.1)	52 (132.1)	Winter precipitation slightly greater than summer.
Lower Great Lakes	6	27 (68.6)	42 (106.7)	Slight summer maximum.
INTERIOR				
Southern Shield	7, 8, 9	19 (48.3)	45 (114.3)	Generally even distribution throughout the year. Summer maximum. Two summer maxima, usually July and September but may be June and August.
Prairies	10, 11	10 (25.4)	24 (61.0)	June maximum.
Northern Interior—Eastern Arctic	12	6 (15.2)	32 (81.3)	Late summer maximum. Most stations record more than 6 inches per year.
Arctic Islands	13	3 (7.6)	6 (15.2)	Late summer maximum. Most stations record less than 6 inches per year. Double maxima.
CORDILLERA				
Southern Cordillera	14	7 (17.8)	52 (132.1)	Summer and winter maxima. Between elevations 3,000 and 4,000 feet, totals are similar to those of the Pacific Coast Region.
Northern Cordillera	15	10 (25.4)	16 (40.6)	Summer maximum comes in late summer. Winter maximum.
PACIFIC COAST				
Coastal British Columbia	16	37 (94.0)	262 (665.5)	Very high winter precipitation. Most stations record more than 36 inches per year.
Southern Straits	17	26 (66.0)	36 (91.4)	Summer very dry. Most stations record less than 36 inches per year.

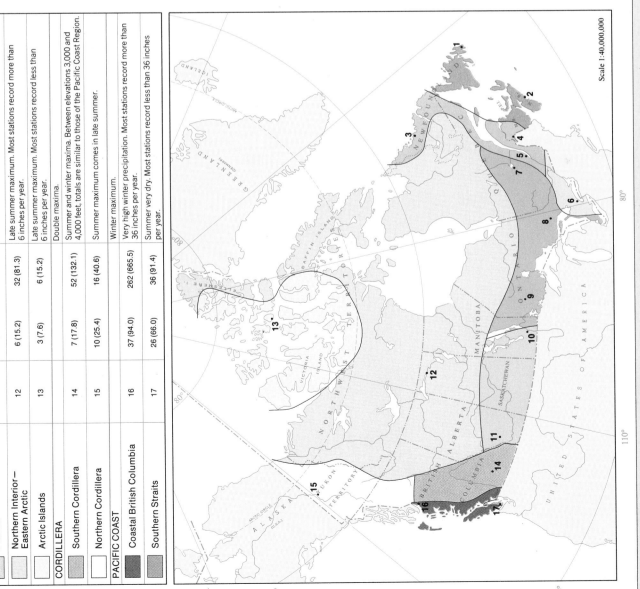

Scale 1:40,000,000

Lambert Conformal Conic Projection Standard Parallels 49°N. and 77°N.

NATIONAL ATLAS OF CANADA

PRECIPITATION

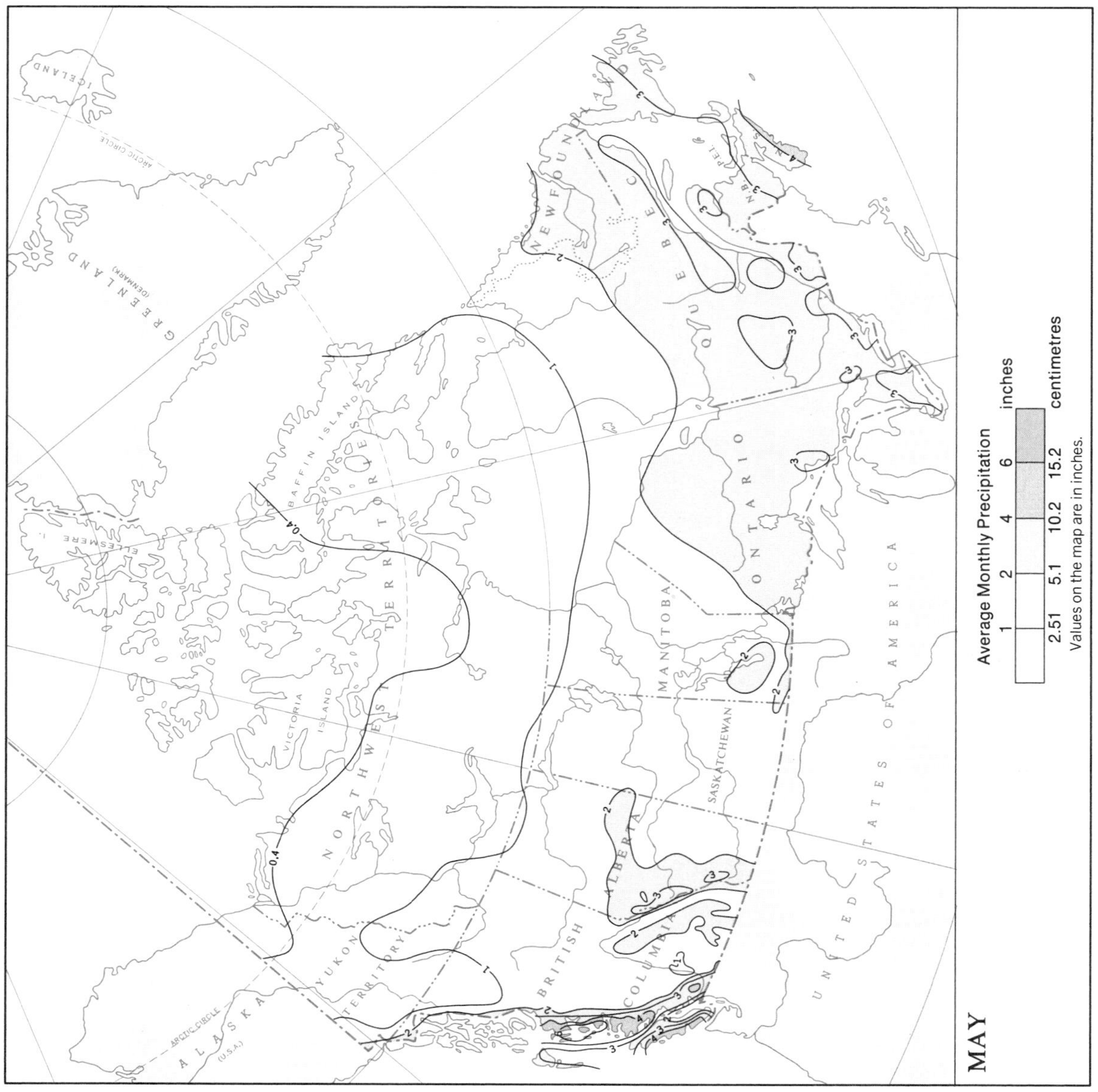

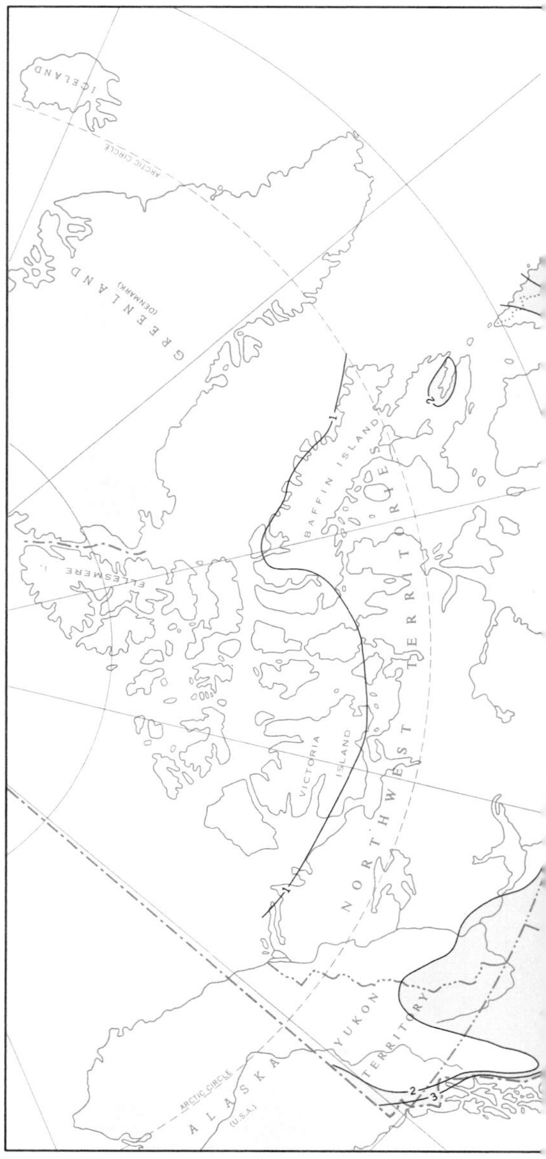

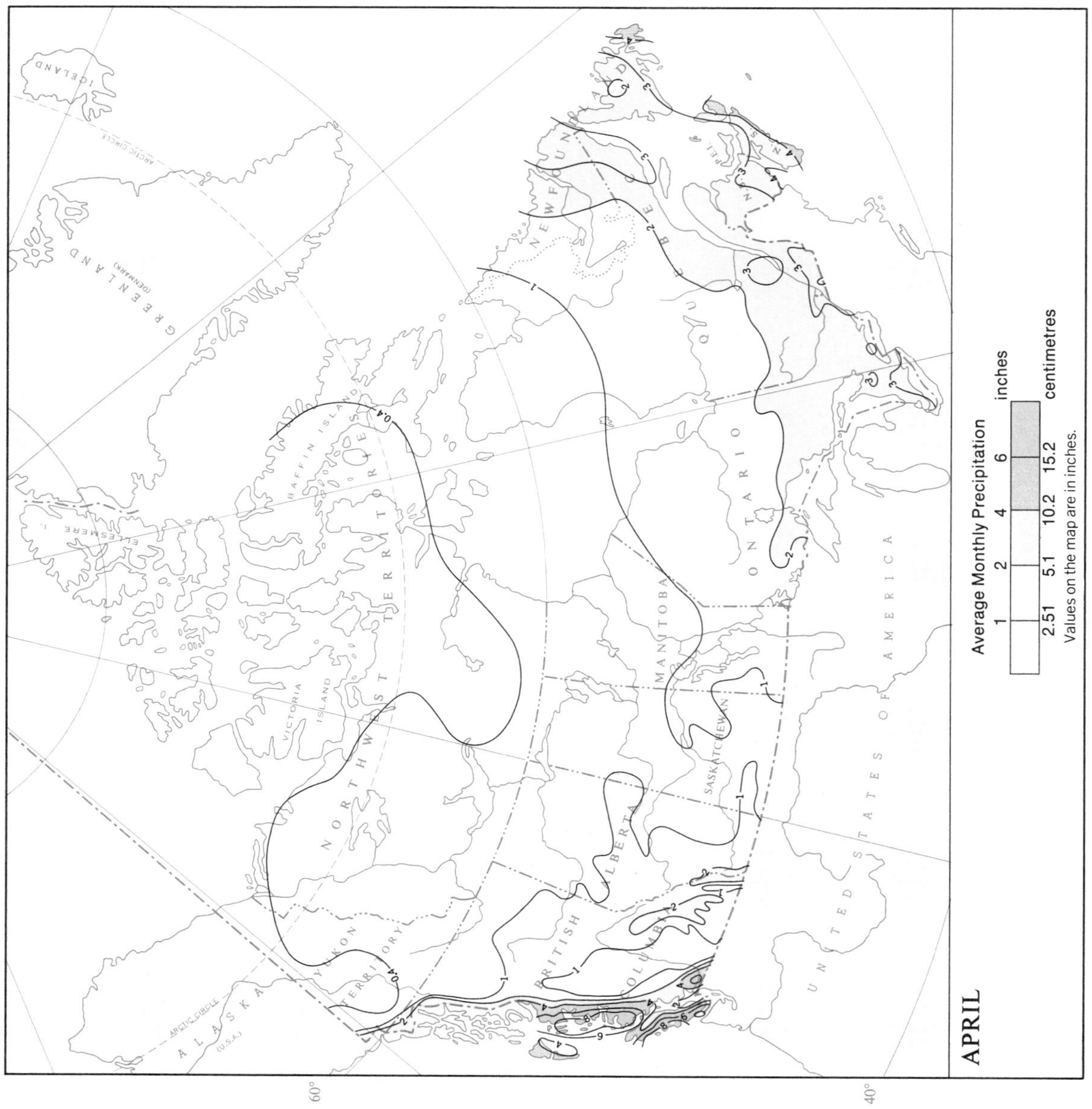

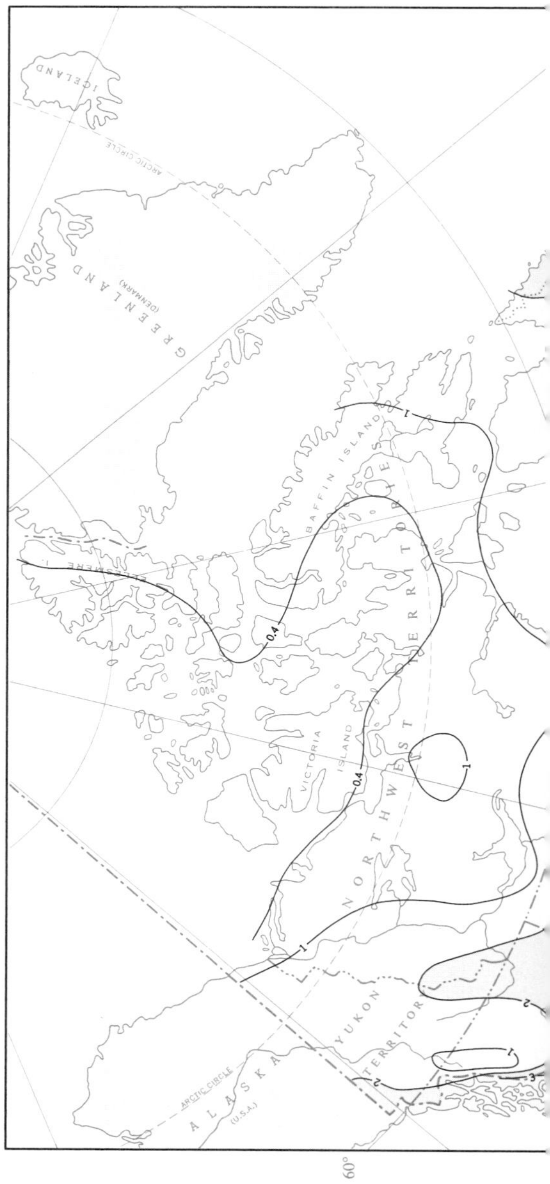

APRIL

Average Monthly Precipitation

inches

| 1 | 2 | 4 | 6 | inches |
| 2.51 | 5.1 | 10.2 | 15.2 | centimetres |

Values on the map are in inches.

MAY

Average Monthly Precipitation

inches

| 1 | 2 | 4 | 6 | inches |
| 2.51 | 5.1 | 10.2 | 15.2 | centimetres |

Values on the map are in inches.

JUNE

JULY

AUGUST

SEPTEMBER

Average Monthly Precipitation

Values on the map are in inches.

Scale 1:35,000,000 or One Inch to 552.40 Miles

Maps supplied by the Meteorological Branch, Department of Transport.

Lambert Conformal Conic Projection Standard Parallels 49°N. and 77°N.

NATIONAL ATLAS OF CANADA

PRECIPITATION

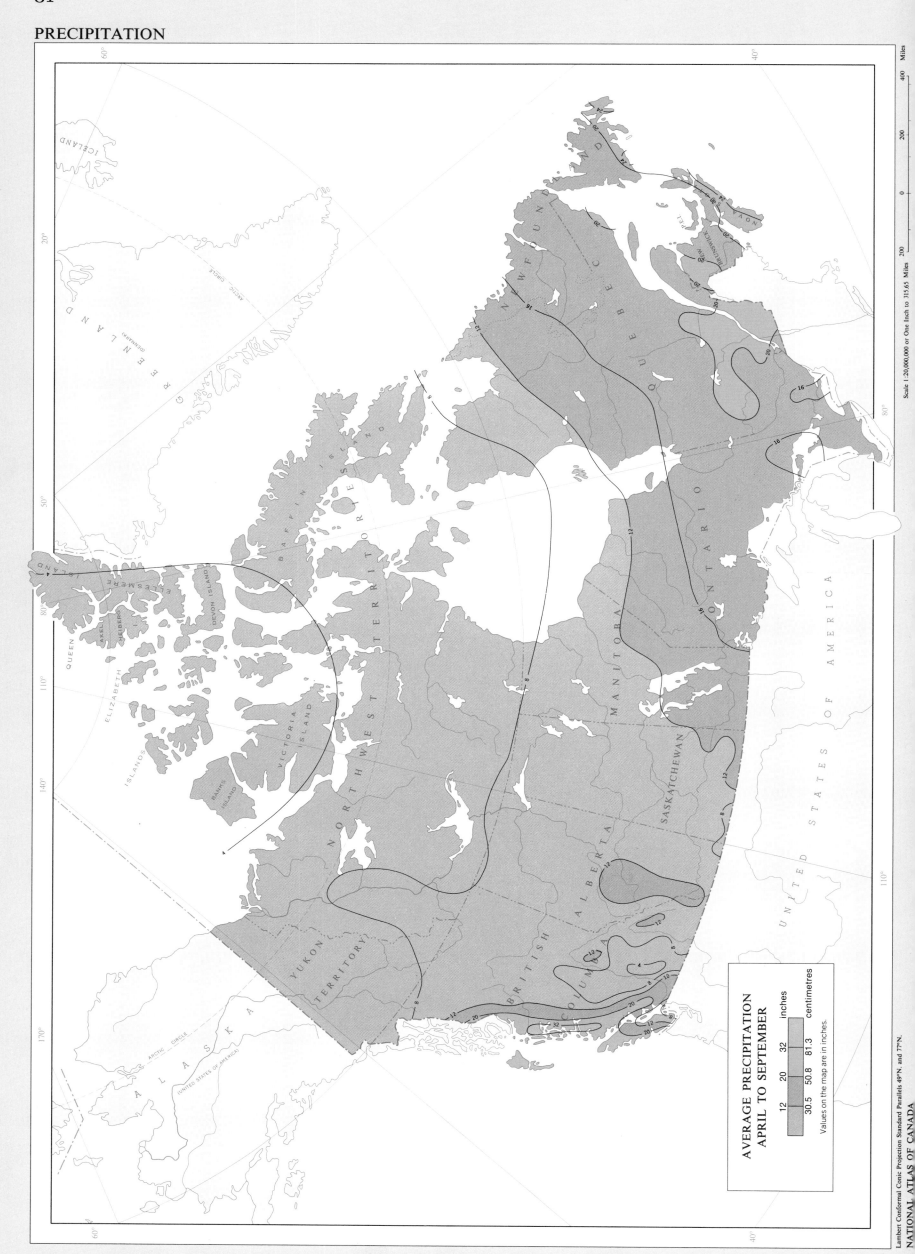

AVERAGE PRECIPITATION
APRIL TO SEPTEMBER

| inches |
| centimetres |

| 12 | 20 | 32 |
| 30.5 | 50.8 | 81.3 |

Values on the map are in inches.

Lambert Conformal Conic Projection Standard Parallels 49°N. and 77°N.

Scale 1:20,000,000 or One Inch to 315.65 Miles

NATIONAL ATLAS OF CANADA

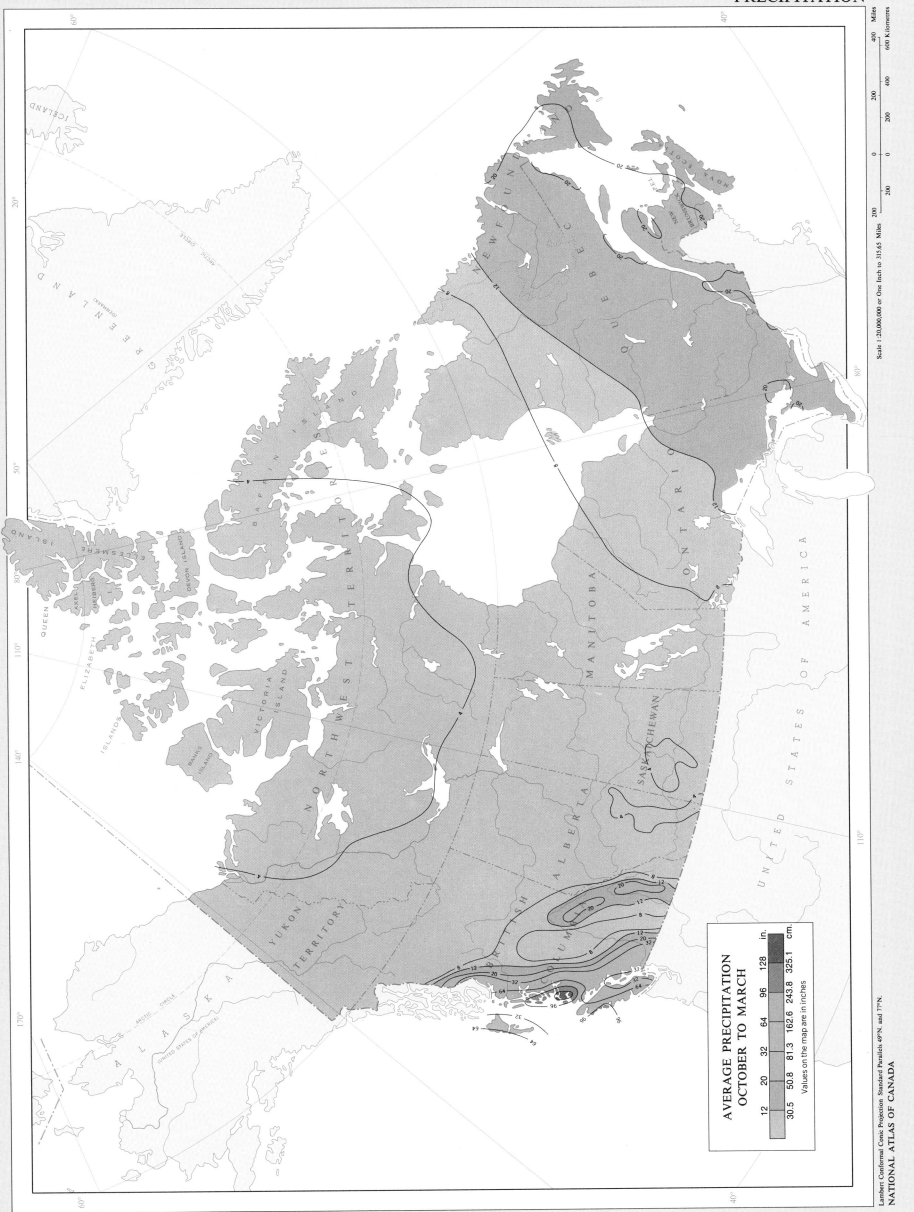

AVERAGE PRECIPITATION
OCTOBER TO MARCH

Values on the map are in inches

Lambert Conformal Conic Projection Standard Parallels 49°N. and 77°N.

NATIONAL ATLAS OF CANADA

Scale 1:20,000,000 or One Inch to 315.65 Miles

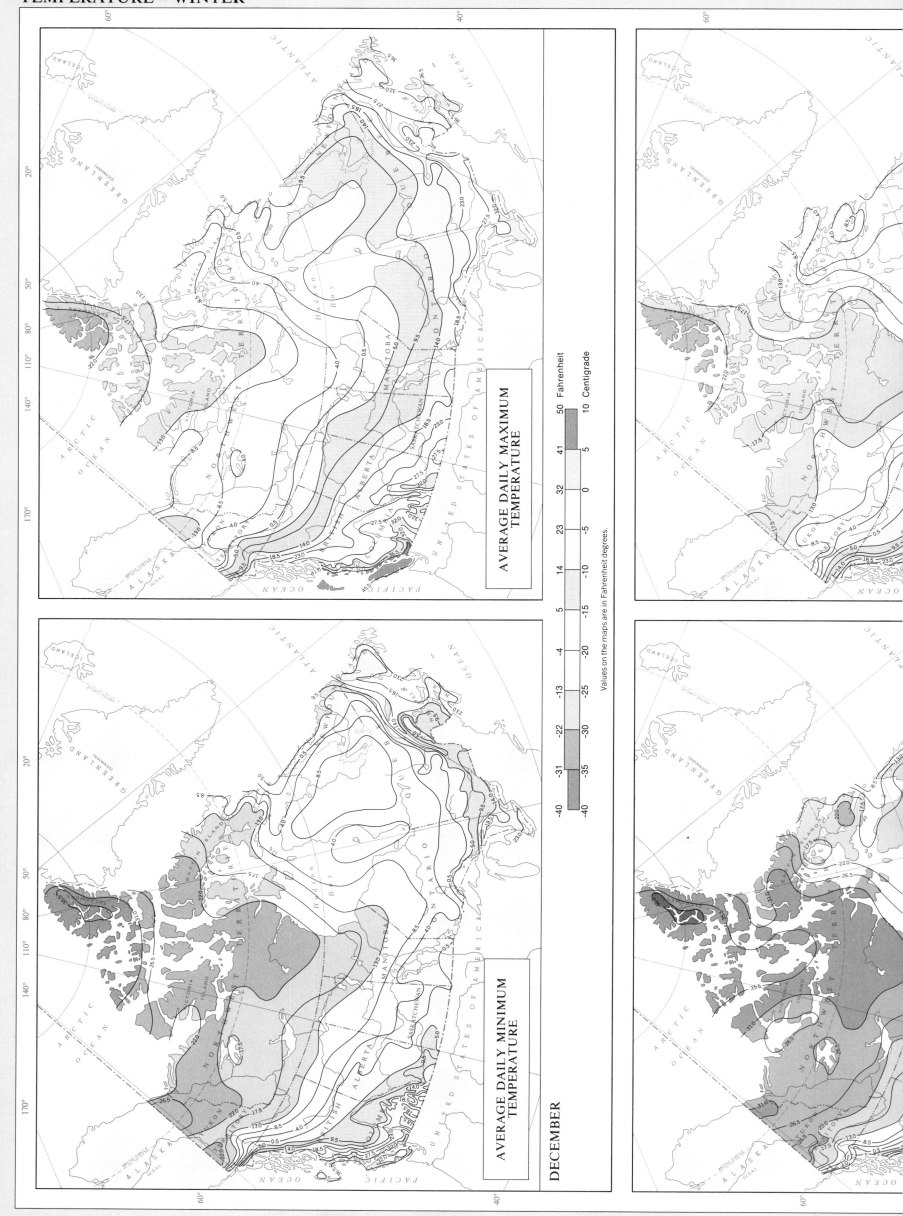

AVERAGE DAILY MAXIMUM
TEMPERATURE

AVERAGE DAILY MINIMUM
TEMPERATURE

DECEMBER

											Fahrenheit
-40	-35	-31	-22	-13	-4	5	14	23	32	41	50
-40	-35	-30	-25	-20	-15	-10	-5	0	5		10 Centigrade

Values on the maps are in Fahrenheit degrees.

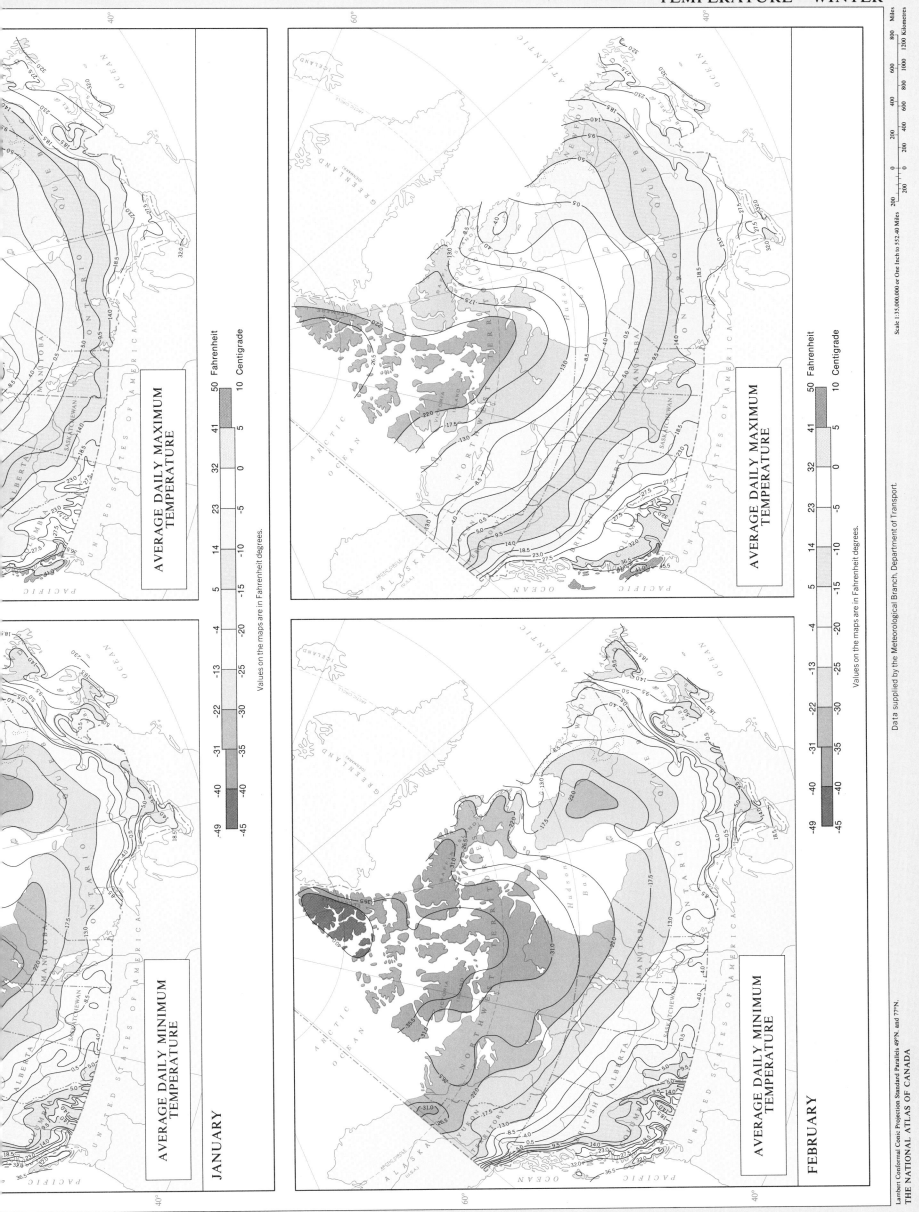

AVERAGE DAILY MAXIMUM
TEMPERATURE

JANUARY

AVERAGE DAILY MINIMUM
TEMPERATURE

AVERAGE DAILY MAXIMUM
TEMPERATURE

FEBRUARY

AVERAGE DAILY MINIMUM
TEMPERATURE

Values on the maps are in Fahrenheit degrees.

Values on the maps are in Fahrenheit degrees.

50	41	32	23	14	5	-4	-13	-22	-31	-40	-49	Fahrenheit
10	5	0	-5	-10	-15	-20	-25	-30	-35	-40	-45	Centigrade

Scale 1:35,000,000 or One Inch to 552.40 Miles

Data supplied by the Meteorological Branch, Department of Transport.

Lambert Conformal Conic Projection Standard Parallels 49°N. and 77°N.

THE NATIONAL ATLAS OF CANADA

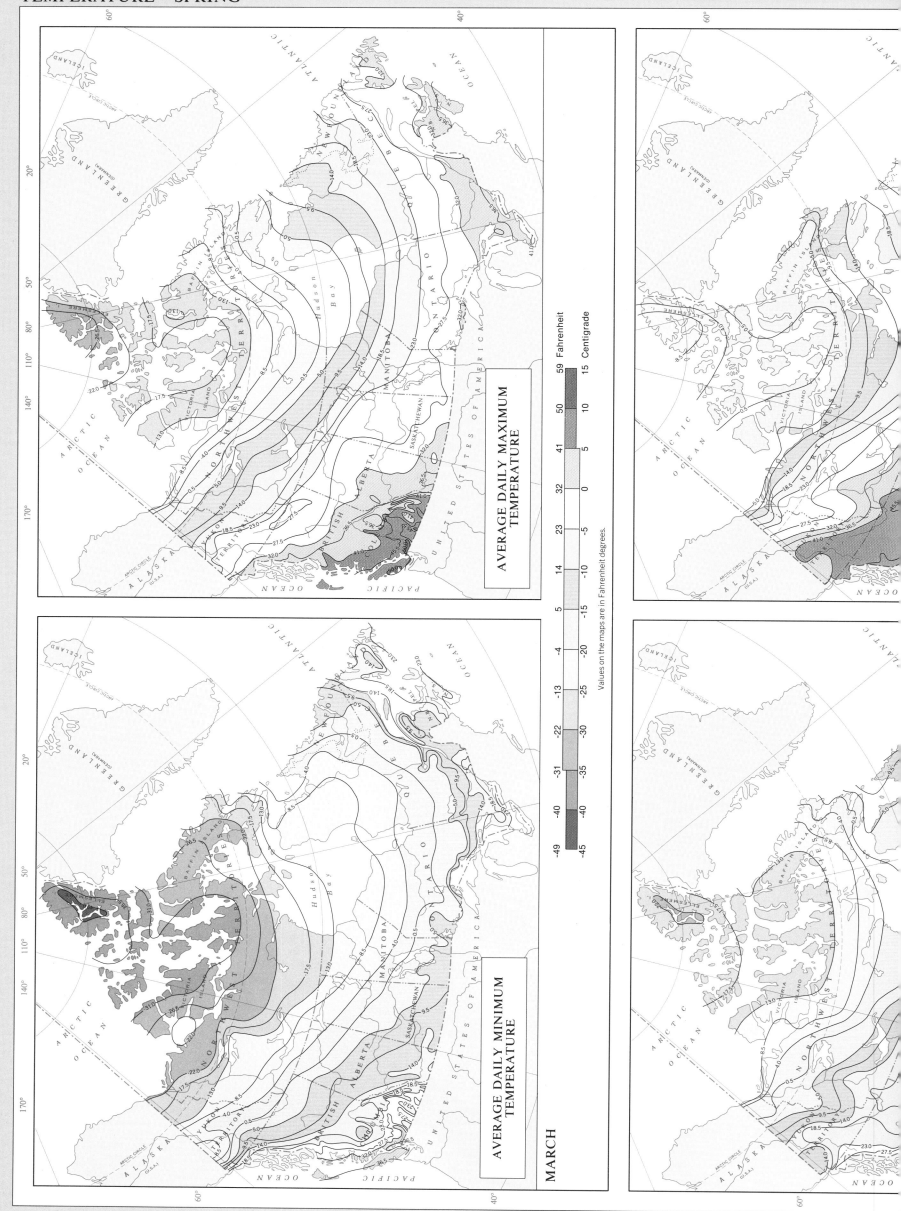

AVERAGE DAILY MAXIMUM
TEMPERATURE

AVERAGE DAILY MINIMUM
TEMPERATURE

MARCH

-49	-40	-31	-22	-13	-4	5	14	23	32	41	50	59	Fahrenheit
-45	-40	-35	-30	-25	-20	-15	-10	-5	0	5	10	15	Centigrade

Values on the maps are in Fahrenheit degrees.

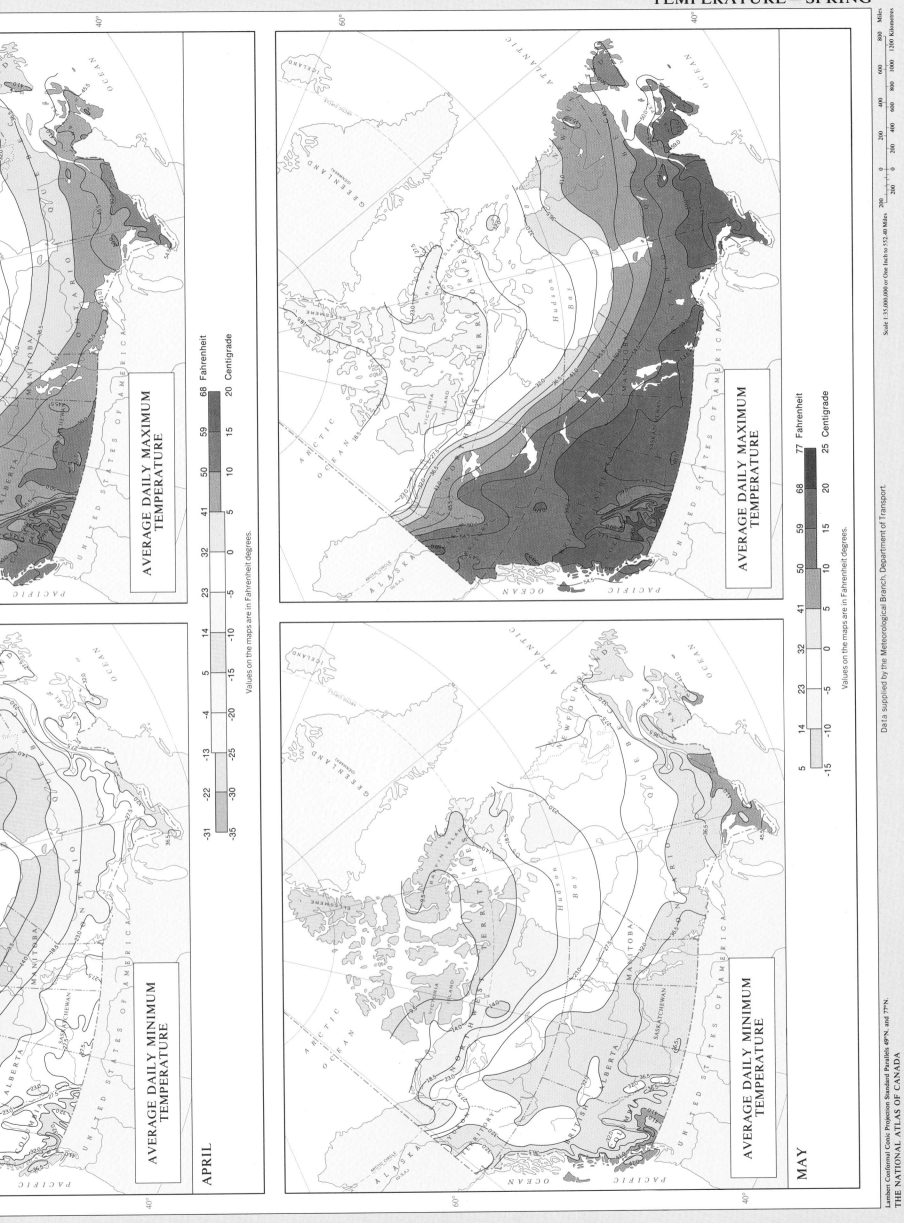

AVERAGE DAILY MAXIMUM
TEMPERATURE

AVERAGE DAILY MAXIMUM
TEMPERATURE

AVERAGE DAILY MINIMUM
TEMPERATURE

AVERAGE DAILY MINIMUM
TEMPERATURE

APRIL

MAY

Fahrenheit

Centigrade

Values on the maps are in Fahrenheit degrees.

Fahrenheit

Centigrade

Values on the maps are in Fahrenheit degrees.

77	Fahrenheit
25	Centigrade
68	20
59	15
50	10
41	5
32	0
23	-5
14	-10
5	-15

Scale 1:35,000,000 or One Inch to 552.40 Miles

Data supplied by the Meteorological Branch, Department of Transport.

Lambert Conformal Conic Projection Standard Parallels 49°N. and 77°N.

THE NATIONAL ATLAS OF CANADA

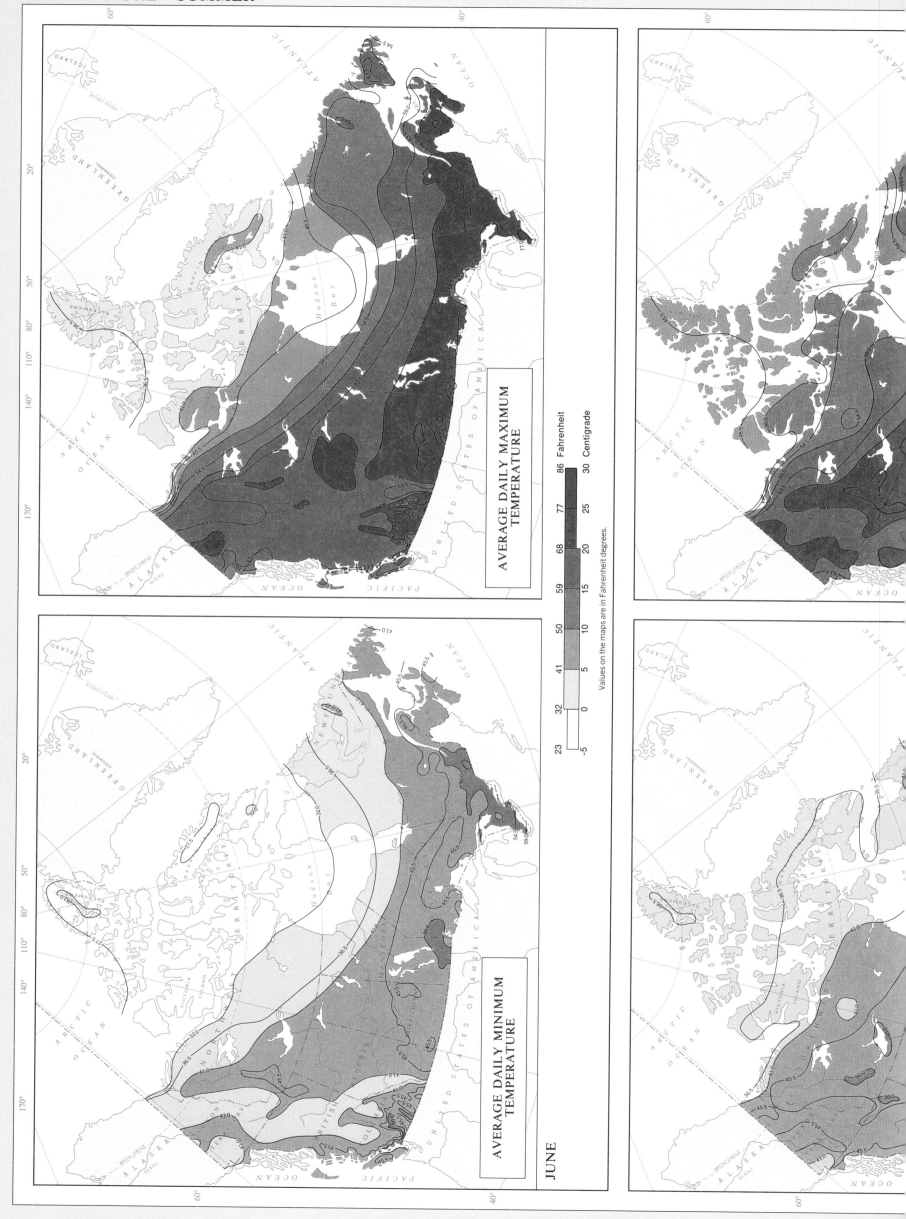

AVERAGE DAILY MAXIMUM
TEMPERATURE

AVERAGE DAILY MINIMUM
TEMPERATURE

JUNE

Fahrenheit	23	32	41	50	59	68	77	86
Centigrade	-5	0	5	10	15	20	25	30

Values on the maps are in Fahrenheit degrees.

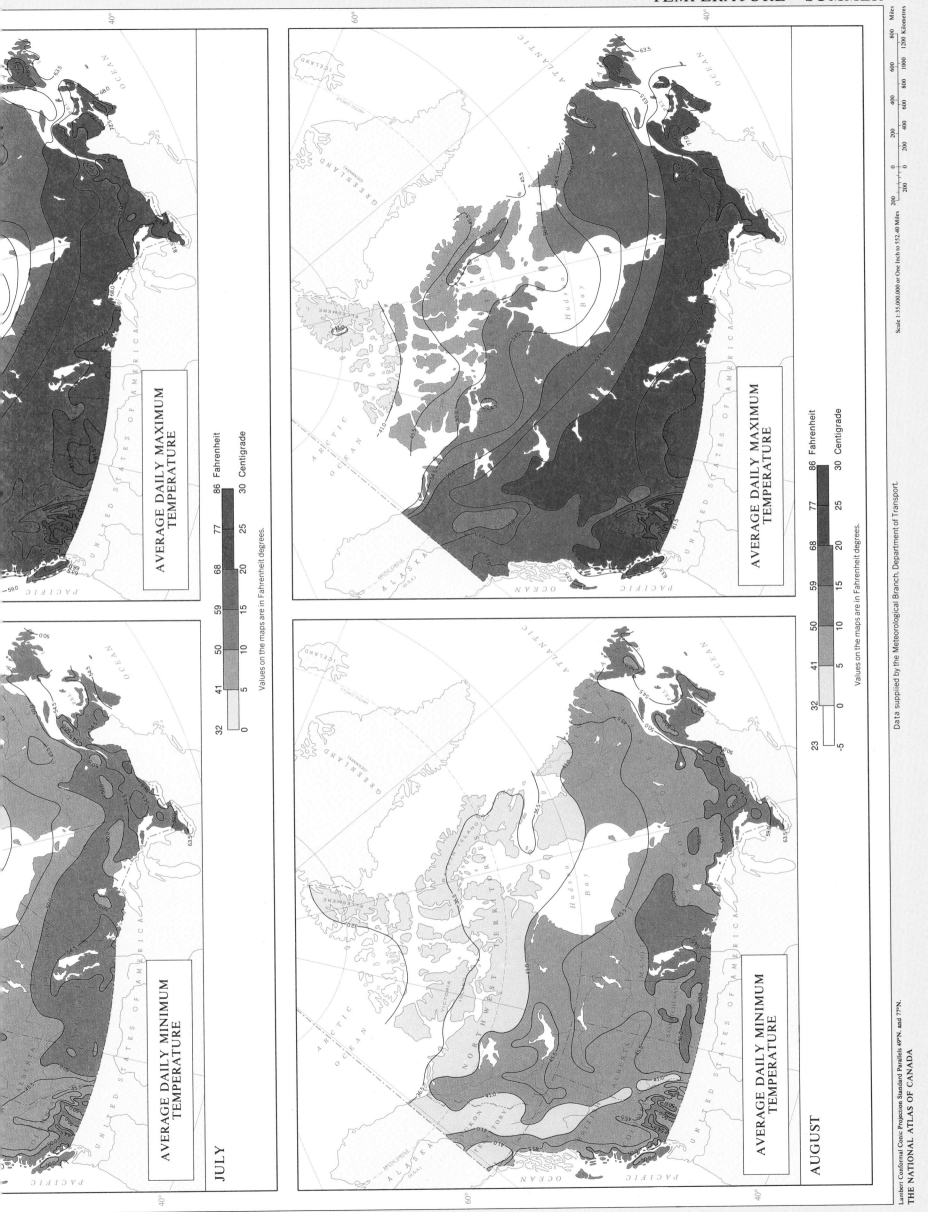

AVERAGE DAILY MAXIMUM
TEMPERATURE

AVERAGE DAILY MAXIMUM
TEMPERATURE

AVERAGE DAILY MINIMUM
TEMPERATURE

AVERAGE DAILY MINIMUM
TEMPERATURE

JULY

AUGUST

86 Fahrenheit	77	68	59	50	41	32
30 Centigrade	25	20	15	10	5	0

Values on the maps are in Fahrenheit degrees.

86 Fahrenheit	77	68	59	50	41	32	23
30 Centigrade	25	20	15	10	5	0	-5

Values on the maps are in Fahrenheit degrees.

Scale 1:35,000,000 or One Inch to 552.40 Miles

Data supplied by the Meteorological Branch, Department of Transport.

Lambert Conformal Conic Projection, Standard Parallels 49°N. and 77°N.

THE NATIONAL ATLAS OF CANADA

AVERAGE DAILY MAXIMUM
TEMPERATURE

AVERAGE DAILY MINIMUM
TEMPERATURE

SEPTEMBER

Fahrenheit	5	14	23	32	41	50	59	68	77
Centigrade	-15	-10	-5	0	5	10	15	20	25

Values on the maps are in Fahrenheit degrees.

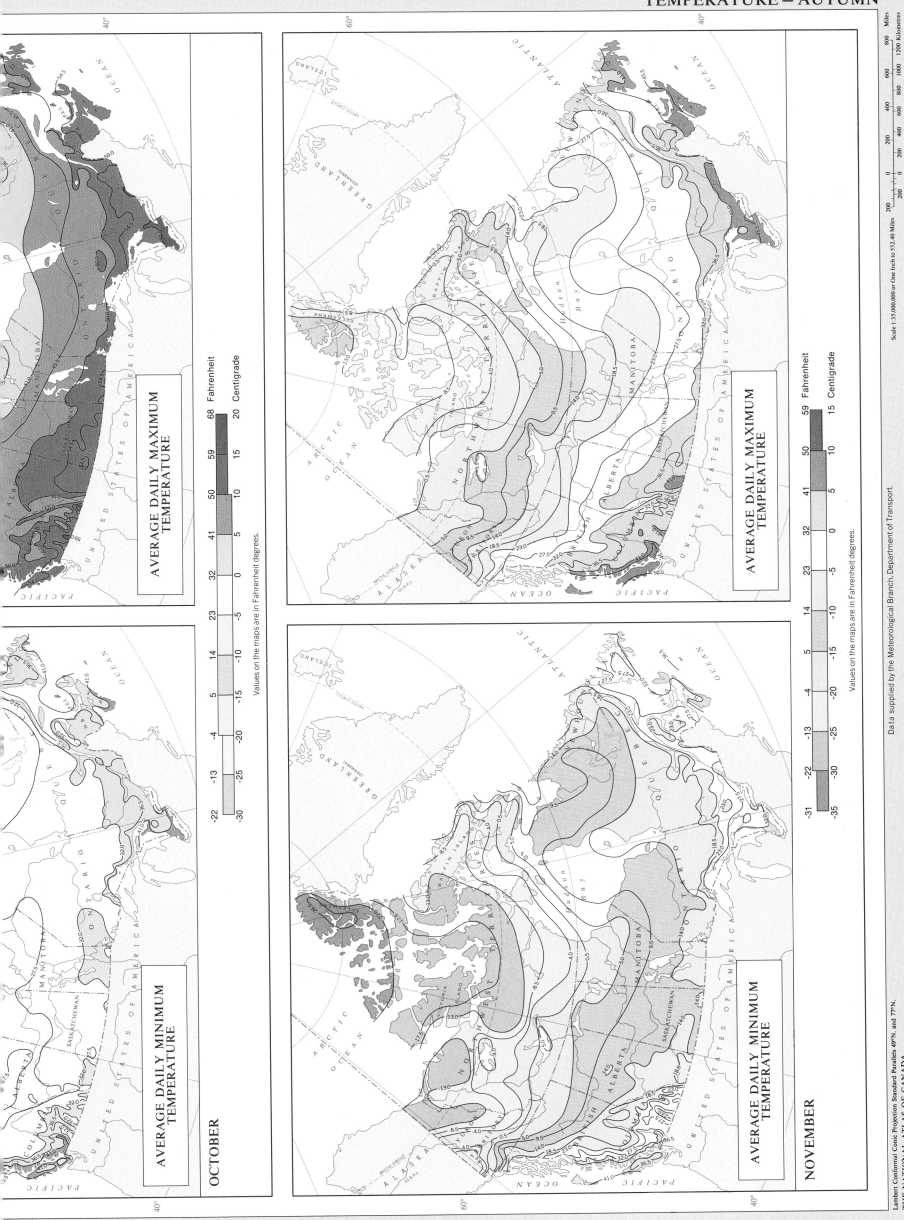

AVERAGE DAILY MAXIMUM
TEMPERATURE

	32	41	50	59	68	Fahrenheit
	0	5	10	15	20	Centigrade

-30	-25	-20	-15	-10	-5	
-22	-13	-4	5	14	23	

Values on the maps are in Fahrenheit degrees.

AVERAGE DAILY MINIMUM
TEMPERATURE

OCTOBER

AVERAGE DAILY MAXIMUM
TEMPERATURE

	23	32	41	50	59	Fahrenheit
	-5	0	5	10	15	Centigrade

-35	-30	-25	-20	-15	-10	
-31	-22	-13	-4	5	14	

Values on the maps are in Fahrenheit degrees.

AVERAGE DAILY MINIMUM
TEMPERATURE

NOVEMBER

Data supplied by the Meteorological Branch, Department of Transport.

Scale 1:35,000,000 or One Inch to 552.40 Miles

Lambert Conformal Conic Projection Standard Parallels 49°N. and 77°N.
THE NATIONAL ATLAS OF CANADA

INDEX OF EXPLORERS

The Index of Explorers lists the persons whose explorations and surveys are shown or mentioned on the maps. The nationality given is that of the explorer at the time of his birth, according to the following specifications. "British" applies to persons born in England, Scotland and Wales after 1707; in Ireland after 1801; in the British American colonies prior to and including 1776; and in present Canadian territory between 1763 and 1867. "Welsh" and "English" refer to Wales and England before 1707. "French" applies to persons born in France after 1488, and in New France prior to 1763. "Florentine" and "Venetian" refer to persons born in Florence and Venice (Italy) before 1870. Other designations of nationality require no further explanation. It should be noted that nationalities given in the legends on the maps apply to the sponsors of the expeditions rather than to the explorers themselves. Bering, for example, conducted explorations for Russia, but was himself a Dane. In this case the expedition is identified on the map as Russian. Ranks and titles given in the index are those held at the time of the explorations. The *Dictionary of Canadian Biography** is used as the authority for the spelling and form of names in the index.   *Brown, G.W., Hayne, D.M., and Halpenny, F.G. gen. eds. 1966-72. *Dictionary of Canadian Biography / Dictionnaire Biographique du Canada.* Toronto: University of Toronto Press, and Québec: Les Presses de l'université Laval.

*The Company of the Merchants Discoverers of the North-West Passage, formed in London in 1612 which appears in this table as The Northwest Company (1612) should not be confused with the fur trade association known as the North West Company (c. 1776) formed in North America.

(n)=note on page 73

INTRODUCTION TO THE HISTORICAL SECTION

The historical section of this edition of the National Atlas is part of a larger undertaking, to be continued in subsequent editions, the purpose of which is to show the sequence of explorations, of instrumental surveys and mapping, and of human occupance through which the land and territorial waters of the country have become known. The subjects selected for study cover specific events in the overall history of Canada, and may be of interest for that reason alone. However, these subjects collectively have another significance in that they indicate the growth of a body of geographical information which, at any given time, would influence political and economic decisions. The historical section can therefore serve to make more intelligible a variety of other historical events which the section does not touch upon. The information given in the historical section is based for the most part on new research into primary sources, supplemented where necessary by secondary sources. The data are plotted on modern base maps which show some features, such as canals and dammed lakes, which were not contemporaneous with the events represented. This leads to some inaccuracies or anomalies such as, for example, where a route is shown on a dammed lake - e.g. Cedar Lake or Gouin Reservoir- which did not exist at that time. The names on the base maps are the modern authorized names which in many cases differ from the names used in the source material.

NATIONALITY	EMPLOYER OR SPONSOR	PAGE
tuguese	Manoel I, King of Portugal	73(n)
tuguese	Manoel I, King of Portugal	73(n)
anish	Government of Spain	75-76(A)
tish	Hudson's Bay Company	78
erican	Canadian Northern Railway	73
tish	Anglican Church of Canada	77
glish	London merchants	74
tish	Royal Navy	75-76(B)
tish	North West Company (c. 1776)	74
tish	Private; North West Company (c. 1776)	74
glish	Muscovy Company; Cathay Company	75-76(B)
tish	Private; North West Company (c. 1776)	74
nch	Government of France	75-76(A)
nch	Private	73
nch	Private	73
nch	Private	73
tuguese	Charles I, King of Spain	73
tish	Corps of Royal Engineers	78
erican	United States Army	77
nch	Private	73
erican	American Geographical and Statistical Society; Government of the United States	75-76(C); 77
tish	Private	78
rman	Der Verein für Erdkunde zu Dresden (The Geographical Society of Dresden)	77
erican	Private	77
tish	Hudson's Bay Company	74
tish	Hudson's Bay Company	74
tish	Hudson's Bay Company	73
gian	Recollet Branch of the Franciscan Order	73
tish	Government of the Province of Canada	78
tch	British Army	78
	Canadian Pacific Railway	78
glish	Private sponsors and merchants	74
tish	Lady Jane Franklin	75-76(C); 77
glish	The Bristol Society of Merchant Venturers	74
	Canadian Pacific Railway	78
tish	British Army	78
nch	Government of New France	73
tish	Government of Great Britain	78
erican	Private societies and organizations	77
tish	Royal Navy	75-76(C)
glish	Hudson's Bay Company	74
tish	Lady Jane Franklin	75-76(C)
nadian	Royal Canadian Mounted Police	75-76(B)
rse	Private	73(n)
	Corps of Royal Engineers	78
nadian	Government of Canada	77
tish	Geological Survey of Canada	78
nadian	Geological Survey of Canada	77; 78
nadian	Canada, Department of the Interior	78
tish	Lady Jane Franklin	75-76(C)
tish	Royal Navy	75-76(B)
nadian	Geological Survey of Canada	78
tish	Hudson's Bay Company	74
nadian	Geological Survey of Canada	78
tish	North West Company (c. 1776)	74
tish	Hudson's Bay Company	73
tish	Hudson's Bay Company	74
	Canadian Pacific Railway	78
erican	National Geographic Society	77
	Geological Survey of Canada	78

NAME OF EXPLORER AND DATE OF EXPEDITION	NATIONALITY	EMPLOYER OR SPONSOR	PAGE
Mahood, James Adams 1871		Canadian Pacific Railway	78
Manning, Thomas Henry 1936-41	British	Royal Geographical Society	77
Marquette, Father Jacques 1673	French	Society of Jesus (Jesuits)	73
Micheau, Daniel 1785		Government of Great Britain	78
Middleton, Commander Christopher 1741		Royal Navy	74
Mitchell, Thomas 1744	British	Hudson's Bay Company	74
Moberly, Walter 1865; 1871	British	Private; Canadian Pacific Railway	78
Monts, see Du Gua de Monts			
Morice, Father Adrien Gabriel 1892; 1895; 1904	French	Missionary Oblates of Mary Immaculate	74
Munk (Munck), Jens Eriksen 1619-20	Danish	Christian IV, King of Denmark	74
Munn, Captain Henry Toke 1916-18	British	Private	77
Murray, Alexander Hunter 1864-66; 1868-72; 1874; 1878	British	Geological Survey of Canada	78
Nares, Captain George Strong (later Sir) 1875-76	British	Royal Navy	77
Nicollet de Belleborne, Jean 1634-35	French	Government of New France	73
Noble, Crawford, Jr. 1902	British	Private	77
Norton, Moses 1762	British	Hudson's Bay Company	74
Noyon, Jacques de 1688	French	Private	73
Ogilvie, William 1888; 1891	Canadian	Canada, Department of the Interior	78
Palliser, Captain John 1857-59	British	Government of Great Britain	78
Palmer, Lieutenant Henry Spencer 1859; 1862	British	Corps of Royal Engineers	78
Parry, Captain William Edward (later Sir) 1819-20; 1821-22	British	Royal Navy	75-76(B)
Peary, Commander Robert Edwin 1898-1902; 1905-06; 1908-09	American	United States Navy	77
Pemberton, Joseph Despard 1856; 1857	British	Hudson's Bay Company	78
Penny, Captain William 1850-51	British	Government of Great Britain	75-76(C)
Pereleshin, Lieutenant 1863		Russian Navy	78
Pérez Hernández, Juan José 1774	Spanish	Government of Spain	75-76(A)
Petitot, Father Émile Fortuné Stanislas Joseph 1864-72; 1878	French	Missionary Oblates of Mary Immaculate	74
Pink, William 1766-67; 1767-68	British	Hudson's Bay Company	74
Pond, Peter 1778-88	British	North West Company (c. 1776)	74
Pope, Franklin L. 1865-66	American	Western Union Telegraph	78
Prichard, Hesketh Vernon Hesketh 1910	British	Private	73
Pullen, Lieutenant William John Samuel 1849-50	British	Royal Navy	75-76(C)
Putnam, George Palmer 1927	American	Private	77
Radisson, Pierre-Esprit 1659-60	French	Private	73
Rae, Dr. John, M.D. 1846-47; 1847-50; 1851; 1854	British	Hudson's Bay Company	75-76(B); (C)
Rasmussen, Knud Johan Victor 1921-24	Danish	Private	75-76(B); 77
Richardson, James 1857-58; 1870	British	Geological Survey of Canada	78
Richardson, Dr. Sir John, M.D. 1825-27; 1847-50	British	Royal Navy	75-76(B); (C)
Ross, Captain Sir James Clark 1848-49	British	Royal Navy	75-76 (C)
Ross, Captain John (later Sir) 1818; 1829-33	British	Royal Navy	75-76 (B)
Rowley, Graham W. 1938-39	British	Cambridge University	77
St. Cyr, Arthur 1897	Canadian	Canada, Department of the Interior	78
Schwatka, Lieutenant Frederick George 1878-79; 1883	American	American Geographical Society; United States Army	75-76(C); 78
Selwyn, Alfred Richard Cecil 1872; 1875	British	Geological Survey of Canada	78
Simpson, Sir George 1824-25; 1841	British	Hudson's Bay Company	74
Simpson, Thomas 1837; 1839	British	Hudson's Bay Company	75-76(B)
Smith, Marcus 1874	British	Canadian Pacific Railway	78
Soper, J. Dewey 1924-26; 1928-29	Canadian	Government of Canada	77
Spicer, Captain John O. 1879-80	American	Private	77
Sproule, Ensign George 1787	British	British Army	78
Stefansson, Vilhjalmur 1913-18	Canadian	Government of Canada	77
Stuart, William 1715	British	Hudson's Bay Company	74
Sverdrup, Captain Otto Neumann 1898-1902	Norwegian	Joint: Government of Norway and merchants	77
Taylor, David 1839		Government of Upper Canada	78
Thompson, David 1792-94; 1796-1802; 1804-05; 1807-12	British	Hudson's Bay Company; North West Company (c. 1776)	78
Thorfinnr karlsefni Thordarson between 1003 and 1015	Icelandic	Private	73(n)
Tibbetts, Hiram 1823		Private	78
Tiedemann, H.O. 1862		Private	78
Tomison, William 1767-68; 1769-70	British	Hudson's Bay Company	74
Troyes, Pierre de 1686	French	Government of New France	73
Turner, Canon John Hudspith 1941	British	Bible Churchman's Missionary Society	77
Turner, William 1780		Moravian Church	73
Turnor, Philip 1778; 1779-82; 1785; 1787; 1790-92	British	Hudson's Bay Company	78
Tyrrell, James Williams 1900	Canadian	Canada, Department of the Interior	78
Tyrrell, Joseph Burr 1892-94; 1898	Canadian	Geological Survey of Canada	78
Valdés y Flores Bazán, Commander Cayetano 1792	Spanish	Government of Spain	75-76(A)
Vancouver, Captain George 1792; 1793; 1794	British	Royal Navy	75-76(A)
Verrazzano, Giovanni da 1524	Florentine	François I, King of France	73
Vondenvelden 1786		Government of Great Britain	78
Wordie, J.M. 1934; 1937	British		77
Wright, Lieutenant Thomas 1766	British	British Army	78

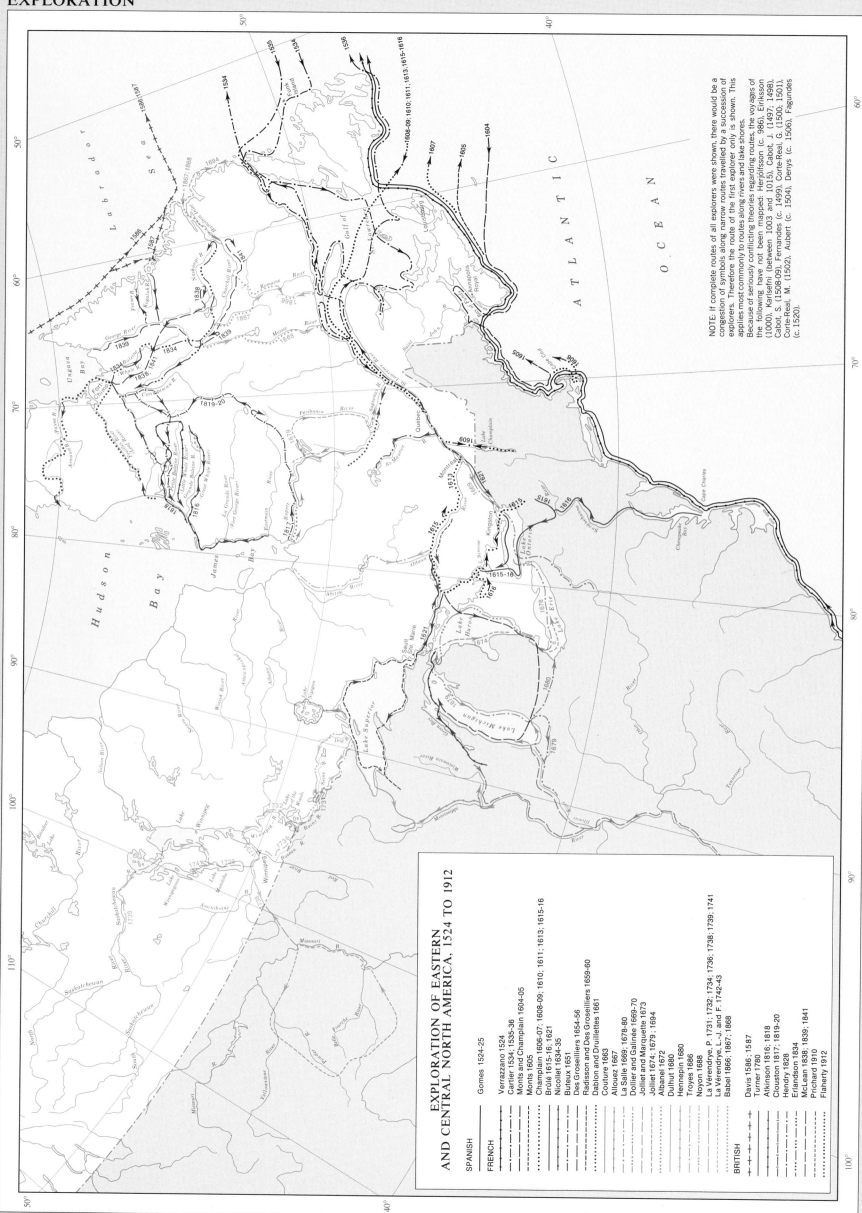

EXPLORATION OF EASTERN AND CENTRAL NORTH AMERICA, 1524 TO 1912

SPANISH
Gomes 1524-25

FRENCH
Verrazzano 1524
Cartier 1534; 1535-36
Monts and Champlain 1604-05
Monts 1605
Champlain 1606-07; 1608-09; 1610; 1611; 1613; 1615-16
Brûlé 1615-16; 1621
Nicollet 1634-35
Buteux 1651
Des Groseilliers 1654-56
Radisson and Des Groseilliers 1659-60
Dablon and Druillettes 1661
Couture 1663
Allouez 1667
La Salle 1669; 1678-80
Dollier and Galinée 1669-70
Jolliet and Marquette 1673
Jolliet 1674; 1679; 1694
Albanel 1672
Dulhut 1680
Hennepin 1680
Troyes 1686
Noyon 1688
La Vérendrye, P. 1731; 1732; 1734; 1736; 1738; 1739; 1741
La Vérendrye, L.-J. and F. 1742-43

BRITISH
Babel 1866; 1867; 1868
Davis 1586; 1587
Turner 1780
Atkinson 1816; 1818
Clouston 1817; 1819-20
Hendry 1828
Erlandson 1834
McLean 1838; 1839; 1841
Prichard 1910
Flaherty 1912

NOTE: If complete routes of all explorers were shown, there would be a congestion of symbols along narrow routes travelled by a succession of explorers. Therefore the route of the first explorer only is shown. This applies most commonly to routes along rivers and lake shores.
Because of seriously conflicting theories regarding routes, the voyages of the following have not been mapped: Herjólfsson (c. 986), Eiriksson (1000), Karlsefni (between 1003 and 1015), Cabot, J. (1497; 1498), Cabot, S. (1508-09), Fernandes (c. 1499), Corte-Real, G. (1500; 1501), Corte-Real, M. (1502), Aubert (c. 1504), Denys (c. 1506), Fagundes (c. 1520).

Lambert Conformal Conic Projection Standard Parallels 49°N. and 77°N.
Scale 1:15,000,000 or One Inch to 236.74 Miles
THE NATIONAL ATLAS OF CANADA

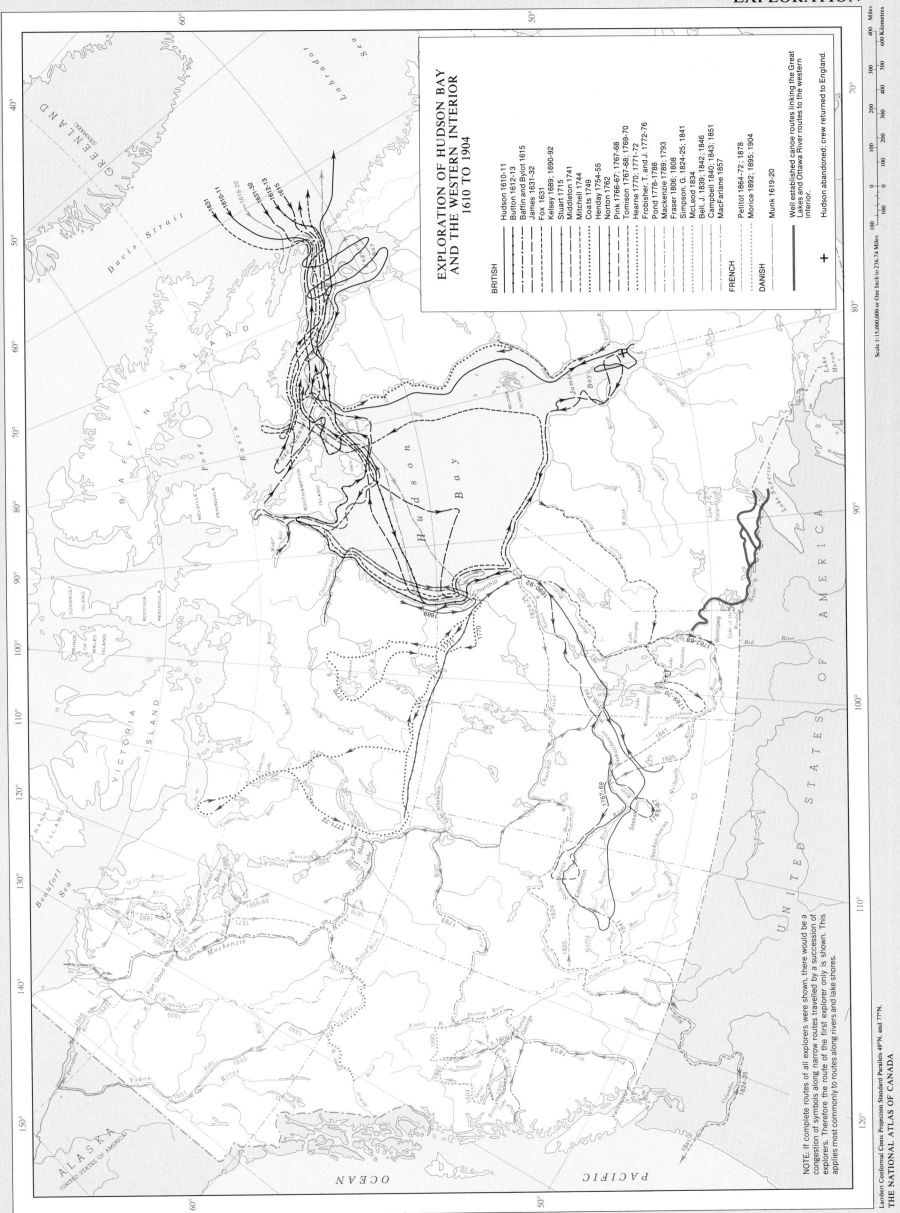

EXPLORATION OF HUDSON BAY
AND THE WESTERN INTERIOR
1610 TO 1904

BRITISH	
Hudson 1610-11	
Button 1612-13	
Baffin and Bylot 1615	
James 1631-32	
Fox 1631	
Kelsey 1689; 1690-92	
Stuart 1715	
Middleton 1741	
Mitchell 1744	
Coats 1749	
Henday 1754-55	
Norton 1762	
Pink 1766-67; 1767-68	
Tomison 1767-68; 1769-70	
Hearne 1770; 1771-72	
Frobisher, T. and J. 1772-76	
Pond 1778-1788	
Mackenzie 1789; 1793	
Fraser 1806; 1808	
Simpson, G. 1824-25; 1841	
McLeod 1834	
Bell, J. 1839; 1842; 1846	
Campbell 1840; 1843; 1851	
MacFarlane 1857	

FRENCH	
Petitot 1864-72; 1878	
Morice 1892; 1895; 1904	

DANISH	
Munk 1619-20	

Well established canoe routes linking the Great
Lakes and Ottawa River routes to the western
interior.

Hudson abandoned; crew returned to England.

NOTE: If complete routes of all explorers were shown, there would be a
congestion of symbols along narrow routes travelled by a succession of
explorers. Therefore the route of the first explorer only is shown. This
applies most commonly to routes along rivers and lake shores.

Scale 1:15,000,000 or One Inch to 236.74 Miles

Lambert Conformal Conic Projection Standard Parallels 49°N. and 77°N.

THE NATIONAL ATLAS OF CANADA

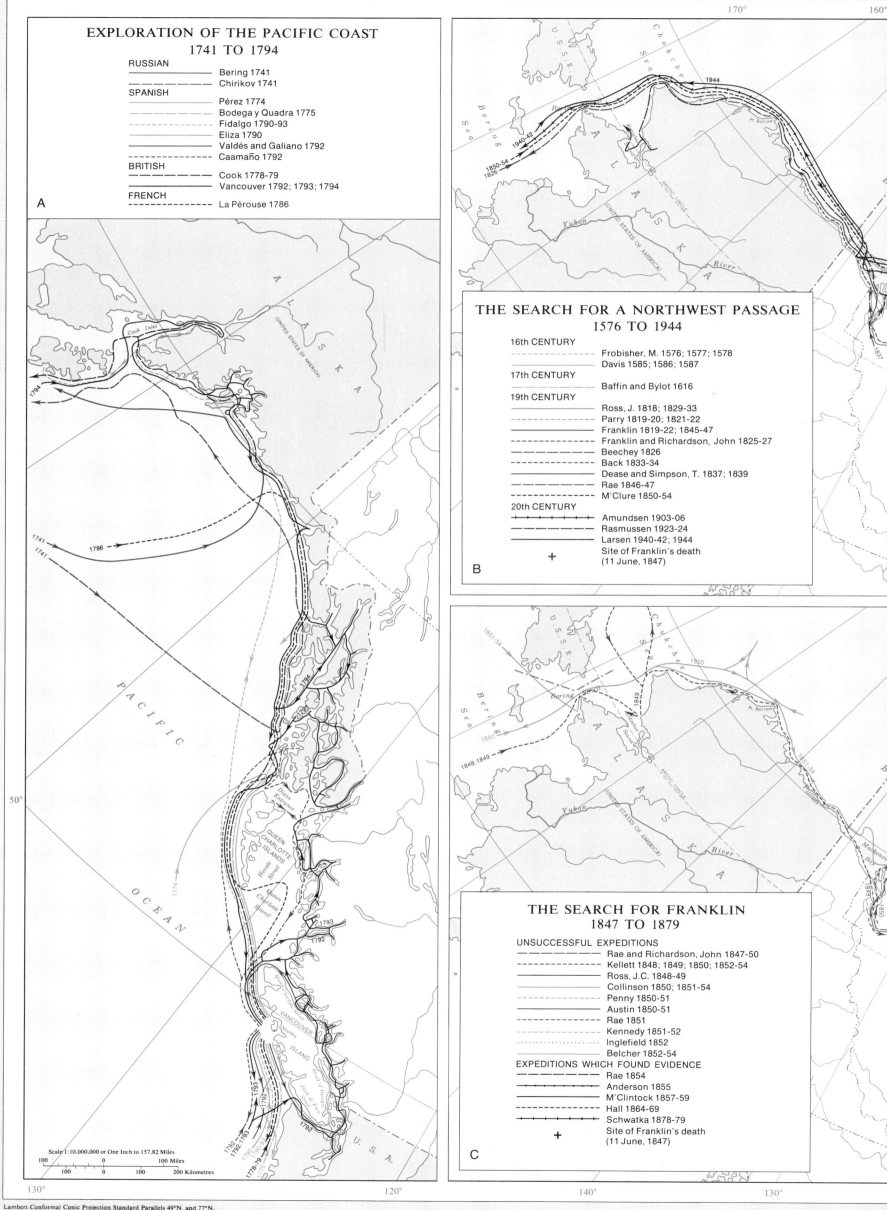

EXPLORATION OF THE PACIFIC COAST 1741 TO 1794

RUSSIAN
——————— Bering 1741
——————— Chirikov 1741

SPANISH
——————— Pérez 1774
- - - - - - - Bodega y Quadra 1775
- - - - - - - Fidalgo 1790-93
——————— Eliza 1790
——————— Valdés and Galiano 1792
——————— Caamaño 1792

BRITISH
——————— Cook 1778-79
——————— Vancouver 1792; 1793; 1794

FRENCH
- - - - - - - La Pérouse 1786

A

THE SEARCH FOR A NORTHWEST PASSAGE 1576 TO 1944

16th CENTURY
- - - - - - - Frobisher, M. 1576; 1577; 1578
——————— Davis 1585; 1586; 1587

17th CENTURY
- - - - - - - Baffin and Bylot 1616

19th CENTURY
——————— Ross, J. 1818; 1829-33
——————— Parry 1819-20; 1821-22
——————— Franklin 1819-22; 1845-47
——————— Franklin and Richardson, John 1825-27
——————— Beechey 1826
- - - - - - - Back 1833-34
——————— Dease and Simpson, T. 1837; 1839
——————— Rae 1846-47
- - - - - - - M'Clure 1850-54

20th CENTURY
—+—+—+— Amundsen 1903-06
——————— Rasmussen 1923-24
——————— Larsen 1940-42; 1944
+ Site of Franklin's death (11 June, 1847)

B

THE SEARCH FOR FRANKLIN 1847 TO 1879

UNSUCCESSFUL EXPEDITIONS
——————— Rae and Richardson, John 1847-50
- - - - - - - Kellett 1848; 1849; 1850; 1852-54
——————— Ross, J.C. 1848-49
——————— Collinson 1850; 1851-54
——————— Penny 1850-51
——————— Austin 1850-51
- - - - - - - Rae 1851
——————— Kennedy 1851-52
· · · · · · · Inglefield 1852
——————— Belcher 1852-54

EXPEDITIONS WHICH FOUND EVIDENCE
——————— Rae 1854
—+—+—+— Anderson 1855
——————— M'Clintock 1857-59
- - - - - - - Hall 1864-69
—+—+—+— Schwatka 1878-79
+ Site of Franklin's death (11 June, 1847)

C

Scale 1:10,000,000 or One Inch to 157.82 Miles

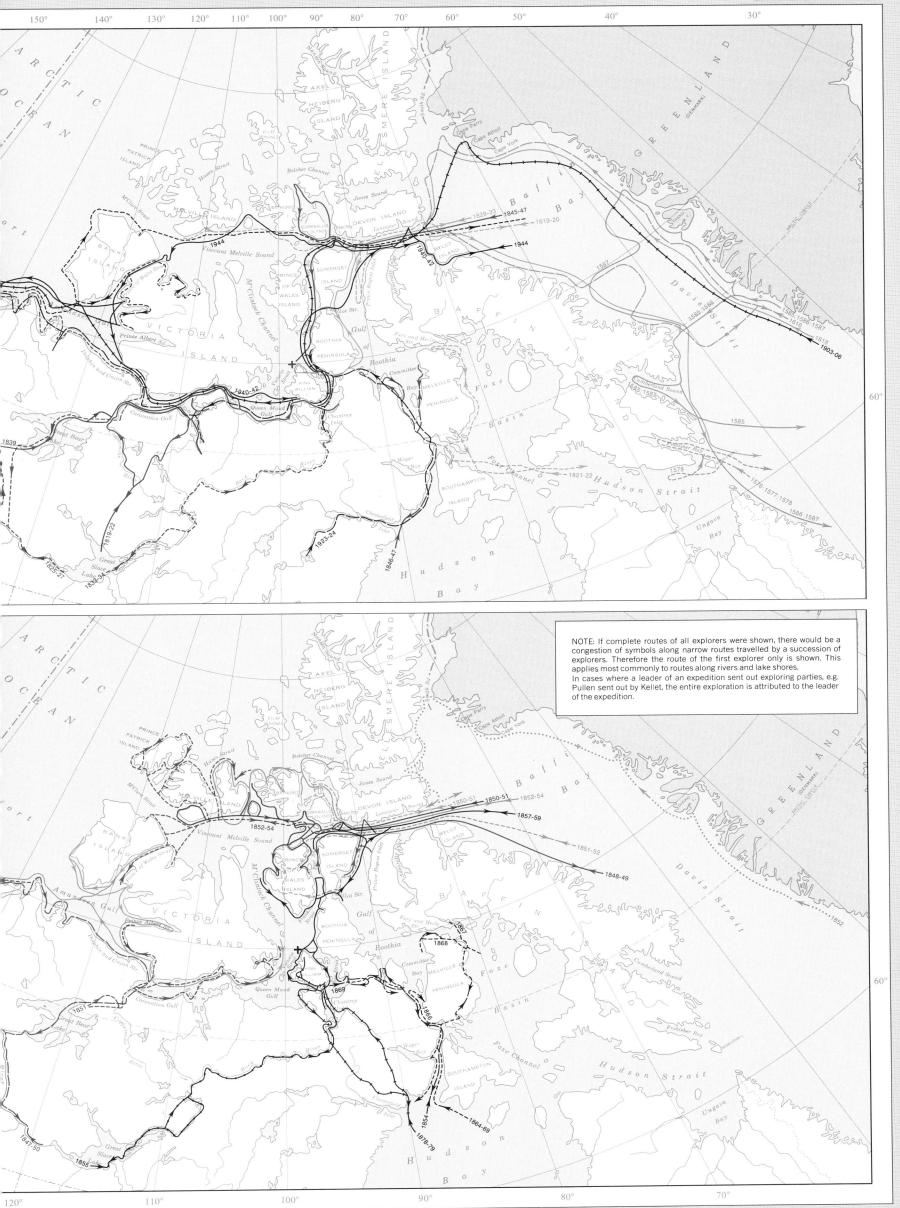

NOTE: If complete routes of all explorers were shown, there would be a congestion of symbols along narrow routes travelled by a succession of explorers. Therefore the route of the first explorer only is shown. This applies most commonly to routes along rivers and lake shores.
In cases where a leader of an expedition sent out exploring parties, e.g. Pullen sent out by Kellet, the entire exploration is attributed to the leader of the expedition.

Scale 1:15,000,000 or One Inch to 236.74 Miles

EXPLORATION

EXPLORATION OF NARES STRAIT

Scale 1:7,500,000

GREENLAND (DENMARK)

ELLESMERE ISLAND

BAFFIN BAY

EXPLORATION OF THE ARCTIC, 1587 TO 1941

BRITISH
- Davis 1587
- Baffin and Bylot 1616
- Inglefield 1852
- Noble 1902
- Munn 1916-18
- Wordie 1934; 1937
- Manning 1936-41
- Rowley 1938-39
- Turner 1941

AMERICAN
- Kane 1853-55
- Hayes 1860-61
- Hall 1871-73
- Spicer 1879-80
- Greely 1881-84
- Peary 1898-1902; 1905-06; 1908-09
- Comer 1907-09; 1910-12
- MacMillan 1913-17
- Putnam 1927

GERMAN
- Boas 1883-84

NORWEGIAN
- Hantzsch 1909-11
- Sverdrup 1898-1902

CANADIAN
- Low 1903-04
- Bernier 1906-07; 1908-09; 1910-11; 1912-13
- Stefansson 1913-18
- Fleming 1911; 1915
- Burwash 1923-24
- Livingstone 1927
- Soper 1924-26; 1928-29

DANISH
- Rasmussen 1921-24

+ Site of Hall's death, 8 November, 1871
+ Site of Hantzsch's death, June, 1911

NOTE: If complete routes of all explorers dealt with on this map were shown there would be severe congestion of symbols in some of the waterways. Only the route of the first explorer is shown in such areas.

The routes of exploration parties belonging to an expedition are shown under the name of the leader of the expedition rather than the name of the leader of the particular exploration party. For example the route of the G. W. Rowley and R.J.O. Bray in 1937 is shown as part of the British Canadian Arctic Expedition of 1936-41 led by T.H. Manning.

Dates in the legend indicate the year or years of the entire expedition. Dates on the map indicate the routes taken in specific years of that expedition.

Lambert Conformal Conic Projection Standard Parallels 49°N. and 77°N.

Scale 1:12,500,000 or One Inch to 197.29 Miles

THE NATIONAL ATLAS OF CANADA

ARCTIC OCEAN

ELIZABETH ISLANDS

VICTORIA ISLAND

BAFFIN ISLAND

Davis Strait

Hudson Strait

Baffin Bay

Labrador Sea

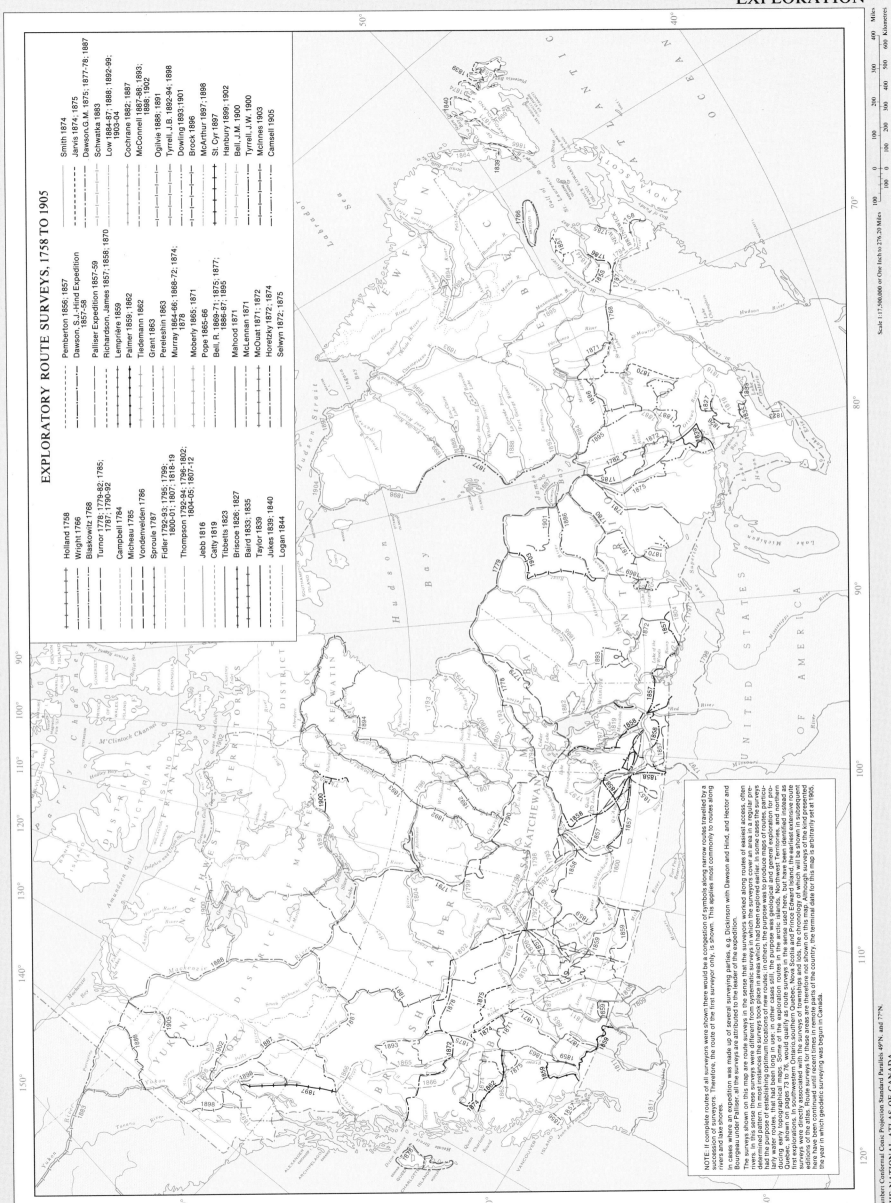

EXPLORATORY ROUTE SURVEYS, 1758 TO 1905

Holland 1758	Pemberton 1856; 1857
Wright 1766	Dawson, S.J.-Hind Expedition 1857-58
Blaskowitz 1768	Palliser Expedition 1857-59
Turner 1778; 1779-82; 1785; 1787; 1790-92	Richardson, James 1857; 1858; 1870
Campbell 1784	Lemprière 1859
Micheau 1785	Palmer 1859; 1862
Vondenvelden 1786	Tiedemann 1862
Sproule 1787	Grant 1863
Fidler 1792-93; 1795; 1799; 1800-01; 1807; 1818-19	Pereleshin 1863
Thompson 1792-94; 1796-1802; 1804-05; 1807-12	Murray 1864-66; 1868-72; 1874; 1878
Jebb 1816	Moberly 1865; 1871
Catty 1819	Pope 1865-66
Tibbetts 1823	Bell, R. 1869-71; 1875; 1877; 1886-87; 1895
Briscoe 1826; 1827	Mahood 1871
Baird 1833; 1835	McLennan 1871
Taylor 1839	McOuat 1871; 1872
Jukes 1839; 1840	Horetzky 1872; 1874
Logan 1844	Selwyn 1872; 1875

Smith 1874	
Jarvis 1874; 1875	
Dawson, G.M. 1875; 1877-78; 1887	
Schwatka 1883	
Low 1884-87; 1888; 1892-99; 1903-04	
Cochrane 1882; 1887	
McConnell 1887-88; 1893; 1898; 1902	
Ogilvie 1888; 1891	
Tyrrell, J.B. 1892-94; 1898	
Dowling 1893;1901	
Brock 1896	
McArthur 1897; 1898	
St. Cyr 1897	
Hanbury 1899; 1902	
Bell, J.M. 1900	
Tyrrell, J.W. 1900	
McInnes 1903	
Camsell 1905	

Scale 1:17,500,000 or One Inch to 276.20 Miles

NOTE: If complete routes of all surveyors were shown there would be a congestion of symbols along routes travelled by a succession of surveyors. Therefore, the route of the first surveyor only, is shown. This applies most commonly to routes along rivers and lake shores.

In cases where an expedition was made up of several surveying parties, e.g. Dickinson with Dawson and Hind, and Hector and Bourgeau under Palliser, all the surveys are attributed to the leader of the expedition.

The surveys shown on this map are route surveys in the sense that the surveyors worked along routes of easiest access, often rivers. In this sense these surveys were different from systematic surveys in which the surveyors cover an area in a regular predetermined pattern. In most instances the surveys took place in areas which had been explored earlier. In some cases the surveys had the purpose of establishing optimum locations of new routes; in others, the purpose was to produce maps of routes, particularly water routes, that had been long in use. In other cases still, the purpose was geological and general exploration for producing early topographical maps. Some of the exploration routes in the arctic islands, Northwest Territories, and northern Quebec, shown on pages 73 to 76, would qualify as route surveys in the sense used here, but have been identified instead as first explorations. In southwestern Ontario, southern Quebec, Nova Scotia and Prince Edward Island, the chronology of which will be shown in subsequent editions of the atlas. Route surveys for these areas are therefore not shown on this map. Although surveys of the kind presented here have been continued until recent times in remote parts of the country, the terminal date for this map is arbitrarily set at 1905, the year in which geodetic surveying was begun in Canada.

Lambert Conformal Conic Projection Standard Parallels 49°N. and 77°N.

POSTS OF THE CANADIAN FUR TRADE

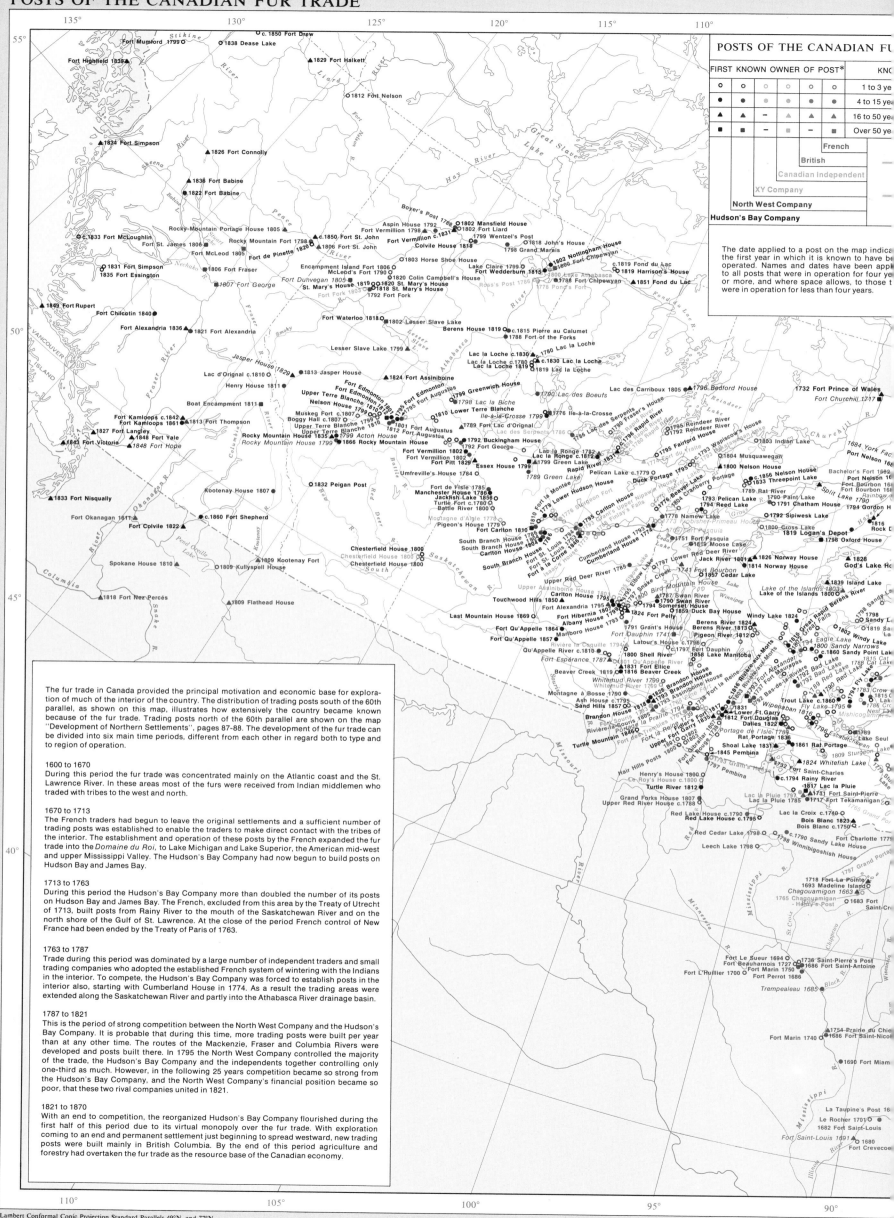

POSTS OF THE CANADIAN FU[R...]

FIRST KNOWN OWNER OF POST*						KNO[WN...]
○	○	○	○	○	○	1 to 3 ye[ars]
●	●	●	●	●	●	4 to 15 yea[rs]
▲	▲	—	▲	▲	▲	16 to 50 yea[rs]
■	■	—	■	—	■	Over 50 yea[rs]
				French		
			British			
		Canadian Independent				
XY Company						
North West Company						
Hudson's Bay Company						

The date applied to a post on the map indica[tes] the first year in which it is known to have be[en] operated. Names and dates have been appli[ed] to all posts that were in operation for four ye[ars] or more, and where space allows, to those t[hat] were in operation for less than four years.

The fur trade in Canada provided the principal motivation and economic base for exploration of much of the interior of the country. The distribution of trading posts south of the 60th parallel, as shown on this map, illustrates how extensively the country became known because of the fur trade. Trading posts north of the 60th parallel are shown on the map "Development of Northern Settlements", pages 87-88. The development of the fur trade can be divided into six main time periods, different from each other in regard both to type and to region of operation.

1600 to 1670
During this period the fur trade was concentrated mainly on the Atlantic coast and the St. Lawrence River. In these areas most of the furs were received from Indian middlemen who traded with tribes to the west and north.

1670 to 1713
The French traders had begun to leave the original settlements and a sufficient number of trading posts was established to enable the traders to make direct contact with the tribes of the interior. The establishment and operation of these posts by the French expanded the fur trade into the *Domaine du Roi*, to Lake Michigan and Lake Superior, the American mid-west and upper Mississippi Valley. The Hudson's Bay Company had now begun to build posts on Hudson Bay and James Bay.

1713 to 1763
During this period the Hudson's Bay Company more than doubled the number of its posts on Hudson Bay and James Bay. The French, excluded from this area by the Treaty of Utrecht of 1713, built posts from Rainy River to the mouth of the Saskatchewan River and on the north shore of the Gulf of St. Lawrence. At the close of the period French control of New France had been ended by the Treaty of Paris of 1763.

1763 to 1787
Trade during this period was dominated by a large number of independent traders and small trading companies who adopted the established French system of wintering with the Indians in the interior. To compete, the Hudson's Bay Company was forced to establish posts in the interior also, starting with Cumberland House in 1774. As a result the trading areas were extended along the Saskatchewan River and partly into the Athabasca River drainage basin.

1787 to 1821
This is the period of strong competition between the North West Company and the Hudson's Bay Company. It is probable that during this time, more trading posts were built per year than at any other time. The routes of the Mackenzie, Fraser and Columbia Rivers were developed and posts built there. In 1795 the North West Company controlled the majority of the trade, the Hudson's Bay Company and the independents together controlling only one-third as much. However, in the following 25 years competition became so strong from the Hudson's Bay Company, and the North West Company's financial position became so poor, that these two rival companies united in 1821.

1821 to 1870
With an end to competition, the reorganized Hudson's Bay Company flourished during the first half of this period due to its virtual monopoly over the fur trade. With exploration coming to an end and permanent settlement just beginning to spread westward, new trading posts were built mainly in British Columbia. By the end of this period agriculture and forestry had overtaken the fur trade as the resource base of the Canadian economy.

ADE, 1600 TO 1870

GTH OF OPERATION OF POST

% of the posts shown on the map)

% of the posts shown on the map)

% of the posts shown on the map)

of the posts shown on the map)

pproximate limit of the *Domaine du oi* as set out in 1653 and 1658.

pproximate limit of the *Domaine du oi* after additions in 1733.

. *(circa)* = about

ange of ownership is not shown. ames in upright type, e.g. **1684 French** eek signify continuous operation. lic type, e.g. *Split Lake 1790* signifies ermittent operation.

FRENCH

In the legend 'French' refers to the ownership of posts by the inhabitants of New France prior to 1763. Several distinct types of posts are included in this category.

First, there were the free posts, such as Fort Détroit, Fort Michilimackinac and Ouiatanon, built and operated by the government, where anyone with a licence could trade. A second type was a post such as Fort Niagara, Fort Presqu'île and Fort Duquesne where trade was carried on, in behalf of the King of France, in an area too unprofitable for general traders, but important for maintaining the goodwill of the Indians. A third type of post was leased by the King to individuals or companies, giving them the exclusive rights to trade within the defined limits of a particular post, such as Témiscamingue, Sault-Sainte-Marie and Camenestigouia. A fourth type was a small post set up by an independent, unlicensed trader where trade with the Indians was carried on. These unlicensed traders were known as the *coureurs de bois.*

The *Domaine du Roi (La Traite de Tadoussac)*, established in 1653 and 1658, and enlarged in 1733, as shown on the map, was an area leased to an individual or company who then enjoyed exclusive trading rights within it for a defined period of time. After the Conquest, the French *Domaine du Roi* became the British King's Domain and continued to operate in the same manner until 1860 when the Hudson's Bay Company's lease of the Domain was terminated.

BRITISH

This term refers mostly to the posts operated by the British Military in order to regulate the operation of the British fur trade. The other posts included in this category are those of the Nova Scotia Government's short-lived experiment of centralized and government supported trading posts in the 1760's.

CANADIAN INDEPENDENT

This term is used to denote any free trader or small trading partnership operating after 1763. These private traders were referred to by the Hudson's Bay Company officers as the 'Pedlars'. They worked from relatively limited resources and were generally forced to sell out to the larger companies.

XY COMPANY

This was the commonly used name of the 'New North West Company', in order to distinguish it from the North West Company. It was formed in 1798 by two firms, Forsyth, Richardson and Company and Leith, Jamieson and Company. In 1800, Sir Alexander Mackenzie joined the XY Company which became known alternatively as Sir Alexander Mackenzie and Company. In 1804 the XY Company was absorbed by the North West Company.

NORTH WEST COMPANY

This company and the Hudson's Bay Company were the two largest groups involved in the Canadian fur trade. The North West Company began as a loose partnership around 1776. The amalgamation with their major rival, Gregory, McLeod and Company, in 1787, resulted in a company capable of competing strongly with the Hudson's Bay Company. Competition became so strong that the existence of both concerns was threatened and in 1821 they united under the name of the Hudson's Bay Company.

HUDSON'S BAY COMPANY

This is the commonly known name for 'The Governor and Company of Adventurers of England trading into Hudson's Bay' which was formed by a royal charter on May 2, 1670. Their amalgamation with the North West Company in 1821 gave them a virtual monopoly of the richest fur-bearing areas in Canada.

This monopoly was gradually broken by the illegal fur trading of free traders which went unchecked and also by the increase in settlement on the Pacific coast and in the Red River district. In 1869, Rupert's Land, the area which the Hudson's Bay Company controlled, was sold to Canada for £300,000 and the rights to one-twentieth of the land in arable areas. The fur trade continued as settlement increased, and many of the old trading posts became retail stores.

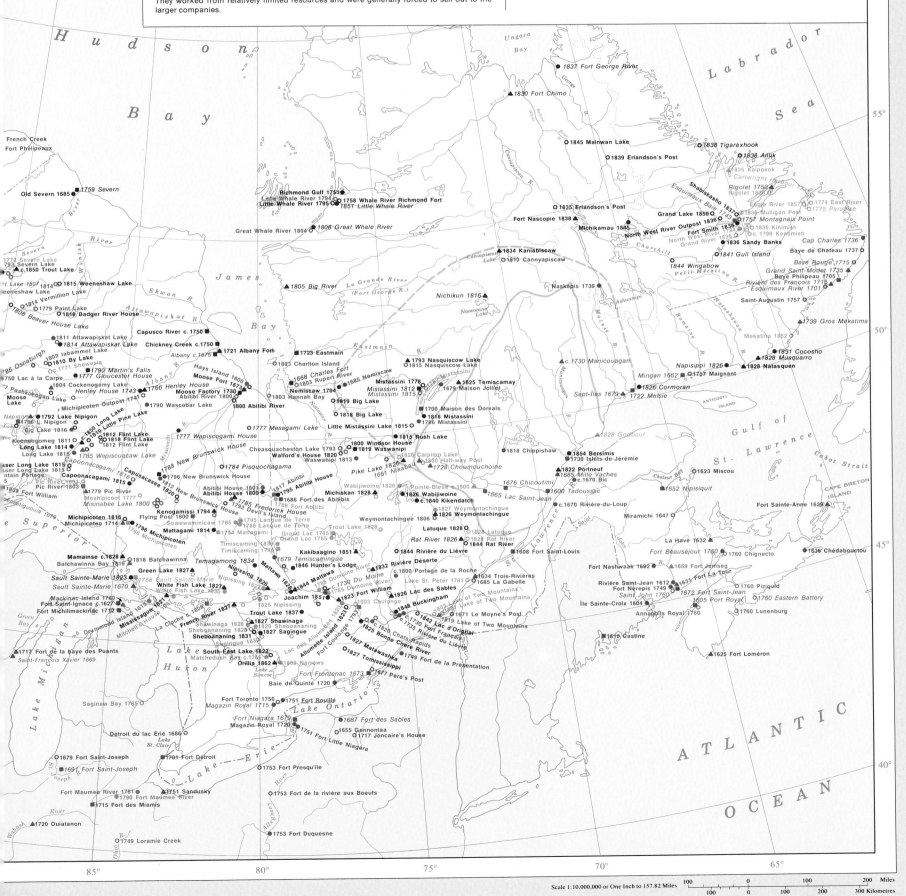

Scale 1:10,000,000 or One Inch to 157.82 Miles

TOPOGRAPHIC MAP COVERAGE

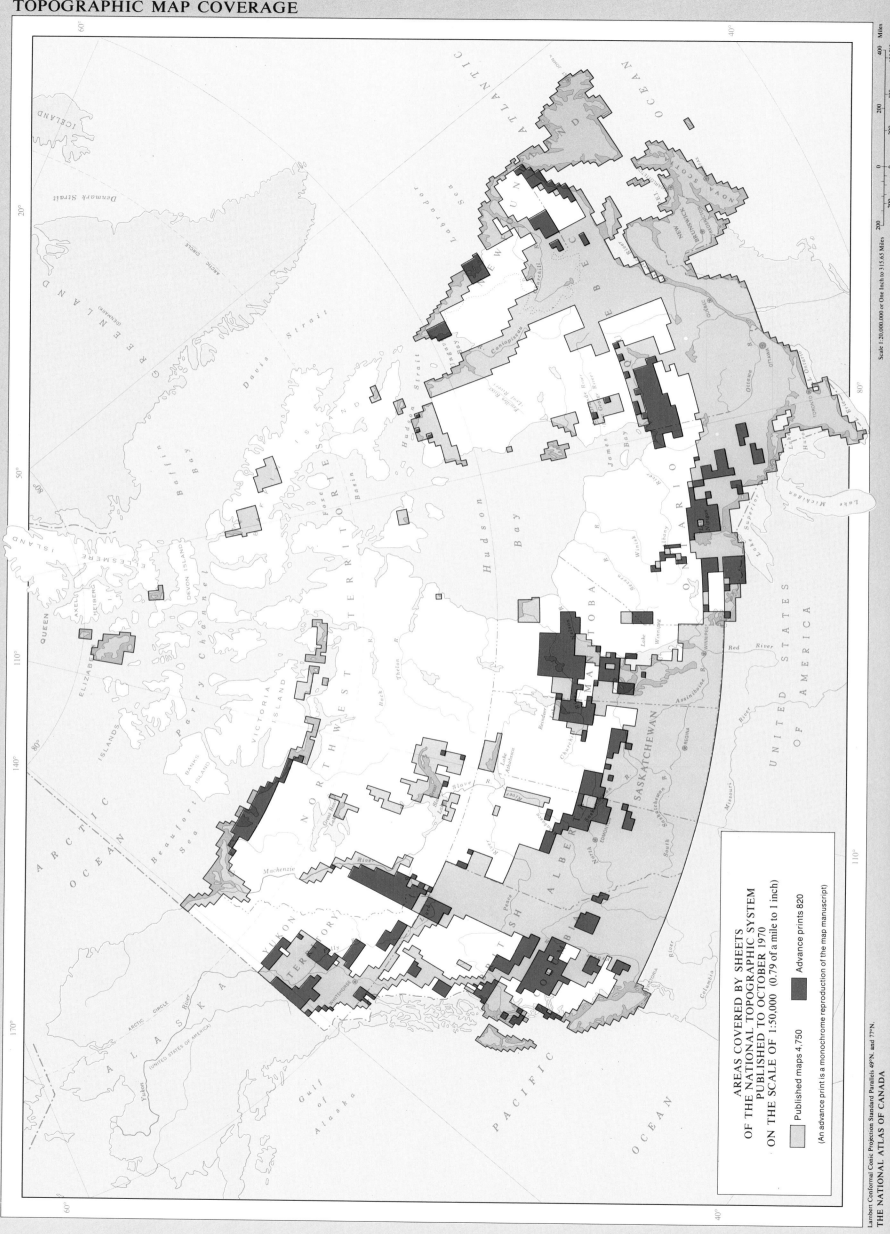

AREAS COVERED BY SHEETS
OF THE NATIONAL TOPOGRAPHIC SYSTEM
PUBLISHED TO OCTOBER 1970
ON THE SCALE OF 1:50,000 (0.79 of a mile to 1 inch)

Published maps 4,750

Advance prints 820

(An advance print is a monochrome reproduction of the map manuscript)

Lambert Conformal Conic Projection Standard Parallels 49°N. and 77°N.

Scale 1:20,000,000 or One Inch to 315.65 Miles

THE NATIONAL ATLAS OF CANADA

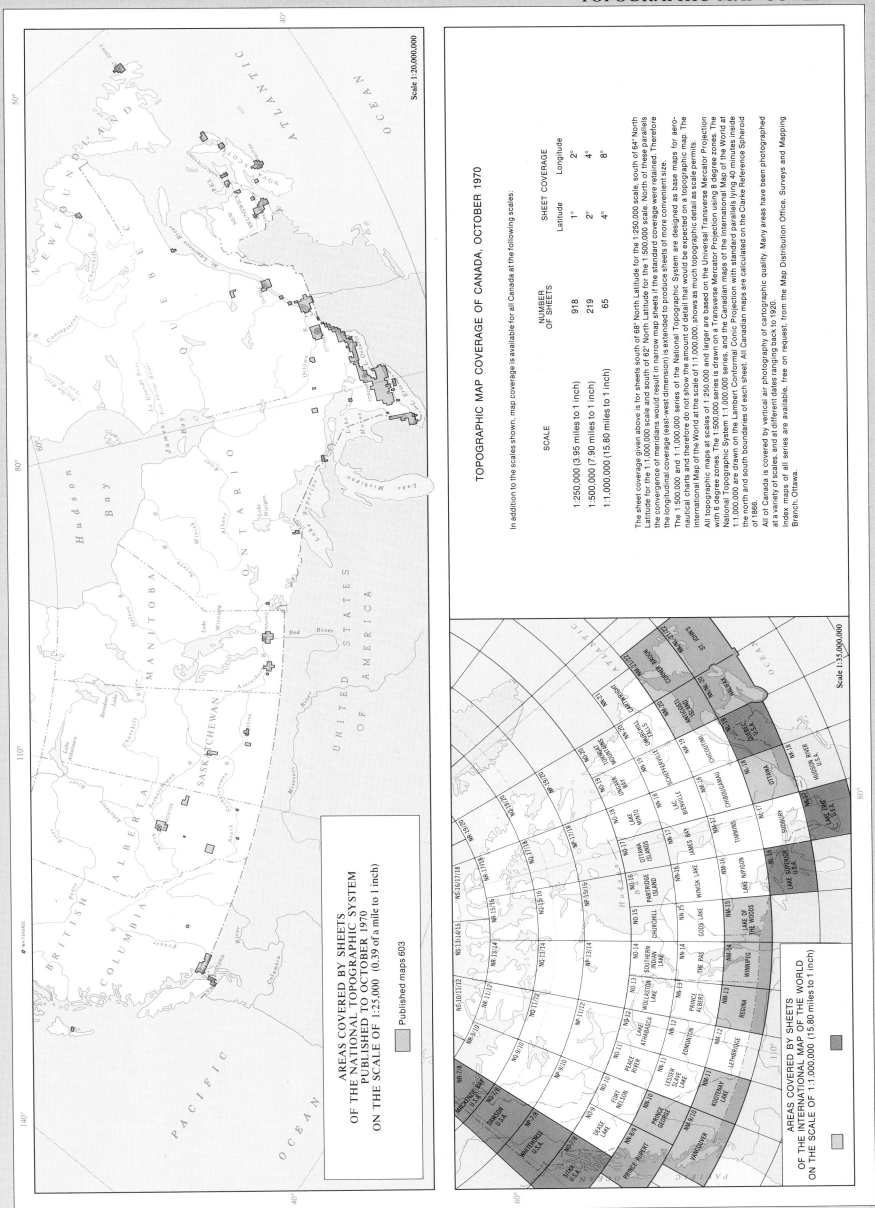

Scale 1:20,000,000

**AREAS COVERED BY SHEETS
OF THE NATIONAL TOPOGRAPHIC SYSTEM
PUBLISHED TO OCTOBER 1970
ON THE SCALE OF 1:25,000 (0.39 of a mile to 1 inch)**

▨ Published maps 603

TOPOGRAPHIC MAP COVERAGE OF CANADA, OCTOBER 1970

In addition to the scales shown, map coverage is available for all Canada at the following scales:

SCALE	NUMBER OF SHEETS	SHEET COVERAGE Latitude	SHEET COVERAGE Longitude
		1°	2°
1:250,000 (3.95 miles to 1 inch)	918	1°	2°
1:500,000 (7.90 miles to 1 inch)	219	2°	4°
1:1,000,000 (15.80 miles to 1 inch)	65	4°	8°

The sheet coverage given above is for sheets south of 68° North Latitude for the 1:250,000 scale, south of 64° North Latitude for the 1:1,000,000 scale and south of 62° North Latitude for the 1:500,000 scale. North of these parallels the convergence of meridians would result in narrow map sheets if the standard coverage were retained. Therefore the longitudinal coverage (east-west dimension) is extended to produce sheets of more convenient size.

The 1:500,000 and 1:1,000,000 series of the National Topographic System are designed as base maps for aeronautical charts and therefore do not show the amount of detail that would be expected on a topographic map. The International Map of the World at the scale of 1:1,000,000, shows as much topographic detail as scale permits.

All topographic maps at scales of 1:250,000 and larger are based on the Universal Transverse Mercator Projection with 6 degree zones. The 1:500,000 series is drawn on a Transverse Mercator Projection using 8 degree zones. The National Topographic System 1:1,000,000 series, and the Canadian maps of the International Map of the World at 1:1,000,000 are drawn on the Lambert Conformal Conic Projection with standard parallels lying 40 minutes inside the north and south boundaries of each sheet. All Canadian maps are calculated on the Clarke Reference Spheroid of 1866.

All of Canada is covered by vertical air photography of cartographic quality. Many areas have been photographed at a variety of scales, and at different dates ranging back to 1920.

Index maps of all series are available, free on request, from the Map Distribution Office, Surveys and Mapping Branch, Ottawa.

Scale 1:35,000,000

**AREAS COVERED BY SHEETS
OF THE INTERNATIONAL MAP OF THE WORLD
ON THE SCALE OF 1:1,000,000 (15.80 miles to 1 inch)**

Lambert Conformal Conic Projection Standard Parallels 49°N. and 77°N.

THE NATIONAL ATLAS OF CANADA

TERRITORIAL EVOLUTION OF CANADA

| ENGLISH |
| FRENCH |
| SPANISH |
| DISPUTED |

1667

First successful French settlements in North America: Port Royal (1606), and Québec (1608). English settlement in Virginia begins (1606-07). French and English territorial claims overlap Acadia. Acadia is recognized as French possession by the Treaty of Breda (1667). A Royal Charter (1670) grants sole trading rights in Hudson Bay drainage basin to the Hudson's Bay Co.

| BRITISH |
| FRENCH |
| DISPUTED |
| DISPUTED |
| SPANISH |

1713

By the Treaty of Utrecht (1713), France cedes Nova Scotia (excluding Cape Breton Island) to Great Britain, relinquishes her interests in Newfoundland and recognizes British rights to Rupert's Land.

| BRITISH |
| DANISH |
| SPANISH |

1763

By the Treaty of Paris (1763), eastern North America becomes British territory except St-Pierre and Miquelon Islands (France). British colonial governments for: Quebec, Newfoundland (with Île d'Anticosti and Îles de la Madeleine), Nova Scotia (including present-day N.B. and P.E.I.). Hudson's Bay Co. still administers Rupert's Land. Louisiana is ceded to Spain by France.

St. John's Island is separated from Nova Scotia (1769). The Quebec Act (1774) enlarges Quebec to include Labrador, Île d'Anticosti, Îles de...

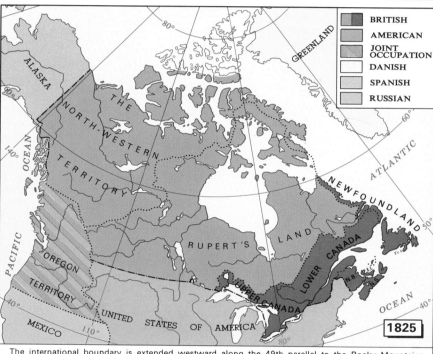

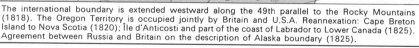

| BRITISH |
| AMERICAN |
| JOINT OCCUPATION |
| DANISH |
| SPANISH |
| RUSSIAN |

1825

The international boundary is extended westward along the 49th parallel to the Rocky Mountains (1818). The Oregon Territory is occupied jointly by Britain and U.S.A. Reannexation: Cape Breton Island to Nova Scotia (1820); Île d'Anticosti and part of the coast of Labrador to Lower Canada (1825). Agreement between Russia and Britain on the description of Alaska boundary (1825).

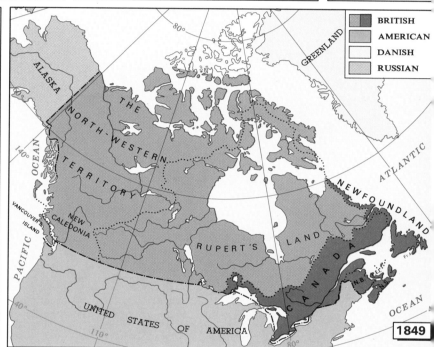

| BRITISH |
| AMERICAN |
| DANISH |
| RUSSIAN |

1849

The Province of Canada is formed by uniting Upper and Lower Canada (1840). The international boundary from the Rocky Mountains to the Pacific is described by the Oregon Treaty (1846). The northern portion of the Oregon Territory is called New Caledonia, a name used by Simon Fraser in 1806. The Hudson's Bay Co. is granted Vancouver's Island to develop a colony (1849).

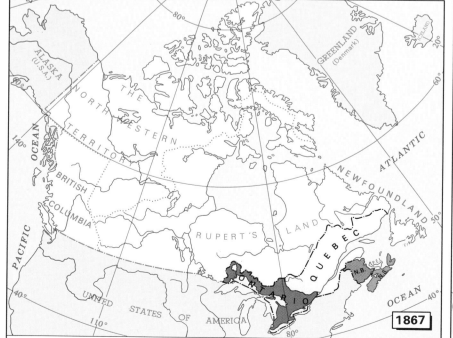

1867

New Brunswick, Nova Scotia and Canada are united in a federal state, the Dominion of Canada, by the British North America Act (July 1, 1867). The province of Canada is divided into Ontario and Quebec. The United States of America proclaims the purchase of Alaska from Russia (June 20).

1870

The North-West Territories (Rupert's Land and the North-Western Territory) are acquired by Canada from the Hudson's Bay Company. From part of them Manitoba is created as the fifth province.

Lambert Conformal Conic Projection Standard Parallels 49°N. and 77°N.

NATIONAL ATLAS OF CANADA

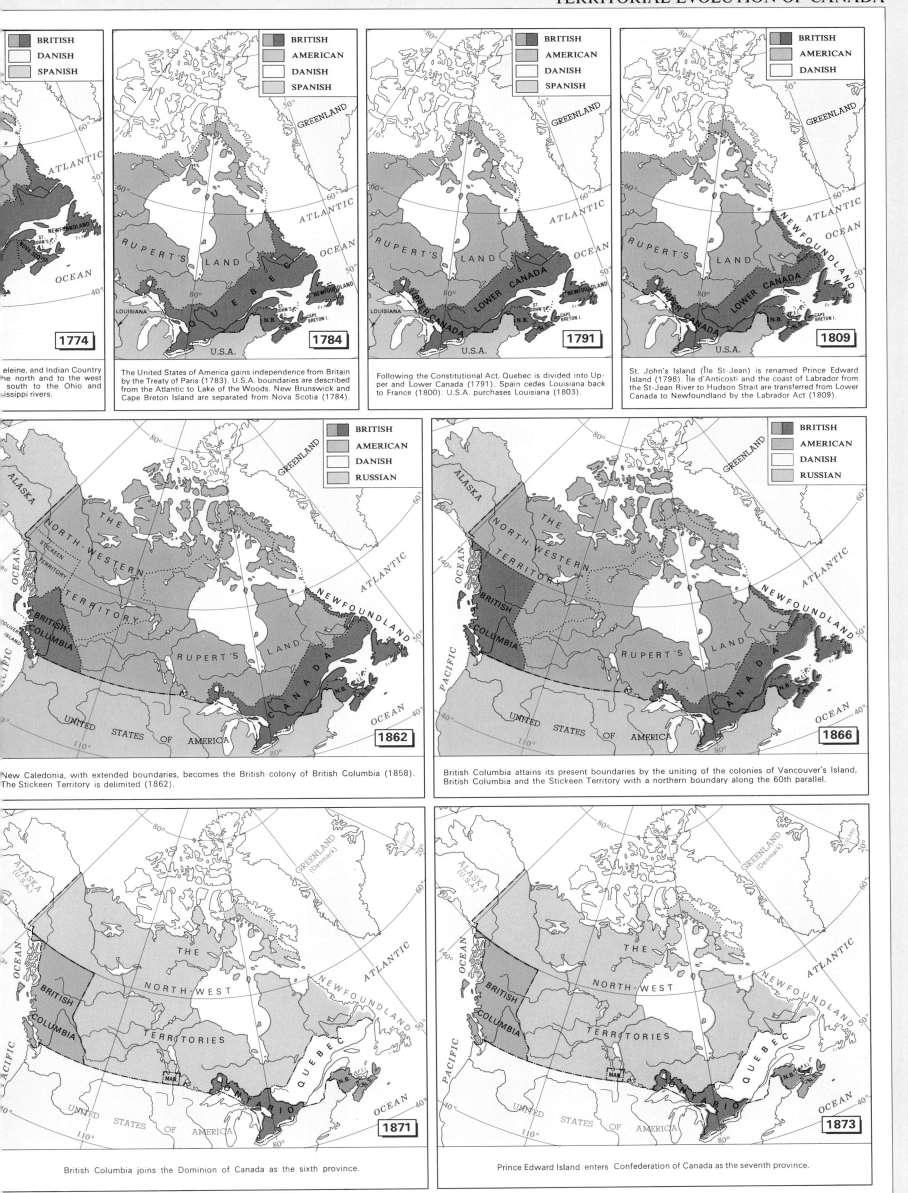

1774

...eleine, and Indian Country ...he north and to the west ...south to the Ohio and ...ississippi rivers.

| BRITISH | | DANISH | | SPANISH |

1784

The United States of America gains independence from Britain by the Treaty of Paris (1783). U.S.A. boundaries are described from the Atlantic to Lake of the Woods. New Brunswick and Cape Breton Island are separated from Nova Scotia (1784).

| BRITISH | AMERICAN | DANISH | SPANISH |

1791

Following the Constitutional Act, Quebec is divided into Upper and Lower Canada (1791). Spain cedes Louisiana back to France (1800). U.S.A. purchases Louisiana (1803).

| BRITISH | AMERICAN | DANISH | SPANISH |

1809

St. John's Island (Île St-Jean) is renamed Prince Edward Island (1798). Île d'Anticosti and the coast of Labrador from the St-Jean River to Hudson Strait are transferred from Lower Canada to Newfoundland by the Labrador Act (1809).

| BRITISH | AMERICAN | DANISH |

1862

New Caledonia, with extended boundaries, becomes the British colony of British Columbia (1858). The Stickeen Territory is delimited (1862).

| BRITISH | AMERICAN | DANISH | RUSSIAN |

1866

British Columbia attains its present boundaries by the uniting of the colonies of Vancouver's Island, British Columbia and the Stickeen Territory with a northern boundary along the 60th parallel.

| BRITISH | AMERICAN | DANISH | RUSSIAN |

1871

British Columbia joins the Dominion of Canada as the sixth province.

1873

Prince Edward Island enters Confederation of Canada as the seventh province.

Scale 1:50,500,000 or 797 Miles to One Inch

TERRITORIAL EVOLUTION OF CANADA

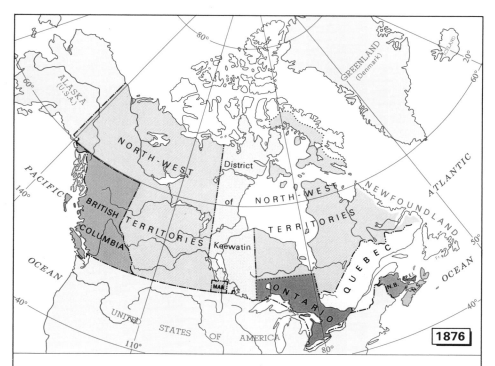

1876

New provisional northern and western boundaries of Ontario are described (1874). From part of the North-West Territories, the District of Keewatin is created (1876).

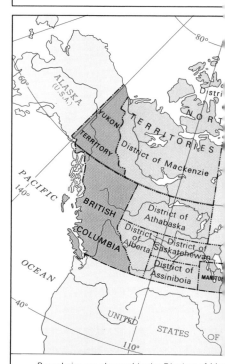

British rights to the arctic islands pass to Ca (1881), but the extension to the east is cont Saskatchewan, Athabaska, and Alberta are cr

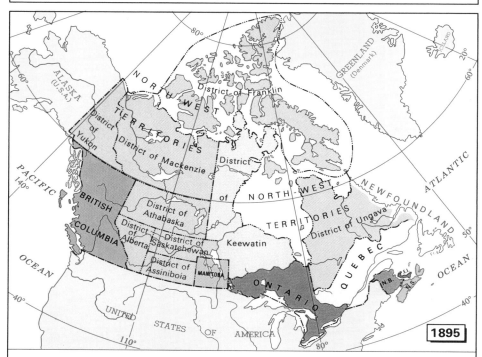

1895

Ungava, Mackenzie, Yukon, and Franklin are established as Districts in the North-West Territories. The creation of the District of Franklin acknowledges the inclusion of the arctic islands in Canada. The Districts of Athabaska and Keewatin are enlarged.

Boundaries are changed in the Districts of Ma The District of Yukon becomes a Territory se boundaries are extended north.

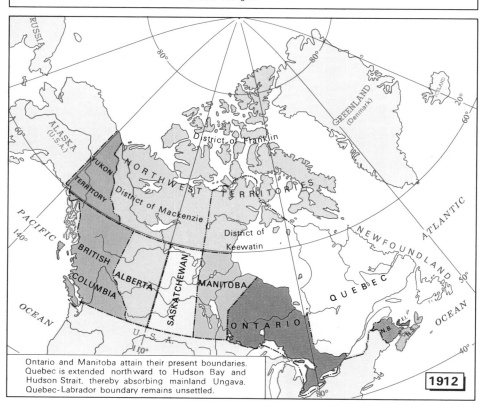

1912

Ontario and Manitoba attain their present boundaries. Quebec is extended northward to Hudson Bay and Hudson Strait, thereby absorbing mainland Ungava. Quebec-Labrador boundary remains unsettled.

Canada's boundaries are extended northward pursu provisions of international law. The Imperial Privy C provides a settlement of the Quebec-Labrador bou question.

1882

). The boundaries of Manitoba are extended
ntario. The provisional Districts of Assiniboia,
2).

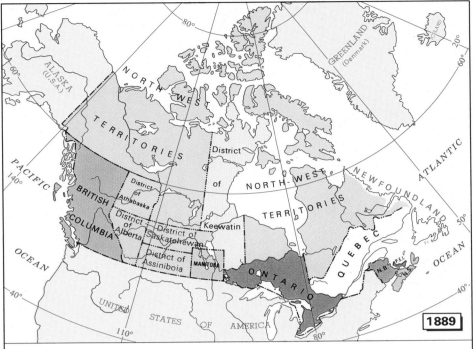

1889

The Ontario-Manitoba boundary dispute is settled by the Ontario Boundary Act. Ontario is enlarged
west to Lake of the Woods and north to the Albany River.

1898

eewatin, Ungava, Franklin, and Yukon (1897).
m the North-West Territories (1898). Quebec

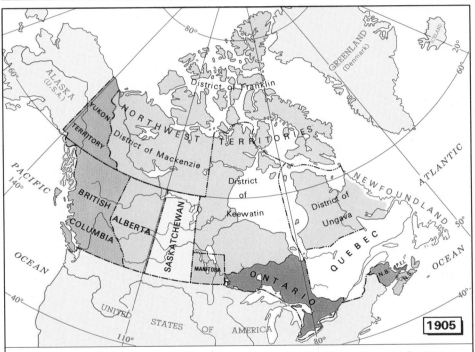

1905

Alberta and Saskatchewan are created as provinces to make a total of nine provinces in the Dominion
of Canada (1905). The District of Keewatin is transferred back to the Northwest Territories. Due to
changes in adjoining areas the boundaries of the Northwest Territories are redefined (1906).

1927

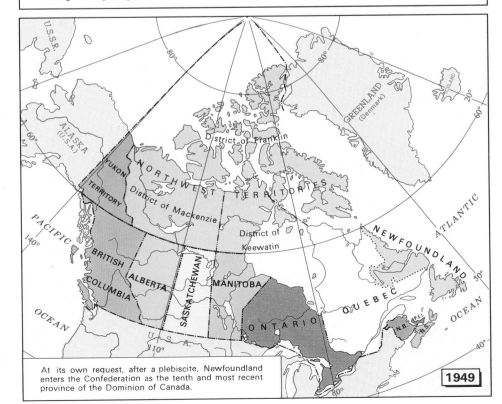

1949

At its own request, after a plebiscite, Newfoundland
enters the Confederation as the tenth and most recent
province of the Dominion of Canada.

Scale 1:50,500,000 or 797 Miles to One Inch

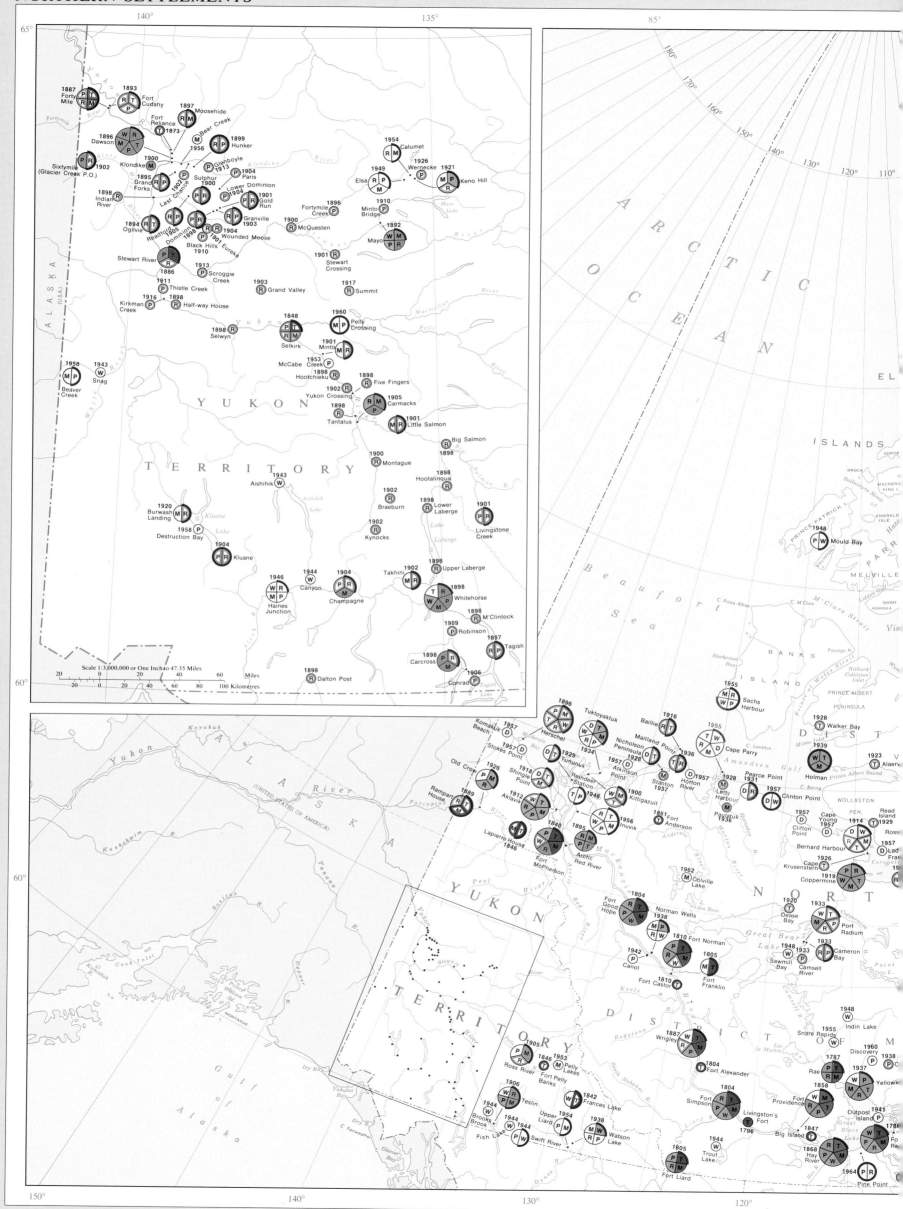

Scale 1:3,000,000 or One Inch to 47.35 Miles

Lambert Conformal Conic Projection Standard Parallels 49°N. and 77°N.

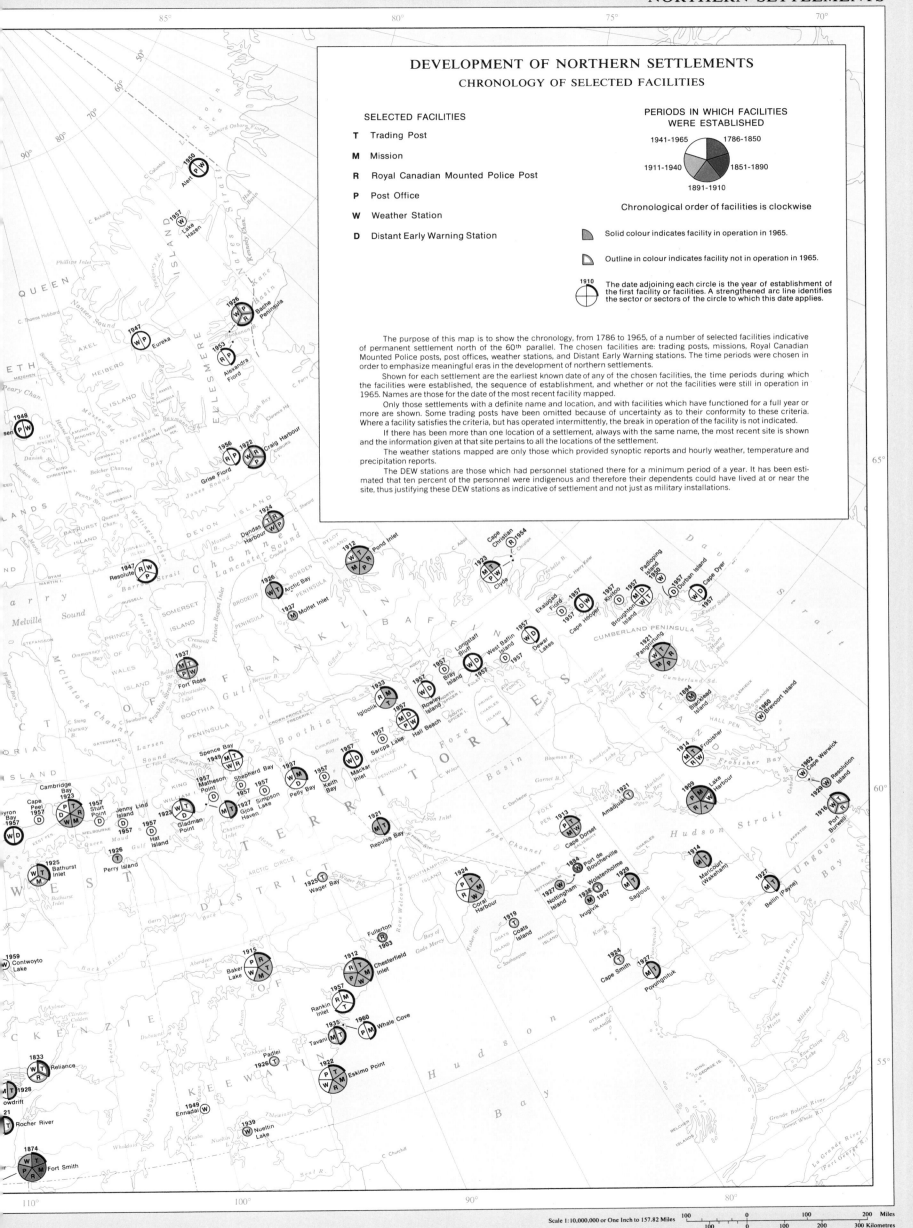

DEVELOPMENT OF NORTHERN SETTLEMENTS
CHRONOLOGY OF SELECTED FACILITIES

SELECTED FACILITIES

T   Trading Post

M   Mission

R   Royal Canadian Mounted Police Post

P   Post Office

W   Weather Station

D   Distant Early Warning Station

PERIODS IN WHICH FACILITIES WERE ESTABLISHED

1941-1965   1786-1850

1911-1940   1851-1890

1891-1910

Chronological order of facilities is clockwise

Solid colour indicates facility in operation in 1965.

Outline in colour indicates facility not in operation in 1965.

1910   The date adjoining each circle is the year of establishment of the first facility or facilities. A strengthened arc line identifies the sector or sectors of the circle to which this date applies.

The purpose of this map is to show the chronology, from 1786 to 1965, of a number of selected facilities indicative of permanent settlement north of the 60th parallel. The chosen facilities are: trading posts, missions, Royal Canadian Mounted Police posts, post offices, weather stations, and Distant Early Warning stations. The time periods were chosen in order to emphasize meaningful eras in the development of northern settlements.

Shown for each settlement are the earliest known date of any of the chosen facilities, the time periods during which the facilities were established, the sequence of establishment, and whether or not the facilities were still in operation in 1965. Names are those for the date of the most recent facility mapped.

Only those settlements with a definite name and location, and with facilities which have functioned for a full year or more are shown. Some trading posts have been omitted because of uncertainty as to their conformity to these criteria. Where a facility satisfies the criteria, but has operated intermittently, the break in operation of the facility is not indicated.

If there has been more than one location of a settlement, always with the same name, the most recent site is shown and the information given at that site pertains to all the locations of the settlement.

The weather stations mapped are only those which provided synoptic reports and hourly weather, temperature and precipitation reports.

The DEW stations are those which had personnel stationed there for a minimum period of a year. It has been estimated that ten percent of the personnel were indigenous and therefore their dependents could have lived at or near the site, thus justifying these DEW stations as indicative of settlement and not just as military installations.

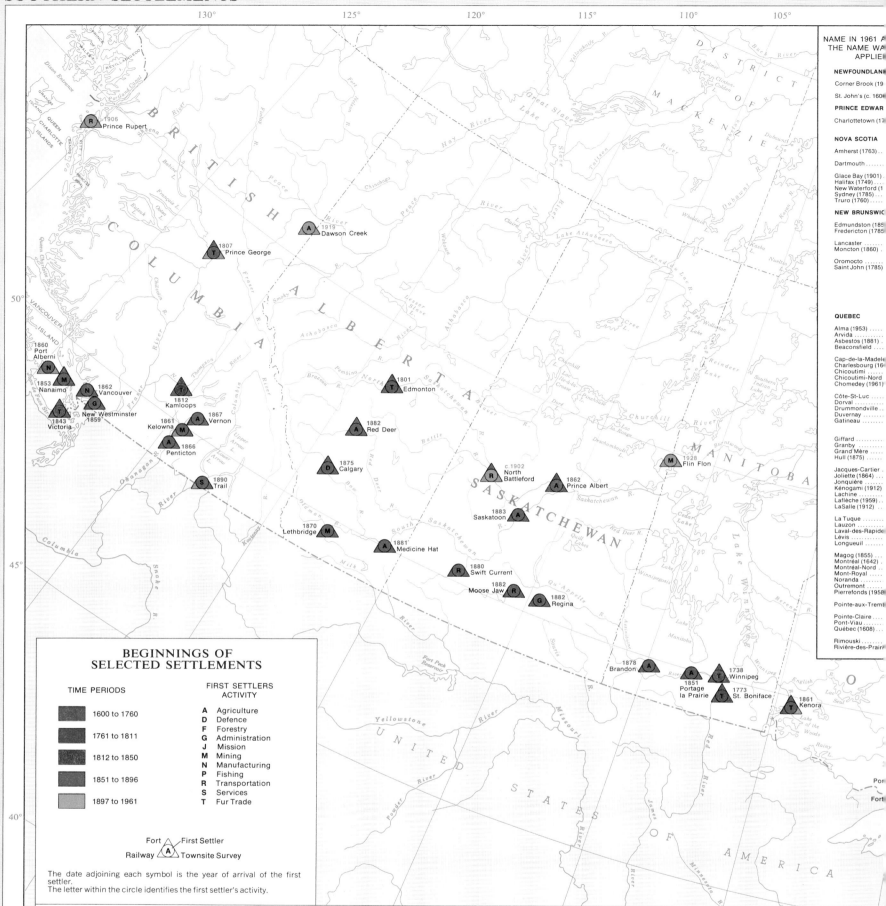

BEGINNINGS OF SELECTED SETTLEMENTS

TIME PERIODS		FIRST SETTLERS ACTIVITY	
	1600 to 1760	A	Agriculture
	1761 to 1811	D	Defence
	1812 to 1850	F	Forestry
	1851 to 1896	G	Administration
	1897 to 1961	J	Mission
		M	Mining
		N	Manufacturing
		P	Fishing
		R	Transportation
		S	Services
		T	Fur Trade

Fort △—First Settler
Railway ⬡—Townsite Survey

The date adjoining each symbol is the year of arrival of the first settler.
The letter within the circle identifies the first settler's activity.

BEGINNINGS OF SELECTED SETTLEMENTS

The material presented on this sheet is part of a larger undertaking, which will be continued in subsequent editions of The National Atlas, to represent the chronology of settlement of Canada. The maps of population distribution in twenty year periods from 1851, beginning on page 91, provide a highly generalized synopsis of the spread of settlement, and pages 87-88 provide detail on settlements north of the 60th parallel where the sparseness of settlement permitted coverage of each settlement. For the more densely settled areas to the south, treatment in this edition of the atlas is necessarily selective, and a decision was made to deal only with incorporated Cities, Towns, and Villages whose population was 10,000 and over in 1961. Strict adherence to these criteria eliminated treatment of many relatively old centres which have not attained a population of 10,000, as well as a few places whose population was over 10,000, such as Kirkland Lake, Ontario, an unincorporated place, and Burnaby, British Columbia, a District Municipality.

The approach here used for chronology of settlement is to show for each place selected, five indicators of origin. These are: the date of arrival of the first settler; the period within which the townsite survey was carried out; the period within which the railway arrived; the period within which the earliest fort was built at the site, if applicable; and the nature of the activity of the first settler. Eleven types of activity are designated.

For large urbanized areas which are composed of a number of immediately adjoining urban municipalities, the map, for reasons of congestion, usually records information for the main nuclear settlement only, for example, information on the city of Montréal only, is shown for the Census Metropolitan Area of Montréal.

In addition to information symbolized on the map, dates of incorporation as a Village, Town, and City are given in the table. The table also lists names by which settlements were previously known, names of the forts or trading posts at that settlement, and the year in which those names were first applied.

FIRST SETTLER

"First Settler" refers to the first non-Indian who settled and began an activity (within the area of the 1961 municipal boundaries) which is judged to have had an influence on the development of subsequent settlement at that site.

In a number of places, a fort or trading post preceded other settlement but was abandoned well before other settlement occurred, and is therefore judged not to have influenced any subsequent settlement at that site. In such cases, the founder of the trading post or fort is not acknowledged as the first settler; nevertheless, the existence of the fort or trading post is symbolized on the map. Where a fort or trading post was the first structure at the site and there was, in fact, continuity of settlement from the establishment of this post, then the founder of the post or fort is considered to be the first settler and the founding activity designated as Trade or Defence. In other places, most particularly the Acadian settlements, the remnants of an abandoned settlement probably facilitated the establishment of a subsequent settlement and the founder of the abandoned settlement is acknowledged as the first settler.

FIRST SETTLER'S ACTIVITY

"First Settler's Activity" refers to the initial activity by which the first settler is judged to have obtained or attempted to obtain his livelihood.

FORT

This term includes trading posts as well as military forts and blockhouses located within the area of the 1961 municipal boundaries.

TOWNSITE SURVEY

Within the Province of Quebec, the period indicated for the townsite survey is actually the period in which the parish register was opened. Elsewhere the term refers to the survey of the townsite.

RAILWAY

The period of the arrival of the railway refers to the period in which the first train arrived at the community rather than to the time of construction of the railway at the place in question.

INCORPORATION DATES

The incorporation dates given in the table are the effective dates of incorporation rather than the dates of enactment of the enabling legislation. Changes after 1961 are not given.

PREVIOUS NAMES

Previously used names given in the table were not necessarily official names at the time they were current, and may in some cases not have had strict reference to the urban place in question so much as to a settled area somewhat larger than the area of the 1961 municipality. Beaubassin, for example, an early name applicable to Amherst, Nova Scotia, referred to an area not totally included in Amherst's 1961 municipal boundaries.

Where a few places became amalgamated under a new name, their names are listed in the table, but where numerous places became amalgamated under the name of the dominant municipality, only the previous names of the dominant municipality are listed.

Village	Town	City	PREVIOUS NAME AND DATE THE NAME WAS FIRST APPLIED
		1956	*[Curling, Corner Brook West, Townsite, Corner Brook East]
	1888		Fort William (1696)
	1855		Port la Joie (1720); Fort Edward (1768)
1889		1961	**Beaubassin (c. 1701); **Les Planches; Amherst Corners
1873		1961	The Sawmill; Quaker Town; Fort Clarence (1754)
1901			Fort William (1746)
1841	1848		The Citadel (1749)
1913			Barrachois; Barrachois Cove
1885	1904		Baie des Espagnols; Spanish Bay
1875			**Cobequid (c. 1701)
1847	1905	1952	Petit Sault
1848			Fort Nashwaak (1692); St. Anne's Point (1732)
	1953		Fairville
1855	1890		Le Coude (c. 1750); Bend of the Petitcodiac; Moncton (1855)
1956			
		1785	Fort Sainte-Marie (1631); Fort La Tour; Fort Charnisay (1645); Fort Martignon (1672); Fort St-Jean (1700); Fort Menagouche (1750); Fort Frederick (1758); Fort Howe (1778); *[Carleton (1783), Parr Town (1783)]
1917	1924	1958	St. Joseph d'Alma
		1926	
1899	1937		
		1910	Thompson's Point (1870); Beaurepaire (1870)
1914	1949	1960	
1863	1879	1930	
1944	1954	1961	*[L'Abord-à-Plouffe, Saint-Martin, Renaud]
		1961	Côte Notre-Dame-de-Liesse
1903	1951	1958	Fort La Présentation (1668)
1892	1903	1956	
1875	1888	1938	
		1958	
1933	1946		Long Point (1807); Pointe-Gatineau (1807); Templeton (1876); Waterloo (1876)
1912		1954	
1859		1916	
1898	1901	1875	Ferme des Chutes; Columbia; Wright (1832); Wrightstown (1851)
1845	1864	1952	L'Industrie
1904	1912	1956	
1912	1920	1958	
1848	1872	1909	Le village du Canal; Mackayville
	1947	1959	Fort Remy (1671); Fort Cuillerier (1676); La Petite Chine; La Chine
1912		1958	
1909	1911		Pointe Lévy
1867	1910	1951	
	1912		
1861		1906	
1874		1920	Chateau de Longueuil (1685); St-Antoine-de-Longueuil (1845)
			Outlet
1888	1890	1950	Ville-Marie (1642)
1792	1832	1959	
	1912		
	1926	1948	
1875	1895	1915	Côte-Sainte-Catherine
1904	1958		Sainte-Geneviève-de-Pierrefonds (1904)
1905	1912	1958	St-Jean-Baptiste-de-la-Pointe-aux-Trembles (1905)
1854	1911	1958	
1926	1946	1958	
1792	1833		Kebec (1608); Fort Saint-Louis (1608); Chateau Saint-Louis (1634)
	1869		St-Germain-de-Rimouski
	1954		

NAME IN 1961 AND DATE THE NAME WAS FIRST APPLIED	Village	Town	City	PREVIOUS NAME AND DATE THE NAME WAS FIRST APPLIED
Rivière-du-Loup (1919)	1850	1874	1910	Fraserville
Rouyn	1926	1927	1948	
Ste-Foy	1845	1949	1955	Notre-Dame-de-Foy
Ste-Thérèse (1916)	1849	1916	1959	Ste-Thérèse-de-Blainville
St-Hubert		1958		
St-Hyacinthe	1849	1850	1857	
St-Jean (1848)	1848	1856	1916	Fort Saint-Jean (1666); Fort Saint John (1760); Dorchester (1815); St-Jean Dorchester (1828)
St-Jérôme (1856)	1856	1881	1950	Dumontville
St-Lambert	1892	1898	1921	Fort de la Prairie (1687); Fort Saint-Lambert (1688)
St-Laurent		1893	1955	
St-Michel (1915)	1912	1915	1952	St-Michel-de-Laval
St-Vincent-de-Paul		1952		
Salaberry de Valleyfield	1874	1904		Catherinestown (1800)
Sept-Iles	1951	1959		L'Ange Gardien (1651)
Shawinigan (1958)	1901	1902	1921	Shawinigan Falls
Shawinigan-Sud	1912	1961		
Sherbrooke (1818)	1823	1839	1875	Big Forks (1794); Hyatt's Mill (1796)
Sillery (1862)	1856		1947	
Sorel (1862)		1860	1889	Fort Richelieu (1642); Fort de Saurel (1665); William Henry (1787); William Henry Bourg (1791)

ONTARIO

NAME IN 1961	Village	Town	City	PREVIOUS NAME
Thetford Mines (1905)	1892	1905	1912	Kingsville
Trois-Rivières	1792	1857		
Val-d'Or	1935	1937		
Verdun (1876)	1876	1907	1912	Côte-des-Argoulets; Rivière-St-Pierre (1874)
Victoriaville	1861	1890		
Westmount (1895)	1873	1890	1908	Priest's Farm (1669); Notre-Dame-de-Grâce (1873); Cote-St-Antoine (1879)
Barrie (1816)	1854	1870	1959	
Belleville (1816)		1850	1877	Thurlow Village (1789); Meyers Creek
Brampton (1834)		1853	1873	
Brantford (1826)		1847	1877	
Brockville (1812)			1850	Buell's Bay (1784); Elizabethtown (1805)
Burlington (1873)	1873		1914	*[Wellington Square (c. 1800), Port Nelson]
Chatham	1851	1855	1895	Raleigh (1820); McGregor's Mills
Cobourg (1819)			1850	Hamilton (1798); Buckville (1808); Hardscrabble
Cornwall (c. 1834)		1847	1945	New Johnstown (1784)
Dundas (1814)		1848		Coote's Paradise (c. 1792)
Eastview (1909)	1909	1913		Janeville; Cummings Island
Forest Hill (1860)		1923		
Fort William (1807)		1892	1907	Fort Camenestigouia (1679); Fort Kaministiquia (1679)
Galt (1827)	1850	1857	1915	Shade's Mills (1817)
Georgetown (1846)	1865	1921		Hungry Hollow
Guelph (1851)	1851	1856	1879	
Hamilton (1813)			1846	Burlington Bay
Kenora (1905)		1892		Rat Portage
Kingston (1788)		1838	1846	Fort Frontenac (1673); Fort Cataraqui (1783); King's Town (1784)
Kitchener (1916)	1854	1870	1912	The Sand Hills; Ben Eby; Ebytown; Berlin (c. 1833)
Leaside (1881)		1913		
Lindsay (1834)		1857		Purdy's Mills (1827)
London		1848	1855	
Long Branch	1930			
Mimico		1911	1917	
New Toronto		1913	1919	
Niagara Falls (1881)		1856	1904	Drummondville; Elgin; Clifton (1856)
North Bay		1890	1925	
Oakville		1857		
Orillia	1867	1875	1924	The Narrows; Newtown
Oshawa (1842)	1850	1879	1924	Skae's Corners (1794)
Ottawa (1855)		1847	1855	Bellows Landing (c. 1810); Richmond Landing (1811); Bytown (1826)
Owen Sound (1857)		1857	1920	Sydenham Village (1837)
Pembroke (1846)	1858	1877		Miramichi; Moffat; Sydenham
Peterborough (1827)		1850	1905	Scott's Plains; Scott's Mills; The Plains; Peterboro
Port Arthur		1884	1907	The Landing; Prince Arthur's Landing (1871); Fort Arthur (1870)
Port Colborne (1870)	1870	1918		Gravelly Bay
Preston (c. 1830)	1852	1900		Cambridge
Richmond Hill (1873)	1873	1957		Mount Pleasant, Miles Hill
Riverside		1921		
St. Catharines (c. 1784)		1850	1876	The Twelve (c. 1784); Shipman's Corners (c. 1784)
St. Thomas (1817)	1852	1861	1881	*[Kettle Creek Village (1810), Hogs Hollow, Stirling]

NAME IN 1961	Village	Town	City	PREVIOUS NAME
Sarnia (1856)		1857	1914	The Rapids (1827); Port Sarnia (1835)
Sault Ste. Marie		1887	1912	Fort Sault Sainte-Marie (1792)
Stratford (1831)	1854	1859	1885	Little Thames (1831)
Sudbury		1893	1930	
Timmins			1912	
Toronto (1834)			1834	Magazin Royal (1720); Fort Toronto (1750); Fort Rouillé (1750); York (1793)
Trenton	1853	1880		River Trent; Trent Port
Waterloo	1857	1876	1948	
Welland (1858)	1858	1878	1917	The Aqueduct (1829); Merrittsville (1842)
Whitby (1855)		1855		*[Windsor Bay, Hamer's Corners, Perry's Corners]
Windsor (1836)		1858	1892	Sandwich; Sandwich Ferry; Richmond
Woodstock (1835)	1851	1857	1901	Oxford (1793)

MANITOBA

NAME IN 1961	Village	Town	City	PREVIOUS NAME
Brandon (1881)		1882		
East Kildonan		1957		
Flin Flon	1939			
Portage la Prairie		1907		
St. Boniface		1883	1908	Dorion's Post (1803)
St. James		1956		
Transcona	1912	1961		
West Kildonan		1961		
Winnipeg (c. 1865)			1873	Fort Rouge (1738); Fort Gibraltar (1807); Fort Douglas (1812); The Forks (1813); Fidler's Fort (1817); Fort Garry (1821); Red River Settlement (1812); McDermotsville (c. 1860)

SASKATCHEWAN

NAME IN 1961	Village	Town	City	PREVIOUS NAME
Moose Jaw		1884	1903	
North Battleford	1906	1906	1913	
Prince Albert (1866)		1885	1904	Sturgeon Fort (1780); Fort Providence (1780); Isbister's Settlement (1862)
Regina		1883	1903	Pile of Bones
Saskatoon (1883)	1901	1903	1906	
Swift Current	1904	1907	1914	

ALBERTA

NAME IN 1961	Village	Town	City	PREVIOUS NAME
Calgary (1876)		1884	1893	The Elbow (1875); Fort Brisebois (1875)
Edmonton		1892	1904	Fort Augustus (1801); Fort Edmonton (1801)
Forest Lawn (1910)	1934	1952		West Jasper Place (1949)
Jasper Place (1950)	1949	1950		
Lethbridge (1885)		1891	1906	Coalbanks (c. 1870); Coalhurst (c. 1870)
Medicine Hat	1894	1898	1906	Fort Normandeau (1883); Red Deer Crossing (c. 1891)
Red Deer	1894	1901	1913	

BRITISH COLUMBIA

NAME IN 1961	Village	Town	City	PREVIOUS NAME
Dawson Creek	1936		1958	
Kamloops (1872)			1893	Fort She Waps (1812); Fort Thompson (1813); Fort Kamloops (c. 1842); The Forks
Kelowna			1905	
Nanaimo (1860)			1874	The Bastion (1853); Colvilletown
New Westminster (1859)			1860	Queensborough (1859)
North Vancouver (1902)			1907	Moodyville (1872)
Penticton			1948	
Port Alberni (1912)			1900	New Alberni (1900)
Prince George (1913)			1915	Fort George (1807)
Prince Rupert (1909)			1910	Knoxville (1907); Baconville (1907); Vickersville (1907)
Trail (1897)		1901		Trail Creek (1891)
Vancouver (1886)			1886	Hastings Mill (1867); Gastown (1867); Granville (1870)
Vernon (1887)			1892	Priest's Valley (1867); Forge Valley (1867); Centreville
Victoria			1862	Fort Albert (1843); Fort Camosun (1843); Fort Victoria (1843)

The name of fort or trading post is shown in italics.

*[ ] Names of places which were amalgamated under a new name.

** Area of settlement which was somewhat larger than the area of the 1961 municipality.

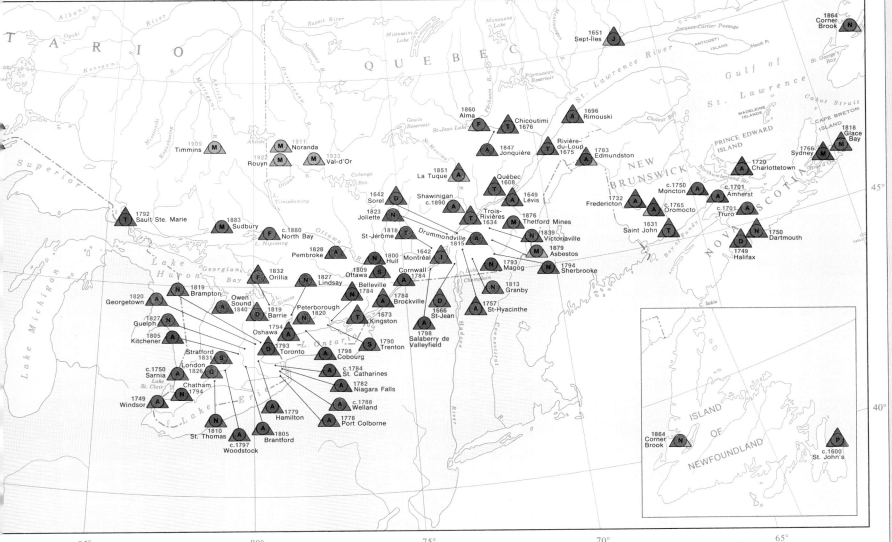

Scale 1:10,000,000 or One Inch to 157.82 Miles

DISTRIBUTION OF POPULATION, 1851 AND 1871

Left map

**BRITISH NORTH AMERICA
1851
(NEWFOUNDLAND, 1857)**

Each dot represents 1000 inhabitants

Population of urban centres of 10,000 and over is shown by circles proportional to the population.

⊙ Montréal Island — — — — 77,381
⊙ Toronto — — — — — — 30,773

NOTE: Distribution of population west of Winnipeg is not shown due to lack of information.

**URBAN CENTRES OF
10,000 AND OVER**

Halifax
Hamilton
Kingston
Montréal*
Québec
Saint John (N.B.)
St. John's (Nfld.)
Toronto

*(Montréal Island)

**PERCENTAGE DISTRIBUTION
OF POPULATION, 1851
(2,560,585)**

CANADA 71.95
N.S. 10.81
N.B. 7.57
NFLD. 4.85
P.E.I. 2.45
RUPERT'S LAND, N.W.T. 2.37
VANCOUVER'S ISLAND

Right map

**CANADA AND PRINCE EDWARD ISLAND
1871
NEWFOUNDLAND, 1869**

Each dot represents 1000 inhabitants

Population of urban centres of 10,000 and over is shown by circles proportional to the population.

⊙ Montréal Island — — — — 144,044
⊙ Toronto — — — — — — 56,092
⊙ Ottawa — — — — — — 21,545

**URBAN CENTRES OF
10,000 AND OVER**

Halifax
Hamilton
Kingston
London
Montréal*
Ottawa
Québec
Saint John (N.B.)
St. John's (Nfld.)
Toronto

*(Montréal Island)

**PERCENTAGE DISTRIBUTION
OF POPULATION, 1871
(3,841,757)**

ONTARIO 42.19
QUEBEC 31.02
N.S. 10.09
N.B. 7.43
NFLD. 3.97
P.E.I. 2.45
B.C. MAN. 1.60
N.W.T. 1.25

Scale 1:20,000,000 or One Inch to 315.65 Miles

Lambert Conformal Conic Projection Standard Parallels 49°N. and 77°N.

THE NATIONAL ATLAS OF CANADA

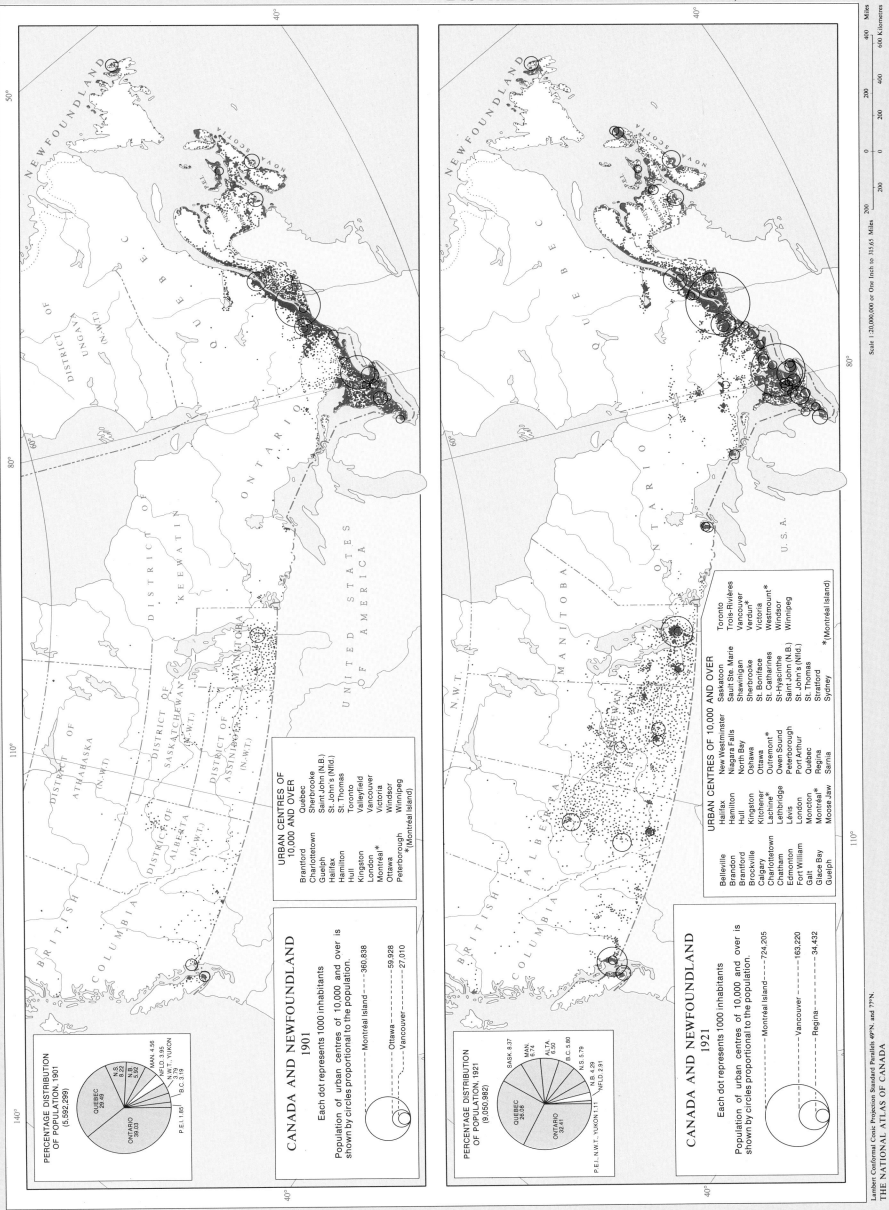

Miles
Kilometres

Scale 1:20,000,000 or One Inch to 315.65 Miles

URBAN CENTRES OF 10,000 AND OVER

Brantford
Charlottetown
Guelph
Halifax
Hamilton
Hull
Kingston
London
Montréal*
Ottawa
Peterborough

Québec
Sherbrooke
Saint John (N.B.)
St. John's (Nfld.)
St. Thomas
Toronto
Valleyfield
Vancouver
Victoria
Windsor
Winnipeg

*(Montréal Island)

CANADA AND NEWFOUNDLAND
1901

Each dot represents 1000 inhabitants

Population of urban centres of 10,000 and over is shown by circles proportional to the population.

Montréal Island————360,838

Ottawa————59,928

Vancouver————27,010

PERCENTAGE DISTRIBUTION OF POPULATION, 1901
(5,592,299)

ONTARIO 39.03
QUEBEC 29.49
N.S. 8.22
N.B. 5.82
MAN. 4.56
NFLD. 3.95
N.W.T. YUKON 3.79
B.C. 3.19
P.E.I. 1.85

URBAN CENTRES OF 10,000 AND OVER

Belleville
Brandon
Brantford
Brockville
Calgary
Charlottetown
Chatham
Edmonton
Fort William
Galt
Glace Bay
Guelph

Halifax
Hamilton
Hull
Kingston
Kitchener
Lachine*
Lévis
London
Moncton
Montréal*
Moose Jaw

New Westminster
Niagara Falls
North Bay
Oshawa
Ottawa
Outremont*
Owen Sound
Peterborough
Port Arthur
Québec
Regina
Sarnia

Saskatoon
Sault Ste. Marie
Shawinigan
Sherbrooke
St. Boniface
St. Catharines
St-Hyacinthe
Saint John (N.B.)
St. John's (Nfld.)
St. Thomas
Stratford
Sydney

Toronto
Trois-Rivières
Vancouver
Verdun*
Victoria
Westmount*
Windsor
Winnipeg

*(Montréal Island)

CANADA AND NEWFOUNDLAND
1921

Each dot represents 1000 inhabitants

Population of urban centres of 10,000 and over is shown by circles proportional to the population.

Montréal Island————724,205

Vancouver————163,220

Regina————34,432

PERCENTAGE DISTRIBUTION OF POPULATION, 1921
(9,050,982)

ONTARIO 32.41
QUEBEC 26.08
SASK. 8.37
MAN. 6.74
ALTA. 6.50
B.C. 5.80
N.S. 5.79
N.B. 4.29
NFLD. 2.91
P.E.I., N.W.T., YUKON 1.11

Lambert Conformal Conic Projection Standard Parallels 49°N. and 77°N.

DISTRIBUTION OF POPULATION, 1941

URBAN CENTRES OF 10,000 AND OVER

Belleville
Brandon
Brantford
Brockville
Calgary
Cap-de-la-Madeleine
Charlottetown
Chatham
Chicoutimi
Cornwall
Dartmouth
Drummondville
Edmonton
Forest Hill
Fort William
Fredericton
Galt
Glace Bay
Granby
Guelph
Halifax
Hamilton
Hull
Joliette
Jonquière
Kingston
Kitchener

Lachine*
Lethbridge
Lévis
London
Medicine Hat
Moncton
Montréal*
Moose Jaw
New Westminster
Niagara Falls
North Bay
Oshawa
Ottawa
Outremont*
Owen Sound
Pembroke
Peterborough
Port Arthur
Prince Albert
Québec
Regina
St. Boniface
St-Hyacinthe
St-Jean (Que.)
St-Jérôme
Saint John (N.B.)

St. John's (Nfld.)
St. Thomas
Sarnia
Saskatoon
Sault Ste. Marie
Shawinigan
Sherbrooke
Sorel
Stratford
Sudbury
Thetford Mines
Timmins
Toronto
Trois-Rivières
Truro
Valleyfield
Vancouver
Verdun*
Victoria
Welland
Westmount*
Windsor
Winnipeg
Woodstock

* (Montréal Island)

CANADA, 1941
NEWFOUNDLAND, 1945
Each dot represents 1000 inhabitants

Population of urban centres of 10,000 and over is shown by circles proportional to the population.

Montréal Island —— 1,116,800
Vancouver —— 275,353
Saskatoon —— 43,027

PERCENTAGE DISTRIBUTION OF POPULATION, 1941
(11,809,955)

ONTARIO 32.07
QUEBEC 28.21
SASK. 7.59
B.C. 6.93
ALTA. 6.74
MAN. 6.18
N.S. 4.89
N.B. 3.87
NFLD. 2.57
P.E.I., N.W.T., YUKON 0.95

Scale 1:20,000,000 or One Inch to 315.65 Miles
Lambert Conformal Conic Projection Standard Parallels 49°N. and 77°N.

THE NATIONAL ATLAS OF CANADA

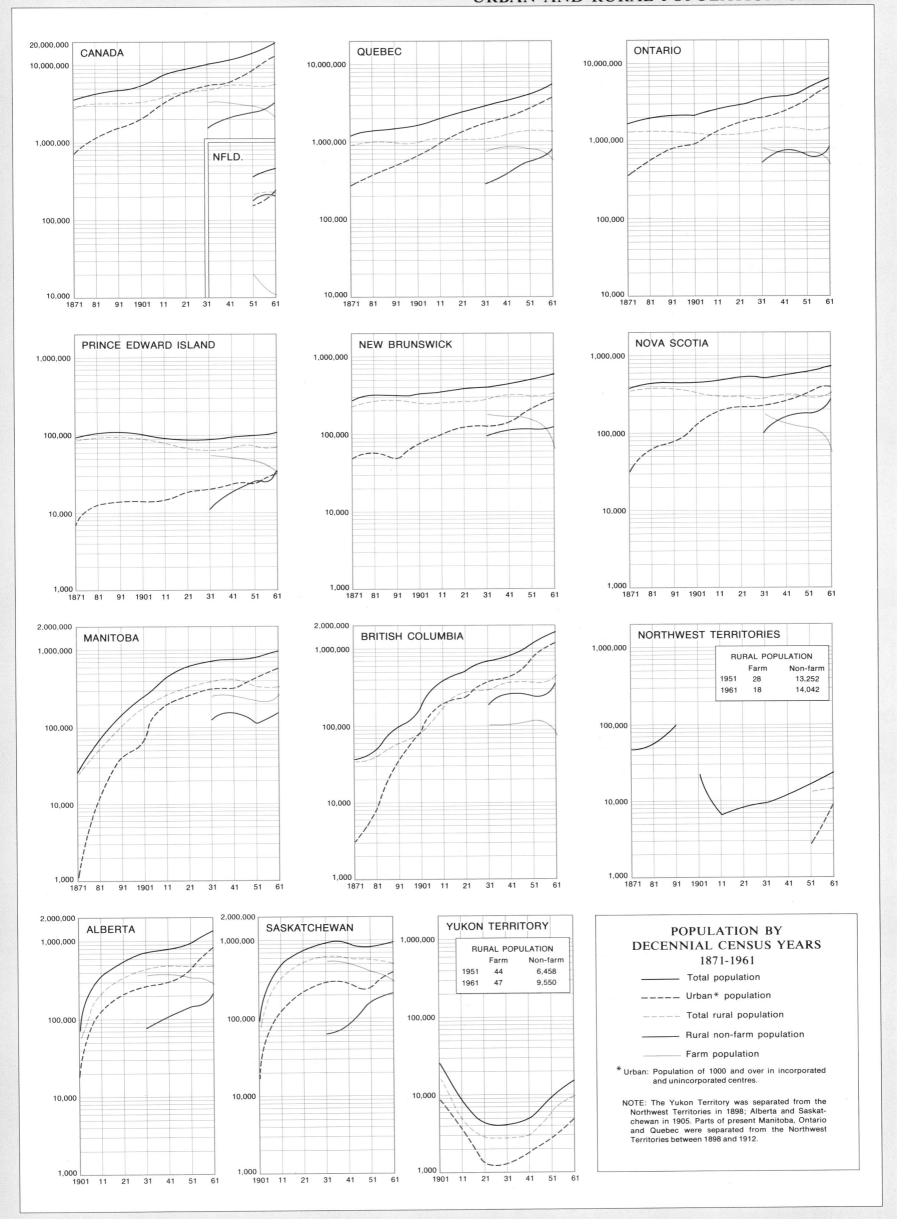

CANADA

QUEBEC

ONTARIO

NFLD.

PRINCE EDWARD ISLAND

NEW BRUNSWICK

NOVA SCOTIA

MANITOBA

BRITISH COLUMBIA

NORTHWEST TERRITORIES

RURAL POPULATION		
	Farm	Non-farm
1951	28	13,252
1961	18	14,042

ALBERTA

SASKATCHEWAN

YUKON TERRITORY

RURAL POPULATION		
	Farm	Non-farm
1951	44	6,458
1961	47	9,550

**POPULATION BY
DECENNIAL CENSUS YEARS
1871-1961**

——————— Total population

- - - - - - - Urban* population

— — — — Total rural population

——————— Rural non-farm population

——————— Farm population

* Urban: Population of 1000 and over in incorporated
   and unincorporated centres.

NOTE: The Yukon Territory was separated from the
Northwest Territories in 1898; Alberta and Saskatchewan in 1905. Parts of present Manitoba, Ontario
and Quebec were separated from the Northwest
Territories between 1898 and 1912.

URBAN COMPLEXES* AND CENTRES**, 5,000 POPULATION AND OVER, 1961

NAME	POP.	***%
1. Montréal, C.M.A., Que.	2,109,509	11.57
2. Toronto, C.M.A., Ont.	1,824,481	21.57
3. Vancouver, C.M.A., B.C.	790,165	25.90
4. Winnipeg, C.M.A., Man.	475,989	28.51
5. Ottawa, C.M.A., Ont./Que.	429,750	30.87
6. Hamilton, C.M.A., Ont.	395,189	33.04
7. Québec, C.M.A., Que.	357,568	35.00
8. Edmonton, C.M.A., Alta.	337,568	36.85
9. Calgary, C.M.A., Alta.	279,062	38.38
10. Windsor, C.M.A., Ont.	193,365	39.44
11. Halifax, C.M.A., N.S.	183,946	40.44
12. London, C.M.A., Ont.	181,283	41.44
13. Kitchener, C.M.A., Ont.	154,864	42.29
14. Victoria, C.M.A., B.C.	154,152	43.13
15. Regina, C., Sask.	112,141	43.75
16. Sudbury, C.M.A., Ont.	110,694	44.36
17. Sydney—Glace Bay, C.M.U.A., N.S.	106,114	44.94
18. Chicoutimi—Jonquière, C.M.U.A., Que.	105,009	45.51
19. St. Catharines, C.M.U.A., Ont.	95,577	46.04
20. Saint John, C.M.A., N.B.	95,563	46.56
21. Saskatoon, C., Sask.	95,526	47.09
22. Fort William—Port Arthur, C.M.U.A., Ont.	93,251	47.60
23. St. John's, C.M.A., Nfld.	90,838	48.09
24. Trois-Rivières, C.M.U.A., Que.	83,659	48.55
25. Oshawa, C.M.A., Ont.	80,914	49.00
26. Sherbrooke, C.M.U.A., Que.	70,253	49.38
27. Shawinigan, C.M.U.A., Que.	63,518	49.73
28. Kingston, C.M.U.A., Ont.	63,419	50.08
29. Sarnia, C.M.U.A., Ont.	61,293	50.41
30. Sault Ste. Marie, C.M.U.A., Ont.	58,460	50.73
31. Brantford, C.M.U.A., Ont.	56,741	51.05
32. Moncton, C.M.U.A., N.B.	55,768	51.35
33. Niagara Falls, C., Ont.	54,649	51.65
34. Peterborough, C.M.U.A., Ont.	49,902	51.92
35. Cornwall, C., Ont.	43,639	52.16
36. Guelph, C.M.U.A., Ont.	41,767	52.39
37. Timmins, C.M.U.A., Ont.	40,121	52.61
38. Drummondville, C.M.U.A., Que.	39,307	52.83
39. Welland, C., Ont.	36,079	53.03
40. Lethbridge, C., Alta.	35,454	53.22
41. St-Jean, C.M.U.A., Que.	34,576	53.41
42. North Bay, C.U.A., Ont.	33,545	53.59
43. Moose Jaw, C., Sask.	33,206	53.78
44. St-Hyacinthe, C.U.A., Que.	31,659	53.95
45. Granby, C., Que.	31,463	54.12
46. Belleville, C., Ont.	30,655	54.29
47. Rouyn, C.U.A., Que.	30,193	54.41
48. Valleyfield, C.M.U.A., Que.	29,849	54.62
49. Chatham, C., Ont.	29,826	54.78
50. St-Jérôme, C.U.A., Que.	29,107	54.94
51. Sorel, C.U.A., Que.	28,906	55.10
52. Brandon, C., Man.	28,166	55.26
53. Thetford Mines, C.U.A., Que.	25,798	55.40

NAME	POP.	***%
54. Corner Brook, C., Nfld.	25,185	55.54
55. Fredericton, C.U.A., N.B.	24,836	55.67
56. Medicine Hat, C., Alta.	24,484	55.81
57. Prince Albert, C., Sask.	24,168	55.94
58. St. Thomas, C., Ont.	22,469	56.06
59. Rimouski, C.U.A., Que.	22,443	56.18
60. New Glasgow, C.U.A., N.S.	22,408	56.31
61. Joliette, C.U.A., Que.	22,198	56.43
62. Victoriaville, C.U.A., Que.	21,697	56.55
63. Barrie, C., Ont.	21,169	56.66
64. Woodstock, C., Ont.	20,486	56.78
65. Stratford, C., Ont.	20,467	56.89
66. Alma, C.U.A., Que.	19,854	57.00
67. Red Deer, C., Alta.	19,612	57.10
68. Pembroke, C.U.A., Ont.	18,811	57.21
69. Kamloops, C.U.A., B.C.	18,700	57.31
70. Brampton, T., Ont.	18,467	57.41
71. Charlottetown, C., P.E.I.	18,318	57.51
72. Orillia, C.U.A., Ont.	18,246	57.61
73. Nanaimo, C.U.A., B.C.	18,031	57.71
74. Brockville, T., Ont.	17,744	57.81
75. Owen Sound, C., Ont.	17,421	57.90
76. Port Colborne, C.U.A., Ont.	16,717	58.00
77. Kirkland Lake, C.U.A., Ont.	16,510	58.09
78. Prince George, C.U.A., B.C.	16,458	58.18
79. Port Alberni, C.U.A., B.C.	16,176	58.27
80. Truro, C., N.S.	15,869	58.35
81. Val-d'Or, C.U.A., Que.	14,327	58.43
82. Kelowna, C.U.A., B.C.	14,243	58.51
83. Magog, C.U.A., Que.	14,233	58.59
84. Sept-Îles, C., Que.	14,196	58.66
85. Penticton, C., B.C.	13,859	58.74
86. Trenton, T., Ont.	13,183	58.81
87. Kenora, T., Ont.	13,101	58.88
88. La Tuque, T., Que.	13,023	58.96
89. Edmundston, C., N.B.	12,791	59.03
90. Portage la Prairie, C., Man.	12,388	59.09
91. Swift Current, C., Sask.	12,186	59.16
92. Oromocto, T., N.B.	12,170	59.23
93. Windsor, C.U.A., Nfld.	12,110	59.29
94. Campbellton, C.U.A., N.B.	12,018	59.36
95. Prince Rupert, C., B.C.	11,987	59.43
96. Trail, C., B.C.	11,580	59.49
97. Lindsay, T., Ont.	11,399	59.55
98. North Battleford, C., Sask.	11,230	59.61
99. Georgetown, C.U.A., Ont.	11,172	59.67
100. Flin Flon, T., Man./Sask.	11,104	59.74
101. Asbestos, T., Que.	11,083	59.80
102. Dawson Creek, C., B.C.	10,946	59.86
103. Wabana, C.U.A., Nfld.	10,919	59.92
104. Rivière-du-Loup, C., Que.	10,835	59.98
105. Amherst, T., N.S.	10,788	60.03
106. Cobourg, T., Ont.	10,646	60.09
107. Vernon, C., B.C.	10,250	60.15
108. Yorkton, C., Sask.	9,995	60.20
109. Elliot Lake, U.P., Ont.	9,950	60.26
110. Smiths Falls, T., Ont.	9,603	60.31
111. Fort Frances, T., Ont.	9,481	60.36
112. Matane, T., Que.	9,190	60.41
113. Weyburn, C., Sask.	9,101	60.46
114. Port-Alfred, T., Que.	9,066	60.51
115. Leamington, T., Ont.	9,030	60.56
116. Fort Erie, T., Ont.	9,027	60.61
117. Renfrew, T., Ont.	8,935	60.66
118. Newmarket, T., Ont.	8,932	60.71
119. Aurora, T., Ont.	8,791	60.76
120. Simcoe, T., Ont.	8,754	60.81
121. Beauharnois, C., Que.	8,704	60.85
122. Hawkesbury, T., Ont.	8,661	60.90

NAME	POP.	***%
123. Midland, T., Ont.	8,656	60.95
124. Yarmouth, T., N.S.	8,636	61.00
125. Summerside, T., P.E.I.	8,611	61.04
126. Selkirk, T., Man.	8,576	61.09
127. Collingwood, T., Ont.	8,385	61.14
128. Grande Prairie, C., Alta.	8,352	61.18
129. Chilliwack, C., B.C.	8,259	61.23
130. Port Hope, T., Ont.	8,091	61.27
131. Baie-Comeau, T., Que.	7,956	61.32
132. Wallaceburg, T., Ont.	7,881	61.36
133. Roberval, C., Que.	7,739	61.40
134. Estevan, C., Sask.	7,728	61.44
135. Lachute, T., Que.	7,560	61.49
136. Buckingham, T., Que.	7,421	61.53
137. Bowmanville, T., Ont.	7,397	61.57
138. Dauphin, T., Man.	7,374	61.61
139. Chatham, T., N.B.	7,109	61.65
140. Nelson, C., B.C.	7,074	61.68
141. Cowansville, T., Que.	7,050	61.72
142. Lac Mégantic, T., Que.	7,015	61.76
143. Malartic, T., Que.	6,998	61.80
144. Camrose, C., Alta.	6,939	61.84
145. Coaticook, C., Que.	6,906	61.88
146. Ingersoll, T., Ont.	6,874	61.91
147. Kapuskasing, T., Ont.	6,870	61.95
148. Montmagny, T., Que.	6,850	61.99
149. Atikokan, U.P., Ont.	6,674	62.03
150. Tillsonburg, T., Ont.	6,600	62.06
151. Windsor, T., Que.	6,589	62.10
152. Plessisville, T., Que.	6,570	62.13
153. Goderich, T., Ont.	6,411	62.17
154. Farnham, C., Que.	6,354	62.20
155. Maniwaki, T., Que.	6,349	62.24
156. Sturgeon Falls, T., Ont.	6,288	62.27
157. Beloeil, T., Que.	6,283	62.31
158. Terrebonne, T., Que.	6,207	62.34
159. Mont-Joli, T., Que.	6,178	62.38
160. Amos, T., Que.	6,080	62.41
161. Dolbeau, T., Que.	6,052	62.44
162. Stephenville, T., Nfld.	6,043	62.48
163. Kimberley, C., B.C.	6,013	62.51
164. Parry Sound, T., Ont.	6,004	62.54
165. Hauterive, T., Que.	5,980	62.57
166. Mont-Laurier, T., Que.	5,859	62.61
167. Dalhousie, T., N.B.	5,856	62.64
168. Springhill, T., N.S.	5,836	62.67
169. Paris, T., Ont.	5,820	62.70
170. Dryden, T., Ont.	5,728	62.73
171. Gander, T., Nfld.	5,725	62.77
172. Ste-Agathe-des-Monts, T., Que.	5,725	62.80
173. Lloydminster, C., Sask./Alta.	5,667	62.83
174. Bagotville, T., Que.	5,629	62.86
175. Cranbrook, C., B.C.	5,549	62.89
176. Bathurst, T., N.B.	5,494	62.92
177. Arnprior, T., Ont.	5,474	62.95
178. Deep River, T., Ont.	5,377	62.98
179. Prescott, T., Ont.	5,366	63.01
180. Perth, T., Ont.	5,360	63.04
181. Espanola, T., Ont.	5,353	63.07
182. Penetanguishene, T., Ont.	5,340	63.10
183. Wetaskiwin, T., Alta.	5,300	63.13
184. Newcastle, T., N.B.	5,236	63.15
185. Melville, C., Sask.	5,191	63.18
186. Dunnville, T., Ont.	5,181	33.21
187. Strathroy, T., Ont.	5,150	63.24
188. Grimsby, T., Ont.	5,148	63.27
189. St-Félicien, T., Que.	5,133	63.30
190. Gananoque, T., Ont.	5,096	63.32
191. Whitehorse, C., Y.T.	5,031	63.35

* Census Metropolitan Areas (*C.M.A.*), Census Major Urban Areas (*C.M.U.A.*), Census Urban Areas (*C.U.A.*), as defined in publications of the Dominion Bureau of Statistics.

** Cities (*C.*), Towns (*T.*) and Unincorporated Places (*U.P.*), not included in or classified as urban complexes.

*** Percentages are of total population, and are cumulative in the list.

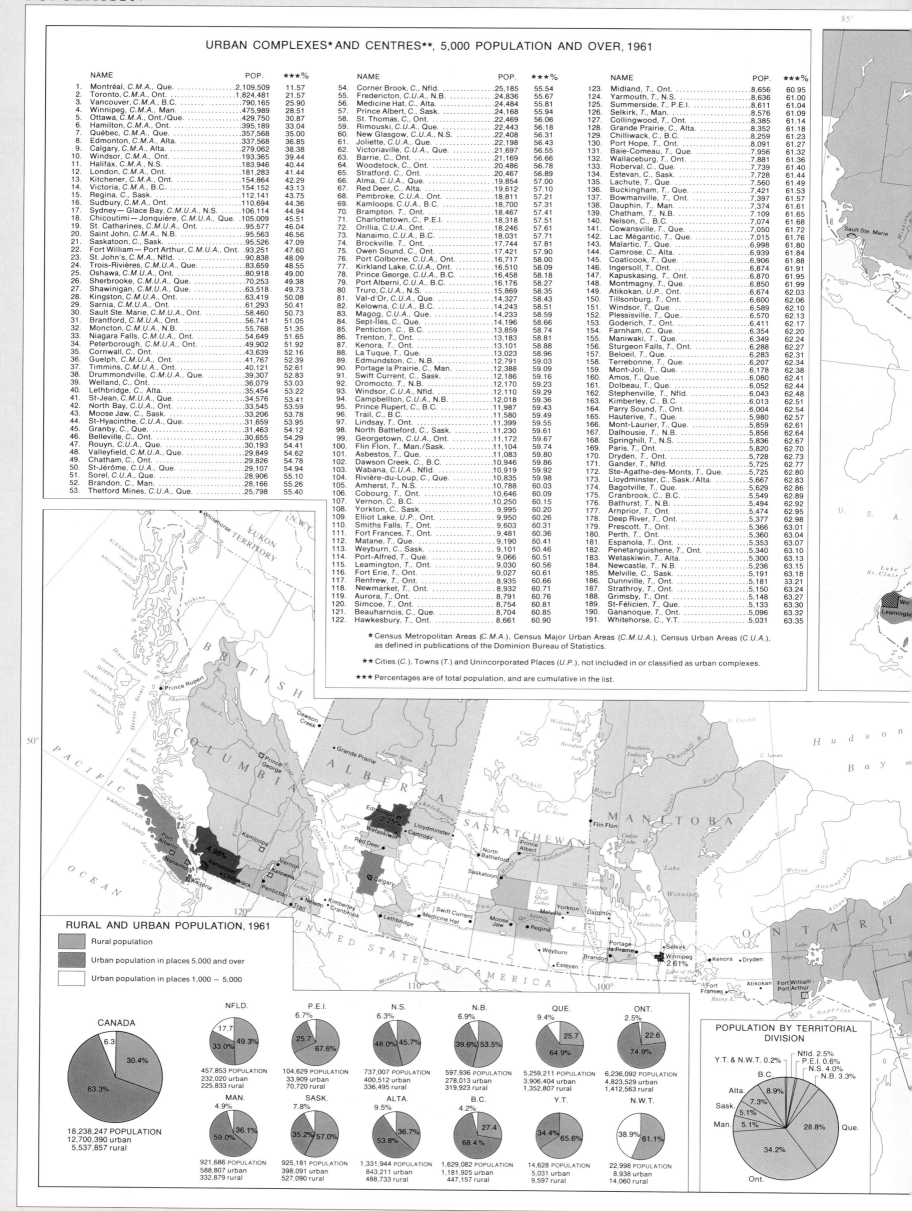

RURAL AND URBAN POPULATION, 1961

Rural population

Urban population in places 5,000 and over

Urban population in places 1,000 – 5,000

CANADA
18,238,247 POPULATION
12,700,390 urban
5,537,857 rural
6.3% / 30.4% / 63.3%

NFLD. 17.7% / 33.0% / 49.3%
457,853 POPULATION
232,020 urban
225,833 rural

P.E.I. 6.7% / 25.7% / 67.6%
104,629 POPULATION
33,909 urban
70,720 rural

N.S. 6.3% / 48.0% / 45.7%
737,007 POPULATION
400,512 urban
336,495 rural

N.B. 6.9% / 39.6% / 53.5%
597,936 POPULATION
278,013 urban
319,923 rural

QUE. 9.4% / 25.7% / 64.9%
5,259,211 POPULATION
3,906,404 urban
1,352,807 rural

ONT. 2.5% / 22.6% / 74.9%
6,236,092 POPULATION
4,823,529 urban
1,412,563 rural

MAN. 4.9% / 36.1% / 59.0%
921,686 POPULATION
588,807 urban
332,879 rural

SASK. 7.8% / 35.2% / 57.0%
925,181 POPULATION
398,091 urban
527,090 rural

ALTA. 9.5% / 36.7% / 53.8%
1,331,944 POPULATION
843,211 urban
488,733 rural

B.C. 4.2% / 27.4% / 68.4%
1,629,082 POPULATION
1,181,925 urban
447,157 rural

Y.T. 34.4% / 65.6%
14,628 POPULATION
5,031 urban
9,597 rural

N.W.T. 38.9% / 61.1%
22,998 POPULATION
8,938 urban
14,060 rural

POPULATION BY TERRITORIAL DIVISION

Y.T. & N.W.T. 0.2%
Nfld. 2.5%
P.E.I. 0.6%
N.S. 4.0%
N.B. 3.3%
B.C. 8.9%
Alta. 7.3%
Sask. 5.1%
Man. 5.1%
Que. 28.8%
Ont. 34.2%

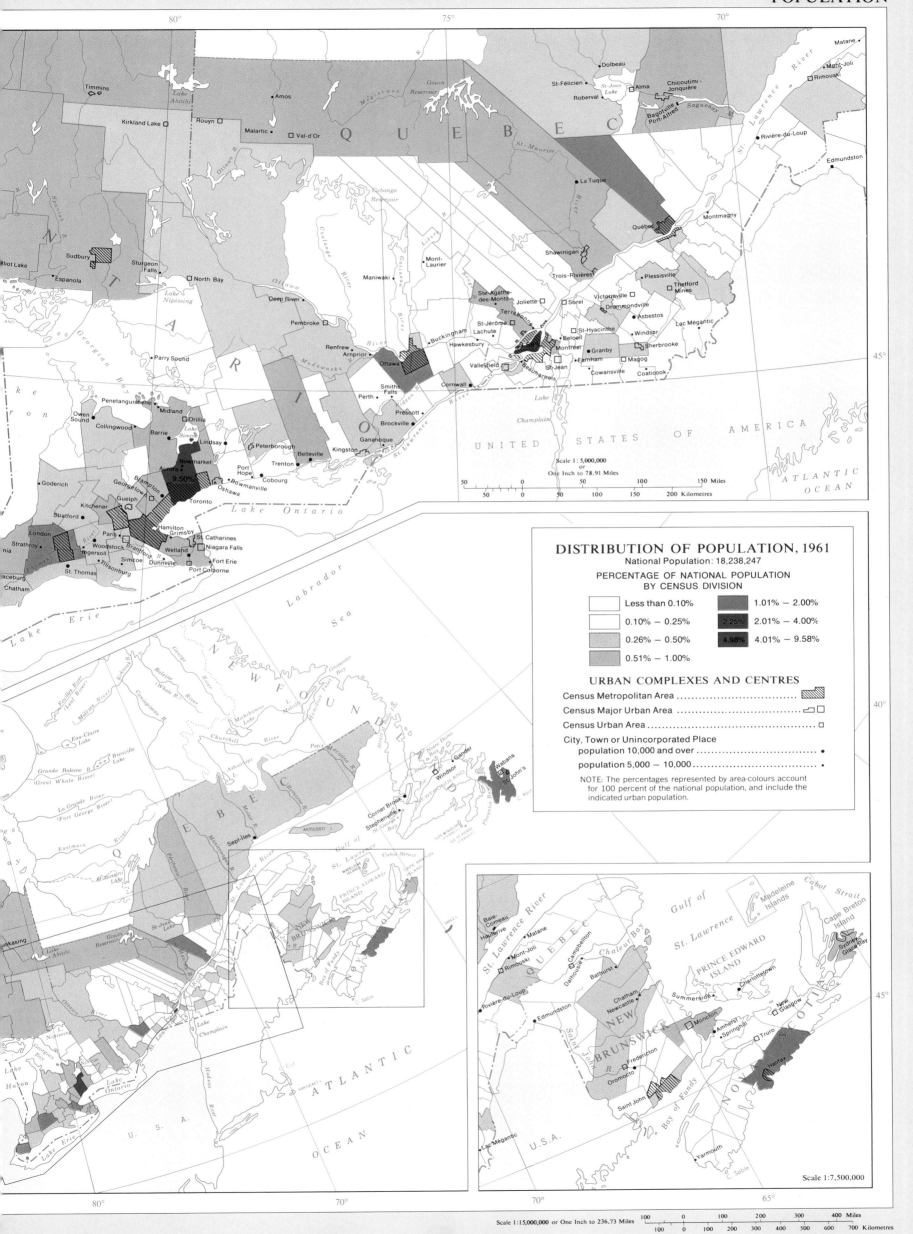

DISTRIBUTION OF POPULATION, 1961
National Population: 18,238,247

PERCENTAGE OF NATIONAL POPULATION BY CENSUS DIVISION

Less than 0.10%

0.10% — 0.25%

0.26% — 0.50%

0.51% — 1.00%

1.01% — 2.00%

2.25% 2.01% — 4.00%

4.98% 4.01% — 9.58%

URBAN COMPLEXES AND CENTRES

Census Metropolitan Area

Census Major Urban Area

Census Urban Area

City, Town or Unincorporated Place
population 10,000 and over

population 5,000 — 10,000

NOTE: The percentages represented by area-colours account
for 100 percent of the national population, and include the
indicated urban population.

Scale 1 : 5,000,000
or
One Inch to 78.91 Miles

50   0   50   100   150 Miles

50   0   50   100   150   200 Kilometres

Scale 1:7,500,000

Scale 1:15,000,000 or One Inch to 236.73 Miles

100   0   100   200   300   400 Miles

100   0   100   200   300   400   500   600   700 Kilometres

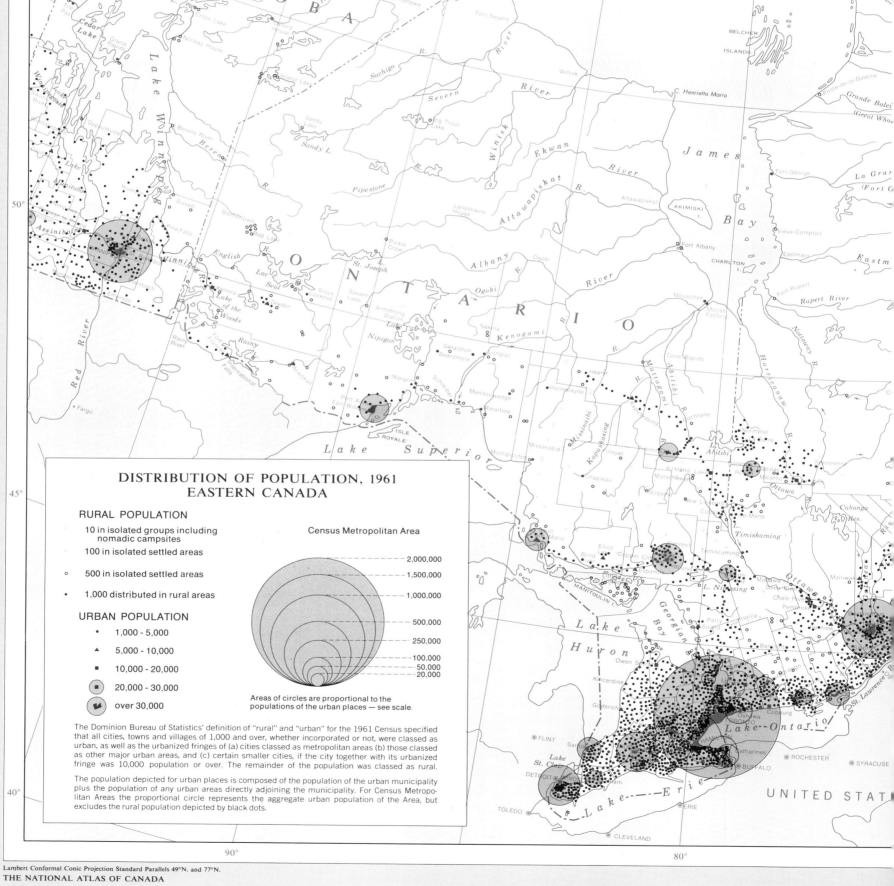

DISTRIBUTION OF POPULATION, 1961
EASTERN CANADA

RURAL POPULATION

· 10 in isolated groups including nomadic campsites

· 100 in isolated settled areas

○ 500 in isolated settled areas

• 1,000 distributed in rural areas

URBAN POPULATION

·   1,000 - 5,000

▲   5,000 - 10,000

■   10,000 - 20,000

⊙   20,000 - 30,000

◉   over 30,000

Census Metropolitan Area

- 2,000,000
- 1,500,000
- 1,000,000
- 500,000
- 250,000
- 100,000
- 50,000
- 20,000

Areas of circles are proportional to the populations of the urban places — see scale.

The Dominion Bureau of Statistics' definition of "rural" and "urban" for the 1961 Census specified that all cities, towns and villages of 1,000 and over, whether incorporated or not, were classed as urban, as well as the urbanized fringes of (a) cities classed as metropolitan areas (b) those classed as other major urban areas, and (c) certain smaller cities, if the city together with its urbanized fringe was 10,000 population or over. The remainder of the population was classed as rural.

The population depicted for urban places is composed of the population of the urban municipality plus the population of any urban areas directly adjoining the municipality. For Census Metropolitan Areas the proportional circle represents the aggregate urban population of the Area, but excludes the rural population depicted by black dots.

Lambert Conformal Conic Projection Standard Parallels 49°N. and 77°N.
THE NATIONAL ATLAS OF CANADA

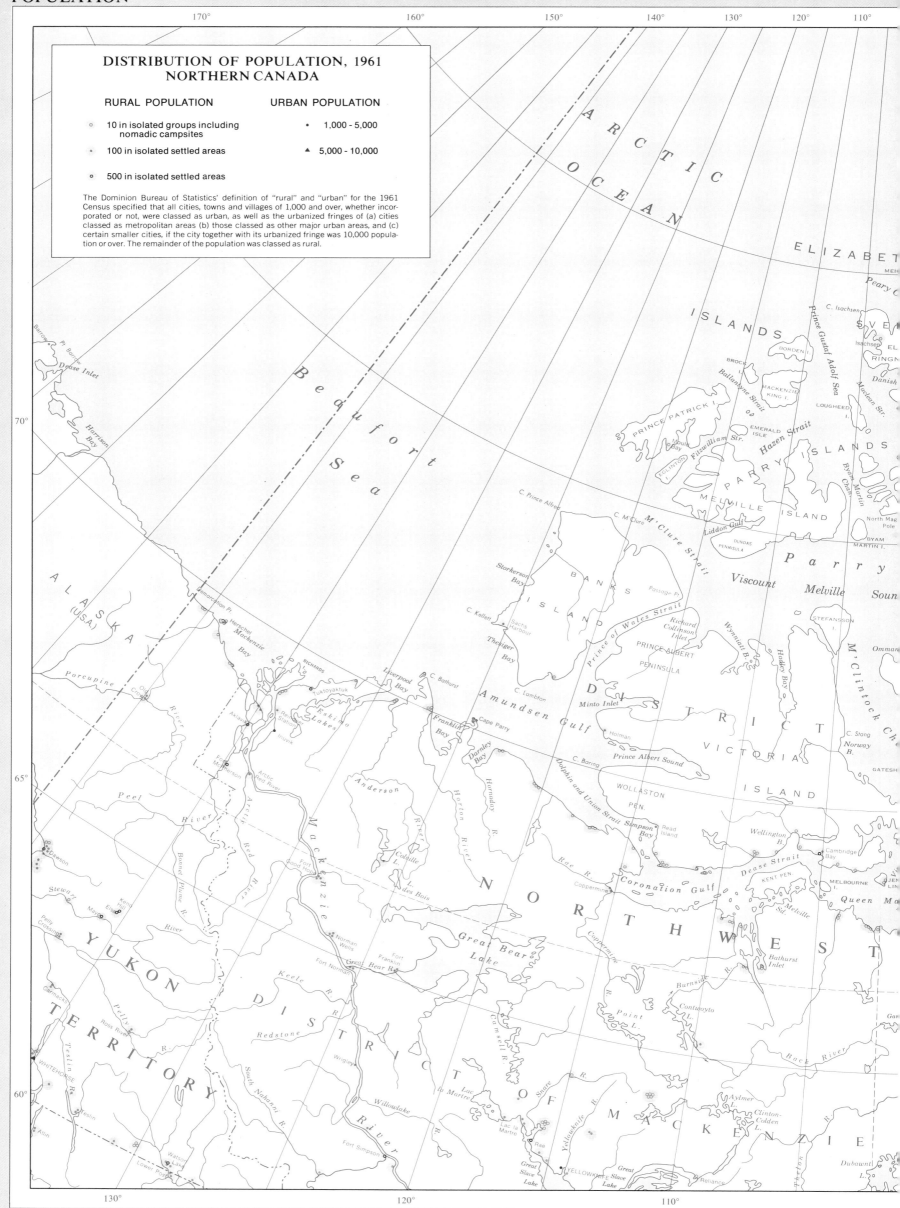

DISTRIBUTION OF POPULATION, 1961
NORTHERN CANADA

RURAL POPULATION   URBAN POPULATION

◦   10 in isolated groups including   •   1,000 - 5,000
      nomadic campsites

•   100 in isolated settled areas   ▲   5,000 - 10,000

◦   500 in isolated settled areas

The Dominion Bureau of Statistics' definition of "rural" and "urban" for the 1961
Census specified that all cities, towns and villages of 1,000 and over, whether incorporated or not, were classed as urban, as well as the urbanized fringes of (a) cities
classed as metropolitan areas (b) those classed as other major urban areas, and (c)
certain smaller cities, if the city together with its urbanized fringe was 10,000 population or over. The remainder of the population was classed as rural.

Lambert Conformal Conic Projection Standard Parallels 49°N. and 77°N.
THE NATIONAL ATLAS OF CANADA

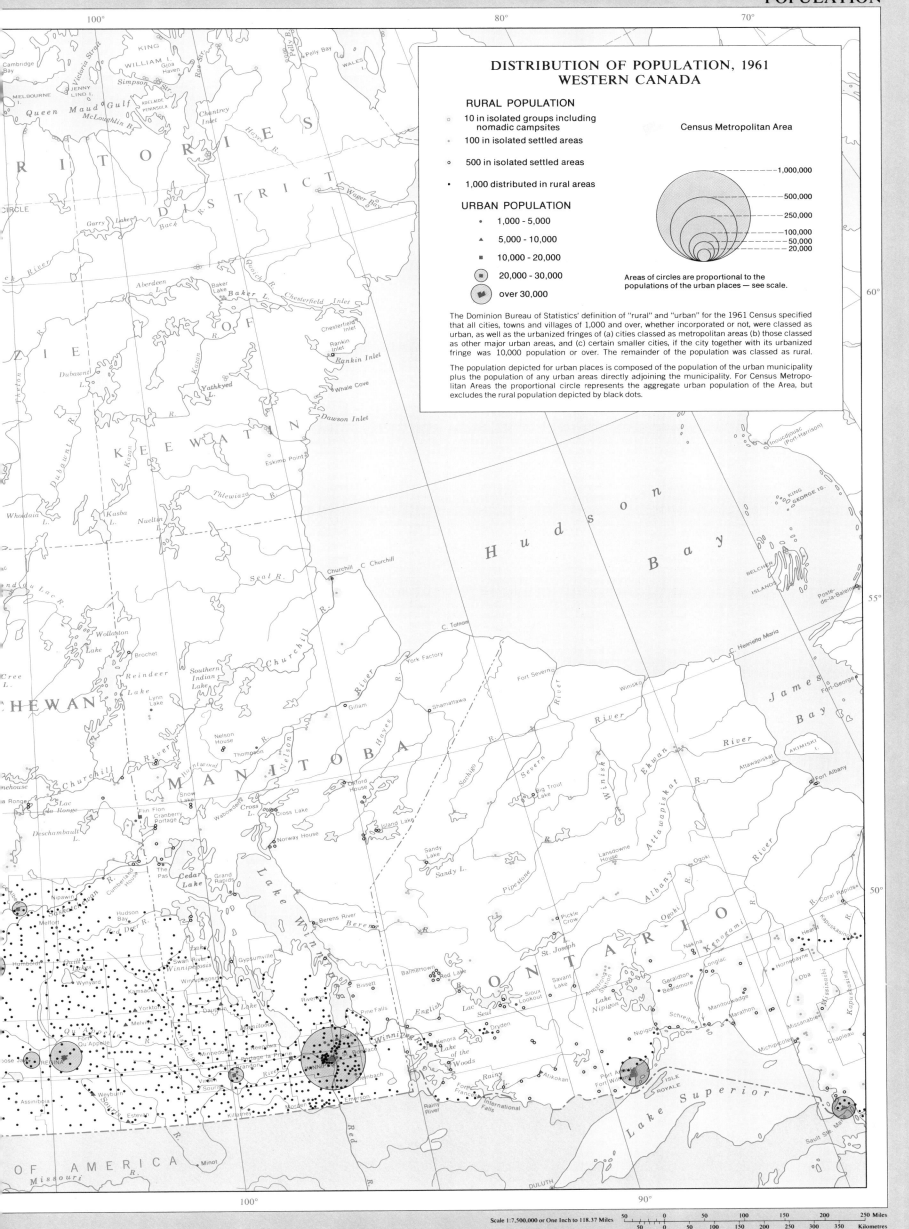

DISTRIBUTION OF POPULATION, 1961
WESTERN CANADA

RURAL POPULATION

○ 10 in isolated groups including nomadic campsites

· 100 in isolated settled areas

○ 500 in isolated settled areas

• 1,000 distributed in rural areas

URBAN POPULATION

· 1,000 - 5,000

▲ 5,000 - 10,000

■ 10,000 - 20,000

⊞ 20,000 - 30,000

⬚ over 30,000

Census Metropolitan Area

—— 1,000,000
—— 500,000
—— 250,000
—— 100,000
—— 50,000
—— 20,000

Areas of circles are proportional to the populations of the urban places — see scale.

The Dominion Bureau of Statistics' definition of "rural" and "urban" for the 1961 Census specified that all cities, towns and villages of 1,000 and over, whether incorporated or not, were classed as urban, as well as the urbanized fringes of (a) cities classed as metropolitan areas (b) those classed as other major urban areas, and (c) certain smaller cities, if the city together with its urbanized fringe was 10,000 population or over. The remainder of the population was classed as rural.

The population depicted for urban places is composed of the population of the urban municipality plus the population of any urban areas directly adjoining the municipality. For Census Metropolitan Areas the proportional circle represents the aggregate urban population of the Area, but excludes the rural population depicted by black dots.

Scale 1:7,500,000 or One Inch to 118.37 Miles

50   0   50   100   150   200   250 Miles

50 0 50 100 150 200 250 300 350 Kilometres

POPULATION CHANGES

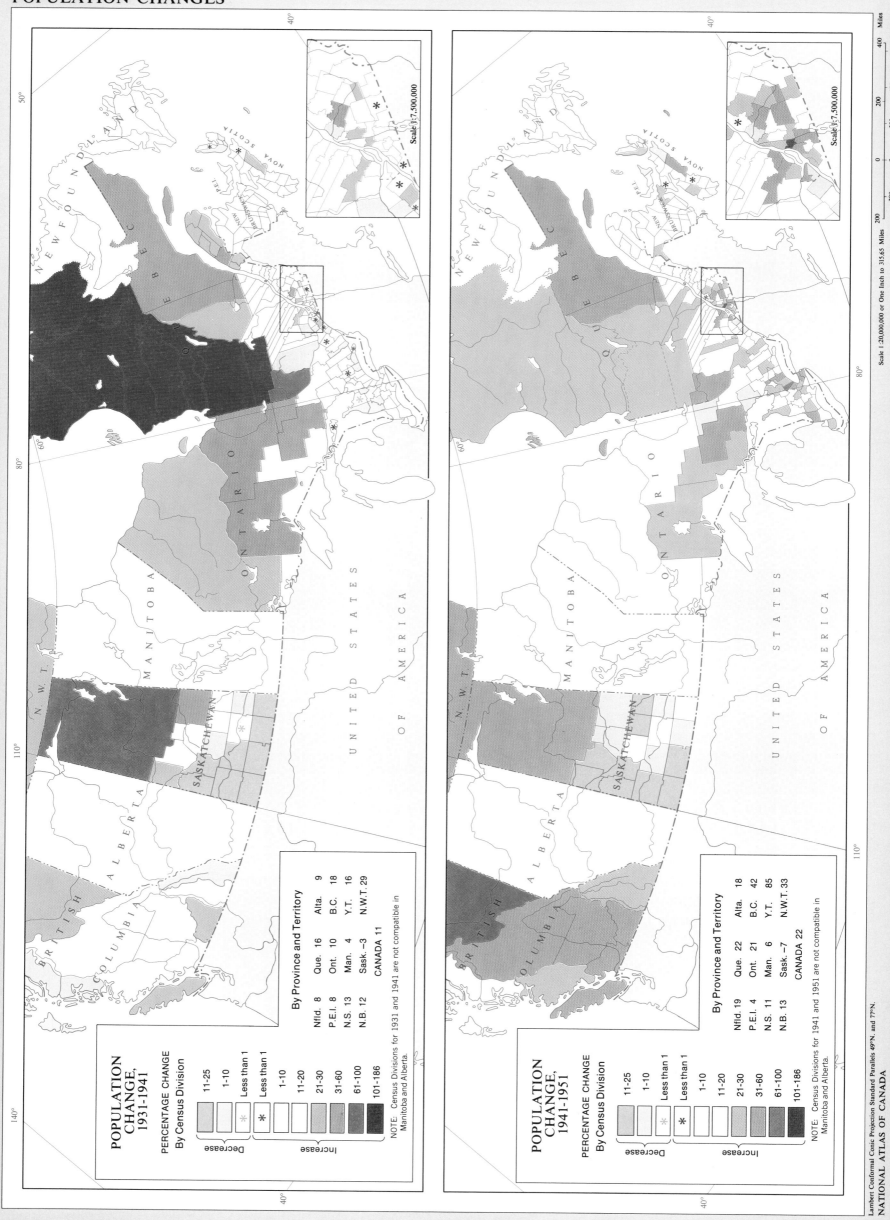

POPULATION CHANGE, 1931-1941

PERCENTAGE CHANGE
By Census Division

Decrease
- 11-25
- 1-10
- Less than 1

- * Less than 1

Increase
- 1-10
- 11-20
- 21-30
- 31-60
- 61-100
- 101-186

NOTE: Census Divisions for 1931 and 1941 are not compatible in Manitoba and Alberta.

By Province and Territory

Nfld. 8	Que. 16	Alta. 9	
P.E.I. 8	Ont. 10	B.C. 18	
N.S. 13	Man. 4	Y.T. 16	
N.B. 12	Sask. -3	N.W.T. 29	
		CANADA 11	

POPULATION CHANGE, 1941-1951

PERCENTAGE CHANGE
By Census Division

Decrease
- 11-25
- 1-10
- Less than 1

- * Less than 1

Increase
- 1-10
- 11-20
- 21-30
- 31-60
- 61-100
- 101-186

NOTE: Census Divisions for 1941 and 1951 are not compatible in Manitoba and Alberta.

By Province and Territory

Nfld. 19	Que. 22	Alta. 18	
P.E.I. 4	Ont. 21	B.C. 42	
N.S. 11	Man. 6	Y.T. 85	
N.B. 13	Sask. -7	N.W.T. 33	
		CANADA 22	

Lambert Conformal Conic Projection Standard Parallels 49°N. and 77°N.

Scale 1:20,000,000 or One Inch to 315.65 Miles

Scale 1:7,500,000

NATIONAL ATLAS OF CANADA

POPULATION CHANGE, 1951-1961

PERCENTAGE CHANGE
By Census Division

Decrease
- 11-25
- 1-10
- Less than 1

Increase
- Less than 1
- 1-10
- 11-20
- 21-30
- 31-60
- 61-100
- 101-186

By Province and Territory

Nfld. 27	Que. 30	Alta. 42	
P.E.I. 6	Ont. 36	B.C. 40	
N.S. 15	Man. 19	Y.T. 61	
N.B. 16	Sask. 11	N.W.T. 44	

CANADA 30

NOTE: Census Divisions for 1951 and 1961 are not compatible in Manitoba and Alberta.

POPULATION CHANGE, 1961-1966

PERCENTAGE CHANGE
By Census Division

Decrease
- 11-25
- 1-10
- Less than 1

Increase
- Less than 1
- 1-10
- 11-20
- 21-30
- 31-60
- 61-100
- 101-186

By Province and Territory

Nfld. 8	Que. 10	Alta. 10	
P.E.I. 4	Ont. 12	B.C. 15	
N.S. 3	Man. 4	Y.T. -2	
N.B. 3	Sask. 3	N.W.T. 25	

CANADA 10

NOTE: Minor changes in Census Division Boundaries in 1966 have not been shown.

Scale 1:7,500,000

Scale 1:7,500,000

Scale 1:20,000,000 or One Inch to 315.65 Miles

Lambert Conformal Conic Projection Standard Parallels 49°N. and 77°N.
NATIONAL ATLAS OF CANADA

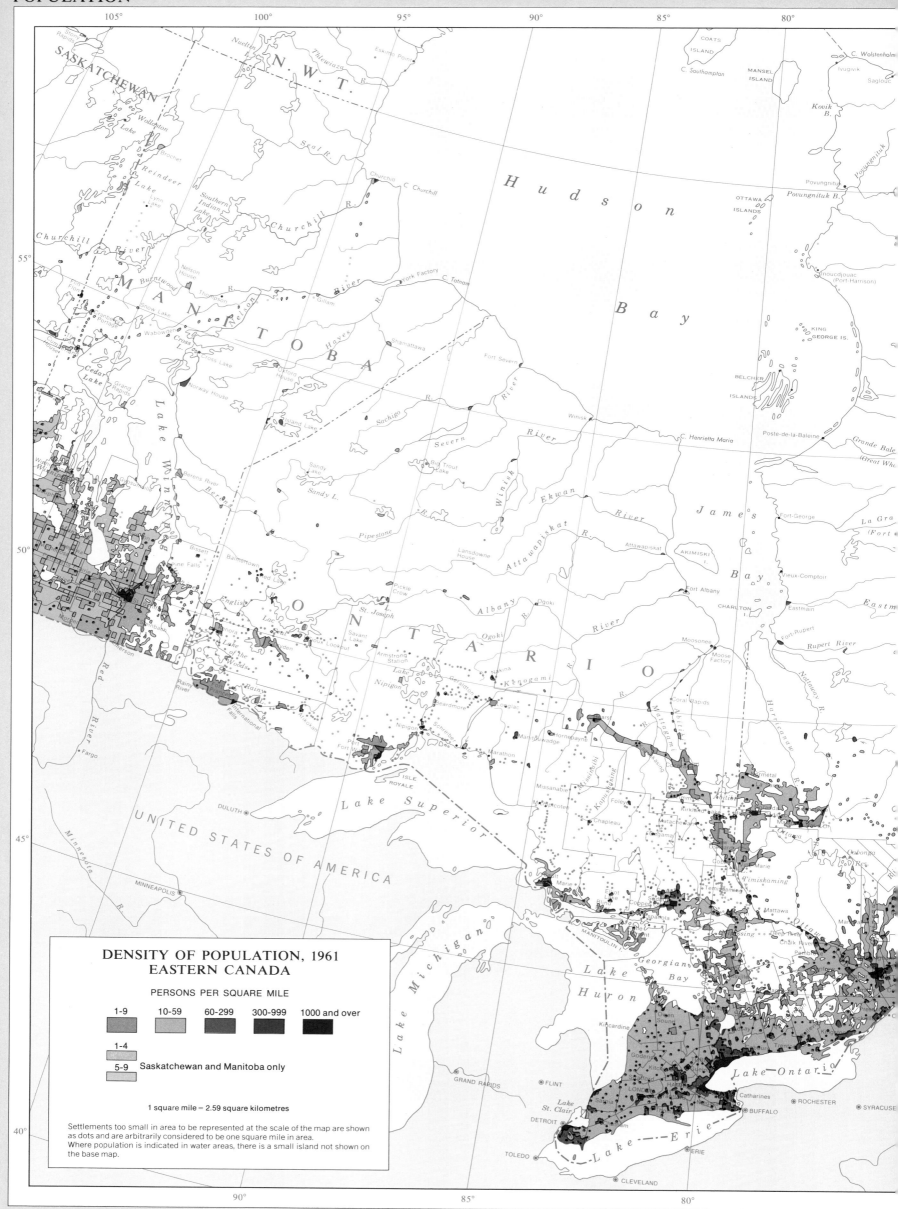

DENSITY OF POPULATION, 1961
EASTERN CANADA

PERSONS PER SQUARE MILE

1-9   10-59   60-299   300-999   1000 and over

1-4
5-9   Saskatchewan and Manitoba only

1 square mile = 2.59 square kilometres

Settlements too small in area to be represented at the scale of the map are shown as dots and are arbitrarily considered to be one square mile in area.
Where population is indicated in water areas, there is a small island not shown on the base map.

Lambert Conformal Conic Projection Standard Parallels 49°N. and 77°N.
THE NATIONAL ATLAS OF CANADA

Scale 1:7,500,000 or One Inch to 118.37 Miles

POPULATION

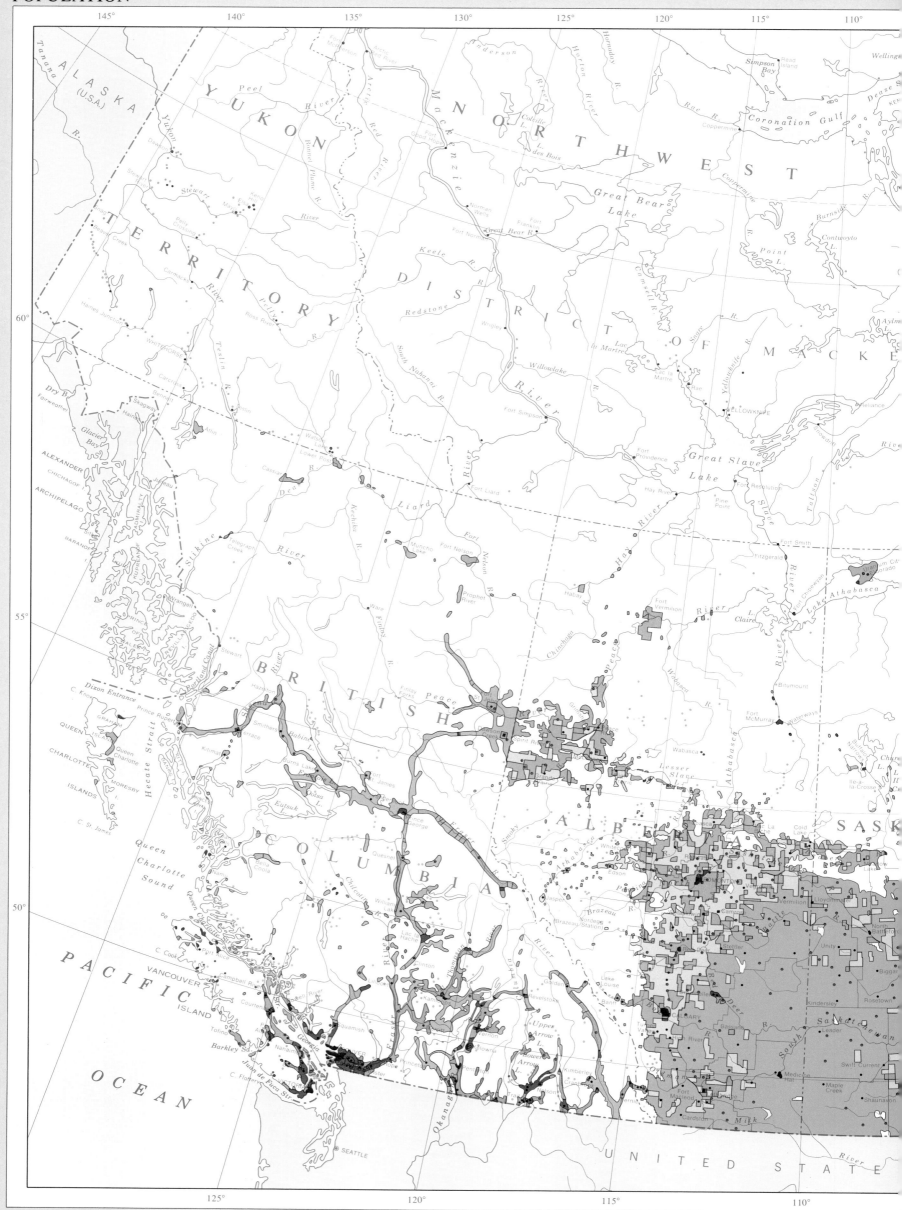

Lambert Conformal Conic Projection Standard Parallels 49°N. and 77°N.
THE NATIONAL ATLAS OF CANADA

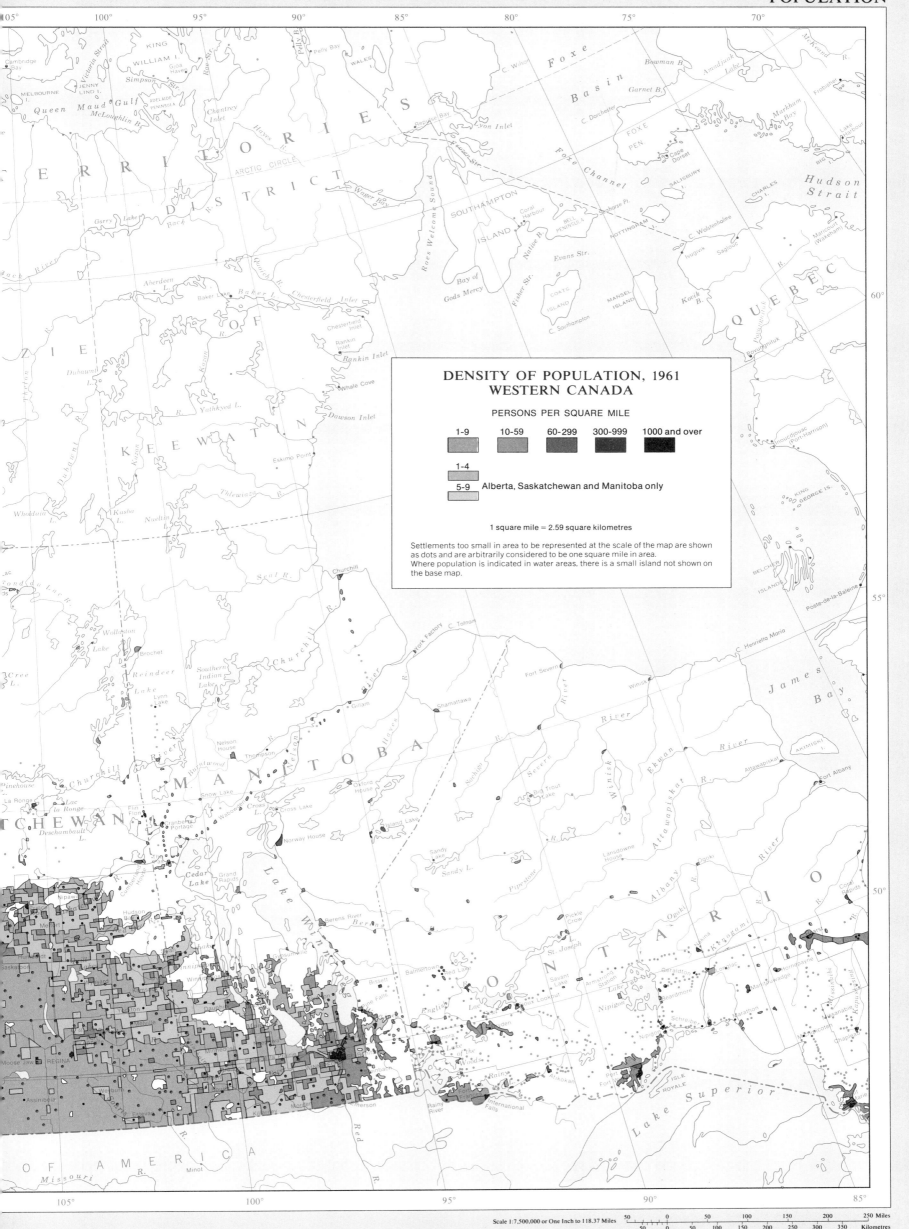

DENSITY OF POPULATION, 1961
WESTERN CANADA

PERSONS PER SQUARE MILE

| 1-9 | 10-59 | 60-299 | 300-999 | 1000 and over |

| 1-4 |
| 5-9 | Alberta, Saskatchewan and Manitoba only

1 square mile = 2.59 square kilometres

Settlements too small in area to be represented at the scale of the map are shown
as dots and are arbitrarily considered to be one square mile in area.
Where population is indicated in water areas, there is a small island not shown on
the base map.

Scale 1:7,500,000 or One Inch to 118.37 Miles

50   0   50   100   150   200   250 Miles
50 0 50 100 150 200 250 300 350 Kilometres

RELIGIONS

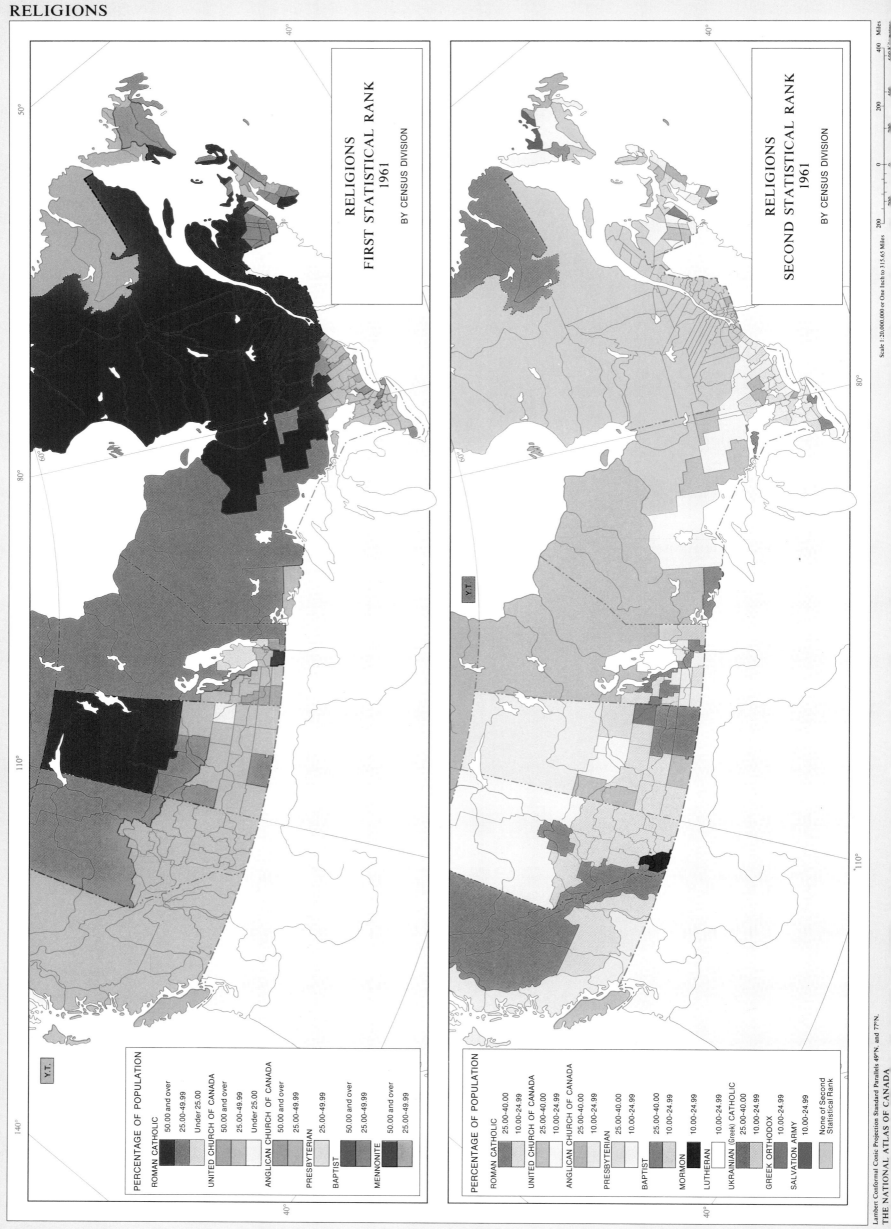

RELIGIONS
FIRST STATISTICAL RANK
1961
BY CENSUS DIVISION

Y.T.

PERCENTAGE OF POPULATION

ROMAN CATHOLIC
50.00 and over
25.00-49.99
Under 25.00

UNITED CHURCH OF CANADA
50.00 and over
25.00-49.99
Under 25.00

ANGLICAN CHURCH OF CANADA
50.00 and over
25.00-49.99

PRESBYTERIAN
25.00-49.99

BAPTIST
50.00 and over
25.00-49.99

MENNONITE
50.00 and over
25.00-49.99

RELIGIONS
SECOND STATISTICAL RANK
1961
BY CENSUS DIVISION

Y.T.

PERCENTAGE OF POPULATION

ROMAN CATHOLIC
25.00-40.00
10.00-24.99

UNITED CHURCH OF CANADA
25.00-40.00
10.00-24.99

ANGLICAN CHURCH OF CANADA
25.00-40.00
10.00-24.99

PRESBYTERIAN
25.00-40.00
10.00-24.99

BAPTIST
25.00-40.00
10.00-24.99

MORMON
10.00-24.99

LUTHERAN
10.00-24.99

UKRAINIAN (Greek) CATHOLIC
25.00-40.00
10.00-24.99

GREEK ORTHODOX
10.00-24.99

SALVATION ARMY
10.00-24.99

None of Second
Statistical Rank

Lambert Conformal Conic Projection Standard Parallels 49°N. and 77°N.

Scale 1:20,000,000 or One Inch to 315.65 Miles

THE NATIONAL ATLAS OF CANADA

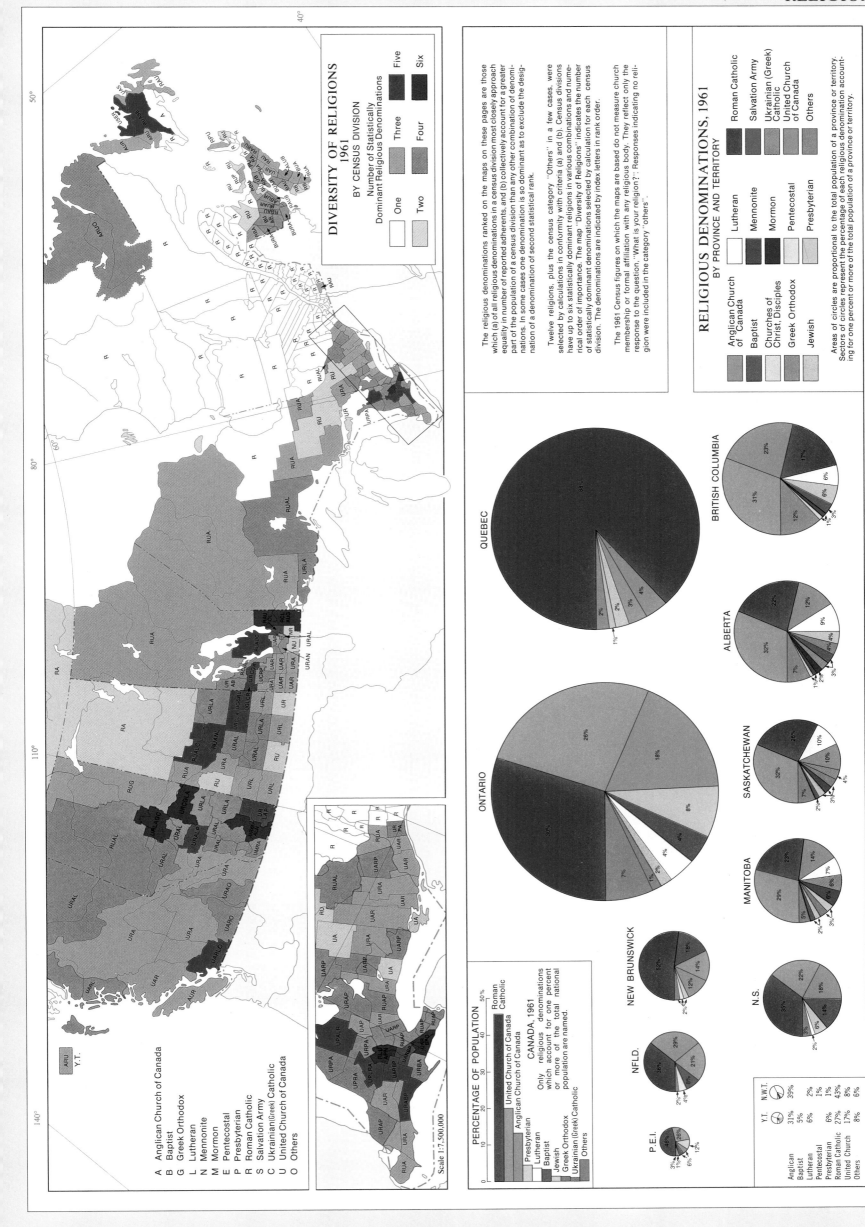

DIVERSITY OF RELIGIONS
1961
BY CENSUS DIVISION

Number of Statistically
Dominant Religious Denominations

- One
- Two
- Three
- Four
- Five
- Six

The religious denominations ranked on the maps on these pages are those which (a) of all religious denominations in a census division most closely approach equality in number of reported adherents, and (b) collectively account for a greater part of the population of a census division than any other combination of denominations. In some cases one denomination is so dominant as to exclude the designation of a denomination of second statistical rank.

Twelve religions, plus the census category "Others" in a few cases, were selected by calculations in conformity with criteria (a) and (b). Census divisions have up to six statistically dominant religions in various combinations and numerical order of importance. The map "Diversity of Religions" indicates the number of statistically dominant denominations selected by calculation for each census division. The denominations are indicated by index letters in rank order.

The 1961 Census figures on which the maps are based do not measure church membership or formal affiliation with any religious body. They reflect only the response to the question, "What is your religion?" Responses indicating no religion were included in the category "others".

RELIGIOUS DENOMINATIONS, 1961
BY PROVINCE AND TERRITORY

- Anglican Church of Canada
- Baptist
- Churches of Christ, Disciples
- Greek Orthodox
- Jewish
- Lutheran
- Mennonite
- Mormon
- Pentecostal
- Presbyterian
- Roman Catholic
- Salvation Army
- Ukrainian (Greek) Catholic
- United Church of Canada
- Others

Areas of circles are proportional to the total population of a province or territory. Sectors of circles represent the percentage of each religious denomination accounting for one percent or more of the total population of a province or territory.

Scale 1:20,000,000 or One Inch to 315.65 Miles

A Anglican Church of Canada
B Baptist
G Greek Orthodox
L Lutheran
N Mennonite
M Mormon
E Pentecostal
P Presbyterian
R Roman Catholic
S Salvation Army
C Ukrainian(Greek) Catholic
U United Church of Canada
O Others

Y.T.

Scale 1:7,500,000

Scale 1:7,500,000

QUEBEC

ONTARIO

BRITISH COLUMBIA

ALBERTA

SASKATCHEWAN

MANITOBA

N.S.

NEW BRUNSWICK

NFLD.

P.E.I.

PERCENTAGE OF POPULATION

CANADA, 1961

Only religious denominations which account for one percent or more of the total national population are named.

Roman Catholic	
United Church of Canada	
Anglican Church of Canada	
Presbyterian	
Lutheran	
Baptist	
Jewish	
Greek Orthodox	
Ukrainian (Greek) Catholic	
Others	

	Y.T.	N.W.T.
Anglican	31%	39%
Baptist	5%	2%
Lutheran	6%	1%
Pentecostal		1%
Presbyterian	6%	1%
Roman Catholic	27%	43%
United Church	17%	8%
Others	8%	6%

Lambert Conformal Conic Projection Standard Parallels 49°N. and 77°N.

THE NATIONAL ATLAS OF CANADA

AGE, SEX, AND MARITAL STATUS, 1961

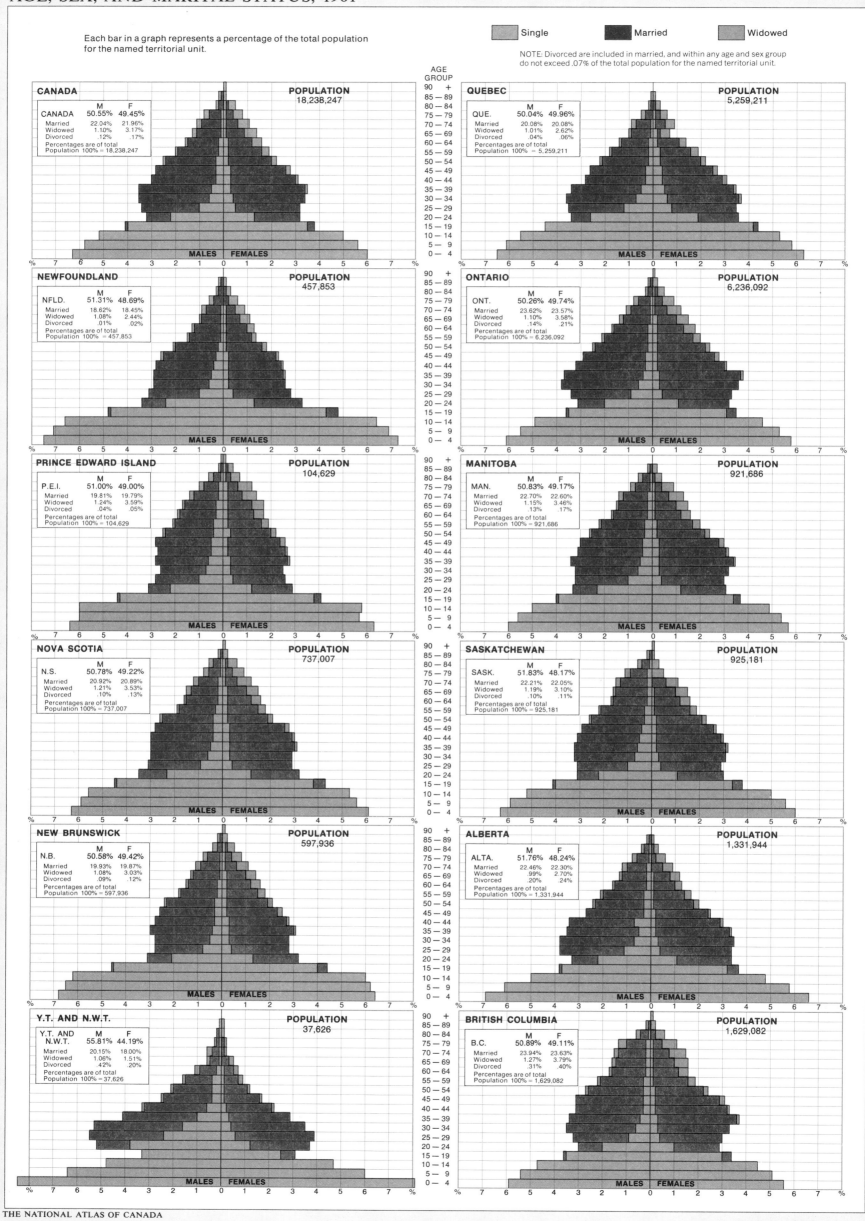

Each bar in a graph represents a percentage of the total population for the named territorial unit.

Single   Married   Widowed

NOTE: Divorced are included in married, and within any age and sex group do not exceed .07% of the total population for the named territorial unit.

CANADA   POPULATION 18,238,247

CANADA	M 50.55%	F 49.45%
Married	22.04%	21.96%
Widowed	1.10%	3.17%
Divorced	.12%	.17%

Percentages are of total Population 100% = 18,238,247

QUEBEC   POPULATION 5,259,211

QUE.	M 50.04%	F 49.96%
Married	20.08%	20.08%
Widowed	1.01%	2.62%
Divorced	.04%	.06%

Percentages are of total Population 100% = 5,259,211

NEWFOUNDLAND   POPULATION 457,853

NFLD.	M 51.31%	F 48.69%
Married	18.62%	18.45%
Widowed	1.08%	2.44%
Divorced	.01%	.02%

Percentages are of total Population 100% = 457,853

ONTARIO   POPULATION 6,236,092

ONT.	M 50.26%	F 49.74%
Married	23.62%	23.57%
Widowed	1.10%	3.58%
Divorced	.14%	.21%

Percentages are of total Population 100% = 6,236,092

PRINCE EDWARD ISLAND   POPULATION 104,629

P.E.I.	M 51.00%	F 49.00%
Married	19.81%	19.79%
Widowed	1.24%	3.59%
Divorced	.04%	.05%

Percentages are of total Population 100% = 104,629

MANITOBA   POPULATION 921,686

MAN.	M 50.83%	F 49.17%
Married	22.70%	22.60%
Widowed	1.15%	3.46%
Divorced	.13%	.17%

Percentages are of total Population 100% = 921,686

NOVA SCOTIA   POPULATION 737,007

N.S.	M 50.78%	F 49.22%
Married	20.92%	20.89%
Widowed	1.21%	3.53%
Divorced	.10%	.13%

Percentages are of total Population 100% = 737,007

SASKATCHEWAN   POPULATION 925,181

SASK.	M 51.83%	F 48.17%
Married	22.21%	22.05%
Widowed	1.19%	3.10%
Divorced	.10%	.11%

Percentages are of total Population 100% = 925,181

NEW BRUNSWICK   POPULATION 597,936

N.B.	M 50.58%	F 49.42%
Married	19.93%	19.87%
Widowed	1.08%	3.03%
Divorced	.09%	.12%

Percentages are of total Population 100% = 597,936

ALBERTA   POPULATION 1,331,944

ALTA.	M 51.76%	F 48.24%
Married	22.46%	22.30%
Widowed	.99%	2.70%
Divorced	.20%	.24%

Percentages are of total Population 100% = 1,331,944

Y.T. AND N.W.T.   POPULATION 37,626

Y.T. AND N.W.T.	M 55.81%	F 44.19%
Married	20.15%	18.00%
Widowed	1.06%	1.51%
Divorced	.42%	.20%

Percentages are of total Population 100% = 37,626

BRITISH COLUMBIA   POPULATION 1,629,082

B.C.	M 50.89%	F 49.11%
Married	23.94%	23.63%
Widowed	1.27%	3.79%
Divorced	.31%	.40%

Percentages are of total Population 100% = 1,629,082

AGE GROUP: 90+, 85—89, 80—84, 75—79, 70—74, 65—69, 60—64, 55—59, 50—54, 45—49, 40—44, 35—39, 30—34, 25—29, 20—24, 15—19, 10—14, 5—9, 0—4

MALES   FEMALES

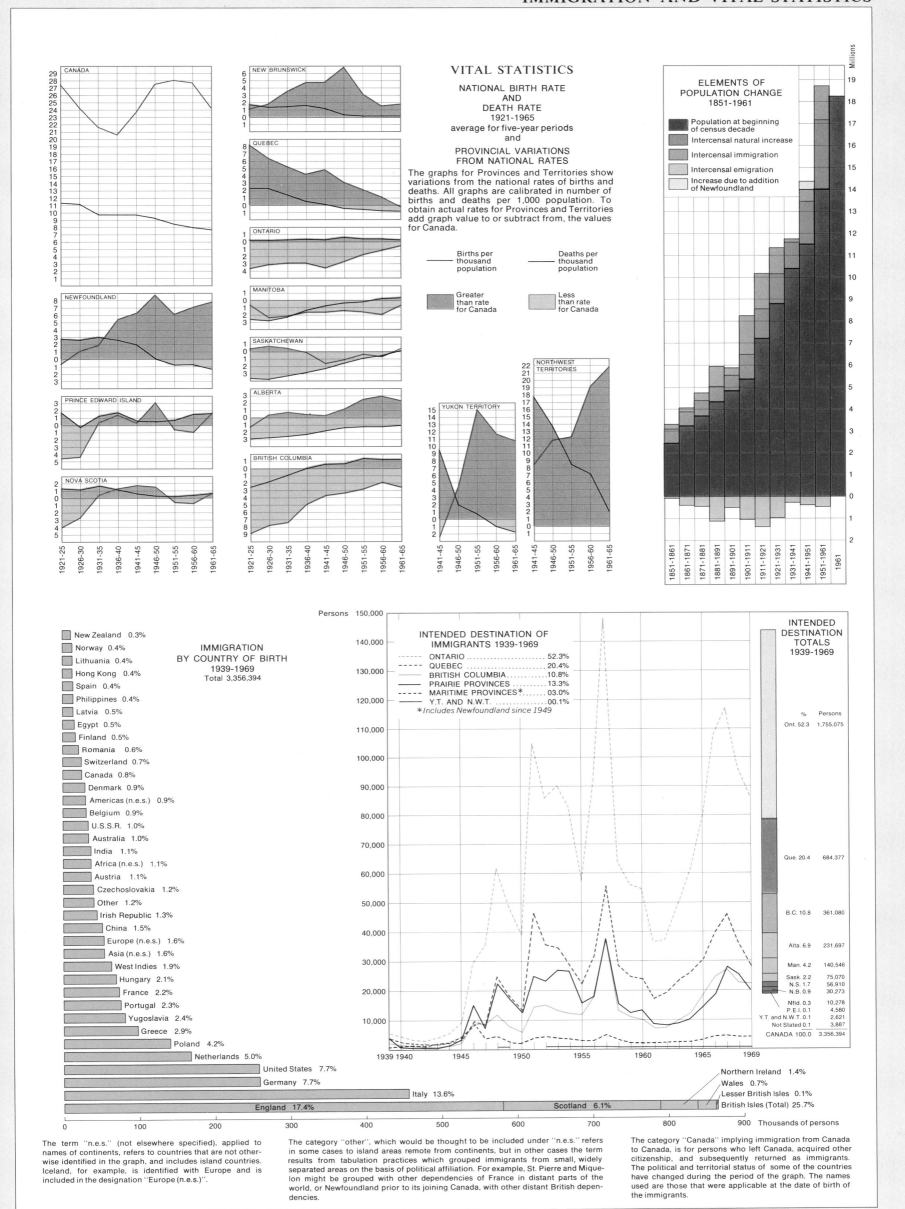

VITAL STATISTICS

NATIONAL BIRTH RATE AND DEATH RATE
1921-1965
average for five-year periods
and

PROVINCIAL VARIATIONS FROM NATIONAL RATES

The graphs for Provinces and Territories show variations from the national rates of births and deaths. All graphs are calibrated in number of births and deaths per 1,000 population. To obtain actual rates for Provinces and Territories add graph value to or subtract from, the values for Canada.

Births per thousand population

Deaths per thousand population

Greater than rate for Canada

Less than rate for Canada

ELEMENTS OF POPULATION CHANGE 1851-1961

Population at beginning of census decade

Intercensal natural increase

Intercensal immigration

Intercensal emigration

Increase due to addition of Newfoundland

IMMIGRATION BY COUNTRY OF BIRTH
1939-1969
Total 3,356,394

New Zealand 0.3%
Norway 0.4%
Lithuania 0.4%
Hong Kong 0.4%
Spain 0.4%
Philippines 0.4%
Latvia 0.5%
Egypt 0.5%
Finland 0.5%
Romania 0.6%
Switzerland 0.7%
Canada 0.8%
Denmark 0.9%
Americas (n.e.s.) 0.9%
Belgium 0.9%
U.S.S.R. 1.0%
Australia 1.0%
India 1.1%
Africa (n.e.s.) 1.1%
Austria 1.1%
Czechoslovakia 1.2%
Other 1.2%
Irish Republic 1.3%
China 1.5%
Europe (n.e.s.) 1.6%
Asia (n.e.s.) 1.6%
West Indies 1.9%
Hungary 2.1%
France 2.2%
Portugal 2.3%
Yugoslavia 2.4%
Greece 2.9%
Poland 4.2%
Netherlands 5.0%
United States 7.7%
Germany 7.7%
Italy 13.6%
England 17.4%   Scotland 6.1%

Northern Ireland 1.4%
Wales 0.7%
Lesser British Isles 0.1%
British Isles (Total) 25.7%

INTENDED DESTINATION OF IMMIGRANTS 1939-1969

ONTARIO 52.3%
QUEBEC 20.4%
BRITISH COLUMBIA 10.8%
PRAIRIE PROVINCES 13.3%
MARITIME PROVINCES* 03.0%
Y.T. AND N.W.T. 00.1%
*Includes Newfoundland since 1949

INTENDED DESTINATION TOTALS 1939-1969

	%	Persons
Ont.	52.3	1,755,075
Que.	20.4	684,377
B.C.	10.8	361,080
Alta.	6.9	231,697
Man.	4.2	140,546
Sask.	2.2	75,070
N.S.	1.7	56,910
N.B.	0.9	30,273
Nfld.	0.3	10,278
P.E.I.	0.1	4,580
Y.T. and N.W.T.	0.1	2,621
Not Stated	0.1	3,887
CANADA	100.0	3,356,394

The term "n.e.s." (not elsewhere specified), applied to names of continents, refers to countries that are not otherwise identified in the graph, and includes island countries. Iceland, for example, is identified with Europe and is included in the designation "Europe (n.e.s.)".

The category "other", which would be thought to be included under "n.e.s." refers in some cases to island areas remote from continents, but in other cases the term results from tabulation practices which grouped immigrants from small, widely separated areas on the basis of political affiliation. For example, St. Pierre and Miquelon might be grouped with other dependencies of France in distant parts of the world, or Newfoundland prior to its joining Canada, with other distant British dependencies.

The category "Canada" implying immigration from Canada to Canada, is for persons who left Canada, acquired other citizenship, and subsequently returned as immigrants. The political and territorial status of some of the countries have changed during the period of the graph. The names used are those that were applicable at the date of birth of the immigrants.

EDUCATION

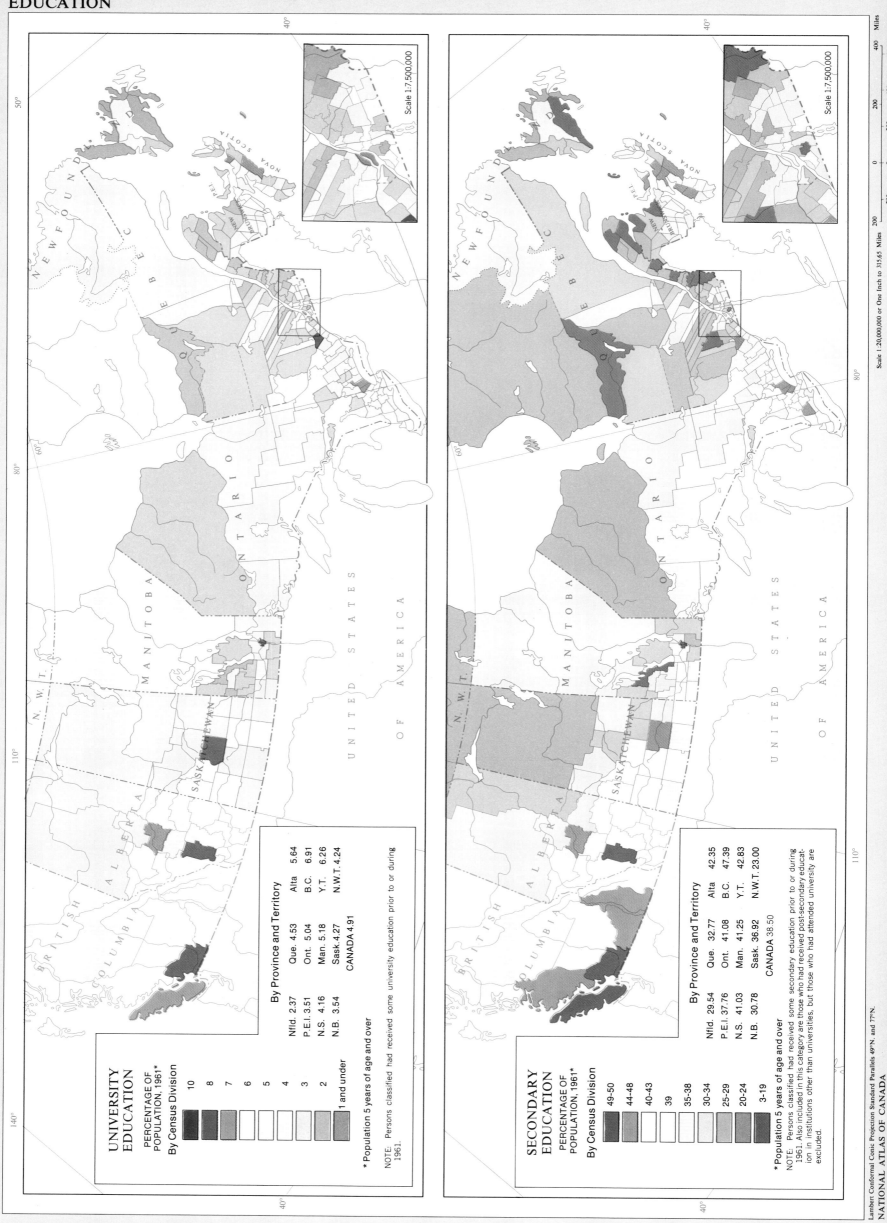

UNIVERSITY EDUCATION

PERCENTAGE OF POPULATION, 1961*

By Census Division

10
8
7
6
5
4
3
2
1 and under

By Province and Territory

Nfld. 2.37	Que. 4.53	Alta 5.64
P.E.I. 3.51	Ont. 5.04	B.C. 6.91
N.S. 4.16	Man. 5.18	Y.T. 6.26
N.B. 3.54	Sask. 4.27	N.W.T. 4.24
		CANADA 4.91

*Population 5 years of age and over

NOTE: Persons classified had received some university education prior to or during 1961.

Scale 1:7,500,000

SECONDARY EDUCATION

PERCENTAGE OF POPULATION, 1961*

By Census Division

49-50
44-48
40-43
39
35-38
30-34
25-29
20-24
3-19

By Province and Territory

Nfld. 29.54	Que. 32.77	Alta 42.35
P.E.I. 37.76	Ont. 41.08	B.C. 47.39
N.S. 41.03	Man. 41.25	Y.T. 42.83
N.B. 30.78	Sask. 36.92	N.W.T. 23.00
		CANADA 38.50

*Population 5 years of age and over

NOTE: Persons classified had received some secondary education prior to or during 1961. Also included in this category are those who had received post-secondary education in institutions other than universities, but those who had attended university are excluded.

Scale 1:7,500,000

Scale 1:20,000,000 or One Inch to 315.65 Miles

Lambert Conformal Conic Projection Standard Parallels 49°N. and 77°N.

NATIONAL ATLAS OF CANADA

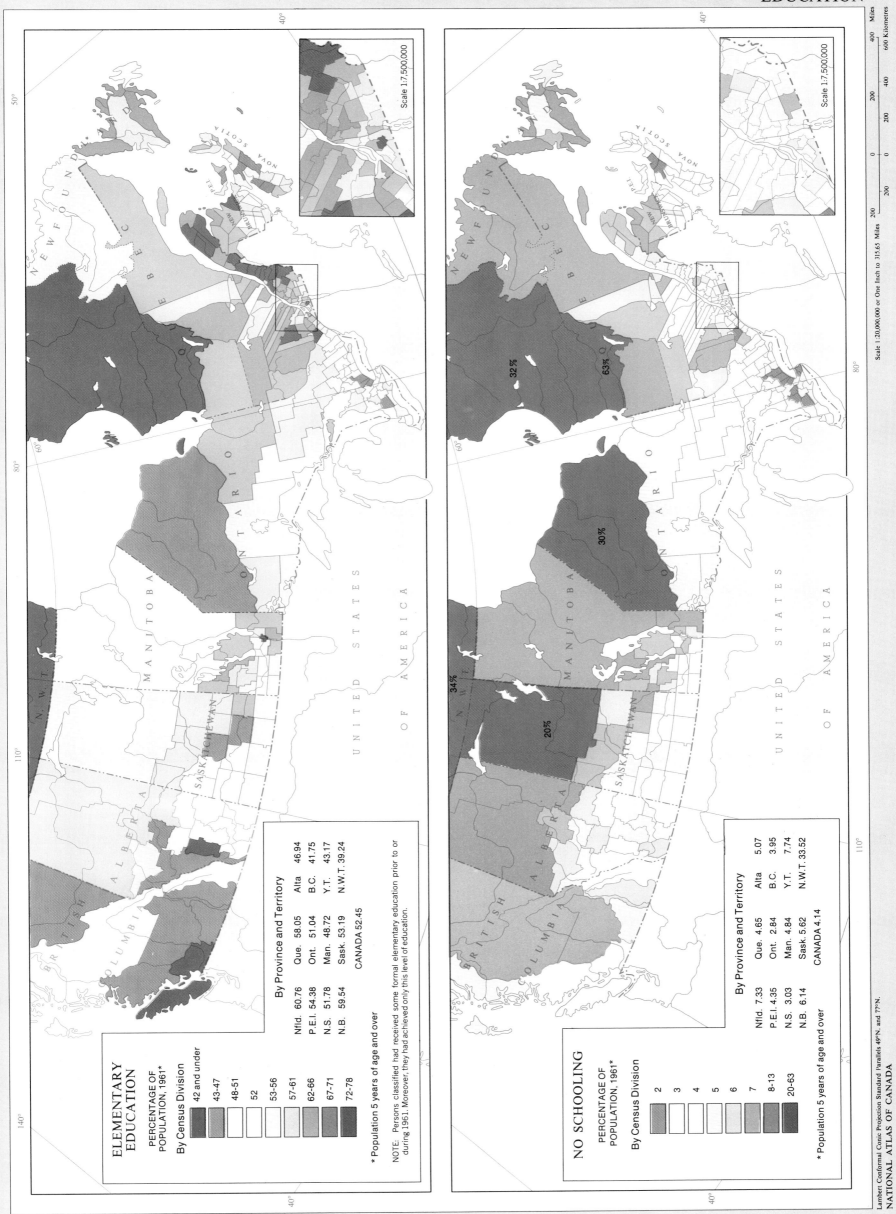

ELEMENTARY EDUCATION

PERCENTAGE OF POPULATION, 1961*

By Census Division

42 and under
43-47
48-51
52
53-56
57-61
62-66
67-71
72-78

By Province and Territory

Nfld. 60.76	Que. 58.05	Alta 46.94	
P.E.I. 54.38	Ont. 51.04	B.C. 41.75	
N.S. 51.78	Man. 48.72	Y.T. 43.17	
N.B. 59.54	Sask. 53.19	N.W.T. 39.24	

CANADA 52.45

* Population 5 years of age and over

NOTE: Persons classified had received some formal elementary education prior to or during 1961. Moreover, they had achieved only this level of education.

Scale 1:7,500,000

NO SCHOOLING

PERCENTAGE OF POPULATION, 1961*

By Census Division

2
3
4
5
6
7
8-13
20-63

By Province and Territory

Nfld. 7.33	Que. 4.65	Alta 5.07	
P.E.I. 4.35	Ont. 2.84	B.C. 3.95	
N.S. 3.03	Man. 4.84	Y.T. 7.74	
N.B. 6.14	Sask. 5.62	N.W.T. 33.52	

CANADA 4.14

* Population 5 years of age and over

Scale 1:7,500,000

Scale 1:20,000,000 or One Inch to 315.65 Miles

Lambert Conformal Conic Projection Standard Parallels 49°N. and 77°N.

NATIONAL ATLAS OF CANADA

UNSCHOOLED POPULATION

UNSCHOOLED POPULATION, 1961
BY AGE GROUP AND SEX

☐ Male ☐ Female

The individual bars express the unschooled population as percentages of the total unschooled population for each territorial unit.

Note: Unschooled persons are not necessarily illiterate.

CANADA

Male	Female	Age
19.4	16.6	65+
15.7	16.0	45-64
5.5	4.9	35-44
5.2	4.6	25-34
2.0	2.0	20-24
2.0	1.6	15-19
2.5	2.0	10-14

184,834=100%

UNSCHOOLED POPULATION BY AGE GROUP, 1961

	AGE GROUP							Total unschooled pop. 10 yrs. old and older	% of total pop. 10 yrs. old and older
	10-14	15-19	20-24	25-34	35-44	45-64	65+		
CANADA	8,310	6,620	7,376	18,116	19,245	58,555	66,612	184,834	1.32
Nfld	284	229	308	1,233	2,257	4,357	4,907	13,575	4.67
P.E.I.	69	34	31	78	80	197	153	642	.81
N.S.	292	247	254	555	702	2,164	2,460	6,674	1.18
N.B.	375	299	248	919	1,327	3,149	3,222	9,539	2.15
Que.	3,101	2,259	2,087	4,138	4,016	9,525	9,866	34,992	.88
Ont.	1,954	1,619	1,944	4,863	4,883	14,772	16,755	46,790	.97
Man.	352	268	413	1,100	1,172	5,363	8,181	16,849	2.36
Sask.	415	389	414	1,267	1,335	6,030	7,668	17,518	2.48
Alta	487	423	507	1,229	1,202	6,055	6,220	16,123	1.62
B.C.	554	460	542	1,459	1,239	5,620	6,636	16,510	1.29
N.W.T.	425	393	621	1,193	916	1,187	396	5,131	31.70
Y.T.	2	0	7	82	116	136	148	491	5.75

NEWFOUNDLAND

Male	Female	Age
21.1	15.0	65+
20.1	11.9	45-64
10.6	6.1	35-44
5.6	3.5	25-34
1.3	1.0	20-24
1.1	0.6	15-19
1.2	0.9	10-14

13,575=100%

NEW-BRUNSWICK

Male	Female	Age
21.3	12.5	65+
22.0	11.0	45-64
8.8	5.1	35-44
6.2	3.4	25-34
1.5	1.1	20-24
2.0	1.2	15-19
2.2	1.7	10-14

9,539=100%

MANITOBA

Male	Female	Age
23.0	25.6	65+
14.0	17.8	45-64
3.5	3.4	35-44
3.6	3.0	25-34
1.2	1.2	20-24
0.9	0.7	15-19
1.2	0.9	10-14

16,849=100%

BRITISH COLUMBIA

Male	Female	Age
23.8	16.3	65+
14.9	19.1	45-64
3.4	4.1	35-44
4.6	4.3	25-34
1.6	1.7	20-24
1.5	1.3	15-19
1.9	1.5	10-14

16,510=100%

PRINCE EDWARD I.

Male	Female	Age
16.7	7.2	65+
21.0	9.7	45-64
8.6	3.9	35-44
7.6	4.5	25-34
3.4	1.4	20-24
3.0	2.2	15-19
6.1	4.7	10-14

642=100%

QUEBEC

Male	Female	Age
15.8	12.4	65+
14.3	12.9	45-64
6.0	5.5	35-44
6.1	5.8	25-34
2.8	3.1	20-24
3.5	2.9	15-19
4.9	4.0	10-14

34,992=100%

SASKATCHEWAN

Male	Female	Age
22.2	21.5	65+
15.0	19.5	45-64
3.9	3.7	35-44
3.9	3.3	25-34
1.3	1.1	20-24
1.2	1.0	15-19
1.4	1.0	10-14

17,518=100%

NORTHWEST TERRITORIES

Male	Female	Age
4.0	3.7	65+
12.4	10.8	45-64
9.8	8.0	35-44
11.6	11.7	25-34
6.2	5.9	20-24
3.9	3.7	15-19
4.5	3.8	10-14

5,131=100%

NOVA SCOTIA

Male	Female	Age
22.4	14.5	65+
19.8	12.6	45-64
6.4	4.1	35-44
5.1	3.2	25-34
2.2	1.6	20-24
2.2	1.5	15-19
2.3	2.1	10-14

6.674=100%

ONTARIO

Male	Female	Age
18.9	16.9	65+
15.0	16.6	45-64
5.2	5.2	35-44
5.2	5.2	25-34
2.1	2.1	20-24
1.9	1.5	15-19
2.4	1.8	10-14

46,790=100%

ALBERTA

Male	Female	Age
19.4	19.2	65+
16.0	21.6	45-64
3.6	3.8	35-44
4.1	3.5	25-34
1.6	1.6	20-24
1.4	1.2	15-19
1.6	1.4	10-14

16,123=100%

YUKON TERRITORY

Male	Female	Age
12.4	17.7	65+
12.4	15.3	45-64
11.0	12.7	35-44
6.5	10.2	25-34
0.8	0.6	20-24
0.0	0.0	15-19
0.0	0.4	10-14

491=100%

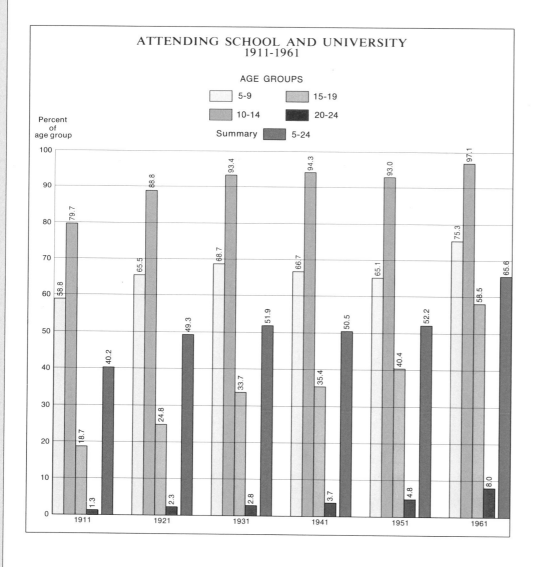

ATTENDING SCHOOL AND UNIVERSITY
1911-1961

AGE GROUPS
☐ 5-9 ☐ 15-19
☐ 10-14 ■ 20-24
Summary ■ 5-24

Percent of age group

Year	5-9	10-14	15-19	20-24	5-24
1911	58.8	79.7	18.7	1.3	40.2
1921	65.5	88.8	24.8	2.3	49.3
1931	68.7	93.4	33.7	2.8	51.9
1941	66.7	94.3	35.4	3.7	50.5
1951	65.1	93.0	40.4	4.8	52.2
1961	75.3	97.1	58.5	8.0	65.6

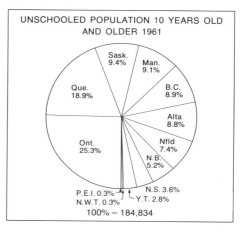

UNSCHOOLED POPULATION 10 YEARS OLD AND OLDER 1961

Sask. 9.4%
Man. 9.1%
B.C. 8.9%
Que. 18.9%
Alta 8.8%
Nfld 7.4%
N.B. 5.2%
Ont. 25.3%
N.S. 3.6%
Y.T. 2.8%
P.E.I. 0.3%
N.W.T. 0.3%

100% = 184,834

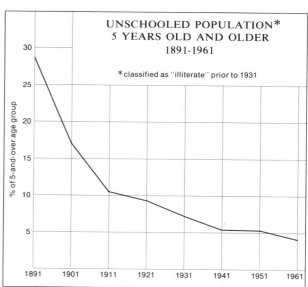

UNSCHOOLED POPULATION*
5 YEARS OLD AND OLDER
1891-1961

*classified as "illiterate" prior to 1931

% of 5-and-over age group

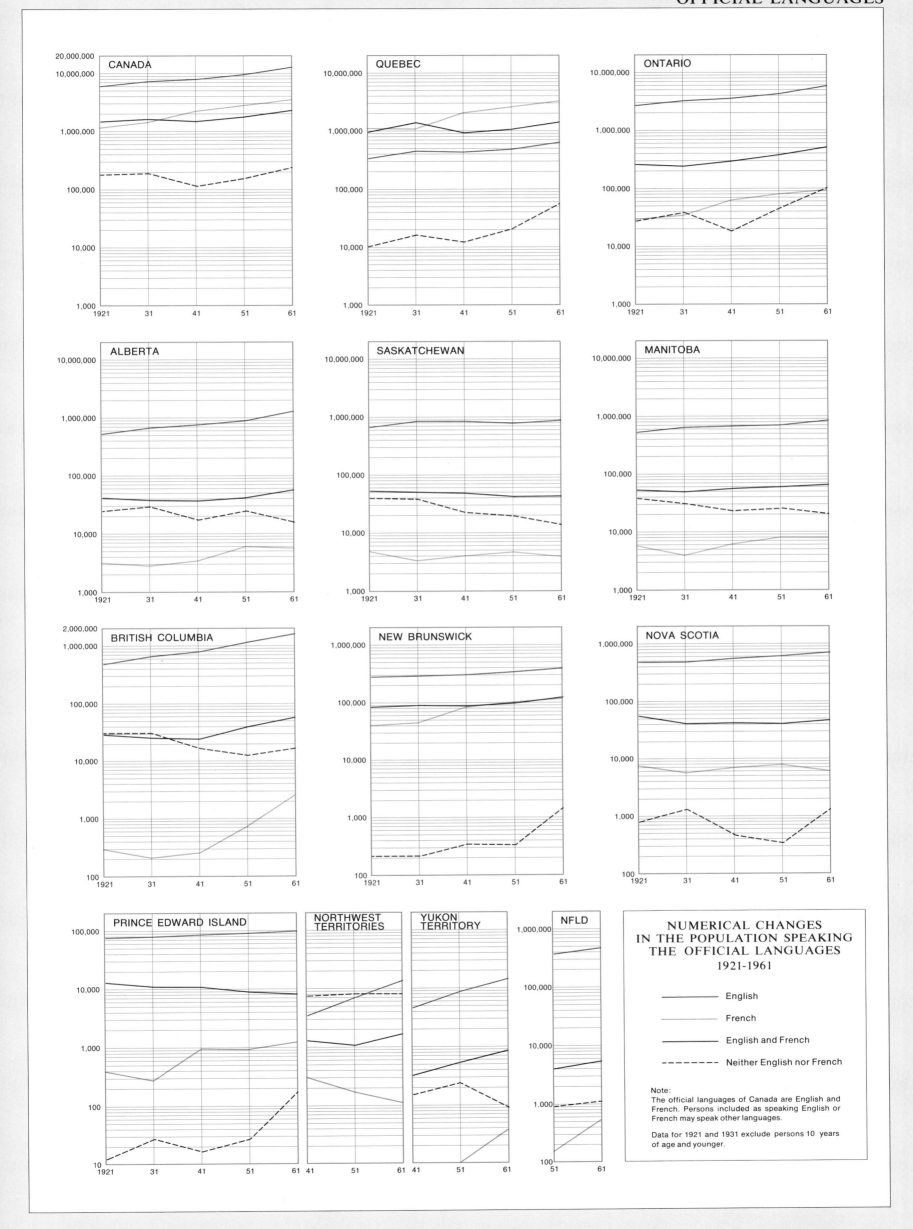

NUMERICAL CHANGES
IN THE POPULATION SPEAKING
THE OFFICIAL LANGUAGES
1921-1961

——————— English

——————— French

——————— English and French

- - - - - - - Neither English nor French

Note:
The official languages of Canada are English and
French. Persons included as speaking English or
French may speak other languages.

Data for 1921 and 1931 exclude persons 10 years
of age and younger.

MOTHER TONGUES

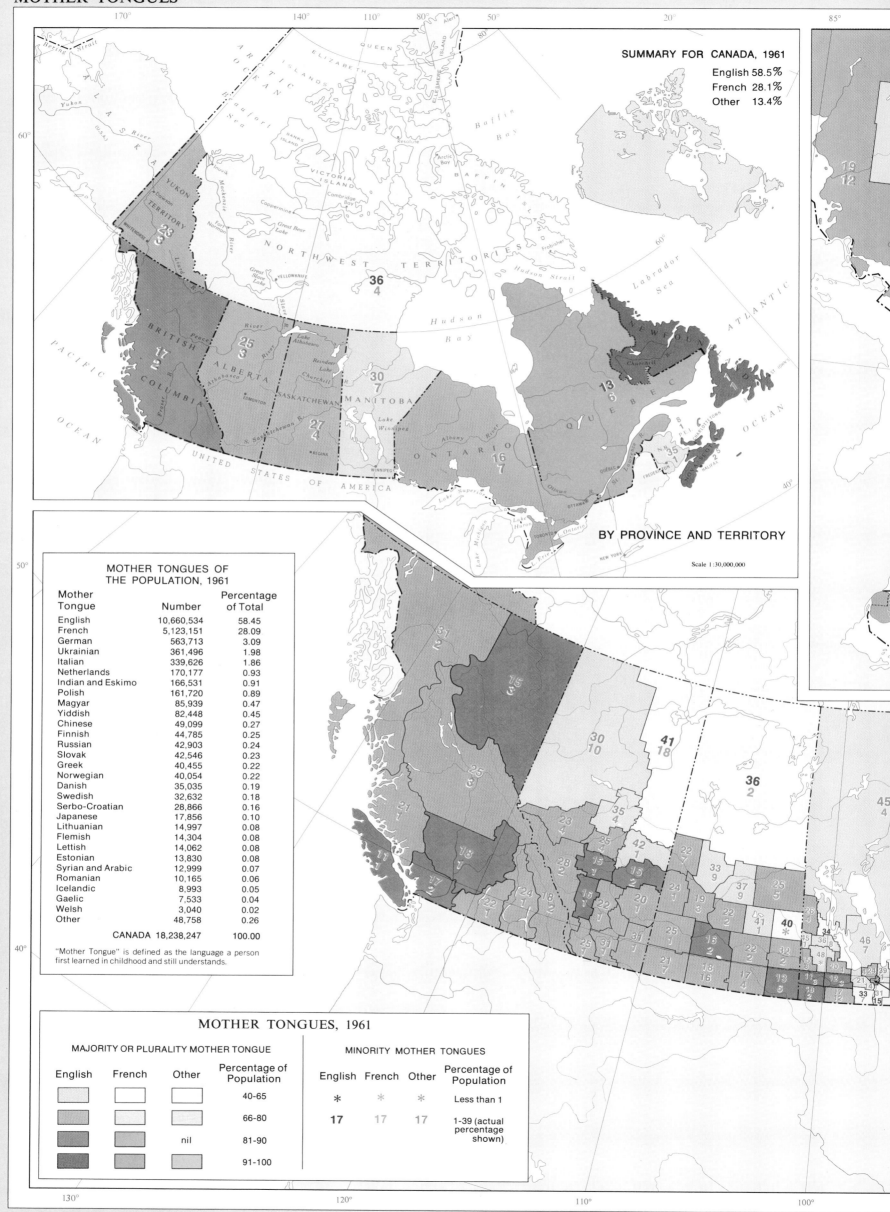

SUMMARY FOR CANADA, 1961

English 58.5%
French 28.1%
Other 13.4%

BY PROVINCE AND TERRITORY

Scale 1:30,000,000

MOTHER TONGUES OF THE POPULATION, 1961

Mother Tongue	Number	Percentage of Total
English	10,660,534	58.45
French	5,123,151	28.09
German	563,713	3.09
Ukrainian	361,496	1.98
Italian	339,626	1.86
Netherlands	170,177	0.93
Indian and Eskimo	166,531	0.91
Polish	161,720	0.89
Magyar	85,939	0.47
Yiddish	82,448	0.45
Chinese	49,099	0.27
Finnish	44,785	0.25
Russian	42,903	0.24
Slovak	42,546	0.23
Greek	40,455	0.22
Norwegian	40,054	0.22
Danish	35,035	0.19
Swedish	32,632	0.18
Serbo-Croatian	28,866	0.16
Japanese	17,856	0.10
Lithuanian	14,997	0.08
Flemish	14,304	0.08
Lettish	14,062	0.08
Estonian	13,830	0.08
Syrian and Arabic	12,999	0.07
Romanian	10,165	0.06
Icelandic	8,993	0.05
Gaelic	7,533	0.04
Welsh	3,040	0.02
Other	48,758	0.26
CANADA	18,238,247	100.00

"Mother Tongue" is defined as the language a person first learned in childhood and still understands.

MOTHER TONGUES, 1961

MAJORITY OR PLURALITY MOTHER TONGUE

English	French	Other	Percentage of Population
			40-65
			66-80
	nil		81-90
			91-100

MINORITY MOTHER TONGUES

English	French	Other	Percentage of Population
*	*	*	Less than 1
17	17	17	1-39 (actual percentage shown)

BY CENSUS DIVISION

Scale 1:5,000,000
or
One Inch to 78.91 Miles

50   0   50   100   150 Miles
50   0   50   100   150   200 Kilometres

BY CENSUS DIVISION

Scale 1:15,000,000 or One Inch to 236.73 Miles

100   0   100   200   300   400 Miles
100   0   100   200   300   400   500   600   700 Kilometres

INDIAN LANDS AND LANGUAGES

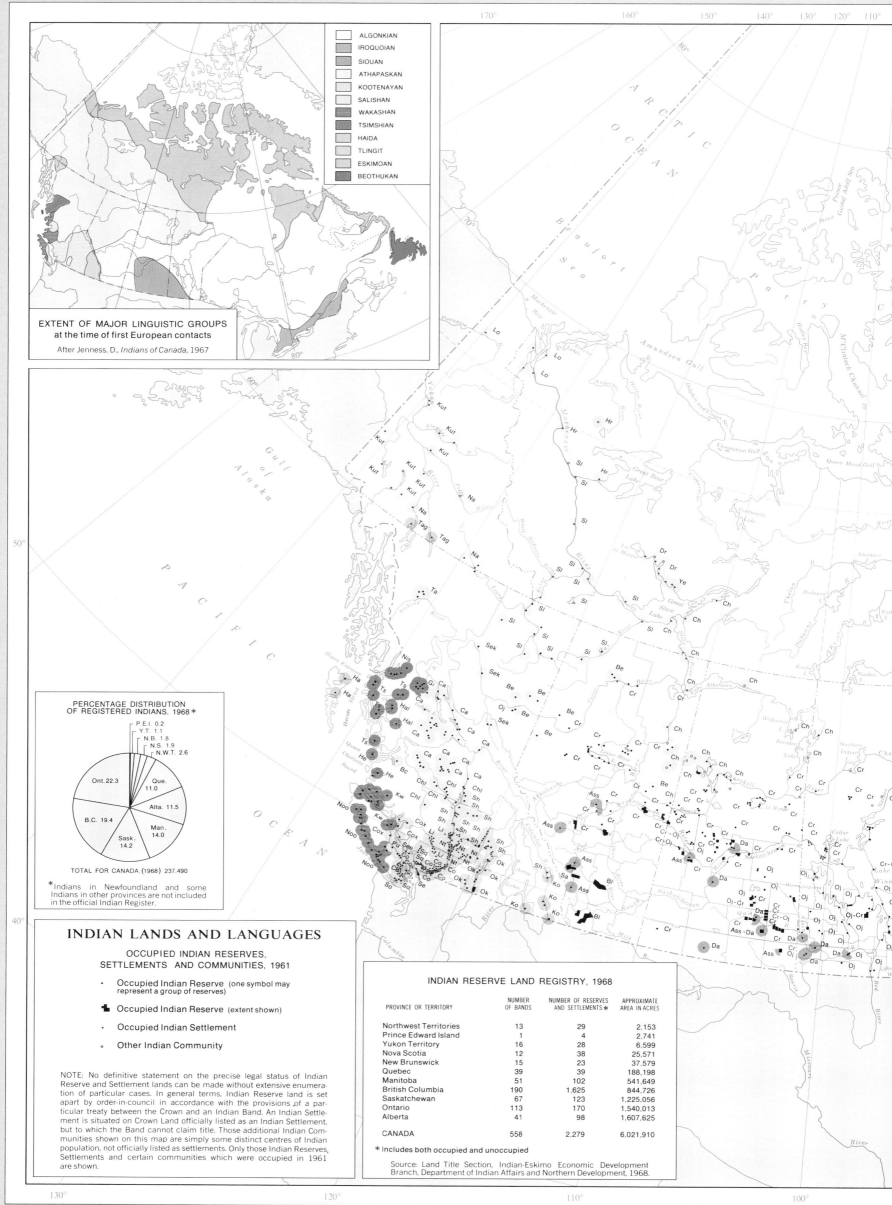

	ALGONKIAN
	IROQUOIAN
	SIOUAN
	ATHAPASKAN
	KOOTENAYAN
	SALISHAN
	WAKASHAN
	TSIMSHIAN
	HAIDA
	TLINGIT
	ESKIMOAN
	BEOTHUKAN

EXTENT OF MAJOR LINGUISTIC GROUPS
at the time of first European contacts

After Jenness, D., *Indians of Canada*, 1967

PERCENTAGE DISTRIBUTION
OF REGISTERED INDIANS, 1968 *

P.E.I. 0.2
Y.T. 1.1
N.B. 1.8
N.S. 1.9
N.W.T. 2.6
Que. 11.0
Ont. 22.3
Alta. 11.5
B.C. 19.4
Man. 14.0
Sask. 14.2

TOTAL FOR CANADA (1968) 237,490

*Indians in Newfoundland and some
Indians in other provinces are not included
in the official Indian Register.

INDIAN LANDS AND LANGUAGES

OCCUPIED INDIAN RESERVES,
SETTLEMENTS AND COMMUNITIES, 1961

· Occupied Indian Reserve (one symbol may
represent a group of reserves)

⬛ Occupied Indian Reserve (extent shown)

· Occupied Indian Settlement

₀ Other Indian Community

NOTE: No definitive statement on the precise legal status of Indian
Reserve and Settlement lands can be made without extensive enumeration of particular cases. In general terms, Indian Reserve land is set
apart by order-in-council in accordance with the provisions of a particular treaty between the Crown and an Indian Band. An Indian Settlement is situated on Crown Land officially listed as an Indian Settlement,
but to which the Band cannot claim title. Those additional Indian Communities shown on this map are simply some distinct centres of Indian
population, not officially listed as settlements. Only those Indian Reserves,
Settlements and certain communities which were occupied in 1961
are shown.

INDIAN RESERVE LAND REGISTRY, 1968

PROVINCE OR TERRITORY	NUMBER OF BANDS	NUMBER OF RESERVES AND SETTLEMENTS *	APPROXIMATE AREA IN ACRES
Northwest Territories	13	29	2,153
Prince Edward Island	1	4	2,741
Yukon Territory	16	28	6,599
Nova Scotia	12	38	25,571
New Brunswick	15	23	37,579
Quebec	39	39	188,198
Manitoba	51	102	541,649
British Columbia	190	1,625	844,726
Saskatchewan	67	123	1,225,056
Ontario	113	170	1,540,013
Alberta	41	98	1,607,625
CANADA	558	2,279	6,021,910

* Includes both occupied and unoccupied

Source: Land Title Section, Indian-Eskimo Economic Development
Branch, Department of Indian Affairs and Northern Development, 1968.

Lambert Conformal Conic Projection Standard Parallels 49°N. and 77°N.

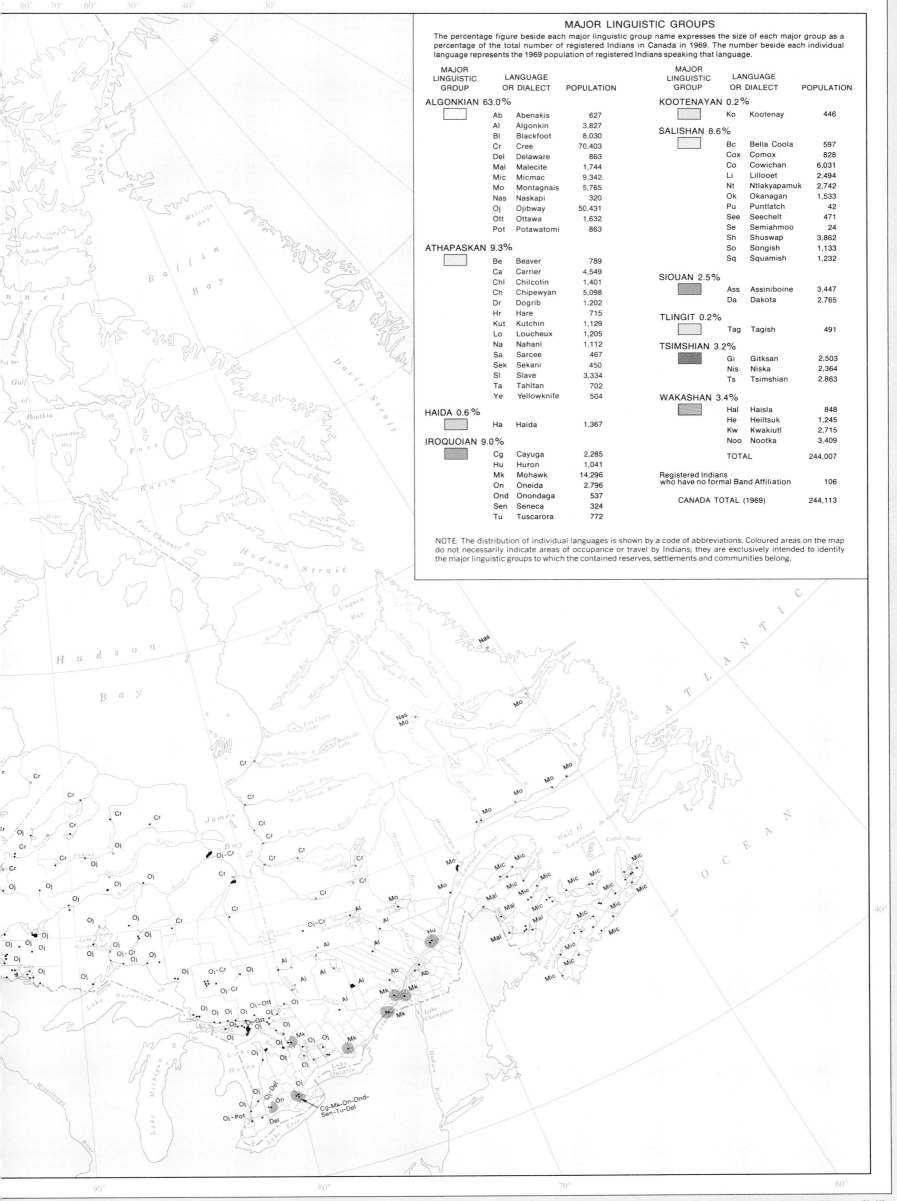

MAJOR LINGUISTIC GROUPS

The percentage figure beside each major linguistic group name expresses the size of each major group as a percentage of the total number of registered Indians in Canada in 1969. The number beside each individual language represents the 1969 population of registered Indians speaking that language.

MAJOR LINGUISTIC GROUP	LANGUAGE OR DIALECT		POPULATION
ALGONKIAN 63.0%			
	Ab	Abenakis	627
	Al	Algonkin	3,827
	Bl	Blackfoot	8,030
	Cr	Cree	70,403
	Del	Delaware	863
	Mal	Malecite	1,744
	Mic	Micmac	9,342
	Mo	Montagnais	5,765
	Nas	Naskapi	320
	Oj	Ojibway	50,431
	Ott	Ottawa	1,632
	Pot	Potawatomi	863
ATHAPASKAN 9.3%			
	Be	Beaver	789
	Ca	Carrier	4,549
	Chl	Chilcotin	1,401
	Ch	Chipewyan	5,098
	Dr	Dogrib	1,202
	Hr	Hare	715
	Kut	Kutchin	1,129
	Lo	Loucheux	1,205
	Na	Nahani	1,112
	Sa	Sarcee	467
	Sek	Sekani	450
	Sl	Slave	3,334
	Ta	Tahltan	702
	Ye	Yellowknife	504
HAIDA 0.6%			
	Ha	Haida	1,367
IROQUOIAN 9.0%			
	Cg	Cayuga	2,285
	Hu	Huron	1,041
	Mk	Mohawk	14,296
	On	Oneida	2,796
	Ond	Onondaga	537
	Sen	Seneca	324
	Tu	Tuscarora	772

MAJOR LINGUISTIC GROUP	LANGUAGE OR DIALECT		POPULATION
KOOTENAYAN 0.2%			
	Ko	Kootenay	446
SALISHAN 8.6%			
	Bc	Bella Coola	597
	Cox	Comox	828
	Co	Cowichan	6,031
	Li	Lillooet	2,494
	Nt	Ntlakyapamuk	2,742
	Ok	Okanagan	1,533
	Pu	Puntlatch	42
	See	Seechelt	471
	Se	Semiahmoo	24
	Sh	Shuswap	3,862
	So	Songish	1,133
	Sq	Squamish	1,232
SIOUAN 2.5%			
	Ass	Assiniboine	3,447
	Da	Dakota	2,765
TLINGIT 0.2%			
	Tag	Tagish	491
TSIMSHIAN 3.2%			
	Gi	Gitksan	2,503
	Nis	Niska	2,364
	Ts	Tsimshian	2,863
WAKASHAN 3.4%			
	Hal	Haisla	848
	He	Heiltsuk	1,245
	Kw	Kwakiutl	2,715
	Noo	Nootka	3,409
		TOTAL	244,007

Registered Indians who have no formal Band Affiliation	106
CANADA TOTAL (1969)	244,113

NOTE: The distribution of individual languages is shown by a code of abbreviations. Coloured areas on the map do not necessarily indicate areas of occupance or travel by Indians; they are exclusively intended to identify the major linguistic groups to which the contained reserves, settlements and communities belong.

Scale 1:15,000,000 or One Inch to 236.74 Miles

INDIAN AND ESKIMO POPULATION

Scale 1:5,000,000

Scale 1:7,500,000

INDIAN AND ESKIMO POPULATION, 1961

INDIAN AND ESKIMO POPULATION
AS A PERCENTAGE OF TOTAL POPULATION, 1961

By Census Division

	INDIANS		ESKIMO
Number of Persons	Living on Reserves	Living off Reserves	
10	—	°	°
50	·	○	○
500	●	○	○
1,000	●	—	—
2,000	▲	—	—

Some symbols represent the aggregate Indian or Eskimo population of an area rather than that of a specific place.

Nil	5-9.9
Less than 1	10-19.9
1-4.9	20-39.9
	40-59.9
	60-79.9
	80-96

CANADA, 1961
Total Population 18,238,247
Native Indians and Eskimos 220,121 (1.2%)

Lambert Conformal Conic Projection Standard Parallels 49°N. and 77°N.
THE NATIONAL ATLAS OF CANADA

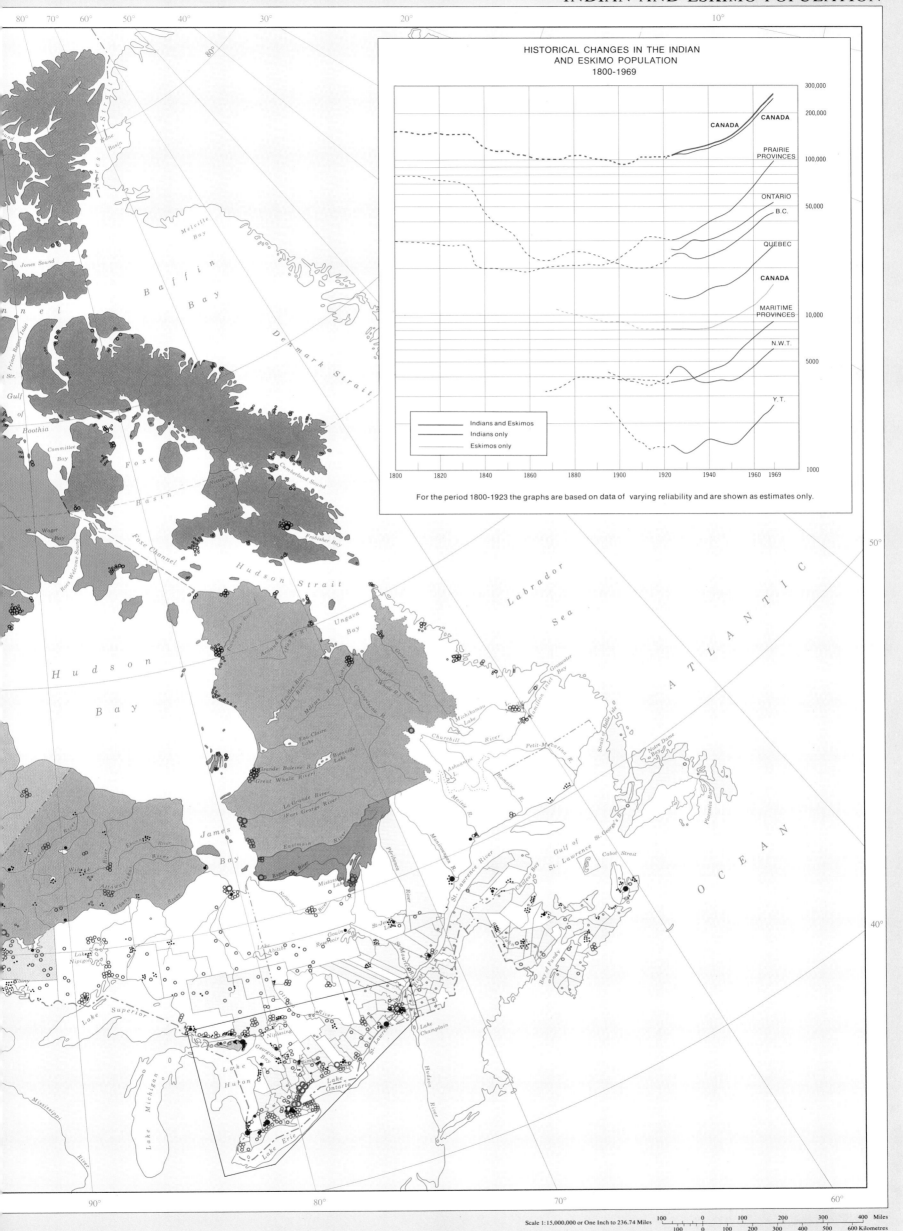

HISTORICAL CHANGES IN THE INDIAN AND ESKIMO POPULATION 1800-1969

CANADA

CANADA

CANADA

PRAIRIE PROVINCES

ONTARIO

B.C.

QUEBEC

CANADA

MARITIME PROVINCES

N.W.T.

Y.T.

300,000

200,000

100,000

50,000

10,000

5000

1000

Indians and Eskimos
Indians only
Eskimos only

1800 1820 1840 1860 1880 1900 1920 1940 1960 1969

For the period 1800-1923 the graphs are based on data of varying reliability and are shown as estimates only.

Scale 1:15,000,000 or One Inch to 236.74 Miles

100   0   100   200   300   400   Miles

100   0   100   200   300   400   500   600 Kilometres

ECONOMIC GEOGRAPHY
INTRODUCTION

The economic geography section of the atlas is ostensibly a mapping of the economy of the country. It is in fact much less than this, and should at best be considered a geography of production.

To speak of mapping the economy is to construe the economy as an entity — a system whose component activities are interrelated and interdependent. The concept is of a spatially distributed value-producing-and-exchanging system which involves the individuals of the population as agents in the system, which converts natural resources and human work into wealth, which is a major factor of human ecology and social structure, and which operates on the face of the land analogously to other environmental systems.

The basic dynamics of the system can be conceived under the headings of production and consumption, or supply and demand, or output and input. The sense of these terms indicates that an undertaking to map the economy would require a geography of consumption complementary to a geography of production. The general outline of the approach would be to map the locations of production of identified commodities, and the locations of their intermediate and final consumption. The intermediate consumption – the consumption of commodities as raw materials in the process of converting them to other commodities — would indicate the interrelationships and interdependencies of the industries of the economy. A geography of consumption so conceived would be extremely complex, and is not feasible at the present time. The reader can gain insight into the complexities that would be involved by consulting *The Input-Output Structure of the Canadian Economy 1961,* vols. 1 and 2, Dominion Bureau of Statistics, Catalogue Nos. 15-501 and 15-502.

Basic to the planning of the section on the economy in the atlas is the Dominion Bureau of Statistics *Standard Industrial Classification* (DBS Catalogue No. 12-501) which classifies all the economic activities of the country under industry titles. The classification is based on the recognition of several thousand types of economic activities which are aggregated into 294 *Classes* which in turn are aggregated into 55 *Major Groups.* The *Major Groups* aggregate into 12 *Divisions.* In comprehending all the economic activities of the country the Classification defines the subject-coverage that a geography of production might attain. Due to a number of limiting factors such as unavailability of suitable data, and due also to judgments related to costs of atlas production, it has not been feasible to transform all the industry titles of the Classification into a corresponding set of maps that would collectively represent the total production of goods and services of the country.

The table that follows names the *Divisions, Major Groups* and some of the *Classes* of the Classification, and otherwise gives the number of *Classes* in each *Major Group.* The industries that are dealt with in the atlas are identified in the table.

The information in the table on labour force and the contribution to the Gross Domestic Product provides an indication of the relative importance of the different industries to the economy. It will be noted that the magnitude of contribution and the detail of the atlas coverage do not necessarily coincide. Trade and the service and financial industries, although accounting for approximately one third of the labour force and one third of the Gross Domestic Product, are treated in less detail than the primary and secondary industries, which is to say that the atlas is biased towards the industries that are most directly related to the physical exploitation of natural resources.

In addition to material dealing directly with industries, the economic geography section of the atlas includes information on the labour force, summary information on the contributions of industries to the national product, a map showing the distribution of personal income, and summary information on Canada's foreign trade. The section is concluded by a map of Economic Regions and an accompanying table in which each of the Economic Regions is briefly described.

STANDARD INDUSTRIAL CLASSIFICATION 1961	NUMBER OF CLASSES Colour indicates coverage in the atlas	LABOUR FORCE AS PERCENTAGE OF TOTAL LABOUR FORCE 1961	OUTPUT AS PERCENTAGE OF GROSS DOMESTIC PRODUCT	
	I	II	1961 III	1967 IV
DIVISION 1 — AGRICULTURE	9	9.90	4.7	4.6
MAJOR GROUP 1 - Experimental and Institutional Farms	2			
MAJOR GROUP 2 - Small Agricultural Holdings — all census farms	1	9.64		
MAJOR GROUP 3 - Commercial Farms	5			
MAJOR GROUP 4 - Services Incidental to Agriculture	1	0.26		
DIVISION 2 — FORESTRY	2	1.68	1.1	1.0
MAJOR GROUP 1 - Logging	1	1.45		
MAJOR GROUP 2 - Forestry Services	1	0.23		
DIVISION 3 — FISHING AND TRAPPING	3	0.57	0.3	0.3
MAJOR GROUP 1 - Fishing	1	0.47		
MAJOR GROUP 2 - Fishery Services	1	0.04		
MAJOR GROUP 3 - Hunting and Trapping	1	0.06		
DIVISION 4 — MINES, QUARRIES AND OIL WELLS	24	1.88	4.3	4.1
MAJOR GROUP 1 - Metal Mines	9	1.06		
MAJOR GROUP 2 - Mineral Fuels	4	0.31		
MAJOR GROUP 3 - Non-Metal Mines except coal	4	0.18		
MAJOR GROUP 4 - Quarries and Sand Pits	2	0.09		
MAJOR GROUP 5 - Services Incidental to Mining	5	0.24		

STANDARD INDUSTRIAL CLASSIFICATION 1961	I	II	III	IV
DIVISION 5 — MANUFACTURING INDUSTRIES	140	21.72	25.5	25.1
MAJOR GROUP 1 - Food and Beverage Industries	19	3.39		
MAJOR GROUP 2 - Tobacco Products Industries	2	0.14		
MAJOR GROUP 3 - Rubber Industries	3	0.29		
MAJOR GROUP 4 - Leather Industries	4	0.51		
MAJOR GROUP 5 - Textile Industries	15	0.96		
MAJOR GROUP 6 - Knitting Mills	2	0.31		
MAJOR GROUP 7 - Clothing Industries	8	1.42		
MAJOR GROUP 8 - Wood Industries	6	1.53		
MAJOR GROUP 9 - Furniture and Fixture Industries	4	0.55		
MAJOR GROUP 10 - Paper and Allied Industries	4	1.57		
MAJOR GROUP 11 - Printing, Publishing and Allied Industries	4	1.31		
MAJOR GROUP 12 - Primary Metal Industries	7	1.40		
MAJOR GROUP 13 - Metal Fabricating Industries	9	1.59		
MAJOR GROUP 14 - Machinery Industries except Electrical	4	0.77		
MAJOR GROUP 15 - Transportation Equipment Industries	8	1.82		
MAJOR GROUP 16 - Electrical Products Industries	8	1.31		
MAJOR GROUP 17 - Non-metallic mineral products Industries	13	0.73		
MAJOR GROUP 18 - Petroleum and Coal Products Industries	2	0.26		
MAJOR GROUP 19 - Chemical and Chemical Products Industries	9	1.07		
MAJOR GROUP 20 - Miscellaneous Industries	9	0.79		
DIVISION 6 — CONSTRUCTION INDUSTRIES	4	6.66	5.5	6.1
MAJOR GROUP 1 - General Contractors	3	3.45		
MAJOR GROUP 2 - Special Trade Contractors	1	3.21		
DIVISION 7 — TRANSPORTATION, COMMUNICATION AND OTHER UTILITIES	23	9.32	12.6	11.9
MAJOR GROUP 1 - Transportation	13	5.89	6.5	5.9
CLASSES — Air Transport	1	0.31		
Services Incidental to Air Transport	1	0.03		
Water Transport	1	0.37		
Services Incidental to Water Transport	1	0.22		
Railway Transport	1	2.16		
Truck Transport	1	1.37		
Bus Transport, Interurban and Rural	1	0.10		
Urban Transit Systems	1	0.28		
Taxicab Operations	1	0.32		
Pipeline Transport	1	0.04		
Highway and Bridge Maintenance	1	0.56		
Other Services Incidental to Transport	1	0.08		
Other Transportation	1	0.05		
MAJOR GROUP 2 - Storage	2	0.27	0.3	0.2
CLASSES — Grain Elevators	1	0.17		
Other Storage and Warehousing	1	0.10		
MAJOR GROUP 3 - Communication	4	2.08	2.4	2.5
CLASSES — Radio and Television Broadcasting	1	0.26		
Telephone Systems	1	1.05		
Telegraph and Cable Systems	1	0.12		
Post Office	1	0.65		
MAJOR GROUP 4 - Electric Power, Gas and Water Utilities	4	1.08	3.4	3.3
CLASSES — Electric Power	1	0.82		
Gas Distribution	1	0.14		
Water Systems	1	0.09		
Other Utilities	1	0.03		
DIVISION 8 — TRADE	44	15.32	13.9	13.6
MAJOR GROUP 1 - Wholesale Trade	20	4.48	4.6	4.8
MAJOR GROUP 2 - Retail Trade	24	10.84	9.3	8.8
DIVISION 9 — FINANCE, INSURANCE, AND REAL ESTATE	5	3.53	10.6	10.2
MAJOR GROUP 1 - Financial Institutions	2	1.71		
MAJOR GROUP 2 - Insurance and Real Estate Industries	3	1.82		
DIVISION 10 — COMMUNITY, BUSINESS AND PERSONAL SERVICES	34	19.52	14.0	15.8
MAJOR GROUP 1 - Education and Related Services	5	4.12		
MAJOR GROUP 2 - Health and Welfare Services	5	4.75		
MAJOR GROUP 3 - Religious Organizations	1	0.82		
MAJOR GROUP 4 - Motion Picture and Recreational Services	3	0.62		
MAJOR GROUP 5 - Services to Business Management	5	1.53		
MAJOR GROUP 6 - Personal Services	9	6.76		
MAJOR GROUP 7 - Miscellaneous Services	6	0.92		
DIVISION 11 — PUBLIC ADMINISTRATION AND DEFENCE	5	7.45	7.5	7.3
MAJOR GROUP 1 - Federal Administration	2	4.40		
MAJOR GROUP 2 - Provincial Administration	1	1.06		
MAJOR GROUP 3 - Local Administration	1	1.91		
MAJOR GROUP 4 - Other Government Offices	1	0.08		
DIVISION 12 — INDUSTRY UNSPECIFIED OR UNDEFINED	1	2.45	No data	

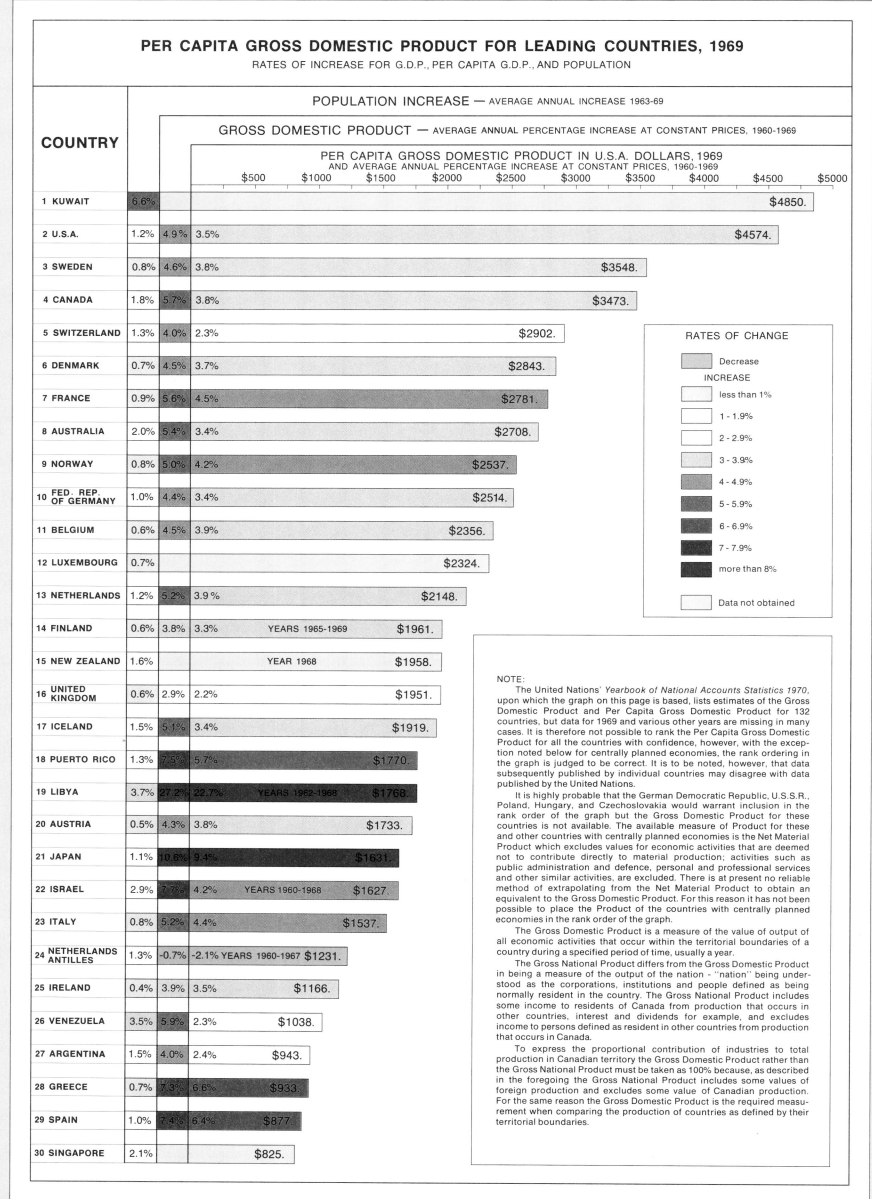

PER CAPITA GROSS DOMESTIC PRODUCT FOR LEADING COUNTRIES, 1969
RATES OF INCREASE FOR G.D.P., PER CAPITA G.D.P., AND POPULATION

POPULATION INCREASE — AVERAGE ANNUAL INCREASE 1963-69

GROSS DOMESTIC PRODUCT — AVERAGE ANNUAL PERCENTAGE INCREASE AT CONSTANT PRICES, 1960-1969

PER CAPITA GROSS DOMESTIC PRODUCT IN U.S.A. DOLLARS, 1969
AND AVERAGE ANNUAL PERCENTAGE INCREASE AT CONSTANT PRICES, 1960-1969

COUNTRY	Pop. incr.	GDP incr.	Per capita GDP incr.	Per Capita GDP
1 KUWAIT	6.6%			$4850.
2 U.S.A.	1.2%	4.9%	3.5%	$4574.
3 SWEDEN	0.8%	4.6%	3.8%	$3548.
4 CANADA	1.8%	5.7%	3.8%	$3473.
5 SWITZERLAND	1.3%	4.0%	2.3%	$2902.
6 DENMARK	0.7%	4.5%	3.7%	$2843.
7 FRANCE	0.9%	5.6%	4.5%	$2781.
8 AUSTRALIA	2.0%	5.4%	3.4%	$2708.
9 NORWAY	0.8%	5.0%	4.2%	$2537.
10 FED. REP. OF GERMANY	1.0%	4.4%	3.4%	$2514.
11 BELGIUM	0.6%	4.5%	3.9%	$2356.
12 LUXEMBOURG	0.7%			$2324.
13 NETHERLANDS	1.2%	5.2%	3.9%	$2148.
14 FINLAND	0.6%	3.8%	3.3%	YEARS 1965-1969 $1961.
15 NEW ZEALAND	1.6%			YEAR 1968 $1958.
16 UNITED KINGDOM	0.6%	2.9%	2.2%	$1951.
17 ICELAND	1.5%	5.1%	3.4%	$1919.
18 PUERTO RICO	1.3%	7.5%	5.7%	$1770.
19 LIBYA	3.7%	27.2%	22.7%	YEARS 1962-1968 $1768.
20 AUSTRIA	0.5%	4.3%	3.8%	$1733.
21 JAPAN	1.1%	10.6%	9.4%	$1631.
22 ISRAEL	2.9%	7.7%	4.2%	YEARS 1960-1968 $1627.
23 ITALY	0.8%	5.2%	4.4%	$1537.
24 NETHERLANDS ANTILLES	1.3%	-0.7%	-2.1% YEARS 1960-1967	$1231.
25 IRELAND	0.4%	3.9%	3.5%	$1166.
26 VENEZUELA	3.5%	5.9%	2.3%	$1038.
27 ARGENTINA	1.5%	4.0%	2.4%	$943.
28 GREECE	0.7%	7.3%	6.6%	$933.
29 SPAIN	1.0%	7.4%	6.4%	$877.
30 SINGAPORE	2.1%			$825.

Scale: $500 $1000 $1500 $2000 $2500 $3000 $3500 $4000 $4500 $5000

RATES OF CHANGE

- Decrease
- INCREASE
- less than 1%
- 1 - 1.9%
- 2 - 2.9%
- 3 - 3.9%
- 4 - 4.9%
- 5 - 5.9%
- 6 - 6.9%
- 7 - 7.9%
- more than 8%
- Data not obtained

NOTE:

The United Nations' *Yearbook of National Accounts Statistics 1970*, upon which the graph on this page is based, lists estimates of the Gross Domestic Product and Per Capita Gross Domestic Product for 132 countries, but data for 1969 and various other years are missing in many cases. It is therefore not possible to rank the Per Capita Gross Domestic Product for all the countries with confidence, however, with the exception noted below for centrally planned economies, the rank ordering in the graph is judged to be correct. It is to be noted, however, that data subsequently published by individual countries may disagree with data published by the United Nations.

It is highly probable that the German Democratic Republic, U.S.S.R., Poland, Hungary, and Czechoslovakia would warrant inclusion in the rank order of the graph but the Gross Domestic Product for these countries is not available. The available measure of Product for these and other countries with centrally planned economies is the Net Material Product which excludes values for economic activities that are deemed not to contribute directly to material production; activities such as public administration and defence, personal and professional services and other similar activities, are excluded. There is at present no reliable method of extrapolating from the Net Material Product to obtain an equivalent to the Gross Domestic Product. For this reason it has not been possible to place the Product of the countries with centrally planned economies in the rank order of the graph.

The Gross Domestic Product is a measure of the value of output of all economic activities that occur within the territorial boundaries of a country during a specified period of time, usually a year.

The Gross National Product differs from the Gross Domestic Product in being a measure of the output of the nation - "nation" being understood as the corporations, institutions and people defined as being normally resident in the country. The Gross National Product includes some income to residents of Canada from production that occurs in other countries, interest and dividends for example, and excludes income to persons defined as resident in other countries from production that occurs in Canada.

To express the proportional contribution of industries to total production in Canadian territory the Gross Domestic Product rather than the Gross National Product must be taken as 100% because, as described in the foregoing the Gross National Product includes some values of foreign production and excludes some value of Canadian production. For the same reason the Gross Domestic Product is the required measurement when comparing the production of countries as defined by their territorial boundaries.

INDUSTRY CONTRIBUTIONS TO THE GROSS DOMESTIC PRODUCT OF SELECTED COUNTRIES

U.S.A. 1969

3%
4%
5%
6%
17%
28%
36%

GDP $925,530 million
Per Capita GDP $4574.

CANADA 1969

5%
7%
6%
9%
12%
24%
37%

GDP $73,243 million
Per Capita GDP $3473.

SERVICES AND MANUFACTURING EMPHASIS

JAPAN 1968

9%
3%
7%
8%
18%
33%
22%

GDP $166,860 million
Per Capita GDP $1631.
(year 1969)

FEDERAL REPUBLIC OF GERMANY 1969

4%
4%
7%
6%
13%
43%
25%

GDP $152,944 million
Per Capita GDP $2514.

MANUFACTURING AND SERVICES EMPHASIS

LIBYA 1968

3%
58%
8%
3%
6%
2
16%

GDP $3,188 million
Per Capita GDP $1768.

KUWAIT 1969

1%
60%
4%
4%
9%
4%
19%

GDP $2,765 million
Per Capita GDP $4850.

OIL PRODUCTION EMPHASIS

INDIA 1965

42%
2
4%
5%
10%
14%
17%

GDP $50,580 million
Per Capita GDP $104.

NIGERIA 1966

52%
5%
5%
4%
13%
6%
9%

GDP $4,219 million
Per Capita GDP $67.

AGRICULTURAL EMPHASIS

INDUSTRIES

- Agriculture, Forestry, Fishing and Hunting
- Other extractive industries (mining, oil wells, electricity, etc)
- Construction
- Transportation and Communication
- Wholesale and Retail Trade
- Manufacturing
- Service Industries

NOTE: The individual bars in each graph express the percentage contribution of the designated industries to the Gross Domestic Product. Money values are in United States dollars.

In instances where percentages do not add up to 100, it is thought that the calculations by which the GDP was determined did not include duties on imports as a value originating within the country in question.

CANADA'S GROSS NATIONAL PRODUCT
AND PER CAPITA GROSS NATIONAL PRODUCT 1926-1971

———————— Gross National Product in Constant (1961) dollars
– – – – – – – Gross National Product in Current (per each year) dollars
———————— Per Capita Gross National Product in Constant dollars
– – – – – – – Per Capita Gross National Product in Current dollars

Values are in Canadian dollars

YEAR 1926   1930   1935   1940   1945   1950   1955   1960   1965   1970

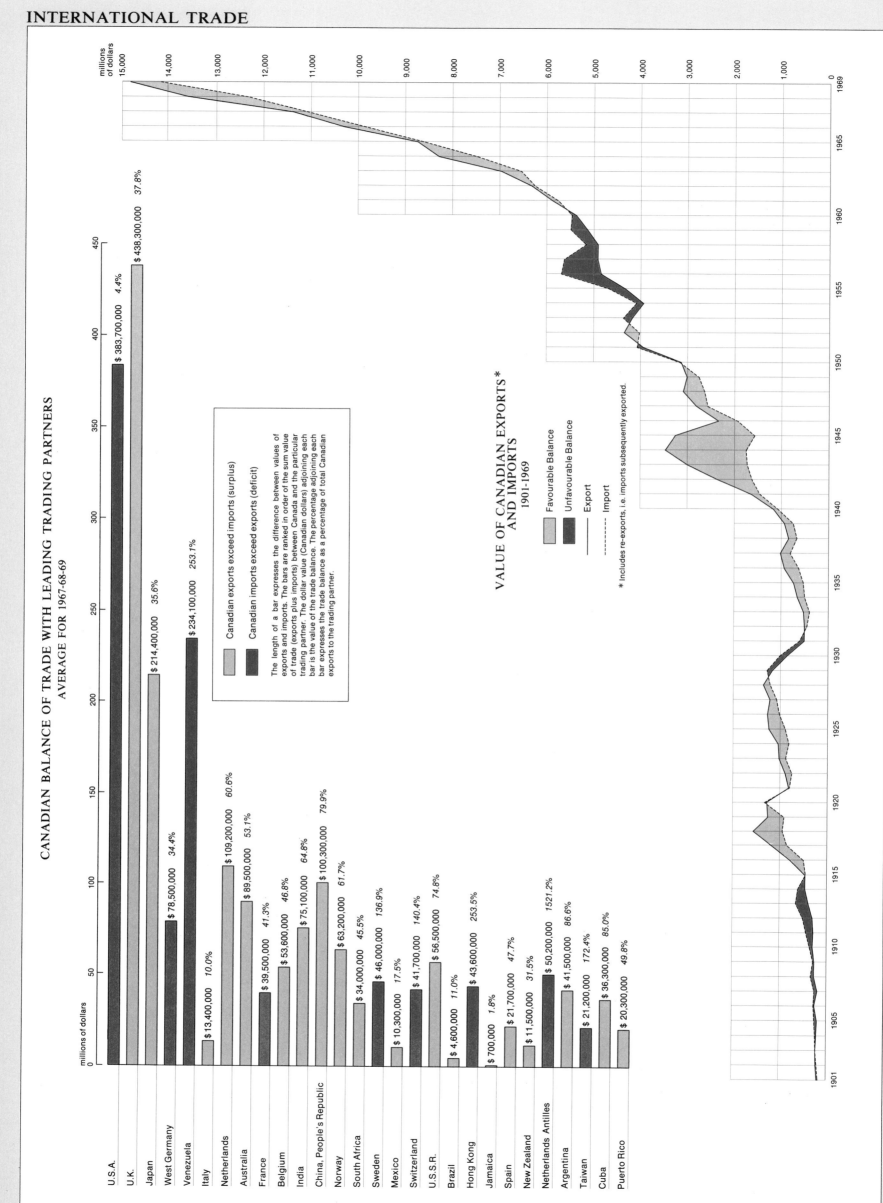

CANADIAN BALANCE OF TRADE WITH LEADING TRADING PARTNERS
AVERAGE FOR 1967-68-69

millions of dollars

U.S.A.	$ 383,700,000	4.4%
U.K.	$ 438,300,000	37.8%
Japan	$ 214,400,000	35.6%
West Germany	$ 78,500,000	34.4%
Venezuela	$ 234,100,000	253.1%
Italy	$ 13,400,000	10.0%
Netherlands	$ 109,200,000	60.6%
Australia	$ 89,500,000	53.1%
France	$ 39,500,000	41.3%
Belgium	$ 53,600,000	46.8%
India	$ 75,100,000	64.8%
China, People's Republic	$ 100,300,000	79.9%
Norway	$ 63,200,000	61.7%
South Africa	$ 34,000,000	45.5%
Sweden	$ 46,000,000	136.9%
Mexico	$ 10,300,000	17.5%
Switzerland	$ 41,700,000	140.4%
U.S.S.R.	$ 56,500,000	74.8%
Brazil	$ 4,600,000	11.0%
Hong Kong	$ 43,600,000	253.5%
Jamaica	$ 700,000	1.8%
Spain	$ 21,700,000	47.7%
New Zealand	$ 11,500,000	31.5%
Netherlands Antilles	$ 50,200,000	1521.2%
Argentina	$ 41,500,000	86.6%
Taiwan	$ 21,200,000	172.4%
Cuba	$ 36,300,000	85.0%
Puerto Rico	$ 20,300,000	49.8%

Canadian exports exceed imports (surplus)

Canadian imports exceed exports (deficit)

The length of a bar expresses the difference between values of exports and imports. The bars are ranked in order of the sum value of trade (exports plus imports) between Canada and the particular trading partner. The dollar value (Canadian dollars) adjoining each bar is the value of the trade balance. The percentage adjoining each bar expresses the trade balance as a percentage of total Canadian exports to the trading partner.

VALUE OF CANADIAN EXPORTS*
AND IMPORTS
1901-1969

millions of dollars

Favourable Balance

Unfavourable Balance

Export

Import

* Includes re-exports, i.e. imports subsequently exported.

COMMODITIES EXPORTED AND IMPORTED
AVERAGE FOR 1967-68-69

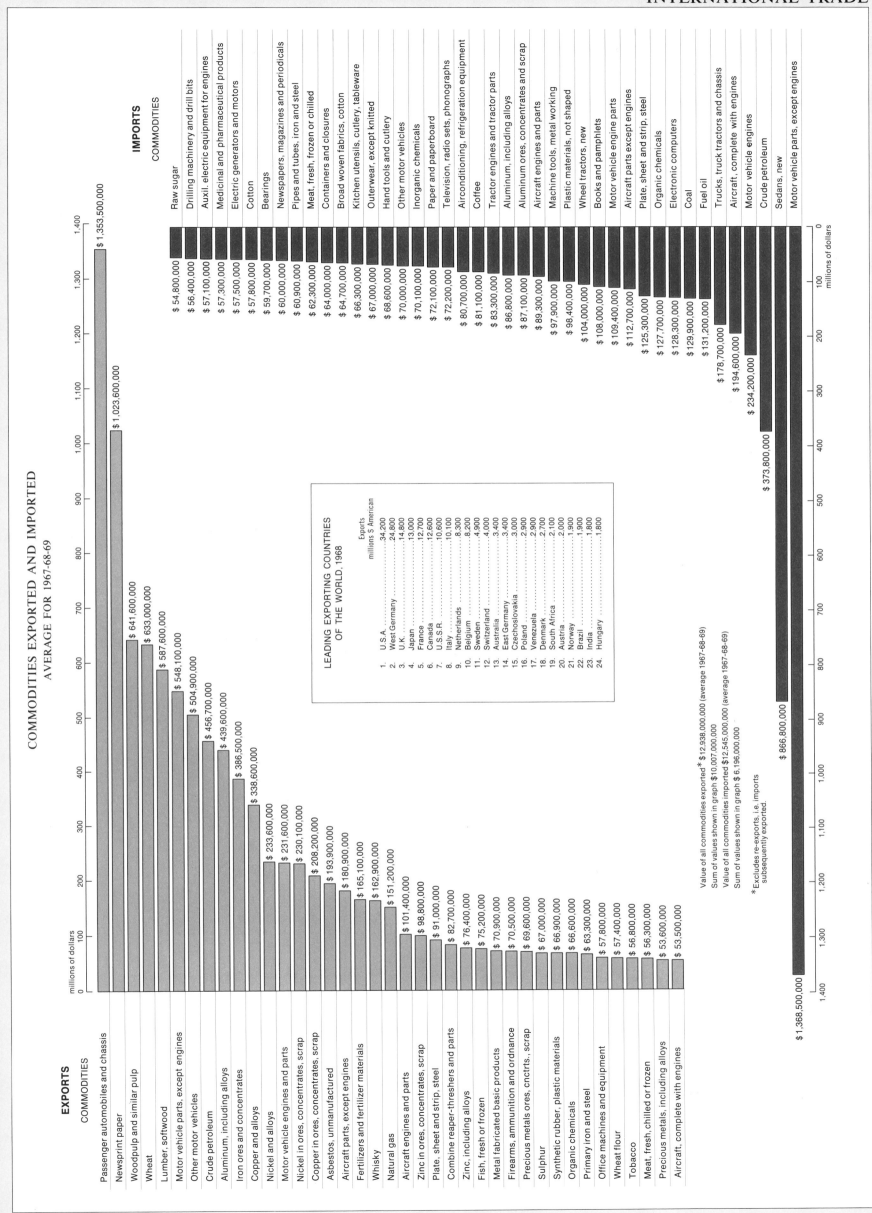

EXPORTS

COMMODITIES

Commodity	Value
Passenger automobiles and chassis	$ 1,353,500,000
Newsprint paper	$ 1,023,600,000
Woodpulp and similar pulp	$ 641,600,000
Wheat	$ 633,000,000
Lumber, softwood	$ 587,600,000
Motor vehicle parts, except engines	$ 548,100,000
Other motor vehicles	$ 504,900,000
Crude petroleum	$ 456,700,000
Aluminum, including alloys	$ 439,600,000
Iron ores and concentrates	$ 386,500,000
Copper and alloys	$ 338,600,000
Nickel and alloys	$ 233,600,000
Motor vehicle engines and parts	$ 231,600,000
Nickel in ores, concentrates, scrap	$ 230,100,000
Copper in ores, concentrates, scrap	$ 208,200,000
Asbestos, unmanufactured	$ 193,900,000
Aircraft parts, except engines	$ 180,900,000
Fertilizers and fertilizer materials	$ 165,100,000
Whisky	$ 162,900,000
Natural gas	$ 151,200,000
Aircraft engines and parts	$ 101,400,000
Zinc in ores, concentrates, scrap	$ 98,800,000
Plate, sheet and strip, steel	$ 91,000,000
Combine reaper-threshers and parts	$ 82,700,000
Zinc, including alloys	$ 76,400,000
Fish, fresh or frozen	$ 75,200,000
Metal fabricated basic products	$ 70,900,000
Firearms, ammunition and ordnance	$ 70,500,000
Precious metals ores, cnctrts., scrap	$ 69,600,000
Sulphur	$ 67,000,000
Synthetic rubber, plastic materials	$ 66,900,000
Organic chemicals	$ 66,600,000
Primary iron and steel	$ 63,300,000
Office machines and equipment	$ 57,800,000
Wheat flour	$ 57,400,000
Tobacco	$ 56,800,000
Meat, fresh, chilled or frozen	$ 56,300,000
Precious metals, including alloys	$ 53,600,000
Aircraft, complete with engines	$ 53,500,000

millions of dollars

IMPORTS

COMMODITIES

Commodity	Value
Motor vehicle parts, except engines	$ 1,368,500,000
Sedans, new	$ 866,800,000
Crude petroleum	$ 373,800,000
Motor vehicle engines	$ 234,200,000
Aircraft, complete with engines	$ 194,600,000
Trucks, truck tractors and chassis	$ 178,700,000
Fuel oil	$ 131,200,000
Coal	$ 129,900,000
Electronic computers	$ 128,300,000
Organic chemicals	$ 127,700,000
Plate, sheet and strip, steel	$ 125,300,000
Aircraft parts except engines	$ 112,700,000
Motor vehicle engine parts	$ 109,400,000
Books and pamphlets	$ 108,000,000
Wheel tractors, new	$ 104,000,000
Plastic materials, not shaped	$ 98,400,000
Machine tools, metal working	$ 97,900,000
Aircraft engines and parts	$ 89,300,000
Aluminum ores, concentrates and scrap	$ 87,100,000
Aluminum, including alloys	$ 86,800,000
Tractor engines and tractor parts	$ 83,300,000
Coffee	$ 81,100,000
Airconditioning, refrigeration equipment	$ 80,700,000
Television, radio sets, phonographs	$ 72,200,000
Paper and paperboard	$ 72,100,000
Inorganic chemicals	$ 70,100,000
Other motor vehicles	$ 70,000,000
Hand tools and cutlery	$ 68,600,000
Outerwear, except knitted	$ 67,000,000
Kitchen utensils, cutlery, tableware	$ 66,300,000
Broad woven fabrics, cotton	$ 64,000,000
Containers and closures	$ 64,000,000
Meat, fresh, frozen or chilled	$ 62,300,000
Pipes and tubes, iron and steel	$ 60,900,000
Newspapers, magazines and periodicals	$ 60,000,000
Bearings	$ 59,700,000
Cotton	$ 57,800,000
Electric generators and motors	$ 57,500,000
Medicinal and pharmaceutical products	$ 57,300,000
Auxil. electric equipment for engines	$ 57,100,000
Drilling machinery and drill bits	$ 56,400,000
Raw sugar	$ 54,800,000

millions of dollars

LEADING EXPORTING COUNTRIES OF THE WORLD, 1968

		Exports millions $ American
1.	U.S.A.	34,200
2.	West Germany	24,800
3.	U.K.	14,800
4.	Japan	13,000
5.	France	12,700
6.	Canada	12,600
7.	U.S.S.R.	10,600
8.	Italy	10,100
9.	Netherlands	8,300
10.	Belgium	8,200
11.	Sweden	4,900
12.	Switzerland	4,000
13.	Australia	3,400
14.	East Germany	3,400
15.	Czechoslovakia	3,000
16.	Poland	2,900
17.	Venezuela	2,900
18.	Denmark	2,700
19.	South Africa	2,100
20.	Austria	2,000
21.	Norway	1,900
22.	Brazil	1,900
23.	India	1,800
24.	Hungary	1,800

Value of all commodities exported* $12,938,000,000 (average 1967-68-69)
Sum of values shown in graph $10,007,000,000
Value of all commodities imported $12,545,000,000 (average 1967-68-69)
Sum of values shown in graph $ 6,196,000,000

*Excludes re-exports, i.e. imports subsequently exported.

PERSONAL INCOME

Personal Income as here mapped is defined as cash income to individuals before taxes. Comparable data were not available for the Yukon and Northwest Territories.

In the data on which the three maps are based some census divisions are grouped. In such cases the boundaries between the census divisions have been deleted.

PER CAPITA PERSONAL INCOME, 1966
BY CENSUS DIVISION

$ 562 - $ 799	$ 1,400 - $ 1,599
$ 800 - $ 999	$ 1,600 - $ 1,799
$ 1,000 - $ 1,199	$ 1,800 - $ 1,999
$ 1,200 - $ 1,399	$ 2,000 - $ 2,199
	$ 2,200 - $ 2,399
	$ 2,400 - $ 2,599
	$ 2,600 - $ 2,756

PROVINCIAL PERSONAL INCOME 1966

Alta. 7.06%
Sask. 4.34%
Man. 4.34%
N.S. 2.83%
N.B. 2.12%
B.C. 10.80%
P.E.I. 0.32%
Nfld. 1.40%
Que. 25.84%
Ont. 40.95%

100% = $ 38,871,224,000

PER CAPITA PERSONAL INCOME, 1966

Ontario	$ 2,286.99
British Columbia	$ 2,241.52
Alberta	$ 1,874.25
Manitoba	$ 1,750.06
Quebec	$ 1,737.79
Saskatchewan	$ 1,712.59
Nova Scotia	$ 1,456.90
New Brunswick	$ 1,335.53
Prince Edward Island	$ 1,148.32
Newfoundland	$ 1,098.94
CANADA	$ 1,942.12

(excluding Y.T. and N.W.T.)

TOTAL PERSONAL INCOME, 1966
BY CENSUS DIVISION
% of national total

.017% - .049%	1.00% - 2.74%
.05% - .099%	6.34%
.10% - .149%	12.50% - 14.30%
.15% - .199%	
.20% - .399%	
.40% - .599%	
.60% - .799%	
.80% - .999%	

100% = $ 38,871,224,000

LEADING CENSUS DIVISIONS, 1966
(each over 1.0% of national *personal income)

Province	Census Division	% of national personal income	% of national population	Major City in Census Division
Ont.	York	14.30	10.11	Toronto
Que.	Montreal & Jesus Is.	12.50	10.57	Montreal
Man.	No. 20	6.34	5.12	Winnipeg
B.C.	No. 4	2.74	1.97	Vancouver
Ont.	Wentworth	2.71	2.04	Hamilton
Ont.	Carleton	2.57	2.38	Ottawa
Alta.	No. 11	2.47	2.15	Edmonton
Alta.	No. 6	2.15	1.90	Calgary
B.C.	Vancouver I.	1.85	1.67	Victoria
Que.	Quebec	1.82	1.92	Québec
Ont.	Essex	1.70	1.41	Windsor
Ont.	Middlesex	1.48	1.25	London
Ont.	Waterloo	1.33	1.09	Kitchener
N.S.	Halifax	1.19	1.23	Halifax
Ont.	Peel	1.17	0.86	Part of Metro. Toronto
		56.37	46.02	

*(excluding Y.T. and N.W.T.)

Scale 1:7,500,000

Scale 1:20,000,000 or One Inch to 315.65 Miles

Lambert Conformal Conic Projection Standard Parallels 49°N. and 77°N.

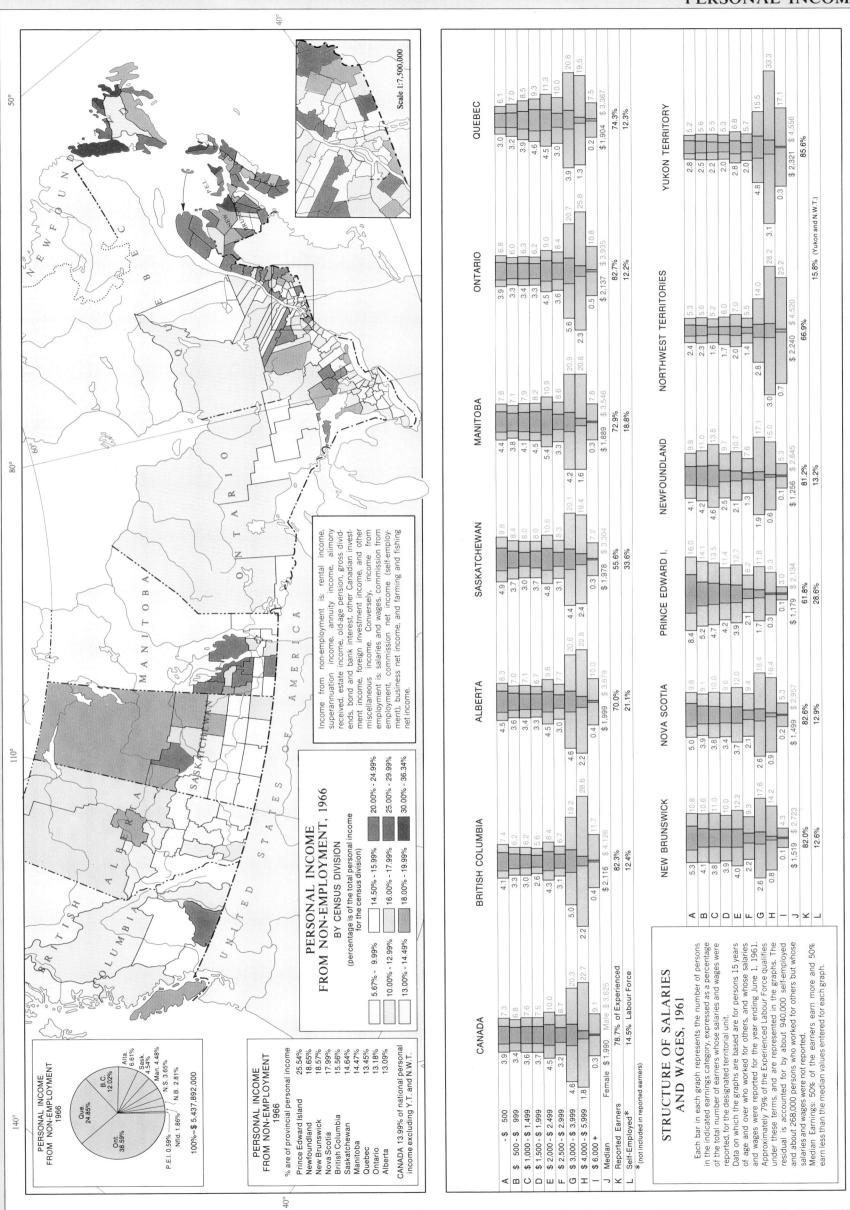

PERSONAL INCOME FROM NON-EMPLOYMENT, 1966
BY CENSUS DIVISION

(percentage is of the total personal income for the census division)

5.67% - 9.99%	20.00% - 24.99%
10.00% - 12.99%	25.00% - 29.99%
13.00% - 14.49%	30.00% - 36.34%
14.50% - 15.99%	
16.00% - 17.99%	
18.00% - 19.99%	

Income from non-employment is: rental income, superannuation income, annuity income, alimony received, estate income, old-age pension, gross dividends, bond and bank interest, other Canadian investment income, foreign investment income, and other miscellaneous income. Conversely, income from employment is: salaries and wages, commission from employment, commission net income (self-employment), business net income, and farming and fishing net income.

PERSONAL INCOME FROM NON-EMPLOYMENT 1966

% are of provincial personal income

Prince Edward Island	25.54%
Newfoundland	18.65%
New Brunswick	18.57%
Nova Scotia	15.56%
British Columbia	15.56%
Saskatchewan	14.64%
Manitoba	14.47%
Quebec	13.45%
Ontario	13.18%
Alberta	13.09%

CANADA 13.99% of national personal income excluding Y.T. and N.W.T.

PERSONAL INCOME FROM NON-EMPLOYMENT 1966

Ont. 38.59%
Que. 24.65%
B.C. 12.02%
Alta. 6.61%
Sask. 4.54%
Man. 4.48%
N.S. 3.65%
N.B. 2.81%
Nfld. 1.86%
P.E.I. 0.59%

100% = $ 5,437,892,000

STRUCTURE OF SALARIES AND WAGES, 1961

Each bar in each graph represents the number of persons in the indicated earnings category, expressed as a percentage of the total number of earners whose salaries and wages were reported, for the designated territorial unit.

Data on which the graphs are based are for persons 15 years of age and over who worked for others, and whose salaries and wages were reported for the year ending June 1, 1961. Approximately 79% of the Experienced Labour Force qualifies under these terms, and are represented in the graphs. The residual is accounted for by about 940,000 self-employed and about 268,000 persons who worked for others but whose salaries and wages were not reported.

Median Earnings: 50% of the earners earn more and 50% earn less than the median values entered for each graph.

	Earnings
A	- $ 500
B	$ 500 - $ 999
C	$ 1,000 - $ 1,499
D	$ 1,500 - $ 1,999
E	$ 2,000 - $ 2,499
F	$ 2,500 - $ 2,999
G	$ 3,000 - $ 3,999
H	$ 4,000 - $ 5,999
I	$ 6,000 +
J	Median
K	Reported Earners
L	Self-Employed*

*(not included in reported earners)

CANADA

A	3.9 / 7.3
B	3.4 / 6.8
C	3.6 / 7.6
D	3.7 / 7.5
E	4.5 / 10.0
F	3.2 / 8.7
G	4.6 / 20.3
H	1.8 / 22.7
I	0.3 / 9.1
J	Male $ 1,990 / Female $ 1,990
K	78.7% of Experienced
L	14.5% Labour Force*

BRITISH COLUMBIA

A	4.1 / 7.4
B	3.3 / 6.2
C	3.0 / 5.6
D	2.6 / 8.4
E	4.3 / 6.7
F	3.1
G	5.0 / 19.2
H	2.2 / 28.6
I	0.4 / 11.7
J	$ 2,116 / $ 4,126
K	82.3%
L	12.4%

ALBERTA

A	4.5 / 8.3
B	3.6 / 7.0
C	3.4 / 7.1
D	3.3 / 6.7
E	4.5 / 9.8
F	3.0 / 7.7
G	20.6
H	22.8
I	0.3 / 10.0
J	$ 1,999 / $ 3,679
K	70.0%
L	21.1%

SASKATCHEWAN

A	4.9 / 9.8
B	3.7 / 8.4
C	3.0 / 8.0
D	3.7 / 8.0
E	4.8 / 10.8
F	3.1 / 8.3
G	4.4 / 20.1
H	2.4 / 19.4
I	0.3 / 7.2
J	$ 1,978 / $ 3,304
K	55.6%
L	33.6%

MANITOBA

A	4.4 / 7.8
B	3.8 / 7.1
C	4.1 / 7.9
D	4.5 / 8.2
E	5.4 / 10.9
F	3.3 / 8.6
G	5.6 / 20.9
H	2.3 / 20.8
I	0.3 / 7.8
J	$ 1,889 / $ 3,546
K	72.9%
L	18.8%

ONTARIO

A	3.9 / 6.8
B	3.3 / 6.0
C	3.4 / 6.3
D	3.3 / 6.2
E	4.5 / 9.0
F	3.6 / 8.4
G	20.7
H	25.8
I	0.5 / 10.8
J	$ 2,137 / $ 3,935
K	82.7%
L	12.2%

QUEBEC

A	3.0 / 6.1
B	3.2 / 7.0
C	3.9 / 8.5
D	4.6 / 9.3
E	4.5 / 11.3
F	3.0 / 10.0
G	3.9 / 20.8
H	1.3 / 19.5
I	0.2 / 7.5
J	$ 1,904 / $ 3,367
K	74.3%
L	12.3%

NEW BRUNSWICK

A	5.3 / 10.8
B	4.1 / 10.6
C	3.8 / 11.0
D	3.9 / 10.0
E	4.0 / 12.2
F	2.2 / 9.3
G	2.6 / 17.6
H	0.9 / 14.2
I	0.1 / 4.3
J	$ 1,519 / $ 2,723
K	82.0%
L	12.6%

NOVA SCOTIA

A	5.0 / 9.8
B	3.9 / 9.1
C	3.8 / 10.0
D	3.4 / 9.6
E	3.7 / 12.0
F	2.1 / 9.4
G	1.7 / 18.4
H	0.8 / 16.4
I	0.1 / 5.3
J	$ 1,499 / $ 2,957
K	82.6%
L	12.9%

PRINCE EDWARD I.

A	8.4 / 16.0
B	5.2 / 14.1
C	4.7 / 13.5
D	4.2 / 11.4
E	3.9 / 12.7
F	2.1 / 8.2
G	1.9 / 11.8
H	0.6 / 9.3
I	0.1 / 3.0
J	$ 1,179 / $ 2,134
K	61.8%
L	28.6%

NEWFOUNDLAND

A	4.1 / 9.8
B	4.2 / 11.0
C	4.6 / 13.8
D	2.5 / 9.7
E	2.0 / 10.7
F	1.3 / 7.6
G	17.1
H	15.0
I	0.1 / 5.3
J	$ 1,256 / $ 2,645
K	66.9%
L	13.2%

NORTHWEST TERRITORIES

A	2.4 / 5.3
B	2.3 / 5.6
C	1.6 / 5.2
D	1.7 / 6.0
E	2.0 / 5.5
F	1.4 / 5.5
G	2.8 / 17.1
H	14.0
I	28.2
J	$ 2,240 / $ 4,520
K	23.2
L	66.9%

YUKON TERRITORY

A	2.8 / 5.2
B	2.5 / 5.6
C	2.0 / 5.5
D	2.0 / 5.3
E	2.8 / 6.8
F	2.0 / 5.7
G	4.8 / 15.5
H	33.3
I	17.1
J	$ 2,321 / $ 4,556
K	85.6%
L	15.8% (Yukon and N.W.T.)

Scale 1:20,000,000 or One Inch to 315.65 Miles

Lambert Conformal Conic Projection Standard Parallels 49°N. and 77°N.

THE NATIONAL ATLAS OF CANADA

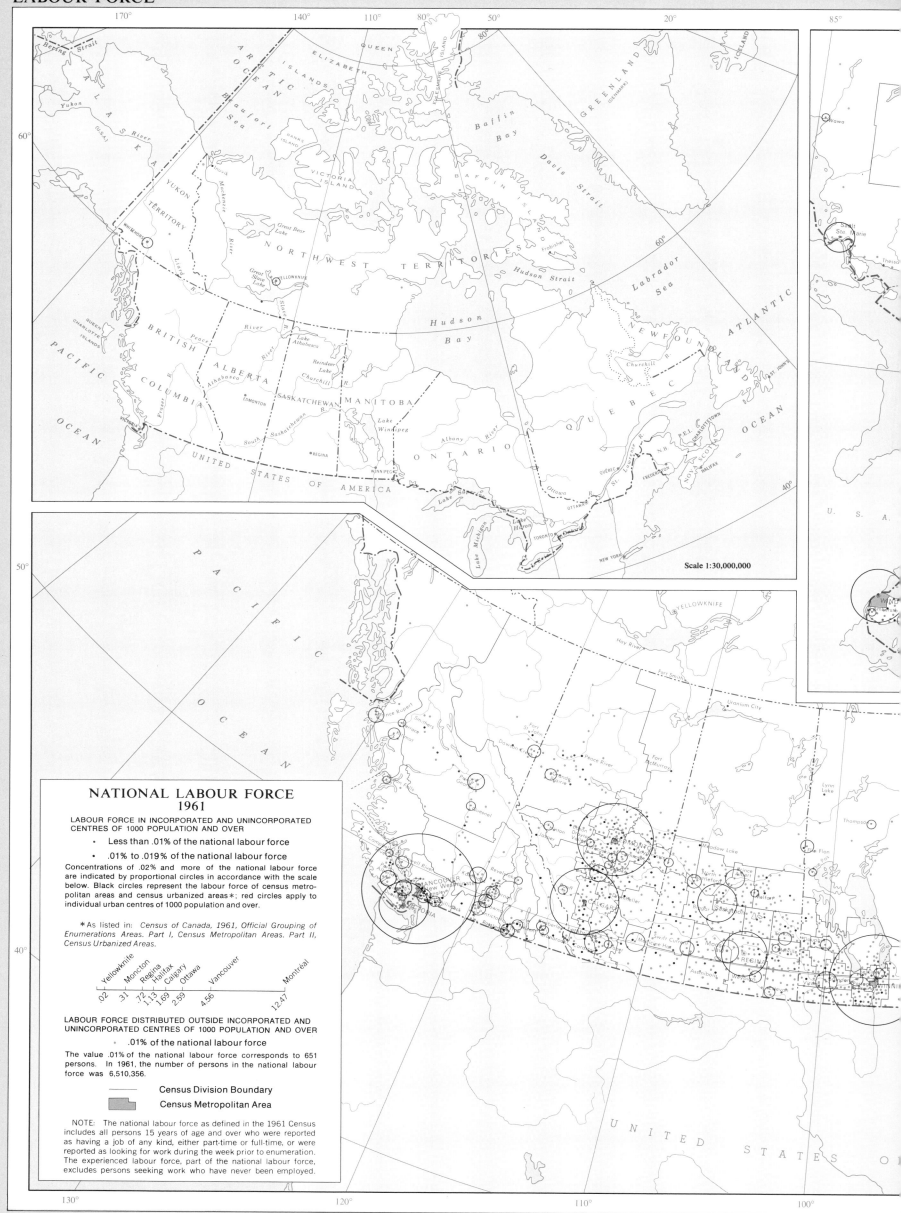

NATIONAL LABOUR FORCE
1961

LABOUR FORCE IN INCORPORATED AND UNINCORPORATED
CENTRES OF 1000 POPULATION AND OVER

• Less than .01% of the national labour force

• .01% to .019% of the national labour force

Concentrations of .02% and more of the national labour force
are indicated by proportional circles in accordance with the scale
below. Black circles represent the labour force of census metropolitan areas and census urbanized areas∗; red circles apply to
individual urban centres of 1000 population and over.

∗As listed in: *Census of Canada, 1961, Official Grouping of
Enumerations Areas. Part I, Census Metropolitan Areas. Part II,
Census Urbanized Areas.*

LABOUR FORCE DISTRIBUTED OUTSIDE INCORPORATED AND
UNINCORPORATED CENTRES OF 1000 POPULATION AND OVER

· .01% of the national labour force

The value .01% of the national labour force corresponds to 651
persons. In 1961, the number of persons in the national labour
force was 6,510,356.

—————— Census Division Boundary

▨ Census Metropolitan Area

NOTE: The national labour force as defined in the 1961 Census
includes all persons 15 years of age and over who were reported
as having a job of any kind, either part-time or full-time, or were
reported as looking for work during the week prior to enumeration.
The experienced labour force, part of the national labour force,
excludes persons seeking work who have never been employed.

Scale 1:30,000,000

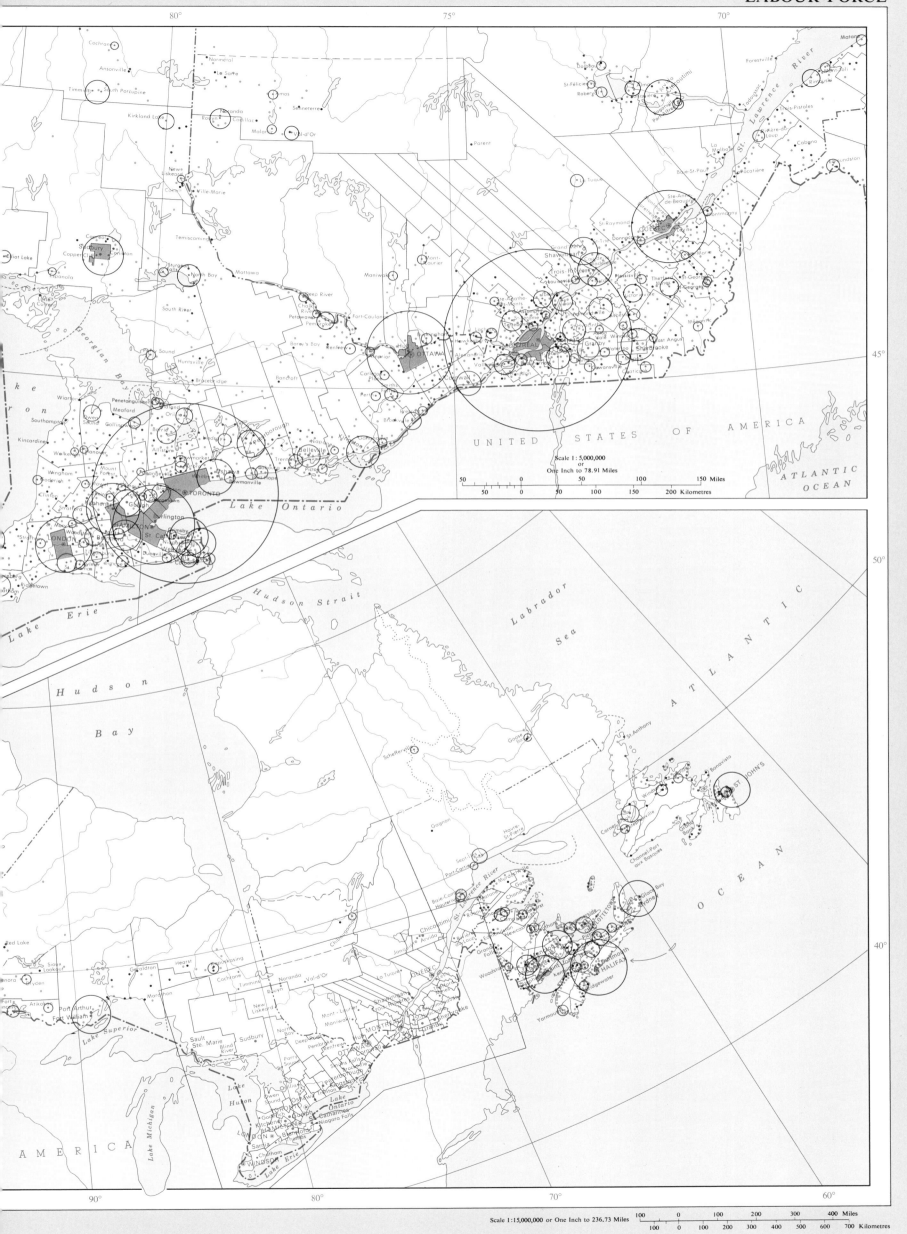

Scale 1: 5,000,000
or
One Inch to 78.91 Miles

50   0   50   100   150 Miles

50   0   50   100   150   200 Kilometres

UNITED STATES OF AMERICA

ATLANTIC OCEAN

Scale 1:15,000,000 or One Inch to 236.73 Miles

100   0   100   200   300   400 Miles

100   0   100   200   300   400   500   600   700 Kilometres

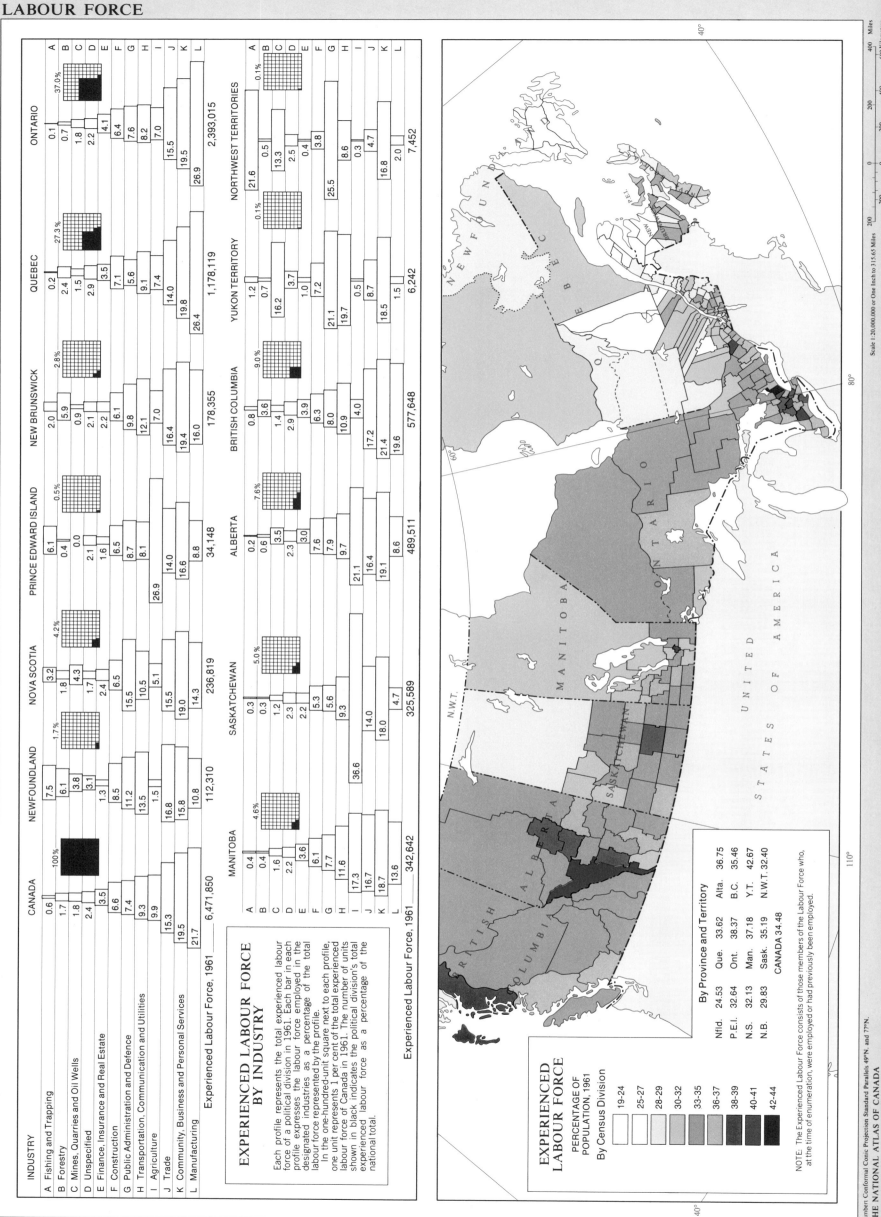

INDUSTRY		CANADA	NEWFOUNDLAND	NOVA SCOTIA	PRINCE EDWARD ISLAND	NEW BRUNSWICK	QUEBEC	ONTARIO
A	Fishing and Trapping	0.6	7.5	3.2	6.1	2.0	0.2	0.1
B	Forestry	1.7	6.1	1.8	0.4	5.9	2.4	0.7
C	Mines, Quarries and Oil Wells	1.8	3.8	4.3	0.0	0.9	1.5	1.8
D	Unspecified	2.4	3.1	1.7	2.1	2.1	2.9	2.2
E	Finance, Insurance and Real Estate	3.5	1.3	2.4	1.6	2.2	3.5	4.1
F	Construction	6.6	8.5	6.5	6.5	6.1	7.1	6.4
G	Public Administration and Defence	7.4	11.2	15.5	8.7	9.8	5.6	7.6
H	Transportation, Communication and Utilities	9.3	13.5	10.5	8.1	12.1	9.1	8.2
I	Agriculture	9.9	1.5	5.1	26.9	7.0	7.4	7.0
J	Trade	15.3	16.8	15.5	14.0	16.4	14.0	15.5
K	Community, Business and Personal Services	19.5	15.8	19.0	16.6	19.4	19.8	19.5
L	Manufacturing	21.7	10.8	14.3	8.8	16.0	26.4	26.9
	Percentage of national total	100%	1.7%	4.2%	0.5%	2.8%	27.3%	37.0%
	Experienced Labour Force, 1961	6,471,850	112,310	236,819	34,148	178,355	1,178,119	2,393,015

		MANITOBA	SASKATCHEWAN	ALBERTA	BRITISH COLUMBIA	YUKON TERRITORY	NORTHWEST TERRITORIES
A		0.4	0.3	0.2	0.8	1.2	21.6
B		0.4	0.3	0.6	3.6	0.7	0.5
C		1.6	1.2	3.5	1.4	16.2	13.3
D		2.2	2.3	2.3	2.9	3.7	2.5
E		3.6	2.2	3.0	3.9	1.0	0.4
F		6.1	5.3	7.6	6.3	7.2	3.8
G		7.7	5.6	7.9	8.0	21.1	25.5
H		11.6	9.3	9.7	10.9	19.7	8.6
I		17.3	36.6	21.1	4.0	0.5	0.3
J		16.7	14.0	16.4	17.2	18.5	16.8
K		18.7	18.0	19.1	21.4	8.7	4.7
L		13.6	4.7	8.6	19.6	1.5	2.0
	Percentage of national total	4.6%	5.0%	7.6%	9.0%	0.1%	0.1%
	Experienced Labour Force, 1961	342,642	325,589	489,511	577,648	6,242	7,452

EXPERIENCED LABOUR FORCE BY INDUSTRY

Each profile represents the total experienced labour force of a political division in 1961. Each bar in each profile expresses the labour force employed in the designated industries as a percentage of the total labour force represented by the profile.

In the one-hundred-unit square next to each profile, one unit represents 1 per cent of the total experienced labour force of Canada in 1961. The number of units shown in black indicates the political division's total experienced labour force as a percentage of the national total.

EXPERIENCED LABOUR FORCE

PERCENTAGE OF POPULATION, 1961
By Census Division

19-24
25-27
28-29
30-32
33-35
36-37
38-39
40-41
42-44

By Province and Territory

Nfld.	24.53	Que.	33.62	Alta.	36.75
P.E.I.	32.64	Ont.	38.37	B.C.	35.46
N.S.	32.13	Man.	37.18	Y.T.	42.67
N.B.	29.83	Sask.	35.19	N.W.T.	32.40

CANADA 34.48

NOTE: The Experienced Labour Force consists of those members of the Labour Force who, at the time of enumeration, were employed or had previously been employed.

Scale 1:20,000,000 or One Inch to 315.65 Miles

Lambert Conformal Conic Projection Standard Parallels 49°N. and 77°N.

THE NATIONAL ATLAS OF CANADA

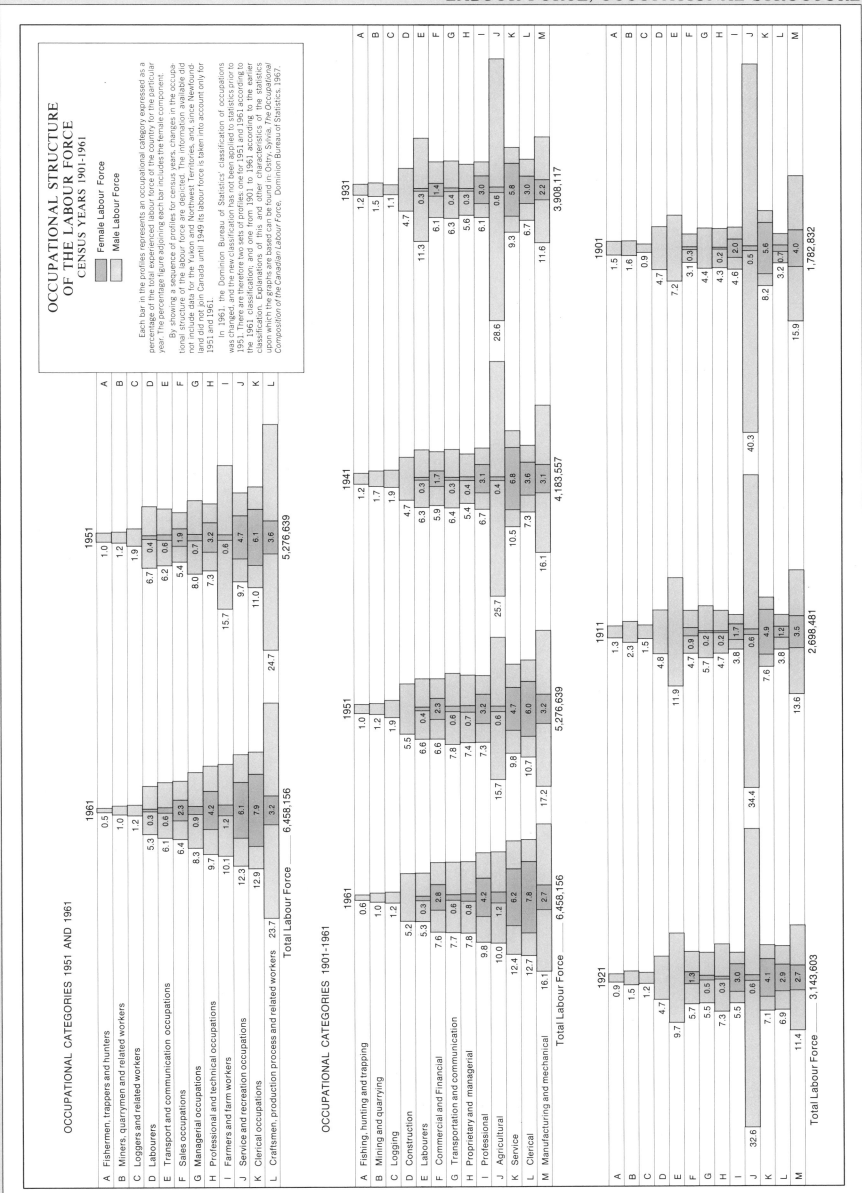

OCCUPATIONAL STRUCTURE
OF THE LABOUR FORCE
CENSUS YEARS 1901-1961

Each bar in the profiles represents an occupational category expressed as a percentage of the total experienced labour force of the country for the particular year. The percentage figure adjoining each bar includes the female component.

By showing a sequence of profiles for census years, changes in the occupational structure of the labour force are depicted. The information available did not include data for the Yukon and Northwest Territories, and, since Newfoundland did not join Canada until 1949 its labour force is taken into account only for 1951 and 1961.

In 1961, the Dominion Bureau of Statistics' classification of occupations was changed, and the new classification has not been applied to statistics prior to 1951. There are therefore two sets of profiles: one for 1951 and 1961 according to the 1961 classification; and one from 1901 to 1961 according to the earlier classification. Explanations of this and other characteristics of the statistics upon which the graphs are based can be found in: Ostry, Sylvia, *The Occupational Composition of the Canadian Labour Force*, Dominion Bureau of Statistics, 1967.

OCCUPATIONAL CATEGORIES 1951 AND 1961

A Fishermen, trappers and hunters
B Miners, quarrymen and related workers
C Loggers and related workers
D Labourers
E Transport and communication occupations
F Sales occupations
G Managerial occupations
H Professional and technical occupations
I Farmers and farm workers
J Service and recreation occupations
K Clerical occupations
L Craftsmen, production process and related workers

OCCUPATIONAL CATEGORIES 1901-1961

A Fishing, hunting and trapping
B Mining and quarrying
C Logging
D Construction
E Labourers
F Commercial and Financial
G Transportation and communication
H Proprietary and managerial
I Professional
J Agricultural
K Service
L Clerical
M Manufacturing and mechanical

AGRICULTURE

Agricultural production is depicted in the atlas by a set of maps each of which shows the value of sales from the farm of a product or group of products. The method of depiction is by percentage dots each of which represents .01% of the national value of sales from the farm for the period June 1, 1960 to May 31, 1961. The presentation indicates the areas of origin of the products and, since the dots have the same value from map to map, makes possible a simple visual assessment of the relative importance of each product. In some instances the values of several products were combined in the available data. In such cases the areas of origin of the individual products cannot be differentiated on the maps showing value of sales. To compensate for this, distribution of seeded acreage is shown on separate maps. On one map the values of sales for all products are accumulated, thereby depicting the total output of the industry and the areal variation of production. In addition to the information conveyed by dots, area-colours are used to show occurrences less than dot-value, to show agricultural areas in which no occurrence of a product is reported, and to show non-agricultural areas.

From a study of the dot maps it is possible to determine the product-combinations, quantitatively expressed in terms of sales, in any part of the agricultural area of the country. The nature of agriculture in an area can be usefully described in terms of its product-combinations, that is, particular combinations can be considered as types. The area of each type can be considered an agricultural region within which the character-istics of agriculture are approximately uniform. In most agricultural areas of Canada there is a wide range of products, and complete product-combinations are therefore complex, but in terms of value many of the products are relatively insignificant. For the *Types of Farming* map product-combinations are used to define types, but the products included are only those of greatest local economic significance. The method by which the types were determined is described in the notes included on the map.

The calculations for *Types of Farming,* in identifying the statistically significant products, provided data for *Diversity of Agriculture.* Diversity is expressed as the number of statistically significant products for each census division.

The detailed information on which the agricultural maps are based is available from the Dominion Bureau of Statistics only for one year in ten, that is, for decennial census years. In order to set the agriculture of the year June 1, 1960 to May 31, 1961 into a context of other years, a page of graphs is included showing the trends over a period of time for a variety of agricultural data. For a similar reason two climatic maps are included which indicate the deviation from average precipitation for the period April to September, in 1960.

AGRICULTURE IN THE NORTHWEST TERRITORIES AND THE YUKON TERRITORY

The small amount of agricultural production in the Northwest Territories and the Yukon did not warrant the large page formats that would be required to cover the area, for this atlas. The 1961 census recorded 26 farms in the two Territories, of which only 3 were classified as commercial. Of 8,590 acres reported as farm land, 1,088 were classified as improved land. Crops occupied 526 acres. In order of size of acreage these were: Other fodder crops (194); Tame hay (136); Oats for grain(85); Wheat (47); Potatoes (35); Vegetables for sale (12); Barley (11); Turnips, Swedes and Mangels (6). A total of 412 cattle were reported of which 16 (two years and over) were being milked or to be milked. The remaining livestock reported was composed of 233 horses and 1320 hens and chickens. The value of sales of agricultural products produced in the Territories for the year covered by the census is estimated at about $20,000.

Although there are considerable friable soils along valleys in the Northwest Territories, the Yukon, and in the non-agricultural areas of northern Alberta and British Columbia, climate and drainage limit the agricultural potential. The areas having the best potential, as indicated by surveys by the federal Department of Agriculture, are shown on page 141. These areas are along the lower Peace and the Slave River, the upper Mackenzie, the Liard River and its tributary the Fort Nelson, the Teslin River and Lake Teslin, and along the Takhini - Dezadeash valleys between Whitehorse and Haines Junction. In most of the northern settlements there are kitchen gardens.

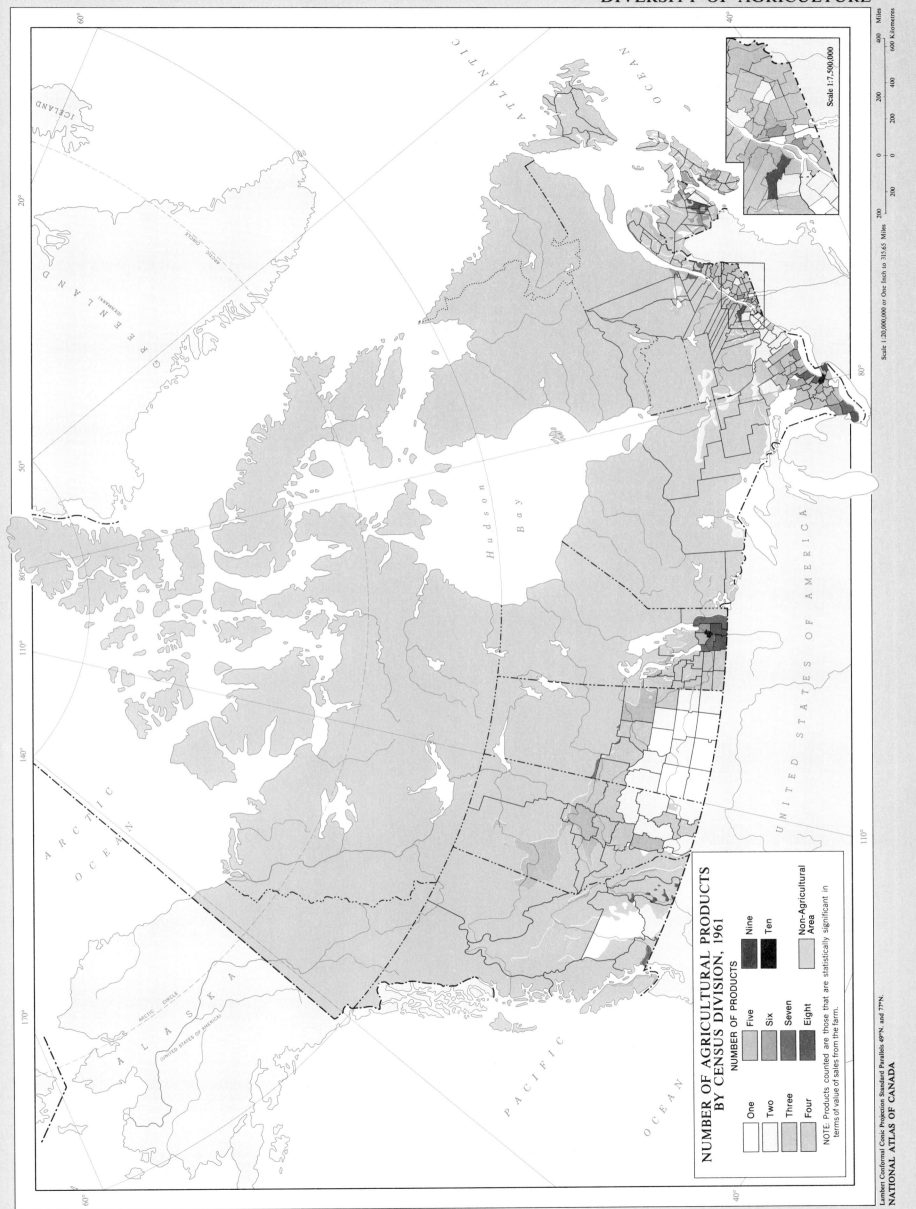

NUMBER OF AGRICULTURAL PRODUCTS
BY CENSUS DIVISION, 1961

NUMBER OF PRODUCTS

One		Five	Nine
Two		Six	Ten
Three		Seven	Non-Agricultural Area
Four		Eight	

NOTE: Products counted are those that are statistically significant in terms of value of sales from the farm.

Scale 1:20,000,000 or One Inch to 315.65 Miles

Lambert Conformal Conic Projection Standard Parallels 49°N. and 77°N.
NATIONAL ATLAS OF CANADA

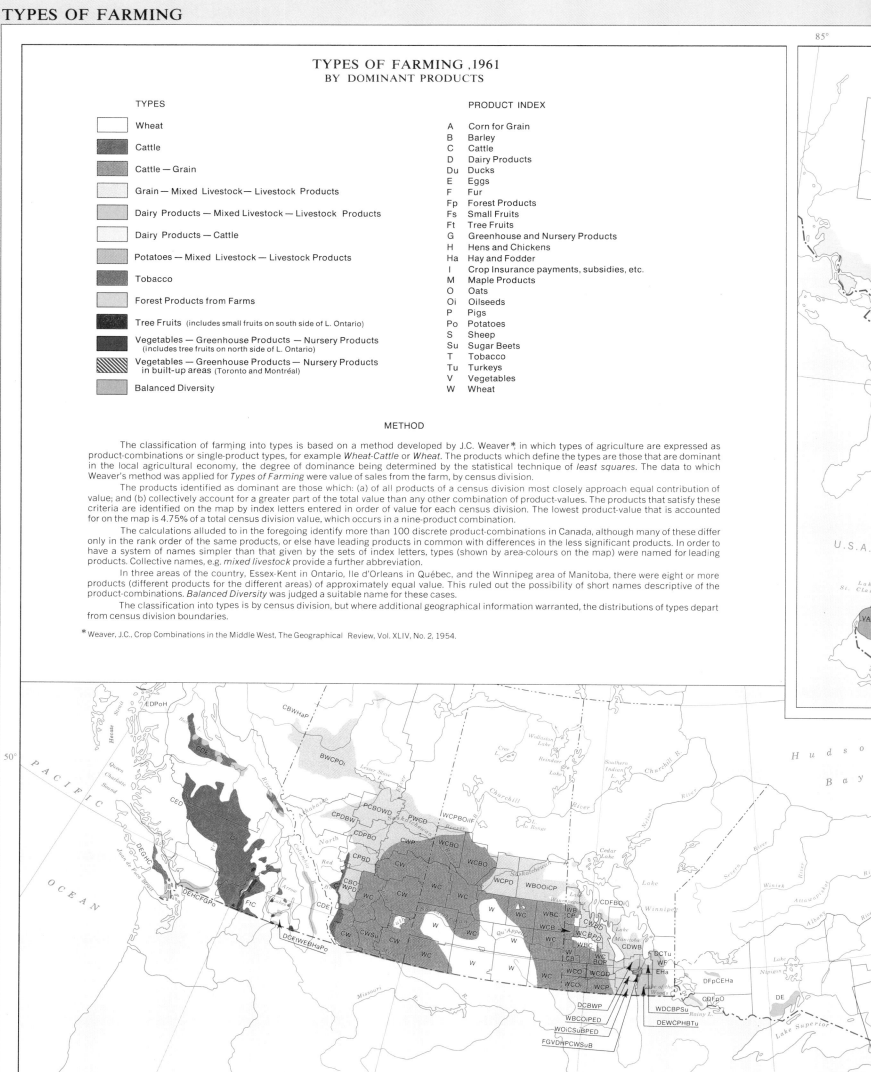

TYPES OF FARMING, 1961
BY DOMINANT PRODUCTS

TYPES

- Wheat
- Cattle
- Cattle — Grain
- Grain — Mixed Livestock — Livestock Products
- Dairy Products — Mixed Livestock — Livestock Products
- Dairy Products — Cattle
- Potatoes — Mixed Livestock — Livestock Products
- Tobacco
- Forest Products from Farms
- Tree Fruits (includes small fruits on south side of L. Ontario)
- Vegetables — Greenhouse Products — Nursery Products (includes tree fruits on north side of L. Ontario)
- Vegetables — Greenhouse Products — Nursery Products in built-up areas (Toronto and Montréal)
- Balanced Diversity

PRODUCT INDEX

A	Corn for Grain
B	Barley
C	Cattle
D	Dairy Products
Du	Ducks
E	Eggs
F	Fur
Fp	Forest Products
Fs	Small Fruits
Ft	Tree Fruits
G	Greenhouse and Nursery Products
H	Hens and Chickens
Ha	Hay and Fodder
I	Crop Insurance payments, subsidies, etc.
M	Maple Products
O	Oats
Oi	Oilseeds
P	Pigs
Po	Potatoes
S	Sheep
Su	Sugar Beets
T	Tobacco
Tu	Turkeys
V	Vegetables
W	Wheat

METHOD

The classification of farming into types is based on a method developed by J.C. Weaver*, in which types of agriculture are expressed as product-combinations or single-product types, for example *Wheat-Cattle* or *Wheat*. The products which define the types are those that are dominant in the local agricultural economy, the degree of dominance being determined by the statistical technique of *least squares*. The data to which Weaver's method was applied for *Types of Farming* were value of sales from the farm, by census division.

The products identified as dominant are those which: (a) of all products of a census division most closely approach equal contribution of value; and (b) collectively account for a greater part of the total value than any other combination of product-values. The products that satisfy these criteria are identified on the map by index letters entered in order of value for each census division. The lowest product-value that is accounted for on the map is 4.75% of a total census division value, which occurs in a nine-product combination.

The calculations alluded to in the foregoing identify more than 100 discrete product-combinations in Canada, although many of these differ only in the rank order of the same products, or else have leading products in common with differences in the less significant products. In order to have a system of names simpler than that given by the sets of index letters, types (shown by area-colours on the map) were named for leading products. Collective names, e.g. *mixed livestock* provide a further abbreviation.

In three areas of the country, Essex-Kent in Ontario, Ile d'Orleans in Québec, and the Winnipeg area of Manitoba, there were eight or more products (different products for the different areas) of approximately equal value. This ruled out the possibility of short names descriptive of the product-combinations. *Balanced Diversity* was judged a suitable name for these cases.

The classification into types is by census division, but where additional geographical information warranted, the distributions of types depart from census division boundaries.

*Weaver, J.C., Crop Combinations in the Middle West, The Geographical Review, Vol. XLIV, No. 2, 1954.

Lambert Conformal Conic Projection Standard Parallels 49°N. and 77°N.

THE NATIONAL ATLAS OF CANADA

AGRICULTURE – SELECTED CHARACTERISTICS

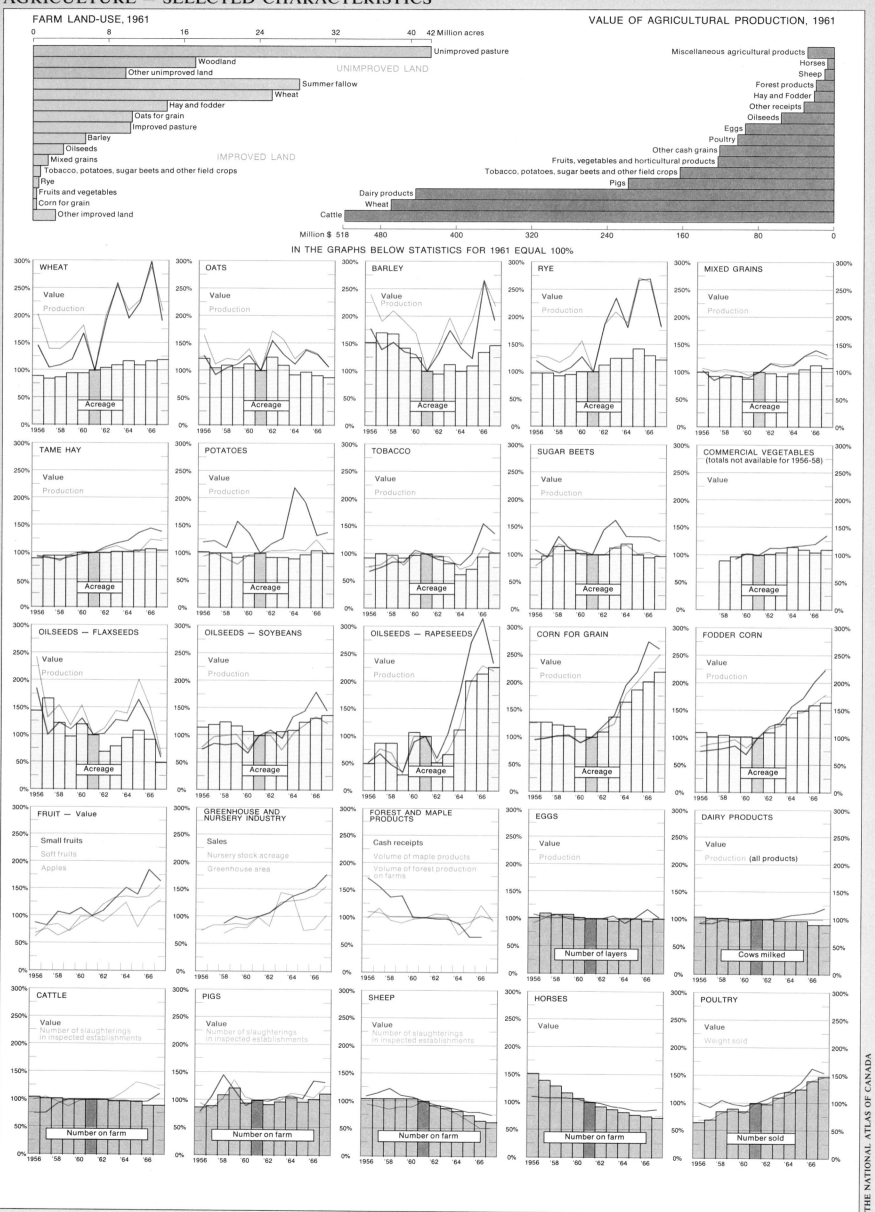

FARM LAND-USE, 1961

0   8   16   24   32   40   42 Million acres

Unimproved pasture
Woodland
Other unimproved land
UNIMPROVED LAND
Summer fallow
Wheat
Hay and fodder
Oats for grain
Improved pasture
Barley
Oilseeds
IMPROVED LAND
Mixed grains
Tobacco, potatoes, sugar beets and other field crops
Rye
Fruits and vegetables
Corn for grain
Other improved land

VALUE OF AGRICULTURAL PRODUCTION, 1961

Miscellaneous agricultural products
Horses
Sheep
Forest products
Hay and Fodder
Other receipts
Oilseeds
Eggs
Poultry
Other cash grains
Fruits, vegetables and horticultural products
Tobacco, potatoes, sugar beets and other field crops
Pigs
Dairy products
Wheat
Cattle

Million $ 518   480   400   320   240   160   80   0

IN THE GRAPHS BELOW STATISTICS FOR 1961 EQUAL 100%

WHEAT — Value, Production, Acreage
OATS — Value, Production, Acreage
BARLEY — Value, Production, Acreage
RYE — Value, Production, Acreage
MIXED GRAINS — Value, Production, Acreage

TAME HAY — Value, Production, Acreage
POTATOES — Value, Production, Acreage
TOBACCO — Value, Production, Acreage
SUGAR BEETS — Value, Production, Acreage
COMMERCIAL VEGETABLES (totals not available for 1956-58) — Value, Acreage

OILSEEDS — FLAXSEEDS — Value, Production, Acreage
OILSEEDS — SOYBEANS — Value, Production, Acreage
OILSEEDS — RAPESEEDS — Value, Production, Acreage
CORN FOR GRAIN — Value, Production, Acreage
FODDER CORN — Value, Production, Acreage

FRUIT — Value — Small fruits, Soft fruits, Apples
GREENHOUSE AND NURSERY INDUSTRY — Sales, Nursery stock acreage, Greenhouse area
FOREST AND MAPLE PRODUCTS — Cash receipts, Volume of maple products, Volume of forest production on farms
EGGS — Value, Production, Number of layers
DAIRY PRODUCTS — Value, Production (all products), Cows milked

CATTLE — Value, Number of slaughterings in inspected establishments, Number on farm
PIGS — Value, Number of slaughterings in inspected establishments, Number on farm
SHEEP — Value, Number of slaughterings in inspected establishments, Number on farm
HORSES — Value, Number on farm
POULTRY — Value, Weight sold, Number sold

THE NATIONAL ATLAS OF CANADA

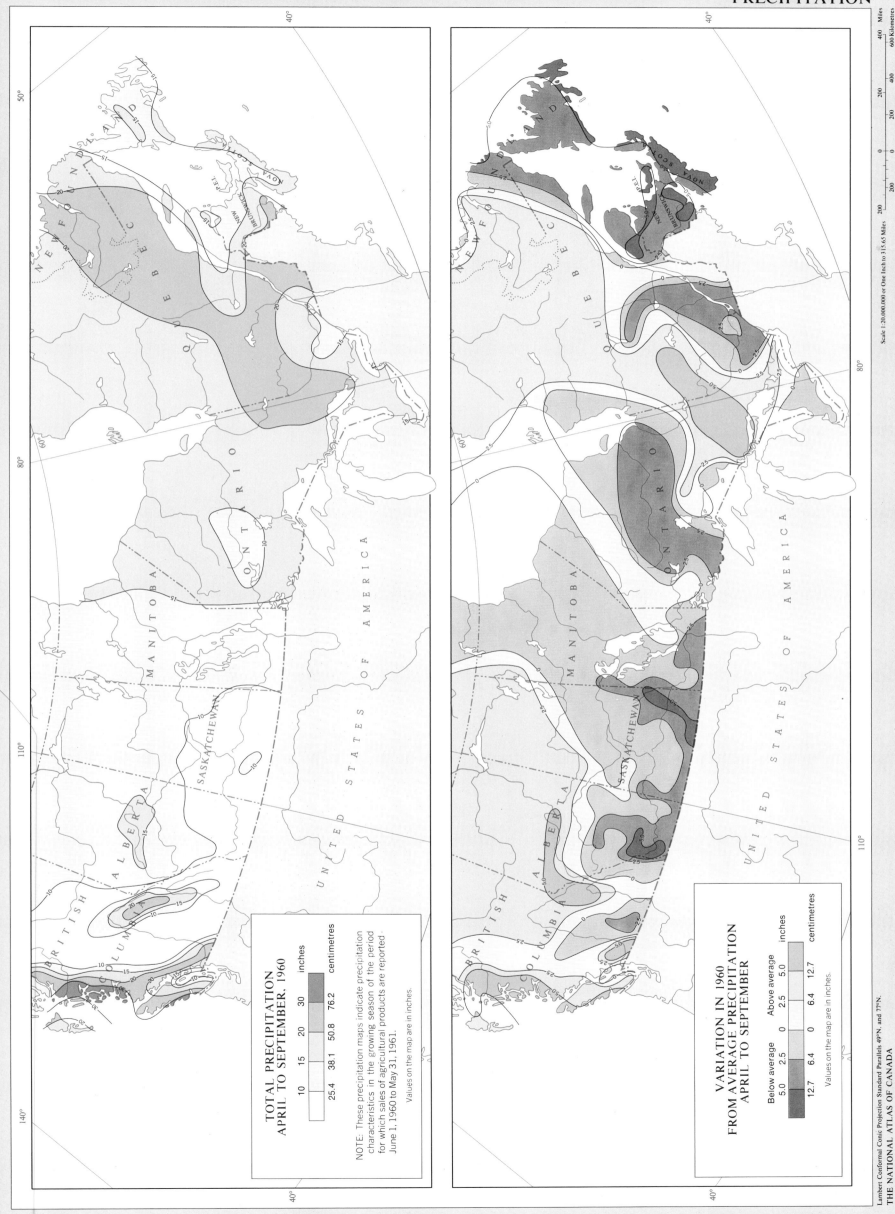

TOTAL PRECIPITATION
APRIL TO SEPTEMBER, 1960

inches	10	15	20	30	
centimetres	25.4	38.1	50.8	76.2	

NOTE: These precipitation maps indicate precipitation characteristics in the growing season of the period for which sales of agricultural products are reported - June 1, 1960 to May 31, 1961.

Values on the map are in inches.

VARIATION IN 1960
FROM AVERAGE PRECIPITATION
APRIL TO SEPTEMBER

Below average 12.7 6.4 2.5 0 0 2.5 5.0 Above average inches

centimetres

Values on the map are in inches.

Lambert Conformal Conic Projection Standard Parallels 49°N. and 77°N.

THE NATIONAL ATLAS OF CANADA

Scale 1:20,000,000 or One Inch to 315.65 Miles

200   0   200   400   Miles
200   0   200   400   600 Kilometres

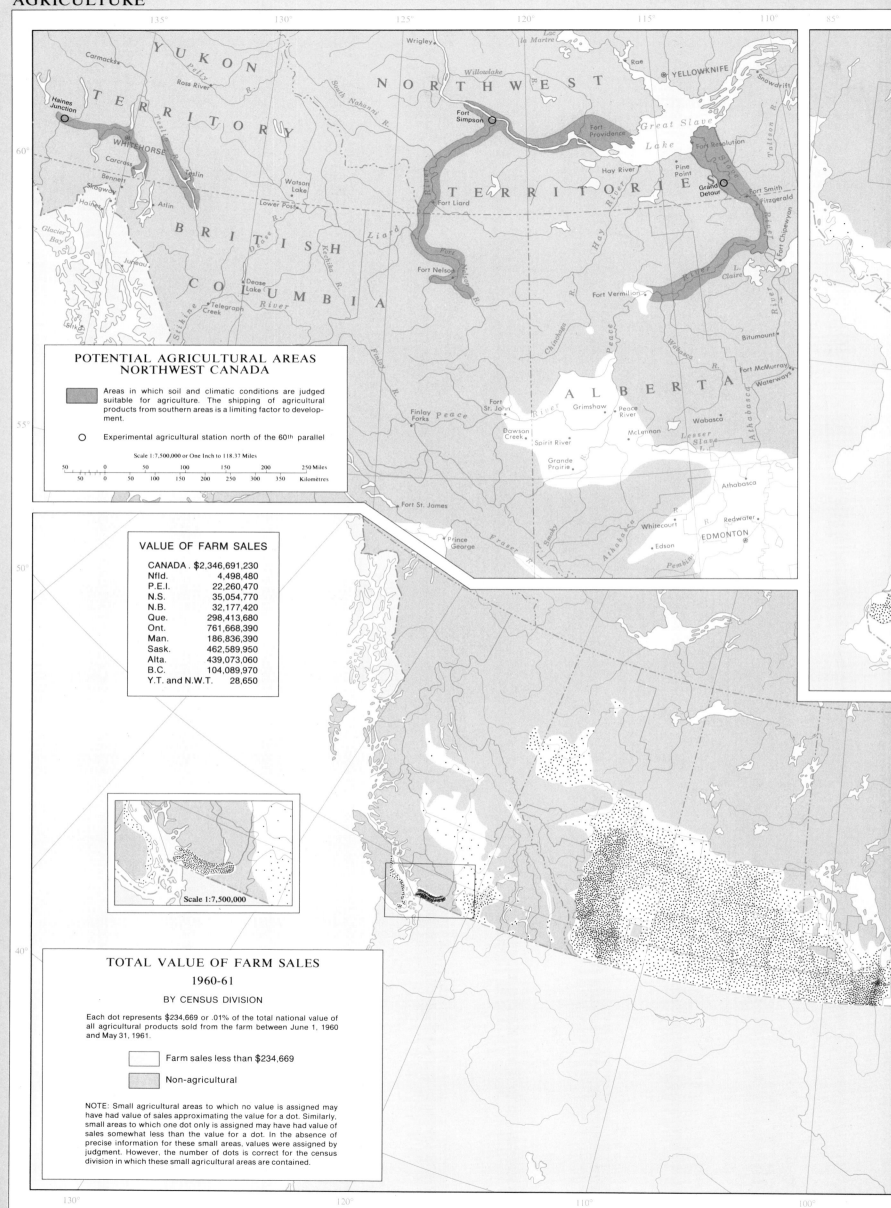

POTENTIAL AGRICULTURAL AREAS NORTHWEST CANADA

Areas in which soil and climatic conditions are judged suitable for agriculture. The shipping of agricultural products from southern areas is a limiting factor to development.

○ Experimental agricultural station north of the 60th parallel

Scale 1:7,500,000 or One Inch to 118.37 Miles

250 Miles
Kilomètres

VALUE OF FARM SALES

CANADA .	$2,346,691,230
Nfld.	4,498,480
P.E.I.	22,260,470
N.S.	35,054,770
N.B.	32,177,420
Que.	298,413,680
Ont.	761,668,390
Man.	186,836,390
Sask.	462,589,950
Alta.	439,073,060
B.C.	104,089,970
Y.T. and N.W.T.	28,650

Scale 1:7,500,000

TOTAL VALUE OF FARM SALES
1960-61
BY CENSUS DIVISION

Each dot represents $234,669 or .01% of the total national value of all agricultural products sold from the farm between June 1, 1960 and May 31, 1961.

☐ Farm sales less than $234,669

☐ Non-agricultural

NOTE: Small agricultural areas to which no value is assigned may have had value of sales approximating the value for a dot. Similarly, small areas to which one dot only is assigned may have had value of sales somewhat less than the value for a dot. In the absence of precise information for these small areas, values were assigned by judgment. However, the number of dots is correct for the census division in which these small agricultural areas are contained.

Lambert Conformal Conic Projection Standard Parallels 49°N. and 77°N.
THE NATIONAL ATLAS OF CANADA

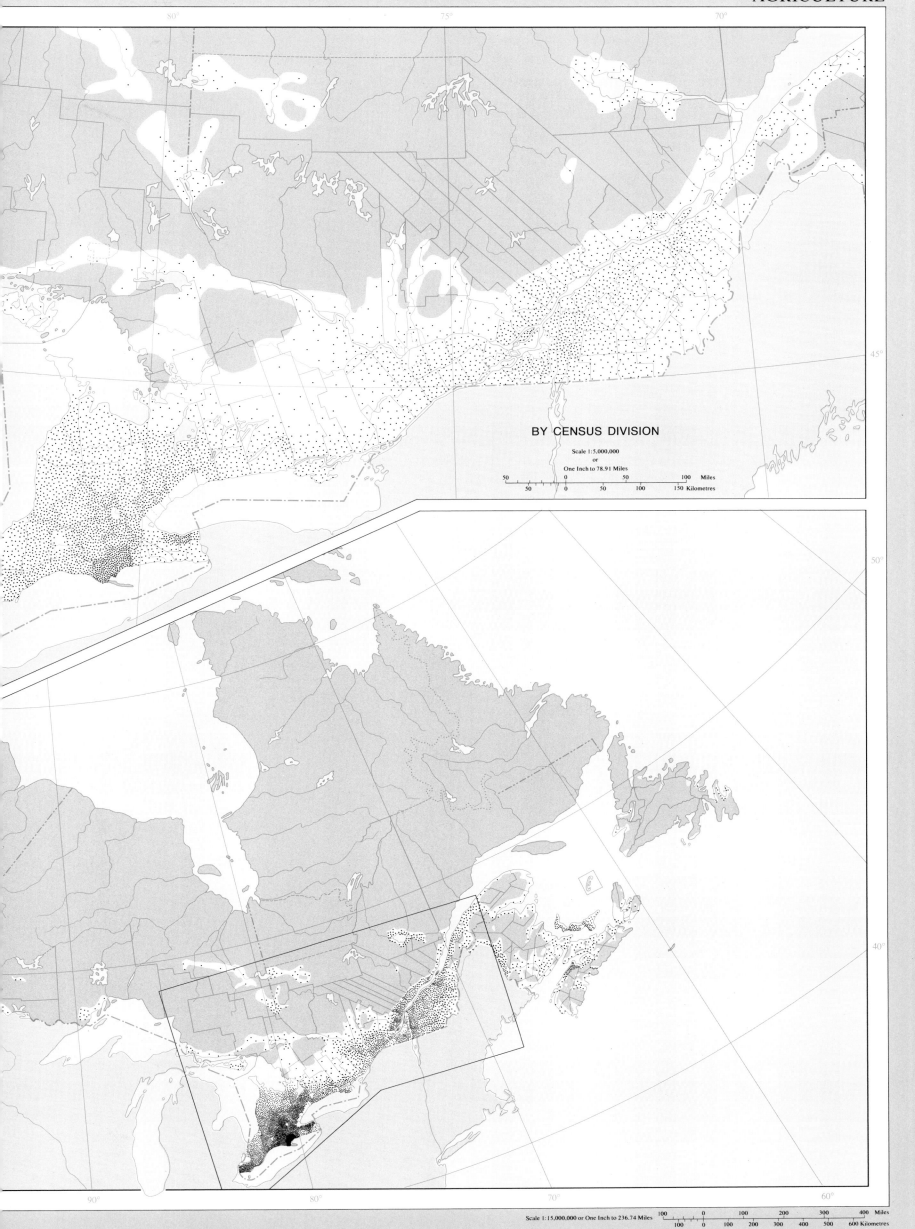

BY CENSUS DIVISION

Scale 1:5,000,000
or
One Inch to 78.91 Miles

50   0   50   100   Miles
50   0   50   100   150 Kilometres

Scale 1:15,000,000 or One Inch to 236.74 Miles   100   0   100   200   300   400 Miles
100   0   100   200   300   400   500   600 Kilometres

VALUE OF FARM SALES

CANADA	$430,861,110
Nfld.	0
P.E.I.	5,700
N.S.	800
N.B.	6,480
Que.	14,040
Ont.	10,410,580
Man.	56,113,990
Sask.	262,988,350
Alta.	99,909,010
B.C.	1,412,160
Y.T. & N.W.T.	0

WHEAT
VALUE OF FARM SALES, 1960-61

BY CENSUS DIVISION

Each dot represents $234,669 or .01% of the total national value of all agricultural products sold from the farm between June 1, 1960 and May 31, 1961.

- Farm sales less than $234,669
- No commercial production
- Non-agricultural

SEEDED ACRES

CANADA	25,315,964
Nfld.	1
P.E.I.	4,056
N.S.	1,359
N.B.	2,527
Que.	10,604
Ont.	581,379
Man.	2,913,795
Sask.	16,082,054
Alta.	5,632,843
B.C.	87,299
Y.T. & N.W.T.	47

WHEAT
SEEDED ACRES, 1961

BY CENSUS DIVISION

- 125,000 acres
- 50,000 acres
- 5000 acres
- Less than 5000 acres
- No acreage
- Non-agricultural

Lambert Conformal Conic Projection Standard Parallels 49°N. and 77°N.
THE NATIONAL ATLAS OF CANADA

Scale 1:20,000,000 or One Inch to 315.65 Miles

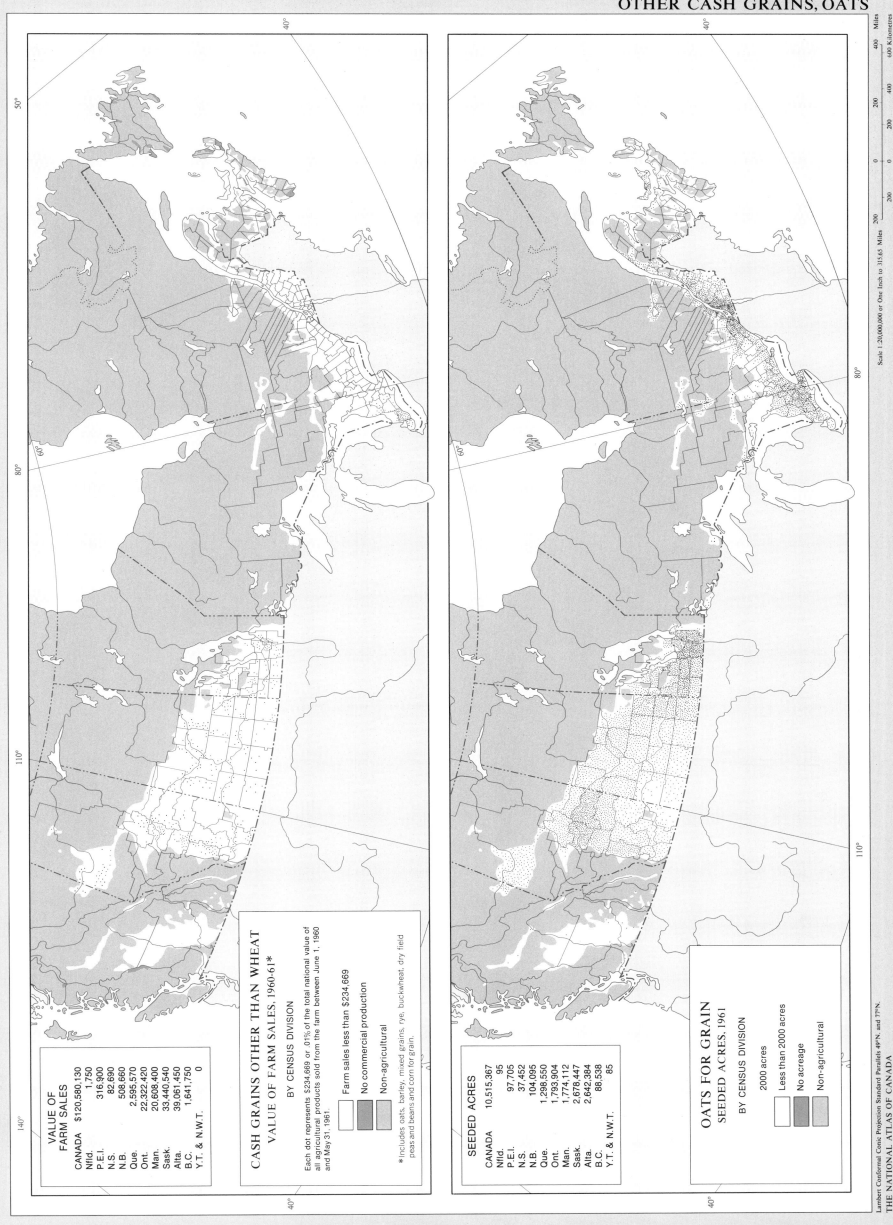

VALUE OF
FARM SALES

CANADA	$120,580,130
Nfld.	1,750
P.E.I.	316,900
N.S.	82,690
N.B.	508,660
Que.	2,595,570
Ont.	22,322,420
Man.	20,608,400
Sask.	33,440,540
Alta.	39,061,450
B.C.	1,641,750
Y.T. & N.W.T.	0

CASH GRAINS OTHER THAN WHEAT
VALUE OF FARM SALES. 1960-61*

BY CENSUS DIVISION

Each dot represents $234,669 or .01% of the total national value of
all agricultural products sold from the farm between June 1, 1960
and May 31, 1961.

Farm sales less than $234,669

No commercial production

Non-agricultural

*Includes oats, barley, mixed grains, rye, buckwheat, dry field
peas and beans and corn for grain.

SEEDED ACRES

CANADA	10,515,367
Nfld.	95
P.E.I.	97,705
N.S.	37,452
N.B.	104,095
Que.	1,298,550
Ont.	1,793,904
Man.	1,774,112
Sask.	2,678,447
Alta.	2,642,384
B.C.	88,538
Y.T. & N.W.T.	85

OATS FOR GRAIN
SEEDED ACRES, 1961

BY CENSUS DIVISION

2000 acres

Less than 2000 acres

No acreage

Non-agricultural

Lambert Conformal Conic Projection Standard Parallels 49°N. and 77°N.

Scale 1:20,000,000 or One Inch to 315.65 Miles

THE NATIONAL ATLAS OF CANADA

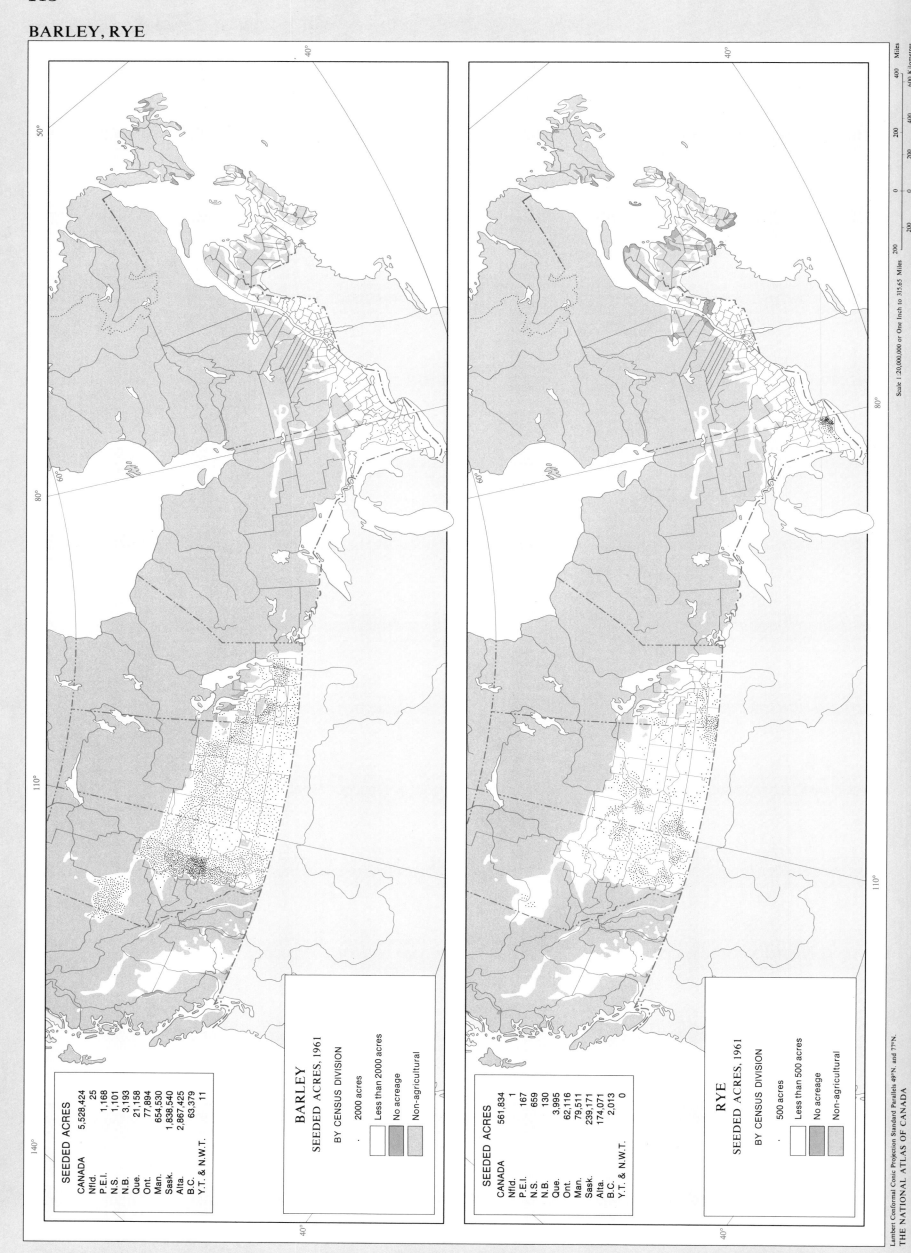

SEEDED ACRES

CANADA	5,528,424
Nfld.	25
P.E.I.	1,168
N.S.	1,101
N.B.	3,193
Que.	21,158
Ont.	77,894
Man.	654,530
Sask.	1,838,540
Alta.	2,867,425
B.C.	63,379
Y.T. & N.W.T.	11

BARLEY
SEEDED ACRES, 1961

BY CENSUS DIVISION

. 2000 acres

Less than 2000 acres
No acreage
Non-agricultural

SEEDED ACRES

CANADA	561,834
Nfld.	1
P.E.I.	167
N.S.	659
N.B.	130
Que.	3,995
Ont.	62,116
Man.	79,511
Sask.	239,171
Alta.	174,071
B.C.	2,013
Y.T. & N.W.T.	0

RYE
SEEDED ACRES, 1961

BY CENSUS DIVISION

. 500 acres

Less than 500 acres
No acreage
Non-agricultural

Lambert Conformal Conic Projection Standard Parallels 49°N. and 77°N.
THE NATIONAL ATLAS OF CANADA

Scale 1:20,000,000 or One Inch to 315.65 Miles

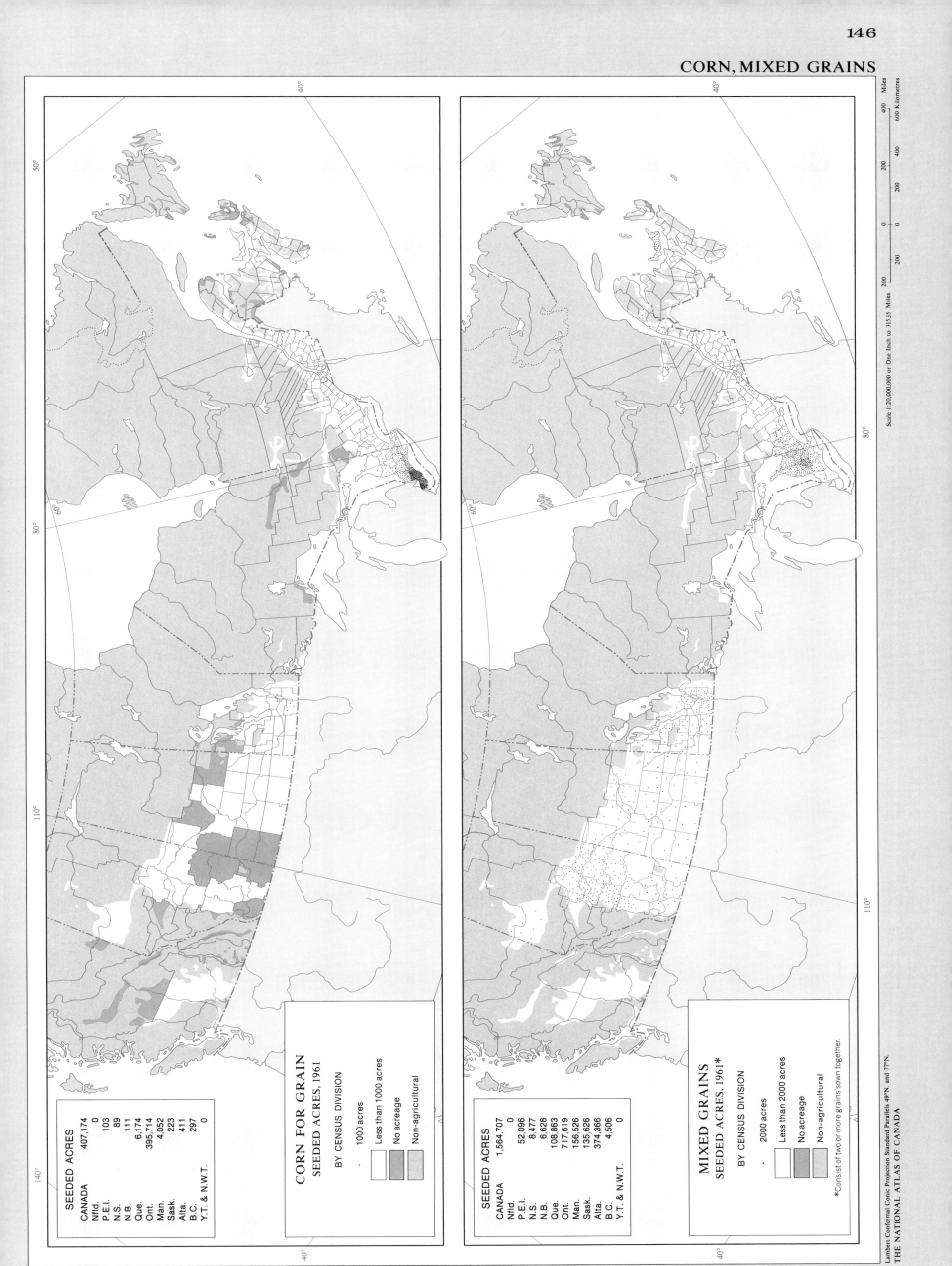

CORN FOR GRAIN

SEEDED ACRES, 1961

BY CENSUS DIVISION

· 1000 acres

Less than 1000 acres

No acreage

Non-agricultural

SEEDED ACRES	
CANADA	407,174
Nfld.	0
P.E.I.	103
N.S.	89
N.B.	111
Que.	6,174
Ont.	395,714
Man.	4,052
Sask.	223
Alta.	411
B.C.	297
Y.T. & N.W.T.	0

MIXED GRAINS

SEEDED ACRES, 1961*

BY CENSUS DIVISION

· 2000 acres

Less than 2000 acres

No acreage

Non-agricultural

*Consist of two or more grains sown together.

SEEDED ACRES	
CANADA	1,564,707
Nfld.	0
P.E.I.	52,096
N.S.	8,477
N.B.	6,628
Que.	108,863
Ont.	717,619
Man.	156,526
Sask.	135,626
Alta.	374,366
B.C.	4,506
Y.T. & N.W.T.	0

Lambert Conformal Conic Projection Standard Parallels 49°N. and 77°N.

THE NATIONAL ATLAS OF CANADA

Scale 1:20,000,000 or One Inch to 315.65 Miles

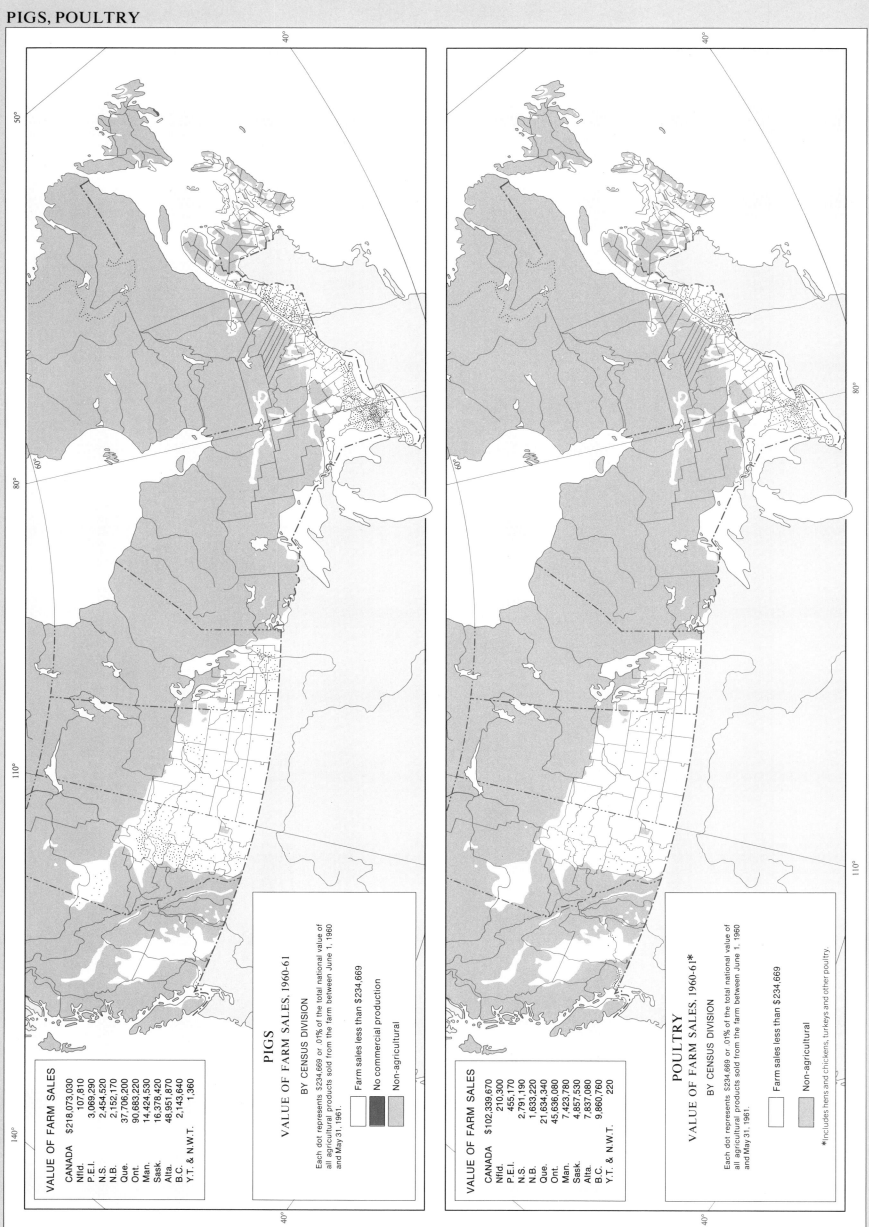

PIGS

VALUE OF FARM SALES, 1960-61

BY CENSUS DIVISION

Each dot represents $234,669 or .01% of the total national value of
all agricultural products sold from the farm between June 1, 1960
and May 31, 1961.

Farm sales less than $234,669

No commercial production

Non-agricultural

VALUE OF FARM SALES

CANADA	$218,073,030
Nfld.	107,810
P.E.I.	3,069,290
N.S.	2,454,520
N.B.	2,152,170
Que.	37,706,200
Ont.	90,683,220
Man.	14,424,530
Sask.	16,378,420
Alta.	48,951,870
B.C.	2,143,640
Y.T. & N.W.T.	1,360

POULTRY

VALUE OF FARM SALES, 1960-61*

BY CENSUS DIVISION

Each dot represents $234,669 or .01% of the total national value of
all agricultural products sold from the farm between June 1, 1960
and May 31, 1961.

Farm sales less than $234,669

Non-agricultural

*Includes hens and chickens, turkeys and other poultry.

VALUE OF FARM SALES

CANADA	$102,339,670
Nfld.	210,300
P.E.I.	455,170
N.S.	2,791,190
N.B.	1,633,220
Que.	21,634,340
Ont.	45,636,080
Man.	7,423,780
Sask.	4,857,530
Alta.	7,837,080
B.C.	9,860,760
Y.T. & N.W.T.	220

Lambert Conformal Conic Projection Standard Parallels 49°N. and 77°N.

THE NATIONAL ATLAS OF CANADA

Scale 1:20,000,000 or One Inch to 315.65 Miles

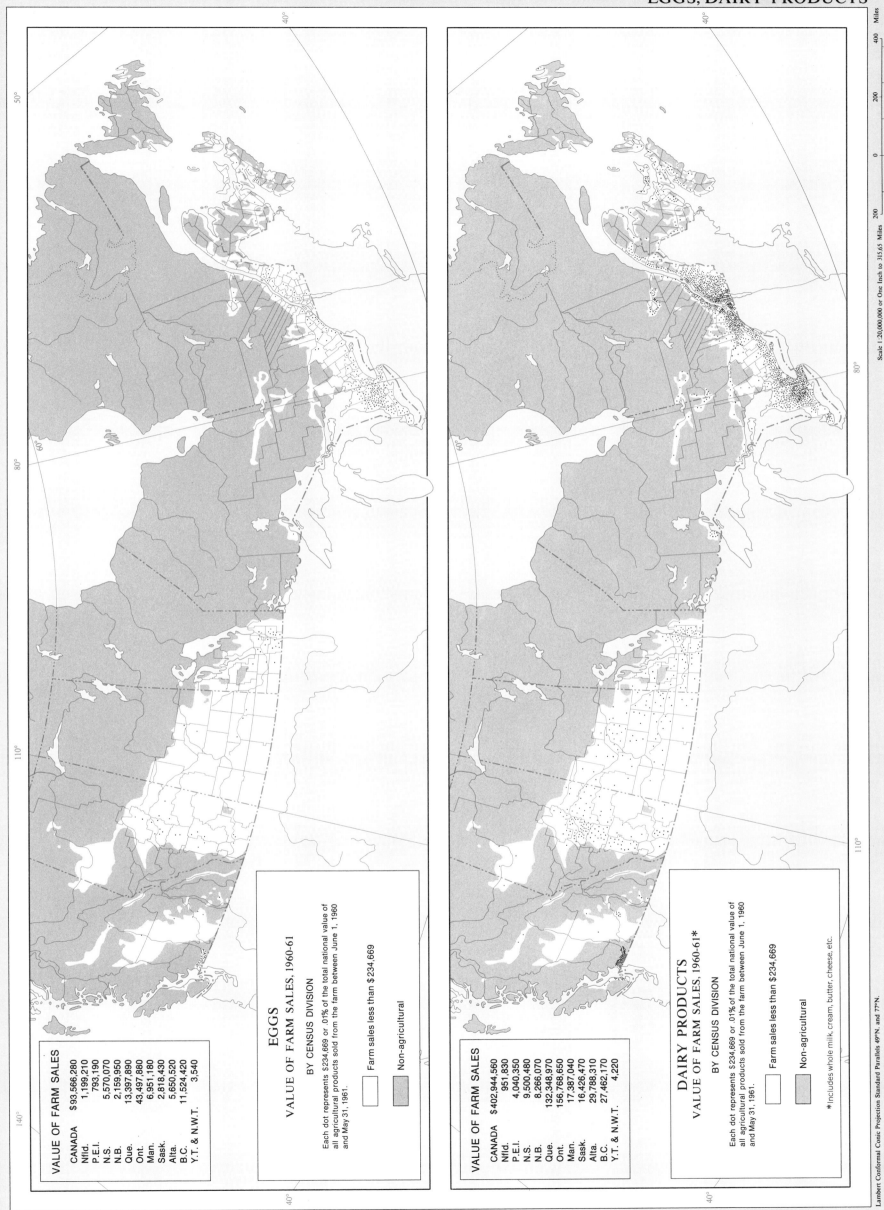

EGGS
VALUE OF FARM SALES, 1960-61
BY CENSUS DIVISION

Each dot represents $234,669 or .01% of the total national value of all agricultural products sold from the farm between June 1, 1960 and May 31, 1961.

Farm sales less than $234,669

Non-agricultural

VALUE OF FARM SALES

CANADA	$93,566,280
Nfld.	1,199,210
P.E.I.	793,190
N.S.	5,570,070
N.B.	2,159,950
Que.	13,397,890
Ont.	43,497,880
Man.	6,951,180
Sask.	2,818,430
Alta.	5,650,520
B.C.	11,524,420
Y.T. & N.W.T.	3,540

DAIRY PRODUCTS
VALUE OF FARM SALES, 1960-61*
BY CENSUS DIVISION

Each dot represents $234,669 or .01% of the total national value of all agricultural products sold from the farm between June 1, 1960 and May 31, 1961.

Farm sales less than $234,669

Non-agricultural

*Includes whole milk, cream, butter, cheese, etc.

VALUE OF FARM SALES

CANADA	$402,944,560
Nfld.	951,830
P.E.I.	4,040,350
N.S.	9,500,480
N.B.	8,266,070
Que.	132,348,970
Ont.	156,768,650
Man.	17,387,040
Sask.	16,426,470
Alta.	29,788,310
B.C.	27,462,170
Y.T. & N.W.T.	4,220

Scale 1:20,000,000 or One Inch to 315.65 Miles

Lambert Conformal Conic Projection Standard Parallels 49°N. and 77°N.

THE NATIONAL ATLAS OF CANADA

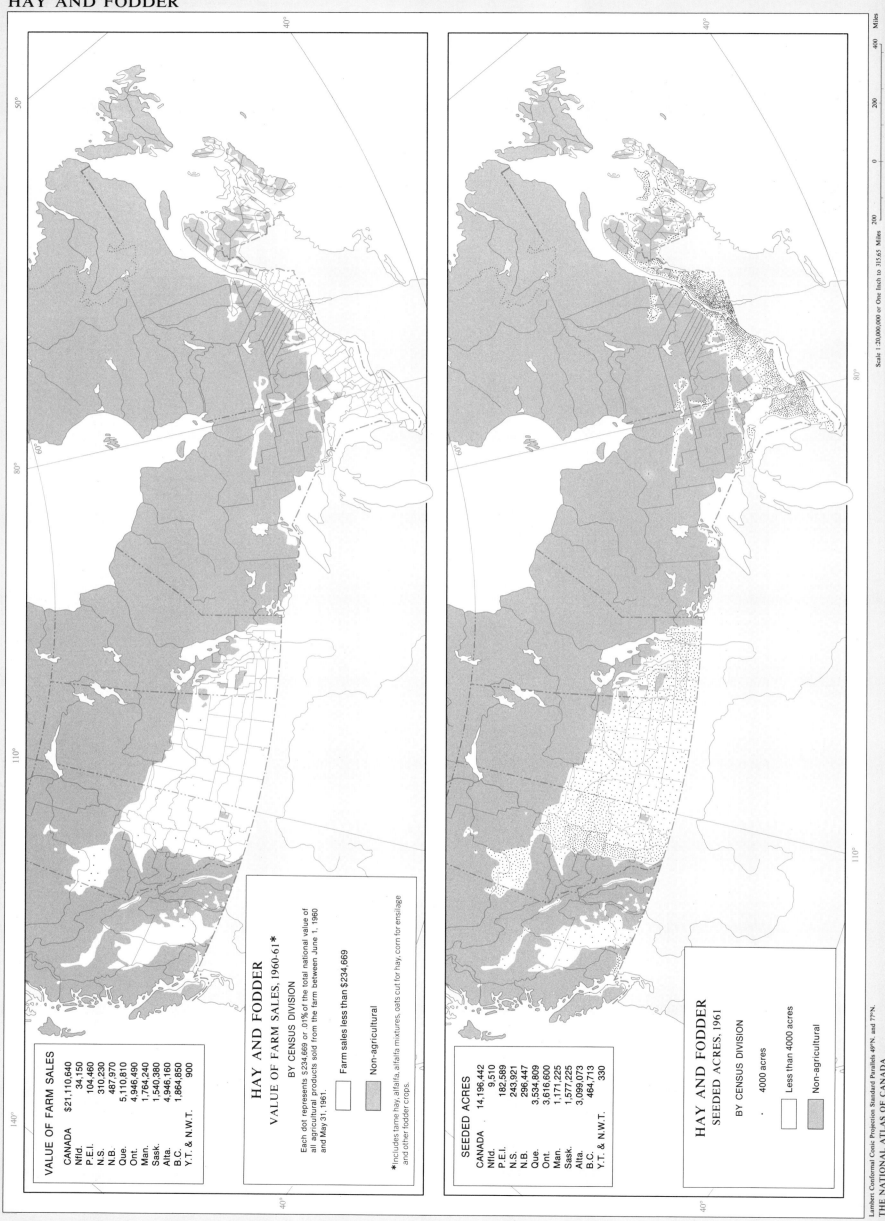

HAY AND FODDER
VALUE OF FARM SALES, 1960-61*
BY CENSUS DIVISION

Each dot represents $234,669 or .01% of the total national value of all agricultural products sold from the farm between June 1, 1960 and May 31, 1961.

☐ Farm sales less than $234,669

▨ Non-agricultural

*Includes tame hay, alfalfa, alfalfa mixtures, oats cut for hay, corn for ensilage and other fodder crops.

VALUE OF FARM SALES	
CANADA	$21,110,640
Nfld.	34,150
P.E.I.	104,460
N.S.	310,230
N.B.	487,970
Que.	5,110,810
Ont.	4,946,490
Man.	1,764,240
Sask.	1,540,380
Alta.	4,946,160
B.C.	1,864,850
Y.T. & N.W.T.	900

HAY AND FODDER
SEEDED ACRES, 1961
BY CENSUS DIVISION

· 4000 acres

☐ Less than 4000 acres

▨ Non-agricultural

SEEDED ACRES	
CANADA	14,196,442
Nfld.	9,510
P.E.I.	182,589
N.S.	243,921
N.B.	296,447
Que.	3,534,809
Ont.	3,616,600
Man.	1,171,225
Sask.	1,577,225
Alta.	3,099,073
B.C.	464,713
Y.T. & N.W.T.	330

Lambert Conformal Conic Projection Standard Parallels 49°N. and 77°N.
Scale 1:20,000,000 or One Inch to 315.65 Miles
THE NATIONAL ATLAS OF CANADA

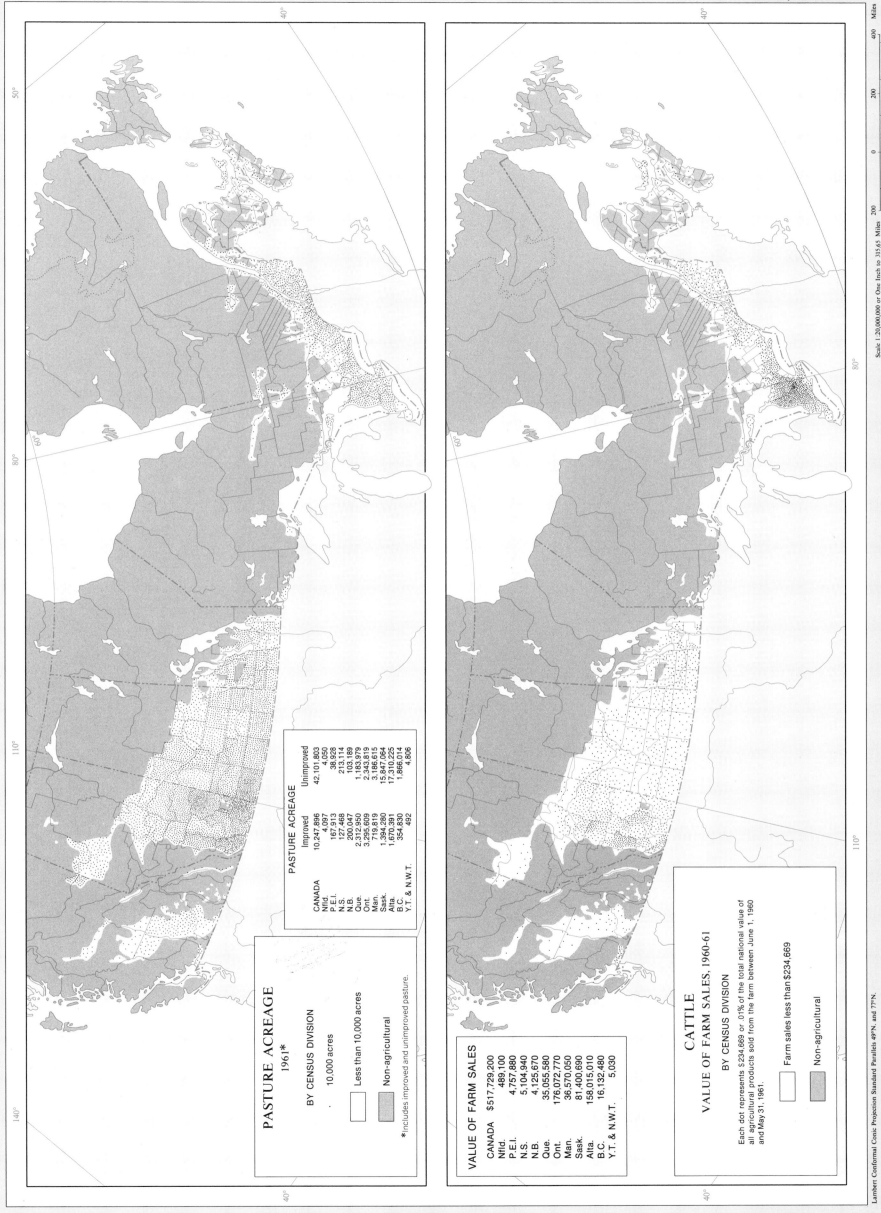

PASTURE ACREAGE
1961*
BY CENSUS DIVISION

· 10,000 acres

	Less than 10,000 acres
	Non-agricultural

*Includes improved and unimproved pasture.

PASTURE ACREAGE

	Improved	Unimproved
CANADA	10,247,896	42,101,803
Nfld.	4,097	4,050
P.E.I.	167,913	38,928
N.S.	127,468	213,114
N.B.	200,047	103,189
Que.	2,312,950	1,183,979
Ont.	3,295,609	2,343,819
Man.	719,819	3,186,615
Sask.	1,394,280	15,847,064
Alta.	1,670,391	17,310,225
B.C.	354,830	1,866,014
Y.T. & N.W.T.	492	4,806

CATTLE
VALUE OF FARM SALES, 1960-61
BY CENSUS DIVISION

Each dot represents $234,669 or .01% of the total national value of all agricultural products sold from the farm between June 1, 1960 and May 31, 1961.

	Farm sales less than $234,669
	Non-agricultural

VALUE OF FARM SALES

CANADA	$517,729,200
Nfld.	489,100
P.E.I.	4,757,880
N.S.	5,104,940
N.B.	4,125,670
Que.	35,055,580
Ont.	176,072,770
Man.	36,570,050
Sask.	81,400,690
Alta.	158,015,010
B.C.	16,132,480
Y.T. & N.W.T.	5,030

Scale 1:20,000,000 or One Inch to 315.65 Miles

Lambert Conformal Conic Projection Standard Parallels 49°N. and 77°N.
THE NATIONAL ATLAS OF CANADA

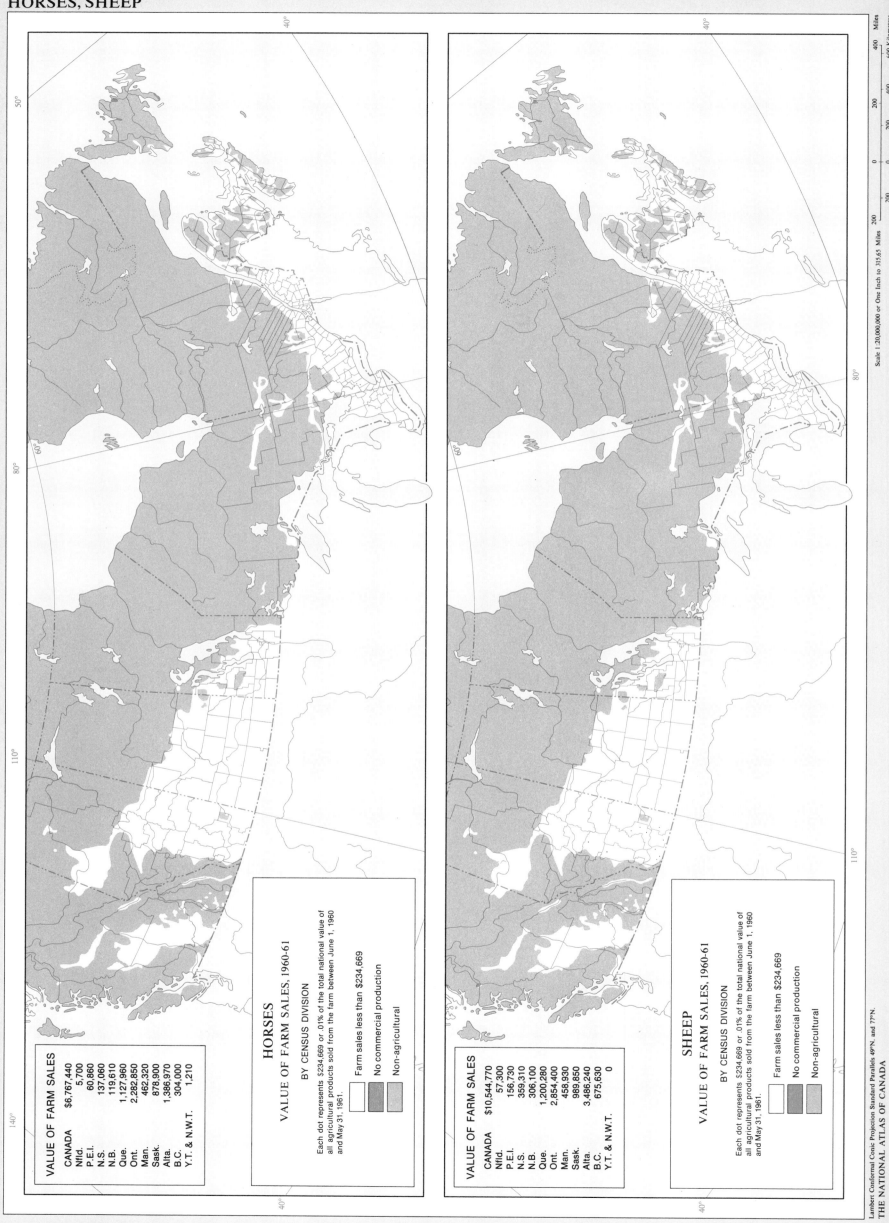

VALUE OF FARM SALES

CANADA	$6,767,440
Nfld.	5,700
P.E.I.	60,860
N.S.	137,060
N.B.	119,610
Que.	1,127,960
Ont.	2,282,850
Man.	462,320
Sask.	878,900
Alta.	1,386,970
B.C.	304,000
Y.T. & N.W.T.	1,210

HORSES
VALUE OF FARM SALES, 1960-61
BY CENSUS DIVISION

Each dot represents $234,669 or .01% of the total national value of
all agricultural products sold from the farm between June 1, 1960
and May 31, 1961.

Farm sales less than $234,669

No commercial production

Non-agricultural

VALUE OF FARM SALES

CANADA	$10,544,770
Nfld.	57,300
P.E.I.	156,730
N.S.	359,310
N.B.	306,100
Que.	1,200,280
Ont.	2,854,400
Man.	458,930
Sask.	989,850
Alta.	3,486,240
B.C.	675,630
Y.T. & N.W.T.	0

SHEEP
VALUE OF FARM SALES, 1960-61
BY CENSUS DIVISION

Each dot represents $234,669 or .01% of the total national value of
all agricultural products sold from the farm between June 1, 1960
and May 31, 1961.

Farm sales less than $234,669

No commercial production

Non-agricultural

Lambert Conformal Conic Projection Standard Parallels 49°N. and 77°N.

Scale 1:20,000,000 or One Inch to 315.65 Miles

THE NATIONAL ATLAS OF CANADA

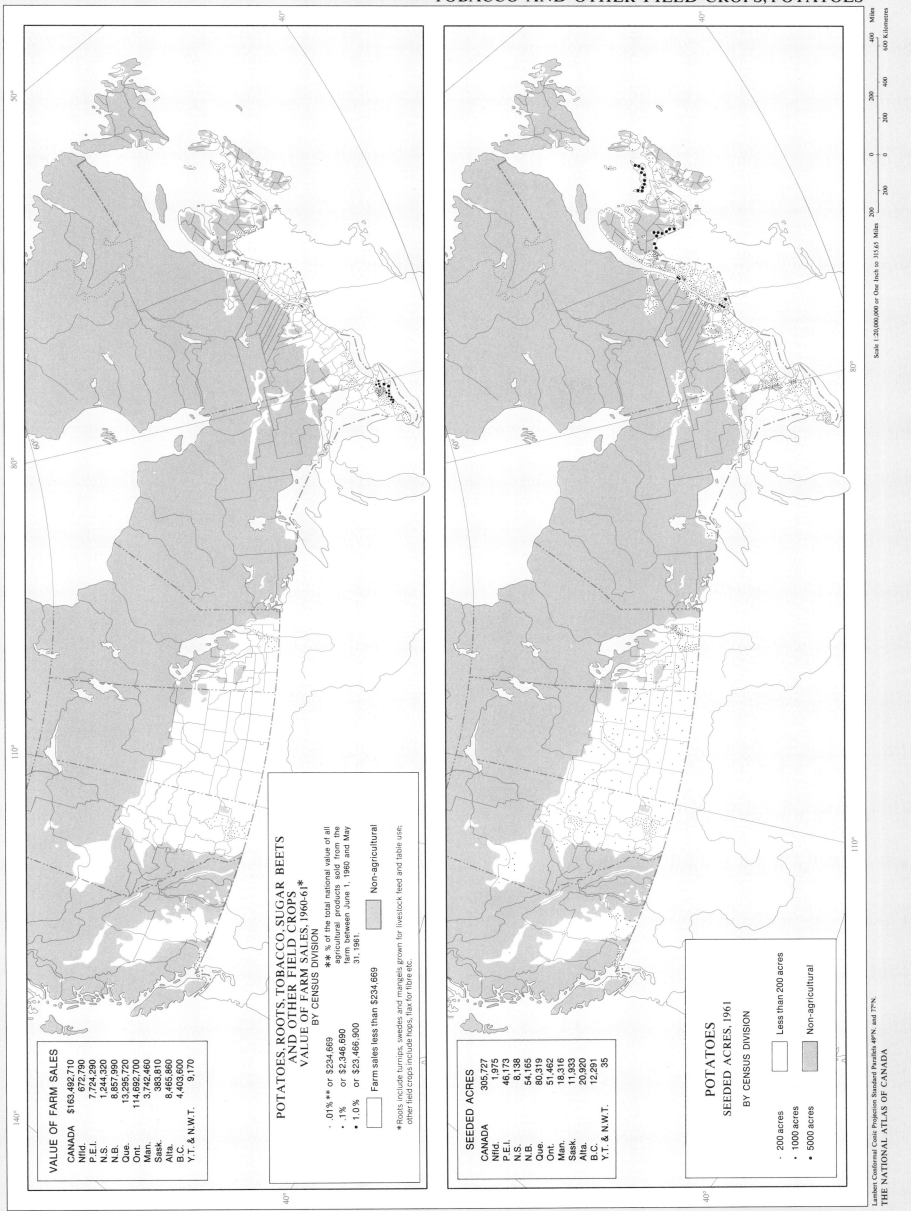

Scale 1:20,000,000 or One Inch to 315.65 Miles

Lambert Conformal Conic Projection Standard Parallels 49°N. and 77°N.
THE NATIONAL ATLAS OF CANADA

VALUE OF FARM SALES	
CANADA	$163,492,710
Nfld.	672,790
P.E.I.	7,724,290
N.S.	1,244,320
N.B.	8,857,990
Que.	13,295,720
Ont.	114,692,700
Man.	3,742,460
Sask.	383,810
Alta.	8,465,860
B.C.	4,403,600
Y.T. & N.W.T.	9,170

POTATOES, ROOTS, TOBACCO, SUGAR BEETS
AND OTHER FIELD CROPS*
VALUE OF FARM SALES, 1960-61*
BY CENSUS DIVISION

· .01%** or $234,669
· .1% or $2,346,690
● 1.0% or $23,466,900

** % of the total national value of all
agricultural products sold from the
farm between June 1, 1960 and May
31, 1961.

Non-agricultural

Farm sales less than $234,669

* Roots include turnips, swedes and mangels grown for livestock feed and table use;
other field crops include hops, flax for fibre etc.

SEEDED ACRES	
CANADA	305,727
Nfld.	1,975
P.E.I.	46,173
N.S.	8,138
N.B.	54,165
Que.	80,319
Ont.	51,462
Man.	18,316
Sask.	11,933
Alta.	20,920
B.C.	12,291
Y.T. & N.W.T.	35

POTATOES
SEEDED ACRES, 1961
BY CENSUS DIVISION

· 200 acres
· 1000 acres
● 5000 acres

Less than 200 acres

Non-agricultural

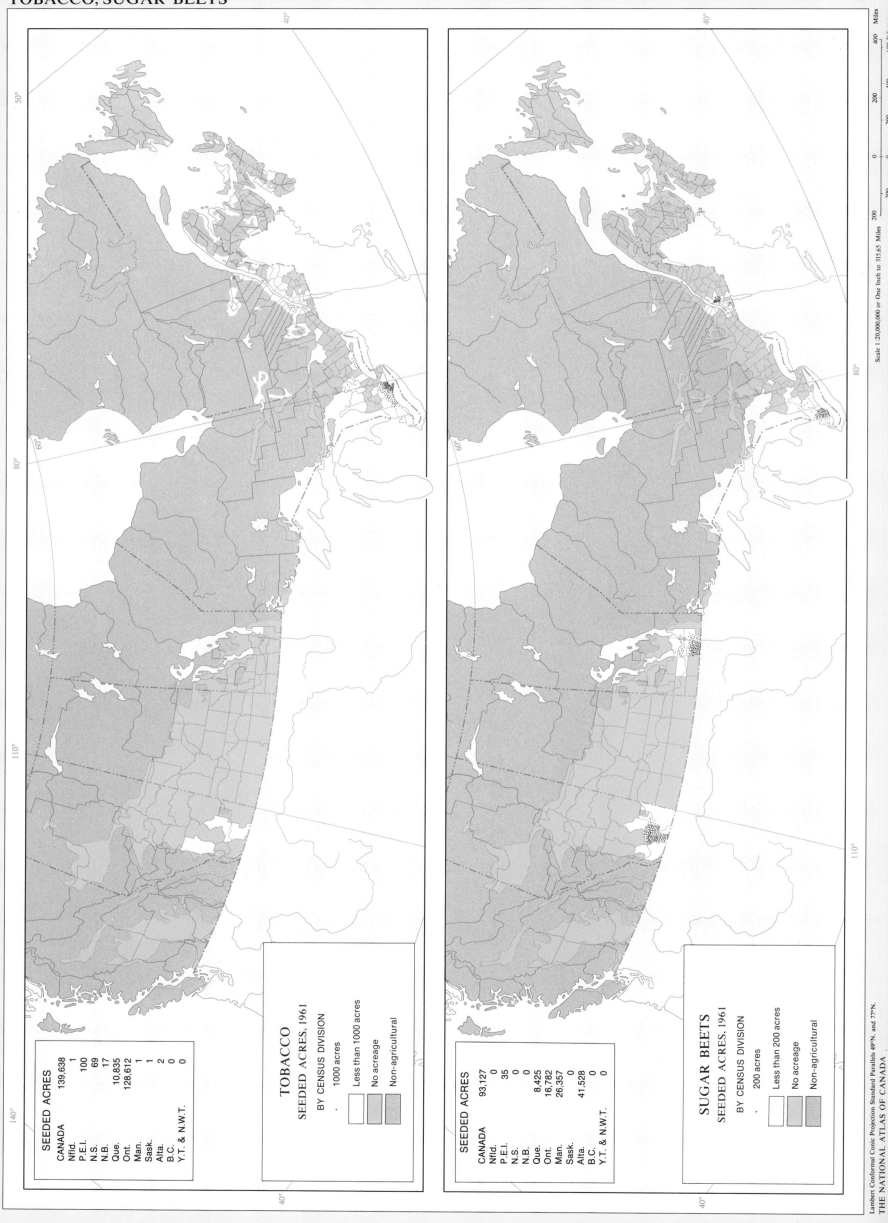

SEEDED ACRES

CANADA	139,638
Nfld.	1
P.E.I.	100
N.S.	69
N.B.	17
Que.	10,835
Ont.	128,612
Man.	1
Sask.	2
Alta.	0
B.C.	0
Y.T. & N.W.T.	0

TOBACCO
SEEDED ACRES, 1961
BY CENSUS DIVISION

- 1000 acres
- Less than 1000 acres
- No acreage
- Non-agricultural

SEEDED ACRES

CANADA	93,127
Nfld.	0
P.E.I.	35
N.S.	0
N.B.	0
Que.	8,425
Ont.	16,782
Man.	26,357
Sask.	0
Alta.	41,528
B.C.	0
Y.T. & N.W.T.	0

SUGAR BEETS
SEEDED ACRES, 1961
BY CENSUS DIVISION

- 200 acres
- Less than 200 acres
- No acreage
- Non-agricultural

Lambert Conformal Conic Projection Standard Parallels 49°N. and 77°N.
THE NATIONAL ATLAS OF CANADA
Scale 1:20,000,000 or One Inch to 315.65 Miles

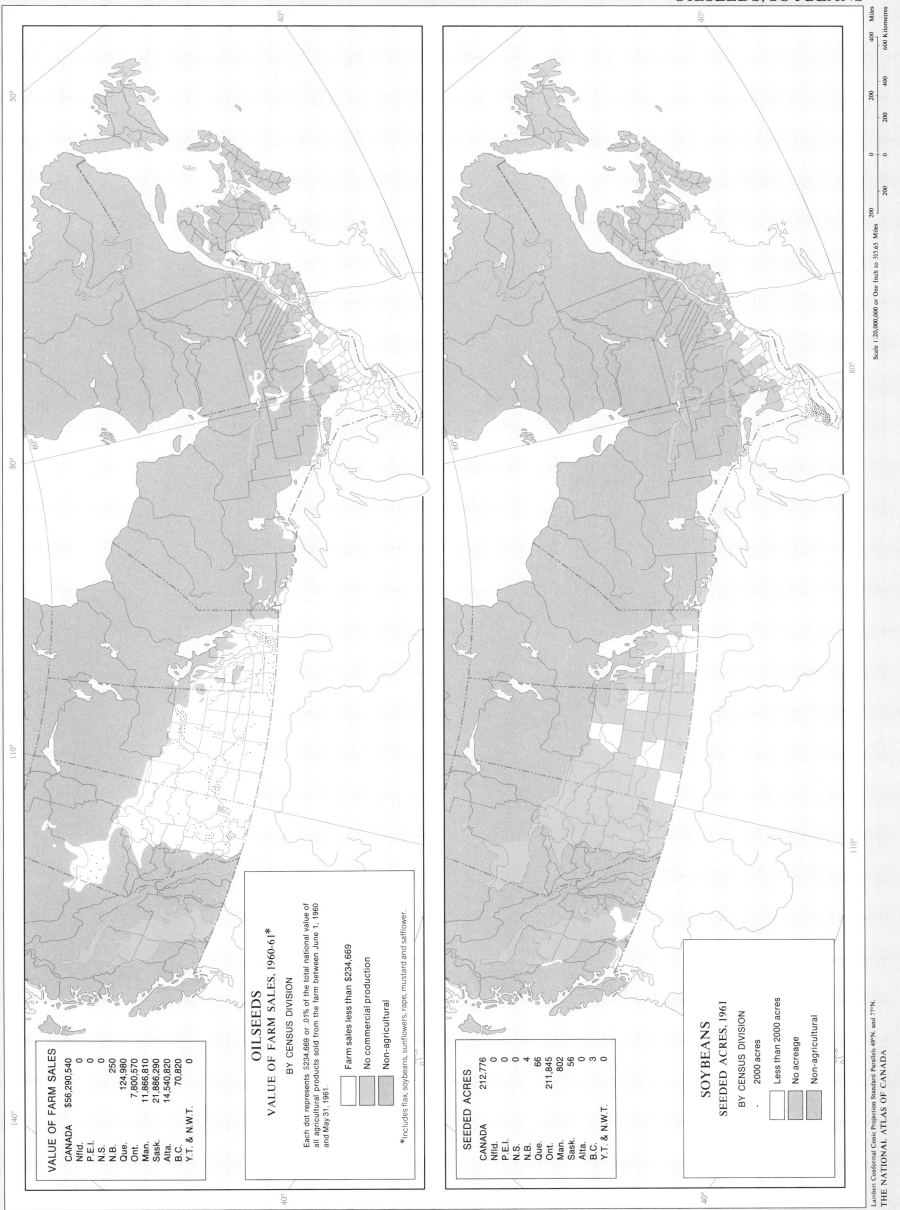

OILSEEDS

VALUE OF FARM SALES, 1960-61*

BY CENSUS DIVISION

Each dot represents $234,669 or .01% of the total national value of all agricultural products sold from the farm between June 1, 1960 and May 31, 1961.

| Farm sales less than $234,669 |
| No commercial production |
| Non-agricultural |

*Includes flax, soybeans, sunflowers, rape, mustard and safflower.

VALUE OF FARM SALES	
CANADA	$56,290,540
Nfld.	0
P.E.I.	0
N.S.	0
N.B.	250
Que.	124,980
Ont.	7,800,570
Man.	11,866,810
Sask.	21,886,290
Alta.	14,540,820
B.C.	70,820
Y.T. & N.W.T.	0

SOYBEANS

SEEDED ACRES, 1961

BY CENSUS DIVISION

| . | 2000 acres |
| Less than 2000 acres |
| No acreage |
| Non-agricultural |

SEEDED ACRES	
CANADA	212,776
Nfld.	0
P.E.I.	0
N.S.	0
N.B.	4
Que.	66
Ont.	211,845
Man.	802
Sask.	56
Alta.	0
B.C.	3
Y.T. & N.W.T.	0

Scale 1:20,000,000 or One Inch to 315.65 Miles

Lambert Conformal Conic Projection Standard Parallels 49°N. and 77°N.

FLAXSEED, FRUITS AND VEGETABLES

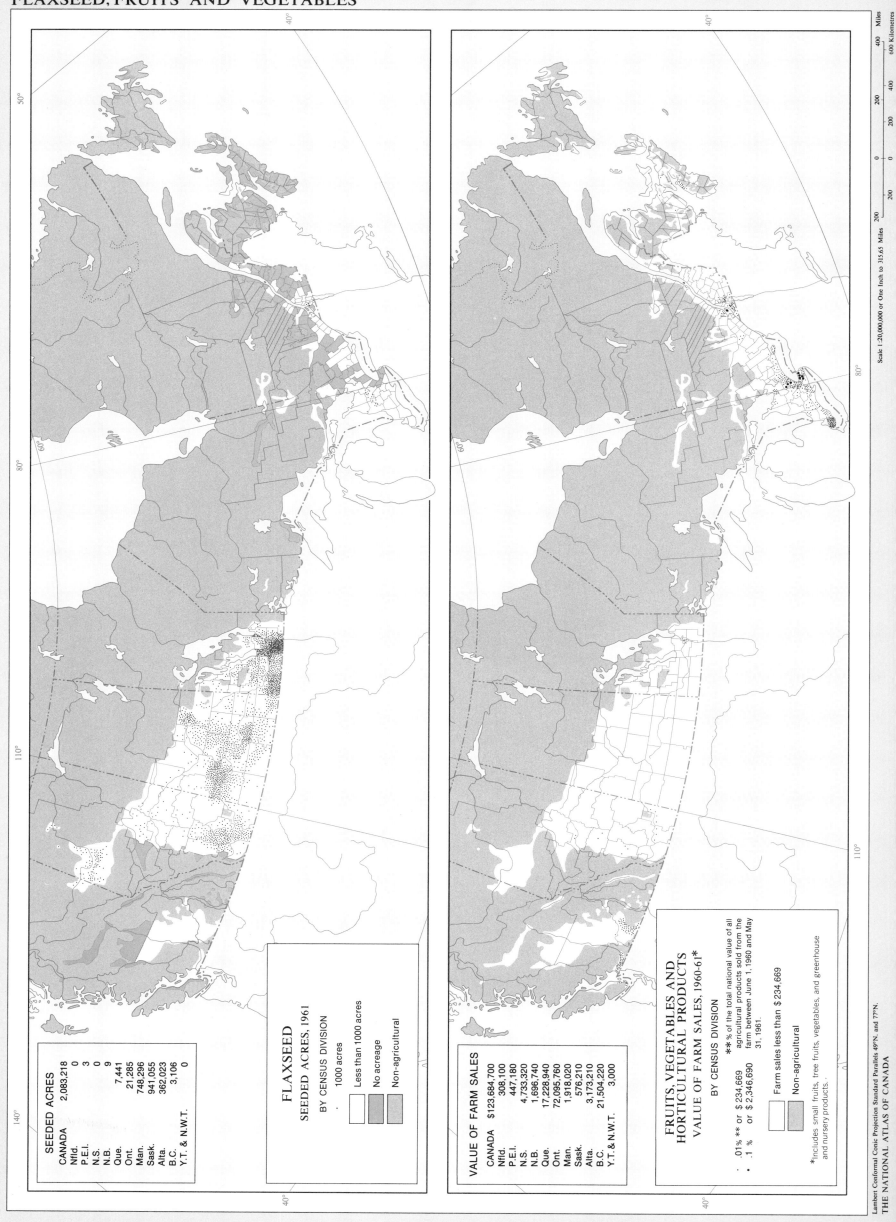

SEEDED ACRES

CANADA	2,083,218
Nfld.	0
P.E.I.	0
N.S.	3
N.B.	0
Que.	9
Ont.	7,441
Man.	21,285
Sask.	748,296
Alta.	941,055
B.C.	362,023
Y.T. & N.W.T.	3,106
	0

FLAXSEED
SEEDED ACRES, 1961

BY CENSUS DIVISION

. 1000 acres

Less than 1000 acres

No acreage

Non-agricultural

VALUE OF FARM SALES

CANADA	$123,684,700
Nfld.	308,100
P.E.I.	447,180
N.S.	4,733,320
N.B.	1,696,740
Que.	17,228,940
Ont.	72,095,760
Man.	1,918,020
Sask.	576,210
Alta.	3,173,210
B.C.	21,504,220
Y.T. & N.W.T.	3,000

FRUITS, VEGETABLES AND HORTICULTURAL PRODUCTS
VALUE OF FARM SALES, 1960-61*

BY CENSUS DIVISION

** % of the total national value of all agricultural products sold from the farm between June 1, 1960 and May 31, 1961.

. .01 % ** or $ 234,669

• .1 % or $ 2,346,690

Farm sales less than $ 234,669

Non-agricultural

*Includes small fruits, tree fruits, vegetables, and greenhouse and nursery products.

Lambert Conformal Conic Projection Standard Parallels 49°N. and 77°N.

Scale 1:20,000,000 or One Inch to 315.65 Miles

THE NATIONAL ATLAS OF CANADA

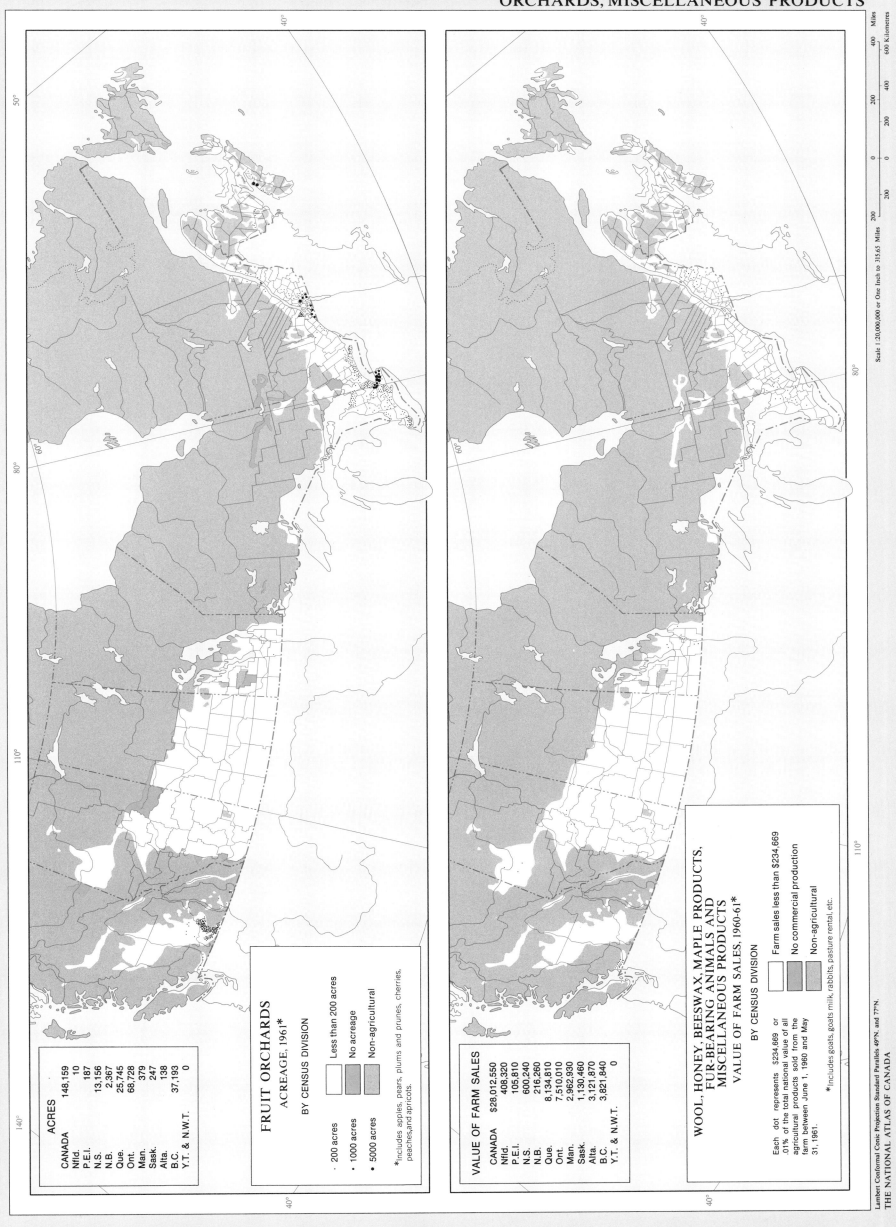

FRUIT ORCHARDS

ACREAGE, 1961*

BY CENSUS DIVISION

ACRES

CANADA	148,159
Nfld.	10
P.E.I.	187
N.S.	13,156
N.B.	2,367
Que.	25,745
Ont.	68,728
Man.	379
Sask.	247
Alta.	138
B.C.	37,193
Y.T. & N.W.T.	0

☐ Less than 200 acres
▨ No acreage
▨ Non-agricultural

· 200 acres
• 1000 acres
● 5000 acres

*Includes apples, pears, plums and prunes, cherries, peaches, and apricots.

WOOL, HONEY, BEESWAX, MAPLE PRODUCTS, FUR-BEARING ANIMALS AND MISCELLANEOUS PRODUCTS

VALUE OF FARM SALES, 1960-61*

BY CENSUS DIVISION

VALUE OF FARM SALES

CANADA	$28,012,550
Nfld.	408,320
P.E.I.	105,810
N.S.	600,240
N.B.	216,260
Que.	8,134,810
Ont.	7,510,010
Man.	2,962,930
Sask.	1,130,460
Alta.	3,121,870
B.C.	3,821,840
Y.T. & N.W.T.	0

☐ Farm sales less than $234,669
▨ No commercial production
▨ Non-agricultural

Each dot represents $234,669 or .01% of the total national value of all agricultural products sold from the farm between June 1, 1960 and May 31, 1961.

*Includes goats, goats milk, rabbits, pasture rental, etc.

Lambert Conformal Conic Projection Standard Parallels 49°N, and 77°N.

Scale 1:20,000,000 or One Inch to 315.65 Miles

THE NATIONAL ATLAS OF CANADA

VALUE OF FARM SALES

CANADA	$18,878,880
Nfld.	47,870
P.E.I.	215,320
N.S.	2,159,620
N.B.	1,638,500
Que.	9,357,590
Ont.	3,884,090
Man.	147,560
Sask.	100,480
Alta.	224,370
B.C.	1,103,480
Y.T. & N.W.T.	0

FOREST PRODUCTS

VALUE OF FARM SALES, 1960-61
BY CENSUS DIVISION

Each dot represents $234,669 or .01% of the total national value of all agricultural products sold from the farm between June 1, 1960 and May 31, 1961.

- Farm sales less than $234,669
- No commercial production
- Non-agricultural

OTHER RECEIPTS

CANADA	$31,815,020
Nfld.	4,250
P.E.I.	7,340
N.S.	5,980
N.B.	1,780
Que.	80,000
Ont.	209,920
Man.	4,034,150
Sask.	16,793,140
Alta.	10,514,310
B.C.	164,150
Y.T. & N.W.T.	0

OTHER RECEIPTS, 1960-61*

BY CENSUS DIVISION

Each dot represents $234,669 or .01% of the total national value of all agricultural products sold from the farm between June 1, 1960 and May 31, 1961.

- Farm sales less than $234,669
- No commercial production
- Non-agricultural

*Includes Prairie Farm Assistance Act payments, Government acreage payments, crop insurance and other similar receipts.

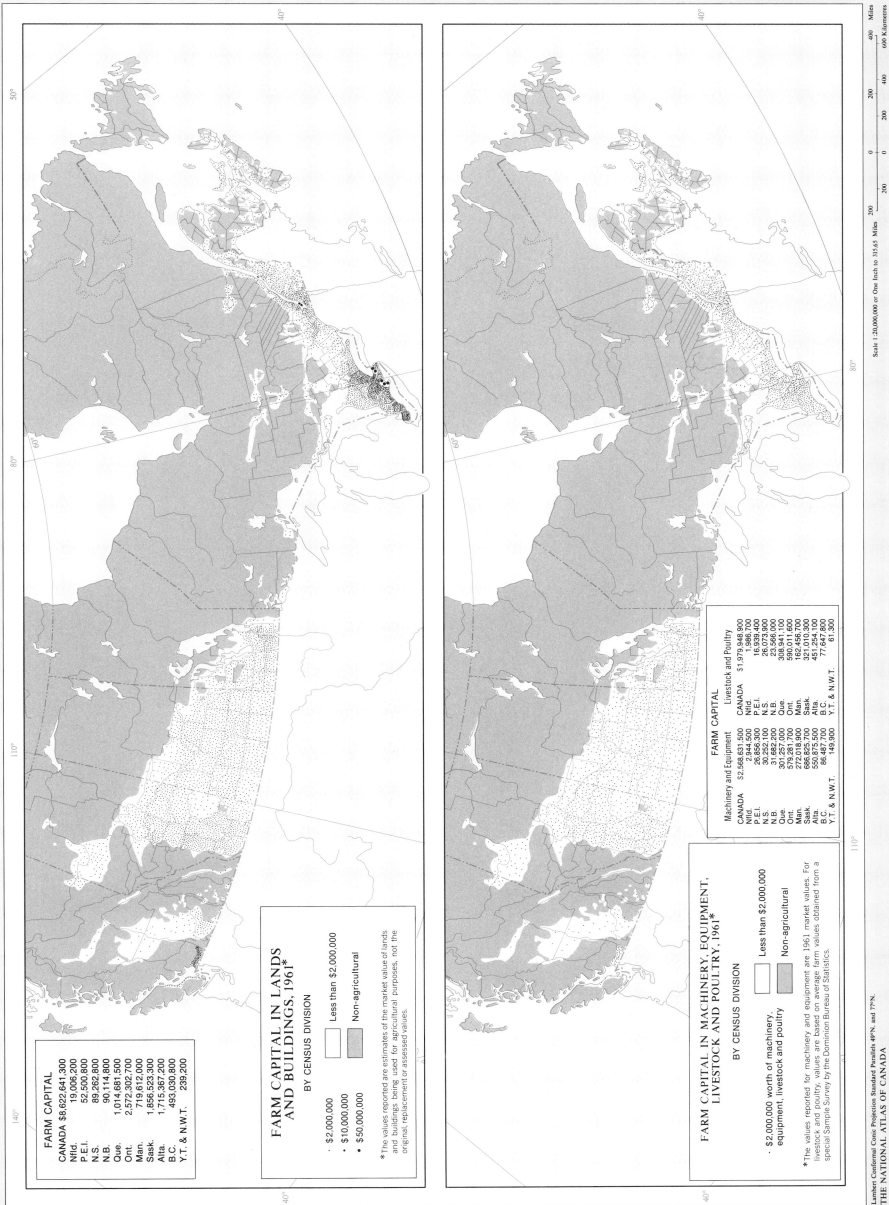

FARM CAPITAL

CANADA	$8,622,641,300
Nfld.	19,006,200
P.E.I.	52,500,800
N.S.	89,262,800
N.B.	90,114,800
Que.	1,014,681,500
Ont.	2,572,302,700
Man.	719,612,000
Sask.	1,856,523,300
Alta.	1,715,367,200
B.C.	493,030,800
Y.T. & N.W.T.	239,200

FARM CAPITAL IN LANDS
AND BUILDINGS, 1961*

BY CENSUS DIVISION

· $2,000,000
· $10,000,000
● $50,000,000

☐ Less than $2,000,000
▨ Non-agricultural

*The values reported are estimates of the market value of lands
and buildings being used for agricultural purposes, not the
original, replacement or assessed values.

FARM CAPITAL

	Machinery and Equipment	Livestock and Poultry
CANADA	$2,568,631,500	$1,979,948,900
Nfld.	2,944,500	1,986,700
P.E.I.	26,856,300	16,939,400
N.S.	30,252,100	26,073,900
N.B.	31,682,200	23,566,000
Que.	301,257,000	308,941,100
Ont.	579,281,700	590,011,600
Man.	272,018,900	162,456,700
Sask.	686,825,700	321,010,300
Alta.	550,875,500	451,254,100
B.C.	86,487,700	77,647,800
Y.T. & N.W.T.	149,900	61,300

FARM CAPITAL IN MACHINERY, EQUIPMENT,
LIVESTOCK AND POULTRY, 1961*

BY CENSUS DIVISION

· $2,000,000 worth of machinery,
equipment, livestock and poultry

☐ Less than $2,000,000
▨ Non-agricultural

*The values reported for machinery and equipment are 1961 market values. For
livestock and poultry, values are based on average farm values obtained from a
special Sample Survey by the Dominion Bureau of Statistics.

Scale 1:20,000,000 or One Inch to 315.65 Miles

Lambert Conformal Conic Projection Standard Parallels 49°N. and 77°N.
THE NATIONAL ATLAS OF CANADA

FORESTRY AND LOGGING – SELECTED CHARACTERISTICS

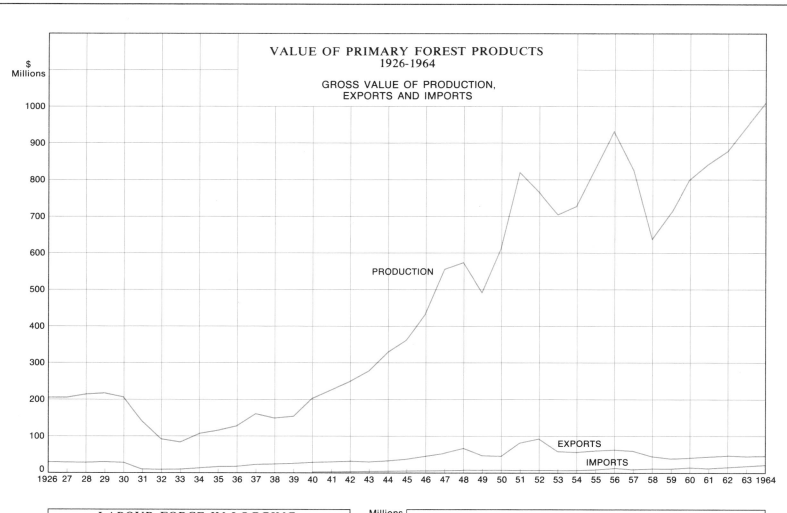

VALUE OF PRIMARY FOREST PRODUCTS
1926-1964

GROSS VALUE OF PRODUCTION,
EXPORTS AND IMPORTS

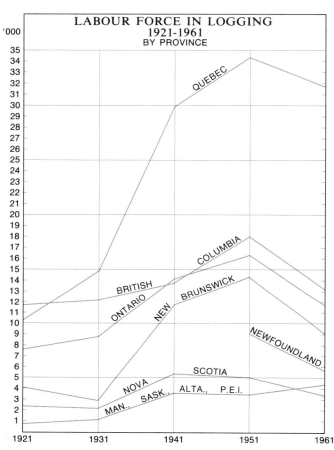

LABOUR FORCE IN LOGGING
1921-1961
BY PROVINCE

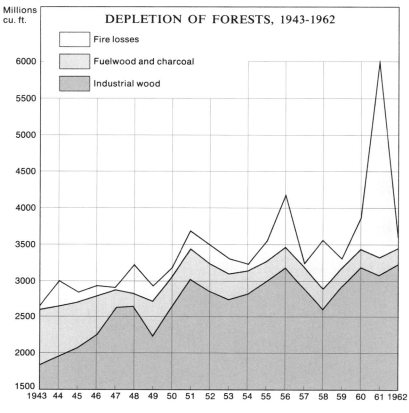

DEPLETION OF FORESTS, 1943-1962

- Fire losses
- Fuelwood and charcoal
- Industrial wood

EXPORTS AND IMPORTS OF PRIMARY FOREST PRODUCTS, 1961

PRODUCTS	EXPORTS		IMPORTS	
	Volume in merchantable timber '000 cu. ft.	Total value $'000	Volume in merchantable timber '000 cu. ft.	Total value $'000
Logs and bolts	17,752	6,198	31,303	8,997
Pulpwood	97,875	27,157	17,572	3,563
Fuelwood	184	36	–	–
Poles and piling	6,597	5,616	772	1,363
Fence posts	3,214	597	–	–
Other products	–	5,830	–	82
Round mining timber	1,553	558	–	–
Total	127,175	45,992	49,647	14,005

CONSUMPTION OF FOREST PRODUCTS 1961

PRODUCTS	Volume in merchantable timber '000 cu. ft.	Total value $'000
Logs and bolts	1,698,542	406,815
Pulpwood	1,227,184	365,330
Fuelwood	239,323	37,709
Poles and piling	18,997	17,806
Round mining timber	5,025	935
Fence posts	9,330	3,238
Hewn ties	136	38
Fence rails	769	301
Wood for charcoal	3,100	533
Miscellaneous roundwood	15,527	6,536
Other products	–	1,468
Total	3,217,933	840,709

VALUE AND VOLUME OF FOREST PRODUCTS, 1961

INDEX OF PRODUCTS

A	Hewn ties	**G**	Other products
B	Fence rails	**H**	Poles and piling
C	Wood for charcoal	**I**	Fuelwood
D	Round mining timber	**J**	Pulpwood
E	Fence posts	**K**	Logs and bolts
F	Miscellaneous roundwood		

Each bar in a graph represents the value of the indexed product expressed as a percentage of the total value for the named territorial unit.

CANADA — Value in $'000: 846,035 — % of national value: 100.00

Index	% of territorial value	Volume in '000 cu. ft.
A	.004	136
B	.03	770
C	.06	3,100
D	.17	6,578
E	.40	12,545
F	.77	15,527
G	.81	*
H	2.03	24,820
I	4.28	239,508
J	43.69	1,315,314
K	47.75	1,684,991

BRITISH COLUMBIA — Value in $'000: 331,174 — % of national value: 39.47

Index	% of territorial value	Volume in '000 cu. ft.
A	.01	136
B	.01	77
C	*	*
D	.02	476
E	.13	1,277
F	.37	2,803
G	.55	*
H	4.07	17,985
I	.15	2,720
J	12.28	191,648
K	82.41	1,077,916

QUEBEC — Value in $'000: 239,529 — % of national value: 28.31

Index	% of territorial value	Volume in '000 cu. ft.
A	*	*
B	.01	45
C	.19	2,900
D	.22	2,592
E	.33	3,528
F	.01	40
G	.52	*
H	.56	2,307
I	8.00	104,000
J	69.04	574,906
K	21.12	223,778

ONTARIO — Value in $'000: 148,434 — % of national value: 17.55

Index	% of territorial value	Volume in '000 cu. ft.
A	*	*
B	.02	57
C	.02	200
D	.13	637
E	.44	1,743
F	.18	641
G	.81	*
H	.65	1,735
I	3.33	38,000
J	68.55	305,915
K	25.87	145,120

NEW BRUNSWICK — Value in $'000: 44,097 — % of national value: 5.21

Index	% of territorial value	Volume in '000 cu. ft.
A	*	*
B	.002	2
C	*	*
D	.77	1,561
E	.05	92
F	.01	59
G	1.72	*
H	.96	795
I	3.84	15,059
J	54.83	95,670
K	37.81	80,108

NEWFOUNDLAND — Value in $'000: 25,961 — % of national value: 3.07

Index	% of territorial value	Volume in '000 cu. ft.
A	*	*
B	.04	45
C	*	*
D	.08	123
E	.04	62
F	*	*
G	.15	*
H	.15	75
I	9.36	19,440
J	83.61	69,757
K	6.56	8,512

ALBERTA — % of national value: 2.64 — Value in $'000: 22,362

Index	Volume in '000 cu. ft.	% of territorial value
A	*	*
B	175	.29
C	*	*
D	34	.03
E	1,470	1.37
F	10,479	21.09
G	*	.60
H	139	.19
I	7,951	4.11
J	25,470	24.39
K	72,672	47.93

NOVA SCOTIA — % of national value: 2.34 — Value in $'000: 19,777

Index	Volume in '000 cu. ft.	% of territorial value
A	*	*
B	151	.27
C	*	*
D	664	.95
E	660	.83
F	95	.05
G	*	7.70
H	69	.17
I	13,972	9.71
J	33,730	35.37
K	47,406	44.95

SASKATCHEWAN — % of national value: 0.78 — Value in $'000: 6,580

Index	Volume in '000 cu. ft.	% of territorial value
A	*	*
B	200	.76
C	*	*
D	*	*
E	2,370	10.50
F	759	2.57
G	*	.96
H	1,175	8.04
I	19,105	34.48
J	2,689	6.98
K	17,738	35.71

MANITOBA — % of national value: 0.74 — Value in $'000: 6,264

Index	Volume in '000 cu. ft.	% of territorial value
A	*	*
B	15	.10
C	*	*
D	488	1.47
E	1,240	4.45
F	559	1.02
G	*	.65
H	435	3.93
I	12,904	24.46
J	13,339	42.59
K	8,622	21.33

PRINCE EDWARD ISLAND — % of national value: 0.19 — Value in $'000: 1,637

Index	Volume in '000 cu. ft.	% of territorial value
A	*	*
B	3	.06
C	*	*
D	3	.06
E	103	1.83
F	92	1.71
G	*	.98
H	*	*
I	5,793	48.69
J	2,190	26.76
K	1,973	19.91

YUKON AND NORTHWEST TERRITORIES — % of national value: 0.03 — Value in $'000: 220

Index	Volume in '000 cu. ft.	% of territorial value
A	*	*
B	*	*
C	*	*
D	*	*
E	*	*
F	*	*
G	*	*
H	105	15.91
I	564	31.82
J	*	*
K	1,146	52.27

* No data

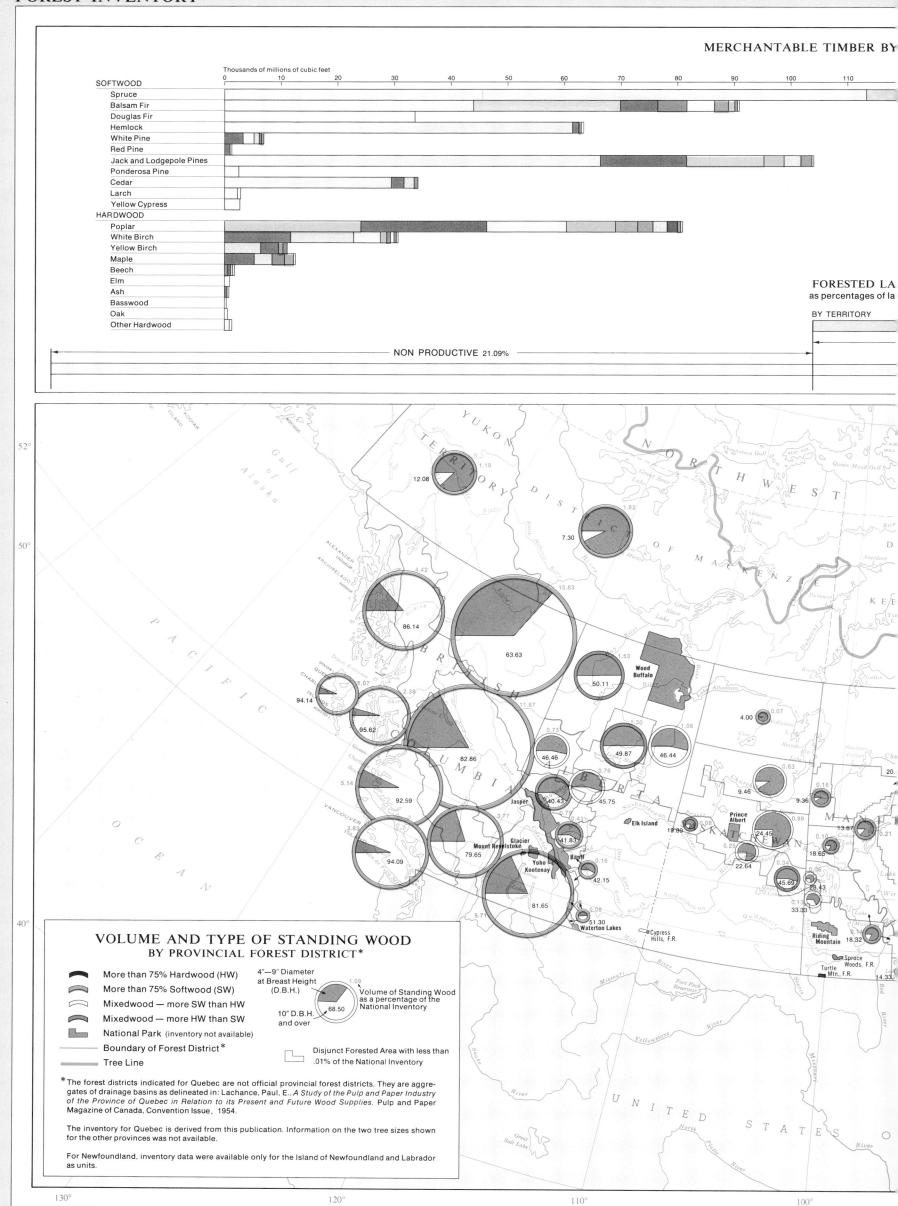

MERCHANTABLE TIMBER BY

Thousands of millions of cubic feet

	0	10	20	30	40	50	60	70	80	90	100	110

SOFTWOOD
Spruce
Balsam Fir
Douglas Fir
Hemlock
White Pine
Red Pine
Jack and Lodgepole Pines
Ponderosa Pine
Cedar
Larch
Yellow Cypress
HARDWOOD
Poplar
White Birch
Yellow Birch
Maple
Beech
Elm
Ash
Basswood
Oak
Other Hardwood

NON PRODUCTIVE 21.09%

FORESTED LA
as percentages of la

BY TERRITORY

VOLUME AND TYPE OF STANDING WOOD
BY PROVINCIAL FOREST DISTRICT*

More than 75% Hardwood (HW)
More than 75% Softwood (SW)
Mixedwood — more SW than HW
Mixedwood — more HW than SW
National Park (inventory not available)
Boundary of Forest District *
Tree Line

4"–9" Diameter
at Breast Height
(D.B.H.)

10" D.B.H.
and over

Volume of Standing Wood
as a percentage of the
National Inventory

Disjunct Forested Area with less than
.01% of the National Inventory

*The forest districts indicated for Quebec are not official provincial forest districts. They are aggregates of drainage basins as delineated in: Lachance, Paul, E.. *A Study of the Pulp and Paper Industry of the Province of Quebec in Relation to its Present and Future Wood Supplies.* Pulp and Paper Magazine of Canada, Convention Issue, 1954.

The inventory for Quebec is derived from this publication. Information on the two tree sizes shown for the other provinces was not available.

For Newfoundland, inventory data were available only for the Island of Newfoundland and Labrador as units.

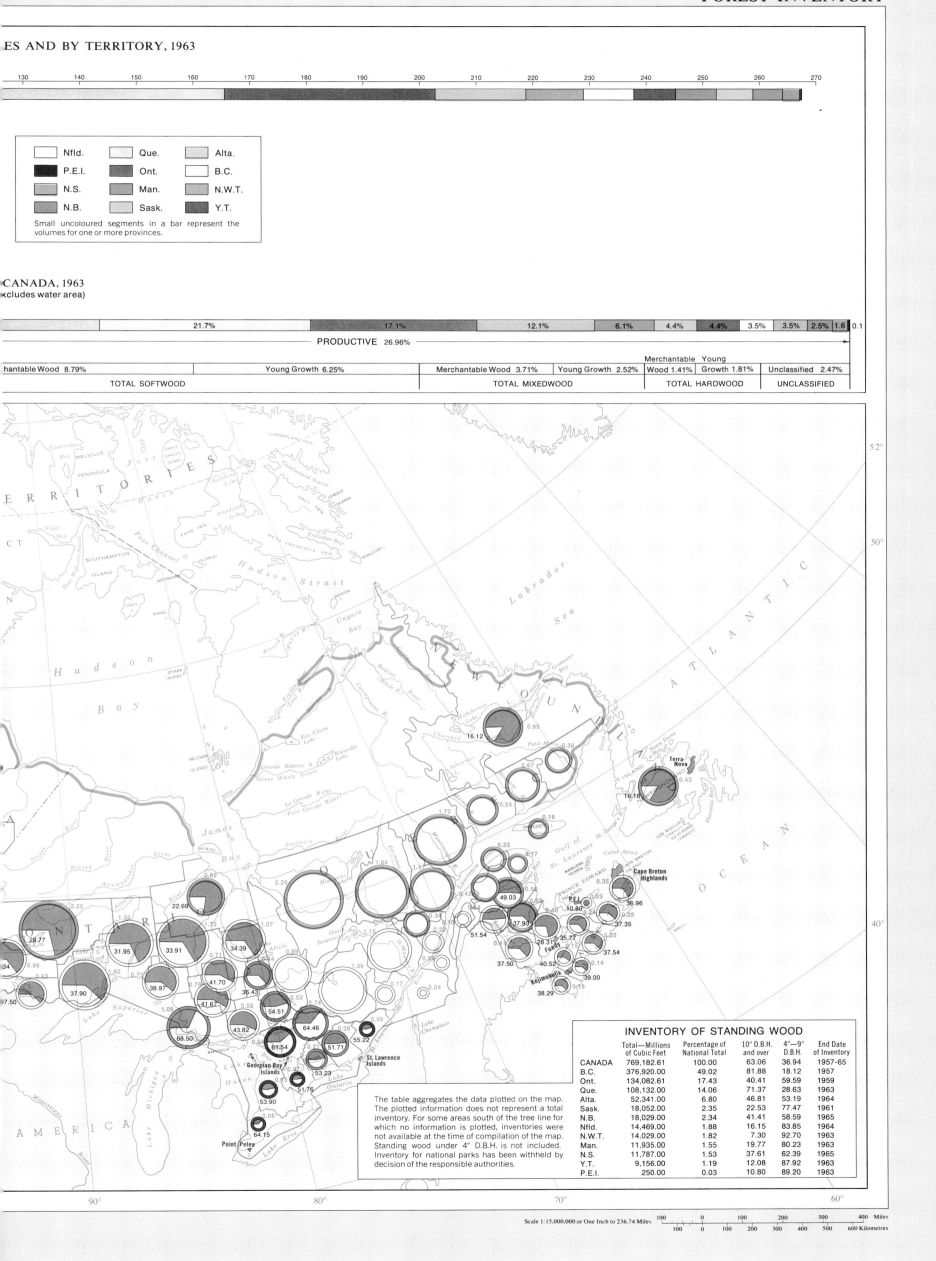

ES AND BY TERRITORY, 1963

| 130 | 140 | 150 | 160 | 170 | 180 | 190 | 200 | 210 | 220 | 230 | 240 | 250 | 260 | 270 |

Nfld.	Que.	Alta.
P.E.I.	Ont.	B.C.
N.S.	Man.	N.W.T.
N.B.	Sask.	Y.T.

Small uncoloured segments in a bar represent the volumes for one or more provinces.

CANADA, 1963
(excludes water area)

| 21.7% | 17.1% | 12.1% | 6.1% | 4.4% | 4.4% | 3.5% | 3.5% | 2.5% | 1.6 | 0.1 |

PRODUCTIVE 26.96%

			Merchantable	Young		
hantable Wood 8.79%	Young Growth 6.25%	Merchantable Wood 3.71%	Young Growth 2.52%	Wood 1.41%	Growth 1.81%	Unclassified 2.47%
TOTAL SOFTWOOD		TOTAL MIXEDWOOD		TOTAL HARDWOOD		UNCLASSIFIED

INVENTORY OF STANDING WOOD

	Total—Millions of Cubic Feet	Percentage of National Total	10" D.B.H. and over	4"—9" D.B.H.	End Date of Inventory
CANADA	769,182.61	100.00	63.06	36.94	1957-65
B.C.	376,920.00	49.02	81.88	18.12	1957
Ont.	134,082.61	17.43	40.41	59.59	1959
Que.	108,132.00	14.06	71.37	28.63	1963
Alta.	52,341.00	6.80	46.81	53.19	1964
Sask.	18,052.00	2.35	22.53	77.47	1961
N.B.	18,029.00	2.34	41.41	58.59	1965
Nfld.	14,469.00	1.88	16.15	83.85	1964
N.W.T.	14,029.00	1.82	7.30	92.70	1963
Man.	11,935.00	1.55	19.77	80.23	1963
N.S.	11,787.00	1.53	37.61	62.39	1965
Y.T.	9,156.00	1.19	12.08	87.92	1963
P.E.I.	250.00	0.03	10.80	89.20	1963

The table aggregates the data plotted on the map. The plotted information does not represent a total inventory. For some areas south of the tree line for which no information is plotted, inventories were not available at the time of compilation of the map. Standing wood under 4" D.B.H. is not included. Inventory for national parks has been withheld by decision of the responsible authorities.

Scale 1:15,000,000 or One Inch to 236.74 Miles

| 100 | 0 | 100 | 200 | 300 | 400 Miles |
| 100 | 0 | 100 | 200 | 300 | 400 | 500 | 600 Kilometres |

PULP AND PAPER

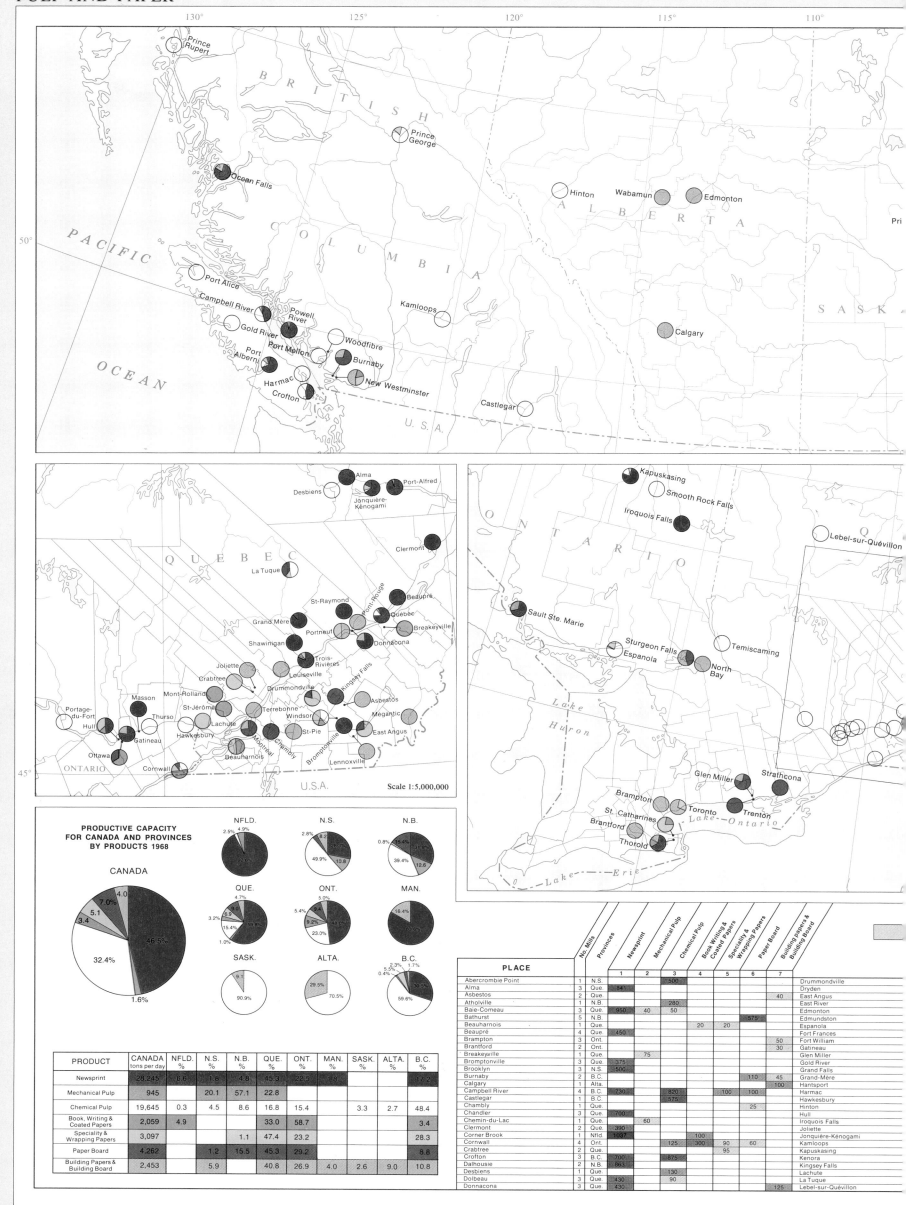

PRODUCTIVE CAPACITY FOR CANADA AND PROVINCES BY PRODUCTS 1968

CANADA · NFLD. · N.S. · N.B. · QUE. · ONT. · MAN. · SASK. · ALTA. · B.C.

PRODUCT	CANADA tons per day	NFLD. %	N.S. %	N.B. %	QUE. %	ONT. %	MAN. %	SASK. %	ALTA. %	B.C. %
Newsprint	28,245	6.6	1.8	4.8	45.3	22.5	1.8			17.2
Mechanical Pulp	945		20.1	57.1	22.8					
Chemical Pulp	19,645	0.3	4.5	8.6	16.8	15.4		3.3	2.7	48.4
Book, Writing & Coated Papers	2,059	4.9			33.0	58.7				3.4
Speciality & Wrapping Papers	3,097			1.1	47.4	23.2				28.3
Paper Board	4,262		1.2	15.5	45.3	29.2				8.8
Building Papers & Building Board	2,453		5.9		40.8	26.9	4.0	2.6	9.0	10.8

PLACE	No. Mills	Provinces	Newsprint 1	Mechanical Pulp 2	Chemical Pulp 3	Book Writing & Coated Papers 4	Speciality & Wrapping Papers 5	Paper Board 6	Building papers & Building Board 7	
Abercrombie Point	1	N.S.			500					Drummondville
Alma	3	Que.	841							Dryden
Asbestos	2	Que.						40		East Angus
Atholville	1	N.B.			280					East River
Baie-Comeau	3	Que.	950	40	50					Edmonton
Bathurst	5	N.B.						575		Edmundston
Beauharnois	1	Que.			20	20				Espanola
Beaupré	4	Que.	450							Fort Frances
Brampton	3	Ont.						50		Fort William
Brantford	2	Ont.						30		Gatineau
Breakeyville	1	Que.		75						Glen Miller
Bromptonville	3	Que.	375							Gold River
Brooklyn	3	N.S.	500							Grand-Mère
Burnaby	2	B.C.					110	45		Hantsport
Calgary	1	Alta.						100		Harmac
Campbell River	4	B.C.	730		820	100	100			Hawkesbury
Castlegar	1	B.C.			575					Hinton
Chambly	1	Que.					25			Hull
Chandler	3	Que.	700							Iroquois Falls
Chemin-du-Lac	1	Que.		60						Joliette
Clermont	2	Que.	390							Jonquière-Kénogami
Corner Brook	1	Nfld.	1037							Kamloops
Cornwall	4	Ont.			125	300	90	60		Kapuskasing
Crabtree	2	Que.				95				Kenora
Crofton	3	B.C.	700		875					Kingsey Falls
Dalhousie	2	N.B.	863							Lachute
Desbiens	1	Que.		130						La Tuque
Dolbeau	3	Que.	430	90						Lebel-sur-Quévillon
Donnacona	3	Que.	430					125		

Scale 1:5,000,000

PULP AND PAPER

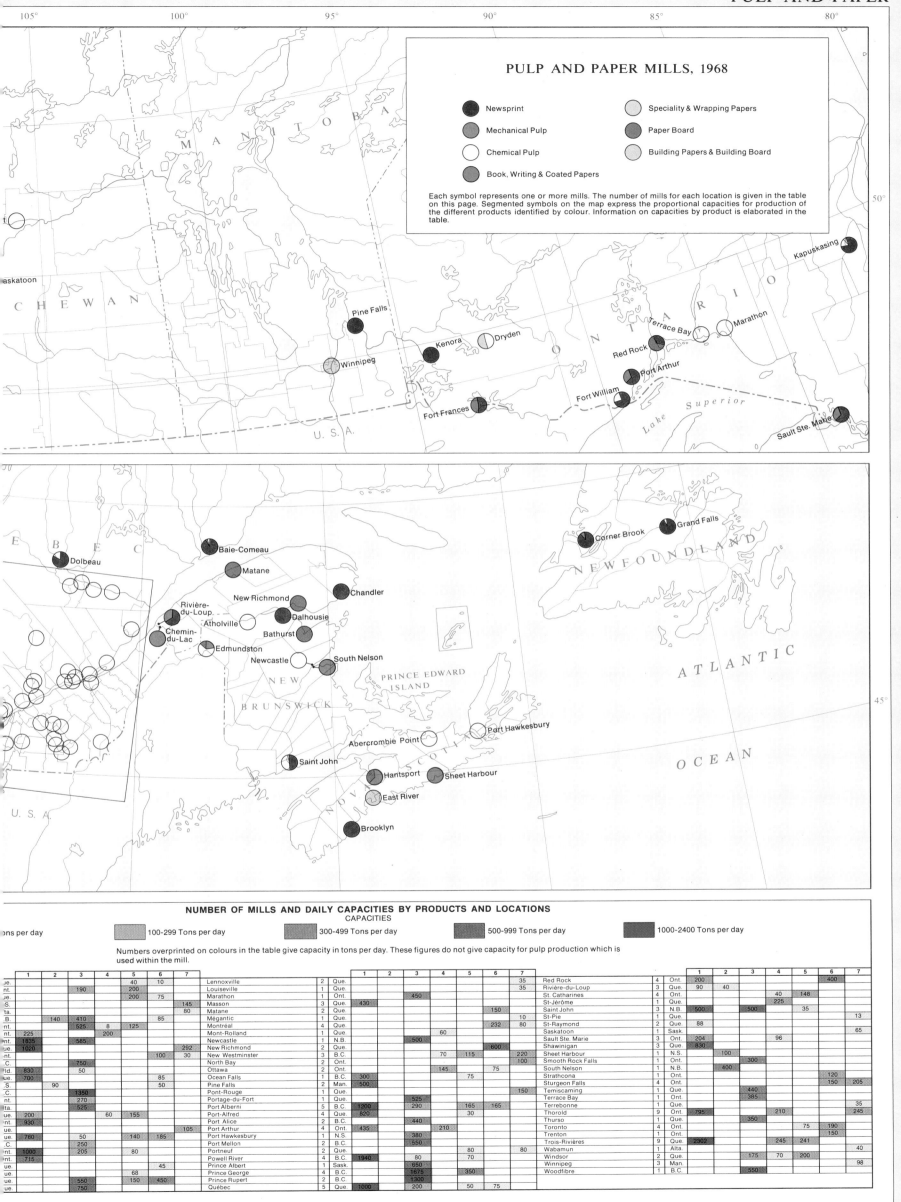

PULP AND PAPER MILLS, 1968

- ● Newsprint
- ● Mechanical Pulp
- ○ Chemical Pulp
- ● Book, Writing & Coated Papers
- ○ Speciality & Wrapping Papers
- ● Paper Board
- ○ Building Papers & Building Board

Each symbol represents one or more mills. The number of mills for each location is given in the table on this page. Segmented symbols on the map express the proportional capacities for production of the different products identified by colour. Information on capacities by product is elaborated in the table.

NUMBER OF MILLS AND DAILY CAPACITIES BY PRODUCTS AND LOCATIONS

CAPACITIES

	100-299 Tons per day
	300-499 Tons per day
	500-999 Tons per day
	1000-2400 Tons per day

Numbers overprinted on colours in the table give capacity in tons per day. These figures do not give capacity for pulp production which is used within the mill.

Location	No.	Prov.	1	2	3	4	5	6	7
Lennoxville	2	Que.					40	10	
Louiseville	1	Que.		190	200				
Marathon	1	Ont.			200		75		450
Masson	3	Que.	430					145	
Matane	2	Que.		140	410		85	80	150
Mégantic	1	Que.			525	8	125		10
Montréal	4	Que.	225			200		232	80
Mont-Rolland	1	Que.	1835	585			60		
Newcastle	1	N.B.	1020		500				
New Richmond	2	Que.				100	30	600	
New Westminster	3	B.C.		750		70	115	292	220
North Bay	2	Ont.	830	50					100
Ottawa	2	Ont.	700			145		75	
Ocean Falls	1	B.C.	300	90		75		85	120
Pine Falls	2	Man.	500		1350			50	150
Pont-Rouge	1	Que.			270				205
Portage-du-Fort	1	Que.			525	60	155		
Port Alberni	5	B.C.	1200	200	290	165	165		35
Port-Alfred	4	Que.	820	930	30			105	245
Port Alice	2	B.C.			440				
Port Arthur	4	Ont.	435	760	210	140	185		
Port Hawkesbury	1	N.S.	380	250				80	
Port Mellon	2	B.C.	1000	205	550				40
Portneuf	2	Que.	715			80	70		
Powell River	4	B.C.	1940		80			45	
Prince Albert	1	Sask.			650	68			
Prince George	4	B.C.		550	1675	350	150	450	
Prince Rupert	2	B.C.		750	1300				
Québec	5	Que.	1000		200		50	75	
Red Rock	4	Ont.	200					400	
Rivière-du-Loup	3	Que.	90	40					
St. Catharines	4	Ont.				40	148		
St-Jérôme	1	Que.			225				
Saint John	3	N.B.	500		500	35			
St-Pie	1	Que.							13
St-Raymond	2	Que.	88						
Saskatoon	1	Sask.							65
Sault Ste. Marie	3	Ont.	204		96				
Shawinigan	3	Que.	830						
Sheet Harbour	1	N.S.		100					
Smooth Rock Falls	1	Ont.		300					
South Nelson	1	N.B.	400						
Strathcona	1	Ont.					120		
Sturgeon Falls	4	Ont.					150	205	
Temiscaming	1	Que.			440				
Terrace Bay	1	Ont.			385				
Terrebonne	1	Que.						35	
Thorold	9	Ont.	795		210			245	
Thurso	1	Que.		350					
Toronto	4	Ont.					75	190	
Trenton	1	Ont.					150		
Trois-Rivières	9	Que.	2302		245	241			
Wabamun	1	Alta.						40	
Windsor	2	Que.		175	70	200			
Winnipeg	3	Man.						98	
Woodfibre	1	B.C.	550						

Scale 1:7,500,000 or One Inch to 118.37 Miles

50 0 50 100 150 200 250 Miles

50 0 50 100 150 200 250 300 350 Kilometres

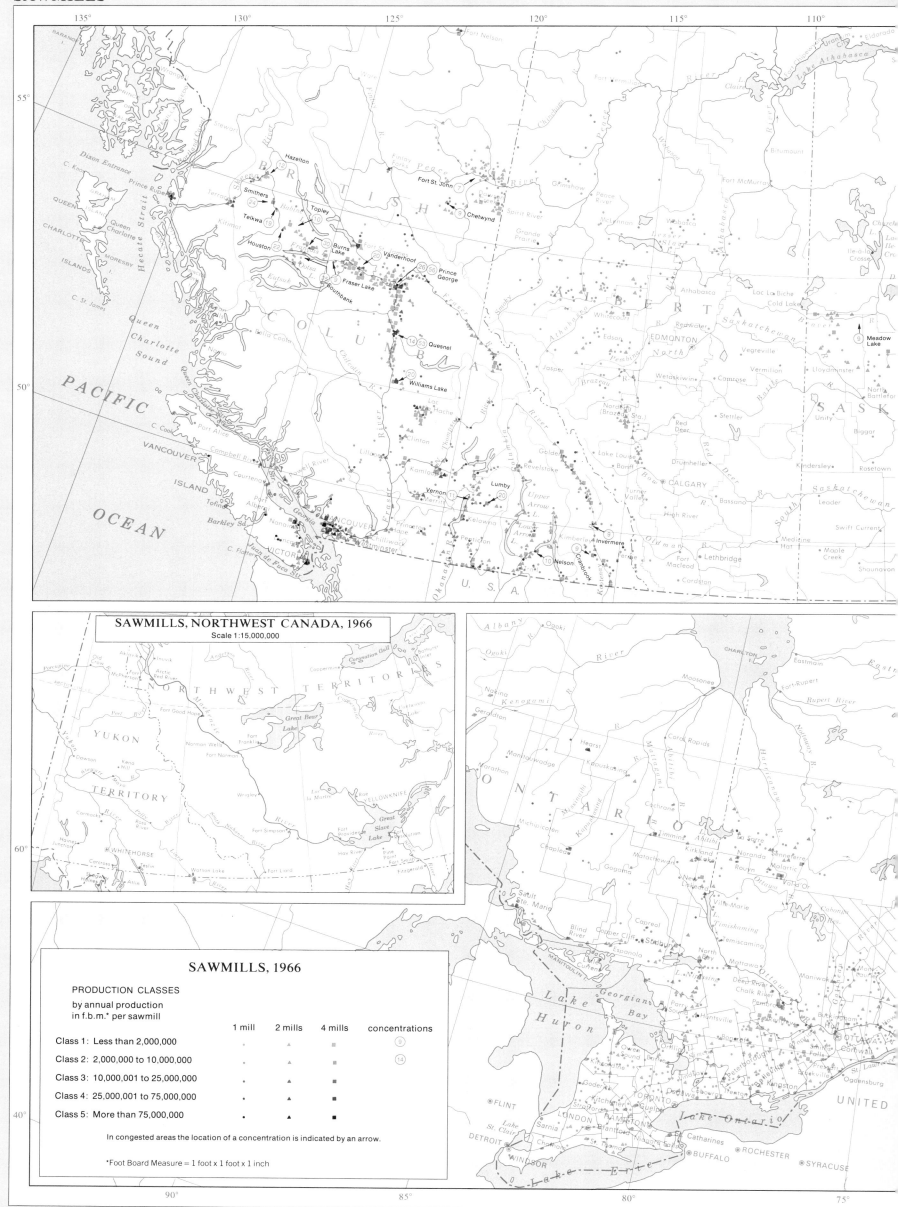

SAWMILLS, NORTHWEST CANADA, 1966
Scale 1:15,000,000

SAWMILLS, 1966

PRODUCTION CLASSES

by annual production
in f.b.m.* per sawmill

	1 mill	2 mills	4 mills	concentrations
Class 1: Less than 2,000,000	·	▴	▪	⑨
Class 2: 2,000,000 to 10,000,000	·	▴	▪	⑭
Class 3: 10,000,001 to 25,000,000	·	▴	▪	
Class 4: 25,000,001 to 75,000,000	·	▴	▪	
Class 5: More than 75,000,000	·	▴	▪	

In congested areas the location of a concentration is indicated by an arrow.

*Foot Board Measure = 1 foot x 1 foot x 1 inch

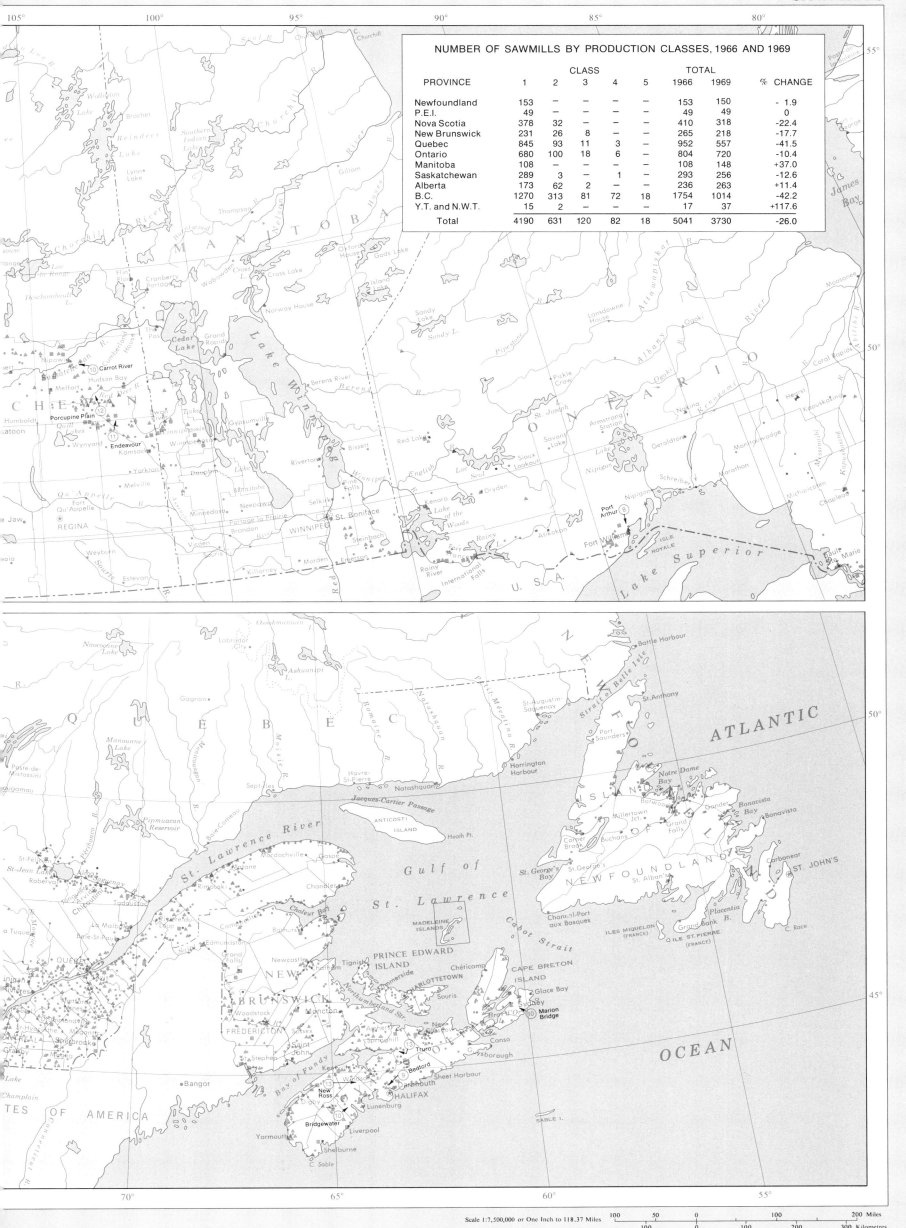

NUMBER OF SAWMILLS BY PRODUCTION CLASSES, 1966 AND 1969

PROVINCE	CLASS 1	2	3	4	5	TOTAL 1966	1969	% CHANGE
Newfoundland	153	–	–	–	–	153	150	- 1.9
P.E.I.	49	–	–	–	–	49	49	0
Nova Scotia	378	32	–	–	–	410	318	-22.4
New Brunswick	231	26	8	–	–	265	218	-17.7
Quebec	845	93	11	3	–	952	557	-41.5
Ontario	680	100	18	6	–	804	720	-10.4
Manitoba	108	–	–	–	–	108	148	+37.0
Saskatchewan	289	3	–	1	–	293	256	-12.6
Alberta	173	62	2	–	–	236	263	+11.4
B.C.	1270	313	81	72	18	1754	1014	-42.2
Y.T. and N.W.T.	15	2	–	–	–	17	37	+117.6
Total	4190	631	120	82	18	5041	3730	-26.0

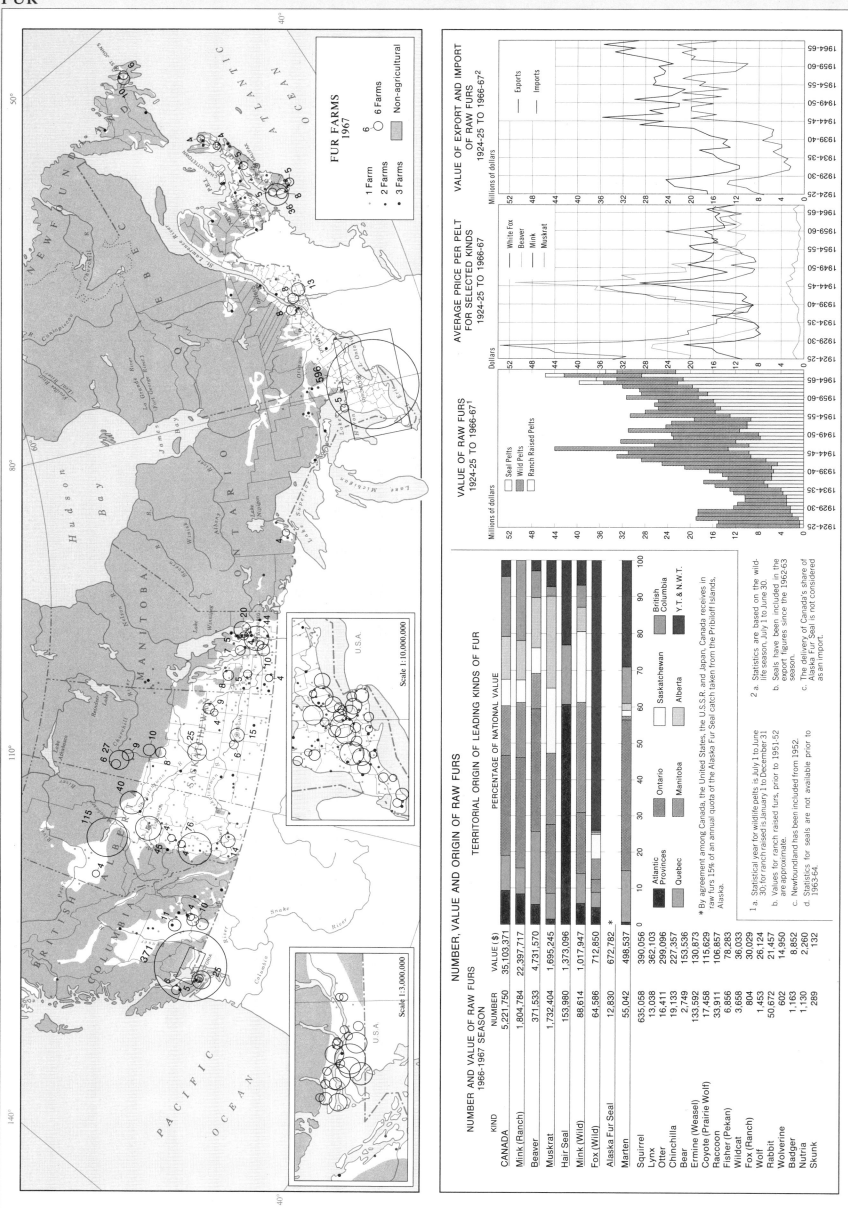

NUMBER, VALUE AND ORIGIN OF RAW FURS

NUMBER AND VALUE OF RAW FURS
1966-1967 SEASON

KIND	NUMBER	VALUE ($)
CANADA	5,221,750	35,103,371
Mink (Ranch)	1,804,784	22,397,717
Beaver	371,533	4,731,570
Muskrat	1,732,404	1,695,245
Hair Seal	153,980	1,373,096
Mink (Wild)	88,614	1,017,947
Fox (Wild)	64,586	712,850
Alaska Fur Seal	12,830	672,782 *
Marten	55,042	498,537
Squirrel	635,058	390,056
Lynx	13,038	362,103
Otter	16,411	299,096
Chinchilla	19,133	227,357
Bear	2,749	153,536
Ermine (Weasel)	133,592	130,873
Coyote (Prairie Wolf)	17,458	115,629
Raccoon	33,911	106,857
Fisher (Pekan)	6,856	78,283
Wildcat	3,658	36,033
Fox (Ranch)	804	30,029
Wolf	1,453	26,124
Rabbit	50,672	21,457
Wolverine	602	14,950
Badger	1,163	8,852
Nutria	1,130	2,260
Skunk	289	132

TERRITORIAL ORIGIN OF LEADING KINDS OF FUR

PERCENTAGE OF NATIONAL VALUE

Legend:
- Atlantic Provinces
- Quebec
- Ontario
- Manitoba
- Saskatchewan
- Alberta
- British Columbia
- Y.T. & N.W.T.

* By agreement among Canada, the United States, the U.S.S.R. and Japan, Canada receives in raw furs 15% of an annual quota of the Alaska Fur Seal catch taken from the Pribiloff Islands, Alaska.

1 a. Statistical year for wildlife pelts is July 1 to June 30; for ranch raised is January 1 to December 31
   b. Values for ranch raised furs, prior to 1951-52 are approximate.
   c. Newfoundland has been included from 1952.
   d. Statistics for seals are not available prior to 1963-64.

2 a. Statistics are based on the wild-life season, July 1 to June 30.
   b. Seals have been included in the export figures since the 1962-63 season.
   c. The delivery of Canada's share of Alaska Fur Seal is not considered as an import.

VALUE OF RAW FURS
1924-25 TO 1966-67[1]

Millions of dollars

Legend:
- Seal Pelts
- Wild Pelts
- Ranch Raised Pelts

AVERAGE PRICE PER PELT
FOR SELECTED KINDS
1924-25 TO 1966-67

Dollars

Legend:
- White Fox
- Beaver
- Mink
- Muskrat

VALUE OF EXPORT AND IMPORT
OF RAW FURS
1924-25 TO 1966-67[2]

Millions of dollars

Legend:
- Exports
- Imports

FUR FARMS
1967

Legend:
- 1 Farm
- 2 Farms
- 3 Farms
- 6 Farms
- Non-agricultural

Scale 1:10,000,000

Scale 1:3,000,000

Lambert Conformal Conic Projection Standard Parallels 49°N. and 77°N.

Scale 1:20,000,000 or One Inch to 315.65 Miles

RANGES OF SELECTED MAMMALS

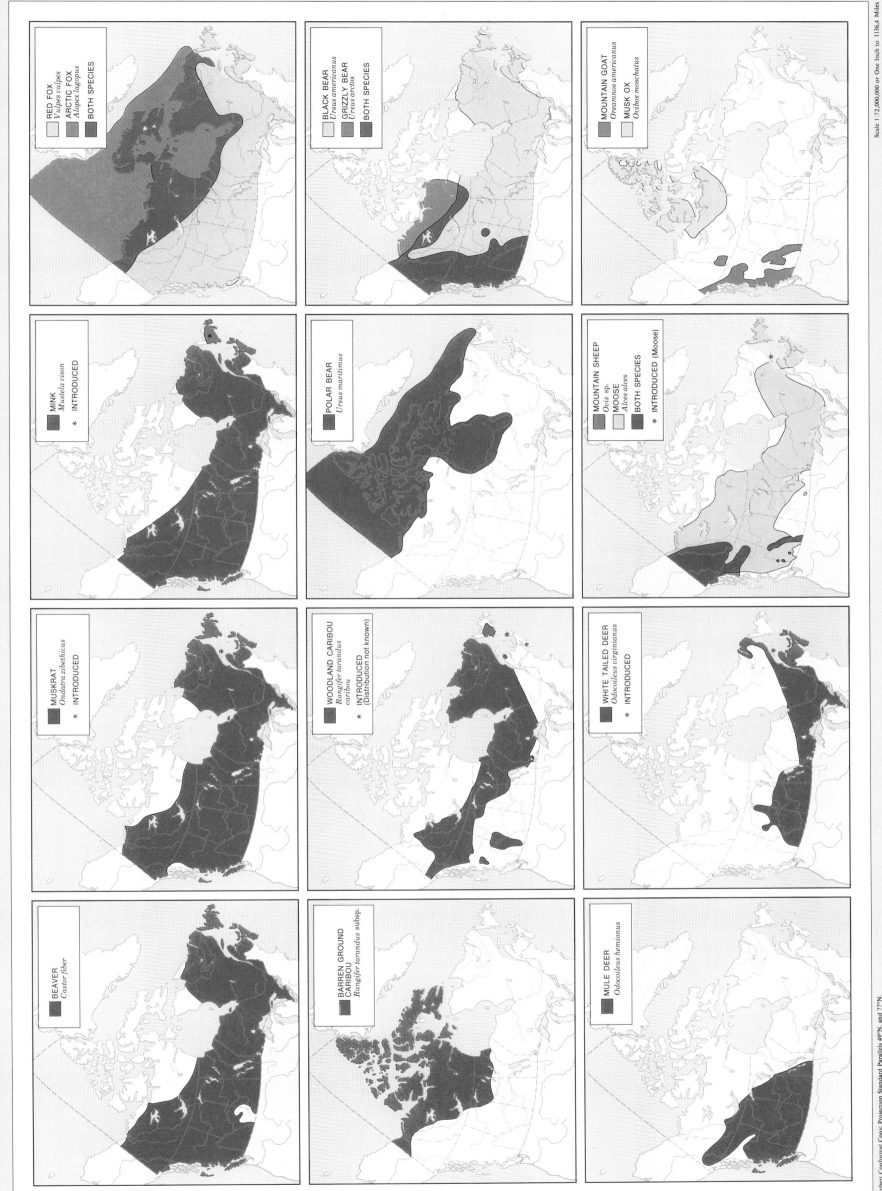

RED FOX
Vulpes vulpes
ARCTIC FOX
Alopex lagopus
BOTH SPECIES

BLACK BEAR
Ursus americanus
GRIZZLY BEAR
Ursus arctos
BOTH SPECIES

MOUNTAIN GOAT
Oreamnos americanus
MUSK OX
Ovibos moschatus

MINK
Mustela vison
* INTRODUCED

POLAR BEAR
Ursus maritimus

MOUNTAIN SHEEP
Ovis sp.
MOOSE
Alces alces
BOTH SPECIES
* INTRODUCED (Moose)

MUSKRAT
Ondatra zibethicus
* INTRODUCED

WOODLAND CARIBOU
Rangifer tarandus caribou
* INTRODUCED
(Distribution not known)

WHITE TAILED DEER
Odocoileus virginianus
* INTRODUCED

BEAVER
Castor fiber

BARREN GROUND CARIBOU
Rangifer tarandus subsp.

MULE DEER
Odocoileus hemionus

Scale 1:72,000,000 or One Inch to 1136.4 Miles

Lambert Conformal Conic Projection Standard Parallels 49°N. and 77°N.

THE NATIONAL ATLAS OF CANADA

FISHERIES – SELECTED CHARACTERISTICS

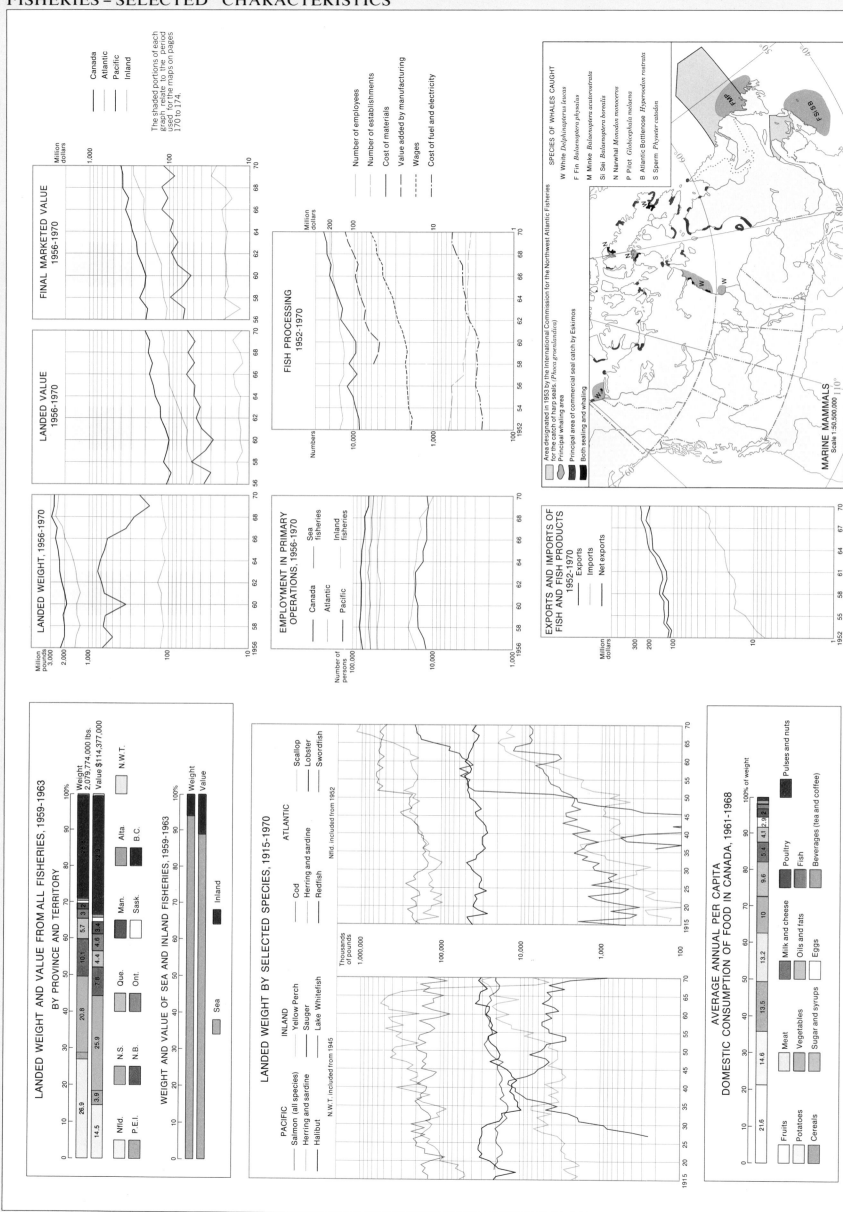

FINAL MARKETED VALUE 1956-1970

LANDED VALUE 1956-1970

LANDED WEIGHT, 1956-1970

FISH PROCESSING 1952-1970

- Number of employees
- Number of establishments
- Cost of materials
- Value added by manufacturing
- Wages
- Cost of fuel and electricity

EMPLOYMENT IN PRIMARY OPERATIONS, 1956-1970

- Canada
- Atlantic
- Pacific
- Sea fisheries
- Inland fisheries

EXPORTS AND IMPORTS OF FISH AND FISH PRODUCTS 1952-1970

- Exports
- Imports
- Net exports

- Canada
- Atlantic
- Pacific
- Inland

The shaded portions of each graph relate to the period used for the maps on pages 170 to 174.

MARINE MAMMALS
Scale 1:50,500,000

Area designated in 1953 by the International Commission for the Northwest Atlantic Fisheries for the catch of harp seals. (*Phoca groenlandica*)
Principal whaling area
Both sealing and whaling

Principal area of commercial seal catch by Eskimos

SPECIES OF WHALES CAUGHT
W White *Delphinapterus leucas*
F Fin *Balaenoptera physalus*
M Minke *Balaenoptera acutorostrata*
Si Sei *Balaenoptera borealis*
N Narwhal *Monodon monoceros*
P Pilot *Globicephala melaena*
B Atlantic Bottlenose *Hyperoodon rostrata*
S Sperm *Physeter catodon*

LANDED WEIGHT AND VALUE FROM ALL FISHERIES, 1959-1963 BY PROVINCE AND TERRITORY

Weight 2,079,774,000 lbs.
Value $114,377,000

Nfld. P.E.I. N.S. N.B. Que. Ont. Man. Sask. Alta. B.C. N.W.T.

WEIGHT AND VALUE OF SEA AND INLAND FISHERIES, 1959-1963

Weight
Value

Sea   Inland

LANDED WEIGHT BY SELECTED SPECIES, 1915-1970

PACIFIC
- Salmon (all species)
- Herring and sardine
- Halibut

INLAND
- Yellow Perch
- Sauger
- Lake Whitefish

ATLANTIC
- Cod
- Herring and sardine
- Redfish
- Scallop
- Lobster
- Swordfish

N.W.T. included from 1945
Nfld. included from 1952

AVERAGE ANNUAL PER CAPITA DOMESTIC CONSUMPTION OF FOOD IN CANADA, 1961-1968

Fruits Potatoes Cereals Meat Vegetables Sugar and syrups Milk and cheese Oils and fats Eggs Poultry Fish Beverages (tea and coffee) Pulses and nuts

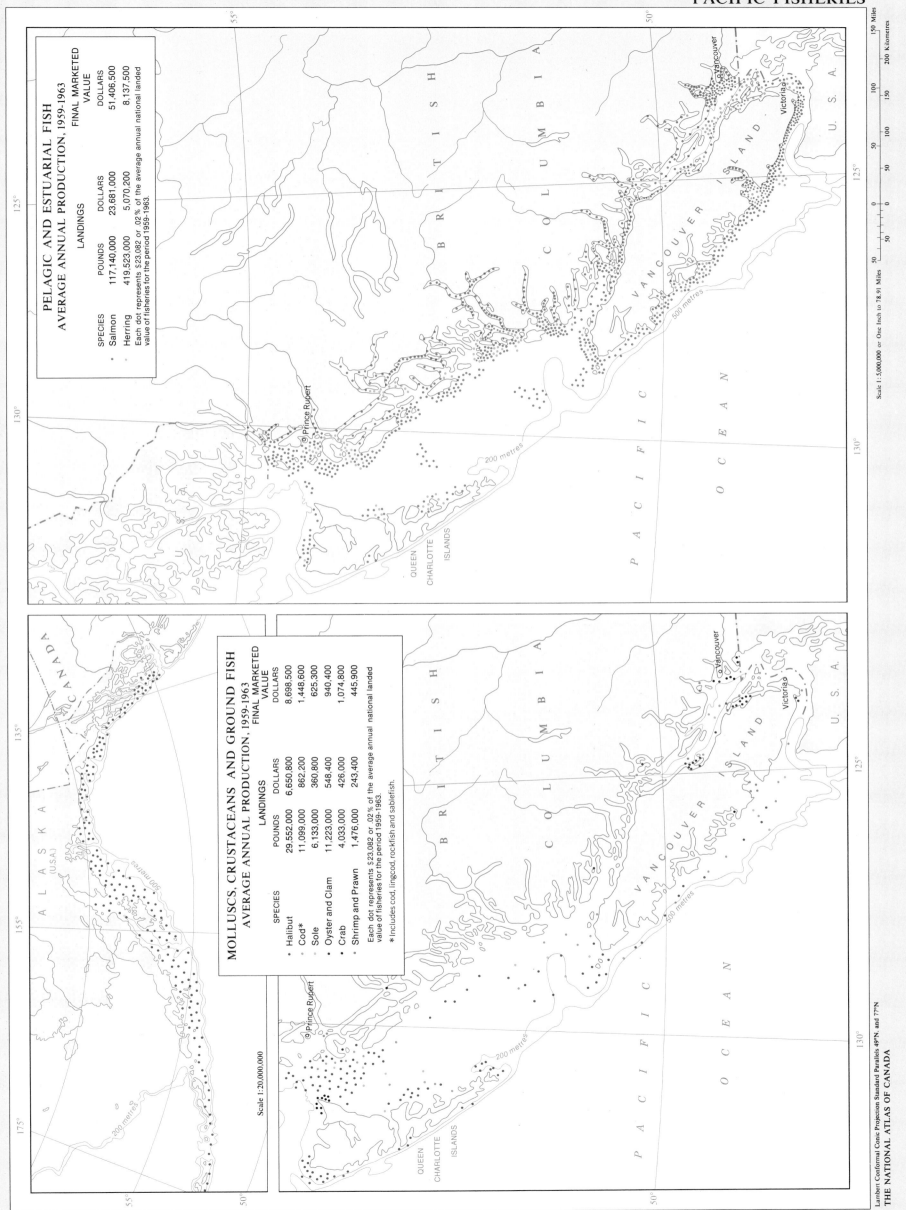

PELAGIC AND ESTUARIAL FISH
AVERAGE ANNUAL PRODUCTION, 1959-1963

SPECIES	LANDINGS		FINAL MARKETED VALUE
	POUNDS	DOLLARS	DOLLARS
Salmon	117,140,000	23,681,000	51,406,500
Herring	419,523,000	5,070,200	8,137,500

Each dot represents $23,082 or .02 % of the average annual national landed value of fisheries for the period 1959-1963.

MOLLUSCS, CRUSTACEANS AND GROUND FISH
AVERAGE ANNUAL PRODUCTION, 1959-1963

SPECIES	LANDINGS		FINAL MARKETED VALUE
	POUNDS	DOLLARS	DOLLARS
Halibut	29,552,000	6,650,800	8,698,500
Cod*	11,099,000	862,200	1,448,600
Sole	6,133,000	360,800	625,300
Oyster and Clam	11,223,000	548,400	940,400
Crab	4,033,000	426,000	1,074,800
Shrimp and Prawn	1,476,000	243,400	445,900

Each dot represents $23,082 or .02 % of the average annual national landed value of fisheries for the period 1959-1963.

* Includes cod, lingcod, rockfish and sablefish.

Scale 1:20,000,000

ATLANTIC FISHERIES

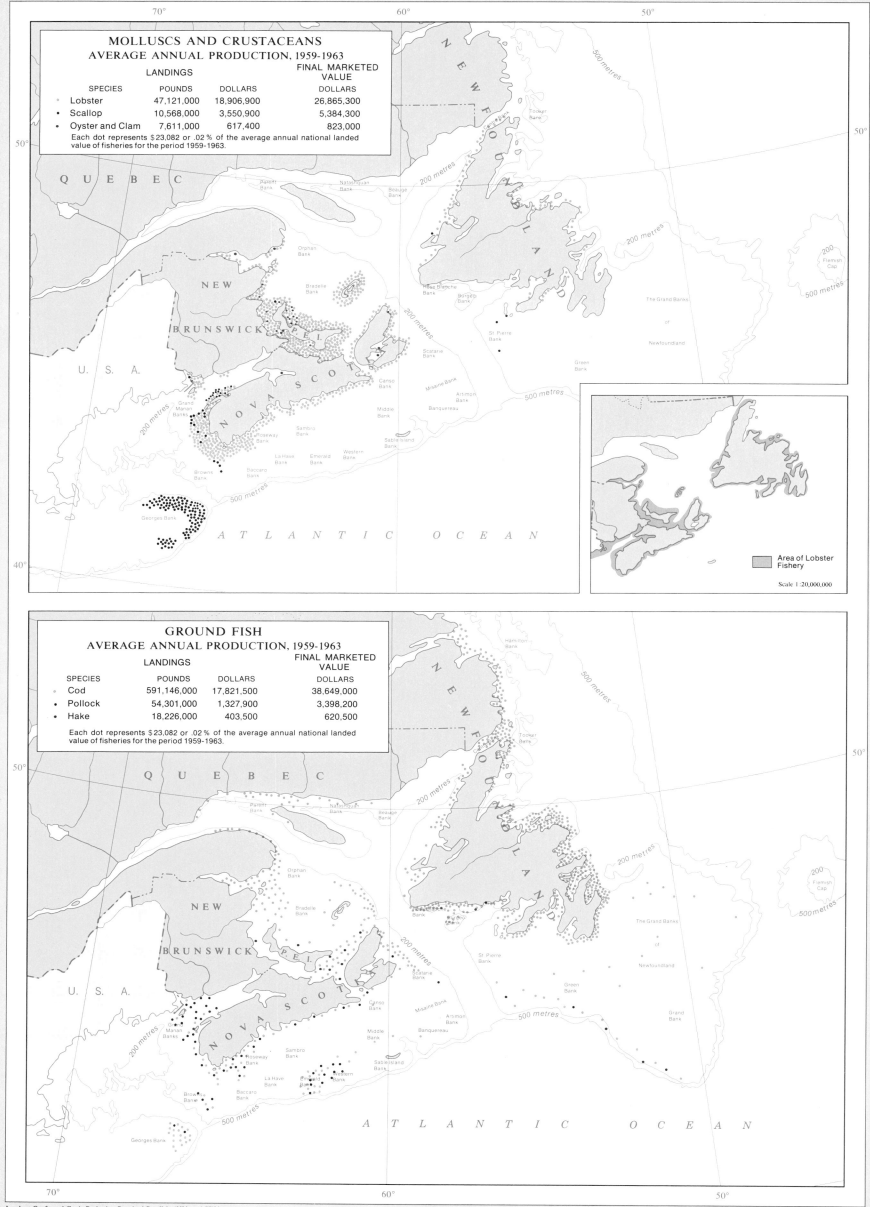

MOLLUSCS AND CRUSTACEANS
AVERAGE ANNUAL PRODUCTION, 1959-1963

SPECIES	LANDINGS		FINAL MARKETED VALUE
	POUNDS	DOLLARS	DOLLARS
Lobster	47,121,000	18,906,900	26,865,300
Scallop	10,568,000	3,550,900	5,384,300
Oyster and Clam	7,611,000	617,400	823,000

Each dot represents $23,082 or .02% of the average annual national landed value of fisheries for the period 1959-1963.

Area of Lobster Fishery

Scale 1:20,000,000

GROUND FISH
AVERAGE ANNUAL PRODUCTION, 1959-1963

SPECIES	LANDINGS		FINAL MARKETED VALUE
	POUNDS	DOLLARS	DOLLARS
Cod	591,146,000	17,821,500	38,649,000
Pollock	54,301,000	1,327,900	3,398,200
Hake	18,226,000	403,500	620,500

Each dot represents $23,082 or .02% of the average annual national landed value of fisheries for the period 1959-1963.

Lambert Conformal Conic Projection Standard Parallels 49°N. and 77°N.

THE NATIONAL ATLAS OF CANADA

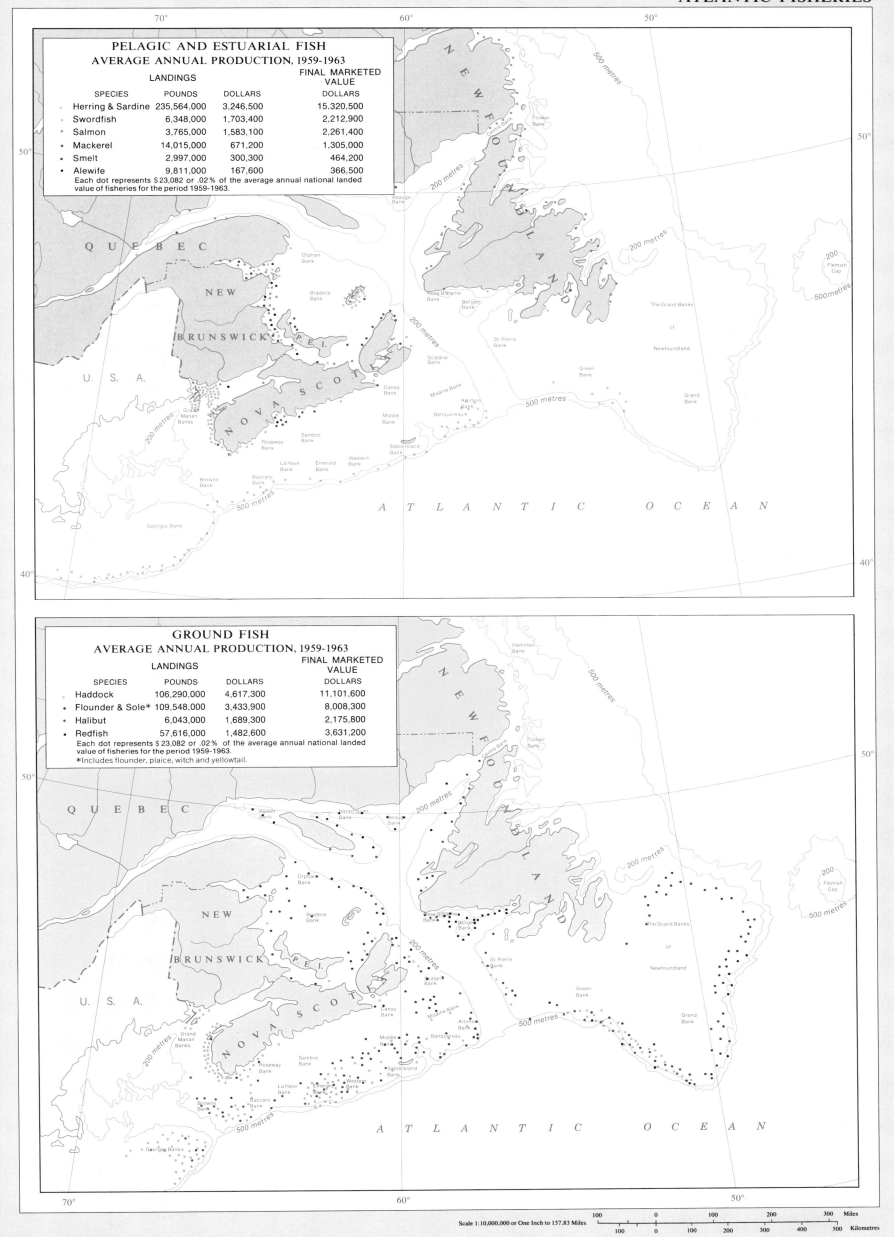

PELAGIC AND ESTUARIAL FISH
AVERAGE ANNUAL PRODUCTION, 1959-1963

| | LANDINGS | | FINAL MARKETED VALUE |
SPECIES	POUNDS	DOLLARS	DOLLARS
Herring & Sardine	235,564,000	3,246,500	15,320,500
Swordfish	6,348,000	1,703,400	2,212,900
Salmon	3,765,000	1,583,100	2,261,400
Mackerel	14,015,000	671,200	1,305,000
Smelt	2,997,000	300,300	464,200
Alewife	9,811,000	167,600	366,500

Each dot represents $23,082 or .02% of the average annual national landed value of fisheries for the period 1959-1963.

GROUND FISH
AVERAGE ANNUAL PRODUCTION, 1959-1963

| | LANDINGS | | FINAL MARKETED VALUE |
SPECIES	POUNDS	DOLLARS	DOLLARS
Haddock	106,290,000	4,617,300	11,101,600
Flounder & Sole*	109,548,000	3,433,900	8,008,300
Halibut	6,043,000	1,689,300	2,175,800
Redfish	57,616,000	1,482,600	3,631,200

Each dot represents $23,082 or .02% of the average annual national landed value of fisheries for the period 1959-1963.

*Includes flounder, plaice, witch and yellowtail.

Scale 1:10,000,000 or One Inch to 157.83 Miles

INLAND FISHERIES

TABLE 1: AVERAGE ANNUAL LANDED VALUE OF INLAND COMMERCIAL FISHERIES, 1959-1963 - LEADING SPECIES

	CANADA	N.W.T.	ALBERTA	SASKATCHEWAN	MANITOBA	
	$'000	$'000	$'000	$'000	$'000	$'000
A	Lake Whitefish *Coregonus clupeaformis*	3,612.3	A 534.2 :::::::::::	A 509.4 ::::::::::	A 734.9 :::::::::::	A 955.4 ::::::::::::::	A 863.4
B	Walleye *Stizostedion vitreum*	3,084.2	B 13.9 *	B 86.5 ::	B 282.2 :::::	B 1,512.1 ::::::::::::::::::::	B 1,119.9
C	Yellow Perch *Perca flavescens*	1,520.3		C 7.0 *		C 53.9 :	C 1,445.8
D	Sauger *Stizostedion canadense*	903.7				D 880.2 :::::::::::::	D 23.5
E	Tullibee *Coregonus artedii*	756.9		E 199.6 :::::*	E 34.4 *	E 46.3 :	E 476.6
F	Lake Trout *Salvelinus namaycush*	557.8	F 173.7 ::::	F 7.5 *	F 208.7 ::::*	F 61.1 :*	F 99.7
G	Northern Pike *Esox lucius*	436.4	G 12.0 *	G 54.7 :	G 57.4 :	G 216.5 :::::*	G 83.4
H	Rainbow Smelt *Osmerus mordax*	406.0					H 397.4
I	Lake Sturgeon *Acipenser fulvescens*	292.6			I 1.6 *	I 19.3 *	I 156.5
J	White Bass *Morone chrysops*	275.2					J 275.2
K	Channel Catfish *Ictalurus punctatus*	205.6				K 7.2 *	K 130.7
L	American Eel *Anguilla rostrata*	140.1					L 19.6
M	Sucker *Catostomus spp*	120.7		M 11.6 *		M 83.0 ::	M 26.0
N	Carp *Cyprinus carpio*	100.6				N 2.4 *	N 84.9
O	Alewife *Alosa pseudoharengus*	85.7					
P	Minnow Family *Cyprinidae*	49.0					
Q	Burbot *Lota lota*	29.5		Q 11.8 *		Q 14.3 *	Q 3.4
R	Atlantic Tomcod *Microgadus tomcod*	26.1					
	TOTAL	12,602.7	733.8	888.1	1,319.2	3,851.7	5,206.1

INLAND COMMERCIAL FISHERIES

Lakes and rivers licensed for commercial
fishing, 1963-1964 ....

Salmon spawning rivers and lakes ....

Fish processing plants, 1966

· 1 Plant   3 Plants

· 2 Plants   · 5 Plants

50°

40°

130°   120°   110°   100°

Lambert Conformal Conic Projection Standard Parallels 49°N. and 77°N.

RIO		QUEBEC $'000		N.B. $'000
::::::::	A	15.0 *		
:::::::::::	B	66.6 :*	B	3.0 *
:::::::::::::::::	C	13.6 *		
	F	7.1 *		
	G	12.4 *		
	H	8.6 *		
	I	113.1 ::*	I	2.0 *
	K	67.7 :*		
	L	119.5 ::*	L	1.0 *
			M	0.1 *
	N	13.3 *		
			O	85.7 ::
	P	49.0 :		
	R	26.1 *		
		512.0		91.8

TABLE 2: AVERAGE ANNUAL LANDED VALUE 1959-1963 – MINOR SPECIES

The following inland species plus "Other" collectively had an average landed value for the period 1959-1963 of $190,100 or 1.4% of the national average value of inland fisheries.

SPECIES	CAN.	N.W.T.	ALTA.	SASK.	MAN.	ONT.	QUE.	N.B.
Atlantic Salmon *Salmo salar*	$15,600							15,600
Goldeye *Hiodon alosoides*	$15,300		400		11,000	3,900		
American Shad *Alosa sapidissima*	$14,700						2,900	11,800
Inconnu *Stenodus Leuciththys*	$13,400	13,400						
Freshwater Drum *Aplodinotus grunniens*	$13,300				13,300			
Striped Bass *Morone saxatilis*	$8,000						1,100	6,900
Crappie *Promoxis spp*	$2,800						2,800	
Other	$107,000	100	700	26,400		77,300	2,500	
TOTAL	$190,100	13,500	1,100	26,400	24,300	81,200	9,300	34,300

The dots shown in Table 1 by species have the same value as the dots distributed on the maps on pages 170, 171, and 172 and are intended to facilitate visual comparisons of the values of inland commercial fisheries with those of the Atlantic and Pacific fisheries. Each dot represents $23,082 or .02% of the average annual national landed value of fisheries for the period 1959-1963.

* Less than the value for one dot.

TERRITORIAL PERCENTAGES OF NATIONAL VALUE OF INLAND COMMERCIAL FISHERIES

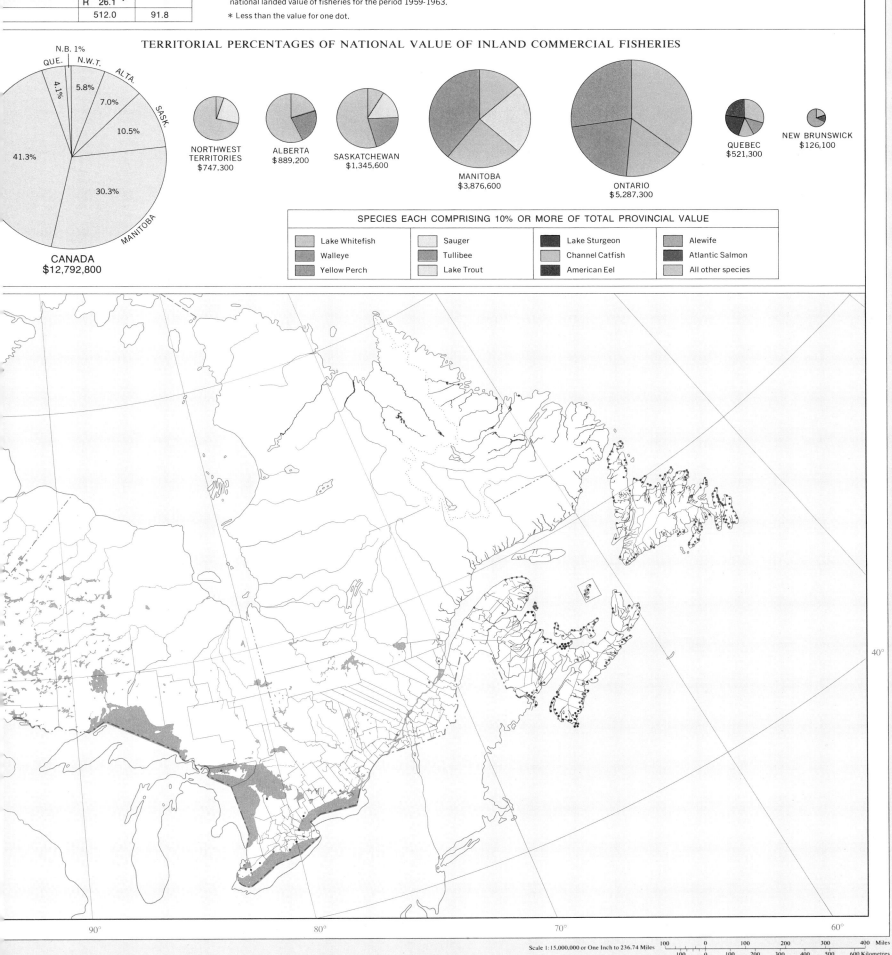

N.B. 1%
QUE. 4.1%
N.W.T. 5.8%
ALTA. 7.0%
SASK. 10.5%
MANITOBA 30.3%
41.3%

CANADA $12,792,800

NORTHWEST TERRITORIES $747,300

ALBERTA $889,200

SASKATCHEWAN $1,345,600

MANITOBA $3,876,600

ONTARIO $5,287,300

QUEBEC $521,300

NEW BRUNSWICK $126,100

SPECIES EACH COMPRISING 10% OR MORE OF TOTAL PROVINCIAL VALUE

- Lake Whitefish
- Walleye
- Yellow Perch
- Sauger
- Tullibee
- Lake Trout
- Lake Sturgeon
- Channel Catfish
- American Eel
- Alewife
- Atlantic Salmon
- All other species

90°   80°   70°   60°

40°

Scale 1:15,000,000 or One Inch to 236.74 Miles
100 0 100 200 300 400 Miles
100 0 100 200 300 400 500 600 Kilometres

RANGES OF PRINCIPAL COMMERCIAL FRESHWATER FISH

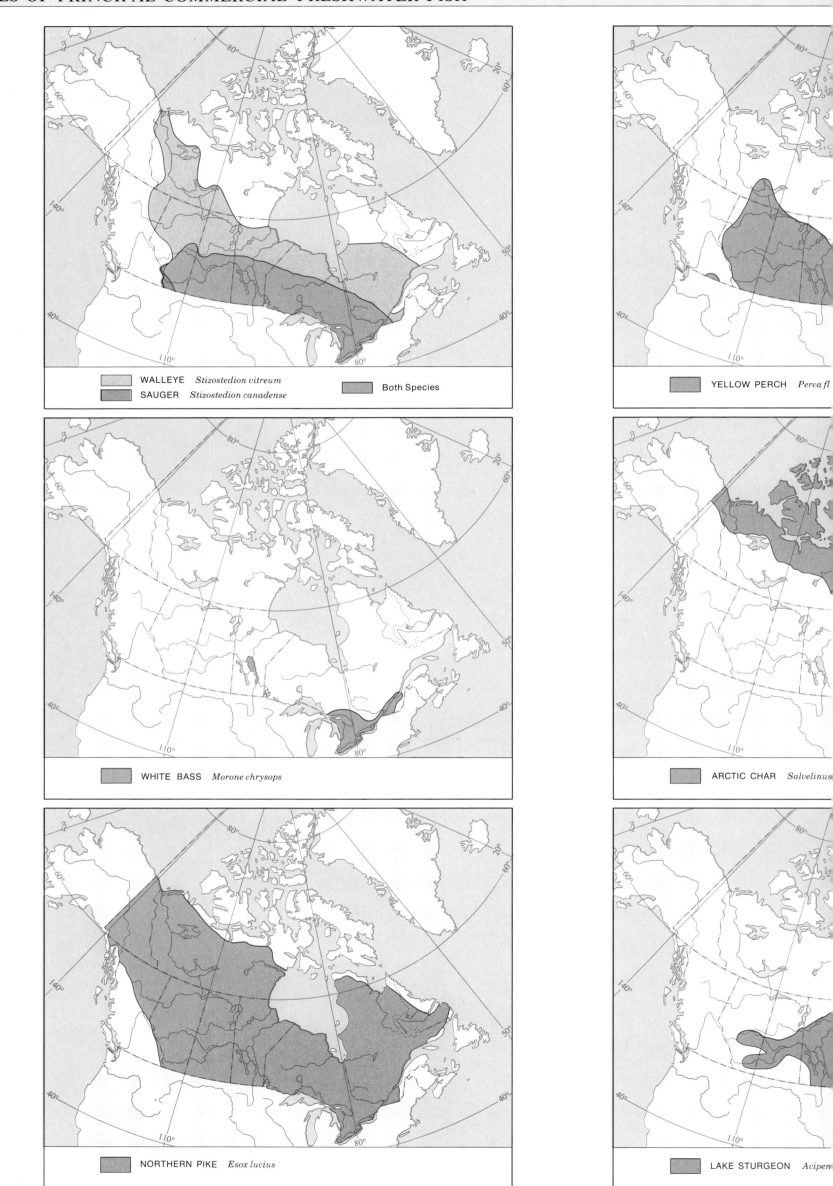

WALLEYE *Stizostedion vitreum*

SAUGER *Stizostedion canadense*

Both Species

YELLOW PERCH *Perca fl*

WHITE BASS *Morone chrysops*

ARCTIC CHAR *Salvelinus*

NORTHERN PIKE *Esox lucius*

LAKE STURGEON *Acipen*

Lambert Conformal Conic Projection Standard Parallels 49°N. and 77°N.

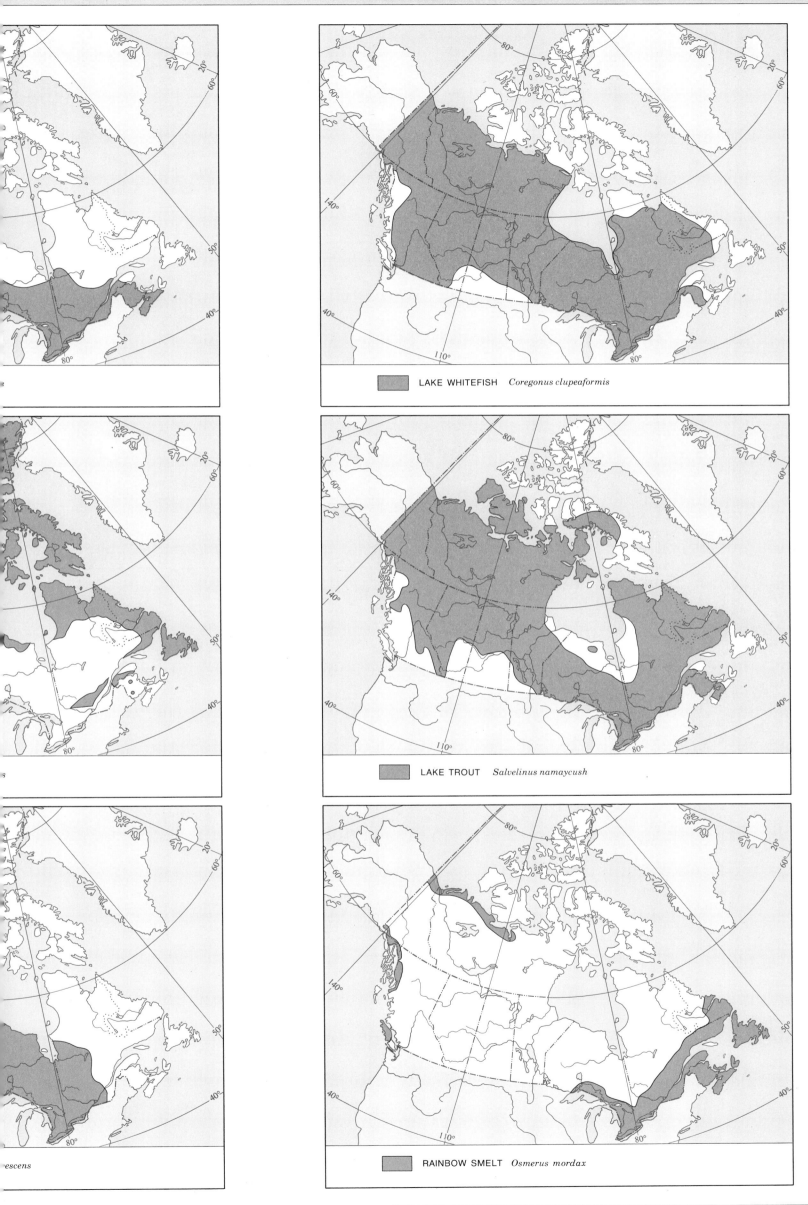

LAKE WHITEFISH *Coregonus clupeaformis*

LAKE TROUT *Salvelinus namaycush*

RAINBOW SMELT *Osmerus mordax*

Scale 1:50,500,000 or 797 Miles to One Inch

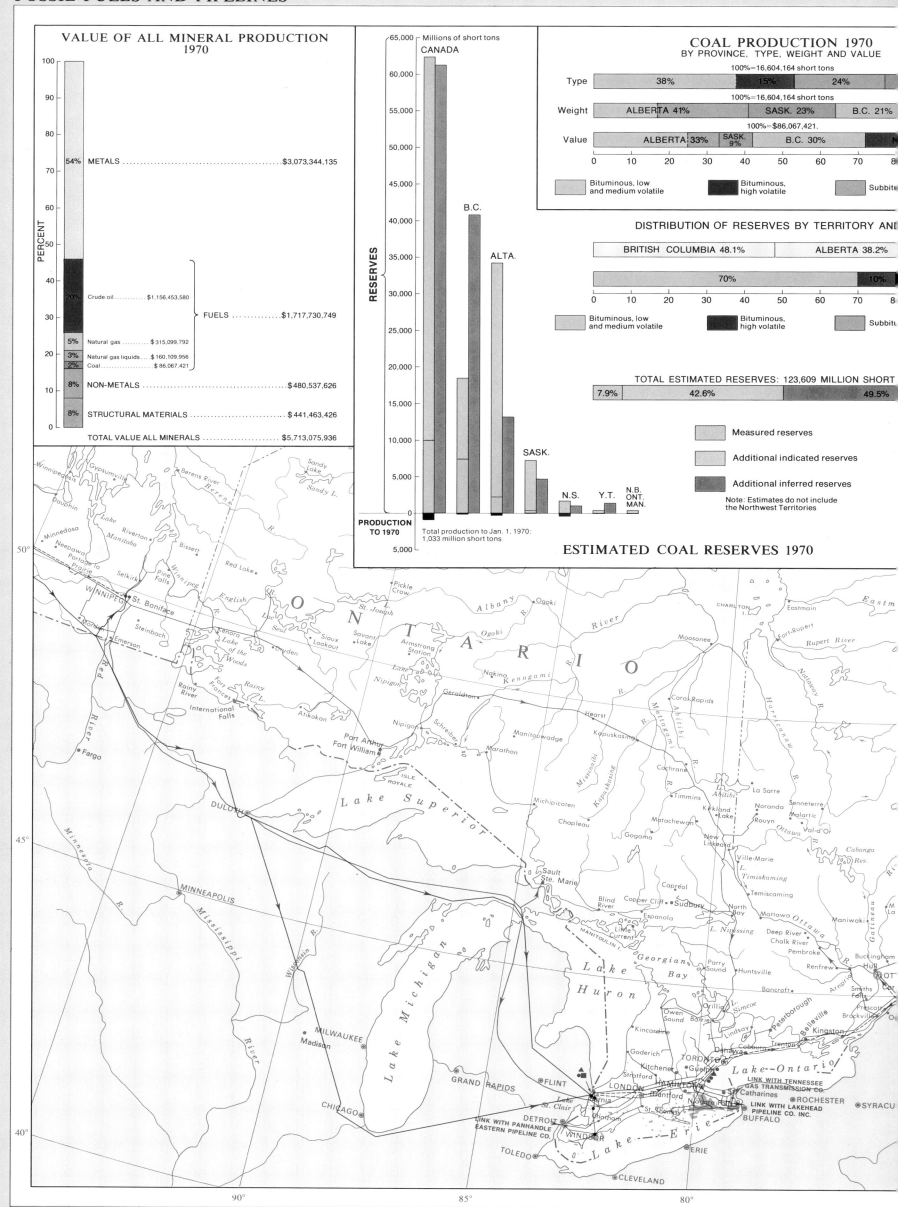

VALUE OF ALL MINERAL PRODUCTION 1970

PERCENT

100 —
54% METALS $3,073,344,135

20% Crude oil $1,156,453,580

5% Natural gas $315,099,792
3% Natural gas liquids $160,109,956
2% Coal $86,067,421

FUELS $1,717,730,749

8% NON-METALS $480,537,626

8% STRUCTURAL MATERIALS $441,463,426

TOTAL VALUE ALL MINERALS $5,713,075,936

COAL PRODUCTION 1970
BY PROVINCE, TYPE, WEIGHT AND VALUE

Type — 100%=16,604,164 short tons — 38% | 15% | 24%

Weight — 100%=16,604,164 short tons — ALBERTA 41% | SASK. 23% | B.C. 21%

Value — 100%=$86,067,421. — ALBERTA 33% | SASK. 9% | B.C. 30% | N

0 10 20 30 40 50 60 70 8

Bituminous, low and medium volatile | Bituminous, high volatile | Subbite

DISTRIBUTION OF RESERVES BY TERRITORY AND

BRITISH COLUMBIA 48.1% | ALBERTA 38.2%

70% | 10%

0 10 20 30 40 50 60 70 8

Bituminous, low and medium volatile | Bituminous, high volatile | Subbitu

TOTAL ESTIMATED RESERVES: 123,609 MILLION SHORT

7.9% | 42.6% | 49.5%

Measured reserves

Additional indicated reserves

Additional inferred reserves

Note: Estimates do not include the Northwest Territories

RESERVES

Millions of short tons — 65,000

CANADA

B.C.

ALTA.

SASK.

N.S. | Y.T. | N.B. ONT. MAN.

PRODUCTION TO 1970

Total production to Jan. 1, 1970: 1,033 million short tons

ESTIMATED COAL RESERVES 1970

Lambert Conformal Conic Projection Standard Parallels 49°N. and 77°N.

THE NATIONAL ATLAS OF CANADA

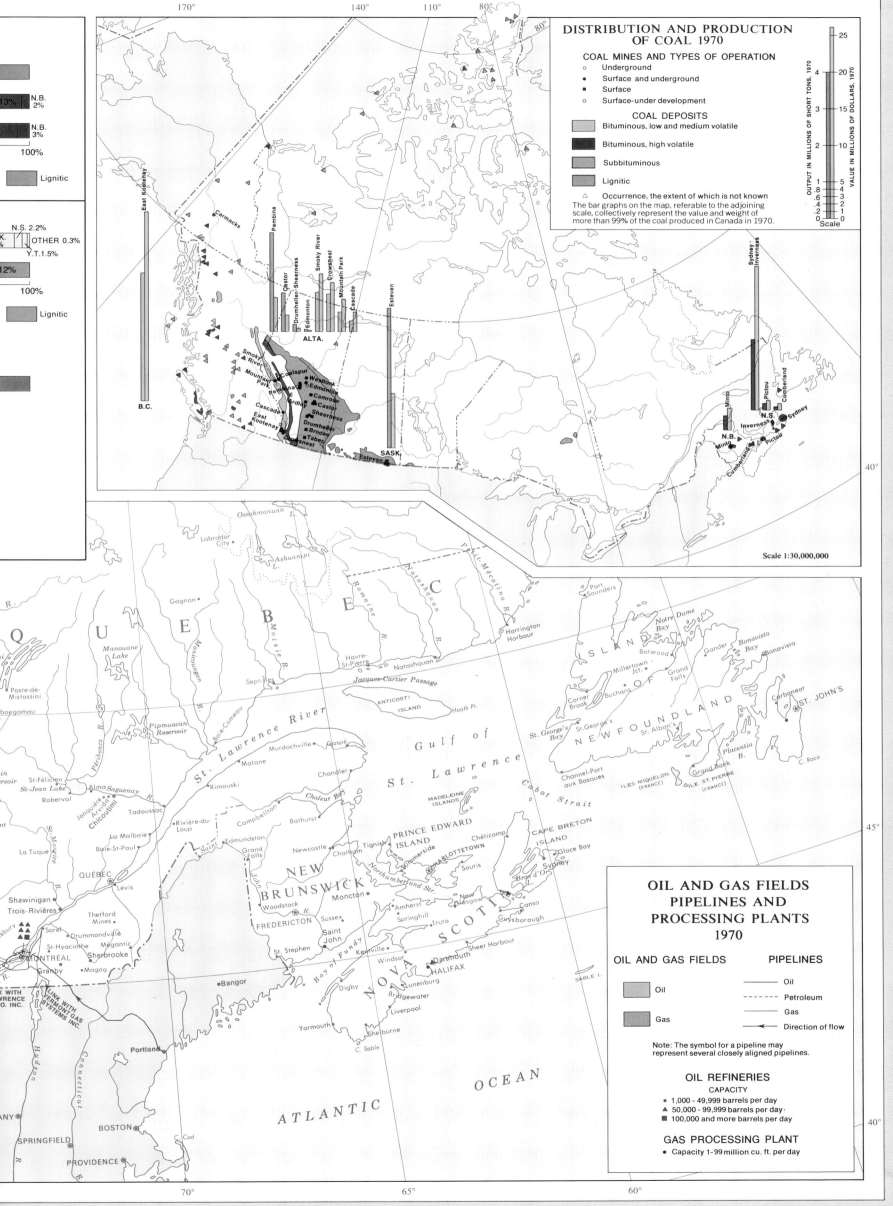

DISTRIBUTION AND PRODUCTION OF COAL 1970

COAL MINES AND TYPES OF OPERATION
- ○ Underground
- ● Surface and underground
- ● Surface
- □ Surface-under development

COAL DEPOSITS
- Bituminous, low and medium volatile
- Bituminous, high volatile
- Subbituminous
- Lignitic
- △ Occurrence, the extent of which is not known

The bar graphs on the map, referable to the adjoining scale, collectively represent the value and weight of more than 99% of the coal produced in Canada in 1970.

OUTPUT IN MILLIONS OF SHORT TONS, 1970
VALUE IN MILLIONS OF DOLLARS, 1970
Scale

Scale 1:30,000,000

OIL AND GAS FIELDS PIPELINES AND PROCESSING PLANTS 1970

OIL AND GAS FIELDS
- Oil
- Gas

PIPELINES
- —— Oil
- ---- Petroleum
- ═══ Gas
- ◄— Direction of flow

Note: The symbol for a pipeline may represent several closely aligned pipelines.

OIL REFINERIES
CAPACITY
- ● 1,000 - 49,999 barrels per day
- ▲ 50,000 - 99,999 barrels per day
- ■ 100,000 and more barrels per day

GAS PROCESSING PLANT
- ● Capacity 1-99 million cu. ft. per day

Scale 1:7,500,000 or One Inch to 118.37 Miles

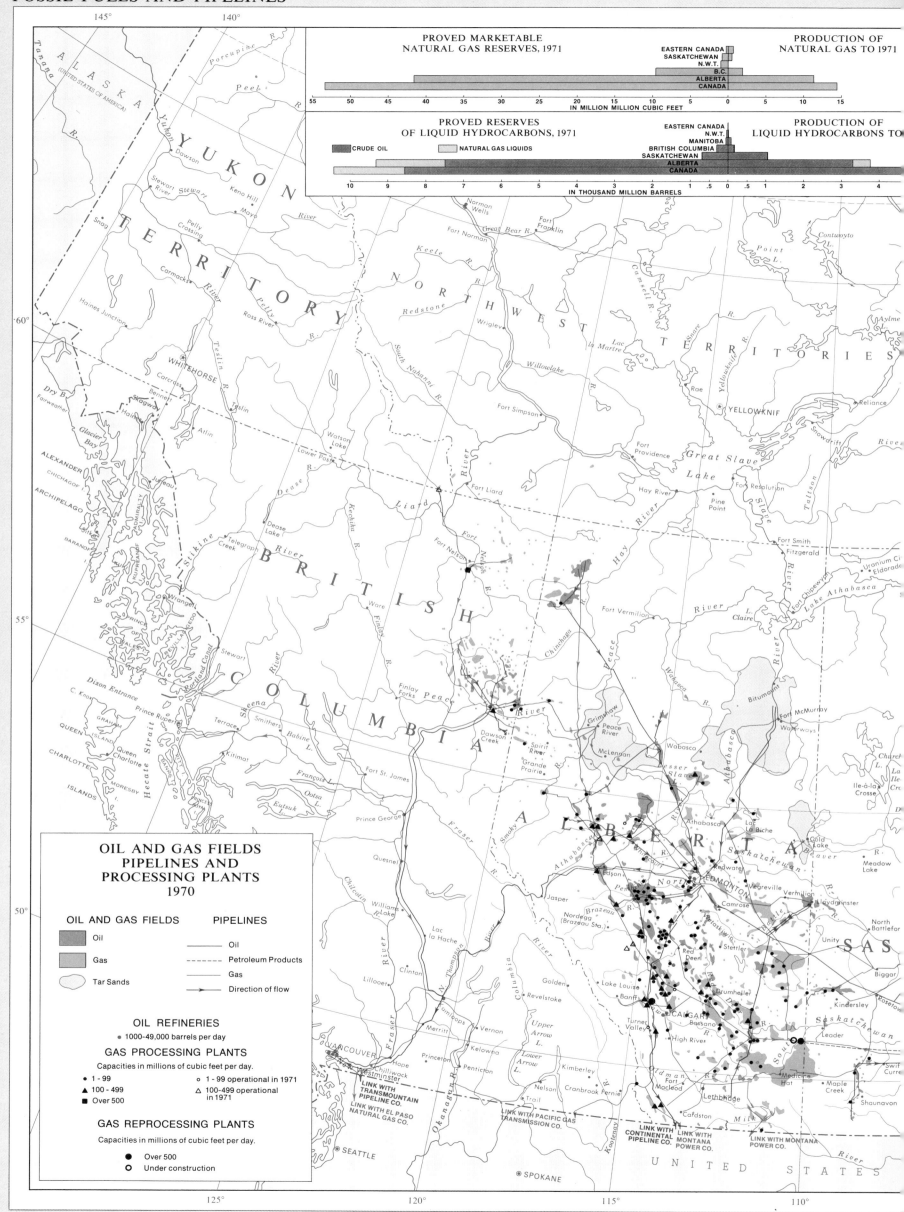

PROVED MARKETABLE
NATURAL GAS RESERVES, 1971

PRODUCTION OF
NATURAL GAS TO 1971

EASTERN CANADA
SASKATCHEWAN
N.W.T.
B.C.
ALBERTA
CANADA

IN MILLION MILLION CUBIC FEET

PROVED RESERVES
OF LIQUID HYDROCARBONS, 1971

PRODUCTION OF
LIQUID HYDROCARBONS TO

CRUDE OIL   NATURAL GAS LIQUIDS

EASTERN CANADA
N.W.T.
MANITOBA
BRITISH COLUMBIA
SASKATCHEWAN
ALBERTA
CANADA

IN THOUSAND MILLION BARRELS

OIL AND GAS FIELDS
PIPELINES AND
PROCESSING PLANTS
1970

OIL AND GAS FIELDS   PIPELINES

Oil   —— Oil
Gas   ----- Petroleum Products
Tar Sands   —— Gas
                       → Direction of flow

OIL REFINERIES
● 1000-49,000 barrels per day

GAS PROCESSING PLANTS
Capacities in millions of cubic feet per day.

● 1 - 99   ○ 1 - 99 operational in 1971
▲ 100 - 499   △ 100-499 operational
■ Over 500   in 1971

GAS REPROCESSING PLANTS
Capacities in millions of cubic feet per day.

● Over 500
○ Under construction

LINK WITH
TRANSMOUNTAIN
PIPELINE CO.

LINK WITH EL PASO
NATURAL GAS CO.

LINK WITH PACIFIC GAS
TRANSMISSION CO.

LINK WITH
CONTINENTAL
PIPELINE CO.

LINK WITH
MONTANA
POWER CO.

LINK WITH MONTANA
POWER CO.

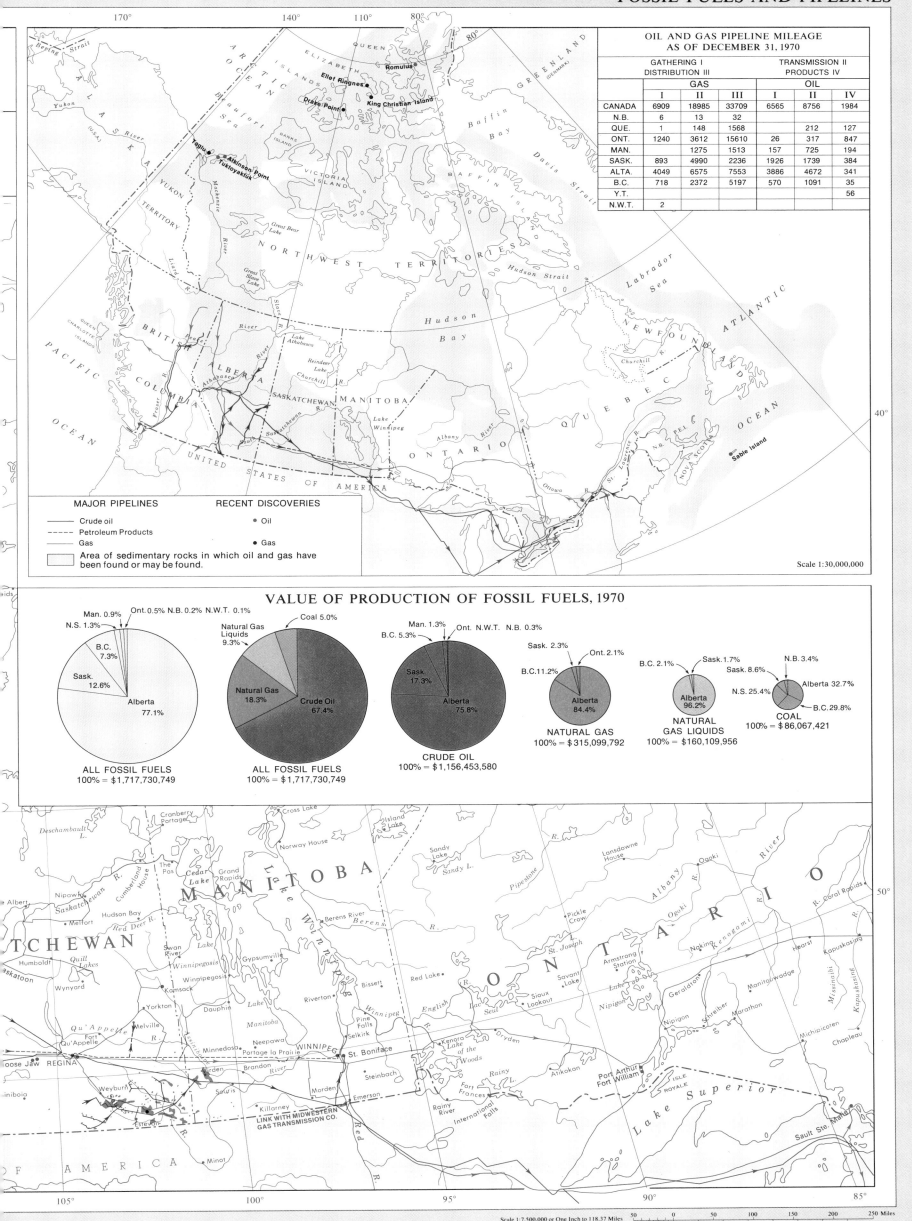

OIL AND GAS PIPELINE MILEAGE AS OF DECEMBER 31, 1970

	GATHERING I DISTRIBUTION III			TRANSMISSION II PRODUCTS IV		
	GAS			OIL		
	I	II	III	I	II	IV
CANADA	6909	18985	33709	6565	8756	1984
N.B.	6	13	32			
QUE.	1	148	1568		212	127
ONT.	1240	3612	15610	26	317	847
MAN.		1275	1513	157	725	194
SASK.	893	4990	2236	1926	1739	384
ALTA.	4049	6575	7553	3886	4672	341
B.C.	718	2372	5197	570	1091	35
Y.T.						56
N.W.T.	2					

MAJOR PIPELINES

—— Crude oil
----- Petroleum Products
—— Gas

Area of sedimentary rocks in which oil and gas have been found or may be found.

RECENT DISCOVERIES

● Oil
● Gas

Scale 1:30,000,000

VALUE OF PRODUCTION OF FOSSIL FUELS, 1970

ALL FOSSIL FUELS
100% = $1,717,730,749

Man. 0.9%
N.S. 1.3%
Ont. 0.5% N.B. 0.2% N.W.T. 0.1%
B.C. 7.3%
Sask. 12.6%
Alberta 77.1%

ALL FOSSIL FUELS
100% = $1,717,730,749

Natural Gas Liquids 9.3%
Coal 5.0%
Natural Gas 18.3%
Crude Oil 67.4%

CRUDE OIL
100% = $1,156,453,580

Man. 1.3%
B.C. 5.3%
Ont. N.W.T. N.B. 0.3%
Sask. 17.3%
Alberta 75.8%

NATURAL GAS
100% = $315,099,792

Sask. 2.3%
B.C. 11.2%
Ont. 2.1%
Alberta 84.4%

NATURAL GAS LIQUIDS
100% = $160,109,956

B.C. 2.1%
Sask. 1.7%
Alberta 96.2%

COAL
100% = $86,067,421

N.B. 3.4%
Sask. 8.6%
N.S. 25.4%
Alberta 32.7%
B.C. 29.8%

Scale 1:7,500,000 or One Inch to 118.37 Miles

50 0 50 100 150 200 250 Miles
50 0 50 100 150 200 250 300 350 Kilometres

PRIMARY IRON AND STEEL

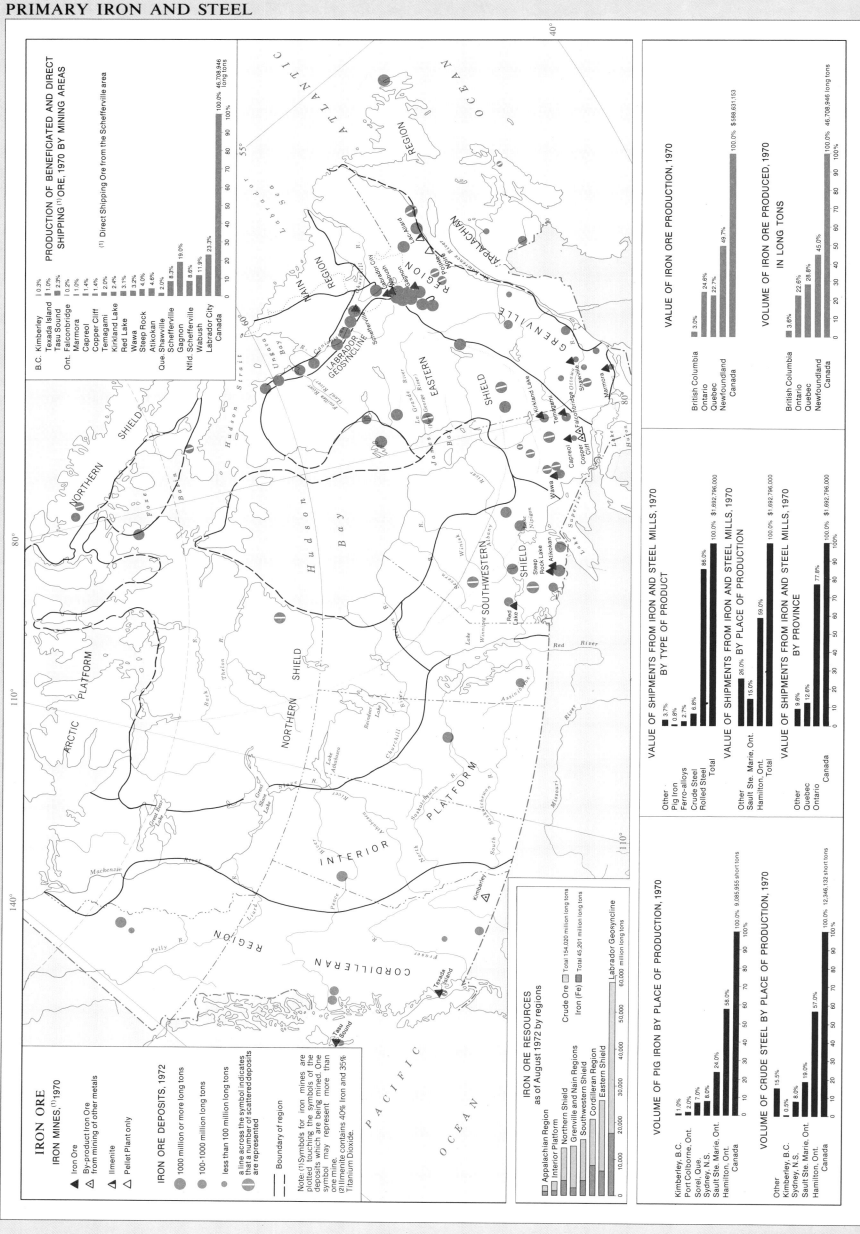

IRON ORE

IRON MINES,(1) 1970

▲ Iron Ore

△ By-product Iron Ore from mining of other metals

▲ Ilmenite

△ Pellet Plant only

IRON ORE DEPOSITS, 1972

● 1000 million or more long tons

● 100-1000 million long tons

◓ less than 100 million long tons

a line across the symbol indicates that a number of scattered deposits are represented

— Boundary of region

Note: (1)Symbols for iron mines are plotted touching the symbols of the deposits which are being mined. One symbol may represent more than one mine.

(2)Ilmenite contains 40% Iron and 35% Titanium Dioxide.

IRON ORE RESOURCES
as of August 1972 by regions

Crude Ore   Total 154,020 million long tons
Iron (Fe)   Total 45,201 million long tons

Appalachian Region
Interior Platform
Northern Shield
Grenville and Nain Regions
Southwestern Shield
Cordilleran Region
Eastern Shield

Labrador Geosyncline

PRODUCTION OF BENEFICIATED AND DIRECT SHIPPING (1) ORE, 1970 BY MINING AREAS

(1) Direct Shipping Ore from the Schefferville area

	%
B.C. Kimberley	0.3%
Texada Island	1.0%
Tasu Sound	2.3%
Ont. Falconbridge	0.2%
Marmora	1.4%
Capreol	1.4%
Copper Cliff	2.0%
Temagami	2.4%
Kirkland Lake	3.1%
Red Lake	3.2%
Wawa	4.0%
Steep Rock	4.6%
Atikokan	2.0%
Que. Shawville	8.3%
Schefferville	8.6%
Gagnon	19.0%
Nfld. Schefferville	11.9%
Wabush	23.3%
Labrador City	100.0% 46,708,846 long tons
Canada	100%

VALUE OF IRON ORE PRODUCTION, 1970

	%
British Columbia	3.0%
Ontario	24.6%
Quebec	22.7%
Newfoundland	49.7%
Canada	100.0% $588,631,153

VOLUME OF IRON ORE PRODUCED, 1970
IN LONG TONS

	%
British Columbia	3.6%
Ontario	22.6%
Quebec	28.8%
Newfoundland	45.0%
Canada	100.0% 46,708,846 long tons

VALUE OF SHIPMENTS FROM IRON AND STEEL MILLS, 1970 BY TYPE OF PRODUCT

	%
Other	3.7%
Pig Iron	0.8%
Ferro-alloys	2.7%
Crude Steel	6.8%
Rolled Steel	86.0%
Total	100.0% $1,692,796,000

VALUE OF SHIPMENTS FROM IRON AND STEEL MILLS, 1970 BY PLACE OF PRODUCTION

	%
Other	26.0%
Sault Ste. Marie, Ont.	15.0%
Hamilton, Ont.	59.0%
Total	100.0% $1,692,796,000

VALUE OF SHIPMENTS FROM IRON AND STEEL MILLS, 1970 BY PROVINCE

	%
Other	9.6%
Quebec	12.6%
Ontario	77.8%
Canada	100.0% $1,692,796,000

VOLUME OF PIG IRON BY PLACE OF PRODUCTION, 1970

	%
Kimberley, B.C.	1.0%
Port Colborne, Ont.	2.0%
Sorel, Que.	7.0%
Sydney, N.S.	8.0%
Sault Ste. Marie, Ont.	24.0%
Hamilton, Ont.	58.0%
Canada	100.0% 9,085,955 short tons

VOLUME OF CRUDE STEEL BY PLACE OF PRODUCTION, 1970

	%
Other	15.5%
Kimberley, B.C.	0.5%
Sydney, N.S.	8.0%
Sault Ste. Marie, Ont.	19.0%
Hamilton, Ont.	57.0%
Canada	100.0% 12,346,132 short tons

Lambert Conformal Conic Projection Standard Parallels 49°N. and 77°N.

Scale 1:20,000,000 or One Inch to 315.65 Miles

THE NATIONAL ATLAS OF CANADA

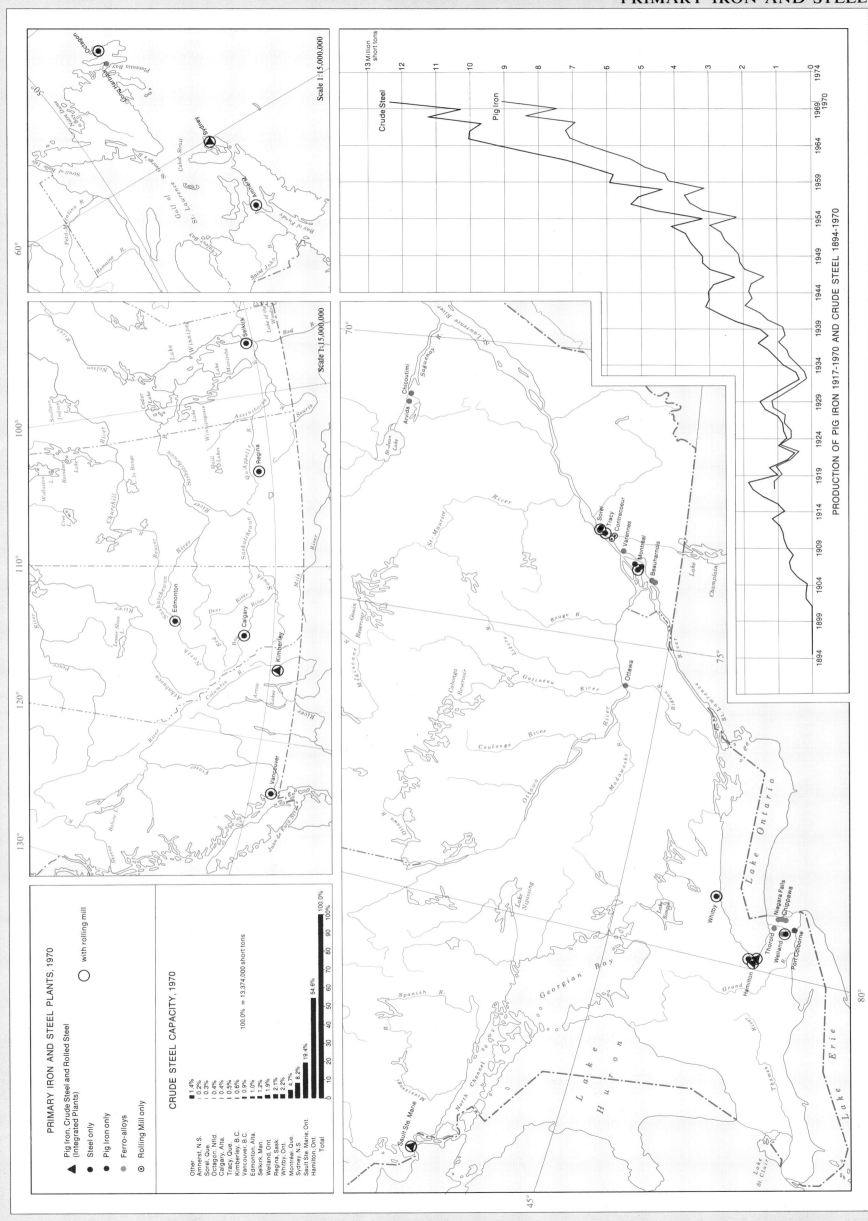

PRODUCTION OF PIG IRON 1917-1970 AND CRUDE STEEL 1894-1970

Scale 1:5,000,000 or One Inch to 78.91 Miles

Scale 1:5,000,000

Scale 1:15,000,000

Scale 1:15,000,000

PRIMARY IRON AND STEEL PLANTS, 1970

○ with rolling mill

Pig Iron, Crude Steel and Rolled Steel
(Integrated Plants)

▲ Steel only

● Pig Iron only

● Ferro-alloys

◉ Rolling Mill only

CRUDE STEEL CAPACITY, 1970

100.0% = 13,374,000 short tons

Other	1.4%
Amherst, N.S.	0.2%
Sorel, Que.	0.3%
Octagon, Nfld.	0.4%
Calgary, Alta.	0.4%
Tracy, Que.	0.5%
Kimberley, B.C.	0.6%
Vancouver, B.C.	0.9%
Edmonton, Alta.	1.0%
Selkirk, Man.	1.2%
Welland, Ont.	1.9%
Regina, Sask.	2.1%
Whitby, Ont.	3.2%
Montreal, Que.	4.7%
Sydney, N.S.	8.2%
Sault Ste. Marie, Ont.	19.4%
Hamilton, Ont.	54.6%
Total	100.0%

Lambert Conformal Conic Projection Standard Parallels 49°N. and 77°N.

THE NATIONAL ATLAS OF CANADA

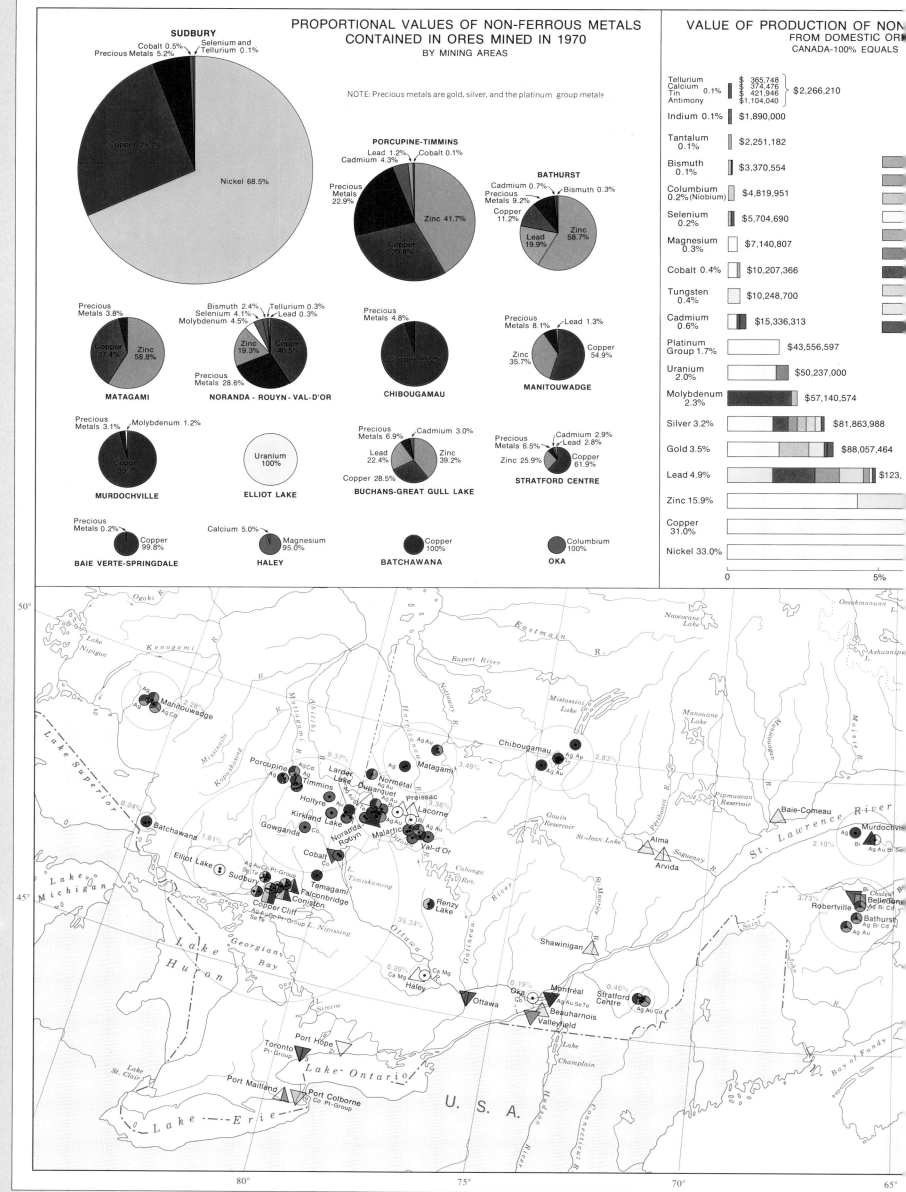

PROPORTIONAL VALUES OF NON-FERROUS METALS CONTAINED IN ORES MINED IN 1970
BY MINING AREAS

NOTE: Precious metals are gold, silver, and the platinum group metals

SUDBURY
- Cobalt 0.5%
- Selenium and Tellurium 0.1%
- Precious Metals 5.2%
- Copper 25.7%
- Nickel 68.5%

PORCUPINE-TIMMINS
- Lead 1.2%
- Cobalt 0.1%
- Cadmium 4.3%
- Precious Metals 22.9%
- Zinc 41.7%
- Copper 29.8%

BATHURST
- Cadmium 0.7%
- Bismuth 0.3%
- Precious Metals 9.2%
- Copper 11.2%
- Zinc 58.7%
- Lead 19.9%

MATAGAMI
- Precious Metals 3.8%
- Copper 37.4%
- Zinc 58.8%

NORANDA - ROUYN - VAL-D'OR
- Bismuth 2.4%
- Tellurium 0.3%
- Selenium 4.1%
- Lead 0.3%
- Molybdenum 4.5%
- Zinc 19.3%
- Copper 40.5%
- Precious Metals 28.6%

CHIBOUGAMAU
- Precious Metals 4.8%
- Copper 95.2%

MANITOUWADGE
- Precious Metals 8.1%
- Lead 1.3%
- Copper 54.9%
- Zinc 35.7%

MURDOCHVILLE
- Precious Metals 3.1%
- Molybdenum 1.2%
- Copper 95.7%

ELLIOT LAKE
- Uranium 100%

BUCHANS-GREAT GULL LAKE
- Precious Metals 6.9%
- Cadmium 3.0%
- Lead 22.4%
- Zinc 39.2%
- Copper 28.5%

STRATFORD CENTRE
- Cadmium 2.9%
- Lead 2.8%
- Precious Metals 6.5%
- Copper 61.9%
- Zinc 25.9%

BAIE VERTE-SPRINGDALE
- Precious Metals 0.2%
- Copper 99.8%

HALEY
- Calcium 5.0%
- Magnesium 95.0%

BATCHAWANA
- Copper 100%

OKA
- Columbium 100%

VALUE OF PRODUCTION OF NON[...]
FROM DOMESTIC OR[...]
CANADA-100% EQUALS [...]

Tellurium	$365,748
Calcium 0.1%	$374,476
Tin	$421,946
Antimony	$1,104,040	$2,266,210
Indium 0.1%	$1,890,000
Tantalum 0.1%	$2,251,182
Bismuth 0.1%	$3,370,554
Columbium 0.2% (Niobium)	$4,819,951
Selenium 0.2%	$5,704,690
Magnesium 0.3%	$7,140,807
Cobalt 0.4%	$10,207,366
Tungsten 0.4%	$10,248,700
Cadmium 0.6%	$15,336,313
Platinum Group 1.7%	$43,556,597
Uranium 2.0%	$50,237,000
Molybdenum 2.3%	$57,140,574
Silver 3.2%	$81,863,988
Gold 3.5%	$88,057,464
Lead 4.9%	$123,[...]
Zinc 15.9%	
Copper 31.0%	
Nickel 33.0%	

0   5%

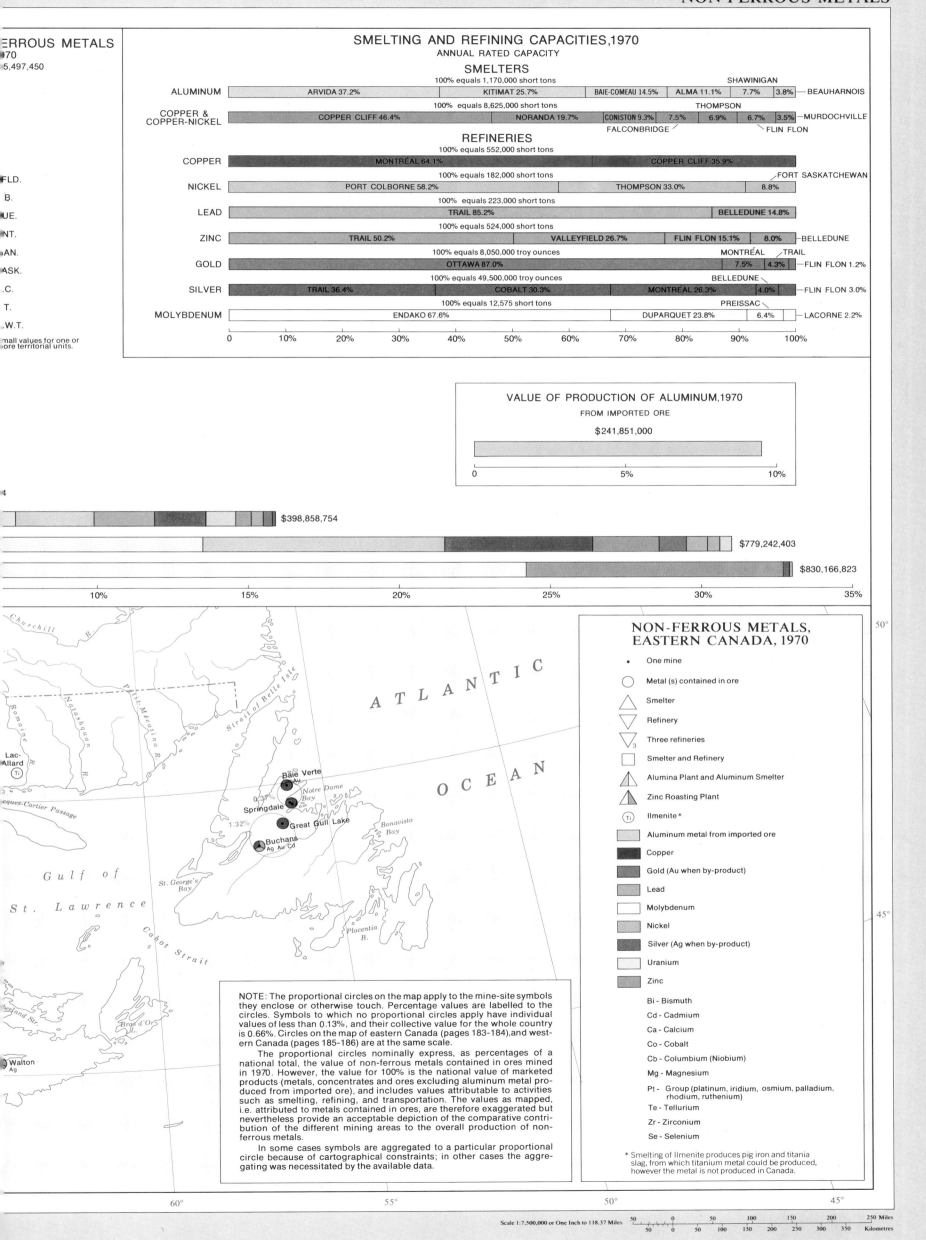

SMELTING AND REFINING CAPACITIES, 1970
ANNUAL RATED CAPACITY
SMELTERS

ALUMINUM — 100% equals 1,170,000 short tons
SHAWINIGAN
| ARVIDA 37.2% | KITIMAT 25.7% | BAIE-COMEAU 14.5% | ALMA 11.1% | 7.7% | 3.8% — BEAUHARNOIS |

COPPER & COPPER-NICKEL — 100% equals 8,625,000 short tons
THOMPSON
| COPPER CLIFF 46.4% | NORANDA 19.7% | CONISTON 9.3% | 7.5% | 6.9% | 6.7% | 3.5% — MURDOCHVILLE |
FALCONBRIDGE   FLIN FLON

REFINERIES

COPPER — 100% equals 552,000 short tons
| MONTRÉAL 64.1% | COPPER CLIFF 35.9% |

FORT SASKATCHEWAN
NICKEL — 100% equals 182,000 short tons
| PORT COLBORNE 58.2% | THOMPSON 33.0% | 8.8% |

LEAD — 100% equals 223,000 short tons
| TRAIL 85.2% | BELLEDUNE 14.8% |

ZINC — 100% equals 524,000 short tons
| TRAIL 50.2% | VALLEYFIELD 26.7% | FLIN FLON 15.1% | 8.0% — BELLEDUNE |

GOLD — 100% equals 8,050,000 troy ounces
MONTRÉAL — TRAIL
| OTTAWA 87.0% | 7.5% | 4.3% — FLIN FLON 1.2% |

SILVER — 100% equals 49,500,000 troy ounces
BELLEDUNE
| TRAIL 36.4% | COBALT 30.3% | MONTRÉAL 26.3% | 4.0% — FLIN FLON 3.0% |

MOLYBDENUM — 100% equals 12,575 short tons
PREISSAC
| ENDAKO 67.6% | DUPARQUET 23.8% | 6.4% — LACORNE 2.2% |

0 10% 20% 30% 40% 50% 60% 70% 80% 90% 100%

VALUE OF PRODUCTION OF ALUMINUM, 1970
FROM IMPORTED ORE
$241,851,000

0 5% 10%

$398,858,754

$779,242,403

$830,166,823

10% 15% 20% 25% 30% 35%

NON-FERROUS METALS, EASTERN CANADA, 1970

- One mine
- Metal (s) contained in ore
- Smelter
- Refinery
- Three refineries
- Smelter and Refinery
- Alumina Plant and Aluminum Smelter
- Zinc Roasting Plant
- (Ti) Ilmenite *
- Aluminum metal from imported ore
- Copper
- Gold (Au when by-product)
- Lead
- Molybdenum
- Nickel
- Silver (Ag when by-product)
- Uranium
- Zinc

Bi - Bismuth
Cd - Cadmium
Ca - Calcium
Co - Cobalt
Cb - Columbium (Niobium)
Mg - Magnesium
Pt - Group (platinum, iridium, osmium, palladium, rhodium, ruthenium)
Te - Tellurium
Zr - Zirconium
Se - Selenium

* Smelting of Ilmenite produces pig iron and titania slag, from which titanium metal could be produced, however the metal is not produced in Canada.

NOTE: The proportional circles on the map apply to the mine-site symbols they enclose or otherwise touch. Percentage values are labelled to the circles. Symbols to which no proportional circles apply have individual values of less than 0.13%, and their collective value for the whole country is 0.66%. Circles on the map of eastern Canada (pages 183-184), and western Canada (pages 185-186) are at the same scale.

The proportional circles nominally express, as percentages of a national total, the value of non-ferrous metals contained in ores mined in 1970. However, the value for 100% is the national value of marketed products (metals, concentrates and ores excluding aluminum metal produced from imported ore), and includes values attributable to activities such as smelting, refining, and transportation. The values as mapped, i.e. attributed to metals contained in ores, are therefore exaggerated but nevertheless provide an acceptable depiction of the comparative contribution of the different mining areas to the overall production of non-ferrous metals.

In some cases symbols are aggregated to a particular proportional circle because of cartographical constraints; in other cases the aggregating was necessitated by the available data.

ATLANTIC OCEAN

Gulf of St. Lawrence

Strait of Belle Isle
Notre Dame Bay
Bonavista Bay
Placentia B.
St. George's Bay

Baie Verte
Au
Springdale 0.37%
1.32% Great Gull Lake
Buchans
Ag Au Cd

Lac-Allard (Ti)
Walton Ag

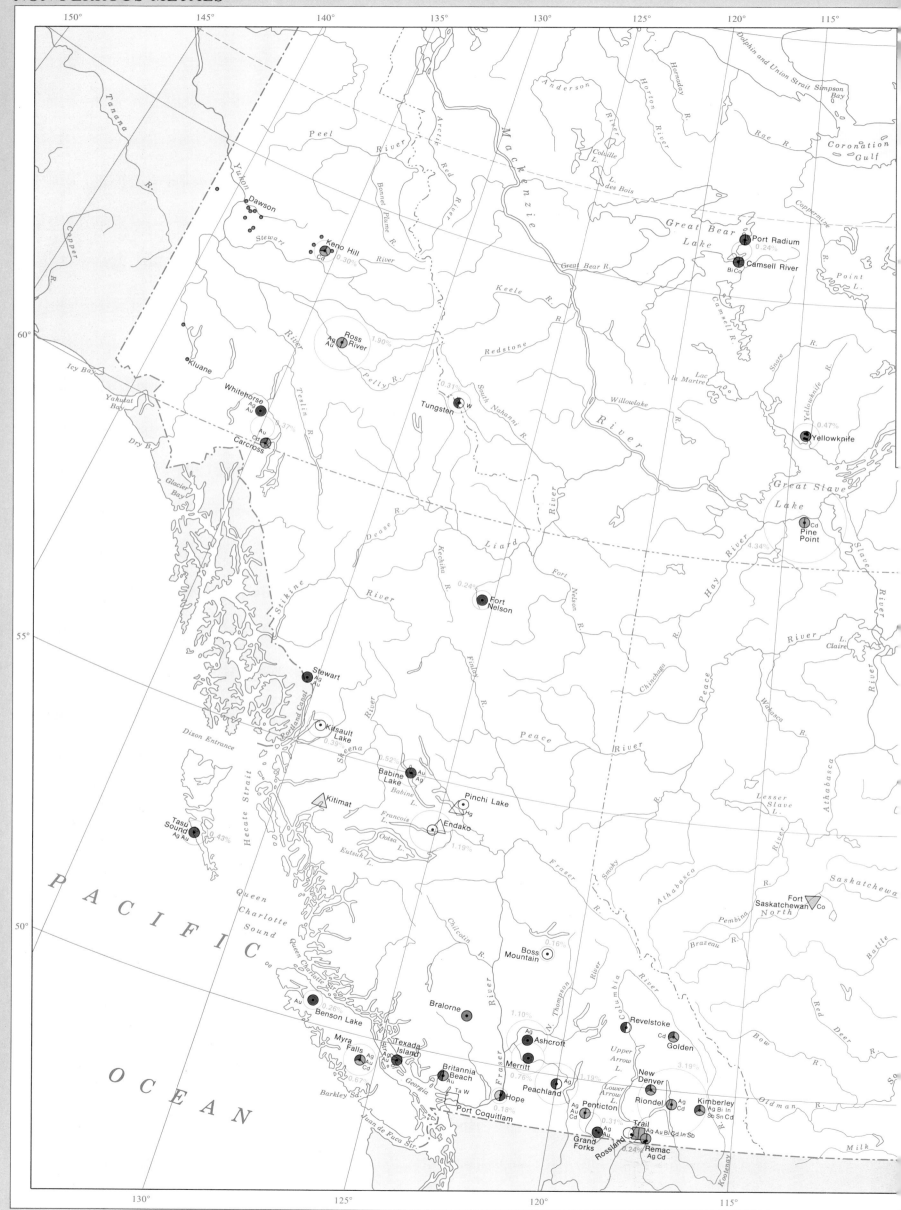

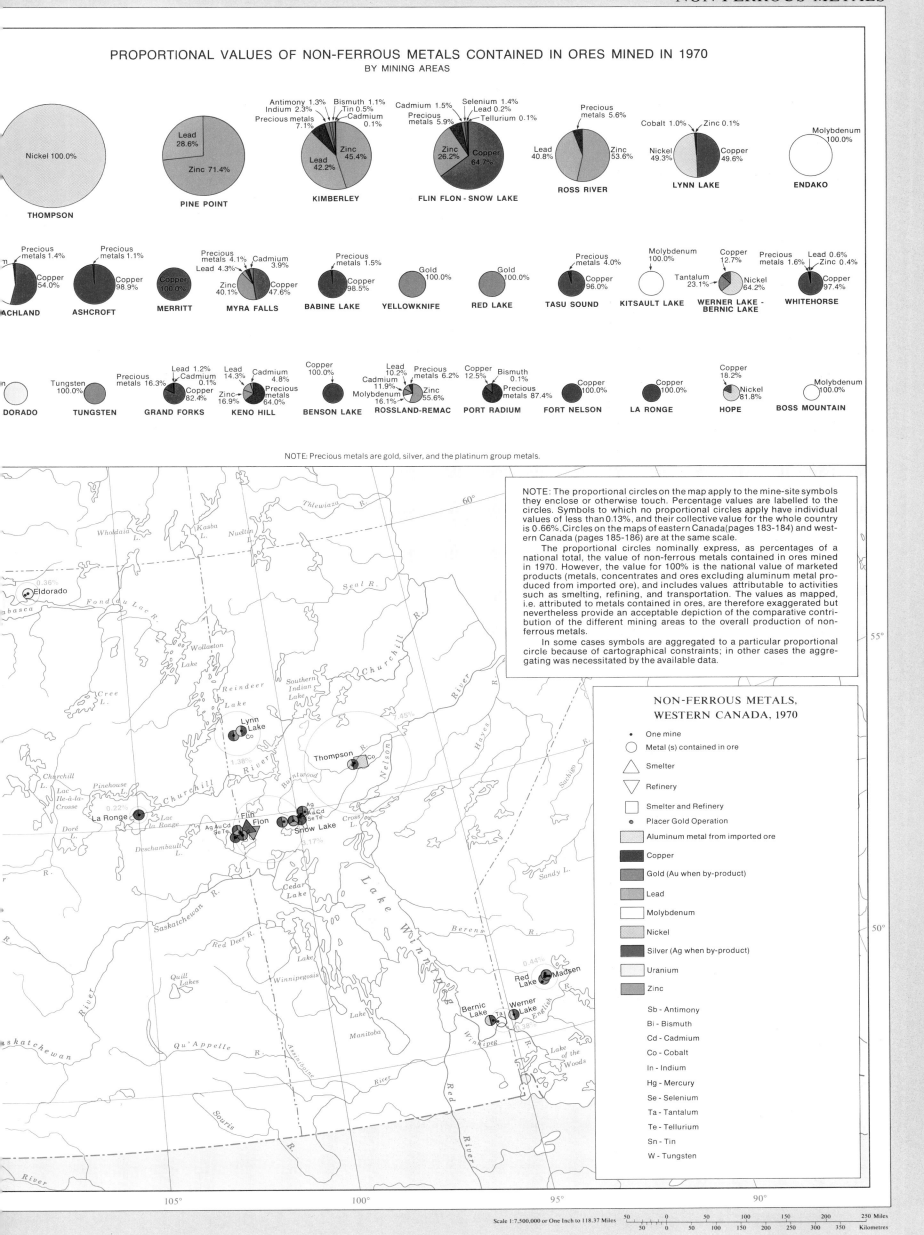

PROPORTIONAL VALUES OF NON-FERROUS METALS CONTAINED IN ORES MINED IN 1970
BY MINING AREAS

Nickel 100.0% — THOMPSON

Lead 28.6% / Zinc 71.4% — PINE POINT

Antimony 1.3% / Indium 2.3% / Precious metals 7.1% / Bismuth 1.1% / Tin 0.5% / Cadmium 0.1% / Zinc 45.4% / Lead 42.2% — KIMBERLEY

Cadmium 1.5% / Precious metals 5.9% / Selenium 1.4% / Lead 0.2% / Tellurium 0.1% / Zinc 26.2% / Copper 64.7% — FLIN FLON - SNOW LAKE

Precious metals 5.6% / Lead 40.8% / Zinc 53.6% — ROSS RIVER

Cobalt 1.0% / Zinc 0.1% / Nickel 49.3% / Copper 49.6% — LYNN LAKE

Molybdenum 100.0% — ENDAKO

Precious metals 1.4% / Copper 54.0% — ACHLAND

Precious metals 1.1% / Copper 98.9% — ASHCROFT

Copper 100.0% — MERRITT

Precious metals 4.1% / Lead 4.3% / Cadmium 3.9% / Zinc 40.1% / Copper 47.6% — MYRA FALLS

Precious metals 1.5% / Copper 98.5% — BABINE LAKE

Gold 100.0% — YELLOWKNIFE

Gold 100.0% — RED LAKE

Precious metals 4.0% / Copper 96.0% — TASU SOUND

Molybdenum 100.0% — KITSAULT LAKE

Copper 12.7% / Tantalum 23.1% / Nickel 64.2% — WERNER LAKE - BERNIC LAKE

Precious metals 1.6% / Lead 0.6% / Zinc 0.4% / Copper 97.4% — WHITEHORSE

Tungsten 100.0% — DORADO

Precious metals 16.3% / Tungsten 100.0% — TUNGSTEN

Lead 1.2% / Cadmium 0.1% / Precious metals 16.3% / Copper 82.4% — GRAND FORKS

Lead 14.3% / Cadmium 4.8% / Zinc 16.9% / Precious metals 64.0% — KENO HILL

Copper 100.0% — BENSON LAKE

Lead 10.2% / Cadmium 11.9% / Molybdenum 16.1% / Precious metals 6.2% / Zinc 55.6% — ROSSLAND-REMAC

Copper 12.5% / Bismuth 0.1% / Precious metals 87.4% — PORT RADIUM

Copper 100.0% — FORT NELSON

Copper 100.0% — LA RONGE

Copper 18.2% / Nickel 81.8% — HOPE

Molybdenum 100.0% — BOSS MOUNTAIN

NOTE: Precious metals are gold, silver, and the platinum group metals.

NOTE: The proportional circles on the map apply to the mine-site symbols they enclose or otherwise touch. Percentage values are labelled to the circles. Symbols to which no proportional circles apply have individual values of less than 0.13%, and their collective value for the whole country is 0.66%. Circles on the maps of eastern Canada (pages 183-184) and western Canada (pages 185-186) are at the same scale.

The proportional circles nominally express, as percentages of a national total, the value of non-ferrous metals contained in ores mined in 1970. However, the value for 100% is the national value of marketed products (metals, concentrates and ores excluding aluminum metal produced from imported ore), and includes values attributable to activities such as smelting, refining, and transportation. The values as mapped, i.e. attributed to metals contained in ores, are therefore exaggerated but nevertheless provide an acceptable depiction of the comparative contribution of the different mining areas to the overall production of non-ferrous metals.

In some cases symbols are aggregated to a particular proportional circle because of cartographical constraints; in other cases the aggregating was necessitated by the available data.

NON-FERROUS METALS,
WESTERN CANADA, 1970

· One mine
○ Metal (s) contained in ore
△ Smelter
▽ Refinery
□ Smelter and Refinery
● Placer Gold Operation

Aluminum metal from imported ore
Copper
Gold (Au when by-product)
Lead
Molybdenum
Nickel
Silver (Ag when by-product)
Uranium
Zinc

Sb - Antimony
Bi - Bismuth
Cd - Cadmium
Co - Cobalt
In - Indium
Hg - Mercury
Se - Selenium
Ta - Tantalum
Te - Tellurium
Sn - Tin
W - Tungsten

Scale 1:7,500,000 or One Inch to 118.37 Miles

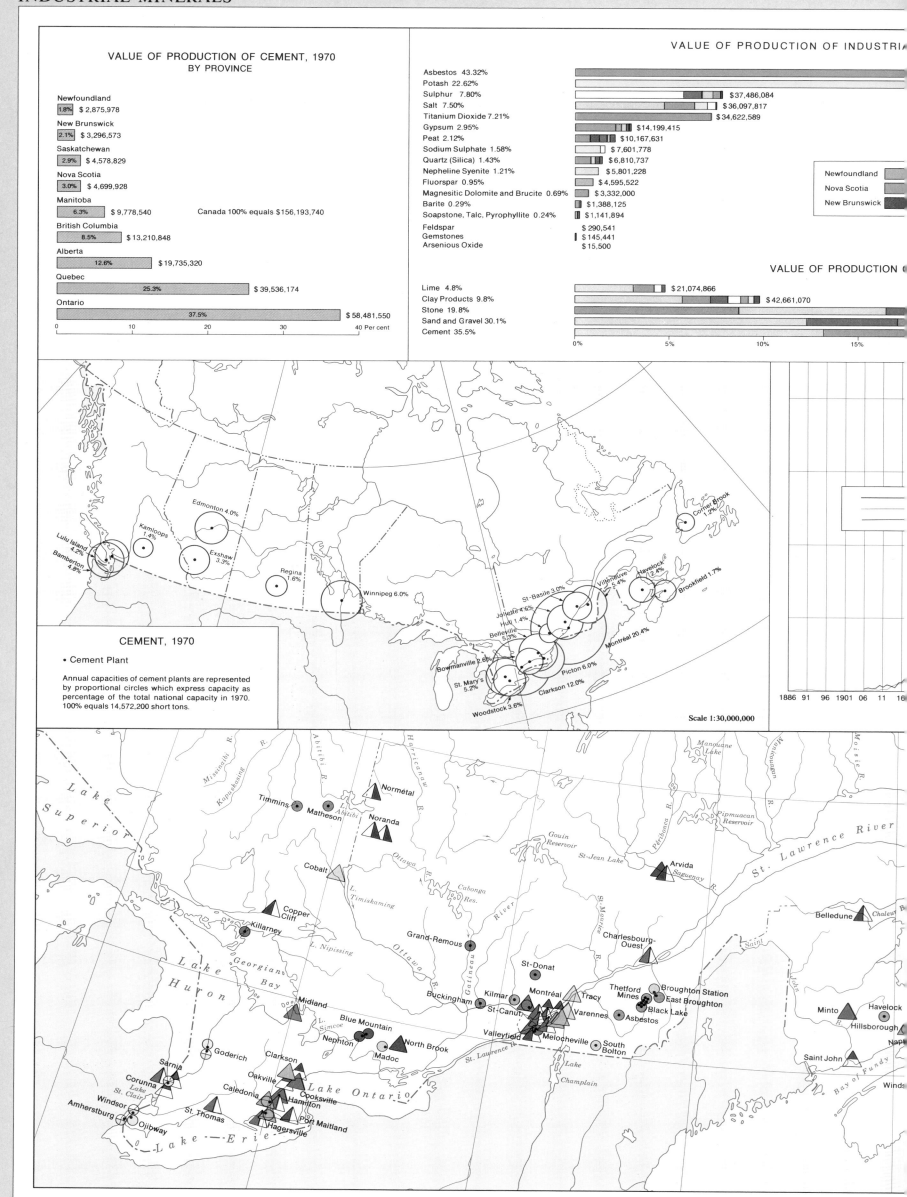

VALUE OF PRODUCTION OF CEMENT, 1970
BY PROVINCE

Newfoundland
1.8% $ 2,875,978

New Brunswick
2.1% $ 3,296,573

Saskatchewan
2.9% $ 4,578,829

Nova Scotia
3.0% $ 4,699,928

Manitoba
6.3% $ 9,778,540

British Columbia
8.5% $ 13,210,848

Alberta
12.6% $ 19,735,320

Quebec
25.3% $ 39,536,174

Ontario
37.5% $ 58,481,550

Canada 100% equals $156,193,740

0 10 20 30 40 Per cent

VALUE OF PRODUCTION OF INDUSTRIA

Asbestos 43.32%	
Potash 22.62%	
Sulphur 7.80%	$37,486,084
Salt 7.50%	$36,097,817
Titanium Dioxide 7.21%	$34,622,589
Gypsum 2.95%	$14,199,415
Peat 2.12%	$10,167,631
Sodium Sulphate 1.58%	$7,601,778
Quartz (Silica) 1.43%	$6,810,737
Nepheline Syenite 1.21%	$5,801,228
Fluorspar 0.95%	$4,595,522
Magnesitic Dolomite and Brucite 0.69%	$3,332,000
Barite 0.29%	$1,388,125
Soapstone, Talc, Pyrophyllite 0.24%	$1,141,894
Feldspar	$ 290,541
Gemstones	$ 145,441
Arsenious Oxide	$ 15,500

Newfoundland
Nova Scotia
New Brunswick

VALUE OF PRODUCTION O

Lime 4.8%	$21,074,866
Clay Products 9.8%	$42,661,070
Stone 19.8%	
Sand and Gravel 30.1%	
Cement 35.5%	

0% 5% 10% 15%

CEMENT, 1970

• Cement Plant

Annual capacities of cement plants are represented by proportional circles which express capacity as percentage of the total national capacity in 1970. 100% equals 14,572,200 short tons.

Scale 1:30,000,000

Edmonton 4.0%
Kamloops 1.4%
Lulu Island 4.2%
Bamberton 4.8%
Exshaw 3.3%
Regina 1.6%
Winnipeg 6.0%
Corner Brook 1.2%
St-Basile 3.0%
Villeneuve 5.4%
Havelock 1.2%
Brookfield 1.7%
Joliette 4.6%
Hull 1.4%
Belleville 5.3%
Montréal 20.4%
Bowmanville 2.6%
St. Mary's 5.2%
Picton 6.0%
Clarkson 12.0%
Woodstock 3.6%

1886 91 96 1901 06 11 16

Lambert Conformal Conic Projection Standard Parallels 49°N. and 77°N.

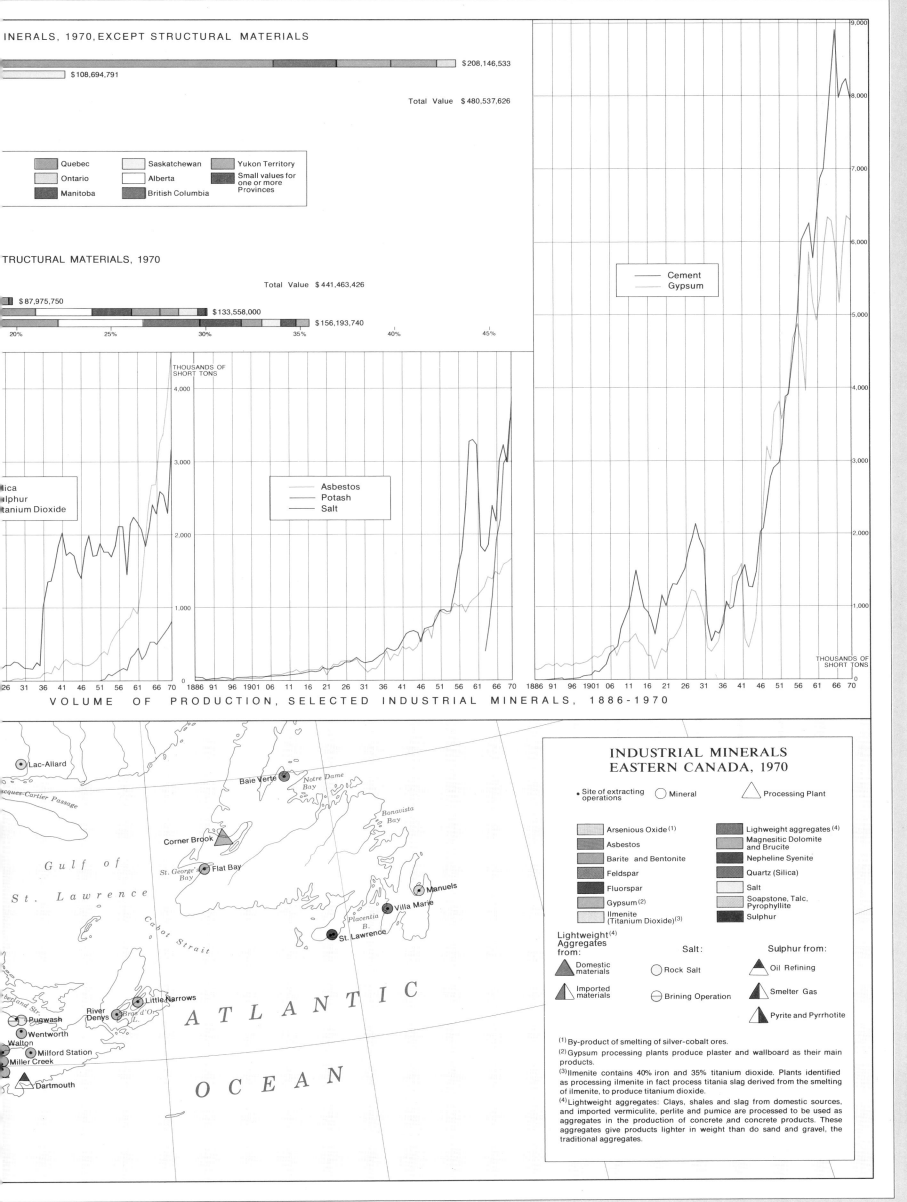

INERALS, 1970, EXCEPT STRUCTURAL MATERIALS

$208,146,533

$108,694,791

Total Value $480,537,626

	Quebec		Saskatchewan		Yukon Territory
	Ontario		Alberta		Small values for one or more Provinces
	Manitoba		British Columbia		

TRUCTURAL MATERIALS, 1970

Total Value $441,463,426

$87,975,750

$133,558,000

$156,193,740

20% 25% 30% 35% 40% 45%

THOUSANDS OF SHORT TONS

4,000

3,000

2,000

1,000

Mica
Sulphur
Titanium Dioxide

Asbestos
Potash
Salt

Cement
Gypsum

9,000

8,000

7,000

6,000

5,000

4,000

3,000

2,000

1,000

THOUSANDS OF SHORT TONS

26 31 36 41 46 51 56 61 66 70   1886 91 96 1901 06 11 16 21 26 31 36 41 46 51 56 61 66 70   1886 91 96 1901 06 11 16 21 26 31 36 41 46 51 56 61 66 70

VOLUME OF PRODUCTION, SELECTED INDUSTRIAL MINERALS, 1886-1970

Lac-Allard

Jacques-Cartier Passage

Baie Verte

Notre Dame Bay

Bonavista Bay

Corner Brook

Gulf of

St. George's Bay   Flat Bay

St. Lawrence

Manuels

Villa Marie

Placentia B.

St. Lawrence

Cabot Strait

Little Narrows

River Denys   Bras d'Or L.

Pugwash

Wentworth

Walton

Milford Station

Miller Creek

Dartmouth

ATLANTIC

OCEAN

INDUSTRIAL MINERALS
EASTERN CANADA, 1970

• Site of extracting operations   ◯ Mineral   △ Processing Plant

Arsenious Oxide [1]		Lighweight aggregates [4]
Asbestos		Magnesitic Dolomite and Brucite
Barite and Bentonite		Nepheline Syenite
Feldspar		Quartz (Silica)
Fluorspar		Salt
Gypsum [2]		Soapstone, Talc, Pyrophyllite
Ilmenite (Titanium Dioxide) [3]		Sulphur

Lightweight [4] Aggregates from:

▲ Domestic materials

◮ Imported materials

Salt:

◯ Rock Salt

⊖ Brining Operation

Sulphur from:

▲ Oil Refining

◣ Smelter Gas

◹ Pyrite and Pyrrhotite

[1] By-product of smelting of silver-cobalt ores.

[2] Gypsum processing plants produce plaster and wallboard as their main products.

[3] Ilmenite contains 40% iron and 35% titanium dioxide. Plants identified as processing ilmenite in fact process titania slag derived from the smelting of ilmenite, to produce titanium dioxide.

[4] Lightweight aggregates: Clays, shales and slag from domestic sources, and imported vermiculite, perlite and pumice are processed to be used as aggregates in the production of concrete and concrete products. These aggregates give products lighter in weight than do sand and gravel, the traditional aggregates.

Scale 1:7,500,000 or One Inch to 118.37 Miles

50 0 50 100 150 200 250 Miles

50 0 50 100 150 200 250 300 350 Kilometres

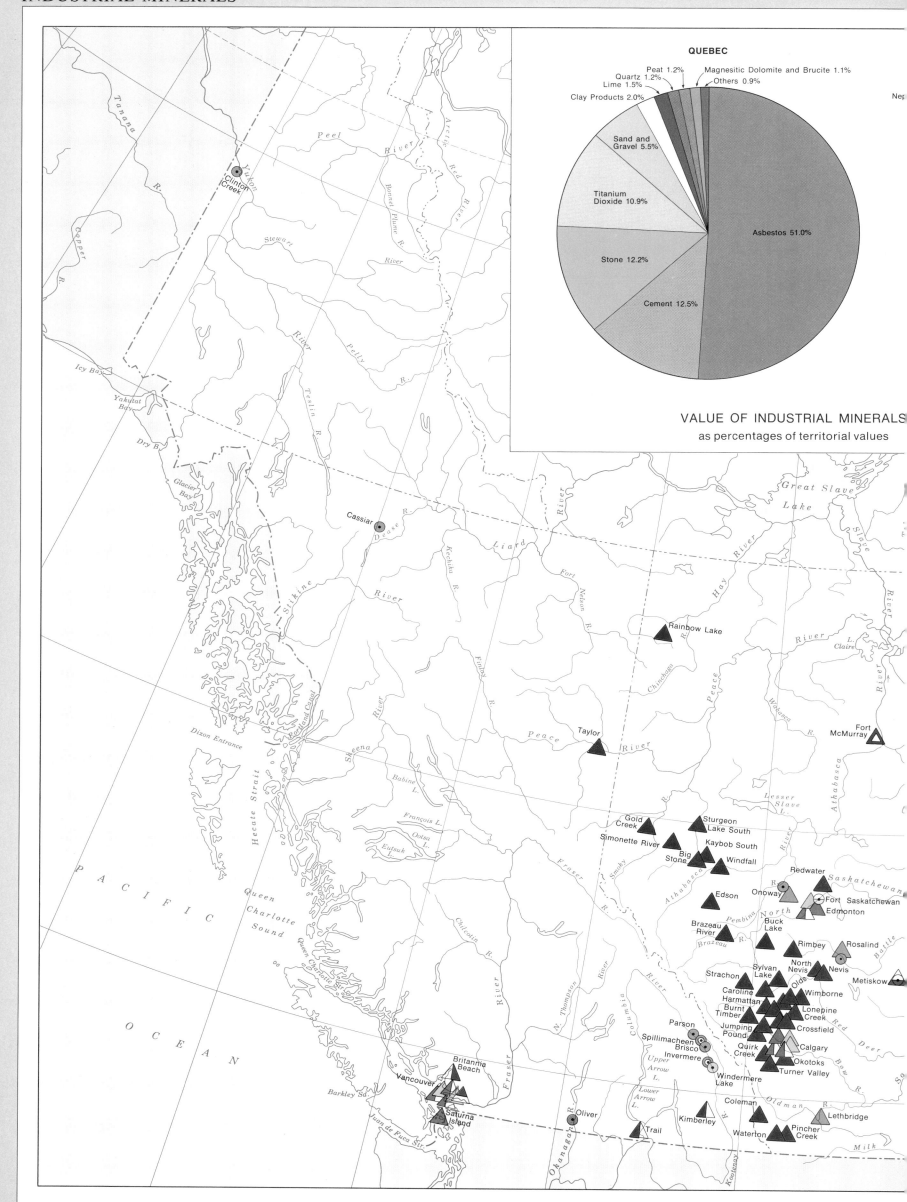

QUEBEC

Peat 1.2%
Quartz 1.2%
Lime 1.5%
Clay Products 2.0%
Magnesitic Dolomite and Brucite 1.1%
Others 0.9%
Sand and Gravel 5.5%
Titanium Dioxide 10.9%
Stone 12.2%
Cement 12.5%
Asbestos 51.0%
Nep

VALUE OF INDUSTRIAL MINERALS
as percentages of territorial values

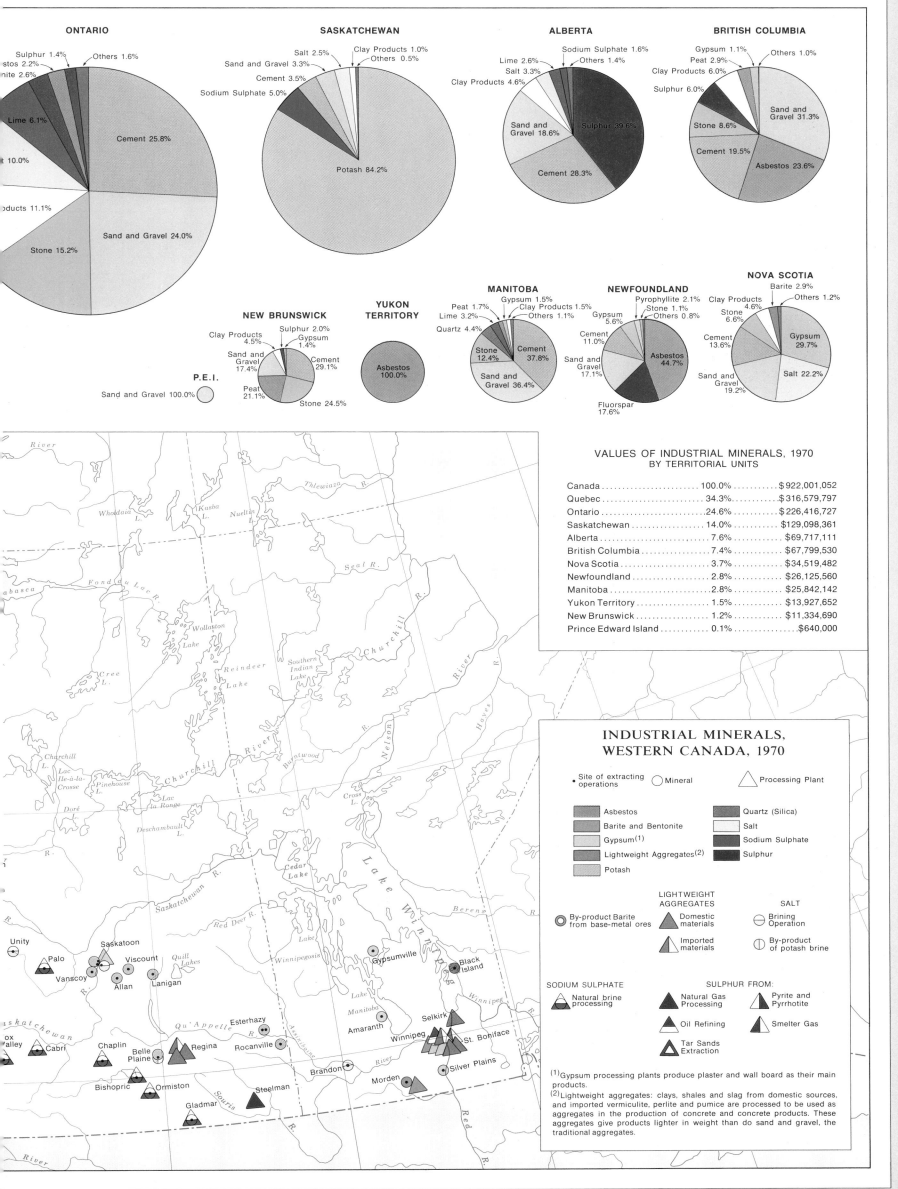

ONTARIO
Sulphur 1.4%
Others 1.6%
...stos 2.2%
...nite 2.6%
Lime 6.1%
...t 10.0%
...oducts 11.1%
Stone 15.2%
Sand and Gravel 24.0%
Cement 25.8%

SASKATCHEWAN
Salt 2.5%
Clay Products 1.0%
Sand and Gravel 3.3%
Others 0.5%
Cement 3.5%
Sodium Sulphate 5.0%
Potash 84.2%

ALBERTA
Sodium Sulphate 1.6%
Lime 2.6%
Others 1.4%
Salt 3.3%
Clay Products 4.6%
Sulphur 39.6%
Sand and Gravel 18.6%
Cement 28.3%

BRITISH COLUMBIA
Gypsum 1.1%
Others 1.0%
Peat 2.9%
Clay Products 6.0%
Sulphur 6.0%
Sand and Gravel 31.3%
Stone 8.6%
Cement 19.5%
Asbestos 23.6%

NEW BRUNSWICK
Clay Products 4.5%
Sulphur 2.0%
Gypsum 1.4%
Sand and Gravel 17.4%
Cement 29.1%
Peat 21.1%
Stone 24.5%

P.E.I.
Sand and Gravel 100.0%

YUKON TERRITORY
Asbestos 100.0%

MANITOBA
Gypsum 1.5%
Peat 1.7%
Clay Products 1.5%
Lime 3.2%
Others 1.1%
Quartz 4.4%
Stone 12.4%
Cement 37.8%
Sand and Gravel 36.4%

NEWFOUNDLAND
Pyrophyllite 2.1%
Stone 1.1%
Gypsum 5.6%
Others 0.8%
Cement 11.0%
Asbestos 44.7%
Sand and Gravel 17.1%
Fluorspar 17.6%

NOVA SCOTIA
Barite 2.9%
Clay Products 4.6%
Others 1.2%
Stone 6.6%
Cement 13.6%
Gypsum 29.7%
Sand and Gravel 19.2%
Salt 22.2%

VALUES OF INDUSTRIAL MINERALS, 1970
BY TERRITORIAL UNITS

Canada	100.0%	$922,001,052
Quebec	34.3%	$316,579,797
Ontario	24.6%	$226,416,727
Saskatchewan	14.0%	$129,098,361
Alberta	7.6%	$69,717,111
British Columbia	7.4%	$67,799,530
Nova Scotia	3.7%	$34,519,482
Newfoundland	2.8%	$26,125,560
Manitoba	2.8%	$25,842,142
Yukon Territory	1.5%	$13,927,652
New Brunswick	1.2%	$11,334,690
Prince Edward Island	0.1%	$640,000

INDUSTRIAL MINERALS, WESTERN CANADA, 1970

- Site of extracting operations
- ○ Mineral
- △ Processing Plant

Asbestos
Barite and Bentonite
Gypsum(1)
Lightweight Aggregates(2)
Potash
Quartz (Silica)
Salt
Sodium Sulphate
Sulphur

By-product Barite from base-metal ores

LIGHTWEIGHT AGGREGATES
Domestic materials
Imported materials

SALT
Brining Operation
By-product of potash brine

SODIUM SULPHATE
Natural brine processing

SULPHUR FROM:
Natural Gas Processing
Pyrite and Pyrrhotite
Oil Refining
Smelter Gas
Tar Sands Extraction

(1)Gypsum processing plants produce plaster and wall board as their main products.
(2)Lightweight aggregates: clays, shales and slag from domestic sources, and imported vermiculite, perlite and pumice are processed to be used as aggregates in the production of concrete and concrete products. These aggregates give products lighter in weight than do sand and gravel, the traditional aggregates.

Scale 1:7,500,000 or One Inch to 118.37 Miles
250 Miles
Kilometres

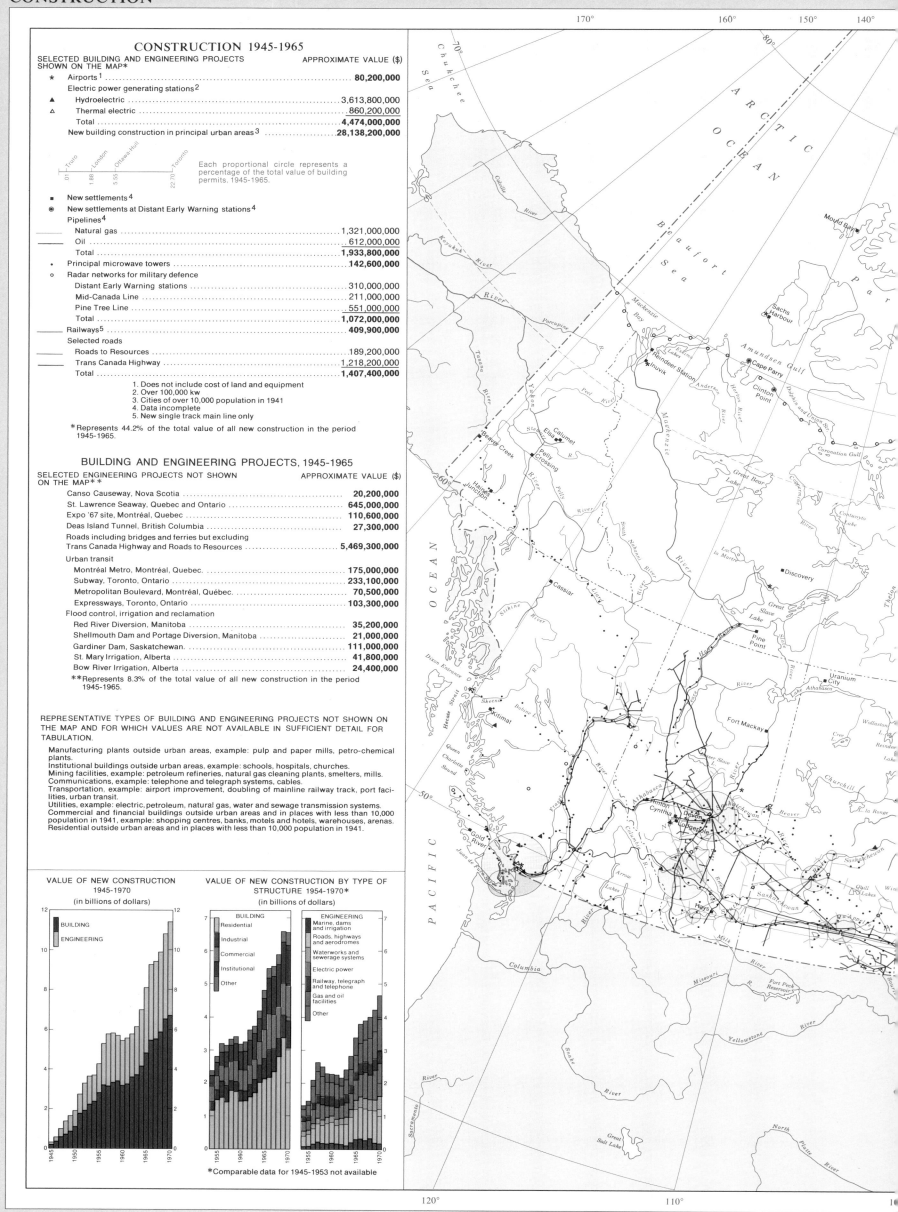

CONSTRUCTION 1945-1965

SELECTED BUILDING AND ENGINEERING PROJECTS
SHOWN ON THE MAP*   APPROXIMATE VALUE ($)

★	Airports[1]	**80,200,000**
	Electric power generating stations[2]	
▲	Hydroelectric	3,613,800,000
△	Thermal electric	860,200,000
	Total	**4,474,000,000**
	New building construction in principal urban areas[3]	**28,138,200,000**

Each proportional circle represents a
percentage of the total value of building
permits, 1945-1965.

■	New settlements[4]	
◉	New settlements at Distant Early Warning stations[4]	
	Pipelines[4]	
	Natural gas	1,321,000,000
	Oil	612,000,000
	Total	**1,933,800,000**
•	Principal microwave towers	**142,600,000**
○	Radar networks for military defence	
	Distant Early Warning stations	310,000,000
	Mid-Canada Line	211,000,000
	Pine Tree Line	551,000,000
	Total	**1,072,000,000**
	Railways[5]	**409,900,000**
	Selected roads	
	Roads to Resources	189,200,000
	Trans Canada Highway	1,218,200,000
	Total	**1,407,400,000**

1. Does not include cost of land and equipment
2. Over 100,000 kw
3. Cities of over 10,000 population in 1941
4. Data incomplete
5. New single track main line only

*Represents 44.2% of the total value of all new construction in the period
1945-1965.

BUILDING AND ENGINEERING PROJECTS, 1945-1965

SELECTED ENGINEERING PROJECTS NOT SHOWN
ON THE MAP**   APPROXIMATE VALUE ($)

Canso Causeway, Nova Scotia	**20,200,000**
St. Lawrence Seaway, Quebec and Ontario	**645,000,000**
Expo '67 site, Montréal, Quebec	**110,600,000**
Deas Island Tunnel, British Columbia	**27,300,000**
Roads including bridges and ferries but excluding Trans Canada Highway and Roads to Resources	**5,469,300,000**
Urban transit	
Montréal Metro, Montréal, Quebec	**175,000,000**
Subway, Toronto, Ontario	**233,100,000**
Metropolitan Boulevard, Montréal, Québec	**70,500,000**
Expressways, Toronto, Ontario	**103,300,000**
Flood control, irrigation and reclamation	
Red River Diversion, Manitoba	**35,200,000**
Shellmouth Dam and Portage Diversion, Manitoba	**21,000,000**
Gardiner Dam, Saskatchewan	**111,000,000**
St. Mary Irrigation, Alberta	**41,800,000**
Bow River Irrigation, Alberta	**24,400,000**

**Represents 8.3% of the total value of all new construction in the period
1945-1965.

REPRESENTATIVE TYPES OF BUILDING AND ENGINEERING PROJECTS NOT SHOWN ON
THE MAP AND FOR WHICH VALUES ARE NOT AVAILABLE IN SUFFICIENT DETAIL FOR
TABULATION.

Manufacturing plants outside urban areas, example: pulp and paper mills, petro-chemical plants.
Institutional buildings outside urban areas, example: schools, hospitals, churches.
Mining facilities, example: petroleum refineries, natural gas cleaning plants, smelters, mills.
Communications, example: telephone and telegraph systems, cables.
Transportation, example: airport improvement, doubling of mainline railway track, port facilities, urban transit.
Utilities, example: electric, petroleum, natural gas, water and sewage transmission systems.
Commercial and financial buildings outside urban areas and in places with less than 10,000 population in 1941, example: shopping centres, banks, motels and hotels, warehouses, arenas.
Residential outside urban areas and in places with less than 10,000 population in 1941.

VALUE OF NEW CONSTRUCTION 1945-1970
(in billions of dollars)

BUILDING
ENGINEERING

VALUE OF NEW CONSTRUCTION BY TYPE OF STRUCTURE 1954-1970*
(in billions of dollars)

BUILDING
Residential
Industrial
Commercial
Institutional
Other

ENGINEERING
Marine, dams and irrigation
Roads, highways and aerodromes
Waterworks and sewerage systems
Electric power
Railway, telegraph and telephone
Gas and oil facilities
Other

*Comparable data for 1945-1953 not available

Lambert Conformal Conic Projection Standard Parallels 49°N. and 77°N.

THE NATIONAL ATLAS OF CANADA

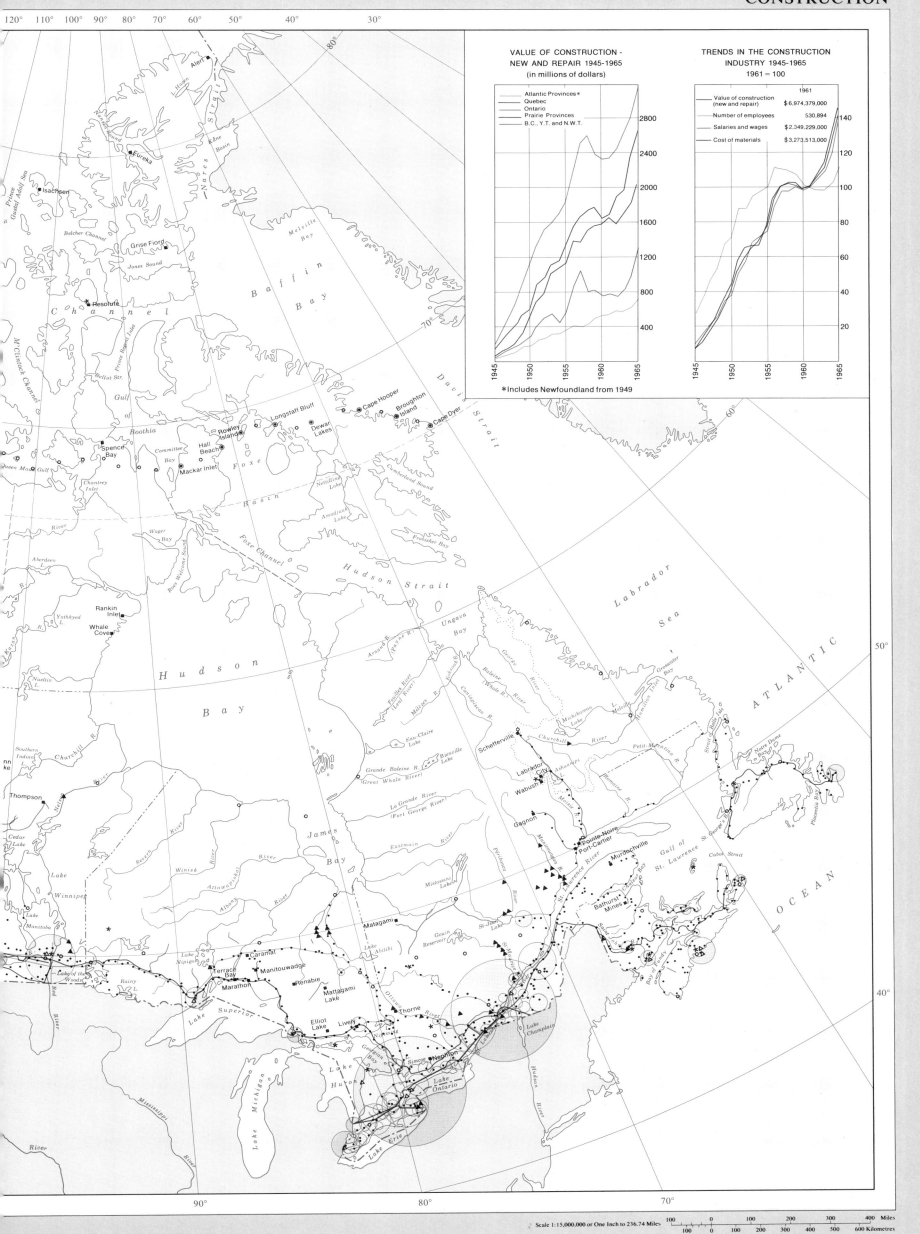

VALUE OF CONSTRUCTION -
NEW AND REPAIR 1945-1965
(in millions of dollars)

Atlantic Provinces*
Quebec
Ontario
Prairie Provinces
B.C., Y.T. and N.W.T.

2800
2400
2000
1600
1200
800
400

1945   1950   1955   1960   1965

*Includes Newfoundland from 1949

TRENDS IN THE CONSTRUCTION
INDUSTRY 1945-1965
1961 = 100

	1961
Value of construction (new and repair)	$6,974,379,000
Number of employees	530,894
Salaries and wages	$2,349,229,000
Cost of materials	$3,273,513,000

140
120
100
80
60
40
20

1945   1950   1955   1960   1965

Scale 1:15,000,000 or One Inch to 236.74 Miles

100   0   100   200   300   400 Miles
100 0   100   200   300   400   500   600 Kilometres

URBAN CENTRES AND COMPLEXES WITH LABOUR FORCE OVER 500 BY PLACE OF RESIDENCE, 1961

RANK	NAME AND TYPE OF AREA*	LABOUR FORCE	%**
1	Montréal, C.M.A., Que.	255,381	18.18
2	Toronto, C.M.A., Ont.	234,511	34.87
3	Hamilton, C.M.A., Ont.	61,090	39.22
4	Vancouver, C.M.A., B.C.	57,485	43.31
5	Winnipeg, C.M.A., Man.	38,537	46.05
6	Kitchener, C.M.A., Ont.	29,294	48.14
7	Windsor, C.M.A., Ont.	24,602	49.89
8	Québec, C.M.A., Que.	23,749	51.58
9	London, C.M.A., Ont.	18,416	52.89
10	Ottawa, C.M.A., Ont.-Que.	17,766	54.16
11	Edmonton, C.M.A., Alta.	17,477	55.40
12	Oshawa, C.M.U.A., Ont.	14,923	56.46
13	St. Catharines, C.M.U.A., Ont.	14,898	57.52
14	Calgary, C.M.A., Alta.	13,064	58.45
15	Trois-Rivières, C.M.U.A., Que.	10,216	59.18
16	Brantford, C.M.U.A., Ont.	9,567	59.86
17	Chicoutimi-Jonquière, C.M.U.A., Que.	9,536	60.54
18	Sault Ste. Marie, C.M.U.A., Ont.	8,545	61.15
19	Sarnia, C.M.U.A., Ont.	8,013	61.72
20	Shawinigan, C.M.U.A., Que.	7,930	62.28
21	Halifax, C.M.A., N.S.	7,472	62.82
22	Peterborough, C.M.U.A., Ont.	7,279	63.33
23	Sherbrooke, C.M.U.A., Que.	7,060	63.84
24	Niagara Falls, C.M.U.A., Ont.	6,746	64.32
25	Saint John, C.M.A., N.B.	6,744	64.80
26	Guelph, C.M.U.A., Ont.	6,274	65.24
27	Welland, centre, Ont.	6,234	65.69
28	Fort William-Port Arthur, C.M.U.A., Ont.	6,027	66.12
29	Victoria, C.M.A., B.C.	5,960	66.54
30	Drummondville, C.M.U.A., Que.	5,958	66.96
31	Granby, centre, Que.	5,702	67.37
32	Sydney-Glace Bay, C.M.U.A., N.S.	5,064	67.73
33	Sudbury, C.M.A., Ont.	4,998	68.09
34	Cornwall, centre, Ont.	4,889	68.43
35	Kingston, C.M.U.A., Ont.	4,886	68.78
36	St-Jean, C.M.U.A., Que.	4,800	69.12
37	Regina, centre, Sask.	4,681	69.46
38	St-Hyacinthe, complex, Que.	4,458	69.77
39	Chilliwack, complex, B.C.	4,264	70.08
40	Sorel, complex, Que.	3,996	70.36
41	Saskatoon, centre, Sask.	3,755	70.63
42	St-Jérôme, complex, Que.	3,754	70.90
43	Valleyfield, complex, Que.	3,658	71.16
44	Rossland-Trail, complex, B.C.	3,443	71.40
45	Port Alberni, complex, B.C.	3,247	71.63
46	Woodstock, centre, Ont.	3,104	71.85
47	Belleville, centre, Ont.	3,021	72.07
48	Victoriaville, complex, Que.	2,985	72.28
49	Chatham, centre, Ont.	2,905	72.49
50	Stratford, centre, Ont.	2,786	72.69
51	Brampton, centre, Ont.	2,728	72.88
52	St. John's, C.M.A., Nfld.	2,693	73.07
53	Magog, complex, Que.	2,620	73.26
54	Brockville, centre, Ont.	2,587	73.44
55	Duncan, complex, B.C.	2,548	73.62
56	Port Colborne, centre, Ont.	2,454	73.80
57	Joliette, complex, Que.	2,302	73.96
58	Moncton, centre, N.B.	2,288	74.12
59	Lachute, complex, Que.	2,196	74.28
60	Corner Brook, centre, Nfld.	2,158	74.44
61	St. Thomas, centre, Ont.	2,052	74.58
62	Powell River, complex, B.C.	2,008	74.72
63	Kitimat, complex, B.C.	1,983	74.87
64	Georgetown, complex, Ont.	1,951	75.00
65	Owen Sound, centre, Ont.	1,861	75.14
66	Orillia, complex, Ont.	1,823	75.27
67	Barrie, centre, Ont.	1,750	75.39
68	La Tuque, centre, Que.	1,674	75.51
69	Medicine Hat, centre, Alta.	1,652	75.63
70	Windsor, complex, Nfld.	1,634	75.74
71	Prince Rupert, complex, B.C.	1,614	75.86
72	Alma, complex, Que.	1,578	75.97
73	Kapuskasing, complex, Ont.	1,575	76.08
74	Lethbridge, centre, Alta.	1,541	76.19
75	Moose Jaw, centre, Sask.	1,523	76.30
76	Prince George, complex, B.C.	1,515	76.41
77	Lindsay, complex, Ont.	1,479	76.52
78	Midland, complex, Ont.	1,439	76.62
79	Nanaimo, complex, B.C.	1,436	76.72
80	Beloeil, complex, Que.	1,426	76.82
81	New Glasgow, complex, N.S.	1,414	76.92
82	Baie-Comeau, complex, Que.	1,304	77.01
83	Pembroke, complex, Ont.	1,297	77.11
84	Cowansville, centre, Que.	1,260	77.20
85	North Bay, complex, Ont.	1,236	77.28
86	Windsor, centre, Que.	1,230	77.37
87	Leamington, centre, Ont.	1,229	77.46
88	Collingwood, centre, Ont.	1,225	77.55
89	Trenton, centre, Ont.	1,213	77.63
90	Port Hope, centre, Ont.	1,191	77.72
91	Wallaceburg, centre, Ont.	1,176	77.80
92	Donnacona, complex, Que.	1,171	77.88
93	Beauharnois, centre, Que.	1,165	77.97
94	Brandon, centre, Man.	1,137	78.05
95	Truro, complex, N.S.	1,117	78.13
96	Paris, centre, Ont.	1,108	78.21
97	Bowmanville, centre, Ont.	1,103	78.29
98	Ocean Falls, centre, B.C.	1,079	78.36
99	Aurora, centre, Ont.	1,071	78.44
100	Edmundston, centre, N.B.	1,071	78.52
101	Cobourg, centre, Ont.	1,048	78.59
102	Ingersoll, centre, Ont.	1,041	78.66
103	Renfrew, centre, Ont.	1,027	78.74
104	Newmarket, centre, Ont.	1,003	78.81
105	Port-Alfred, complex, Que.	997	78.88
106	Coaticook, centre, Que.	987	78.95
107	Prince Albert, centre, Sask.	984	79.02
108	Plessisville, centre, Que.	983	79.09
109	Fredericton, complex, N.B.	967	79.16
110	Hawkesbury, centre, Ont.	960	79.23
111	Amherst, centre, N.S.	955	79.29
112	Fort Erie, centre, Ont.	937	79.36
113	Simcoe, centre, Ont.	932	79.43
114	Charlottetown, centre, P.E.I.	929	79.49
115	Acton Vale, centre, Que.	910	79.56
116	Farnham, centre, Que.	879	79.62
117	Fort Frances, centre, Ont.	877	79.68
118	Bathurst, complex, N.B.	874	79.75
119	Kamloops, complex, B.C.	872	79.81
120	Dryden, centre, Ont.	867	79.87
121	Acton, centre, Ont.	866	79.93
122	L'Assomption, complex, Que.	862	79.99
123	Dalhousie, centre, N.B.	853	80.05
124	Waterloo, centre, Que.	848	80.11
125	Buckingham, centre, Que.	836	80.17
126	Montmagny, centre, Que.	836	80.23
127	Dunnville, centre, Ont.	824	80.29
128	East Angus, centre, Que.	822	80.35
129	Arnprior, centre, Ont.	818	80.41
130	Kenora, centre, Ont.	804	80.47
131	Campbell River, complex, B.C.	795	80.52
132	Kelowna, complex, B.C.	794	80.58
133	Prescott, centre, Ont.	794	80.64
134	Marieville, complex, Que.	782	80.69
135	Espanola, centre, Ont.	760	80.74
136	Perth, centre, Ont.	716	80.80
137	Rock Island, complex, Que.	708	80.85
138	St-Georges, complex, Que.	707	80.90
139	Rimouski, complex, Que.	706	80.95
140	Vernon, complex, B.C.	691	81.00
141	Hanover, centre, Ont.	689	81.04
142	Selkirk, centre, Man.	689	81.09
143	Fergus, centre, Ont.	682	81.14
144	Gananoque, centre, Ont.	678	81.19
145	Terrebonne, centré, Que.	667	81.24
146	Louiseville, centre, Que.	661	81.28
147	Grimsby, centre, Ont.	658	81.33
148	Marathon, centre, Ont.	658	81.38
149	Strathroy, centre, Ont.	655	81.43
150	Chambly, centre, Que.	651	81.47
151	Tillsonburg, centre, Ont.	651	81.52
152	Ste-Marie, centre, Que.	644	81.56
153	Yarmouth, centre, N.S.	644	81.61
154	Kinnaird, complex, B.C.	642	81.66
155	Timmins, C.M.U.A., Ont.	642	81.70
156	Kimberley, complex, B.C.	640	81.75
157	Lac Mégantic, centre, Que.	624	81.79
158	Elmira, centre, Ont.	609	81.83
159	Amherstburg, centre, Ont.	608	81.88
160	St. Mary's, centre, Ont.	600	81.92
161	Smiths Falls, centre, Ont.	582	81.96
162	Richmond, centre, Que.	571	82.00
163	Newcastle, complex, Ont.	569	82.04
164	Thetford Mines, complex, Que.	566	82.08
165	Asbestos, centre, Que.	557	82.12
166	Thurso, centre, Que.	557	82.16
167	Terrace Bay, complex, Ont.	555	82.20
168	Red Rock, complex, Ont.	536	82.24
169	Temiscaming, centre, Que.	534	82.28
170	Campbellton, complex, N.B.	531	82.32
171	Rouyn, complex, Que.	515	82.35
172	Red Deer, centre, Alta.	514	82.39
173	Listowel, centre, Ont.	513	82.43
174	Princeville, centre, Que.	513	82.46

* Types of area

Centre:	The area within the municipal boundaries of a city, town or village; and disjunct unincorporated places.
Complex:	Two or more centres close to each other on the map. An urban municipality with an unincorporated urban fringe adjoining the municipal boundary is designated as a complex.
C.M.A.-C.M.U.A.:	Census Metropolitan Area; Census Major Urban Area; - a complex delineated by the Dominion Bureau of Statistics centred on a major city.

** Percentages are of the national labour force in manufacturing and are cumulative in the table.

RURAL AND URBAN LABOUR FORCE IN MANUFACTURING, 1961

Urban Rural Female

For the purposes of these graphs the term "urban" applies to Centres and Complexes (defined elsewhere on this page) which have a population of 1,000 and over.

CANADA
66.6% 11.9% 19.2% 2.3%

TOTAL - 1,404,865
RURAL - 199,356
URBAN - 1,205,509

NFLD.
61.1 27.9 2.9 8.1
Total - 12,168
Rural - 3,754
Urban - 8,414

P.E.I.
33.1 38.3 2.9 10.1 18.5 9.9
Total - 3,014
Rural - 1,712
Urban - 1,302

N.S.
48.2 36.1 5.8 9.9
Total - 34,081
Rural - 14,276
Urban - 19,805

N.B.
45.3 37.3 8.5 8.9
Total - 28,508
Rural - 13,170
Urban - 15,338

QUE.
66.4 22.5 8.8 2.3
Total - 466,443
Rural - 51,883
Urban - 414,560

ONT.
68.4 19.7 10.0 1.9
Total - 643,284
Rural - 76,609
Urban - 566,675

MAN.
68.6 22.2 7.6 1.6
Total - 46,713
Rural - 4,258
Urban - 42,455

SASK.
73.4 15.2 9.8 1.6
Total - 15,177
Rural - 1,729
Urban - 13,448

ALTA.
73.9 16.4 8.8 0.9
Total - 42,217
Rural - 4,081
Urban - 38,136

B.C.
64.4 22.8 11.0 1.8
Total - 113,019
Rural - 27,758
Urban - 85,261

Y.T.
45.3 31.6 6.3 16.8
Total - 95
Rural - 36
Urban - 59

N.W.T.
33.6 43.8 5.5 17.1
Total - 146
Rural - 89
Urban - 57

LABOUR FORCE IN MANUFACTURING BY TERRITORIAL DIVISION

Y.T. & N.W.T. 0.02% Nfld. 0.87%
B.C. 8.04% P.E.I. 0.22%
Alta. 3.00% N.S. 2.43%
Sask. 1.08% N.B. 2.03%
Man. 3.32% Que. 33.20%
Ont. 45.79%

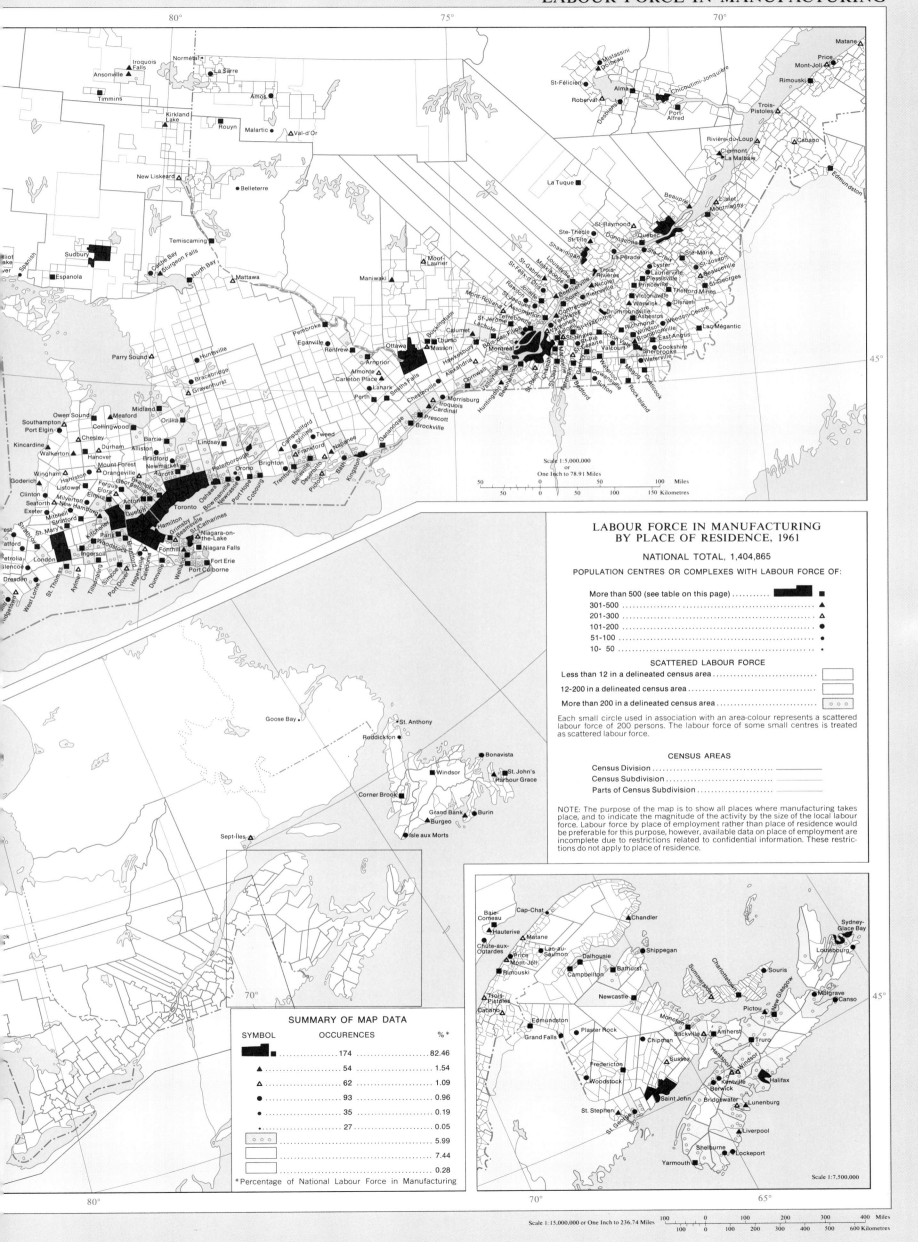

LABOUR FORCE IN MANUFACTURING BY PLACE OF RESIDENCE, 1961

NATIONAL TOTAL, 1,404,865

POPULATION CENTRES OR COMPLEXES WITH LABOUR FORCE OF:

More than 500 (see table on this page) .... ■

301-500 .... ▲

201-300 .... △

101-200 .... ●

51-100 .... •

10- 50 .... ·

SCATTERED LABOUR FORCE

Less than 12 in a delineated census area .... ·

12-200 in a delineated census area ....

More than 200 in a delineated census area .... ○○○

Each small circle used in association with an area-colour represents a scattered labour force of 200 persons. The labour force of some small centres is treated as scattered labour force.

CENSUS AREAS

Census Division ....

Census Subdivision ....

Parts of Census Subdivision ....

NOTE: The purpose of the map is to show all places where manufacturing takes place, and to indicate the magnitude of the activity by the size of the local labour force. Labour force by place of employment rather than place of residence would be preferable for this purpose, however, available data on place of employment are incomplete due to restrictions related to confidential information. These restrictions do not apply to place of residence.

Scale 1:5,000,000
or
One Inch to 78.91 Miles

50   0   50   100 Miles
50   0   50   100   150 Kilometres

SUMMARY OF MAP DATA

SYMBOL	OCCURENCES	% *
■	174	82.46
▲	54	1.54
△	62	1.09
●	93	0.96
•	35	0.19
·	27	0.05
○○○		5.99
		7.44
		0.28

*Percentage of National Labour Force in Manufacturing

Scale 1:7,500,000

Scale 1:15,000,000 or One Inch to 236.74 Miles

100   0   100   200   300   400 Miles
100   0   100   200   300   400   500   600 Kilometres

MANUFACTURING CENTRES

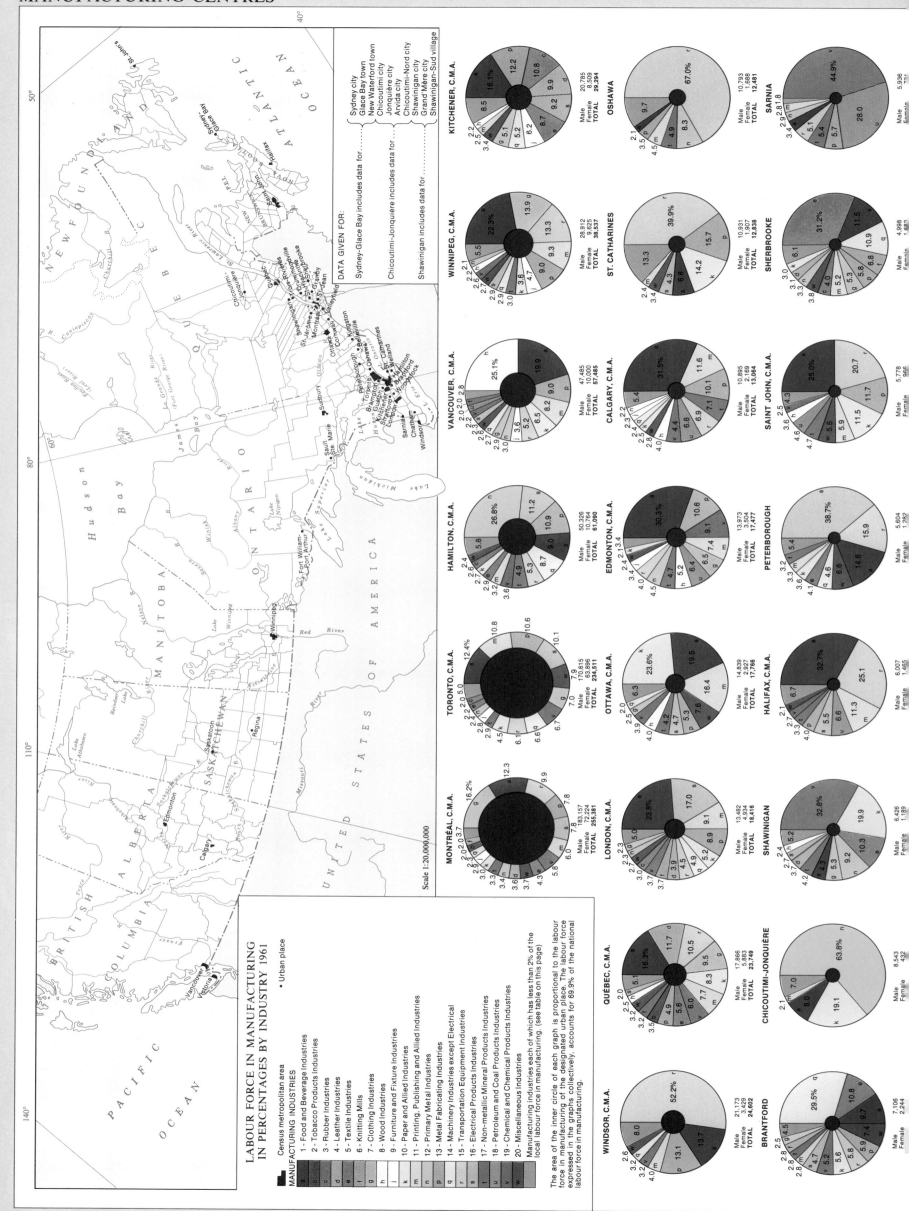

DATA GIVEN FOR:

Sydney-Glace Bay includes data for......
Sydney city
Glace Bay town
New Waterford town

Chicoutimi-Jonquiere includes data for......
Chicoutimi city
Jonquiere city
Arvida city
Chicoutimi-Nord city

Shawinigan includes data for......
Shawinigan city
Grand'Mère city
Shawinigan-Sud village

Scale 1:20,000,000

LABOUR FORCE IN MANUFACTURING IN PERCENTAGES BY INDUSTRY 1961

- Census metropolitan area
- Urban place

MANUFACTURING INDUSTRIES

1 - Food and Beverage Industries
2 - Tobacco Products Industries
3 - Rubber Industries
4 - Leather Industries
5 - Textile Industries
6 - Knitting Mills
7 - Clothing Industries
8 - Wood Industries
9 - Furniture and Fixture Industries
10 - Paper and Allied Industries
11 - Printing, Publishing and Allied Industries
12 - Primary Metal Industries
13 - Metal Fabricating Industries
14 - Machinery Industries except Electrical
15 - Transportation Equipment Industries
16 - Electrical Products Industries
17 - Non-metallic Mineral Products Industries
18 - Petroleum and Coal Products Industries
19 - Chemical and Chemical Products Industries
20 - Miscellaneous Industries

The area of the inner circle of each graph is proportional to the labour force in manufacturing of the designated urban place. The labour force expressed in the graphs collectively, accounts for 69.9% of the national labour force in manufacturing.

Manufacturing industries each of which has less than 2% of the local labour force in manufacturing. (see table on this page)

Pie charts (Manufacturing labour force by city)

SUDBURY, C.M.A. — 64.3%, 13.3 (a), 4.5 (m), 4.2 (p), 3.8 (g), 3.0, 2.1 (n)
Male 4,697 / Female 301 / TOTAL 4,998

VALLEYFIELD — 51.3%, 14.6 (v), 14.1 (a), 6.3 (g), 4.2, 3.8, 2.6 (e)
Male 2,563 / Female 773 / TOTAL 3,336

ST. JOHN'S, C.M.A. — 48.9%, 11.8 (m), 6.9, 6.5 (r), 5.6, 5.1 (e), 4.1 (h), 3.7, 3.1, 2.3, 2.0 (q)
Male 2,120 / Female 573 / TOTAL 2,693

GRANBY — 28.0% (e), 15.2 (s), 11.9, 9.5, 9.0 (b), 8.2, 4.1 (q), 4.0 (w), 2.8, 2.7
Male 3,878 / Female 1,824 / TOTAL 5,702

SASKATOON — 53.6%, 12.6 (m), 6.9, 5.3 (p), 7.7, 3.3 (h), 2.7, 2.0
Male 3,079 / Female 676 / TOTAL 3,755

BRAMPTON — 20.0%, 11.3 (m), 10.4, 9.3, 8.8 (k), 8.5, 7.6 (w), 5.4, 4.0 (q), 3.7, 2.8 (m), 2.7
Male 2,153 / Female 575 / TOTAL 2,728

FORT WILLIAM-PORT ARTHUR — 45.8% (k), 17.1 (r), 14.1 (a), 7.0 (h), 5.4 (m), 4.7, 3.8, 2.1
Male 5,309 / Female 523 / TOTAL 5,832

ST-JEAN — 34.7% (s), 13.2, 7.4 (r), 6.2 (f), 6.6, 6.1, 5.9, 5.9, 5.7, 5.3 (v), 3.0
Male 2,850 / Female 1,031 / TOTAL 3,881

STRATFORD — 19.7%, 16.7 (a), 10.5, 10.4 (j), 6.8, 5.7 (w), 5.5, 5.4, 5.1 (r), 4.0, 3.4
Male 1,927 / Female 859 / TOTAL 2,786

VICTORIA, C.M.A. — 28.3% (h), 24.4, 17.6 (m), 12.9, 7.2 (p), 7.7, 4.2 (q), 3.1 (d), 2.3, 2.0
Male 5,187 / Female 773 / TOTAL 5,960

SYDNEY-GLACE BAY — 65.8% (a), 15.4 (p), 7.7 (m), 7.1, 4.0
Male 3,769 / Female 270 / TOTAL 4,039

CHATHAM — 34.1% (r), 29.3, 7.7 (q), 5.6 (m), 4.9, 4.0 (j), 3.7 (h), 2.5, 2.2, 2.0
Male 2,489 / Female 416 / TOTAL 2,905

GUELPH — 25.5%, 11.1 (s), 10.4, 10.1 (n), 8.5, 7.4, 7.2 (m), 5.1 (q), 3.2, 2.9, 2.4, 2.2, 2.0, 2.0
Male 4,446 / Female 1,661 / TOTAL 6,107

KINGSTON — 34.9% (n), 25.5, 8.5 (a), 7.6, 5.1, 4.3, 3.6, 3.6, 2.2
Male 3,730 / Female 714 / TOTAL 4,444

BELLEVILLE — 31.6% (s), 17.4, 8.3, 7.1 (a), 6.5, 6.0 (w), 5.5, 4.7 (g), 3.9, 3.5, 3.3 (m), 2.2
Male 2,143 / Female 878 / TOTAL 3,021

TROIS-RIVIÈRES — 30.9%, 17.1 (k), 11.0, 9.3 (s), 7.2, 6.9 (m), 6.1, 3.4, 3.1 (q), 3.0, 2.0
Male 4,595 / Female 1,521 / TOTAL 6,116

DRUMMONDVILLE — 59.8% (e), 6.8, 6.3 (k), 5.3 (g), 5.6, 3.6 (m), 3.4 (f), 3.5, 2.3
Male 3,242 / Female 1,249 / TOTAL 4,491

WOODSTOCK — 20.5%, 14.7 (f), 13.2 (k), 9.1, 7.9, 6.1 (m), 5.6 (h), 4.6 (g), 4.0 (t), 2.3
Male 2,344 / Female 760 / TOTAL 3,104

WELLAND — 52.4% (n), 13.4 (p), 7.2 (q), 6.0 (p), 4.7, 4.5, 4.1, 3.2
Male 5,343 / Female 891 / TOTAL 6,234

REGINA — 30.7%, 13.1 (m), 12.1 (u), 10.2 (p), 7.3, 7.0 (f), 14.8, 3.0 (k), 2.7, 2.5, 2.3, 2.0
Male 3,988 / Female 693 / TOTAL 4,681

ST-HYACINTHE — 24.0% (e), 20.9, 12.3, 8.7 (d), 8.0 (a), 7.6 (h), 4.9 (k), 2.4, 2.2
Male 2,110 / Female 1,120 / TOTAL 3,230

SAULT STE. MARIE — 74.3%, 8.2 (a), 6.3, 3.6 (h), 2.5 (n), 2.4, 2.4 (p m)
Male 5,972 / Female 423 / TOTAL 6,395

CORNWALL — 35.0%, 32.1, 11.3, 7.8, 6.7 (a), 4.9, 2.2
Male 4,125 / Female 764 / TOTAL 4,889

ST-JÉRÔME — 28.4% (c), 15.2, 14.2 (k), 8.8 (d), 8.1 (a), 4.2 (p), 3.8, 3.7, 2.9, 2.7
Male 2,368 / Female 958 / TOTAL 3,326

MANUFACTURING INDUSTRIES EACH OF WHICH HAS LESS THAN 2% OF THE LOCAL LABOUR FORCE IN MANUFACTURING

NOTE: Where percentage values are not shown the value is less than 0.1% of the local labour force in manufacturing.

MANUFACTURING INDUSTRIES

1) Food and Beverage
2) Tobacco Products
3) Rubber
4) Leather
5) Textile
6) Knitting Mills
7) Clothing
8) Wood
9) Furniture and Fixture
10) Paper and Allied
11) Printing, Publishing and Allied
12) Primary Metal
13) Metal Fabricating
14) Machinery except Electrical
15) Transportation Equipment
16) Electrical Products
17) Non-metallic Mineral Products
18) Petroleum and Coal Products
19) Chemical and Chemical Products
20) Miscellaneous

Lambert Conformal Conic Projection Standard Parallels 49°N. and 77°N.
THE NATIONAL ATLAS OF CANADA

MANUFAC

SELECTED CHARACTERISTICS
AND LOCATION OF ESTABLI

	RANK BY VALUE ADDED				STANDARD INDUSTRIAL CLASSIFICATION CODE			FEMALE PRODUCTION WORKERS AS A PERCE TOTAL PRODUCTION WORKERS IN THE INDU
	RANK BY GROSS VALUE				PERCENTAGE OF NATIONAL VALUE ADDED BY MANUFACTURING			PRODUCTION WORKERS AS A PERCENTAGE OF TOTAL EMPLOYEES IN THE INDUSTRY
		RANK BY NUMBER OF EMPLOYEES				CUMULATIVE PERCENTAGE		LABOUR FORCE IN THE INDUSTRY AS A PERCENTAGE OF NATIONAL LABOUR FORCE IN MANUFACTURING

COST STRUCTURE

COST FACTORS AS PERCENTAGES OF GROSS VALUE

				RANK BY NUMBER OF ESTABLISHMENTS				Salary and Wages %	Depreciation, profits, etc. %	Raw Materials %	Power %
				INDUSTRY				VALUE ADDED			
								GROSS VALUE			
I	II	III	IV	V	VI	VII	VIII	IX			
				ALL MANUFACTURING							
1	1	1	60	PULP AND PAPER	10-2710	7.89	7.89	20.50%	30.73%	41.61%	7.16% $1,639,671,340.
2	2	7	138	SMELTING AND REFINING	12-2950	4.96	12.85	10.60%	25.44%	60.63%	$1,471,048,021.
3	6	4	111	IRON AND STEEL MILLS	12-2910	3.85	16.70	24.36%	27.57%	44.32%	$792,574,921.
4	5	15	154	MOTOR VEHICLES	15-3230	2.60	19.30	13.65%	17.65%	68.13%	$885,584,796.
5	3	31	106	PETROLEUM REFINING	18-3651	2.59	21.89	6.86%	16.42%	75.81%	$1,186,928,752.
6	13	5	9	PRINTING AND PUBLISHING	11-2890	2.56	24.45	39.93%	33.79%	25.46%	$370,303,367.
7	8	24	57	INDUSTRIAL CHEMICALS	19-3780	2.37	26.82	18.55%	34.94%	37.79%	8.72% $481,677,708.
8	7	2	1	SAWMILLS	8-2513	2.04	28.86	27.00%	13.73%	57.15%	$535,846,444.
9	11	9	19	MISCELLANEOUS MACHINERY AND EQUIPMENT	14-3150	1.95	30.81	31.35%	21.90%	45.62%	$391,498,556.
10	22	53	97	BREWERIES	1-1450	1.85	32.66	15.73%	60.27%	22.73%	$259,759,979.
11	14	3	2	BAKERIES	1-1291	1.82	34.48	31.30%	21.26%	44.51%	$369,793,018.
12	16	8	73	AIRCRAFT AND PARTS	15-3210	1.80	36.28	40.21%	14.22%	44.72%	$352,946,738.
13	4	11	30	SLAUGHTERING AND MEAT PACKING	1-1011	1.71	37.99	10.42%	6.46%	82.52%	$1,083,064,453.
14	12	19	17	METAL STAMPING, PRESSING AND COATING	13-3040	1.58	39.57	22.61%	22.27%	54.10%	$375,739,996.
15	23	12	61	COMMUNICATION EQUIPMENT	16-3350	1.53	41.10	42.41%	20.76%	36.26%	$258,530,324.
16	15	17	58	MOTOR VEHICLE PARTS AND ACCESSORIES	15-3250	1.51	42.61	29.24%	16.43%	52.81%	$352,143,141.
17	10	36	29	MISCELLANEOUS FOOD	1-1392	1.43	44.04	10.52%	26.67%	61.73%	$409,416,837.
18	27	13	3	PRINTING AND BOOKBINDING	11-2861	1.37	45.41	38.06%	25.21%	35.87%	$231,013,338.
19	9	14	10	PASTEURIZING PLANTS	1-1053	1.28	46.69	20.47%	12.60%	64.82%	$411,895,269.
20	17	22	23	FRUIT AND VEGETABLE CANNERS AND PRESERVERS	1-1120	1.23	47.92	14.80%	24.49%	59.47%	$334,047,507.
21	32	23	66	ELECTRICAL INDUSTRIAL EQUIPMENT	16-3360	1.21	49.13	37.04%	22.15%	39.73%	$218,491,201.
22	21	10	11	WOMEN'S CLOTHING	7-2441	1.20	50.33	26.64%	19.06%	54.05%	$279,577,186.

RING, 1961

IANUFACTURING INDUSTRIES
ITS BY ECONOMIC REGIONS.

SUMMARY STATISTICS

GROSS VALUE OF MANUFACTURING	$24,243,294,949
VALUE ADDED BY MANUFACTURING	$10,682,137,680
LABOUR FORCE IN MANUFACTURING	1,264,946
NUMBER OF PRODUCTION WORKERS	969,276

XII:)F
XIII: PER CAPITA VALUE ADDED BY PRODUCTION WORKERS (Total value added) ÷ (Number of production workers)
XIV: AVERAGE WAGES OF PRODUCTION WORKERS
XV: NUMBER OF ESTABLISHMENTS

I	XII	XIII	XIV	XV
2	21.77	$11,020.	$3,762.	32,415
9	1.95	$15,767.	$5,077.	125
25	0.01	$22,549.	$5,142.	24
5	6.13	$14,428.	$5,362.	42
2	2.05	$17,182.	$5,249.	17
3	0.07	$38,001.	$5,642.	44
2	12.42	$17,301.	$4,686.	752
39	0.56	$23,785.	$5,171.	128
24	0.56	$6,223.	$3,428.	3,260
13	4.07	$11,845.	$4,236.	420
55	0.69	$35,155.	$4,908.	54
99	23.98	$6,341.	$3,151.	2,529
32	2.05	$9,976.	$4,561.	80
34	19.13	$9,285.	$4,230.	447
45	10.95	$11,865.	$4,346.	542
03	47.21	$10,543.	$3,714.	125
35	13.19	$10,112.	$4,553.	126
66	39.93	$20,003.	$3,296.	268
38	27.17	$9,096.	$3,742.	1,688
47	3.46	$7,616.	$3,845.	732
96	47.58	$9,722.	$2,560.	335
60	16.26	$13,008.	$4,404.	97
99	77.94	$5,599.	$2,509.	633

LOCATION OF ESTABLISHMENTS BY ECONOMIC REGION

PERCENTAGE OF TOTAL ESTABLISHMENTS IN CANADA (to nearest whole number)

Less than 1% · 1% · 2% · 3% · 4% · 5-7% · 8-70% · Not an economic region

The two digit number (e.g. **00**) in the upper left corner of a cell is the code for an Economic Region as shown on the map of Economic Regions, page 202.

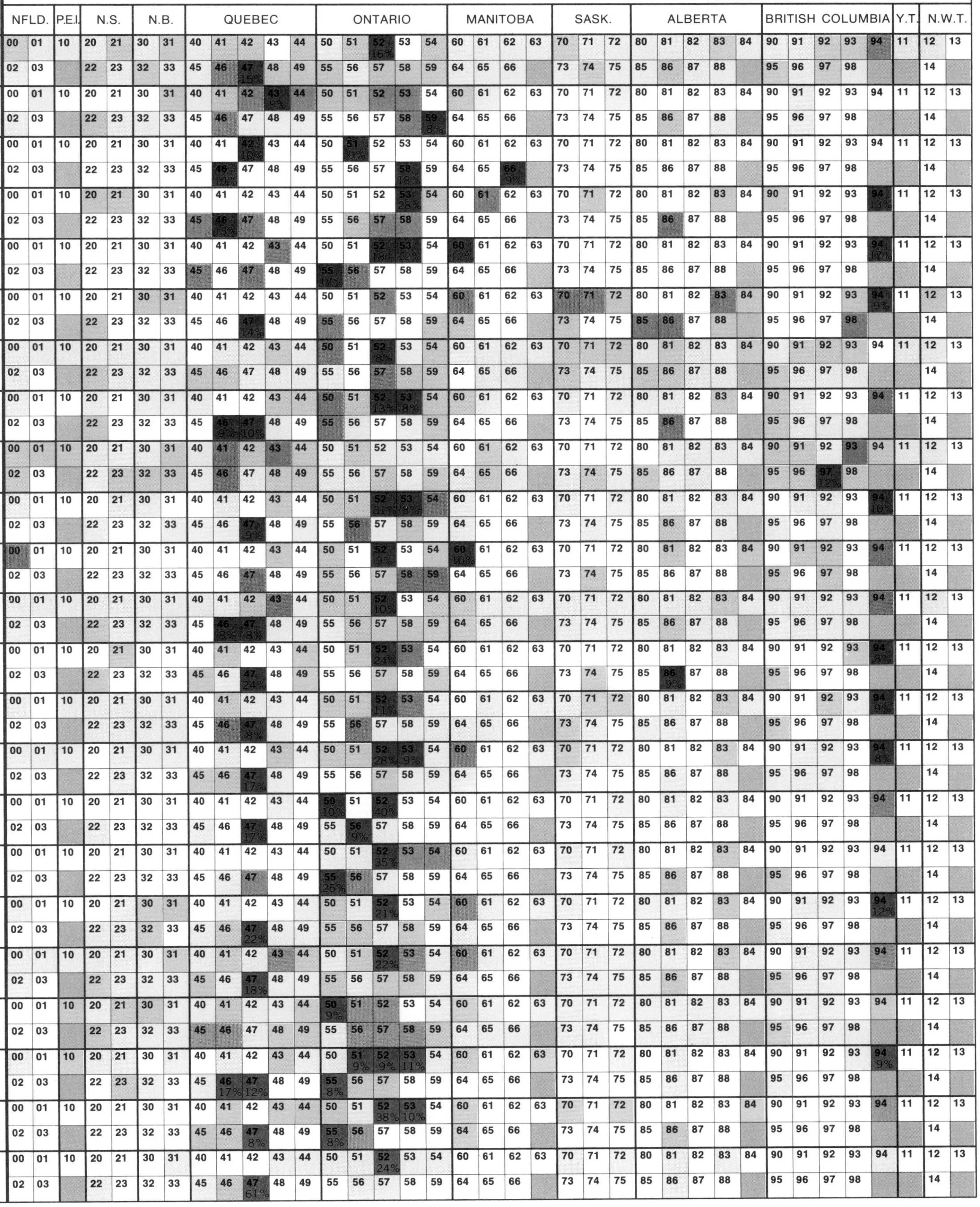
NFLD.
P.E.I.
N.S.
N.B.
QUEBEC
ONTARIO
MANITOBA
SASK.
ALBERTA
BRITISH COLUMBIA
Y.T.
N.W.T.

MANUFACTUR...

I	II	III	IV	V	VI	VII	VIII	IX	X
23	20	6	15	MEN'S CLOTHING	7-2431	1.16	51.49	28.40% / 15.38% / 55.86% — $282,398,689.	2.
24	24	26	93	SYNTHETIC TEXTILE MILLS	5-2010	1.16	52.65	24.06% / 25.97% / 47.93% — $246,830,376.	1.
25	31	28	24	MISCELLANEOUS METAL FABRICATING	13-3090	1.10	53.75	28.85% / 25.36% / 43.95% — $216,800,901.	1.
26	44	54	42	PHARMACEUTICALS AND MEDICINES	19-3740	1.10	54.85	18.89% / 50.87% / 29.62% — $168,035,552.	0.
27	40	51	14	SOFT DRINKS	1-1410	1.09	55.94	17.17% / 49.81% / 30.50% — $163,320,538.	0.
28	43	78	147	DISTILLERIES	1-1430	1.07	57.01	12.26% / 54.29% / 32.15% — $171,161,300.	0.
29	28	52	141	TOBACCO PRODUCTS	2-1530	1.01	58.02	14.71% / 31.90% / 53.09% — $230,650,825.	0.
30	35	18	4	HOUSEHOLD FURNITURE	9-2610	0.98	59.00	32.05% / 18.46% / 48.45% — $206,393,693.	1.5
31	25	20	115	COTTON YARN AND CLOTH MILLS	5-1830	0.90	59.90	23.55% / 17.08% / 57.50% — $236,883,136.	1.
32	33	29	74	FABRICATED STRUCTURAL METAL	13-3020	0.90	60.80	32.56% / 13.16% / 53.32% — $210,060,531.	1.
33	26	25	5	DOORS AND SASHES ETC. (except hardwood flooring)	8-2541	0.88	61.68	23.22% / 16.46% / 58.67% — $236,188,387.	1.2
34	34	35	108	MANUFACTURERS OF MAJOR APPLIANCES (electrical and non-electrical)	16-3320	0.87	62.55	22.84% / 22.27% / 53.58% — $205,096,579.	0.
35	29	33	34	WIRE AND WIRE PRODUCTS	13-3050	0.86	63.41	25.83% / 15.85% / 56.94% — $220,070,222.	0.9
36	39	16	31	SHOE FACTORIES	4-1740	0.84	64.25	32.75% / 18.63% / 48.17% — $173,318,335.	1.
37	41	79	59	SOAP AND CLEANING COMPOUNDS	19-3760	0.81	65.06	12.76% / 37.88% / 48.39% — $171,268,131.	0.
38	56	27	86	SHIPBUILDING AND REPAIRS	15-3270	0.81	65.87	46.68% / 16.78% / 35.23% — $136,598,363.	1.
39	38	57	174	RUBBER TIRES AND TUBES	3-1630	0.79	66.66	21.75% / 26.83% / 49.89% — $174,704,701.	0.5
40	36	39	37	OTHER PAPER CONVERTERS	10-2740	0.77	67.43	21.08% / 22.86% / 55.07% — $187,284,116.	0.7
41	54	38	25	LITHOGRAPHING	11-2862	0.75	68.18	32.66% / 24.16% / 42.48% — $140,647,203.	0.8
42	37	21	129	RAILROAD ROLLING STOCK	15-3260	0.74	68.92	39.96% / 54.49% — $181,945,694.	1.3
43	47	68	50	PAINT AND VARNISH	19-3750	0.72	69.64	16.82% / 33.27% / 49.23% — $153,071,802.	0.4
44	70	99	144	CEMENT	17-3410	0.72	70.36	15.59% / 55.81% / 13.41% / 15.19% — $107,044,107.	0.2
45	66	44	27	HARDWARE, TOOLS AND CUTLERY	13-3060	0.70	71.06	32.18% / 33.83% / 32.66% — $112,676,582.	0.6
46	52	43	53	MISCELLANEOUS ELECTRICAL PRODUCTS	16-3390	0.69	71.75	24.10% / 27.43% / 47.48% — $142,979,253.	0.7
47	48	71	26	OTHER CHEMICAL INDUSTRIES, N.E.S. (not elsewhere specified)	19-3799	0.68	72.43	15.43% / 32.34% / 50.68% — $152,623,895.	0.4
48	58	40	13	ORNAMENTAL AND ARCHITECTURAL METAL	13-3030	0.66	73.09	29.27% / 23.55% / 46.07% — $132,705,729.	0.7
49	53	42	35	CONFECTIONERY	1-1310	0.64	73.73	19.90% / 28.55% / 50.47% — $141,143,810.	0.7
50	62	59	75	OTHER RUBBER INDUSTRIES	3-1690	0.63	74.36	26.42% / 30.35% / 41.38% — $118,542,043.	0.5
51	65	45	12	CONCRETE PRODUCTS	17-3470	0.61	74.97	27.76% / 29.85% / 39.21% — $113,326,403.	0.6
52	59	50	69	INSTRUMENTS AND RELATED PRODUCTS	20-3811	0.60	75.57	30.26% / 21.11% / 48.02% — $124,323,370.	0.6

1961 (Continued)

XI	XII	XIII	XIV	XV
.07	69.19	$4,833.	$2,416.	488
.85	21.91	$10,138.	$3,257.	56
.51	9.88	$10,658.	$3,990.	331
.81	49.71	$27,623.	$3,260.	175
.71	5.63	$22,875.	$3,182.	502
.06	30.40	$37,602.	$4,477.	19
.03	58.14	$16,556.	$4,057.	22
.84	9.33	$6,450.	$3,057.	1580
.18	31.21	$6,574.	$2,939.	39
.42	0.43	$9,485.	$4,668.	78
.80	1.12	$7,349.	$3,139.	1356
.50	5.68	$11,483.	$3,929.	43
.71	9.33	$10,095.	$4,416.	199
.01	50.98	$4,876.	$2,471.	237
.61	18.59	$36,305.	$4,726.	126
.49	0.23	$7,162.	$4,152.	63
.84	4.67	$15,245.	$4,894.	10
.31	33.60	$11,067.	$3,554.	190
.07	26.24	$10,215.	$4,202.	326
.20	0.19	$5,525.	$4,122.	29
.27	9.12	$24,896.	$3,830.	136
.13	0.07	$29,887.	$5,053.	20
.77	16.21	$11,040.	$3,876.	308
.98	43.81	$10,610.	$3,282.	133
.23	18.03	$22,979.	$3,634.	314
.68	3.66	$10,286.	$3,754.	549
.95	56.02	$49,290.	$2,781.	194
.74	21.53	$10,364.	$3,837.	77
.77	0.53	$10,194.	$3,524.	616
.15	28.50	$12,701.	$4,229.	93

Provincial grid column headers: NFLD. | P.E.I. | N.S. | N.B. | QUEBEC | ONTARIO | MANITOBA | SASK. | ALBERTA | BRITISH COLUMBIA | Y.T. | N.W.T.

Cell codes per header band:
- NFLD.: 00, 01
- P.E.I.: 10
- N.S.: 20, 21, 22, 23
- N.B.: 30, 31, 32, 33
- QUEBEC: 40, 41, 42, 43, 44, 45, 46, 47, 48, 49
- ONTARIO: 50, 51, 52, 53, 54, 55, 56, 57, 58, 59
- MANITOBA: 60, 61, 62, 63, 64, 65, 66
- SASK.: 70, 71, 72, 73, 74, 75
- ALBERTA: 80, 81, 82, 83, 84, 85, 86, 87, 88
- BRITISH COLUMBIA: 90, 91, 92, 93, 94, 95, 96, 97, 98
- Y.T.: 11
- N.W.T.: 12, 13, 14

MANUFACTURING, 1961

MANUFACTURING, 1961 (Continued)

The 52 industries of the foregoing table (pages 197-200) account for 75.57% of the value added by manufacturing in Canada (1961). The 128 industries below constitute the remainder of the manufacturing industries listed in *General Review of Manufacturing Industries of Canada 1961* (Dominion Bureau of Statistics Catalogue No 31-201). They are tabulated in order of value added, in continuity with the foregoing table, and the cumulative percentage column is also continued.

RANK BY VALUE ADDED	INDUSTRY	STANDARD INDUSTRIAL CLASSIFICATION CODE	CUMULATIVE PERCENTAGE
53	ELECTRIC WIRE AND CABLE	16-3380	76.15
54	VENEER AND PLYWOOD MILLS	8-2520	76.71
55	OTHER KNITTING MILLS	6-2390	77.27
56	AGRICULTURAL IMPLEMENTS	14-3110	77.83
57	ANIMAL FEED	1-1230	78.39
58	FISH PRODUCTS	1-1110	78.95
59	OTHER FURNITURE	9-2660	79.49
60	IRON FOUNDRIES	12-2940	80.00
61	PLASTIC FABRICATIONS, N.E.S.	20-3850	80.47
62	CORRUGATED BOXES	10-2732	80.94
63	PUBLISHING ONLY	11-2880	81.40
64	OFFICE AND STORE MACHINERY	14-3180	81.85
65	FOLDING BOXES AND SET-UP BOXES	10-2731	82.30
66	STEEL PIPE AND TUBE MILLS	12-2920	82.75
67	MACHINE SHOPS	13-3080	83.19
68	PLASTICS AND SYNTHETIC RESINS	19-3730	83.63
69	TOILET PREPARATIONS	19-3770	84.06
70	FLOUR MILLS	1-1240	84.48
71	BISCUITS	1-1280	84.90
72	BUTTER AND CHEESE	1-1051	85.32
73	GLASS	17-3561	85.74
74	HOUSEHOLD RADIO AND TELEVISION RECEIVERS	16-3340	86.15
75	HEATING EQUIPMENT	13-3070	86.55
85	CHILDREN'S CLOTHING	7-2450	89.77
86	MISCELLANEOUS TEXTILES, N.E.S.	5-2299	90.05
87	COPPER AND ALLOY ROLLING, CASTING AND EXTRUDING	12-2970	90.33
88	PAPER BAGS	10-2733	90.60
89	SIGNS AND DISPLAY INDUSTRY	20-3970	90.84
90	JEWELLERY AND SILVERWARE	20-3820	91.08
91	SPORTING GOODS	20-3931	91.31
92	CLAY PRODUCTS (from domestic clay)	17-3511	91.54
93	BREAKFAST CEREALS	1-1250	91.72
94	METAL ROLLING, CASTING AND EXTRUDING, N.E.S.	12-2980	91.97
95	FUR GOODS	7-2460	92.18
96	GLASS PRODUCTS	17-3562	92.39
97	TRUCK BODIES AND TRAILERS	15-3240	92.59
98	ABRASIVES	17-3570	92.79
99	LEAF TOBACCO PROCESSING	2-1510	92.99
100	ASBESTOS PRODUCTS	17-3550	93.19
101	FOUNDATION GARMENTS	7-2480	93.38
102	MISCELLANEOUS LEATHER PRODUCTS	4-1799	93.57
103	ASPHALT ROOFING	10-2720	93.75
104	LEATHER TANNERIES	4-1720	93.93
105	RUBBER FOOTWEAR	3-1610	94.11
106	BATTERIES	16-3370	94.29
107	CONDENSERIES	1-1055	94.47
117	MEN'S CLOTHING CONTRACTORS	7-2432	96.02
118	OTHER MISCELLANEOUS INDUSTRIES	20-3999	96.14
119	WOMEN'S CLOTHING CONTRACTORS	7-2442	96.26
120	CLAY PRODUCTS (from imported clay)	17-3512	96.38
121	BROOMS, BRUSHES AND MOPS	20-3830	96.50
122	COMMERCIAL REFRIGERATION AND AIR CONDITIONING EQUIPMENT	14-3160	96.62
123	NARROW FABRIC MILLS	5-2140	96.73
124	ICE CREAM	1-1056	96.84
125	TEXTILE DYEING AND FINISHING	5-2180	96.95
126	WOODEN BOXES	8-2560	97.06
127	SAUSAGES AND SAUSAGE CASINGS	1-1013	97.17
128	CARPETS, MATS AND RUGS	5-2160	97.28
129	PRINTING INKS	19-3791	97.38
130	WINERIES	1-1470	97.47
131	MINERAL WOOL	17-3540	97.56
132	WOOL YARN MILLS	5-1930	97.65
133	TRADE COMPOSITION AND TYPESETTING	11-2872	97.74
134	LIME KILNS	17-3430	97.82
135	OTHER PETROLEUM AND COAL PRODUCTS	18-3690	97.90
136	REFRACTORIES MANUFACTURERS	17-3520	97.98
137	VEGETABLE OIL MILLS	1-1350	98.06
138	MACARONI	1-1391	98.14
139	FOUNTAIN PENS AND PENCILS	20-3989	98.22
149	BOAT BUILDING AND REPAIRS	15-3280	98.90
150	EMBROIDERY, PLEATING AND HEMSTITCHING	5-2292	98.96
151	CORDAGE AND TWINE	5-2130	99.02
152	BOOT AND SHOE FINDINGS	4-1792	99.08
153	HARDWOOD FLOORING	8-2542	99.14
154	ELECTRICAL LAMPS AND SHADES	9-2680	99.19
155	LUBRICATING OILS AND GREASES	18-3652	99.24
156	FIBRE PREPARING MILLS	5-2110	99.29
157	FUR DRESSING AND DYEING	20-3950	99.34
158	LEATHER GLOVES	4-1750	99.39
159	AUTOMOBILE FABRIC ACCESSORIES	5-2291	99.44
160	ANIMAL OILS AND FATS	1-1012	99.49
161	OTHER NON-METALLIC MINERAL PRODUCTS	17-3590	99.54
162	MISCELLANEOUS VEHICLES	15-3290	99.58
163	MISCELLANEOUS CLOTHING, N.E.S.	7-2499	99.62
164	STAMPS AND STENCILS (rubber and metal)	20-3995	99.66
165	WOOD HANDLES AND TURNINGS	8-2592	99.70
166	OPHTHALMIC GOODS	20-3814	99.74
167	STATUARY, ART GOODS, REGALIA AND NOVELTIES	20-3996	99.77
168	TYPEWRITER SUPPLIES	20-3988	99.80
169	PRESSED AND PUNCHED FELT MILLS	5-2150	99.83
170	FABRIC GLOVES	7-2491	99.86
171	VENETIAN BLINDS	20-3840	99.88

78	READY-MIX CONCRETE	17-3480	87.66
79	ALUMINUM ROLLING, CASTING AND EXTRUDING	12-2960	87.98
80	SMALL ELECTRICAL APPLIANCES	16-3310	88.29
81	ENGRAVING AND DUPLICATING PLATES	11-2871	88.60
82	WOOL CLOTH MILLS	5-1970	88.90
83	EXPLOSIVES AND AMMUNITION	19-3710	89.20
84	BOILER AND PLATE WORKS	13-3010	89.49

110	PROCESS CHEESE	1-1070	94.98
111	HATS AND CAPS	7-2470	95.15
112	OFFICE FURNITURE	9-2640	95.32
113	LINOLEUM AND COATED FABRICS INDUSTRY	5-2190	95.48
114	MUSICAL INSTRUMENTS AND SOUND RECORDING	20-3986	95.62
115	MANUFACTURING OF MIXED FERTILIZERS	19-3720	95.76
116	TOYS AND GAMES	20-3932	95.89

142	BUTTONS, BUCKLES AND FASTENERS	20-3981	98.46
143	SHINGLE MILLS	8-2511	98.53
144	MODEL AND PATTERN MANUFACTURING	20-3985	98.60
145	THREAD MILLS	5-2120	98.66
146	STONE PRODUCTS	17-3530	98.72
147	COFFINS AND CASKETS	8-2580	98.78
148	COTTON AND JUTE BAGS	5-2230	98.84

174	CANDLE MAKERS	20-3982	99.94
175	WOODENWARE	8-2593	99.96
176	ARTIFICIAL FLOWERS AND FEATHER GOODS	20-3984	99.98
177	ARTIFICIAL ICE	20-3998	99.99
178	SMOKERS' SUPPLIES	20-3993	99.99
179	UMBRELLAS	20-3997	99.99
180	HAIR GOODS	20-3983	100.0

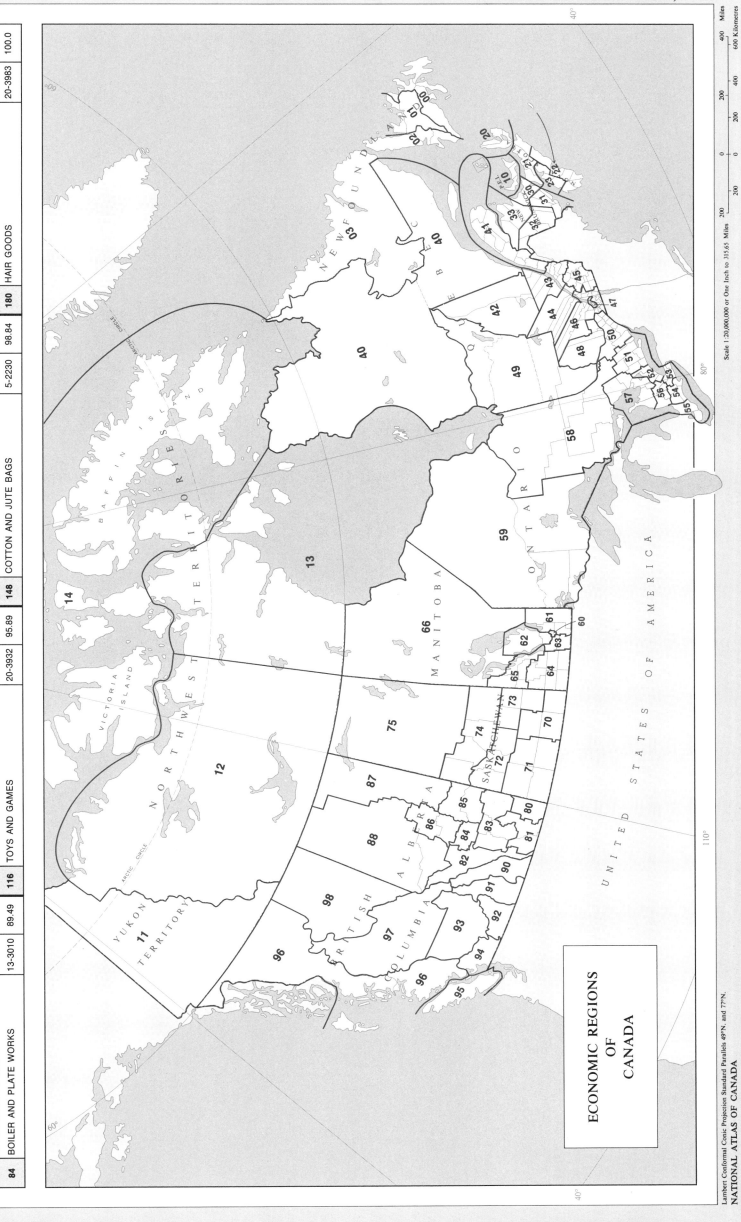

ECONOMIC REGIONS
OF
CANADA

Scale 1:20,000,000 or One Inch to 315.65 Miles

Lambert Conformal Conic Projection Standard Parallels 49°N. and 77°N.

RAILWAYS AND CANALS

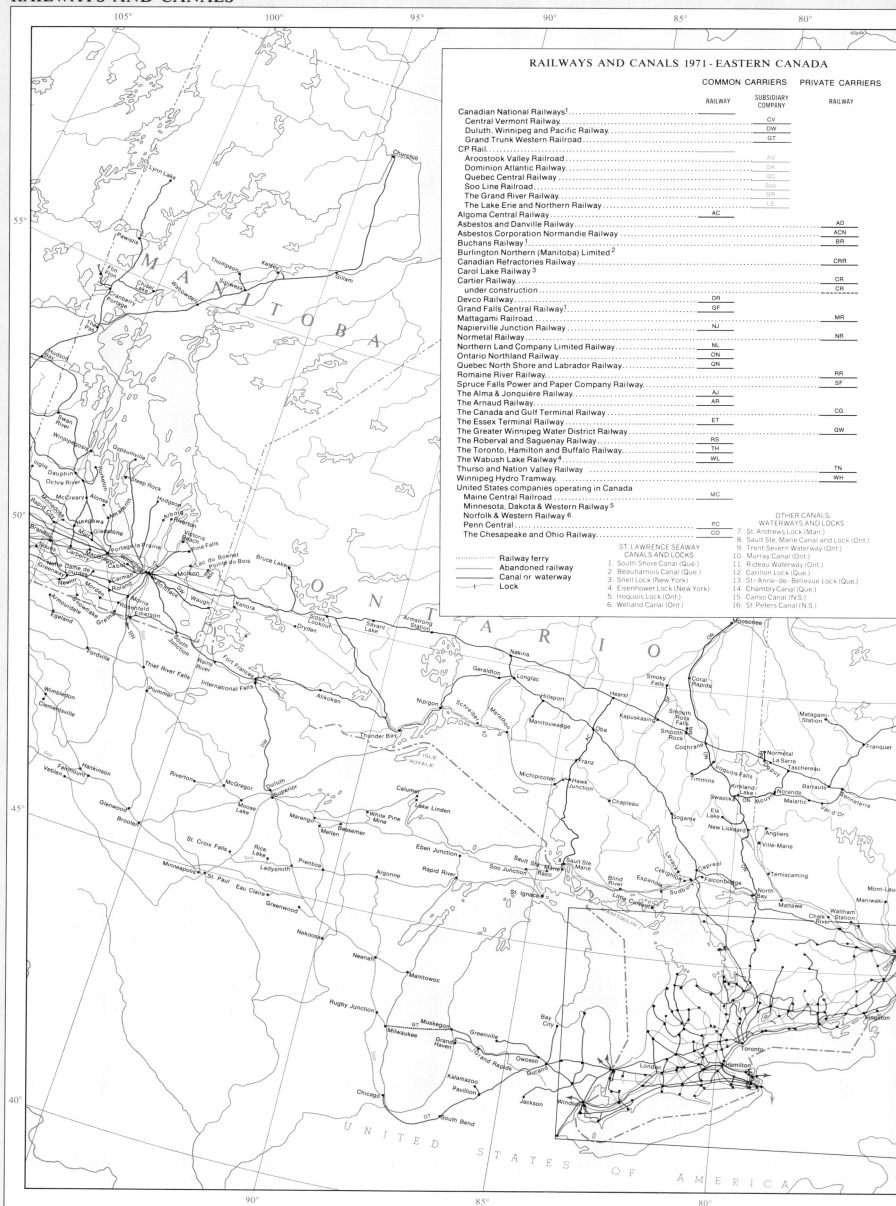

RAILWAYS AND CANALS 1971 - EASTERN CANADA

	COMMON CARRIERS		PRIVATE CARRIERS
	RAILWAY	SUBSIDIARY COMPANY	RAILWAY
Canadian National Railways[1]			
Central Vermont Railway		CV	
Duluth, Winnipeg and Pacific Railway		DW	
Grand Trunk Western Railroad		GT	
CP Rail			
Aroostook Valley Railroad		AV	
Dominion Atlantic Railway		DA	
Quebec Central Railway		QC	
Soo Line Railroad		Soo	
The Grand River Railway		GR	
The Lake Erie and Northern Railway		LE	
Algoma Central Railway	AC		
Asbestos and Danville Railway			AD
Asbestos Corporation Normandie Railway			ACN
Buchans Railway[1]			BR
Burlington Northern (Manitoba) Limited[2]			
Canadian Refractories Railway			CRR
Carol Lake Railway[3]			
Cartier Railway			CR
under construction			CR
Devco Railway	DR		
Grand Falls Central Railway[1]	GF		
Mattagami Railroad			MR
Napierville Junction Railway	NJ		
Normetal Railway			NR
Northern Land Company Limited Railway	NL		
Ontario Northland Railway	ON		
Quebec North Shore and Labrador Railway	QN		
Romaine River Railway			RR
Spruce Falls Power and Paper Company Railway			SF
The Alma & Jonquière Railway	AJ		
The Arnaud Railway	AR		
The Canada and Gulf Terminal Railway			CG
The Essex Terminal Railway	ET		
The Greater Winnipeg Water District Railway			GW
The Roberval and Saguenay Railway	RS		
The Toronto, Hamilton and Buffalo Railway	TH		
The Wabush Lake Railway[4]	WL		
Thurso and Nation Valley Railway			TN
Winnipeg Hydro Tramway			WH
United States companies operating in Canada			
Maine Central Railroad	MC		
Minnesota, Dakota & Western Railway[5]			
Norfolk & Western Railway[6]			
Penn Central	PC		
The Chesapeake and Ohio Railway	CO		

.... Railway ferry
--- -- Abandoned railway
——— Canal or waterway
——|— Lock

ST. LAWRENCE SEAWAY CANALS AND LOCKS
1. South Shore Canal (Que.)
2. Beauharnois Canal (Que.)
3. Snell Lock (New York)
4. Eisenhower Lock (New York)
5. Iroquois Lock (Ont.)
6. Welland Canal (Ont.)

OTHER CANALS, WATERWAYS AND LOCKS
7. St. Andrews Lock (Man.)
8. Sault Ste. Marie Canal and Lock (Ont.)
9. Trent-Severn Waterway (Ont.)
10. Murray Canal (Ont.)
11. Rideau Waterway (Ont.)
12. Carillon Lock (Que.)
13. St.-Anne-de-Bellevue Lock (Que.)
14. Chambly Canal (Que.)
15. Canso Canal (N.S.)
16. St. Peters Canal (N.S.)

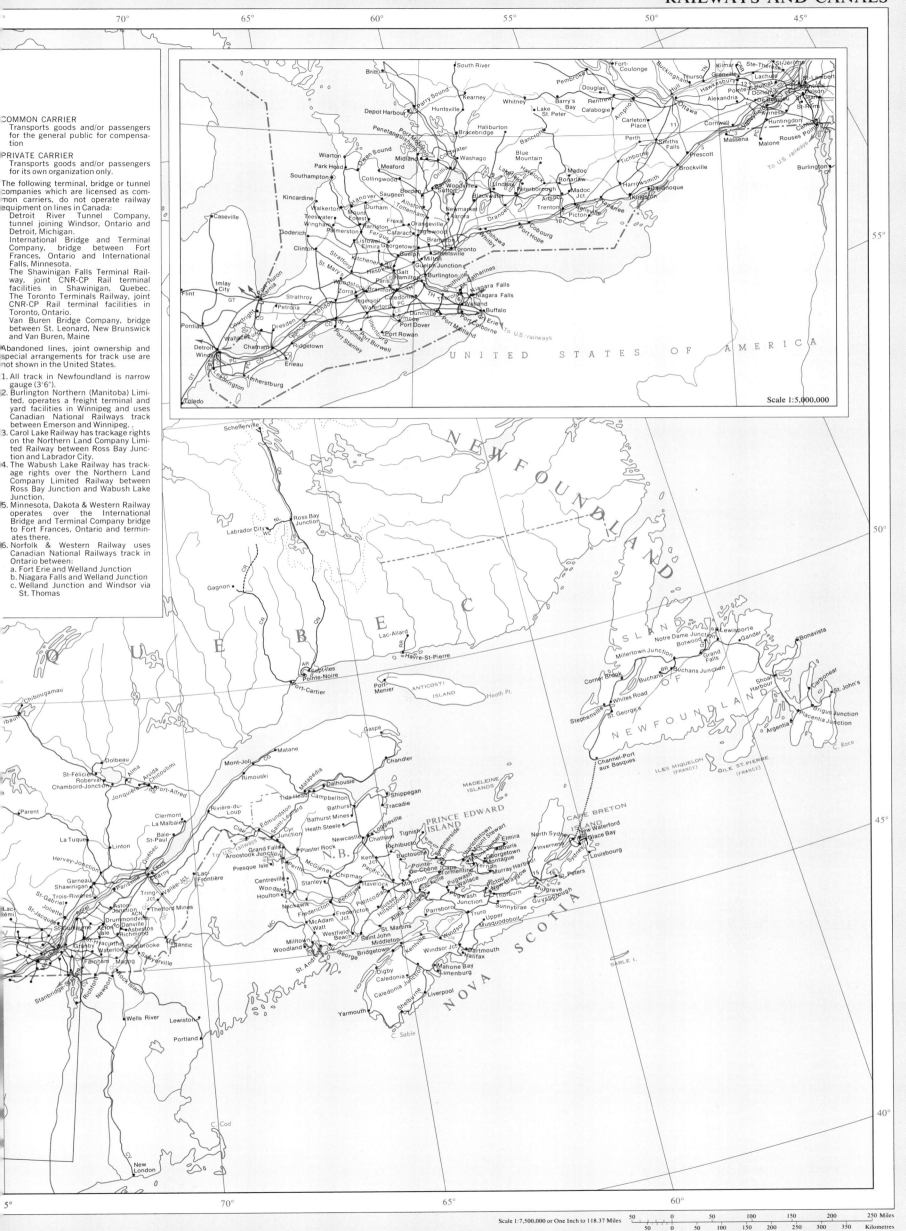

COMMON CARRIER
Transports goods and/or passengers for the general public for compensation

PRIVATE CARRIER
Transports goods and/or passengers for its own organization only.

The following terminal, bridge or tunnel companies which are licensed as common carriers, do not operate railway equipment on lines in Canada:
Detroit River Tunnel Company, tunnel joining Windsor, Ontario and Detroit, Michigan.
International Bridge and Terminal Company, bridge between Fort Frances, Ontario and International Falls, Minnesota.
The Shawinigan Falls Terminal Railway, joint CNR-CP Rail terminal facilities in Shawinigan, Quebec.
The Toronto Terminals Railway, joint CNR-CP Rail terminal facilities in Toronto, Ontario.
Van Buren Bridge Company, bridge between St. Leonard, New Brunswick and Van Buren, Maine

Abandoned lines, joint ownership and special arrangements for track use are not shown in the United States.

1. All track in Newfoundland is narrow gauge (3'6").
2. Burlington Northern (Manitoba) Limited, operates a freight terminal and yard facilities in Winnipeg and uses Canadian National Railways track between Emerson and Winnipeg.
3. Carol Lake Railway has trackage rights on the Northern Land Company Limited Railway between Ross Bay Junction and Labrador City.
4. The Wabush Lake Railway has trackage rights over the Northern Land Company Limited Railway between Ross Bay Junction and Wabush Lake Junction.
5. Minnesota, Dakota & Western Railway operates over the International Bridge and Terminal Company bridge to Fort Frances, Ontario and terminates there.
6. Norfolk & Western Railway uses Canadian National Railways track in Ontario between:
   a. Fort Erie and Welland Junction
   b. Niagara Falls and Welland Junction
   c. Welland Junction and Windsor via St. Thomas

Scale 1:5,000,000

Scale 1:7,500,000 or One Inch to 118.37 Miles

250 Miles

Kilometres

Scale 1:2,000,000

Lambert Conformal Conic Projection Standard Parallels 49°N. and 77°N.
THE NATIONAL ATLAS OF CANADA

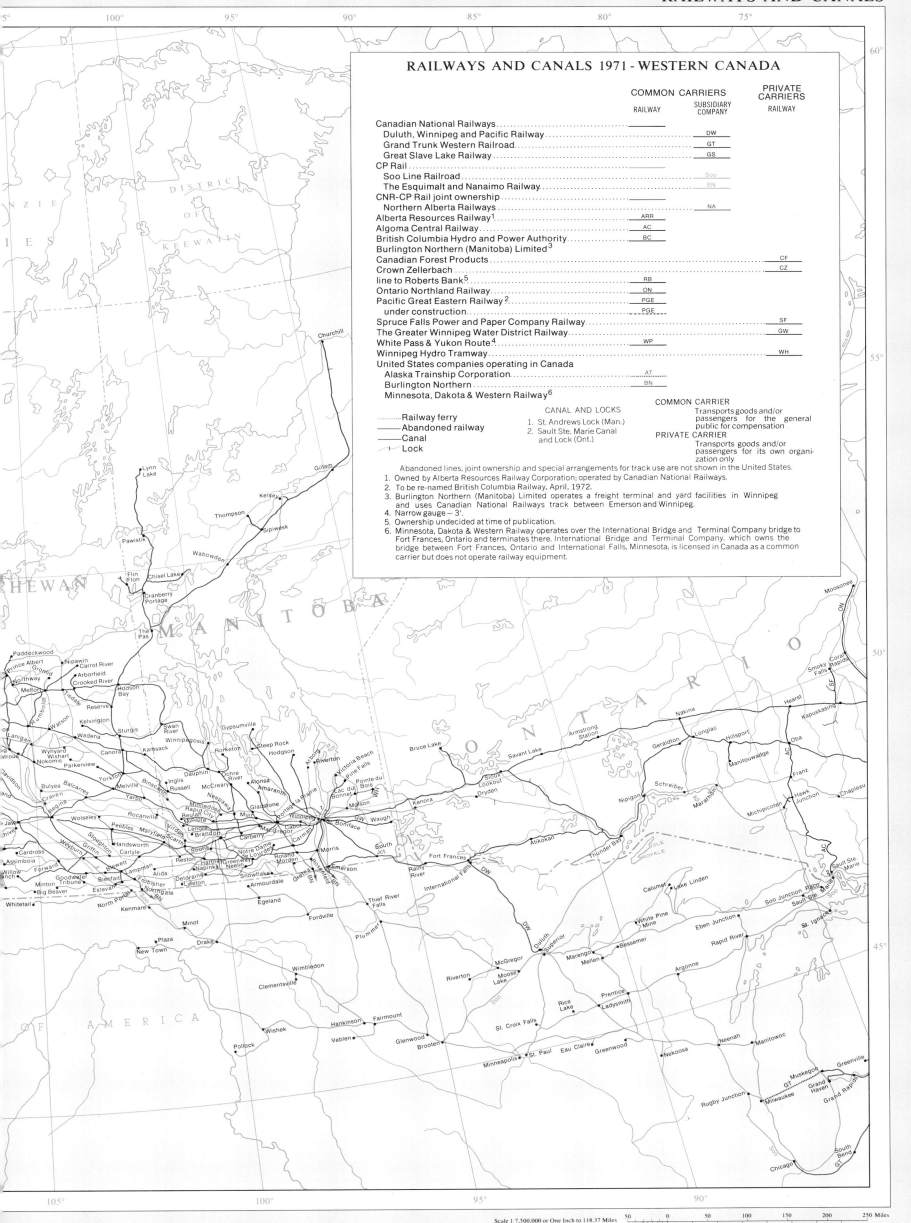

RAILWAYS AND CANALS 1971 - WESTERN CANADA

	COMMON CARRIERS		PRIVATE CARRIERS
	RAILWAY	SUBSIDIARY COMPANY	RAILWAY
Canadian National Railways			
Duluth, Winnipeg and Pacific Railway		DW	
Grand Trunk Western Railroad		GT	
Great Slave Lake Railway		GS	
CP Rail			
Soo Line Railroad		Soo	
The Esquimalt and Nanaimo Railway		EN	
CNR-CP Rail joint ownership			
Northern Alberta Railways		NA	
Alberta Resources Railway[1]	ARR		
Algoma Central Railway	AC		
British Columbia Hydro and Power Authority	BC		
Burlington Northern (Manitoba) Limited[3]			
Canadian Forest Products			CF
Crown Zellerbach			CZ
line to Roberts Bank[5]	RB		
Ontario Northland Railway	ON		
Pacific Great Eastern Railway[2]	PGE		
under construction	PGE		
Spruce Falls Power and Paper Company Railway			SF
The Greater Winnipeg Water District Railway			GW
White Pass & Yukon Route[4]	WP		
Winnipeg Hydro Tramway			WH
United States companies operating in Canada			
Alaska Trainship Corporation	AT		
Burlington Northern	BN		
Minnesota, Dakota & Western Railway[6]			

.... Railway ferry
———— Abandoned railway
———— Canal
├ Lock

CANAL AND LOCKS
1. St. Andrews Lock (Man.)
2. Sault Ste. Marie Canal and Lock (Ont.)

COMMON CARRIER
Transports goods and/or passengers for the general public for compensation
PRIVATE CARRIER
Transports goods and/or passengers for its own organization only

Abandoned lines, joint ownership and special arrangements for track use are not shown in the United States.
1. Owned by Alberta Resources Railway Corporation; operated by Canadian National Railways.
2. To be re-named British Columbia Railway, April, 1972.
3. Burlington Northern (Manitoba) Limited operates a freight terminal and yard facilities in Winnipeg and uses Canadian National Railways track between Emerson and Winnipeg.
4. Narrow gauge – 3'.
5. Ownership undecided at time of publication.
6. Minnesota, Dakota & Western Railway operates over the International Bridge and Terminal Company bridge to Fort Frances, Ontario and terminates there. International Bridge and Terminal Company, which owns the bridge between Fort Frances, Ontario and International Falls, Minnesota, is licensed in Canada as a common carrier but does not operate railway equipment.

Scale 1:7,500,000 or One Inch to 118.37 Miles

EXTENSION OF THE RAILWAY NETWORK
1836-1971

PERIOD*

1836-1852
1853-1880
1881-1905
1906-1918
1919-1935
1936-1952
1953-1971

*Based on first operating dates of railways

Scale 1:20,000,000

REDUCTION OF TRAVEL TIME

	APPROXIMATE TIME*
TRAIN	
1893 Wood and coal	115 hours
1935 Coal	93 hours
1971 Diesel	70 hours
AIRCRAFT	
1939 Propellor driven	18 hours
1971 Jet	5 hours

*Based on the distance Montreal to Vancouver

TRANSCONTINENTAL RAILWAY
PASSENGER ROUTES, 1972

Canadian National Railways
CP Rail
Ferry

Scale 1:35,000,000

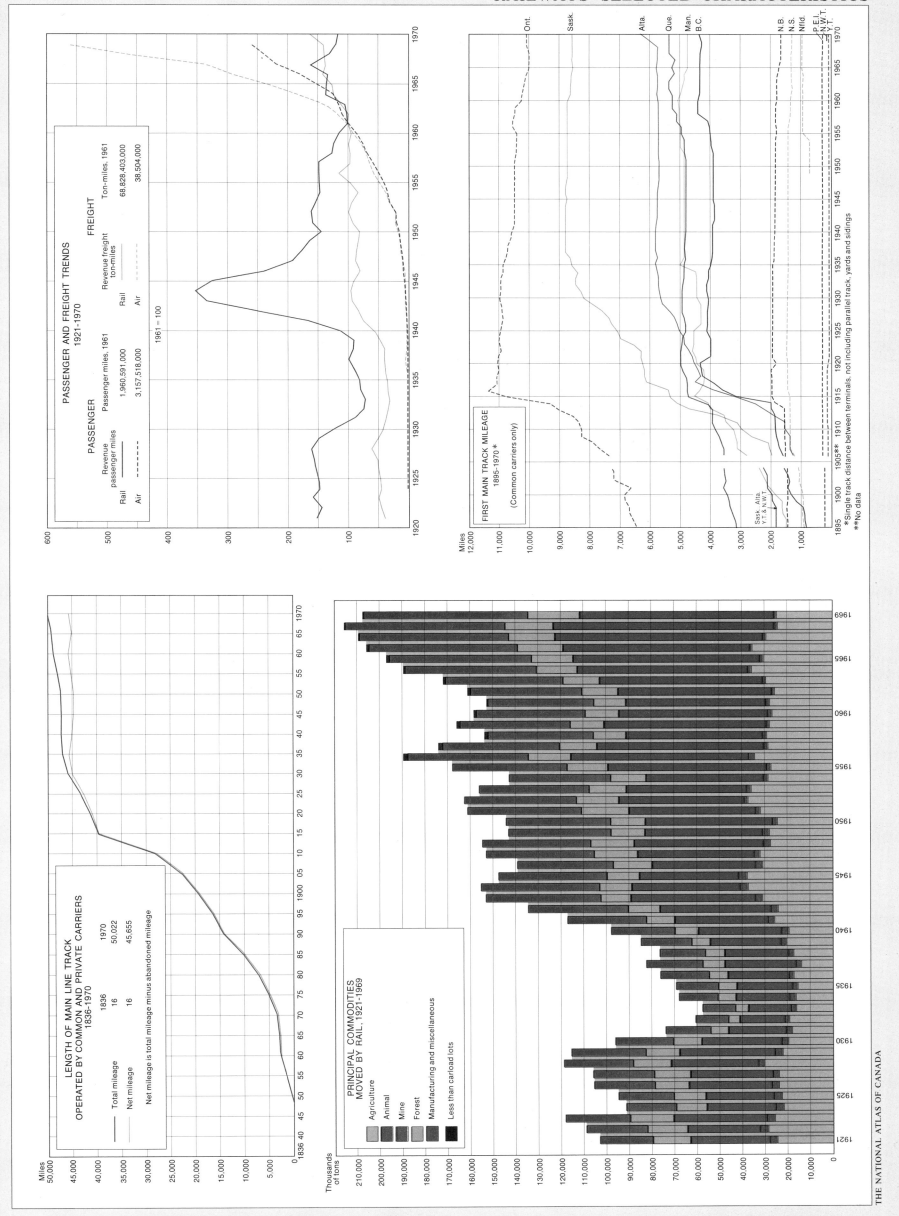

PASSENGER AND FREIGHT TRENDS
1921-1970

1961 = 100

PASSENGER

Rail — Revenue passenger miles — Passenger miles, 1961 — 1,960,591,000
Air --- Revenue passenger miles --- 3,157,518,000

FREIGHT

Rail — Revenue freight ton-miles — Ton-miles, 1961 — 68,828,403,000
Air --- ton-miles --- 38,504,000

FIRST MAIN TRACK MILEAGE
1895-1970 *

(Common carriers only)

*Single track distance between terminals, not including parallel track, yards and sidings
**No data

Sask. Alta.
Y.T. & N.W.T

*1905**

LENGTH OF MAIN LINE TRACK
OPERATED BY COMMON AND PRIVATE CARRIERS
1836-1970

	1836	1970
Total mileage	16	50,022
Net mileage	16	45,655

Net mileage is total mileage minus abandoned mileage

PRINCIPAL COMMODITIES
MOVED BY RAIL, 1921-1969

Agriculture
Animal
Mine
Forest
Manufacturing and miscellaneous
Less than carload lots

PORTS AND HARBOURS

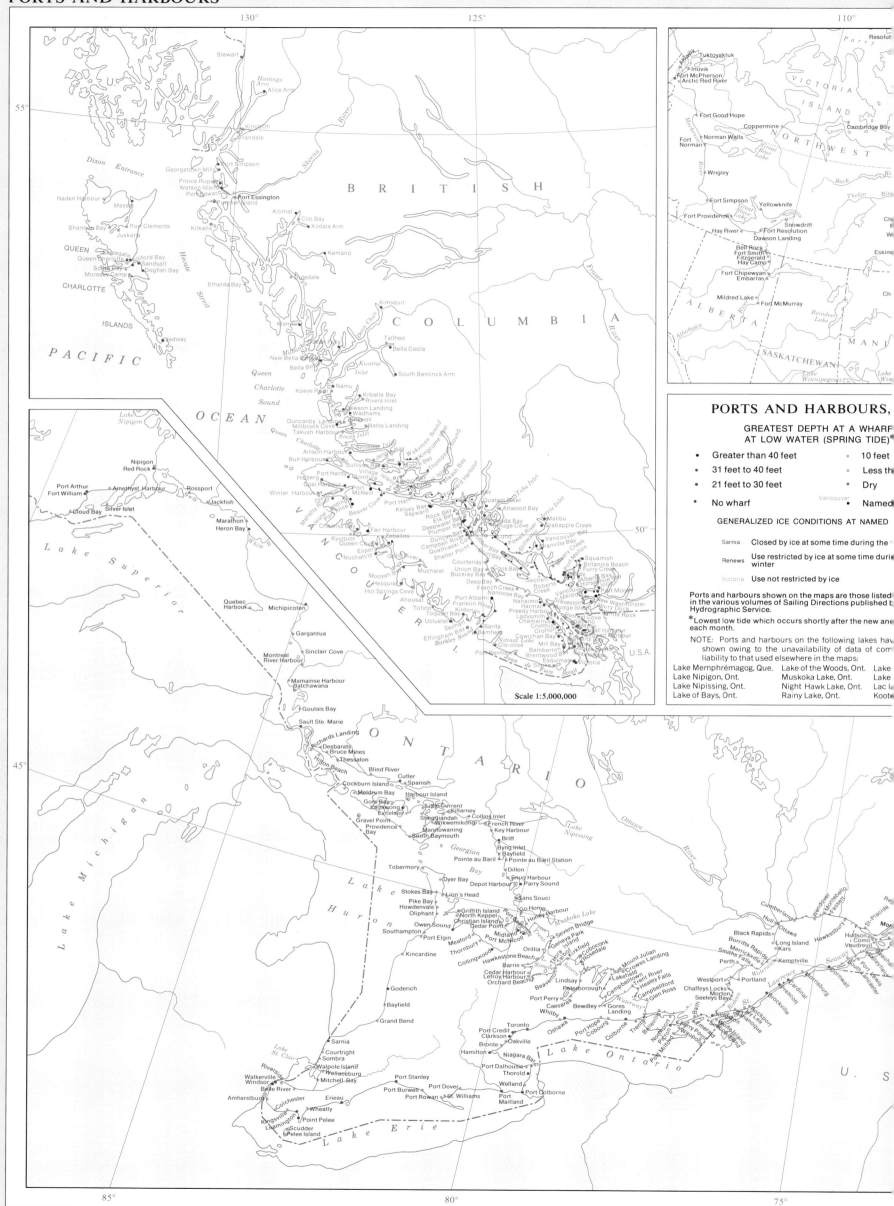

Scale 1:25,000,000

Scale 1:5,000,000

Scale 1:5,000,000 or One Inch to 78.91 Miles

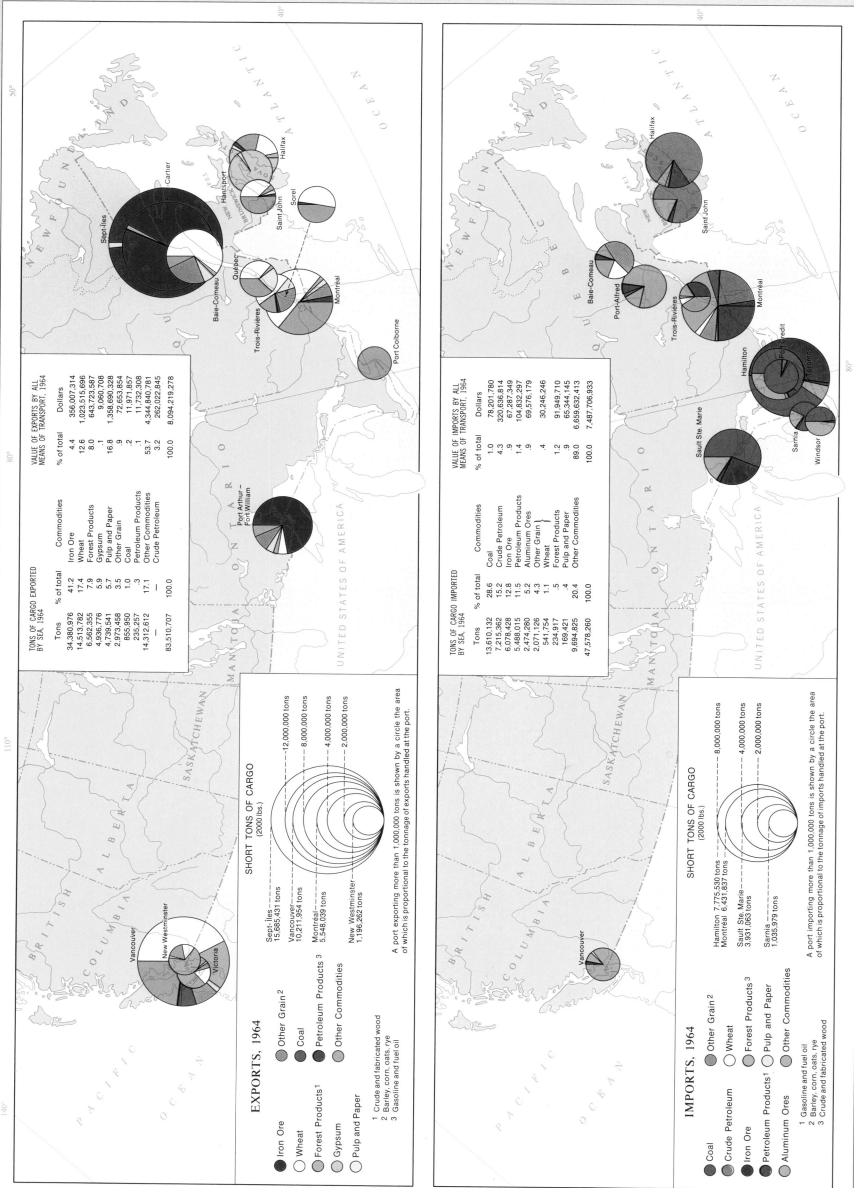

EXPORTS, 1964

TONS OF CARGO EXPORTED BY SEA, 1964		
Tons	% of total	Commodities
34,380,976	41.2	Iron Ore
14,513,782	17.4	Wheat
6,562,355	7.9	Forest Products
4,936,776	5.9	Gypsum
4,739,541	5.7	Pulp and Paper
2,973,458	3.5	Other Grain
855,950	1.0	Coal
235,257	.3	Petroleum Products
14,312,612	17.1	Other Commodities
—	—	Crude Petroleum
83,510,707	100.0	

VALUE OF EXPORTS BY ALL MEANS OF TRANSPORT, 1964	
% of total	Dollars
4.4	356,007,314
12.6	1,023,515,696
8.0	643,723,587
.1	9,060,708
16.8	1,358,690,328
.9	72,653,854
.1	11,971,857
.1	11,732,308
53.7	4,344,840,781
3.2	262,022,845
100.0	8,094,219,278

SHORT TONS OF CARGO
(2000 lbs.)

— 12,000,000 tons
— 8,000,000 tons
— 4,000,000 tons
— 2,000,000 tons

A port exporting more than 1,000,000 tons is shown by a circle the area of which is proportional to the tonnage of exports handled at the port.

Sept-Iles — 15,685,431 tons
Vancouver — 10,211,954 tons
Montréal — 5,548,039 tons
New Westminster — 1,196,262 tons

Iron Ore
Wheat
Forest Products [1]
Gypsum
Pulp and Paper
Other Grain [2]
Coal
Petroleum Products [3]
Other Commodities

1 Crude and fabricated wood
2 Barley, corn, oats, rye
3 Gasoline and fuel oil

IMPORTS, 1964

TONS OF CARGO IMPORTED BY SEA, 1964		
Tons	% of total	Commodities
13,610,132	28.6	Coal
7,215,362	15.2	Crude Petroleum
6,078,428	12.8	Iron Ore
5,488,015	11.5	Petroleum Products
2,474,280	5.2	Aluminum Ores
2,071,126	4.3	Other Grain
541,754	1.1	Wheat
234,917	.5	Forest Products
169,421	.4	Pulp and Paper
9,694,825	20.4	Other Commodities
47,578,260	100.0	

VALUE OF IMPORTS BY ALL MEANS OF TRANSPORT, 1964	
% of total	Dollars
1.0	78,201,780
4.3	320,636,814
.9	67,287,349
1.4	104,832,297
.9	69,576,179
.4	30,246,246
1.2	91,949,710
.9	65,344,145
89.0	6,659,632,413
100.0	7,487,706,933

SHORT TONS OF CARGO
(2000 lbs.)

— 8,000,000 tons
— 4,000,000 tons
— 2,000,000 tons

A port importing more than 1,000,000 tons is shown by a circle the area of which is proportional to the tonnage of imports handled at the port.

Hamilton — 7,775,530 tons
Montréal — 6,431,837 tons
Sault Ste. Marie — 3,931,063 tons
Sarnia — 1,035,979 tons

Coal
Crude Petroleum
Iron Ore
Petroleum Products [1]
Aluminum Ores
Wheat
Other Grain [2]
Forest Products [3]
Pulp and Paper
Other Commodities

1 Gasoline and fuel oil
2 Barley, corn, oats, rye
3 Crude and fabricated wood

Lambert Conformal Conic Projection Standard Parallels 49°N. and 77°N.
THE NATIONAL ATLAS OF CANADA

Scale 1:20,000,000 or One Inch to 315.65 Miles

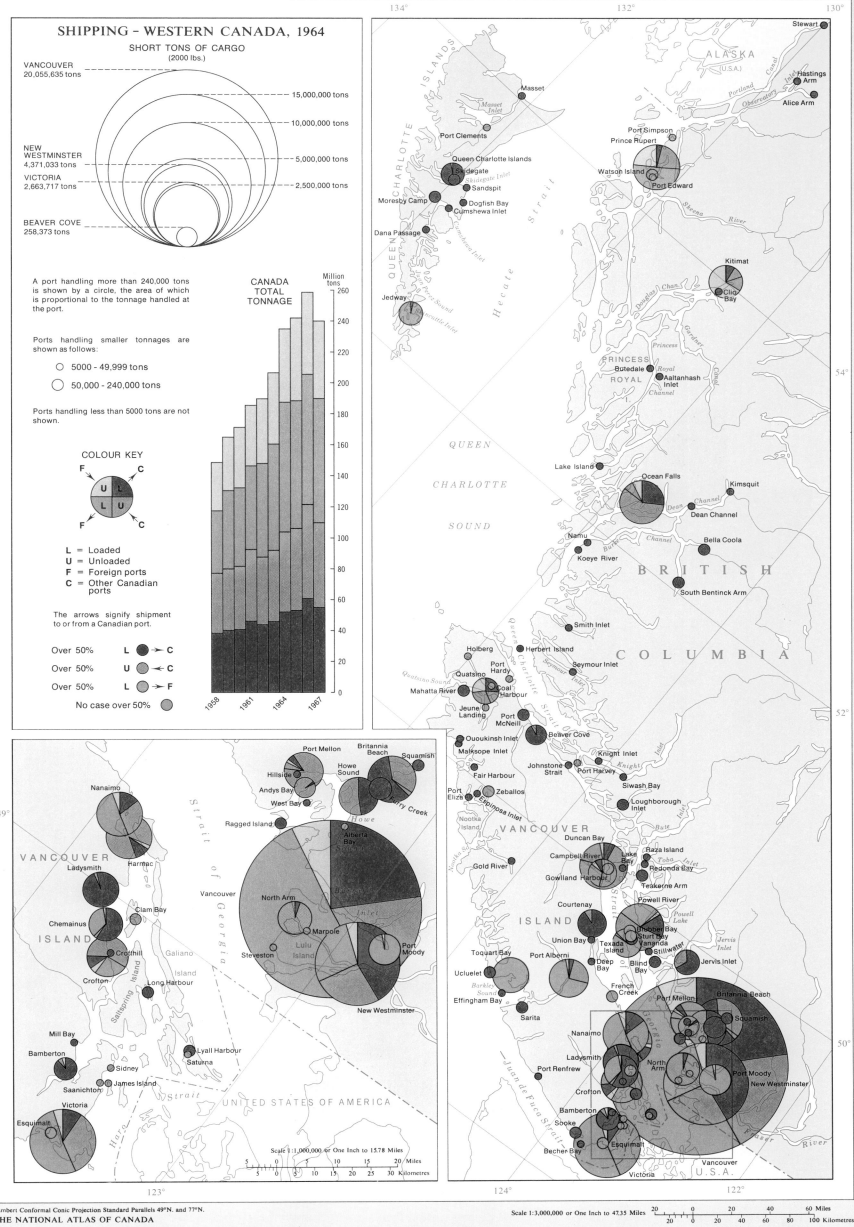

SHIPPING - WESTERN CANADA, 1964

SHORT TONS OF CARGO
(2000 lbs.)

VANCOUVER
20,055,635 tons

— 15,000,000 tons

— 10,000,000 tons

NEW
WESTMINSTER
4,371,033 tons

— 5,000,000 tons

VICTORIA
2,663,717 tons

— 2,500,000 tons

BEAVER COVE
258,373 tons

A port handling more than 240,000 tons is shown by a circle, the area of which is proportional to the tonnage handled at the port.

Ports handling smaller tonnages are shown as follows:

○ 5000 - 49,999 tons

○ 50,000 - 240,000 tons

Ports handling less than 5000 tons are not shown.

COLOUR KEY

F   C
 U L
 L U
F   C

L = Loaded
U = Unloaded
F = Foreign ports
C = Other Canadian ports

The arrows signify shipment to or from a Canadian port.

Over 50%   L ● → C

Over 50%   U ● ← C

Over 50%   L ● → F

No case over 50% ●

CANADA TOTAL TONNAGE

Million tons

260
240
220
200
180
160
140
120
100
80
60
40
20
0

1958   1961   1964   1967

Scale 1:1,000,000 or One Inch to 15.78 Miles

Scale 1:3,000,000 or One Inch to 47.35 Miles

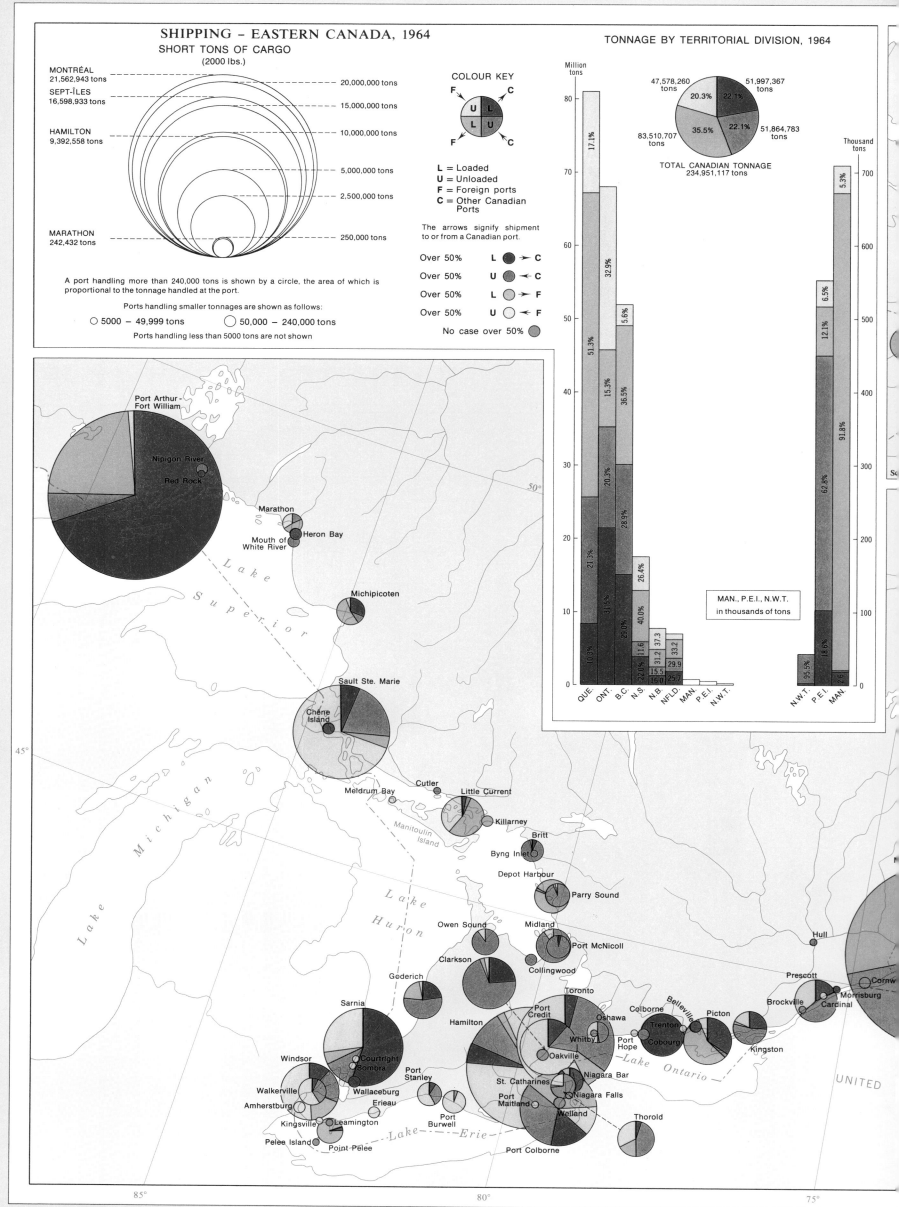

SHIPPING – EASTERN CANADA, 1964
SHORT TONS OF CARGO
(2000 lbs.)

MONTRÉAL
21,562,943 tons — — — — — — 20,000,000 tons

SEPT-ÎLES
16,598,933 tons — — — — — — 15,000,000 tons

HAMILTON
9,392,558 tons — — — — — — 10,000,000 tons

— — — — — — 5,000,000 tons

— — — — — — 2,500,000 tons

MARATHON
242,432 tons — — — — — — 250,000 tons

A port handling more than 240,000 tons is shown by a circle, the area of which is proportional to the tonnage handled at the port.

Ports handling smaller tonnages are shown as follows:

◯ 5000 – 49,999 tons   ◯ 50,000 – 240,000 tons

Ports handling less than 5000 tons are not shown

COLOUR KEY

F — C
U L
L U
F — C

L = Loaded
U = Unloaded
F = Foreign ports
C = Other Canadian Ports

The arrows signify shipment to or from a Canadian port.

Over 50%   L ● → C
Over 50%   U ● ← C
Over 50%   L ◐ → F
Over 50%   U ◯ ← F
No case over 50%   ◓

TONNAGE BY TERRITORIAL DIVISION, 1964

47,578,260 tons   51,997,367 tons
20.3%   22.1%
35.5%   22.1%
83,510,707 tons   51,864,783 tons

TOTAL CANADIAN TONNAGE
234,951,117 tons

MAN., P.E.I., N.W.T.
in thousands of tons

THE NATIONAL ATLAS OF CANADA

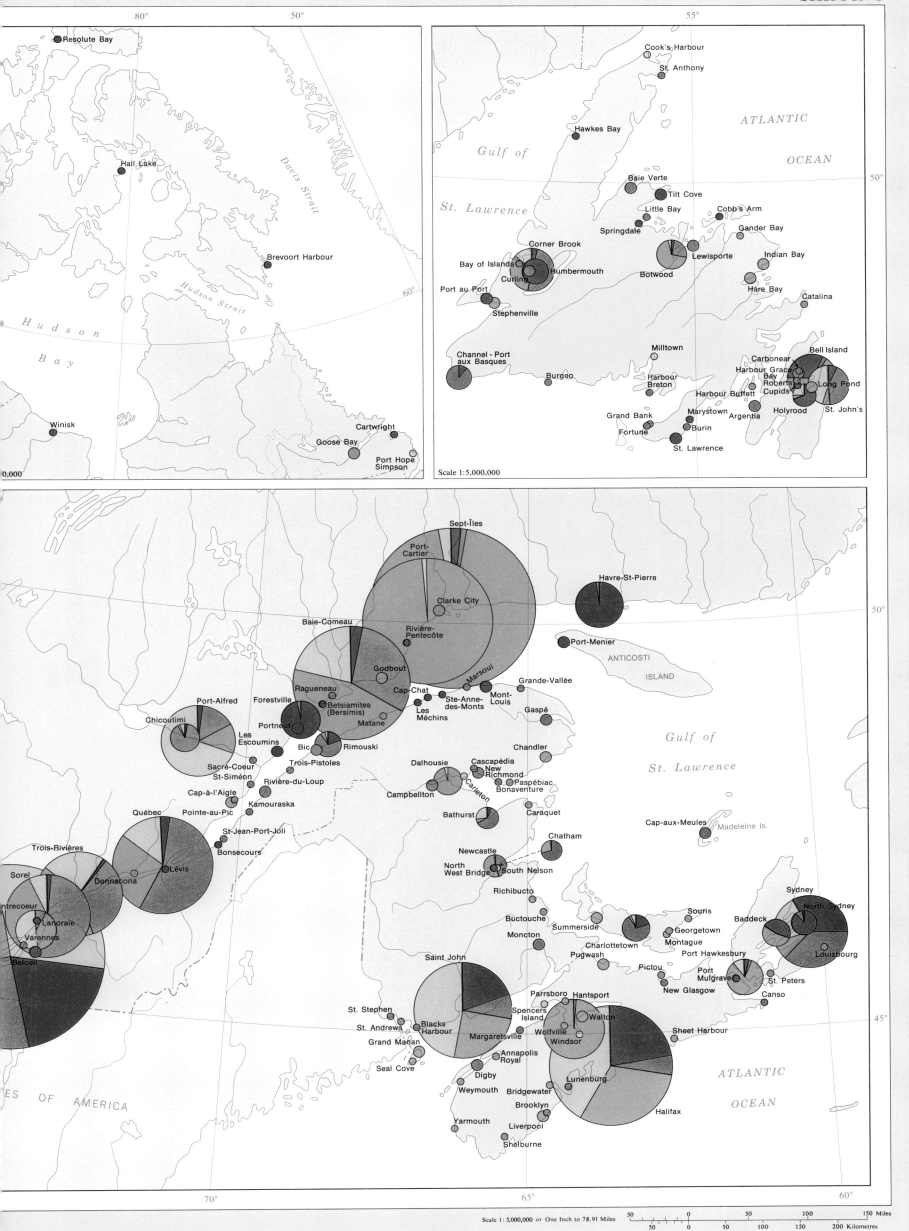

Resolute Bay

Hall Lake

Davis Strait

Brevoort Harbour

Hudson Strait

H u d s o n

B a y

Winisk

Cartwright

Goose Bay

Port Hope
Simpson

Cook's Harbour
St. Anthony

ATLANTIC

Hawkes Bay

Gulf of

OCEAN

St. Lawrence

Baie Verte
Tilt Cove
Little Bay
Cobb's Arm
Springdale
Gander Bay
Corner Brook
Lewisporte
Indian Bay
Bay of Islands
Humbermouth
Botwood
Curling
Hare Bay
Port au Port
Catalina
Stephenville

Channel - Port
aux Basques
Milltown
Bell Island
Carbonear
Harbour Grace
Burgeo
Harbour
Breton
Bay
Roberts
Long Pond
Harbour Buffett
Cupids
Grand Bank
Marystown
Holyrood
St. John's
Fortune
Burin
Argentia
St. Lawrence

Sept-Îles
Port-
Cartier
Havre-St-Pierre
Clarke City
Baie-Comeau
Rivière-
Pentecôte
Port-Menier
Godbout
ANTICOSTI
Marsoui
ISLAND
Port-Alfred
Forestville
Ragueneau
Cap-Chat
Grande-Vallée
Chicoutimi
Betsiamites
Ste-Anne-
Mont-
Gaspé
(Bersimis)
des-Monts
Louis
Les
Portneuf
Matane
Méchins
Gulf of
Les Escoumins
Bic
Sacré-Coeur
Rimouski
Chandler
St-Siméon
Trois-Pistoles
Dalhousie
Cascapédia
St. Lawrence
Cap-à-l'Aigle
Rivière-du-Loup
New
Richmond
Québec
Kamouraska
Campbellton
Paspébiac
Pointe-au-Pic
Carleton
Bonaventure
Trois-Rivières
St-Jean-Port-Joli
Bathurst
Caraquet
Sorel
Bonsecours
Lévis
Cap-aux-Meules
Madeleine Is.
Donnacona
Chatham
ntrecoeur
Lanoraie
Newcastle
Varennes
North
Sydney
West Bridge
South Nelson
North Sydney
Beloeil
Richibucto
Baddeck
Souris
Buctouche
Georgetown
Louisbourg
Summerside
Montague
Moncton
Port Hawkesbury
Charlottetown
Saint John
Pugwash
St. Peters
Pictou
Port
Canso
St. Stephen
Parrsboro Hantsport
Mulgrave
New Glasgow
Spencers
St. Andrews
Blacks
Island
Walton
Sheet Harbour
Harbour
Margaretsville
Wolfville
Grand Manan
Windsor
Annapolis
ATLANTIC
Royal
Seal Cove
Digby
Lunenburg
Weymouth
Bridgewater
OCEAN
Brooklyn
Yarmouth
Halifax
Liverpool
Shelburne

EXPORTS BY MODE OF TRANSPORT, 1966

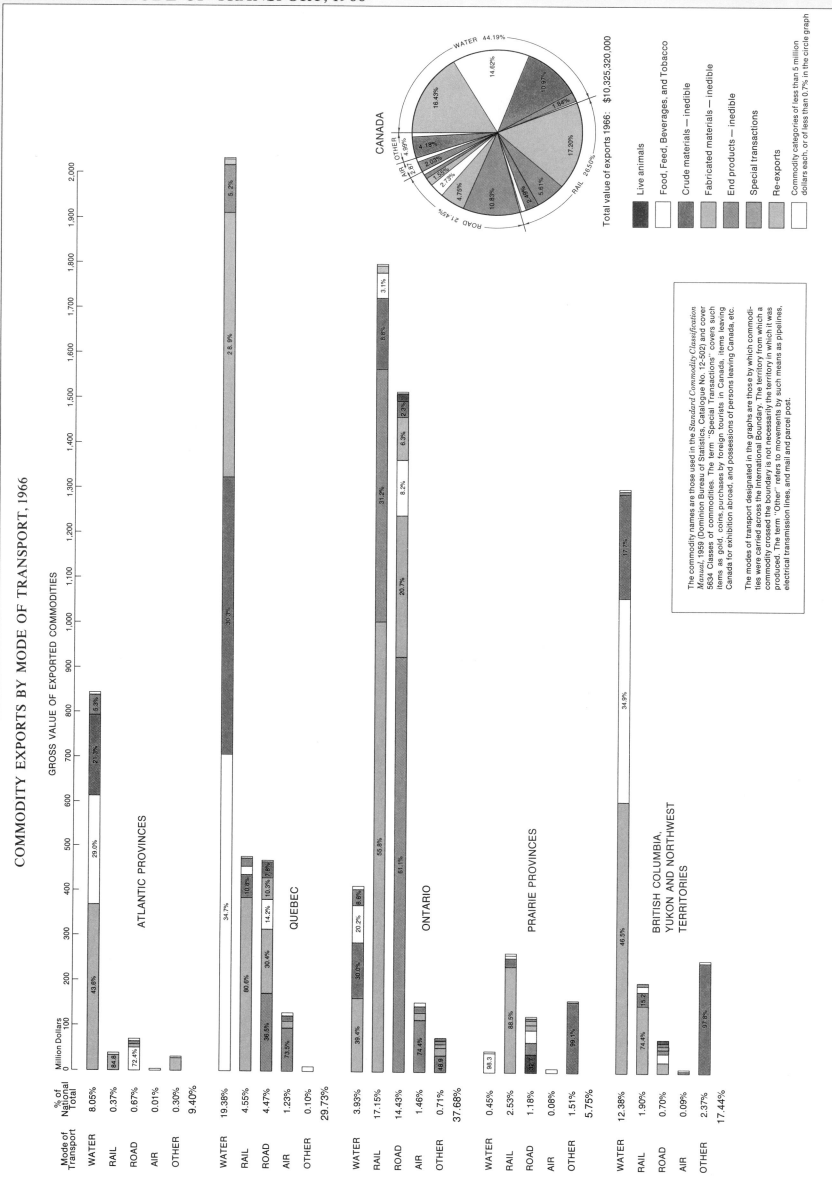

COMMODITY EXPORTS BY MODE OF TRANSPORT, 1966

GROSS VALUE OF EXPORTED COMMODITIES

Million Dollars

ATLANTIC PROVINCES

QUEBEC

ONTARIO

PRAIRIE PROVINCES

BRITISH COLUMBIA, YUKON AND NORTHWEST TERRITORIES

Mode of Transport	% of National Total
WATER	8.05%
RAIL	0.37%
ROAD	0.67%
AIR	0.01%
OTHER	0.30%
	9.40%
WATER	19.38%
RAIL	4.55%
ROAD	4.47%
AIR	1.23%
OTHER	0.10%
	29.73%
WATER	3.93%
RAIL	17.15%
ROAD	14.43%
AIR	1.46%
OTHER	0.71%
	37.68%
WATER	0.45%
RAIL	2.53%
ROAD	1.18%
AIR	0.08%
OTHER	1.51%
	5.75%
WATER	12.38%
RAIL	1.90%
ROAD	0.70%
AIR	0.09%
OTHER	2.37%
	17.44%

CANADA

WATER 44.19%

RAIL 26.50%

ROAD 21.45%

AIR OTHER 4.99%

14.62%

10.97%

1.84%

17.20%

5.61%

2.49%

10.83%

4.75%

2.73%

1.55%

2.03%

4.18%

16.43%

Total value of exports 1966: $10,325,320,000

Live animals

Food, Feed, Beverages, and Tobacco

Crude materials — inedible

Fabricated materials — inedible

End products — inedible

Special transactions

Re-exports

Commodity categories of less than 5 million dollars each, or of less than 0.7% in the circle graph

The commodity names are those used in the *Standard Commodity Classification Manual*, 1959 (Dominion Bureau of Statistics, Catalogue No. 12-502) and cover 5634 Classes of commodities. The term "Special Transactions" covers such items as gold, coins, purchases by foreign tourists in Canada, items leaving Canada for exhibition abroad, and possessions of persons leaving Canada, etc.

The modes of transport designated in the graphs are those by which commodities were carried across the International Boundary. The territory from which a commodity crossed the boundary is not necessarily the territory in which it was produced. The term "Other" refers to movements by such means as pipelines, electrical transmission lines, and mail and parcel post.

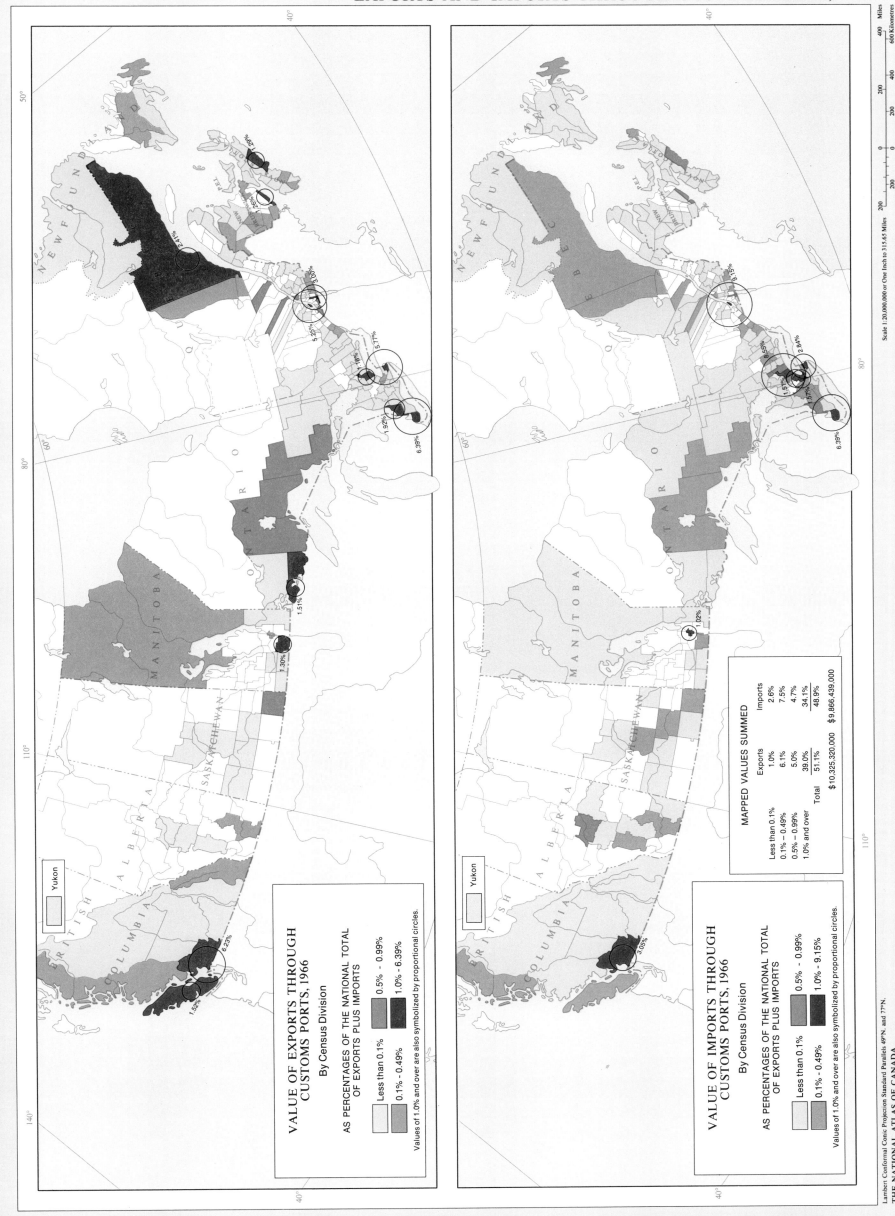

**VALUE OF EXPORTS THROUGH
CUSTOMS PORTS, 1966**

By Census Division

AS PERCENTAGES OF THE NATIONAL TOTAL
OF EXPORTS PLUS IMPORTS

Less than 0.1% 0.5% - 0.99%

0.1% - 0.49% 1.0% - 6.39%

Values of 1.0% and over are also symbolized by proportional circles.

**VALUE OF IMPORTS THROUGH
CUSTOMS PORTS, 1966**

By Census Division

AS PERCENTAGES OF THE NATIONAL TOTAL
OF EXPORTS PLUS IMPORTS

Less than 0.1% 0.5% - 0.99%

0.1% - 0.49% 1.0% - 9.15%

Values of 1.0% and over are also symbolized by proportional circles.

MAPPED VALUES SUMMED		
	Exports	Imports
Less than 0.1%	1.0%	2.6%
0.1% - 0.49%	6.1%	7.5%
0.5% - 0.99%	5.0%	4.7%
1.0% and over	39.0%	34.1%
Total	51.1%	48.9%
	$10,325,320,000	$9,866,439,000

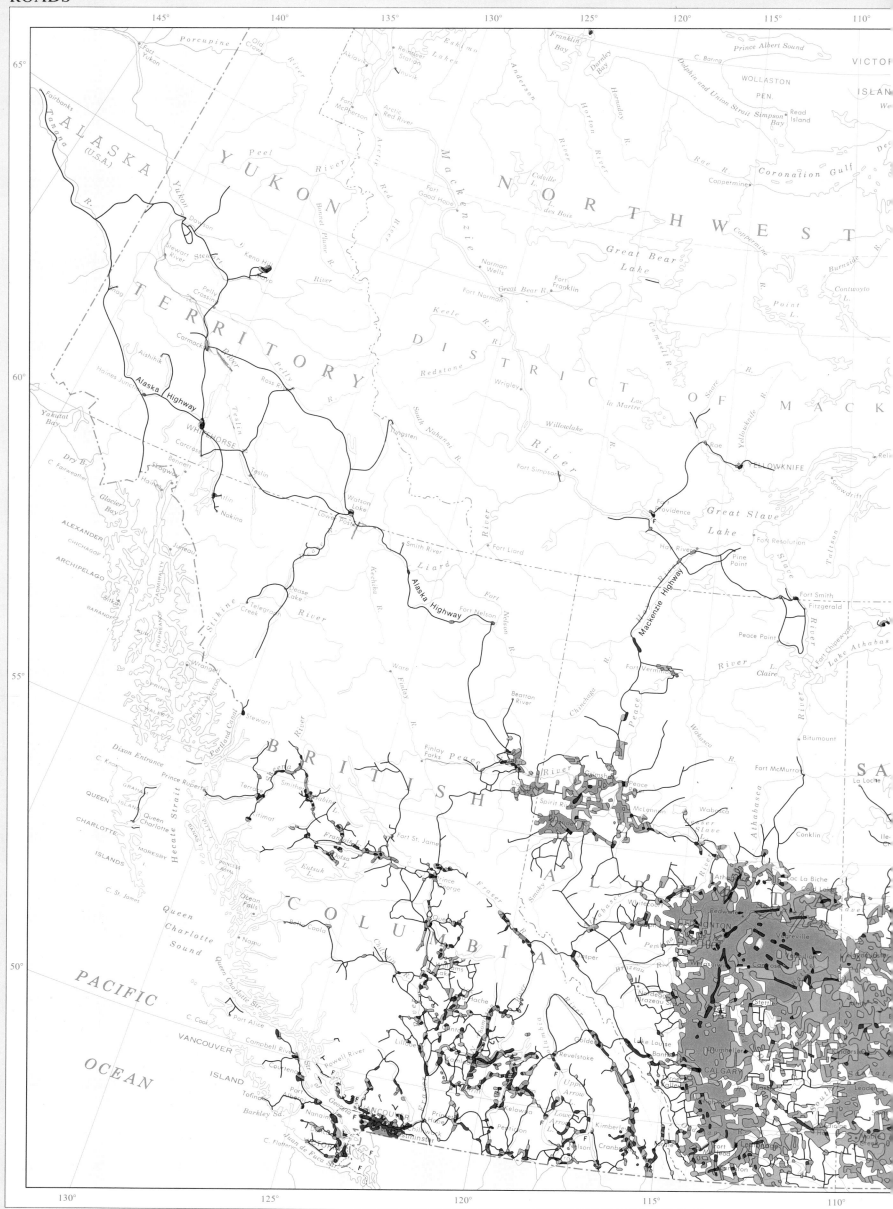

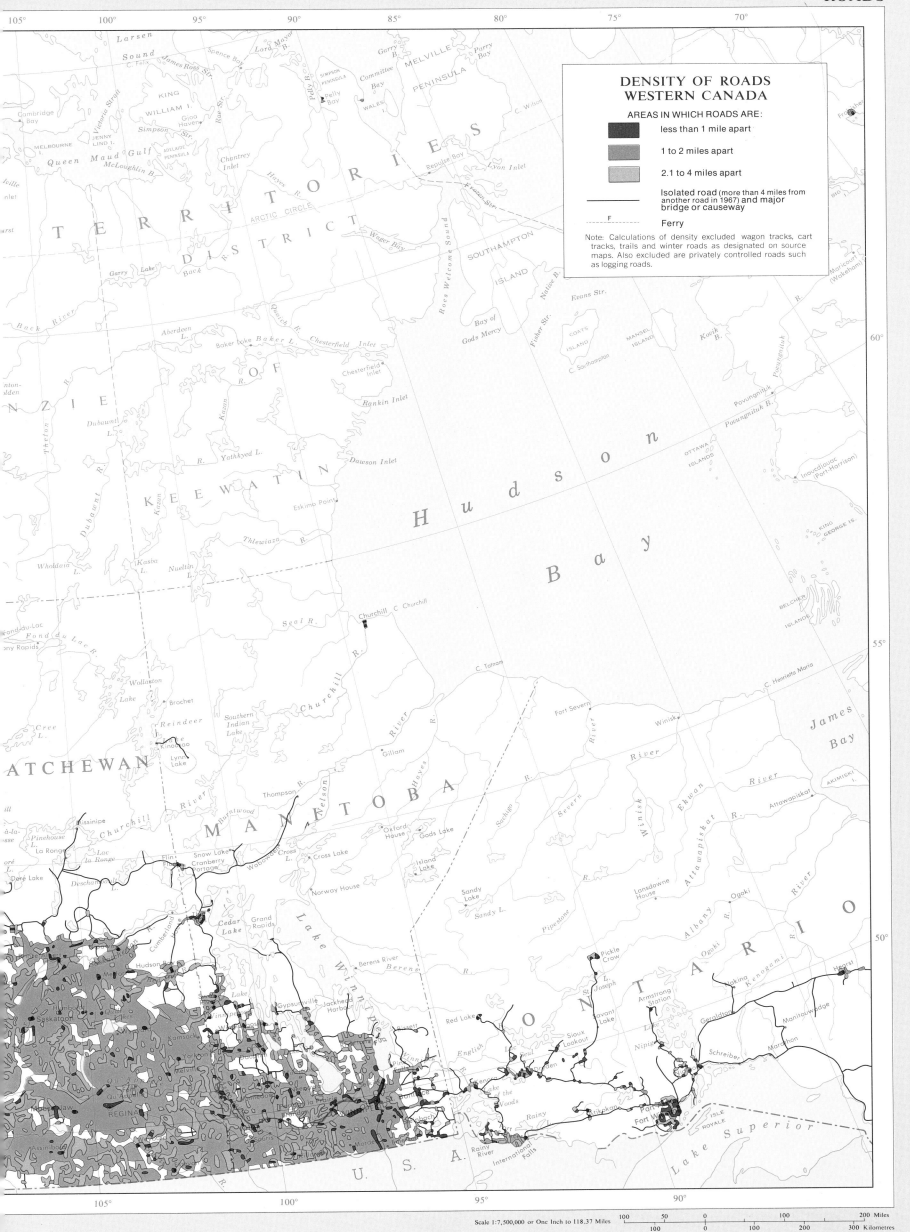

DENSITY OF ROADS
WESTERN CANADA

AREAS IN WHICH ROADS ARE:

less than 1 mile apart

1 to 2 miles apart

2.1 to 4 miles apart

Isolated road (more than 4 miles from another road in 1967) and major bridge or causeway

F   Ferry

Note: Calculations of density excluded wagon tracks, cart tracks, trails and winter roads as designated on source maps. Also excluded are privately controlled roads such as logging roads.

Scale 1:7,500,000 or One Inch to 118.37 Miles

ROADS

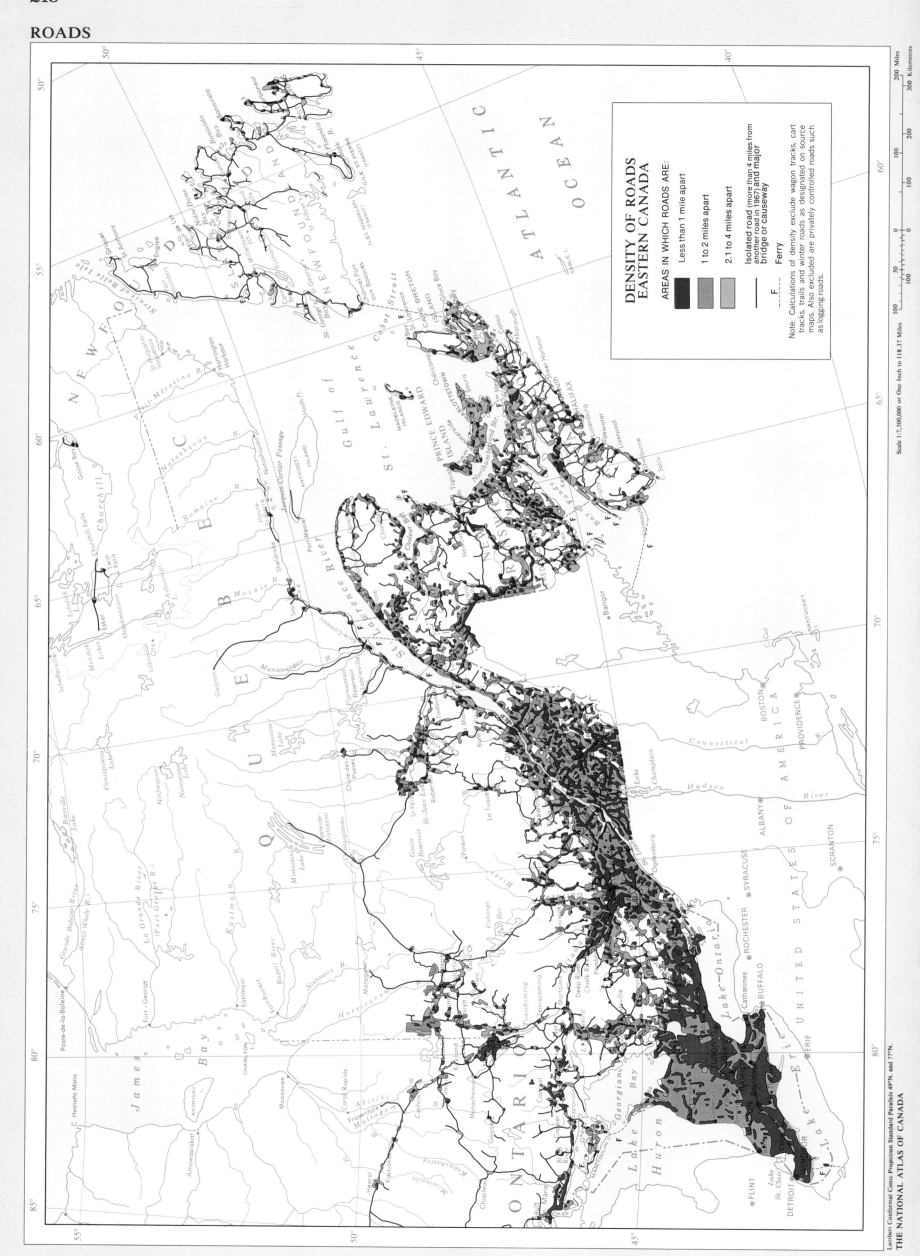

DENSITY OF ROADS
EASTERN CANADA

AREAS IN WHICH ROADS ARE:

Less than 1 mile apart

1 to 2 miles apart

2.1 to 4 miles apart

Isolated road (more than 4 miles from
another road in 1967) and major
bridge or causeway

F — — — Ferry

Note: Calculations of density exclude wagon tracks, cart
tracks, trails and winter roads as designated on source
maps. Also excluded are privately controlled roads such
as logging roads.

Lambert Conformal Conic Projection Standard Parallels 49°N. and 77°N.

Scale 1:7,500,000 or One Inch to 118.37 Miles

THE NATIONAL ATLAS OF CANADA

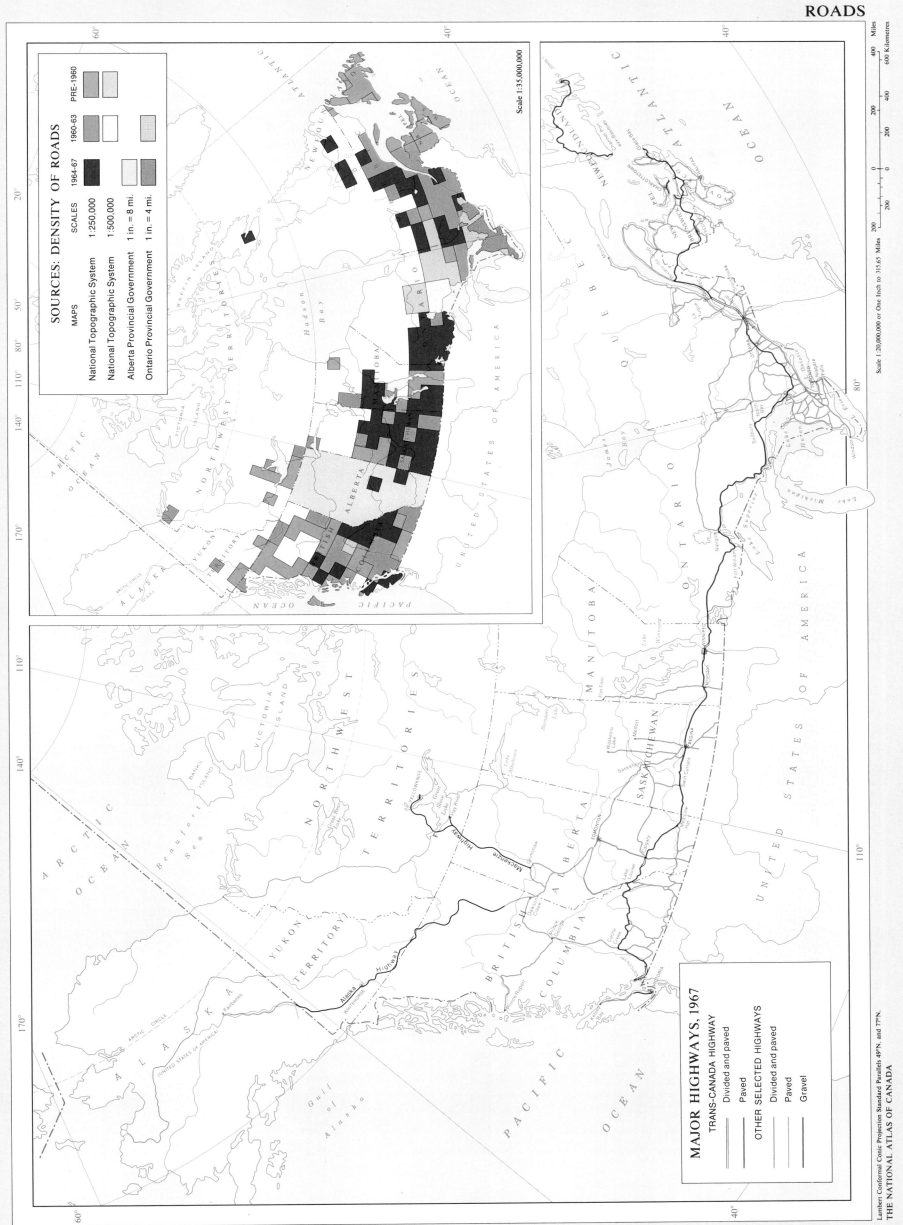

SOURCES: DENSITY OF ROADS

MAPS   SCALES   1964-67   1960-63   PRE-1960

National Topographic System   1:250,000
National Topographic System   1:500,000
Alberta Provincial Government   1 in. = 8 mi.
Ontario Provincial Government   1 in. = 4 mi.

Scale 1:35,000,000

MAJOR HIGHWAYS, 1967

TRANS-CANADA HIGHWAY
    Divided and paved
    Paved
OTHER SELECTED HIGHWAYS
    Divided and paved
    Paved
    Gravel

Lambert Conformal Conic Projection Standard Parallels 49°N. and 77°N.

THE NATIONAL ATLAS OF CANADA

Scale 1:20,000,000 or One Inch to 315.65 Miles

Miles
400   200   0   200   400
600   400   200   0   200   Kilometres

GRAIN ELEVATORS

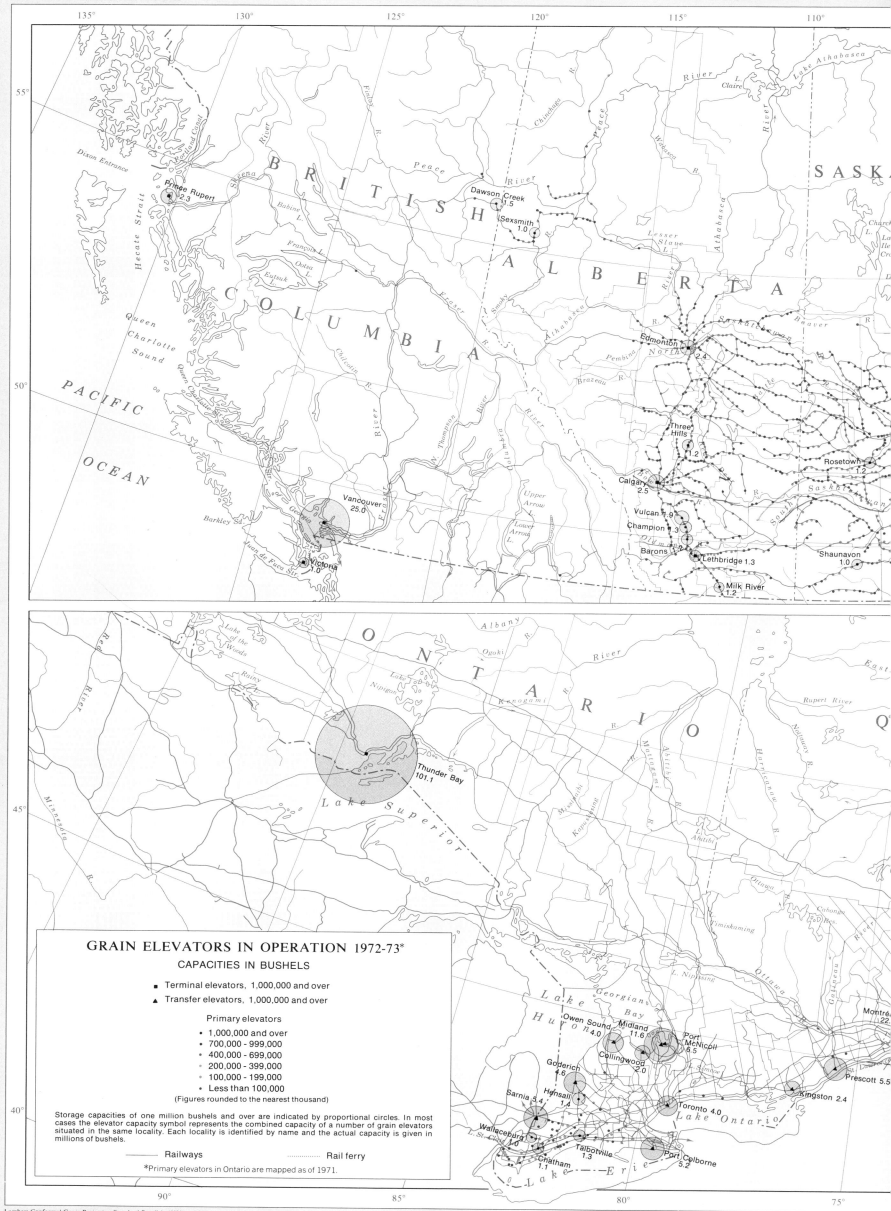

Prince Rupert 2.3

Dawson Creek 1.5
Sexsmith 1.0

BRITISH COLUMBIA

ALBERTA

SASK

Edmonton North 2.4

Three Hills 1.2

Rosetown 1.2

Calgary 2.5

Vulcan 7.9
Champion 4.3
Barons

Shaunavon 1.0

Lethbridge 1.3

Vancouver 25.0

Victoria 1.0

Milk River 1.2

ONTARIO

Q

Thunder Bay 101.1

Lake Superior

GRAIN ELEVATORS IN OPERATION 1972-73*

CAPACITIES IN BUSHELS

- ■ Terminal elevators, 1,000,000 and over
- ▲ Transfer elevators, 1,000,000 and over

Primary elevators
- • 1,000,000 and over
- • 700,000 - 999,000
- • 400,000 - 699,000
- · 200,000 - 399,000
- · 100,000 - 199,000
- · Less than 100,000
(Figures rounded to the nearest thousand)

Storage capacities of one million bushels and over are indicated by proportional circles. In most cases the elevator capacity symbol represents the combined capacity of a number of grain elevators situated in the same locality. Each locality is identified by name and the actual capacity is given in millions of bushels.

———— Railways   ·········· Rail ferry

*Primary elevators in Ontario are mapped as of 1971.

Owen Sound 4.0
Midland 11.6
Port McNicoll 6.5
Collingwood
Goderich 4.6
Sarnia 5.4
Hensall 1.4
Wallaceburg 1.0
Chatham 1.1
Talbotville 1.3
Toronto 4.0
Kingston 2.4
Prescott 5.5
Port Colborne 5.2
Montréal 22.

Lake Huron
Georgian Bay
Lake Ontario
Lake Erie

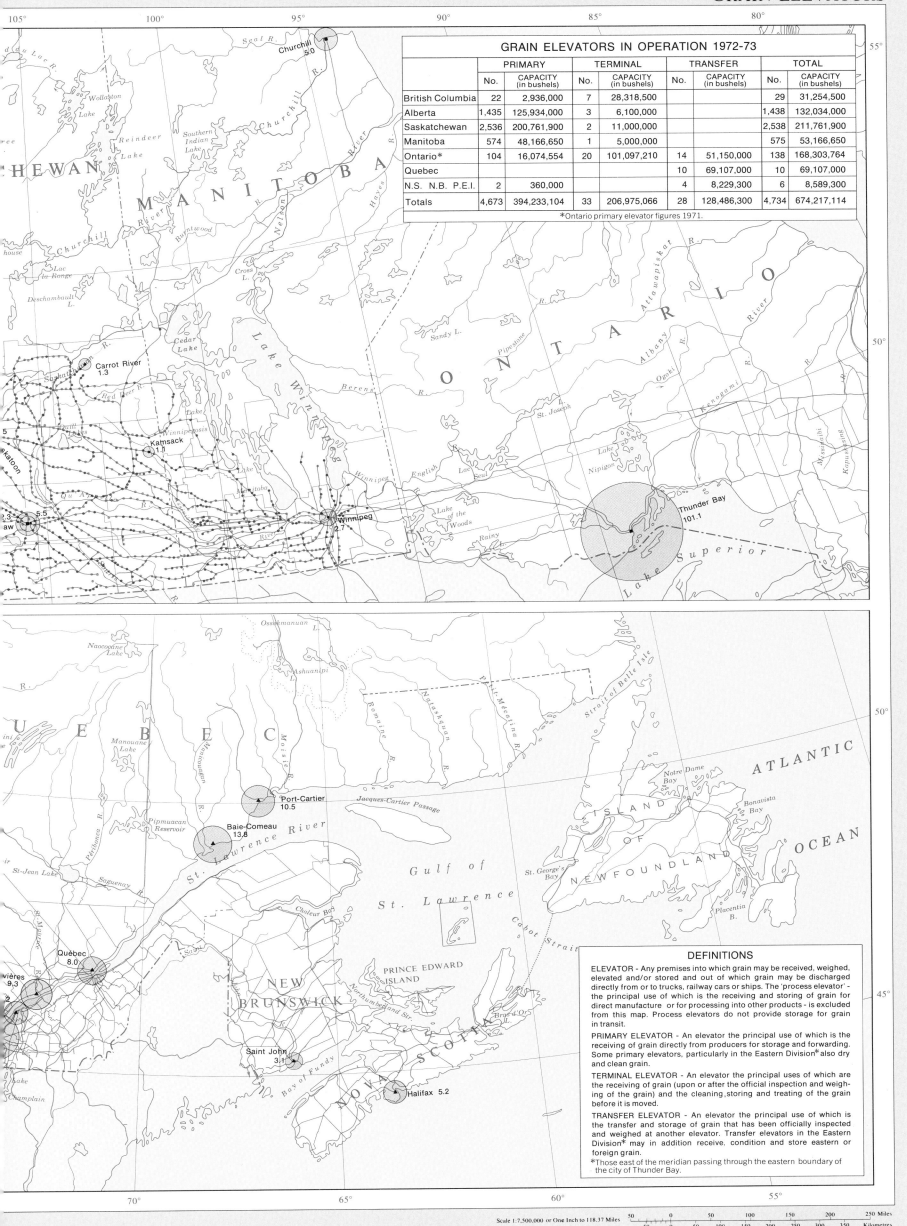

GRAIN ELEVATORS IN OPERATION 1972-73

	PRIMARY		TERMINAL		TRANSFER		TOTAL	
	No.	CAPACITY (in bushels)	No.	CAPACITY (in bushels)	No.	CAPACITY (in bushels)	No.	CAPACITY (in bushels)
British Columbia	22	2,936,000	7	28,318,500			29	31,254,500
Alberta	1,435	125,934,000	3	6,100,000			1,438	132,034,000
Saskatchewan	2,536	200,761,900	2	11,000,000			2,538	211,761,900
Manitoba	574	48,166,650	1	5,000,000			575	53,166,650
Ontario*	104	16,074,554	20	101,097,210	14	51,150,000	138	168,303,764
Quebec					10	69,107,000	10	69,107,000
N.S. N.B. P.E.I.	2	360,000			4	8,229,300	6	8,589,300
Totals	4,673	394,233,104	33	206,975,066	28	128,486,300	4,734	674,217,114

*Ontario primary elevator figures 1971.

DEFINITIONS

ELEVATOR - Any premises into which grain may be received, weighed, elevated and/or stored and out of which grain may be discharged directly from or to trucks, railway cars or ships. The 'process elevator' - the principal use of which is the receiving and storing of grain for direct manufacture or for processing into other products - is excluded from this map. Process elevators do not provide storage for grain in transit.

PRIMARY ELEVATOR - An elevator the principal use of which is the receiving of grain directly from producers for storage and forwarding. Some primary elevators, particularly in the Eastern Division* also dry and clean grain.

TERMINAL ELEVATOR - An elevator the principal uses of which are the receiving of grain (upon or after the official inspection and weighing of the grain) and the cleaning, storing and treating of the grain before it is moved.

TRANSFER ELEVATOR - An elevator the principal use of which is the transfer and storage of grain that has been officially inspected and weighed at another elevator. Transfer elevators in the Eastern Division* may in addition receive, condition and store eastern or foreign grain.

*Those east of the meridian passing through the eastern boundary of the city of Thunder Bay.

Scale 1:7,500,000 or One Inch to 118.37 Miles

**SELECTED AIR SERVICES,
DECEMBER 1967**

	Canadian	Foreign[1]
SCHEDULED SERVICES	————	————
REGULAR SPECIFIC POINT SERVICES[2]	————	————

[1] Available only for travel and/or shipment originating or terminating outside Canada.

[2] Regular service is available to designated points on a route pattern. When service is not required, points may be by-passed.

NOTE: The air services shown are those that carry passengers, mail and/or freight. Non-scheduled services are not shown. The flight lines are diagrammatic and do not necessarily represent actual routes.

Lambert Conformal Conic Projection Standard Parallels 49°N. and 77°N.

NATIONAL ATLAS OF CANADA

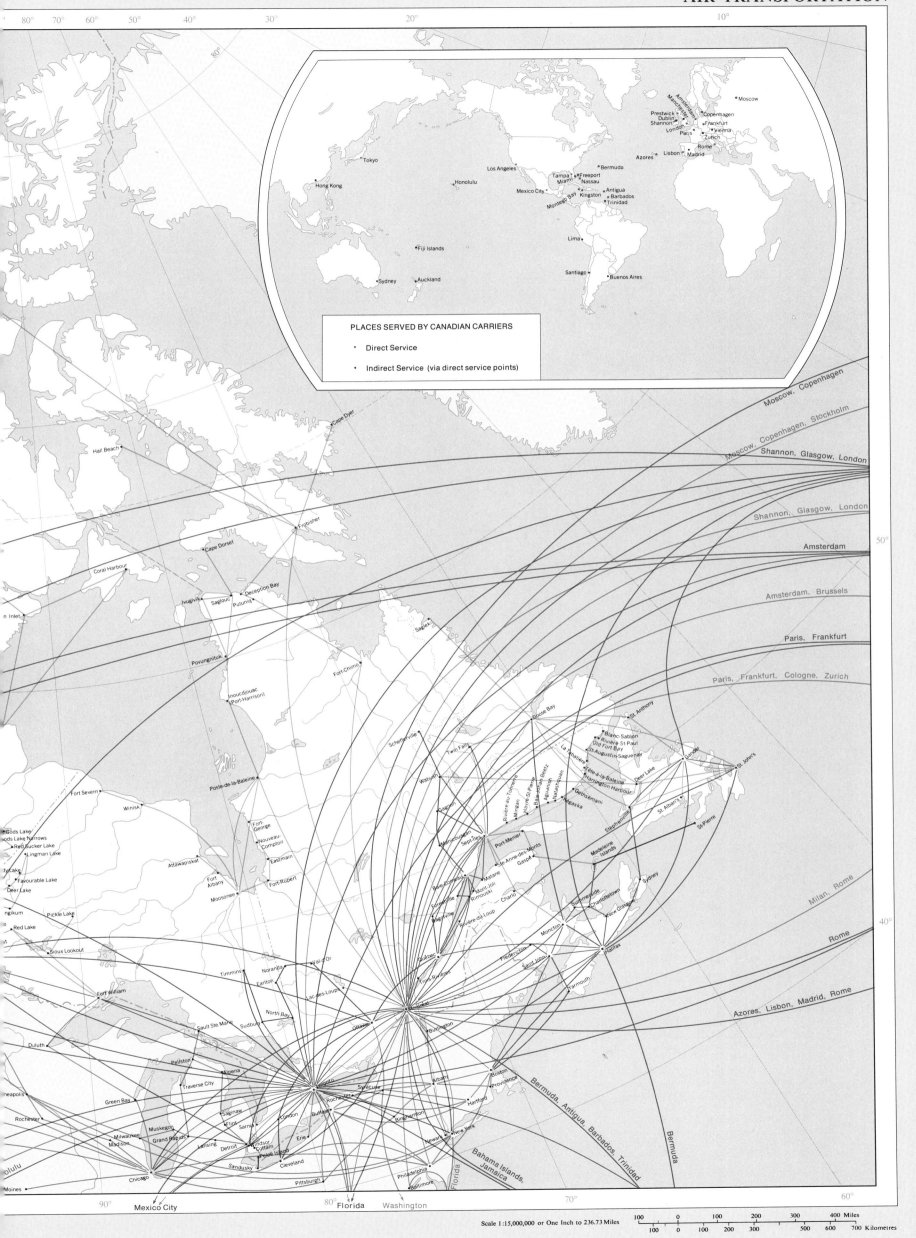

PLACES SERVED BY CANADIAN CARRIERS

· Direct Service

· Indirect Service (via direct service points)

Scale 1:15,000,000 or One Inch to 236.73 Miles

100   0   100   200   300   400 Miles

100   0   100   200   300   400   500   600   700 Kilometres

AIRPORTS, AERODROMES AND TIME ZONES

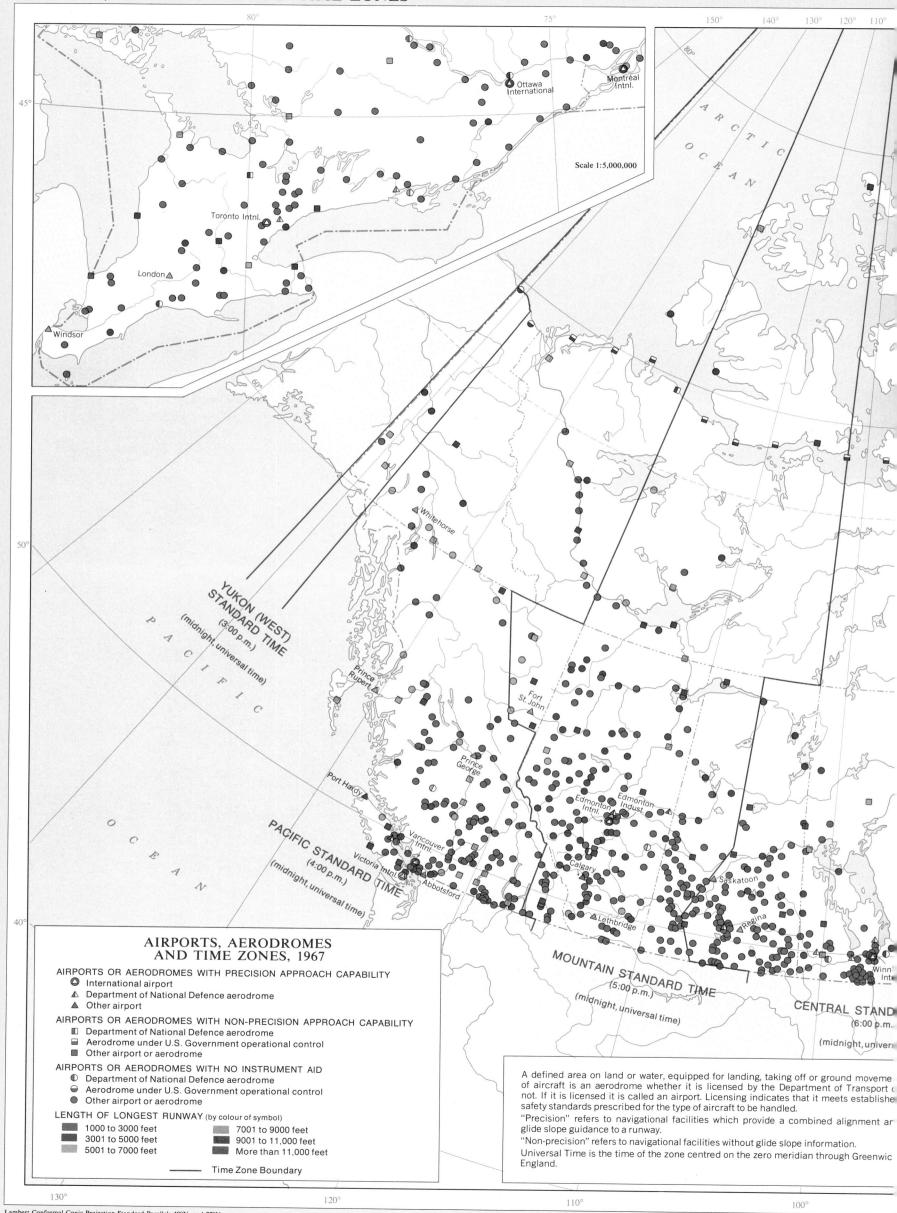

Scale 1:5,000,000

YUKON (WEST) STANDARD TIME
(3:00 p.m.)
(midnight, universal time)

PACIFIC STANDARD TIME
(4:00 p.m.)
(midnight, universal time)

MOUNTAIN STANDARD TIME
(5:00 p.m.)
(midnight, universal time)

CENTRAL STAND
(6:00 p.m.

(midnight, univers

Whitehorse

Prince Rupert

Port Hardy

Prince George

Fort St. John

Edmonton Intnl.
Edmonton Indust.

Vancouver Intnl.

Victoria Intnl.
Abbotsford

Calgary

Saskatoon

Lethbridge

Regina

Winn
Int

Ottawa International

Montréal Intnl.

Toronto Intnl.

London

Windsor

AIRPORTS, AERODROMES AND TIME ZONES, 1967

AIRPORTS OR AERODROMES WITH PRECISION APPROACH CAPABILITY
- International airport
- Department of National Defence aerodrome
- Other airport

AIRPORTS OR AERODROMES WITH NON-PRECISION APPROACH CAPABILITY
- Department of National Defence aerodrome
- Aerodrome under U.S. Government operational control
- Other airport or aerodrome

AIRPORTS OR AERODROMES WITH NO INSTRUMENT AID
- Department of National Defence aerodrome
- Aerodrome under U.S. Government operational control
- Other airport or aerodrome

LENGTH OF LONGEST RUNWAY (by colour of symbol)
- 1000 to 3000 feet
- 3001 to 5000 feet
- 5001 to 7000 feet
- 7001 to 9000 feet
- 9001 to 11,000 feet
- More than 11,000 feet

—— Time Zone Boundary

A defined area on land or water, equipped for landing, taking off or ground moveme of aircraft is an aerodrome whether it is licensed by the Department of Transport o not. If it is licensed it is called an airport. Licensing indicates that it meets establishe safety standards prescribed for the type of aircraft to be handled.

"Precision" refers to navigational facilities which provide a combined alignment ar glide slope guidance to a runway.

"Non-precision" refers to navigational facilities without glide slope information.

Universal Time is the time of the zone centred on the zero meridian through Greenwic England.

Lambert Conformal Conic Projection Standard Parallels 49°N. and 77°N.
NATIONAL ATLAS OF CANADA

Water aerodrome
Heliport
A heliport is an aerodrome for the exclusive use of helicopters.

Scale 1:35,000,000

NEWFOUNDLAND
STANDARD TIME
(8:30 p.m.)

(midnight,
universal time)

Gander
International

Torbay

Frobisher

Sept-Îles

Charlottetown

Sydney

Moncton

Halifax International

Fredericton

Saint John

Québec

Yarmouth

ATLANTIC STANDARD TIME
(8:00 p.m.)

(midnight, universal time)

Lakehead
(Port Arthur-Fort William)

TIME

Sault
Ste.Marie

North Bay

Ottawa
Intnl.

Montreal
International

Toronto International

EASTERN STANDARD TIME
(7:00 p.m.)

(midnight, universal time)

Scale 1:15,000,000 or One Inch to 236.73 Miles

100   0   100   200   300   400 Miles

100 0 100 200 300 400 500 600 700 Kilometres

COMMUNICATIONS

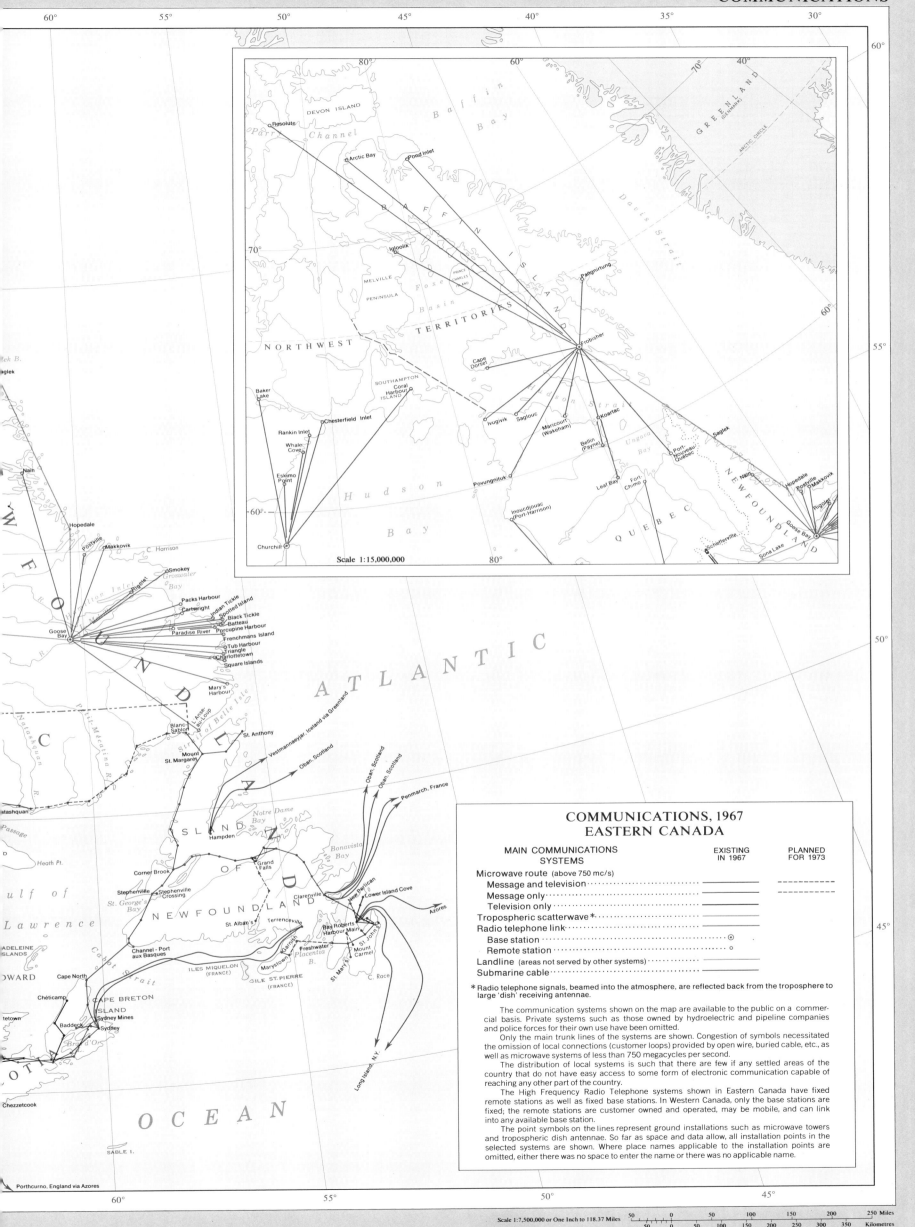

Scale 1:15,000,000

COMMUNICATIONS, 1967
EASTERN CANADA

MAIN COMMUNICATIONS SYSTEMS	EXISTING IN 1967	PLANNED FOR 1973
Microwave route (above 750 mc/s)		
Message and television	———	- - - - -
Message only	———	- - - - -
Television only	———	
Tropospheric scatterwave *	———	
Radio telephone link		
Base station	⊙	
Remote station	○	
Landline (areas not served by other systems)	———	
Submarine cable	———	

*Radio telephone signals, beamed into the atmosphere, are reflected back from the troposphere to large 'dish' receiving antennae.

The communication systems shown on the map are available to the public on a commercial basis. Private systems such as those owned by hydroelectric and pipeline companies and police forces for their own use have been omitted.

Only the main trunk lines of the systems are shown. Congestion of symbols necessitated the omission of local connections (customer loops) provided by open wire, buried cable, etc., as well as microwave systems of less than 750 megacycles per second.

The distribution of local systems is such that there are few if any settled areas of the country that do not have easy access to some form of electronic communication capable of reaching any other part of the country.

The High Frequency Radio Telephone systems shown in Eastern Canada have fixed remote stations as well as fixed base stations. In Western Canada, only the base stations are fixed; the remote stations are customer owned and operated, may be mobile, and can link into any available base station.

The point symbols on the lines represent ground installations such as microwave towers and tropospheric dish antennae. So far as space and data allow, all installation points in the selected systems are shown. Where place names applicable to the installation points are omitted, either there was no space to enter the name or there was no applicable name.

Scale 1:7,500,000 or One Inch to 118.37 Miles

50   0   50   100   150   200   250 Miles

50   0   50   100   150   200   250   300   350 Kilometres

COMMUNICATIONS

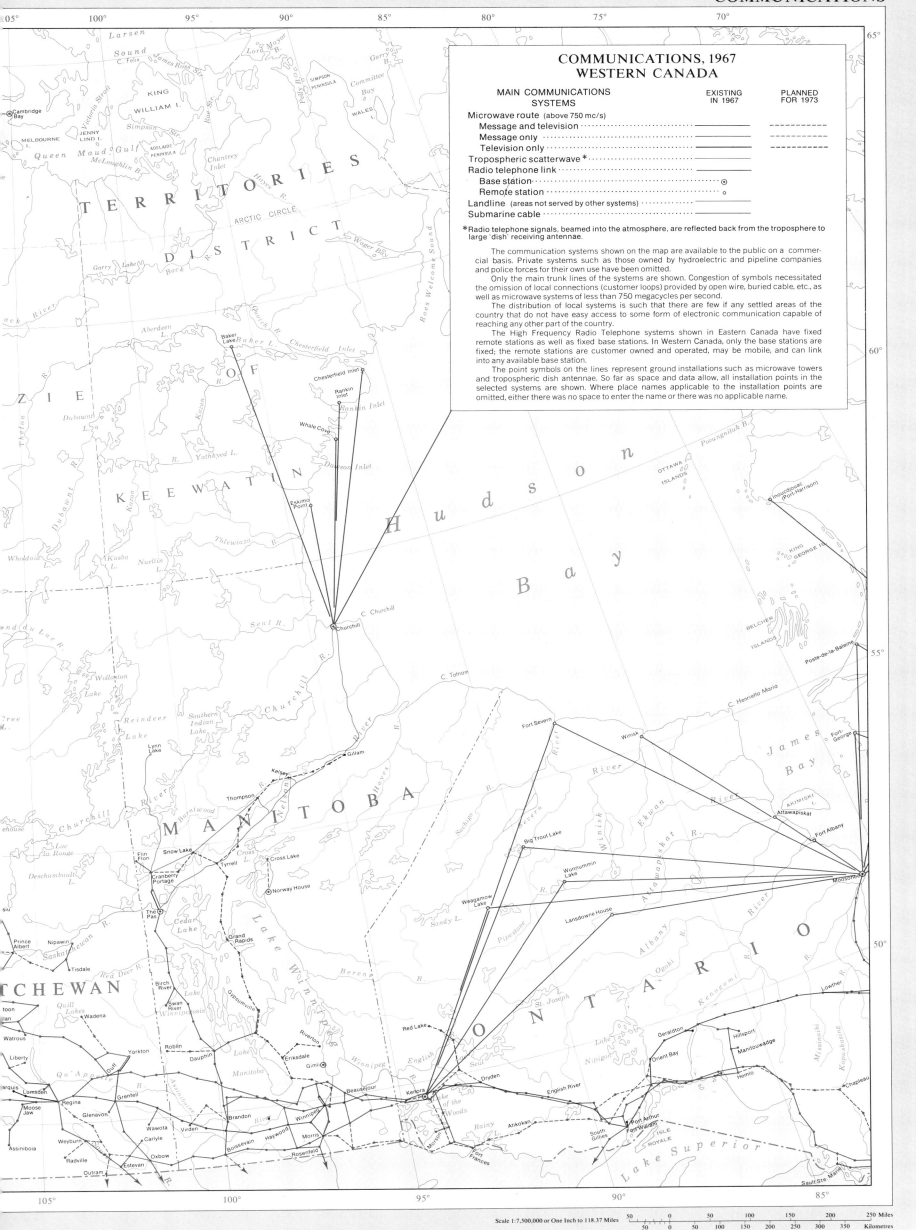

COMMUNICATIONS, 1967
WESTERN CANADA

MAIN COMMUNICATIONS SYSTEMS	EXISTING IN 1967	PLANNED FOR 1973
Microwave route (above 750 mc/s)		
Message and television		
Message only		
Television only		
Tropospheric scatterwave *		
Radio telephone link		
Base station		
Remote station		
Landline (areas not served by other systems)		
Submarine cable		

*Radio telephone signals, beamed into the atmosphere, are reflected back from the troposphere to large 'dish' receiving antennae.

The communication systems shown on the map are available to the public on a commercial basis. Private systems such as those owned by hydroelectric and pipeline companies and police forces for their own use have been omitted.

Only the main trunk lines of the systems are shown. Congestion of symbols necessitated the omission of local connections (customer loops) provided by open wire, buried cable, etc., as well as microwave systems of less than 750 megacycles per second.

The distribution of local systems is such that there are few if any settled areas of the country that do not have easy access to some form of electronic communication capable of reaching any other part of the country.

The High Frequency Radio Telephone systems shown in Eastern Canada have fixed remote stations as well as fixed base stations. In Western Canada, only the base stations are fixed; the remote stations are customer owned and operated, may be mobile, and can link into any available base station.

The point symbols on the lines represent ground installations such as microwave towers and tropospheric dish antennae. So far as space and data allow, all installation points in the selected systems are shown. Where place names applicable to the installation points are omitted, either there was no space to enter the name or there was no applicable name.

Scale 1:7,500,000 or One Inch to 118.37 Miles

50   0   50   100   150   200   250 Miles
50   0   50   100   150   200   250   300   350 Kilometres

RADIO STATIONS

YUKON TERRITORY
Whitehorse	CFWH-AM

NORTHWEST TERRITORIES
Fort Simpson	CFSP-FM
Inuvik	CHAK-AM
Yellowknife	CFYK-AM

BRITISH COLUMBIA
Abbotsford	CFVR-AM
Burns Lake	CFLD-AM
Campbell River	CFWB-AM
Chilliwack	CHWK-AM
Clearwater	CFFM-FM-2
Clinton	CFFM-FM-4
Courtenay	CFCP-AM
Cranbrook	CKEK-AM
Dawson Creek	CJDC-AM
Duncan	CKAY-AM
Fort Nelson	CFNL-AM
Fort St. John	CKNL-AM
Kamloops	CFJC-AM
Kamloops	CHUB-AM
Kelowna	CKOV-AM
Kimat	CKTK-AM
Langley	CJJC-AM
Merritt	CFFM-FM-3
Mount Timothy	CFFM-FM-5
Nanaimo	CHUB-AM
Nelson	CKKC-AM
New Westminster	CKNW-AM
North Vancouver	CKLG-AM
Penticton	CKOK-AM
Port Alberni	CJAV-AM
Powell River	CHQB-AM
Prince George	CKPG-AM
Prince Rupert	CFPR-AM
Quesnel	CKCQ-AM
Revelstoke	CKCR-AM
Salmon Arm	CKXR-AM
Smithers	CFBV-AM
Terrace	CFTK-AM
Trail	CJAT-AM
Vancouver	CBU-AM
	CBU-FM
	CHQM-AM
	CJOR-AM
	CKWX-AM
	CKLG-FM
	CHQM-FM
Vernon	CJIB-AM
Victoria	CFAX-AM
	CJVI-AM
	CKDA-AM
Williams Lake	CKWL-AM

ALBERTA
Calgary	CBR-AM
	CFAC-AM
	CFCN-AM
	CHQR-AM
	CKXL-AM
	CHFM-FM
Camrose	CFCW-AM
Drumheller	CJDV-AM
Edmonton	CBX-AM
	CHED-AM
	CHFA-AM
	CHQT-AM
	CJCA-AM
	CKUA-AM
	CKXM-FM
Grande Prairie	CFGP-AM
Lethbridge	CHEC-AM
	CJOC-AM
Lloydminster	CKSA-AM
Medicine Hat	CHAT-AM
Peace River	CKYL-AM
Red Deer	CKRD-AM
	CKRD-FM

SASKATCHEWAN
Estevan	CJSL-AM
Gravelbourg	CFRG-AM
Melfort	CJVR-AM
Moose Jaw	CHAB-AM
North Battleford	CJNB-AM
Prince Albert	CKBI-AM
Regina	CBK-AM
	CJME-AM
	CKCK-AM
	CKRM-AM
	CFMQ-FM
Rosetown	CKKR-AM
Saskatoon	CFQC-AM
	CKOM-AM
	CFMC-FM
	CJUS-FM
Shaunavon	CJSN-AM
Swift Current	CKSW-AM
Weyburn	CFSL-AM
Yorkton	CJGX-AM

MANITOBA
Altona	CFAM-AM
Brandon	CKX-AM
	CKX-FM
Churchill	CHFC-AM
Dauphin	CKDM-AM
Flin Flon	CFAR-AM
Portage la Prairie	CFRY-AM
St. Boniface	CKSB-AM
Steinbach	CHSM-AM
Thompson	CHTM-AM
Winnipeg	CBW-AM
	CFRW-AM
	CJOB-AM
	CKRC-AM
	CKY-AM
	CBW-FM
	CJOB-FM
	CKY-FM

ONTARIO
Ajax	CHOO-AM
Barrie	CKBB-AM
Belleville	CJBQ-AM
Blind River	CJNR-AM
Brampton	CHIC-AM
Brantford	CKPC-AM
	CKPC-FM
Brockville	CFJR-AM
Callander	CFCH-AM
Chatham	CFCO-AM
Collingwood	CKCB-AM
Cornwall	CFML-AM
	CJSS-AM
	CJSS-FM
Dryden	CKDR-AM
Elliot Lake	CKNR-AM
Fort Frances	CKFM-AM
Fort William	CKPR-AM
	CFPA-AM
Galt	CHYR-AM
Guelph	CJOY-AM
Hamilton	CHAM-AM
	CHML-AM
	CHUM-AM
	CKOC-AM
	CKLB-AM
	CKGB-AM
	CBO-AM
Hearst	CKAR-AM
Huntsville	CKAP-AM
Kapuskasing	CFRC-AM
Kenora	CJRL-AM
Kingston	CKLC-AM
	CFRC-FM
Kirkland Lake	CKWS-AM
Kitchener	CHYM-AM
	CKKW-AM
	CHYM-FM
Leamington	CHIR-AM
Lindsay	CKLY-AM
London	CFPL-AM
	CJOE-AM
	CKSL-AM
	CFPL-FM
Midland	CKMP-AM
Niagara Falls	CJRN-AM
North Bay	CKAT-AM
	CFCH?
Oakville	CHWO-AM
Orillia	CFOR-AM
Oshawa	CKLB-AM
	CKGB-FM
Ottawa	CBO-AM
	CBO-FM
	CFRA-AM
	CKOY-AM
	CKPM-AM
	CBO-FM
	CKOS-FM
Owen Sound	CFOS-AM
Parry Sound	CKAR-AM-1
Pembroke	CHOV-AM
Peterborough	CKPT-AM
	CFPA-AM
Port Arthur	CKPR-FM
Richmond Hill	CFGM-AM

ONTARIO (cont.)
St. Catharines	CKTB-AM
	CHSC-FM
St. Thomas	CHLO-AM
Sarnia	CHOK-AM
	CKJD-FM
Sault Ste. Marie	CJIC-AM
	CHAS-FM
Simcoe	CFRS-AM
Smiths Falls	CJET-AM
Stratford	CJCS-AM
Sudbury	CFBR-AM
	CHNO-AM
	CKSO-AM
	CKCB-FM
	CKSO-FM
	CKOT-FM
Tillsonburg	CKOT-AM
Timmins	CFCL-AM
	CKGB-AM
Toronto	CBL-AM
	CFRB-AM
	CHFI-AM
	CHUM-AM
	CKEY-AM
	CKFH-AM
	CHIN-FM
	CHFI-FM
	CHUM-FM
	CJRT-FM
	CKFM-FM
	CFRX-SW
	CJWA-AM
Wawa	CHOW-AM
Welland	

QUEBEC
Alma	CKGT-AM
Amos	CHAD-AM
Cabano	CJAF-AM
Causapscal	CJBR-AM
Chicoutimi	CBJ-AM
Dolbeau	CHMT-AM
Drummondville	CHEF-AM
Granby	CHLC-AM
Hauterive	CHLT-AM
Hull	CKCH-AM
Joliette	CJLM-AM
Jonquière	CKRS-AM
La Pocatière	CHGB-AM
La Sarre	CKLS-AM
La Tuque	CFLM-AM
Lévis	CFLS-AM
Maniwaki	CKBL-AM
Matane	CKBL-AM
Mont-Laurier	CKML-AM
Montmagny	CKBM-AM
Montréal	CBM-AM
	CBF-FM
	CFCF-AM
	CJAD-AM
	CJMS-AM
	CKAC-AM
	CKGM-AM
	CKLM-AM
	CKVL-AM
	CKVL-FM
	CKOI-FM

QUEBEC (cont.)
Montréal	CKGM-AM
	CBF-FM
	CBM-FM
	CFQR-FM
	CJFM-FM
	CKGM-FM
	CHLT-FM
	CKVL-SW
	CHAY-SW
	CHLR-SW
	CHRX-SW
	CHSB-SW
	CKCX-SW
	CKLP-SW
	CKUS-SW
	CKVU-SW
	CKYT-SW
New Carlisle	CFCH-AM
Pointe-Claire	CFOX-AM
Québec	CBV-AM
	CFOM-AM
	CHRC-AM
	CJRP-AM
	CKCV-AM
	CBV-FM
	CHRC-FM
	CKCV-FM
Rimouski	CJBR-AM
Rivière-du-Loup	CJFP-AM
Roberval	CHRL-AM
Rouyn	CKRN-AM

Montréal
Ste-Agathe-des-Monts	CJSA-AM
St-Georges	CKBS-AM
St-Hyacinthe	CKBM-AM
St-Jean	CBF-FM
St-Jérôme	CFGR-FM
Schefferville	CFNB-FM
Sept-Iles	CKCN-FM
Shawinigan	CKSM-AM
Sherbrooke	CKGM-FM
	CHAY-SW
	CHLT-FM
Sorel	CKTS-SW
	CHLT-FM
Thetford Mines	CKLD-AM
Trois-Rivières	CKTR-AM
Val-d'Or	CKVD-AM
Valleyfield	CKVL-FM
Verdun...Bilingual	CKVL-AM
Victoriaville	CFDA-AM
Ville-Marie...Bilingual	CKVM-AM

NEW BRUNSWICK
Bathurst	CKBC-AM
Campbellton	CKNB-AM
Edmundston	CJEM-AM
Fredericton	CBZ-AM
	CFNB-AM
Moncton	CBA-AM
	CKCW-AM
	CKMR-AM
Newcastle	CBA-AM
Sackville	CBD-AM
Saint John	CFBC-AM
	CHSJ-AM
	CHSJ-FM
	CJCJ-AM

NOVA SCOTIA
Amherst	CKDH-AM
Antigonish	CJFX-AM
Bridgewater	CKBW-AM
Dartmouth	CFDR-AM
Halifax	CBH-AM
	CHNS-AM
	CJCH-AM
	CHNS-FM
	CHNX-SW
Kentville	CKEN-AM
Middleton	CKAD-AM
New Glasgow	CKEC-AM
Sydney	CBI-AM
	CHER-AM
	CJCB-AM
	CJCB-FM
	CJCX-SW
Truro	CKCL-AM
Windsor	CFAB-AM
Yarmouth	CJLS-AM

PRINCE EDWARD ISLAND
Charlottetown	CFCY-AM
Summerside	CJRW-AM

NEWFOUNDLAND
Corner Brook	CBY-AM
Gander	CBG-AM
Goose Bay	CFGB-AM
Grand Bank	CJOX-AM
Grand Falls	CBT-AM
	CJCN-AM
	CKCM-AM
	CBN-AM
	CBN-FM
St. John's	VOAR-AM
	VOCM-AM
	VOWR-AM
	CKZN-SW
	CFSX-SW

RADIO BROADCASTING, DECEMBER 1967

	English	French	Bilingual
AM Broadcasting Station *	●	○	
AM Rebroadcasting Station *			
FM Broadcasting Station	▲	△	▲
FM Rebroadcasting Station			
Shortwave Station (SW) *	★		
More than one station	3		

Area of usual daytime coverage by AM broadcasting station or low power relay transmitter**

* A station which does not originate its programming but rebroadcasts the programmes of a parent station simultaneously or at a later time.

** The limit of AM coverage, under average conditions, as here delineated is the line along which the signal strength during the day is normally 0.5 millivolt per metre.

Scale 1:7,500,000

Scale 1:20,000,000 or One Inch to 315.65 Miles

Lambert Conformal Conic Projection Standard Parallels 49°N. and 77°N.

THE NATIONAL ATLAS OF CANADA

TELEVISION BROADCASTING STATIONS

NORTHWEST TERRITORIES
Yellowknife .... CFYK-TV

BRITISH COLUMBIA
Burnaby .... CHAN-TV
Cranbrook .... CJPM-TV
Dawson Creek .... CJDC-TV
Kamloops .... CFCR-TV
Kelowna .... CHBC-TV
Prince George .... CFCT-TV
Terrace .... CFTK-TV
Trail .... CBUT
Vancouver .... CBUT
Victoria .... CHEK-TV

ALBERTA
Calgary .... CHCT-TV
Edmonton .... CBXT
Grande Prairie .... CBXAT
Lethbridge .... CJLH-TV
Lloydminster .... CKSA-TV
Medicine Hat .... CHAT-TV
Red Deer .... CKRD-TV

SASKATCHEWAN
Carlyle Lake .... CFSS-TV
Marcuis .... CKX-TV
Moose Jaw .... CHAB-TV
Prince Albert .... CKBI-TV
Regina .... CHRE-TV
Saskatoon .... CFQC-TV
Swift Current .... CJFB-TV
Wynyard .... CHSS-TV
Yorkton .... CKOS-TV

MANITOBA
Baldy Mountain .... CKSS-TV
Brandon .... CKX-TV
Churchill .... CBWBT
Flin Flon .... CHGH-TV
Lynn Lake .... CBWBT
Winnipeg .... CBWT

ONTARIO
Barrie .... CKVR-TV
Callander .... CKX-TV
Dryden .... CBWDT
Fort Frances .... CBWCT
Geraldton .... CBLAT
Hamilton .... CHCH-TV
Kenora .... CBWAT
Kingston .... CKWS-TV
Kitchener .... CKCO-TV
London .... CFPL-TV
Ottawa .... CBOT
Pembroke .... CHOV-TV
Peterborough .... CHEX-TV
Port Arthur .... CKPR-TV
Red Lake .... CBWET
Sault Ste. Marie .... CJIC-TV
Sturgeon Falls .... CICO-TV
Sudbury .... CKSO-TV
Timmins .... CFCL-TV
Toronto .... CBLT
Windsor .... CKLW-TV
Wingham .... CKNX-TV

QUEBEC
Carleton .... CHAU-TV
Chicoutimi .... CJPM-TV
Jonquière .... CKRS-TV
Matane .... CBGT
Montreal .... CBFT / CFCF-TV / CFTM-TV
Quebec .... CFCM-TV / CKMI-TV
Rimouski .... CJBR-TV
Rivière-du-Loup .... CKRT-TV
Rouyn .... CKRN-TV
Schefferville .... Bilingual CFRL-TV
Sherbrooke .... CHLT-TV
Trois-Rivières .... CKTM-TV

NEW BRUNSWICK
Campbellton .... CKCW-TV
Moncton .... CKCW-TV
Saint John .... CHSJ-TV
Upsalquitch Lake .... CKAM-TV

NOVA SCOTIA
Chelicamp .... CBFCT
Halifax .... CBHT
Sydney .... CJCB-TV

PRINCE EDWARD ISLAND
Charlottetown .... CFCY-TV

NEWFOUNDLAND
Argentia .... CJOX-TV
Channel-Port aux Basques .... CBYBT
Corner Brook .... CKY
Deer Lake .... CBYAT
Goose Bay .... CFLA-TV
Grand Falls .... CBNAT
Labrador City .... Bilingual CJCL-TV
St. John's .... CJON-TV

TV REBROADCASTING STATIONS

BRITISH COLUMBIA

Station		Transmission received from
Adams River	CFZO-TV-2	Kamloops
Ashcroft	CFCR-TV-2	
Avola	CFCR-TV-13	
Boss Mountain	CFCR-TV-16	Mount Timothy
Boston Bar	CFCR-TV-9	Lillooet
Bowen Island	CBUT-4	Vancouver
Bralorne	CHAN-TV-2	Burnaby
Bulkhead Mountain	CFCR-TV-15	Mount Timothy
Burns Lake	CJDC-TV-2	Dawson Creek
Canoe	CHBC-TV-8	Salmon Arm
Canoe Mountain	CHBC-TV-8	Mount Timothy
Castlegar	CBUAT-2	Trail
Cawston	CHKC-TV-9	Olalla
Celista	CHBC-TV-6	Salmon Arm
Cherryville	CJWR-TV-1	Kelowna
Chilliwack	CHEK-TV-5	Victoria
Clearwater	CFCR-TV-10	Kamloops
Clinton	CBUT-1	Vancouver
Courtenay	CBUT-3	
Crawford Bay	CHMS-TV-1	Nelson
Crescent Valley	CBUAT-3	Trail
Creston	CBUAT-4	Crawford Bay
Enderby	CFEN-TV-1	Kelowna
Falkland	CHBC-TV-2	
Fort Fraser	CKVS-TV-1	Terrace
Grand Forks	CBUAT-5	Trail
Hixon	CKPG-TV-1	Prince George
Houston	CFTK-TV-10	Smithers
Hudson Hope	CJDC-TV-1	Dawson Creek
Invermere	CFWL-TV-1	Calgary CFCN-TV (Alta.)
Jubilee Mountain	CFWL-TV-2	
Juskatla	CFTK-TV-5	Prince Rupert
Kemano	CFTK-TV-6	Kildala Arm
Kildala Arm	CHKC-TV-4	Kelowna
Kokish	CFKB-TV-2	Sointula
Lillooet	CKUP-TV-1	Burnaby
Lookout Ridge	CHBC-TV-2	Vancouver
Lumby	CHID-TV-1	Kelowna
Mabel Lake	CHPP-TV-1	Mount Timothy
Malakwa	CFPJ-TV-1	
Merritt	CFCR-TV-3	Kamloops

Station		Transmission received from
Mica Creek	CFZO-TV-2	Revelstoke
Midway	CKMY-TV-1	Kelowna
Mount Parizeau	CFTK-TV-8	Terrace
Mount Poole	CHOC-TV-6	Prince Rupert
Mount Timothy	CFCR-TV-6	Clinton
Moyie	CKVS-TV-1	Lethbridge (Alta.)
Nakusp	CJNP-TV-1	Vancouver
Nass Camp	CFCR-TV-15	Mount Timothy
Nelson	CJDC-TV-2	Dawson Creek
Newcastle Ridge	CHBC-TV-8	Houston
New Denver	CBUAT-1	Mount Timothy
Nimpkish Camp	CHSL-TV-1	Victoria
Ocean Falls	CFTK-TV-9	Woss Camp
Oliver	CHKC-TV-2	Mount Parizeau
Olalla	CHBC-TV-3	Keremeos
Passmore	CHKS-TV-1	Penticton
Pavillon	CHPT-TV-1	Crescent Valley
Penticton	CHBC-TV-1	Kelowna
Perrys	CHMS-TV-3	Passmore
Port Alberni	CBUT-1	Vancouver
Port Alice	CBUAT-3	Nelson
Prince Rupert	CHMS-TV-1	Newcastle Ridge
Princeton	CKPA-TV-1	Kelowna
Promontory Mountain	CFEN-TV-1	
Quesnel	CFTK-TV-1	Terrace
Revelstoke	CFCR-TV-12	Kamloops
Salmon Arm	CKCQ-TV-1	Hixon
Savona	CFZO-TV-1	Kelowna
Skaha Lake	CHBC-TV-4	
Smithers	CFCR-TV-7	
Sointula	CFCR-TV-2	Terrace
Spences Bridge	CJFB-TV-1	Prince Rupert
Squamish	CJNA-TV-1	Kelowna
Ucluelet	CBUT-5	Bowen Island
Vernon	CHAN-TV-3	Burnaby
Westbank	CKUP-TV-1	Burnaby
Westwold	CHBC-TV-2	Kelowna
Williams Lake	CFWS-TV-5	Falkland
Woss Camp	CFCR-TV-5	Mount Timothy
Yuill Mountain	CKBF-TV-1	Spokane KXLY-TV (U.S.A.)

ALBERTA

Station		Transmission received from
Athabasca	CFRN-TV-4	Edmonton
Banff	CBXT-1	Calgary
Bonnyville	CHCT-TV-2	Red Deer
Brooks	CKRD-TV-1	Lloydminster
Burmis	CKVS-TV-1	Drumheller
Coleman	CLH-TV-3	Kelowna
Coronation	CLH-TV-1	Red Deer
Drumheller	CKRD-TV-1	
High Prairie	CFCN-TV-1	Calgary
Hinton	CBXAT-2	Victoria
Jasper	CBXT-3	Whitecourt
Lake Louise	CFLL-TV-1	Banff
Peace River	CBXAT-1	Grande Prairie
Pivot	CHAT-TV-1	Medicine Hat
Waterton Park	CJWP-TV-1	Lethbridge
Whitecourt	CBXT-2	Edmonton

SASKATCHEWAN

Station		Transmission received from
Alticane	CKBI-TV-1	Prince Albert
Big River	CKBI-TV-5	
Colgate	CKCK-TV-1	Regina
Eastend	CJFB-TV-1	Swift Current
Greenwater Lake	CKBI-TV-3	Prince Albert
Meadow Lake	CKSA-TV-1	Lloydminster
Nipawin	CKBI-TV-4	Prince Albert
North Battleford	CFQC-TV-1	Saskatoon
Riverhurst	CFQC-TV-1	Swift Current
Stranraer	CFQC-TV-1	Saskatoon
Val Marie	CJFB-TV-1	Swift Current
Willow Bunch	CKCK-TV-2	Regina

MANITOBA

Station		Transmission received from
Fisher Branch	CBWT-1	Winnipeg
Foxwarren	CKX-TV-1	Brandon
Melita	CBWBT-1	Flin Flon
The Pas		

ONTARIO

Station		Transmission received from
Ashmont	CBWCT	Fort Frances
Atikokan	CHEX-TV-4	Peterborough
Bancroft	CFCL-TV-6	Timmins
Chapleau	CJSS-TV	Cornwall
Cornwall	CBFT-3	Ottawa CJOH-TV
Elliot Lake	CKSO-TV-1	Sudbury CKSO-TV
Haliburton	CKVR-TV-3	Barrie
Hearst	CBFOT-TV	Kapuskasing
Huntsville	CKVR-TV-2	Barrie
Kapuskasing	CFCL-TV-1	Timmins
Kearns	CFCL-TV-3	
Minden	CBLAT-1	Peterborough
Parry Sound	CKVR-TV-2	Barrie
Sioux Lookout	CBWDT-1	Dryden
Sudbury	CBLAT-1	White River
Wawa	CBLAT-2	Manitouwadge
White River		

QUEBEC

Station		Transmission received from
Baie-St-Paul	CKRT-TV-4	Rivière-du-Loup
Cabano	CKRT-TV-1	
Causapscal	CHAU-TV-4	Matane
Chandler	CHAU-TV-3	Percé
Chicoutimi	CKRS-TV-2	Jonquière
Cloridorme	CHAU-TV-6	Rivière-au-Renard
Gaspé	CHAU-TV-7	Percé
Grande-Vallée	CKBL-TV-5	Matane
Îles-de-la-Madeleine	CBFGT-1	Chelicamp (N.S.)
L'Anse-à-Valleau	CHAU-TV-9	Rivière-au-Renard
Malartic	CFCL-TV-5	Kearns (Ont.)
Manicouagan-Cinq	CFCY-TV-1	Matane
Matagami	CKRD-TV-1	Rouyn
Matane	CKBL-TV-6	Matane
Micoua	CKHQ-TV-1	Rimouski
Mont-Bécharvals	CFGW-TV-1	Mont-Blanc-Percé
Mont-Blanc-Percé	CFGW-TV-2	Upsalquitch Lake (N.B.)
Mont-Climont	CKBL-TV-1	Matane
Mont-Georges	CKBL-TV-5	Manicouagan-Cinq
Mont-Laurier	CBFT-1	Mont-Tremblant
Mont-Louis	CHAU-TV-5	Matane
Mont-Tremblant	CKBF-TV-1	Montreal

TRANSMISSION RECEIVED FROM

ONTARIO (TV Rebroadcasting)

Murdochville	CKBL-TV-2	Matane
Outardes-Trois	CKMU-TV-1	Upsalquitch Lake (N.B.)
Outardes-Quatre	CKHQ-TV-2	Rimouski
Perce	CHAU-TV-3	
Port-Alfred	CKRS-TV-1	Jonquière
Port-Daniel	CHAU-TV-2	Carleton
Rivière-au-Renard	CHAU-TV-1	Percé
Rivière-du-Loup	CKRS-TV-1	Jonquière
Roberval	CKRS-TV-3	
Ste-Marguerite-Marie	CHAU-TV-1	
Ste-Rose-du-Dégelis	CKRT-TV-1	Rivière-du-Loup
St-Georges	CBVT-1	Quebec
Sennetere	CKRN-TV-1	Rouyn
Temiscaming	CJTK-TV-1	Sturgeon Falls (Ont.)
Val-d'Or	CKRN-TV-1	Callander (Ont.)
Ville-Marie	CKRN-TV-3	Rouyn

NEW BRUNSWICK

Bon Accord	CHSJ-TV-1	Saint John
Edmundston	CKBR-TV-1	Rimouski (Que.)
Newcastle	CKAM-TV-1	Upsalquitch Lake (N.B.)
St-Quentin	CHAU-TV-2	Carleton (Que.)

NOVA SCOTIA

Amherst	CJCH-TV-3	Canning
Antigonish	CKMJ-TV-2	Halifax
Bay View	CJCH-TV-2	Canning
Canning	CJCH-TV-1	Halifax
Inverness	CJCB-TV-1	Sydney
Liverpool	CBHT-1	Halifax
New Glasgow	CFCY-TV-1	Charlottetown (P.E.I.)
Sheet Harbour	CBHT-4	Halifax
Shelburne	CBHT-3	
Yarmouth	CBHT-2	

NEWFOUNDLAND

Bonavista	CJON-TV-2	St. John's
Corner Brook	CJON-TV-1	
Grand Bank	CJOX-TV-1	Argentia
Lawn	CJOX-TV-2	
Marystown	CBNT-2	Placentia
Placentia	CBNT-1	St. John's
Port Rexton	CBNT-1	
St. Andrew's	CBYBT-1	Corner Brook
Stephenville		

TELEVISION BROADCASTING, DECEMBER 1967

	English	French	Bilingual
TV Broadcasting Station	■	■	■
TV Rebroadcasting Station *	■	■	■
More than one station	■	■	■

☐ Area enclosed by Grade 'B' Service Contour **

*A station which does not originate its programming but rebroadcasts the programmes of a parent station simultaneously or at a later time.

**Grade 'B' service can be received with a simple outdoor antenna. The limit of television coverage as delineated on the map is the line along which the signal strength is 0.22 millivolt per metre for channels 2 to 6, and 0.63 millivolt per metre for channels 7 to 13.

Scale 1:20,000,000 or One Inch to 315.65 Miles

Lambert Conformal Conic Projection Standard Parallels 49°N. and 77°N.

THE NATIONAL ATLAS OF CANADA

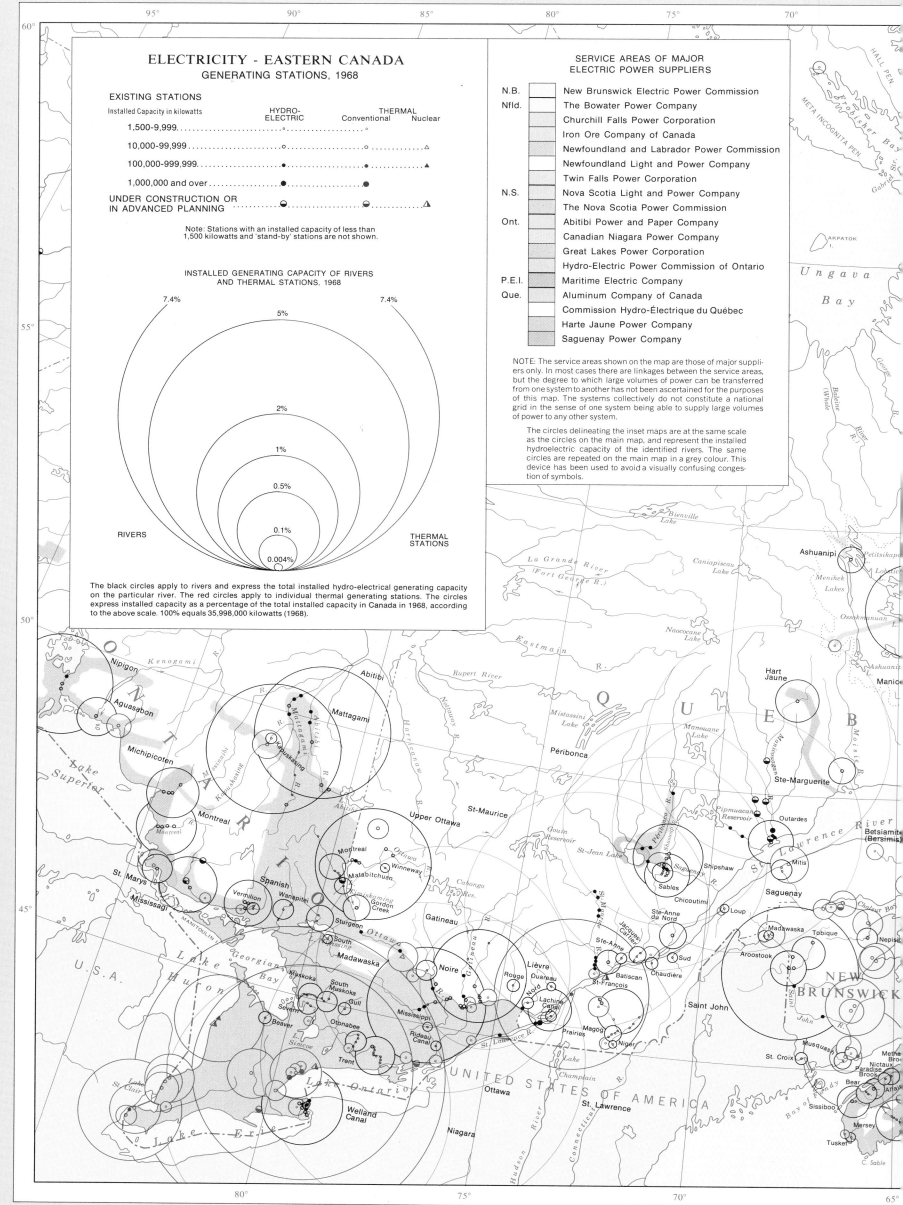

ELECTRICITY - EASTERN CANADA
GENERATING STATIONS, 1968

EXISTING STATIONS

Installed Capacity in kilowatts

	HYDRO-ELECTRIC	THERMAL Conventional	Nuclear
1,500-9,999			
10,000-99,999			
100,000-999,999			
1,000,000 and over			

UNDER CONSTRUCTION OR
IN ADVANCED PLANNING

Note: Stations with an installed capacity of less than
1,500 kilowatts and 'stand-by' stations are not shown.

INSTALLED GENERATING CAPACITY OF RIVERS
AND THERMAL STATIONS, 1968

7.4%   5%   7.4%
2%
1%
0.5%
0.1%
RIVERS   0.004%   THERMAL
STATIONS

The black circles apply to rivers and express the total installed hydro-electrical generating capacity
on the particular river. The red circles apply to individual thermal generating stations. The circles
express installed capacity as a percentage of the total installed capacity in Canada in 1968, according
to the above scale. 100% equals 35,998,000 kilowatts (1968).

SERVICE AREAS OF MAJOR
ELECTRIC POWER SUPPLIERS

N.B.   New Brunswick Electric Power Commission
Nfld.   The Bowater Power Company
          Churchill Falls Power Corporation
          Iron Ore Company of Canada
          Newfoundland and Labrador Power Commission
          Newfoundland Light and Power Company
          Twin Falls Power Corporation
N.S.   Nova Scotia Light and Power Company
          The Nova Scotia Power Commission
Ont.   Abitibi Power and Paper Company
          Canadian Niagara Power Company
          Great Lakes Power Corporation
          Hydro-Electric Power Commission of Ontario
P.E.I.   Maritime Electric Company
Que.   Aluminum Company of Canada
          Commission Hydro-Électrique du Québec
          Harte Jaune Power Company
          Saguenay Power Company

NOTE: The service areas shown on the map are those of major suppliers only. In most cases there are linkages between the service areas,
but the degree to which large volumes of power can be transferred
from one system to another has not been ascertained for the purposes
of this map. The systems collectively do not constitute a national
grid in the sense of one system being able to supply large volumes
of power to any other system.

The circles delineating the inset maps are at the same scale
as the circles on the main map, and represent the installed
hydroelectric capacity of the identified rivers. The same
circles are repeated on the main map in a grey colour. This
device has been used to avoid a visually confusing congestion of symbols.

PÉRIBONCA RIVER

SAGUENAY RIVER

ST-MAURICE RIVER

BETSIAMITES (BERSIMIS) RIVER

GATINEAU RIVER

OTTAWA RIVER

MANICOUAGAN RIVER

NIAGARA RIVER

ST. LAWRENCE RIVER

Scale 1:7,500,000 or One Inch to 118.37 Miles

50 0 50 100 150 200 250 Miles

50 0 50 100 150 200 250 300 350 Kilometres

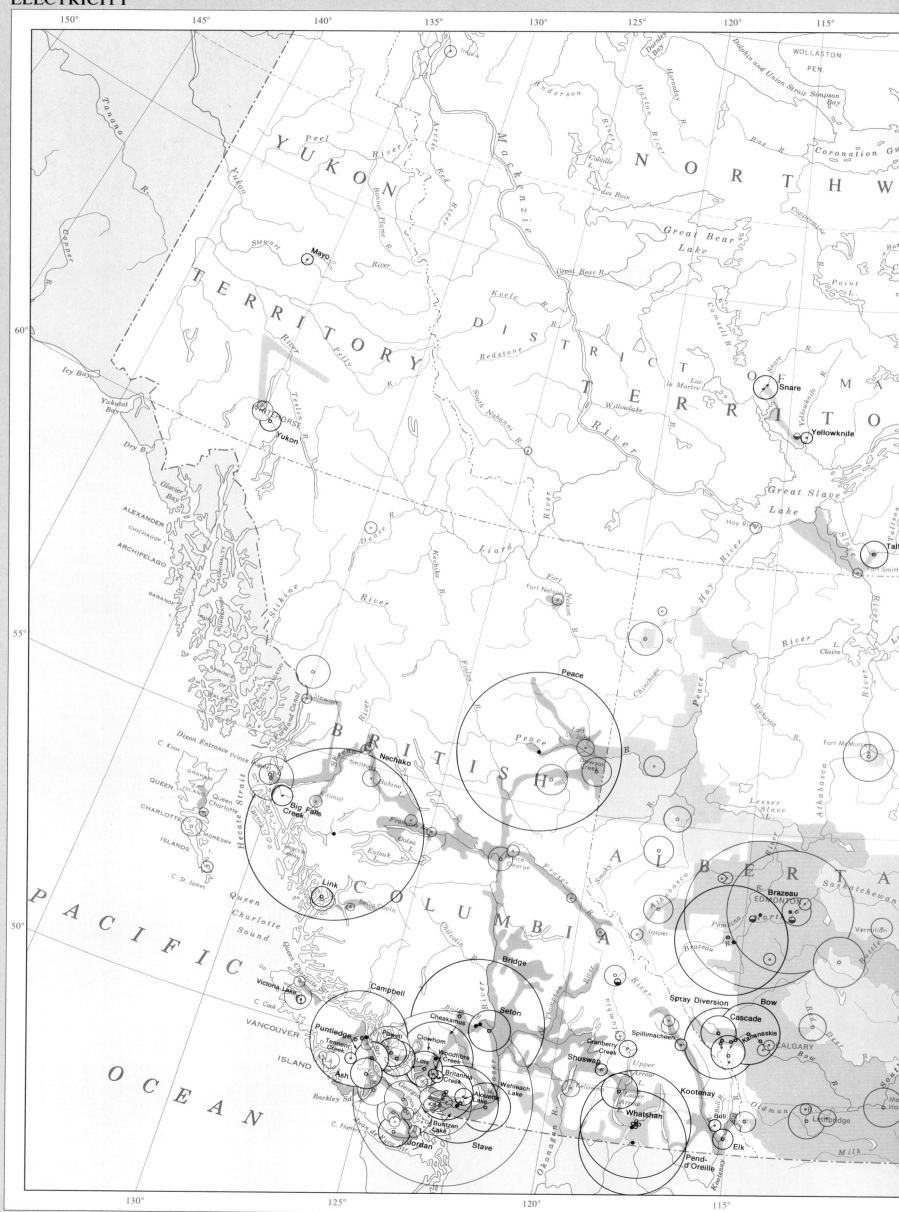

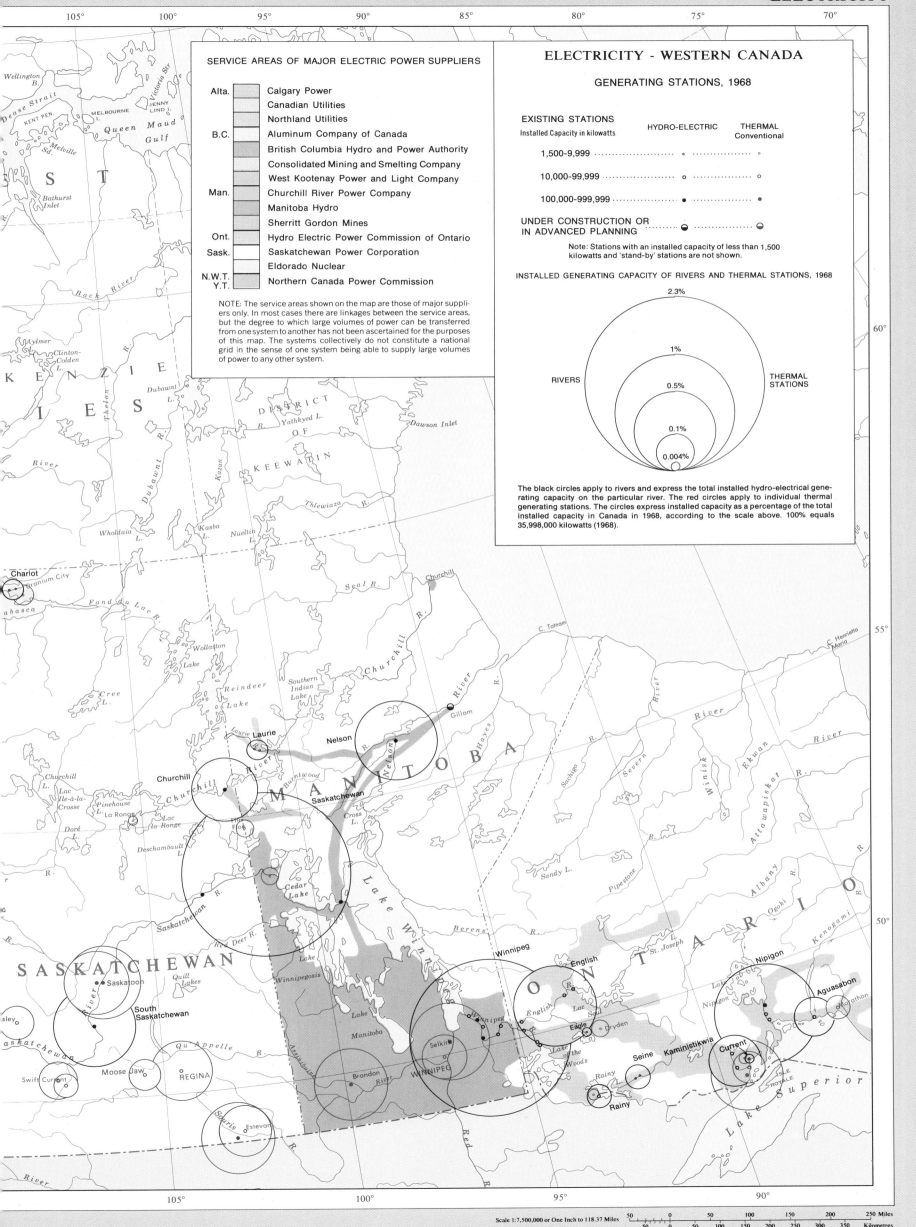

SERVICE AREAS OF MAJOR ELECTRIC POWER SUPPLIERS

Alta.	Calgary Power
	Canadian Utilities
	Northland Utilities
B.C.	Aluminum Company of Canada
	British Columbia Hydro and Power Authority
	Consolidated Mining and Smelting Company
	West Kootenay Power and Light Company
Man.	Churchill River Power Company
	Manitoba Hydro
	Sherritt Gordon Mines
Ont.	Hydro Electric Power Commission of Ontario
Sask.	Saskatchewan Power Corporation
	Eldorado Nuclear
N.W.T. Y.T.	Northern Canada Power Commission

NOTE: The service areas shown on the map are those of major suppliers only. In most cases there are linkages between the service areas, but the degree to which large volumes of power can be transferred from one system to another has not been ascertained for the purposes of this map. The systems collectively do not constitute a national grid in the sense of one system being able to supply large volumes of power to any other system.

ELECTRICITY - WESTERN CANADA

GENERATING STATIONS, 1968

EXISTING STATIONS
Installed Capacity in kilowatts — HYDRO-ELECTRIC — THERMAL Conventional

1,500-9,999

10,000-99,999

100,000-999,999

UNDER CONSTRUCTION OR IN ADVANCED PLANNING

Note: Stations with an installed capacity of less than 1,500 kilowatts and 'stand-by' stations are not shown.

INSTALLED GENERATING CAPACITY OF RIVERS AND THERMAL STATIONS, 1968

2.3%

1%

0.5%

RIVERS — THERMAL STATIONS

0.1%

0.004%

The black circles apply to rivers and express the total installed hydro-electrical generating capacity on the particular river. The red circles apply to individual thermal generating stations. The circles express installed capacity as a percentage of the total installed capacity in Canada in 1968, according to the scale above. 100% equals 35,998,000 kilowatts (1968).

Scale 1:7,500,000 or One Inch to 118.37 Miles

RETAIL TRADE

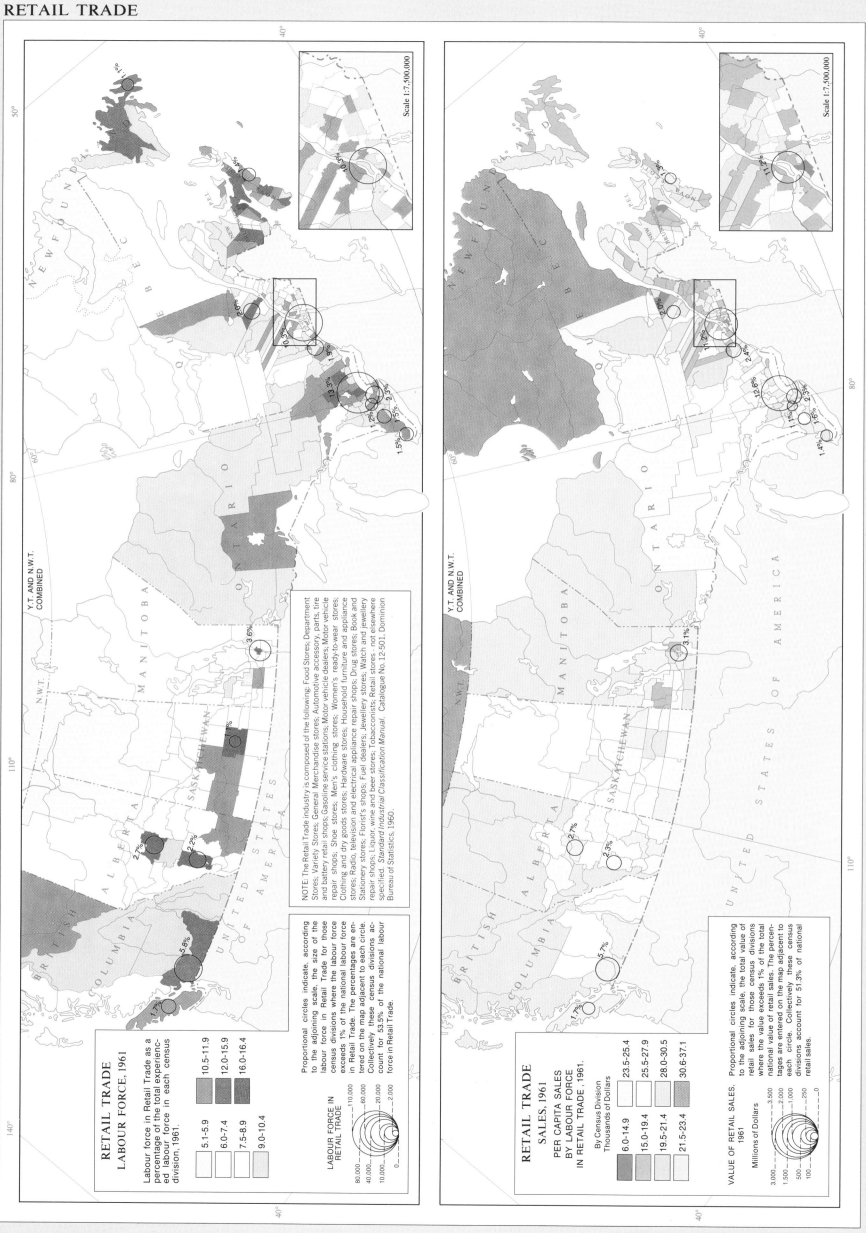

NOTE: The Retail Trade industry is composed of the following: Food Stores; Department Stores; Variety Stores; General Merchandise stores; Automotive accessory, parts, tire and battery retail shops; Gasoline service stations; Motor vehicle dealers; Motor vehicle repair shops; Shoe stores; Men's clothing stores; Women's ready-to-wear stores; Clothing and dry goods stores; Hardware stores; Household furniture and appliance stores; Radio, television and electrical appliance repair shops; Drug stores; Book and Stationery stores; Florist's shops; Fuel dealers; Jewellery stores; Watch and jewellery repair shops; Liquor, wine and beer stores; Tobacconists; Retail stores - not elsewhere specified. *Standard Industrial Classification Manual.* Catalogue No. 12-501, Dominion Bureau of Statistics, 1960.

RETAIL TRADE
LABOUR FORCE, 1961

Labour force in Retail Trade as a percentage of the total experienced labour force in each census division, 1961.

	5.1-5.9
	6.0-7.4
	7.5-8.9
	9.0-10.4
	10.5-11.9
	12.0-15.9
	16.0-16.4

Proportional circles indicate, according to the adjoining scale, the size of the labour force in Retail Trade for those census divisions where the labour force in Retail Trade exceeds 1% of the national labour force in Retail Trade. The percentages are entered on the map adjacent to each circle. Collectively these census divisions account for 53.5% of the national labour force in Retail Trade.

LABOUR FORCE IN RETAIL TRADE

Scale 1:7,500,000

RETAIL TRADE
SALES, 1961
PER CAPITA SALES BY LABOUR FORCE IN RETAIL TRADE, 1961.

By Census Division
Thousands of Dollars

	6.0-14.9
	15.0-19.4
	19.5-21.4
	21.5-23.4
	23.5-25.4
	25.5-27.9
	28.0-30.5
	30.6-37.1

VALUE OF RETAIL SALES, 1961
Millions of Dollars

Proportional circles indicate, according to the adjoining scale, the total value of retail sales for those census divisions where the value exceeds 1% of the total national value of retail sales. The percentages are entered on the map adjacent to each circle. Collectively these census divisions account for 51.3% of national retail sales.

Scale 1:7,500,000

Lambert Conformal Conic Projection Standard Parallels 49°N. and 77°N.

THE NATIONAL ATLAS OF CANADA

Scale 1:20,000,000 or One Inch to 315.65 Miles

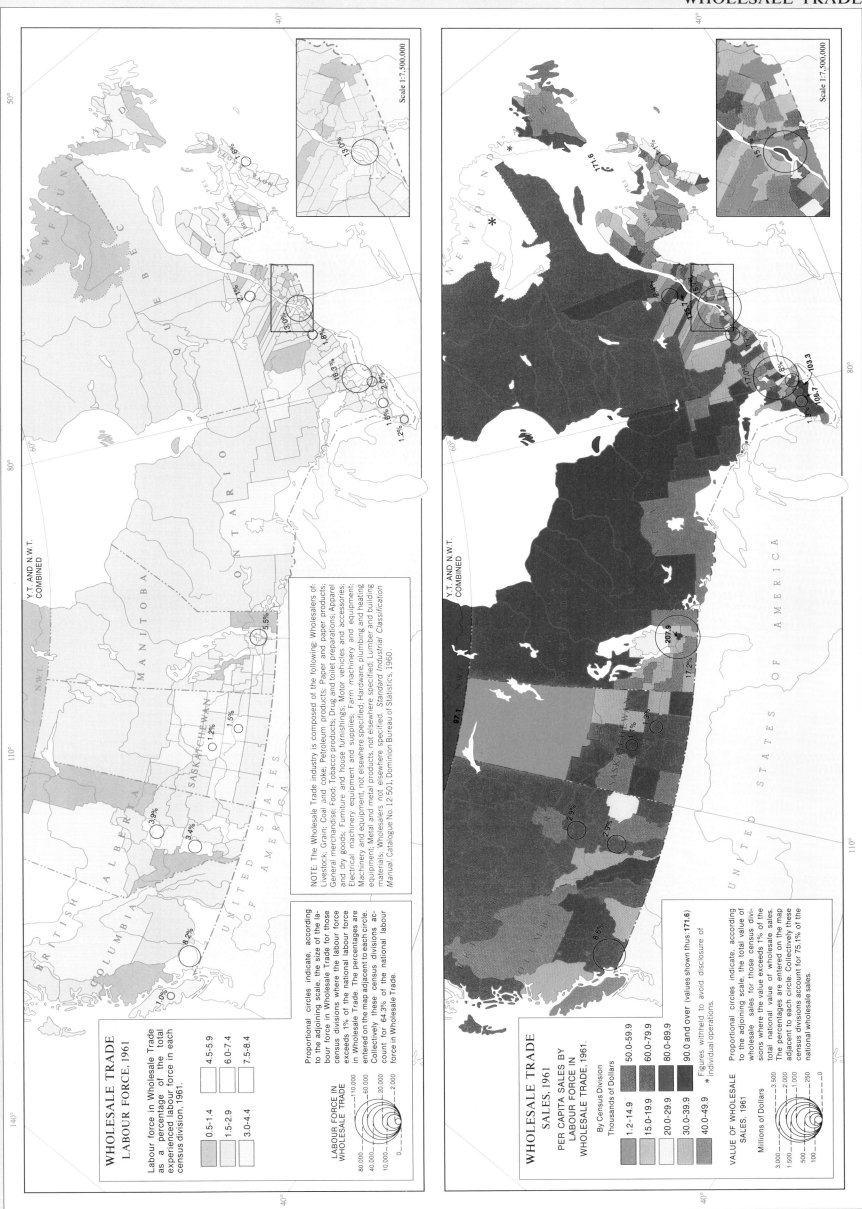

WHOLESALE TRADE
LABOUR FORCE, 1961

Labour force in Wholesale Trade as a percentage of the total experienced labour force in each census division, 1961.

0.5-1.4	4.5-5.9
1.5-2.9	6.0-7.4
3.0-4.4	7.5-8.4

Proportional circles indicate, according to the adjoining scale, the size of the labour force in Wholesale Trade for those census divisions where the labour force in Wholesale Trade exceeds 1% of the national labour force in Wholesale Trade. The percentages are entered on the map adjacent to each circle. Collectively these census divisions account for 64.3% of the national labour force in Wholesale Trade.

LABOUR FORCE IN WHOLESALE TRADE

110,000
80,000
60,000
40,000
20,000
10,000
2,000
0

NOTE: The Wholesale Trade industry is composed of the following: Wholesalers of: Livestock; Grain; Coal and coke; Petroleum products; Paper and paper products; General merchandise; Food; Tobacco products; Drug and toilet preparations; Apparel and dry goods; Furniture and house furnishings; Motor vehicles and accessories; Electrical machinery equipment and supplies; Farm machinery and equipment; Machinery and equipment, not elsewhere specified; Hardware, plumbing and heating equipment; Metal and metal products, not elsewhere specified; Lumber and building materials; Wholesalers not elsewhere specified. *Standard Industrial Classification Manual,* Catalogue No. 12-501, Dominion Bureau of Statistics, 1960.

WHOLESALE TRADE
SALES, 1961

PER CAPITA SALES BY LABOUR FORCE IN WHOLESALE TRADE, 1961.

By Census Division
Thousands of Dollars

1.2-14.9	50.0-59.9
15.0-19.9	60.0-79.9
20.0-29.9	80.0-89.9
30.0-39.9	90.0 and over (values shown thus:171.6)
40.0-49.9	

* Figures withheld to avoid disclosure of individual operations.

Proportional circles indicate, according to the adjoining scale, the total value of wholesale sales for those census divisions where the value exceeds 1% of the total national value of wholesale sales. The percentages are entered on the map adjacent to each circle. Collectively these census divisions account for 75.1% of the national wholesale sales.

VALUE OF WHOLESALE SALES, 1961
Millions of Dollars

3,500
3,000
2,000
1,500
1,000
500
250
100
0

Lambert Conformal Conic Projection Standard Parallels 49°N. and 77°N.

THE NATIONAL ATLAS OF CANADA

Scale 1:20,000,000 or One Inch to 315.65 Miles

FINANCE, DEFENCE AND PUBLIC ADMINISTRATION

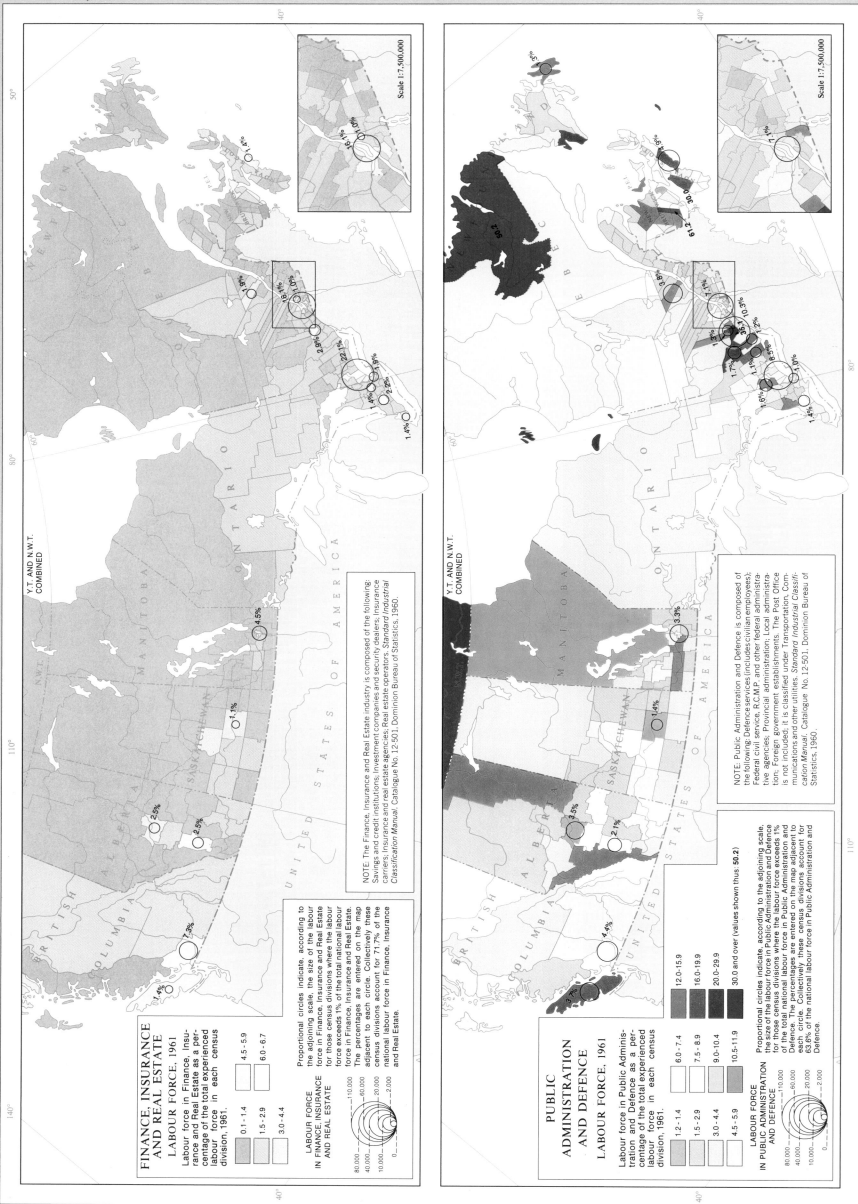

FINANCE, INSURANCE AND REAL ESTATE
LABOUR FORCE, 1961

Labour force in Finance, Insurance and Real Estate as a percentage of the total experienced labour force in each census division, 1961.

0.1 - 1.4	4.5 - 5.9
1.5 - 2.9	6.0 - 6.7
3.0 - 4.4	

LABOUR FORCE IN FINANCE, INSURANCE AND REAL ESTATE

110,000
60,000
20,000
2,000

80,000
40,000
10,000
0

Proportional circles indicate, according to the adjoining scale, the size of the labour force in Finance, Insurance and Real Estate for those census divisions where the labour force exceeds 1% of the total national labour force in Finance, Insurance and Real Estate. The percentages are entered on the map adjacent to each circle. Collectively these census divisions account for 71.7% of the total national labour force in Finance, Insurance and Real Estate.

NOTE: The The Finance, Insurance and Real Estate industry is composed of the following: Savings and credit institutions; Investment companies and security dealers; Insurance carriers; Insurance and real estate agencies; Real estate operators. *Standard Industrial Classification Manual*. Catalogue No. 12-501, Dominion Bureau of Statistics, 1960.

Scale 1:7,500,000

PUBLIC ADMINISTRATION AND DEFENCE
LABOUR FORCE, 1961

Labour force in Public Administration and Defence as a percentage of the total experienced labour force in each census division, 1961.

1.2 - 1.4	6.0 - 7.4
1.5 - 2.9	7.5 - 8.9
3.0 - 4.4	9.0 - 10.4
4.5 - 5.9	10.5 - 11.9
12.0 - 15.9	
16.0 - 19.9	
20.0 - 29.9	
30.0 and over (values shown thus: 50.2)	

LABOUR FORCE IN PUBLIC ADMINISTRATION AND DEFENCE

110,000
60,000
20,000
2,000

80,000
40,000
10,000
0

Proportional circles indicate, according to the adjoining scale, the size of the labour force in Public Administration and Defence for those census divisions where the labour force exceeds 1% of the total national labour force in Public Administration and Defence. The percentages are entered on the map adjacent to each circle. Collectively these census divisions account for 63.6% of the national labour force in Public Administration and Defence.

NOTE: Public Administration and Defence is composed of the following: Defence services (includes civilian employees); Federal civil service, R.C.M.P. and other federal administration; Provincial administration; Local administration; Foreign government establishments. The Post Office is not included; it is classified under Transportation, Communications and other utilities. *Standard Industrial Classification Manual*. Catalogue No. 12-501, Dominion Bureau of Statistics, 1960.

Scale 1:7,500,000

Scale 1:20,000,000 or One Inch to 315.65 Miles

Lambert Conformal Conic Projection Standard Parallels 49°N. and 77°N.
THE NATIONAL ATLAS OF CANADA

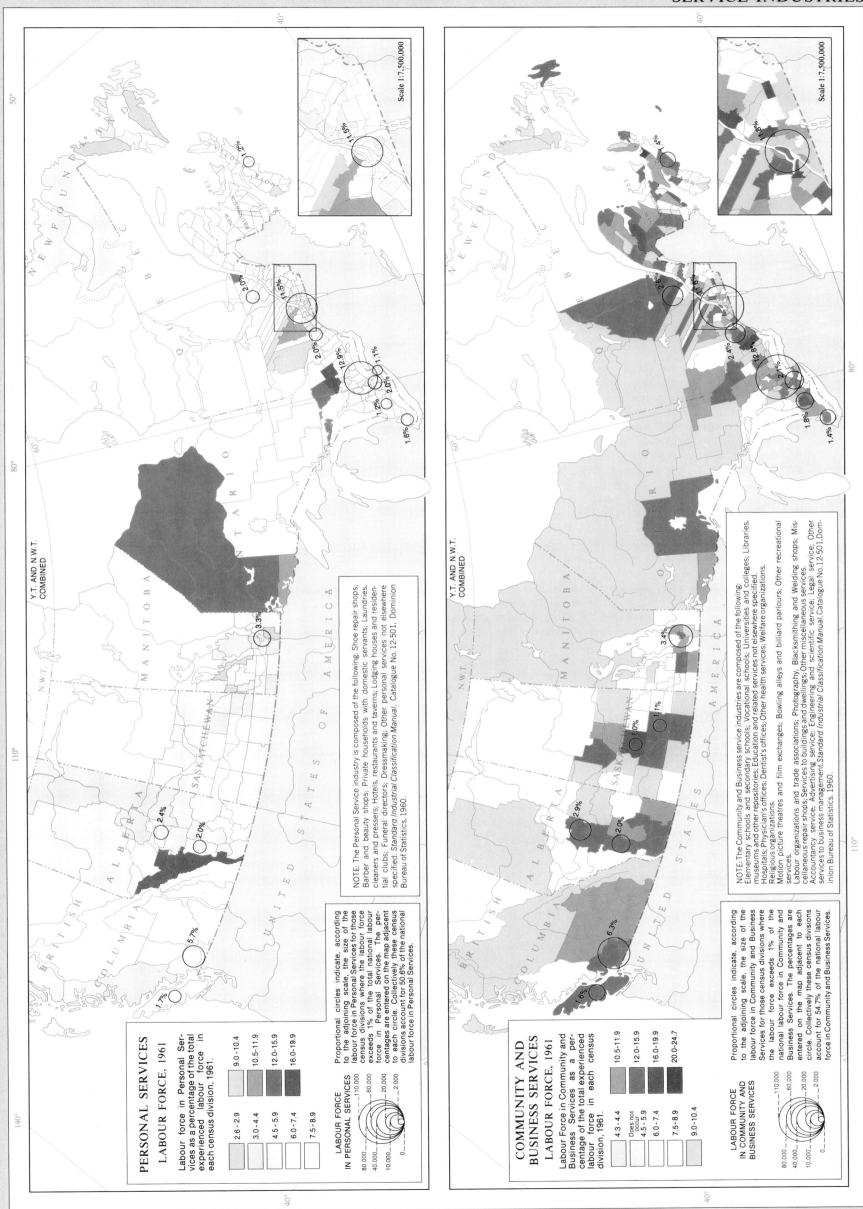

PERSONAL SERVICES

LABOUR FORCE, 1961

Labour force in Personal Services as a percentage of the total experienced labour force in each census division, 1961.

2.6 - 2.9	9.0 - 10.4
3.0 - 4.4	10.5 - 11.9
4.5 - 5.9	12.0 - 15.9
6.0 - 7.4	16.0 - 19.9
7.5 - 8.9	

LABOUR FORCE IN PERSONAL SERVICES

Proportional circles indicate, according to the adjoining scale, the size of the labour force in Personal Services for those census divisions where the labour force exceeds 1% of the total national labour force in Personal Services. The percentages are entered on the map adjacent to each circle. Collectively these census divisions account for 50.6% of the national labour force in Personal Services.

NOTE: The Personal Service industry is composed of the following: Shoe repair shops; Barber and beauty shops; Private households with domestic servants; Laundries, cleaners and pressers; Hotels, restaurants and taverns; Lodging houses and residential clubs; Funeral directors; Dressmaking; Other personal services not elsewhere specified. *Standard Industrial Classification Manual,* Catalogue No.12-501, Dominion Bureau of Statistics, 1960.

COMMUNITY AND BUSINESS SERVICES

LABOUR FORCE, 1961

Labour Force in Community and Business Services as a percentage of the total experienced labour force in each census division, 1961.

4.3 - 4.4	10.5 - 11.9
Does not occur	12.0 - 15.9
4.5 - 5.9	16.0 - 19.9
6.0 - 7.4	20.0 - 24.7
7.5 - 8.9	
9.0 - 10.4	

LABOUR FORCE IN COMMUNITY AND BUSINESS SERVICES

Proportional circles indicate, according to the adjoining scale, the size of the labour force in Community and Business Services for those census divisions where the labour force exceeds 1% of the national labour force in Community and Business Services. The percentages are entered on the map adjacent to each circle. Collectively these census divisions account for 54.7% of the national labour force in Community and Business Services.

NOTE: The Community and Business service industries are composed of the following: Elementary schools and secondary schools; Vocational schools; Universities and colleges; Libraries, museums and other repositories; Education and related services not elsewhere specified. Hospitals; Physician's offices; Dentist's offices; Other health services; Welfare organizations. Religious organizations. Motion picture theatres and film exchanges; Bowling alleys and billiard parlours; Other recreational services. Labour organizations and trade associations; Photography, Blacksmithing and Welding shops; Miscellaneous repair shops; Services to buildings and dwellings; Other miscellaneous services. Accountancy service; Advertising service; Engineering and scientific service; Legal service; Other services to business management. *Standard Industrial Classification Manual.* Catalogue No.12-501.Dominion Bureau of Statistics, 1960.

Lambert Conformal Conic Projection Standard Parallels 49°N. and 77°N.

THE NATIONAL ATLAS OF CANADA

ECONOMIC REGIONS

The map of sixty-eight economic regions of Canada and the table describing them are taken from *Economic Geography of Canada* by P. Camu, E.P. Weeks, and Z.W. Sametz, published in 1964 by MAC-MILLAN OF CANADA, Toronto; MACMILLAN & CO. LTD. London; and ST. MARTIN'S PRESS, New York. The material is presented in this atlas by permission of the publishers.

The principles upon which the economic regions are based are discussed at length in *Economic Geography of Canada*. Physiographic factors, transportation and communication, population and labour force, and production and marketing factors have been taken into account in delineating the regions. To maintain compatibility with a large body of census information the regions are, in most cases, aggregates of intact *census divisions* - the smallest areas for which there is a variety of official data on demographic and economic phenomena. Because census division boundaries were created in the past and without clear regard even to the then-current economic and demographic phenomena, the shape of a region may not precisely accord with the distribution of the present economic and demographic phenomena by which the entire region is descriptively characterized.

One of the main intentions of the authors was to delineate the largest possible sub-provincial areas for which certain useful economic generalizations can be stated. If this purpose has been attained, each region would be expected to respond to economic changes more or less as a unit, in the sense that economic changes at places within a region would have effects throughout the region but not necessarily in adjoining regions. This is not to say that changes outside a region would not affect the region, since there are many economic relationships between even widely separated regions.

The table entitled *Analytical Description of Economic Regions* provides brief descriptive notes on each of the sixty-eight regions. The content and organization of the notes is for the most part self-explanatory, but some explanation is required for terms under the headings *Functional Factors* and *Marketing Factors*.

The heading *Functional Factors* refers to the activities and conditions that tend to tie an area together as a cohesive unit, specifically transportation, communication, and the population distributions and production-areas among which transportation and communication take place.

The notes under *Functional Factors* mention *local offices, zones,* and first to fifth order *centres*. These terms have direct reference to the distribution and size of the labour force, and indirect reference to the distribution and size of the population. The *centres* mentioned in the table are shown on the map.

A *local office* is an office of the National Employment Service * which has the duty of maintaining records of local employment opportunities and of directing applicants to jobs. These offices are distributed in relation to population in such a way as to minimize travelling distance to the *local office* for the greatest number of persons from all parts of the area served. Because of its centrality to labour force and places of employment the *local office* is an important indicator of the centre of a unit-area or zone of economic activity.

---

* Since 1966, National Employment Service Offices have been called Canada Manpower Centres.

A zone (1st-order, 2nd-order etc.) is the area served by a *local office*. A *centre* (1st-order, 2nd-order etc.) is the town or city in which the *local office* is situated. In a few cases zones without local offices have been created. In the table these are referred to as *district zones*.

1st-order zones are small *local office* areas that have a labour force of under 10,000.

2nd-order zones are minor *local office areas* that have a labour force of 10,000 to 25,000, whether principally of an agricultural or non - agricultural nature.

3rd-order zones are *local office areas* with a labour force of 25,000 to 75,000, of which over forty per cent is engaged in agriculture. *3rd-order zones* are always major agricultural areas. A *3rd-order centre* tends to be a commercial rather than a manufacturing centre.

4th-order zones are *local office areas* with a labour force of 25,000 to 75,000, of which over sixty per cent is employed in non-agricultural industries. A *4th-order centre* tends to be a manufacturing rather than a commercial centre, and is usually the functional centre of the region.

5th-order centres are those *census metropolitan areas* which have a labour force of over 75,000. A *census metropolitan area* is a statistical area created by the Dominion Bureau of Statistics covering closely grouped municipalities which collectively make up a large urban complex. A *5th-order centre* contains a major *local office,* and is the functional centre of the region.

The six largest *5th-order centres*, Montréal, Toronto, Vancouver, Québec, Winnipeg, and Edmonton have multi-regional functions significantly greater than other *centres*. To signify this characteristic the regions to which these *centres* belong are designated as *Metropolitan Regions*.

In the case of Winnipeg and of Montréal the *Metropolitan Region* approximately coincides with the *census metropolitan area*. In the other cases the *Metropolitan Region* includes the *census divisions* of which the *census metropolitan area* forms a part. The *census divisions* in which the *census metropolitan area* of Ottawa is located would qualify as a *Metropolitan Region*, but because it would be divided by a provincial boundary it has not been designated as such.

The *market index* listed under the heading *Marketing Factors* is an indicator of personal purchasing power within a region. The market index is obtained by expressing the regional per capita disposable personal income as a percentage of the national per capita disposable personal income. A marketing index of 62, for example, indicates that for the particular region per capita disposable personal income was 62 per cent of the national per capita disposable personal income in the year preceding the census of 1961.

ANALYTICAL DESCRIPTION OF ECONOMIC REGIONS

REGIONAL CODE	NAME OF REGION	STRUCTURAL FACTORS	FUNCTIONAL FACTORS	PRODUCTION FACTORS	MARKETING FACTORS
	Regions of the Atlantic Provinces				
00	St. John's–South-eastern Newfoundland	A combination of two similar physiographic areas: the Avalon Peninsula and the southern and north-eastern coastal areas. The Grand Banks fishing is so important that it may be regarded as an extension of this region.	Coastal shipping and peninsular highways. St. John's is dominant as a 5th-order centre, commercially and administratively serving coastal settlements. Single local office at St. John's. Four zones are involved, the Southern Coast Districts and the Bonavista Bay District being somewhat isolated.	Secondary industries in St. John's, and iron-ore mining at Wabana on Bell Island. Otherwise a fishing hinterland, producing salt, fresh, and fresh-filleted fish. Fresh and fresh-filleted becoming dominant along South Shore to St. John's because of year-round open water. Two-thirds of provincial fish landings are in this region.	St. John's is the dominant marketing centre. *Market index 56.*
01	Central Newfoundland	Central plateau physiographic area.	Grand Falls is a 2nd-order centre. The Notre Dame District zone is still to some extent functionally related to St. John's, particularly in the north-east fishing sector. The Green Bay District zone is a fishing area tied more to central and western Newfoundland.	Pulp and paper, forestry, non-ferrous metal mining, and the salt fishery of Notre Dame Bay District. Much of the timber for the pulp-and-paper operations comes from the Notre Dame Bay District, thus helping to tie that district into this region. The port of Botwood is also a tying factor.	Grand Falls is increasingly becoming the marketing centre, although the Notre Dame Bay District has coastal contact with St. John's. The Trans-Canada Highway will help to tie the area more thoroughly to Grand Falls as marketing centre. *Market index 62.*
02	Western Newfoundland	Western highlands physiographic area.	Corner Brook is a 4th-order centre. French Shore fishing ties make it preferable to treat that area still as a separate district.	Manufacturing (pulp and paper, cement), forestry, and some fishing, mining (gypsum), and mixed farming.	Corner Brook is the marketing centre, on railway and coastal routes. *Market index 73.*
03	Labrador	Part of the Canadian Shield. Separated from the rest of Newfoundland. An obvious geographic and economic region.	A district with no local office (inadequately tied to St. John's local office). Has only isolated non-dominant small communities except in the iron-mining area, where the centres of Wabush and Labrador City have emerged.	Primary industries—fishing, trapping, iron-ore mining. Possible future forestry.	Scattered coastal trading posts are supplied from St. John's. There are new lines of supply by rail from Sept-Îles and by air from Montreal. *Market index 100.*
10	Prince Edward Island	A separate spatial entity and a homogeneous geographic area.	A functional unit revolving round two local office centres, Charlottetown (a 3rd-order centre) and Summerside (a 2nd-order centre).	Two primary industries, agriculture (mixed farming and potatoes) and fishing, are dominant.	A natural marketing unit, with limited access lines of supply and export. *Market index 66.*
20	Sydney–Cape Breton Island	A separate spatial entity and a recognized geographic region.	Historically and sociologically distinct. A functional unit in transportation. Sydney is a 4th-order centre. Inverness is a 1st-order centre.	Iron and steel manufacturing, based on coal mining, most significant. Fishing also important, and scattered mixed farming.	The Canso bottleneck makes this a natural marketing unit. *Market index 84.*
21	Northern Nova Scotia	Mostly comprises the North Shore Lowlands of Nova Scotia physiographic area.	New Glasgow is a 4th-order centre. There is a chain of smaller local offices at Truro (2nd-order centre), Amherst, and Springhill (both 1st-order centres). Transportation tie-in with Truro.	Manufacturing (steel products and textiles) important. There are also mining (coal, salt, gypsum), mixed agriculture, and fishing. Hants County is not included in this region despite some functional ties, because its agricultural and mining activities closely resemble those of adjacent parts of Region 23.	The functional centres may be taken as a marketing chain. Guysborough County, though topographically part of the South Shore physiographic region, is included in this region for reasons of access and marketing. *Market index 68.*
22	Halifax–South Shore	Most of the Nova Scotia South Shore physiographic area.	Halifax is important as a 4th-order centre, although the other local offices are somewhat independent, with 2nd-order centres at Bridgewater and Yarmouth, and a 1st-order centre at Liverpool.	Manufacturing (shipbuilding, electronics, automobile assembly, textiles, etc.) and fishing important. Forestry of minor importance. Agriculture poor.	Halifax is the marketing centre, though not completely dominant. It also serves as a major national port. *Market index 87.*
23	Annapolis Valley	Annapolis Lowland, a physiographic area.	Single local office at Kentville, a 2nd-order centre.	Specialized agriculture (especially apples), food processing, and mining (gypsum and barite).	A natural marketing unit. *Market index 72.*
30	Moncton–South-eastern New Brunswick	Part of the Southern New Brunswick geographic area.	Single local office at Moncton, a 4th-order centre which is a dominant railway centre performing distributing functions for the Maritime Provinces. The marginal district of Kent County could have been tied structurally with Region 33 to the north, but it is functionally integrated with Region 30.	Services, manufacturing (especially foundries, food packing, textiles), lobster fishing, and mixed farming.	Moncton is a wholesale marketing centre for a wide area. This region could be structurally tied to the Southern New Brunswick region, but the wider marketing functions favour separate treatment. *Market index 77.*

ANALYTICAL DESCRIPTION OF ECONOMIC REGIONS

REGIONAL CODE	NAME OF REGION	STRUCTURAL FACTORS	FUNCTIONAL FACTORS	PRODUCTION FACTORS	MARKETING FACTORS
31	Saint John–Southern New Brunswick	Most of the Southern New Brunswick geographic area.	Saint John is a dominant 4th-order centre. Sussex, Minto, and St. Stephen are subsidiary 1st-order centres.	A diversified economy, with manufacturing (shipbuilding, oil and sugar refining, pulp, food processing, etc.), mixed agriculture and dairying, fishing (particularly in Charlotte County), and coal mining.	Saint John is the marketing centre and a major national port. *Market index 77.*
32	Upper Saint John Valley	Saint John Valley geographic area.	Railway and highway transportation along the Saint John River routes. Fredericton, Woodstock, and Edmundston are 2nd-order centres. Fredericton is the largest and most dominant.	Specialized agriculture (potatoes), forestry, and manufacturing (pulp and paper, wood-working, textiles).	A marketing chain, with Fredericton as the most important link. *Market index 69.*
33	North-eastern New Brunswick	A combination of two physiographic regions, New Brunswick Highlands and New Brunswick Lowlands.	A string of smaller 2nd-order centres at Newcastle, Bathurst, and Campbellton.	Manufacturing (pulp and paper, lumber), forestry, fishing, a little agriculture and mining.	Weak marketing links. Could be regarded as a marketing chain. *Market index 61.*
	Regions of Quebec				
40	North Shore/New Quebec	Part of the Canadian Shield, and a fairly uniform physiographic area, but determined primarily by its being the single county of Saguenay.	A marginal primary producing area, isolated, with communications by water, air, and a new railway line. Sept-Îles, Forestville, and Baie-Comeau are 1st-order centres.	Primary industries—forestry, iron-ore mining, fishing, and trapping.	A marginal marketing belt, characterized by difficult access. Three remote district zones are involved: Anticosti, New Quebec–Labrador, and New Quebec–West. *Market index 88.*
41	Gaspé Peninsula/South Shore	A combination of 3 geographic areas: Appalachian Highlands, South Shore Coastal Lowlands, and the Gaspé Peninsula.	A string of non-dominant local office centres. Rivière-du-Loup is a 3rd-order centre; Montmagny, Rimouski, and Gaspé are 2nd-order centres; Chandler, New Richmond, Causapscal, and Matane are 1st-order centres.	Primary industries—forestry, fishing, and mixed agriculture. Tourism important in the Gaspé Peninsula.	A chain of small marketing centres, mainly supplied from Québec. The isolated Magdalen Islands are serviced largely from Moncton. *Market index 46.*
42	Saguenay Valley/Lake St. John	Approximately coincides with the widely recognized geographic region of the Saguenay, although with two geographic sub-zones: the Chicoutimi-Saguenay belt and the Lake St. John Basin.	A string of local office areas. Chicoutimi-Jonquière is a 4th-order centre; Port-Alfred and Alma are 2nd-order centres; Roberval and Dolbeau are 1st-order centres.	Manufacturing (aluminum and pulp and paper), forestry, mixed agriculture, and dairying.	A marketing unit supplied in the main from Québec. *Market index 73.*
43	Québec Metropolitan–Eastern Laurentians	A combination of two geographic types: the Québec Plains and the Eastern Laurentians, plus part of the South Shore Appalachians.	Greater Québec is a functionally dominant 5th-order centre, with two local offices (including Lévis). La Malbaie and Saint-Georges are subsidiary 2nd-order centres.	Manufacturing (pulp and paper, shipbuilding, small industries), tourism, and agriculture (dairying and market gardening for the metropolitan area).	Québec is the dominant marketing centre for eastern Quebec, and a major national port. The South Shore Appalachian zones are functionally tied in with this region despite structural similarities with Regions 41 and 45. *Market index 72.*
44	Trois-Rivières–St-Maurice Valley	A combination of two geographic areas: the Trois-Rivières Plain and the East-Central Laurentians.	Trois-Rivières and Shawinigan are 4th-order centres; Louiseville and La Tuque are 1st-order centres.	Manufacturing (pulp and paper, chemicals, textiles), forestry, and some agriculture.	Trois-Rivières is the key marketing centre. Berthier District has more structural and functional ties with the Trois-Rivières Plain and the interior uplands than with the Montréal Environs. *Market index 73.*
45	Sherbrooke–Eastern Townships	Approximately coincides with the Lower Québec Appalachian geographic area, consisting of the Piedmont of the South Shore and the Interior Plateaux.	Recognized as a functional unit despite absence of complete dominance by a regional centre. Sherbrooke and Granby are 4th-order centres; Thetford Mines is a 3rd-order centre; Victoriaville and Drummondville are 2nd-order centres; Lac-Mégantic, Asbestos, and Magog are 1st-order centres.	Manufacturing (textiles dominant), agriculture (mixed farming, dairying, livestock), and mining (especially asbestos).	The marketing pattern is tri-focal, with Sherbrooke dominant only within its fairly immediate area, Montréal impinging on the north and west sides, and Québec exerting its influence in the northeastern part. *Market index 71.*
46	Montréal Environs	A combination of the Montréal Plain and West Central Laurentians, excluding the Montréal Metropolitan Region lying within it.	A constellation of smaller local office centres surrounding Montréal, with close functional ties with that centre. Joliette and Farnham are 4th-order centres; Sorel, Saint-Jean, Beauharnois, Valleyfield, Sainte-Thérèse, Saint-Jérôme, Sainte-Agathe-des-Monts, and Lachute are 2nd-order centres; Mont-Laurier and Cowansville are 1st-order centres.	Highly diversified manufacturing, market gardening, tobacco. Important year-round tourism in the Laurentians.	There are strong marketing and production ties with Montréal. Missisquoi County is in this region because of functional ties, despite some structural similarities with adjacent counties of Region 45. *Market index 77.*

ANALYTICAL DESCRIPTION OF ECONOMIC REGIONS

REGIONAL CODE	NAME OF REGION	STRUCTURAL FACTORS	FUNCTIONAL FACTORS	PRODUCTION FACTORS	MARKETING FACTORS
47	Montréal Metropolitan Region	Montréal and Jésus islands and the South Shore county of Chambly. Metropolitan structure.	This is the strongest 5th-order centre in the country, with national functions. These functions warrant separate analysis for this region, independent of its environs. There are two local offices, one (with sub-offices) for Montréal and one at Sainte-Anne-de-Bellevue for the western part.	Very extensive and varied manufacturing.	This is a dominant wholesale and retail centre. *Market index 114.*
48	Hull–Western Laurentians	Approximately coincides with the Western Laurentians geographic area, plus the narrow riverside plain.	Functional relations extend to and along the Ottawa River. Hull is a 4th-order centre; Buckingham and Maniwaki are 1st-order centres.	Manufacturing (pulp and paper), forestry, and marginal agriculture.	Hull is the dominant marketing centre. *Market index 83.*
49	Western Quebec	A geographic area consisting of the western part of the Canadian Shield within Quebec.	A string of mining communities. Rouyn and Val-d'Or are 4th-order centres.	Mining (non-ferrous metals, gold) very important; lumbering, and pulp and paper.	This is a marginal marketing area with no dominant centre, being supplied from wholesale firms in Québec, Montréal, and Toronto. Mistassini District is included because of census units, but eastern Mistassini District could be integrated with Region 42. *Market index 76.*

Regions of Ontario

REGIONAL CODE	NAME OF REGION	STRUCTURAL FACTORS	FUNCTIONAL FACTORS	PRODUCTION FACTORS	MARKETING FACTORS
50	Ottawa/Kingston–Eastern Ontario	A recognized geographic area. East of the Pembroke-Kingston front, the Eastern Ontario Lowlands is topographically uniform.	A constellation of local offices along two axes, the Ottawa River valley and the St. Lawrence River valley, bordering on a common hinterland. Ottawa is a 5th-order centre; Kingston and Cornwall are 4th-order centres; Pembroke is a 2nd-order centre; Renfrew, Arnprior, Carleton Place, Perth, Smiths Falls, Hawkesbury, Prescott, Brockville, and Gananoque are 1st-order centres.	The region is a dairy-farming unit. Governmental and other services in Ottawa. Varied manufacturing (pulp and paper, textiles, some small industries) in the other centres.	Ottawa is the main marketing centre although the St. Lawrence River string of localities is supplied by goods moving along the Montréal-Toronto route. *Market index 108.*
51	Peterborough–Central Lake Ontario	The portion of the St. Lawrence Lowlands which is on the eastern section of the northern shore of Lake Ontario, plus part of the Canadian Shield which protrudes diagonally across the northern part.	Peterborough is a 4th-order centre. Otherwise, mainly a string of local office centres along the lake. Belleville, Trenton, and Lindsay are 2nd-order centres; Napanee, Picton, and Cobourg are 1st-order centres. Haliburton County is included in this region rather than with the adjacent structurally related Georgian Bay counties because its communications are through this area.	Secondary industries in the centres referred to, agriculture (ranging from intensive fruit and vegetable canning and dairy farming to general farming and marginal operations), and tourism (important in the Shield portion).	A chain of marketing centres, falling within the dominant Toronto wholesale area. Durham County is a district zone because of the encroachment of the Oshawa urban fringe, but largely belongs in this region. *Market index 95.*
52	Toronto Metropolitan Region	A highly organized portion of the north shore of the Lake Ontario Plains.	A metropolitan conurbation area centred on Toronto, a 5th-order centre, with related manufacturing suburbs in an arc from Oshawa (a 4th-order centre) to Oakville (1st-order), including Brampton (2nd-order) and Newmarket (1st-order). In addition there are local offices at Weston and New Toronto as well as within the Toronto area.	Very extensive and varied manufacturing; truck gardening, fruit growing, and milk-shed activities in an agricultural hinterland. Ontario County is included in this region rather than in Region 51 because the post-war growth of automobile manufacturing at Toronto and Oakville has led to Oshawa having new ties with this region; and including Ontario County facilitates analysis of the area impact of automobile production trends.	Toronto is predominant as a marketing centre, both wholesale and retail. *Market index 129.*
53	Hamilton/St. Catharines–Niagara	The Niagara Peninsula is a unique geographic area and requires a separate region. To it are tied the uplands in the Hamilton orbit. Brant County is structurally not part of the Peninsula, but is integrated into this region because of its functional ties.	Hamilton is a 5th-order centre. The following 4th-order major centres are in a southern crescent: St. Catharines, Niagara Falls, Welland, Brantford. Also in this string are the 1st-order centres of Fort Erie and Port Colborne. This is a traditional functional region, influenced by its position with respect to the Toronto area and the United States, and the Welland Canal. Wentworth County is included in the region because Hamilton is a functional centre for the region (although some definitions of the region do not include Hamilton). Burlington in Halton County could also be included because it is part of Metropolitan Hamilton, but since the rest of the county is in the Toronto orbit the whole county is zoned to Region 52. If Halton County were to be redefined, Burlington should be transferred to Wentworth and Region 53.	Manufacturing (diversified; especially steel, steel products, and other heavy manufacturing related to the strategic location of the region). Specialized agriculture (peaches, grapes, other fruit, and dairying). Hydro-electric-power production at Niagara Falls exerts a great influence.	Hamilton is the dominant marketing centre, though St. Catharines is also important. *Market index 126.*

ANALYTICAL DESCRIPTION OF ECONOMIC REGIONS

REGIONAL CODE	NAME OF REGION	STRUCTURAL FACTORS	FUNCTIONAL FACTORS	PRODUCTION FACTORS	MARKETING FACTORS
54	London–Lake Erie	Western Ontario Plains are the central portion of the South-western Ontario geographic area.	London, a 4th-order centre, is the regional capital, being dominant in finance, transportation, and education. Woodstock, Simcoe, and St. Thomas are 2nd-order satellite centres; Tillsonburg is a 1st-order centre.	Manufacturing (diverse, though tending to be heavy), specialized agriculture (tobacco, dairy products, fruit), mixed farming, and fishing (in Lake Erie).	London is the commercial centre, though eastern fringes may be pulled toward Hamilton. *Market index 109.*
55	Windsor/Sarnia– Lake St. Clair	The 'corn belt' area, plus the mixed farming belt in Lambton County—in other words the south-western portion of the South-western Ontario geographic area.	The influence of lake-front industrial sites and of the proximity of the United States border is dominant. Windsor and Sarnia are 4th-order centres; Chatham, Leamington, and Wallaceburg are, respectively, 3rd-order, 2nd-order, and 1st-order centres.	Heavy manufacturing (automobiles, chemicals, petroleum, rubber, etc.), specialized agriculture (vegetables) and (in the north) mixed farming.	Windsor is the dominant marketing centre, though Sarnia and Chatham have local marketing roles. *Market index 116.*
56	Kitchener-Midlands	The northern part of the South-western Ontario geographic area.	A constellation of significant local office centres adjacent to the Toronto-Hamilton axis. Kitchener and Guelph are 4th-order centres; Galt, Stratford, Listowel, and Goderich are 2nd-order centres. Huron County is tied to this region functionally, but structural factors are indeterminate (e.g. soil characteristics are like those of Bruce County but the production pattern is like that of the Midlands).	Manufacturing (diverse) and agriculture (this region is an important part of the major metropolitan milkshed).	The centres tend to be independent as markets, though they are all affected by the proximity of Toronto and Hamilton. *Market index 107.*
57	Lake Huron/ Georgian Bay	A combination of two physiographic areas, the Western Ontario and the Central Ontario Highlands. Manitoulin Island is not considered to be part of this region, although physiographically it is an extension of Bruce County and its two principal activities, livestock-raising and tourism, closely resemble the general pattern of the region. It has predominant functional ties with Region 58 (e.g. Little Current is the coal port for Sudbury), and it is therefore set up as a district zone in that region.	A constellation of counties fronting on Lake Huron and Georgian Bay. Barrie is a 3rd-order centre; Walkerton, Owen Sound, and Bracebridge are 2nd-order centres; Collingwood, Orillia, Midland, and Parry Sound are 1st-order centres.	Manufacturing (flour and feed, lake vessels, foods), agriculture (livestock mixed farming products), and tourism. Dufferin County is in this region for production and structural reasons, though its functional relationships are southward rather than northward.	A string of minor marketing centres. *Market index 83.*
58	Sudbury–North-eastern Ontario	The eastern portion of the Canadian Shield in Ontario, plus Manitoulin Island (see Region 57).	A constellation of mining and pulp-and-paper centres. Sudbury, Timmins, and Kirkland Lake are 4th-order centres; North Bay and Sault Ste. Marie are 2nd-order centres; Sturgeon Falls, Elliot Lake and Kapuskasing are 1st-order centres.	Mining (nickel, gold, copper, iron, uranium), manufacturing (steel, non-ferrous metals, pulp and paper), forestry, and agriculture (clay belt).	North Bay is the dominant distribution centre, but Sudbury and Sault Ste. Marie are marketing centres for their immediate areas. *Market index 116.*
59	Lakehead–North-western Ontario	The western portion of the Canadian Shield in Ontario, separated from North-eastern Ontario by a broad non-productive gap.	Functionally tied together by transportation factors, including lake shipping. Fort William and Port Arthur are 4th-order centres; Sioux Lookout and Kenora are 2nd-order centres; Fort Frances is a 1st-order centre.	Manufacturing (flour, buses and trucks, pulp and paper), mining (iron and gold), forestry, and trapping.	The Lakehead cities of Fort William and Port Arthur constitute the dominant marketing centre, although the north-western fringes of the region have some ties with Winnipeg. *Market index 112.*
	Regions of the Prairie Provinces				
60	Winnipeg Metropolitan Region	A small homogeneous metropolitan region.	The 5th-order metropolitan area of Winnipeg is functionally dominant as a communications, financial, and educational centre for all of Manitoba as well as for its own environs. Furthermore, as an entrepôt or transportation focus for the Prairies the metropolis performs many general functions for many of the Prairie regions. It must, therefore, be differentiated as a separate metropolitan region.	Manufacturing (diverse—meat, clothing, steel products) and services.	A great commercial centre with a two-way marketing flow in relation to many Prairie regions as well as those of Manitoba. *Market index 112.*
61	South-eastern Manitoba	A largely homogeneous region on the fringe of the Canadian Shield, plus the eastern Red River Valley.	Dominated by Winnipeg.	Agriculture (mixed, and 'pioneer' in nature) and (in the north) pulp and paper.	Dominated from Winnipeg. *Market index 84.*

ANALYTICAL DESCRIPTION OF ECONOMIC REGIONS

REGIONAL CODE	NAME OF REGION	STRUCTURAL FACTORS	FUNCTIONAL FACTORS	PRODUCTION FACTORS	MARKETING FACTORS
62	Manitoba Inter-Lakes	A largely homogeneous region on the fringe of the Canadian Shield to the north of Winnipeg, plus the North Winnipeg plains.	Dominated by Winnipeg.	Agriculture (mixed), forestry, and fishing (out of Gimli).	Dominated from Winnipeg. *Market index 71.*
63	South Central Manitoba	Rich Red River Valley, west side, and lower Assiniboine Valley.	Dominated by Winnipeg, although the north-western portion has a 2nd-order centre at Portage la Prairie.	Agriculture (wheat, special crops, dairy products).	Dominated by Winnipeg and Portage la Prairie. *Market index 68.*
64	Manitoba South-western Plains	A geographic area consisting of the drier uplands.	Brandon is a 3rd-order centre, though the eastern districts are part of the Portage la Prairie and Winnipeg hinterlands.	Agriculture (wheat farming predominant); some manufacturing of agricultural products.	Brandon is the marketing centre, except for the eastern portions of Census District 3, influenced by Winnipeg, and Census Districts 7 and 10, influenced by Portage la Prairie. *Market index 80.*
65	Manitoba Parklands	A geographic area called the Park Belt. It is an area of transition from plains to forest.	Dauphin is a 2nd-order centre.	Agriculture (mixed), manufacturing (minor and related to the agriculture), fishing, and forestry.	There is no strong marketing pattern, but Dauphin performs much of the marketing function. *Market index 66.*
66	Northern Manitoba	A combination of two physiographic areas: the Manitoba sector of the Canadian Shield and the Manitoba sector of the Hudson Bay Lowlands.	Activity is concentrated along two railway lines, except for intermittent activities served by air and water. The Pas and Flin Flon are 1st-order centres.	Primary industries: nickel-copper mining (including a smelter), fishing, forestry, and trapping.	The pioneer southern fringe around Lake Winnipeg and the areas served by air are tied to Winnipeg. Otherwise, marketing takes place along the two railway lines. *Market index 122.*
70	Regina-South-eastern Saskatchewan Plains	The southern portion of the mixed-grass, dark-brown-soil prairie, plus the Oxbow portion of the black-soil belt.	Regina is a dominant 3rd-order centre, but it has satellite centres each with a local office, Weyburn (2nd order) and Estevan (1st order). The Moosomin District zone (south Census District 5) could be included in this region because of marketing and communication ties with Regina, but structurally most of	Agriculture (wheat dominant, mixed farming on the north-eastern fringes), governmental services and manufacturing (both at Regina), and coal mining (at Estevan). ⎯⎯⎯⎯⎯ Census District 5 is part of the black-soil Park Belt (Region 73).	Regina is the dominant marketing centre. *Market index 92.*
71	Saskatchewan Palliser	A dry south-west belt of short-grass, brown-soil prairie. It is the Saskatchewan section of the Palliser Triangle.	Moose Jaw is a 3rd-order centre and an entrepôt; Swift Current is also a 3rd-order centre.	Agriculture (varies from wheat in the north-east to ranch livestock in the south-west), some manufacturing (flour and oil refining at Moose Jaw), and minor mining (clay).	Moose Jaw and Swift Current are the marketing centres. *Market index 73.*
72	Saskatoon-Central Plains	The northern portion of the mixed-grass, dark-brown-soil prairie.	Saskatoon is a 3rd-order centre also performing functions such as distribution and education; Battleford district zone should be included in Region 74 (an anomaly which can be corrected by redefinition of census districts).	Agriculture (wheat) and manufacturing (mainly agricultural products).	Saskatoon is the dominant marketing centre. In fact, its market influence stretches northwards into Region 74 and eastward into Region 73. On the other hand, the southern district is influenced by Regina. *Market index 89.*
73	Saskatchewan South-eastern Parklands	Black soil. This is a richly cultivated portion of the Saskatchewan Parkland Belt.	A reason for separation of this region from the other Saskatchewan regions is that it is to a large extent functionally related with Manitoba centres east of it. Yorkton is a 3rd-order centre, but its grip on the west, east, and south fringes is weak, though it has a strong effect to the north.	Agriculture (wheat, feed grains and livestock) is predominant.	The region is largely serviced from Winnipeg, Brandon, and Dauphin rather than from Saskatchewan wholesale centres (except in the case of District Zone 733 south of the Qu'Appelle, which is more accessible from Regina — again, redefinition of census districts should correct this). *Market index 63.*
74	Saskatchewan Parklands	A geographic area of aspen groves and mixed woods.	Prince Albert is a 3rd-order centre, but North Battleford controls the south-western portion and Lloydminster the south-western corner (both 1st-order).	Agriculture (gradually changing from wheat along the southern fringe to mixed farming products; the northern fringe has pioneer farming). There is forestry potential in the northern fringe.	The region has an important marketing centre in Prince Albert, but it only dominates the central portion. The influence of Saskatoon as a wholesale centre reaches out through this area. *Market index 62.*
75	Northern Saskatchewan	The Saskatchewan portion of the northern coniferous forest of the Canadian Shield.	This is a residual northern region, functionally disjointed, with no local office of its own; it is served by four centres — Prince Albert, North Battleford, Flin Flon, and Edmonton.	Primary industries: mining (non-ferrous metal, especially uranium), fishing, trapping, forestry.	The region has no marketing focus. It is largely served by air from Prince Albert. *Market index 90.*
80	Medicine Hat Palliser	Short-grass, brown-soil prairie, semi-arid. It is the Alberta section of the Palliser Triangle.	Medicine Hat is a 2nd-order centre. The Northern Palliser area is marginal, not well tied in functionally to the region, and is, therefore, in Region 83.	Agriculture (ranching in natural areas, sugar beets and greenhouse products in irrigated areas), manufacturing (flour, sugar, pottery, other clay products).	Medicine Hat is the principal marketing centre. *Market index 95.*

ANALYTICAL DESCRIPTION OF ECONOMIC REGIONS

REGIONAL CODE	NAME OF REGION	STRUCTURAL FACTORS	FUNCTIONAL FACTORS	PRODUCTION FACTORS	MARKETING FACTORS
81	Lethbridge Prairie	Mid-grass prairie, with intensive agriculture fostered by irrigation.	Lethbridge, a 3rd-order centre, and the third largest centre in Alberta, is dominant; it has a distinct zone of influence.	Agriculture (mixed farming products and sugar beets in irrigated areas, ranch livestock towards the foot-hills).	A separate marketing area dominated by Lethbridge, except for Newell County, which should be tied to Census District I and Region 80. *Market index 93.*
82	Alberta Rocky Mountain/Foothills	Predominantly a structural region characterized by mountains and foothills.	Functionally diffused, with Blairmore, a 1st-order centre, serving the main or Crowsnest zone, Calgary dominating the central or Banff zone, Red Deer serving the north-eastern zone along the Red Deer spur, and Jasper zone tied to Edson.	Mining (coal), forestry and tourism.	A heterogeneous marketing area. *Marketing index 116.*
83	Calgary–South Central Alberta	Largely mid-grass prairie, though it extends into the foothills (High River district).	Calgary is a 5th-order centre; Drumheller is a 2nd-order centre.	Manufacturing (agricultural products such as meat and flour, oil and other chemical products), agriculture (livestock and mixed farming), and mining (coal and oil).	Calgary is the dominant wholesale marketing centre for Southern Alberta, as well as reaching into Region 90. *Market index 116.*
84	Red Deer	Largely a 'badlands' region with adjacent mixed farming.	Red Deer is a 3rd-order centre.	Agriculture (mixed).	The Red Deer area is a 'watershed' between the Calgary and Edmonton areas of influence. *Market index 91.*
85	East Central Alberta Prairie	A structural region comprising the northern portion of the Alberta Prairie, and the adjacent fringe of the Park Belt.	Lloydminster is a 1st-order centre. The rest of the region has strong ties with Edmonton except for Stettler's ties with Red Deer.	Agriculture (mixed).	The region is touched by Saskatoon from the east, but dominated by Edmonton from the west. *Market index 84.*
86	Edmonton Metropolitan–Parklands	A rich farming belt stretching from the northern portion of the Alberta Prairie through the cultivated Park Belt.	Functionally a well-defined region characterized by the dominance of Edmonton (a 5th-order centre) as a transportation, trade, and service focus.	Agriculture (mixed), manufacturing (agricultural and oil refinery products), mining (oil, gas, and coal), and (along the region's northern fringe) forestry.	Edmonton is the dominant marketing centre. It also performs wholesale functions for all regions to the north and north-west. *Market index 112.*
87	North-eastern Alberta	A physiographic area, although the Canadian Shield intrudes in the eastern part.	The Lower Athabasca zone is functionally unorganized except for the railway to Fort McMurray from Edmonton. The southern Beaver River District zone is developing.	Largely a marginal area. There is some activity in forestry, fishing, and trapping. The Athabasca tarsands have vast oil possibilities. Agriculture in the south.	The region depends largely on Edmonton as its marketing centre. *Market index 83.*
88	North-western Alberta/Peace River	The Peace River is a distinct geographic area, an isolated extension of the Great Plains Belt and the Park Belt, surrounded by parklands.	Few lines of communication. A distinct region, with growing small centres, serviced from the Edson and Grande Prairie local offices.	Agriculture (wheat and mixed farming products), mining (oil, gas, and coal), and forestry.	Distinct marketing units, although tied to Edmonton wholesale functions. *Market index 81.*
Regions of British Columbia					
90	East Kootenay	The eastern part of the geographic area of south-eastern British Columbia.	Functionally tied along the Kootenay Valley. There are production and functional ties with Region 91 because the Kimberley metals are smelted and refined at Trail, but these ties are offset by other factors such as marketing patterns and the independent growth potential of the region. Cranbrook is a 2nd-order centre.	Mining (lead, zinc, coal), forestry, and tourism.	The considerable marketing influence of Calgary warrants separating this region from Region 91. *Market index 138.*
91	West Kootenay	The western part of the geographic area of South-eastern British Columbia.	A major mining area integrated around the Trail smelting and refining facilities. Trail is a 2nd-order centre. It is supplemented by Nelson, also a 2nd-order centre. The Revelstoke District is treated as a distinct zone because of difficulty of access; if this zone could be separated from Census District 2 it would be preferable to link it to Census District 6 in Region 93.	Manufacturing (smelting and refining, pulp and paper), mining (silver, tungsten), and forestry (along the Arrow Lakes) serving the integrated pulp and lumber facilities at Castlegar.	Trail is the principal marketing centre, but it is not completely dominant. *Market index 134.*
92	Okanagan Valley	The southern part of the Fraser Plateau physiographic area.	A string of 2nd-order centres at Vernon, Kelowna, and Penticton; a 1st-order centre at Princeton; and a marginal sub-zone at Grand Forks.	Agriculture (specialized: fruit and vegetables in the irrigated portions along the lake, ranch livestock elsewhere because of the arid climate), and mining (silver, copper).	There is no dominant marketing centre. Each of the zones may be taken as a separate marketing unit in a chain. *Market index 96.*

ANALYTICAL DESCRIPTION OF ECONOMIC REGIONS

REGIONAL CODE	NAME OF REGION	STRUCTURAL FACTORS	FUNCTIONAL FACTORS	PRODUCTION FACTORS	MARKETING FACTORS
93	South Central British Columbia	The northern portion of the Fraser Plateau physiographic area.	Although the region is structurally and topographically a unit, functionally it is not a unit because the PGE Districts in the north are tied along the Pacific Great Eastern line. Also the Merritt area is structurally and functionally more closely related to Region 92, particularly to Princeton. Therefore, while Kam-	Agriculture (vegetables, livestock, dairy products) and mining (gold). loops is the 2nd-order centre for the region, there are, in the present system, three somewhat independent districts tied in.	Not an integrated marketing unit, though Kamloops is to some extent a marketing centre. *Market index 115.*
94	Vancouver Metropolitan-Lower Fraser	A distinct geographical area, comprising the Coastal Trench Lowlands.	A fundamental unit tied to the 5th-order metropolitan centre of Vancouver, with a satellite 2nd-order centre at Chilliwack and a 1st-order centre at Mission City. There is an additional local office in New Westminster to facilitate servicing the region.	Manufacturing (varied, but especially forest products and foods) and agriculture (specialized dairy and fruit farming).	Vancouver is the dominant marketing centre, not only for this region but for much of Regions 95 and 96. *Market index 117.*
95	Victoria-Vancouver Island	A separate geographic area, consisting of two physical areas, the coastal lowlands in the south-east and the Coast mountains in the remainder of the island.	A distinct functional unit with a regional personality. The principal centre is Victoria, a 4th-order centre. Duncan, Nanaimo, Port Alberni, and Courtenay are 2nd-order centres, and are somewhat independent. The Northern District in particular tends to independence, being more closely related to Vancouver than to Victoria.	Manufacturing (lumber, pulp and paper, ships), mining (coal), and fishing.	Victoria is the principal marketing centre, though not dominant. Vancouver performs a major wholesaling role for much of the island. *Market index 118.*
96	North-western British Columbia	The coastal area, plus the north-western section of British Columbia.	The region is not functionally integrated internally, its coastal nature stressing the importance of shipping services tied in with Vancouver. Nevertheless, Prince Rupert and Kitimat are 2nd-order centres, the	Manufacturing (lumber, pulp and paper, fish products, aluminum), forestry, fishing. former having wide outlying districts.	Prince Rupert, in its own hinterlands, is an important marketing centre, but the rest of the region is within the Vancouver marketing area. *Market index 132.*
97	North Central British Columbia	A distinct physiographic area, termed the Nechako Plateau.	Most activity is tied to the immediate environs of the two transportation routes, the Canadian National Railway Northern Line and the Pacific Great Eastern extension. Prince George is a 2nd-order centre, Quesnel a 1st-order centre.	Agriculture (ranch livestock and mixed farming products – the latter marginal) and forestry.	The marketing pattern is not integrated; it is scattered along the railway lines. Northern development may, however, have an integrating effect. *Market index 114.*
98	North-eastern British Columbia	The region consists predominantly of the extension of Region 88, but it also includes the separate mountainous Finlay-Parsnip District.	Dawson Creek is a 2nd-order centre.	Agriculture (mixed farming products) and mining (oil and gas).	The marketing pattern is similar to that of Region 88, access being provided by the Alaska Highway. With the extension of the Pacific Great Eastern into this area formerly isolated from the rest of the province, there may be some reorientation of the pattern. *Market index 108.*

Northern Canada

REGIONAL CODE	NAME OF REGION	STRUCTURAL FACTORS	FUNCTIONAL FACTORS	PRODUCTION FACTORS	MARKETING FACTORS
11	Yukon	A mountainous separate physiographic area.	A distinct functional and political unit, with a 1st-order centre at Whitehorse.	Mining (gold, silver, lead) and trapping.	A separate isolated marketing unit. *Marketing index 146.*
12	Mackenzie	A combination of two physiographic regions: the Mackenzie Lowlands and a portion of the Arctic mainland.	This political region can be treated also as a functional unit because of economic and population factors. Yellowknife, Fort Norman, and Inuvik are district centres.	Mining (gold, radium, oil), fishing, and trapping.	A separate marketing unit (because of distinct access problems). Dominated by Edmonton wholesaling. *Market index 120.*
13	Keewatin				*Market index 91.*

This eastern portion of the Arctic mainland is treated as a single region because it is structurally homogeneous, a functional unit, a production unit involving mining and Eskimo livelihood, and a marketing unit.

REGIONAL CODE	NAME OF REGION				MARKETING FACTORS
14	Franklin				*Market index 136.*

The northern islands are also treated as a single distinctive region. This regional distinction would be maintained even with the combination of Keewatin District and Franklin District in a single administrative unit, provided that data was still presented separately for the two regions. Otherwise they would have to become zones of a new Region 13.

ECONOMIC REGIONS

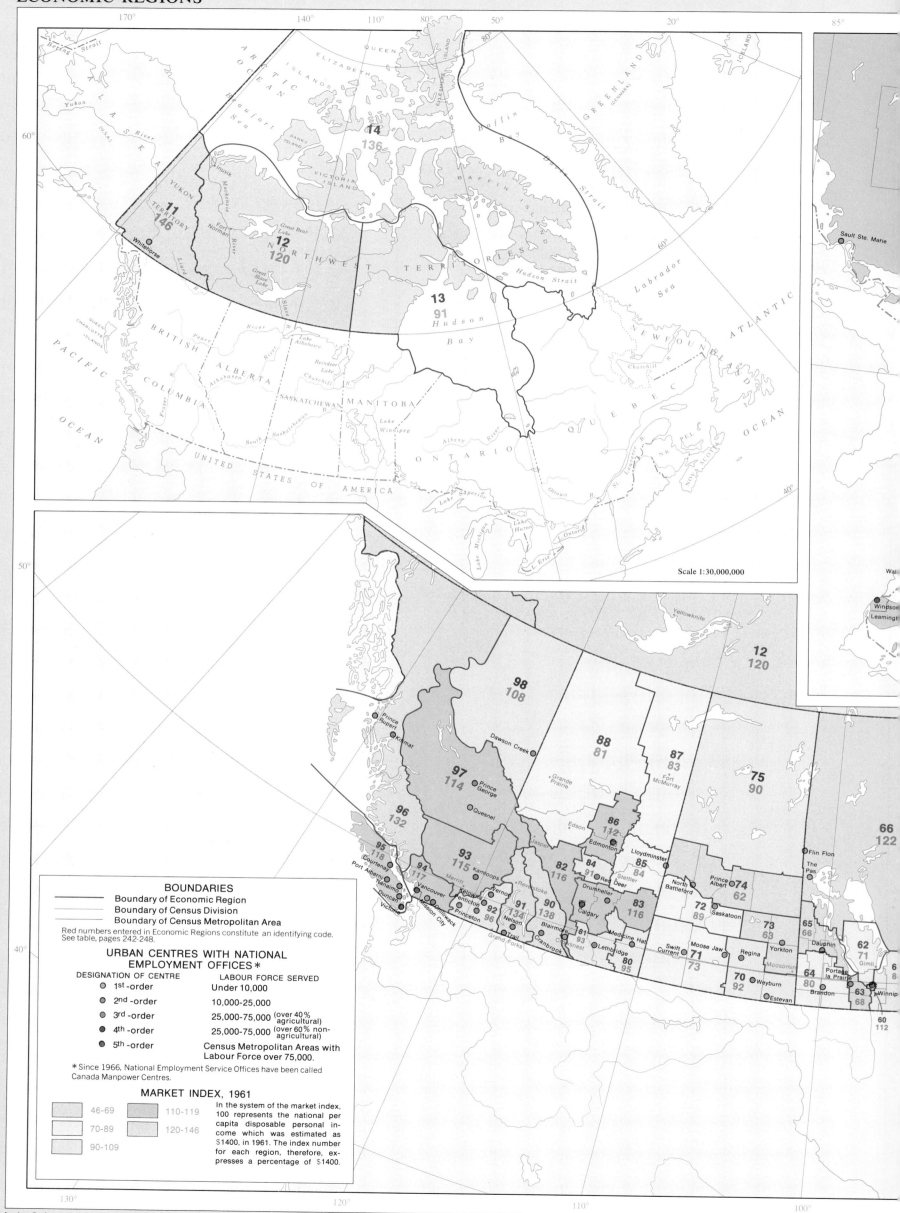

Scale 1:30,000,000

BOUNDARIES

—————— Boundary of Economic Region
—————— Boundary of Census Division
—————— Boundary of Census Metropolitan Area

Red numbers entered in Economic Regions constitute an identifying code.
See table, pages 242-248.

URBAN CENTRES WITH NATIONAL EMPLOYMENT OFFICES *

DESIGNATION OF CENTRE	LABOUR FORCE SERVED
◉ 1st -order	Under 10,000
◉ 2nd -order	10,000-25,000
◉ 3rd -order	25,000-75,000 (over 40% agricultural)
● 4th -order	25,000-75,000 (over 60% non-agricultural)
● 5th -order	Census Metropolitan Areas with Labour Force over 75,000.

* Since 1966, National Employment Service Offices have been called Canada Manpower Centres.

MARKET INDEX, 1961

46-69	110-119
70-89	120-146
90-109	

In the system of the market index, 100 represents the national per capita disposable personal income which was estimated as $1400, in 1961. The index number for each region, therefore, expresses a percentage of $1400.

Lambert Conformal Conic Projection Standard Parallels 49°N. and 77°N.

Scale 1 : 5,000,000
or
One Inch to 78.91 Miles

Scale 1:15,000,000 or One Inch to 236.73 Miles

CENSUS DIVISIONS AND SUBDIVISIONS, 1961.

The Yukon Territory and the Northwest Territories are treated as census divisions, but are not identified by numbers. The Districts of Franklin, Mackenzie and Keewatin are treated as census subdivisions of the Northwest Territories. Islands in Hudson Bay, James Bay, Hudson Strait and Ungava Bay are part of the Northwest Territories.

Scale 1:30,000,000

INDEX TO CENSUS DIVISIONS

PRINCE EDWARD ISLAND

1. Kings
2. Prince
3. Queens

NOVA SCOTIA

1. Annapolis
2. Antigonish
3. Cape Breton
4. Colchester
5. Cumberland
6. Digby
7. Guysborough
8. Halifax
9. Hants
10. Inverness
11. Kings
12. Lunenburg
13. Pictou
14. Queens
15. Richmond
16. Shelburne
17. Victoria
18. Yarmouth

NEW BRUNSWICK

1. Albert
2. Carleton
3. Charlotte
4. Gloucester
5. Kent
6. Kings
7. Madawaska
8. Northumberland
9. Queens
10. Restigouche
11. St. John
12. Sunbury
13. Victoria
14. Westmorland
15. York

QUEBEC

1a. Abitibi County
1b. Territory of Abitibi
1c. Territory of Mistassini
2. Argenteuil
3. Arthabaska
4. Bagot
5. Beauce
6. Beauharnois
7. Bellechasse
8. Berthier
9. Bonaventure
10. Brome
11. Chambly
12. Champlain
13. Charlevoix-Est
14. Charlevoix-Ouest
15. Châteauguay
16. Chicoutimi
17. Compton
18. Deux-Montagnes
19. Dorchester
20. Drummond
21. Frontenac
22. Gaspé-Est
23. Gaspé-Ouest
24. Îles-de-la-Madeleine
25. Gatineau
26. Hull

QUEBEC

27. Huntingdon
28. Iberville
29. Joliette
30. Kamouraska
31. Labelle
32. Lac-St-Jean-Est
33. Lac-St-Jean-Ouest
34. Laprairie
35. L'Assomption
36. Lévis
37. L'Islet
38. Lotbinière
39. Maskinongé
40. Matane
41. Matapédia
42. Mégantic
43. Missisquoi
44. Montcalm
45. Montmagny
46. Montmorency No. 1
47. Montmorency No. 2
48. Île-Jésus
49. Île-de-Montréal
50. Napierville
51. Nicolet
52. Papineau
53. Pontiac
54. Portneuf
55. Québec
56. Richelieu
57. Richmond
58. Rimouski
59. Rouville
60a. Saguenay County
60b. Territory of New Quebec
61. Shefford
62. Sherbrooke
63. Soulanges
64. Stanstead
65. St-Hyacinthe
66. St-Jean
67. St-Maurice
68. Témiscamingue
69. Témiscouata
70. Rivière-du-Loup
71. Terrebonne
72. Vaudreuil
73. Verchères
74. Wolfe
75. Yamaska

ONTARIO

1. Algoma
2. Brant
3. Bruce
4. Carleton
5. Cochrane
6. Dufferin
7. Dundas
8. Durham
9. Elgin
10. Essex
11. Frontenac
12. Glengarry
13. Grenville
14. Grey
15. Haldimand
16. Haliburton

ONTARIO

17. Halton
18. Hastings
19. Huron
20. Kenora Territorial District
20(a) Kenora
20(b) Patricia Portion
21. Kent
22. Lambton
23. Lanark
24. Leeds
25. Lennox and Addington
26. Lincoln
27. Manitoulin
28. Middlesex
29. Muskoka
30. Nipissing
31. Norfolk
32. Northumberland
33. Ontario
34. Oxford

35. Parry Sound
36. Peel
37. Perth
38. Peterborough
39. Prescott
40. Prince Edward
41. Rainy River
42. Renfrew
43. Russell
44. Simcoe
45. Stormont
46. Sudbury
47. Thunder Bay
48. Timiskaming
49. Victoria
50. Waterloo
51. Welland
52. Wellington
53. Wentworth
54. York

NOTE: Census Divisions in Newfoundland, Manitoba, Saskatchewan, Alberta and British Columbia are identified by number only.

CENSUS DIVISIONS AND SUBDIVISIONS, 1961.

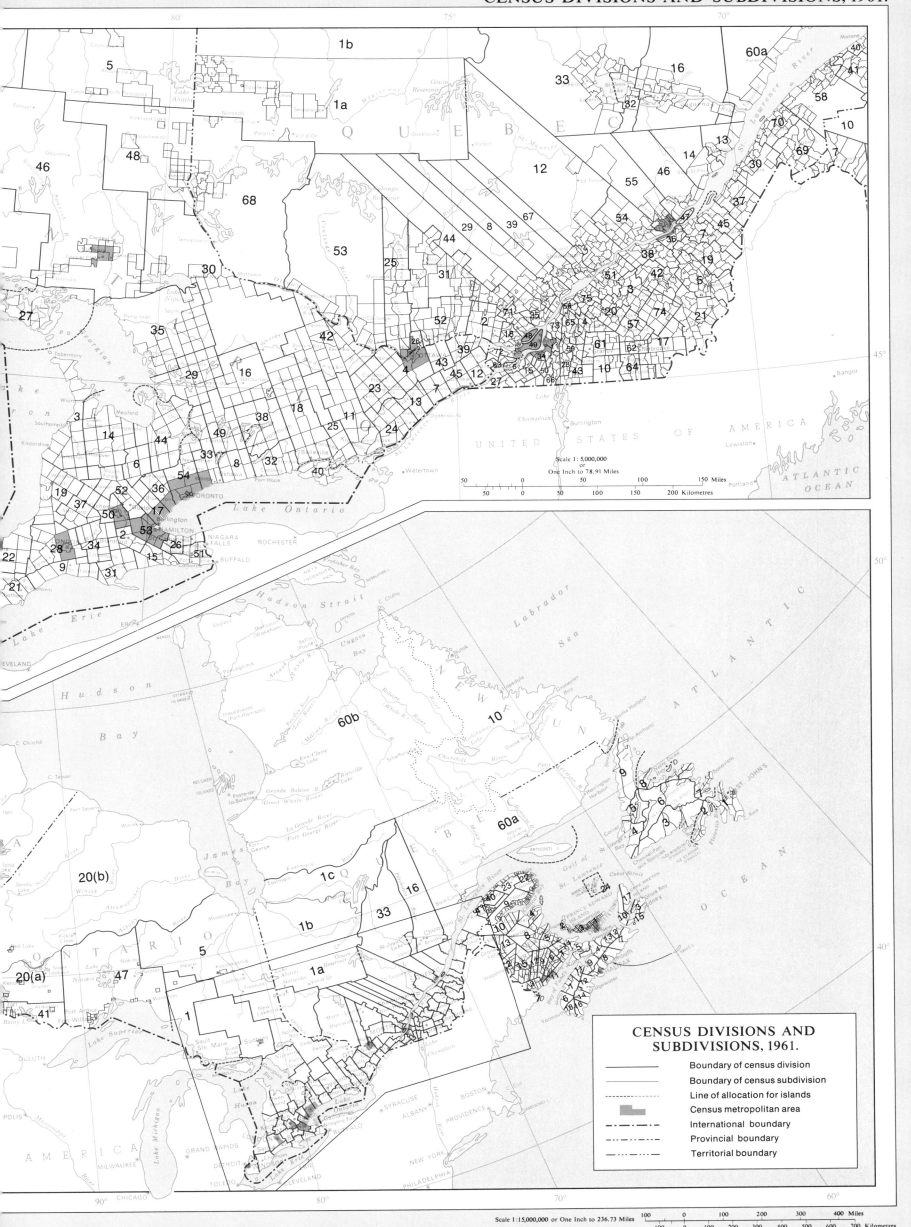

CENSUS DIVISIONS AND
SUBDIVISIONS, 1961.

Boundary of census division
Boundary of census subdivision
Line of allocation for islands
Census metropolitan area
International boundary
Provincial boundary
Territorial boundary

Scale 1 : 5,000,000
or
One Inch to 78.91 Miles

Scale 1:15,000,000 or One Inch to 236.73 Miles

CENSUS DIVISIONS, 1961

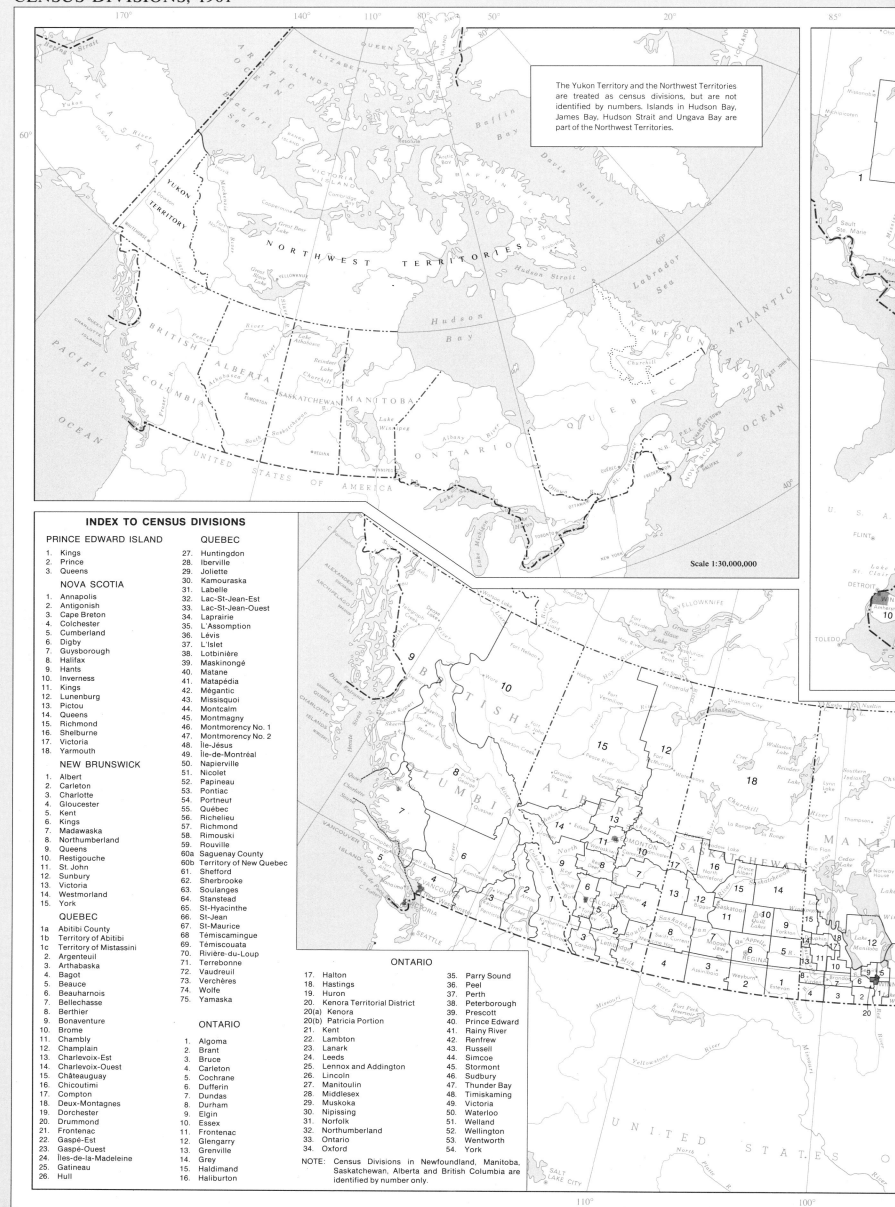

The Yukon Territory and the Northwest Territories are treated as census divisions, but are not identified by numbers. Islands in Hudson Bay, James Bay, Hudson Strait and Ungava Bay are part of the Northwest Territories.

Scale 1:30,000,000

INDEX TO CENSUS DIVISIONS

PRINCE EDWARD ISLAND

1. Kings
2. Prince
3. Queens

NOVA SCOTIA

1. Annapolis
2. Antigonish
3. Cape Breton
4. Colchester
5. Cumberland
6. Digby
7. Guysborough
8. Halifax
9. Hants
10. Inverness
11. Kings
12. Lunenburg
13. Pictou
14. Queens
15. Richmond
16. Shelburne
17. Victoria
18. Yarmouth

NEW BRUNSWICK

1. Albert
2. Carleton
3. Charlotte
4. Gloucester
5. Kent
6. Kings
7. Madawaska
8. Northumberland
9. Queens
10. Restigouche
11. St. John
12. Sunbury
13. Victoria
14. Westmorland
15. York

QUEBEC

1a. Abitibi County
1b. Territory of Abitibi
1c. Territory of Mistassini
2. Argenteuil
3. Arthabaska
4. Bagot
5. Beauce
6. Beauharnois
7. Bellechasse
8. Berthier
9. Bonaventure
10. Brome
11. Chambly
12. Champlain
13. Charlevoix-Est
14. Charlevoix-Ouest
15. Châteauguay
16. Chicoutimi
17. Compton
18. Deux-Montagnes
19. Dorchester
20. Drummond
21. Frontenac
22. Gaspé-Est
23. Gaspé-Ouest
24. Îles-de-la-Madeleine
25. Gatineau
26. Hull

QUEBEC

27. Huntingdon
28. Iberville
29. Joliette
30. Kamouraska
31. Labelle
32. Lac-St-Jean-Est
33. Lac-St-Jean-Ouest
34. Laprairie
35. L'Assomption
36. Lévis
37. L'Islet
38. Lotbinière
39. Maskinongé
40. Matane
41. Matapédia
42. Mégantic
43. Missisquoi
44. Montcalm
45. Montmagny
46. Montmorency No. 1
47. Montmorency No. 2
48. Île-Jésus
49. Île-de-Montréal
50. Napierville
51. Nicolet
52. Papineau
53. Pontiac
54. Portneuf
55. Québec
56. Richelieu
57. Richmond
58. Rimouski
59. Rouville
60a Saguenay County
60b Territory of New Quebec
61. Shefford
62. Sherbrooke
63. Soulanges
64. Stanstead
65. St-Hyacinthe
66. St-Jean
67. St-Maurice
68. Témiscamingue
69. Témiscouata
70. Rivière-du-Loup
71. Terrebonne
72. Vaudreuil
73. Verchères
74. Wolfe
75. Yamaska

ONTARIO

1. Algoma
2. Brant
3. Bruce
4. Carleton
5. Cochrane
6. Dufferin
7. Dundas
8. Durham
9. Elgin
10. Essex
11. Frontenac
12. Glengarry
13. Grenville
14. Grey
15. Haldimand
16. Haliburton

ONTARIO

17. Halton
18. Hastings
19. Huron
20. Kenora Territorial District
20(a) Kenora
20(b) Patricia Portion
21. Kent
22. Lambton
23. Lanark
24. Leeds
25. Lennox and Addington
26. Lincoln
27. Manitoulin
28. Middlesex
29. Muskoka
30. Nipissing
31. Norfolk
32. Northumberland
33. Ontario
34. Oxford
35. Parry Sound
36. Peel
37. Perth
38. Peterborough
39. Prescott
40. Prince Edward
41. Rainy River
42. Renfrew
43. Russell
44. Simcoe
45. Stormont
46. Sudbury
47. Thunder Bay
48. Timiskaming
49. Victoria
50. Waterloo
51. Welland
52. Wellington
53. Wentworth
54. York

NOTE: Census Divisions in Newfoundland, Manitoba, Saskatchewan, Alberta and British Columbia are identified by number only.

Lambert Conformal Conic Projection Standard Parallels 49°N. and 77°N.

NATIONAL ATLAS OF CANADA

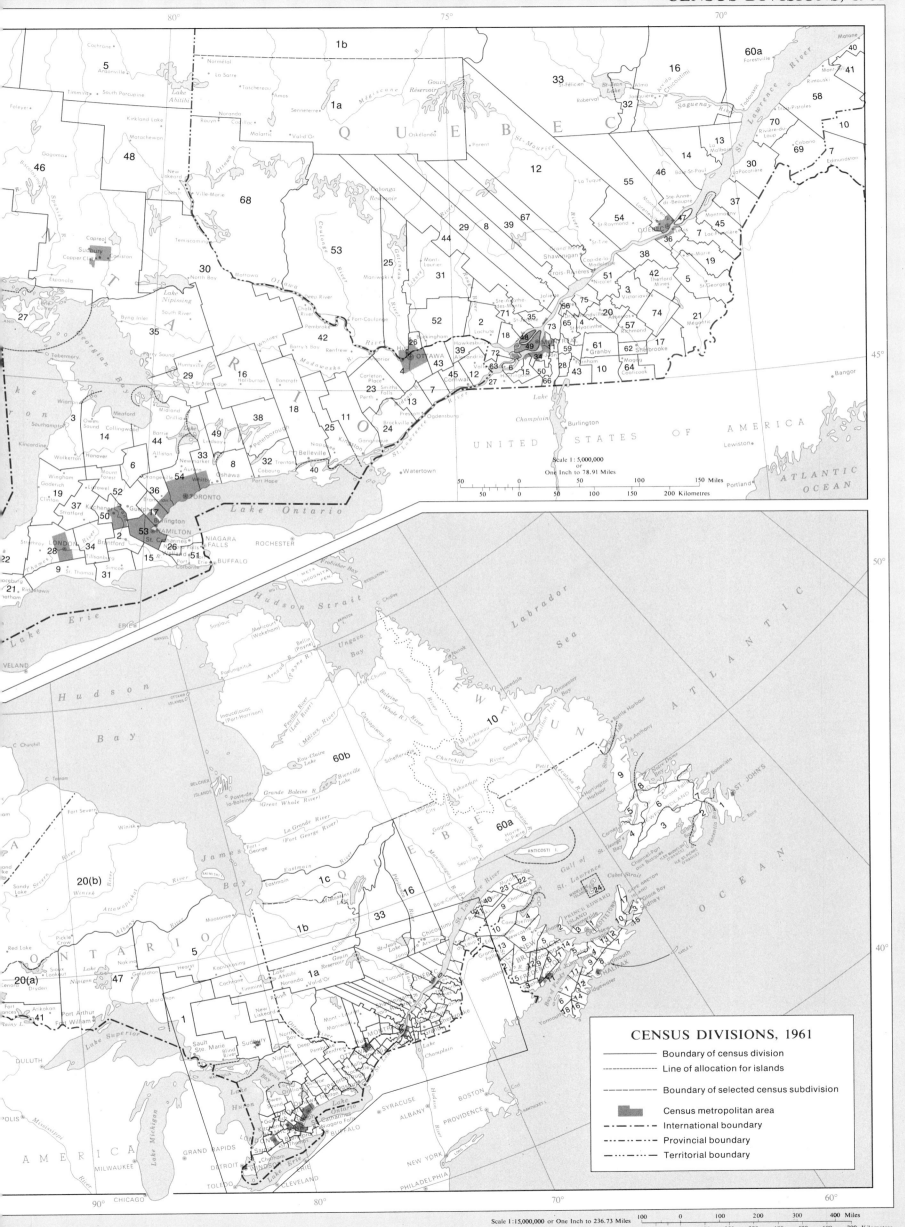

CENSUS DIVISIONS, 1961

	Boundary of census division
	Line of allocation for islands
	Boundary of selected census subdivision
	Census metropolitan area
	International boundary
	Provincial boundary
	Territorial boundary

Scale 1:5,000,000
or
One Inch to 78.91 Miles

Scale 1:15,000,000 or One Inch to 236.73 Miles

SOURCES

The Sources lists most of the published material from which the data of the atlas have been derived. Unpublished material is listed when it conforms to the following: (a) it is routinely available from the originating agency, or it is in a repository such as an archives to which the public has access; (b) it is a map manuscript compiled specifically for the atlas in an agency other than the Surveys and Mapping Branch. The term "Personal Communication" refers to persons who have supplied large quantities of unpublished information other than a map manuscript, derived from their personal research, specifically for the atlas, and upon which the atlas map is substantially based; and to a few persons, otherwise uncredited, whose specialist advice crucially affected the concept and contents of an atlas map.

Unlisted material may be classified as follows:

(a) Current maps of the National Topographic System and similar provincial maps, unless they are the major source of data for an atlas map, in which case they are collectively cited.

(b) Miscellaneous early topographical maps in archival collections (about 100 maps).

(c) Miscellaneous current thematic maps, covering an agency's service area, usually unpublished (about 50 maps). In cases where an atlas map is substantially based on such maps, the supplying agencies are listed.

(d) Short unpublished lists of data or single items of information, provided by public and private agencies, and individually forming a relatively small part of the data used for an atlas map. In cases where an atlas map is very substantially based on such information, the supplying agencies are listed (about 225 receipts of information).

(e) Answered questionnaires (75).

(f) Personal communications from individuals on one or a few items of information derived from their personal research (about 50 instances).

The agency (author) most frequently cited is: CANADA, Dominion Bureau of Statistics. This is abbreviated to: CANADA, DBS. Similarly, *Census of Canada/Recensement du Canada,* published by the Dominion Bureau of Statistics (now Statistics Canada), is abbreviated to: *Census/Recensement.* The catalogue numbers given in these citations are referable to the catalogue maintained by Statistics Canada, and in many cases provide reference approximately to the level of a chapter in a book.

1 - 2   RELIEF

CANADA, Department of Energy, Mines and Resources, Surveys and Mapping Branch. Map series MCR 5 (1:2,000,000). Ottawa.

—————. National Topographic System maps. Ottawa.

—————. World Aeronautical Charts (1:1,000,000). Ottawa.

CANADA, Department of the Environment, Marine Sciences Directorate, Canadian Hydrographic Service. Bathymetric charts 800-A (revised) and 896. Ottawa.

INTERNATIONAL HYDROGRAPHIC BUREAU. *General Bathymetric Chart of the Oceans (GEBCO).* Charts, plotting sheets.

UNITED STATES, Department of Commerce, Coast and Geodetic Survey. Hydrographic chart 5052.

3 - 4   RELIEF PROFILES

CANADA, Department of Energy, Mines and Resources, Surveys and Mapping Branch. National Topographic System maps. Ottawa.

5 - 6   PHYSIOGRAPHIC REGIONS

BOSTOCK, H.S. 1967. *Physiographic Regions of Canada.* Map no. 1254A. Ottawa: Geological Survey of Canada.

7 - 8   FRESH WATER

HARE, F.K., FERGUSON, H.L., ANDERSON, J.C. and SCHWARTZ, J. Forthcoming. *Mean Evapotranspiration over Canada, Part 1: Cover and Land Form.* Climatological Series. Department of the Environment, Atmospheric Environment Service.

9 - 10   LAKES, RIVERS AND GLACIERS

CANADA, Department of Energy, Mines and Resources, Surveys and Mapping Branch. National Topographic System maps. Ottawa.

11 - 12   PERMAFROST

BROWN, R.J.E. 1967. *Permafrost in Canada.* Map no. 1246A. Ottawa: Geological Survey of Canada.

—————. 1970. *Permafrost in Canada (Its Influence on Northern Development).* Canadian Building Series no. 41. Sponsored by Division of Building Research, National Research Council, Ottawa. Toronto: University of Toronto Press.

CANADA, Department of Energy, Mines and Resources, Geological Survey of Canada. 1960. *Surficial Geology, North-central District of Mackenzie, N.W.T.* Map no. 24-1960. Ottawa.

FYLES, J.G. 1963. *Surficial Geology of Victoria and Stefansson Islands, District of Franklin, N.W.T.* Map in Bulletin no. 101. Ottawa: Geological Survey of Canada.

HUGHES, O.L. 1969. *Distribution of Open-System Pingos in Central Yukon Territory with respect to Glacial Limits.* Paper no. 69-34. Ottawa: Geological Survey of Canada.

MACKAY, J. ROSS. 1963. Pingos in Canada. *Proceedings.* Permafrost International Conference, 11-15 November, at Purdue University, Lafayette, Indiana. National Academy of Sciences - National Research Council, publication no. 1287.

—————. 1963. *The Mackenzie Delta Area, N.W.T.* Geographical Branch Memoir no. 8. Ottawa: Department of Mines and Technical Surveys.

—————. 1967. Permafrost Depths, Lower Mackenzie Delta. *Arctic* 20: 21-26.

PISSART, A. 1967. Les Pingos de l'île Prince Patrick, (76°N-120°O). *Geographical Bulletin* 9: 189-217.

11 - 12 (cont'd.)

THOMPSON, H.A. 1963. Air Temperatures in Northern Canada, with Emphasis on Freezing and Thawing Indices. *Proceedings.* Permafrost International Conference, 11-15 November, at Purdue University, Lafayette, Indiana. National Academy of Sciences - National Research Council, publication no. 1287.

13 - 14   ICE

ALLEN, W.T.R. 1964. *Break-up and Freeze-up Dates in Canada.* Technical Circular no. CIR-4116 ICE-17. Ottawa: Department of Transport.

DUNBAR, M. Department of National Defence, Defence Research Board. Manuscript maps. Ottawa.

15 - 16   DRAINAGE BASINS

CANADA, Department of Energy, Mines and Resources, Surveys and Mapping Branch. National Topographic System maps. Ottawa.

CANADA, DBS. *Canada Year Book, 1968.* Ottawa.

CANADA, Canadian National Committee for the International Hydrological Decade. Forthcoming. *Hydrological Atlas of Canada.* Preliminary maps. Ottawa.

DIONNE, JEAN-CLAUDE. 1963. Vers une définition plus adéquate de l'estuaire du Saint-Laurent. *Zeitschrift für Geomorphologie* 7: 36-44.

INTERNATIONAL COLUMBIA RIVER ENGINEERING BOARD. 1959. *Report to the International Joint Commission, United States and Canada: Water Resources of the Columbia River Basin.* Abstract. (n.p.)

ONTARIO, Department of Lands and Forests. 1966. *Location of Dams on Principal Watersheds: Ontario 1966.* Toronto.

17 - 18   SEASONAL RUNOFF

CANADA, Department of Energy, Mines and Resources, Inland Waters Branch. 1965-67. *Surface Water Data.* Ottawa.

CANADA, succession of Departments. 1918-64. *Water Resources Papers.* Ottawa.

19   AVERAGE ANNUAL RUNOFF

20   MONTHLY DISTRIBUTION OF RUNOFF

CANADA, Canadian National Committee for the International Hydrological Decade. Forthcoming. *Hydrological Atlas of Canada.* Preliminary map. Ottawa.

21 - 22   RIVER DISCHARGE

CANADA, Canadian National Committee for the International Hydrological Decade. Forthcoming. *Hydrological Atlas of Canada.* Preliminary maps. Ottawa.

CANADA, Department of Energy, Mines and Resources, Inland Waters Branch. 1965-67. *Surface Water Data.* Ottawa.

CANADA, succession of Departments. 1918-64. *Water Resources Papers.* Ottawa.

QUEBEC, Ministère des Richesses naturelles. *Annuaire hydrologique.* Selected issues. Québec.

INTERNATIONAL COLUMBIA RIVER ENGINEERING BOARD. 1959. *Report to the International Joint Commission, United States and Canada: Water Resources of the Columbia River Basin.* Appendix 5. (n.p.)

UNITED STATES SENATE, Select Committee on National Water Resources. 1960. *Water Resources Activities in the United States: Surface Water Resources of the United States.* 86th Cong., 2nd sess. Committee print no. 4. Washington.

23 - 24   RIVER PROFILES

AITKINSON, C.H., MCCONNELL, A.D., HAMILTON, W. and KEEPING, P.A.T. 1970. Flood Analysis and Design of Flood Control Facilities for the Churchill Falls Power Project. *Engineering Journal* 53: 21-27.

CANADA, Department of Energy, Mines and Resources, Marine Sciences Branch. 1967. *Great Lakes Pilot.* Vol. 1, 6th ed. Ottawa.

————. 1966. *St. Lawrence River Pilot.* 1st ed. Ottawa.

————. Hydrographic charts. Ottawa.

————, Surveys and Mapping Branch. National Topographic System maps. Ottawa.

CANADA, Department of External Affairs and Department of Northern Affairs and Natural Resources. 1964. *The Columbia River Treaty and Protocol - A Presentation.* Ottawa.

CANADA, Department of Transport, St. Lawrence Seaway Authority. (n.d.) *The St. Lawrence Seaway.* Pamphlet. Ottawa.

————. (n.d.) *2,342 Miles into the Heart of a Continent.* Pamphlet. Ottawa.

CANADIAN NATIONAL COMMITTEE OF THE INTERNATIONAL COMMITTEE ON LARGE DAMS. 1970. *Register of Dams in Canada/ Répertoire des barrages du Canada.* Montréal .

HEARTS, R.E. 1957. Rapide Beaumont - Important Addition on St. Maurice. *Electrical Digest* 26: 56.

INTERNATIONAL COLUMBIA RIVER ENGINEERING BOARD. 1959. *Report to the International Joint Commission, United States and Canada: Water Resources of the Columbia River Basin.* Appendix 1. (n.p.)

LEE, W.S. 1925. Hydroelectric Development of the Saguenay River. *Transactions of the American Institute of Electrical Engineers* 44: 722-736.

MACKENZIE, G.L. 1960. The South Saskatchewan River Dam. *Engineering Journal* 43: 50-55.

MCMORDIE, C. and MORGAN, C. 1970. The Columbia River Development - A Geotechnical Review. *Engineering Journal* 53: 9-17.

MILES, W.F. 1969. From Feasibility Report to First Power Output. *Engineering Journal* 52: 12-24.

Power in Pictures: Churchill Falls. *Canadian Geographical Journal* 78: 54-61.

25 - 26   GEOLOGY

DOUGLAS, R.J.W. 1967. *Geological Map of Canada.* Map no. 1250A. Ottawa: Geological Survey of Canada.

27 - 28   GEOLOGICAL PROVINCES

DOUGLAS, R.J.W. Department of Energy, Mines and Resources, Geological Survey of Canada. Manuscript map.

29 - 30   TECTONICS

CANADA, Department of Energy, Mines and Resources, Geological Survey of Canada. 1968. *Tectonic Map of Canada.* Map no. 1251A. Prepared by The Tectonic Map of Canada Committee, C.H. Stockwell, Chairman. Ottawa.

Personal Communication:

DOUGLAS, R.J.W. Department of Energy, Mines and Resources, Geological Survey of Canada. Ottawa.

31 - 32   RETREAT OF THE LAST ICE SHEET

PREST, V.K. 1970. Quaternary Geology of Canada, Fig. XII - 15, Stages in the deglaciation of Wisconsin ice. Map. In *Geology and Economic Minerals of Canada.* Economic Geology Report no. 1. Ottawa: Geological Survey of Canada.

33 - 34   GLACIAL GEOLOGY

PREST, V.K., GRANT, D.R. and RAMPTON, V.N. 1968. *Glacial Map of Canada.* Map no. 1253A. Ottawa: Geological Survey of Canada.

35 - 36   POST GLACIAL REBOUND

ANDREWS, J.T. Institute of Arctic and Alpine Research, University of Colorado. Manuscript maps and text. Boulder, Colorado.

37 - 38   SURFACE MATERIALS

CANADA, Department of Energy, Mines and Resources, Geological Survey of Canada. Bulletins, Memoirs, Papers. Ottawa.

CANADA, Department of Mines and Technical Surveys, Geographical Branch. Bulletins, Memoirs, Papers. Ottawa.

HARE, F.K. 1959. *A Photo-Reconnaissance Survey of Labrador-Ungava.* Geographical Branch Memoir no. 6. Ottawa: Department of Mines and Technical Surveys.

UNITED STATES AIR FORCE PROJECT RAND. 1962, 1963. *Reports on areas of the Northwest Territories, Canada.* Series prepared by the Department of Geography, McGill University. Santa Monica, California: The RAND Corporation.

WILSON, J. TUZO, et al. 1954-57. Maps of physiography and surface materials of northern Canada. Unpublished.

39 - 40   WETLANDS

HARE, F.K., FERGUSON, H.L., ANDERSON, J.C. and SCHWARTZ, J. Forthcoming. *Mean Evapotranspiration over Canada, Part 1: Cover and Land Form.* Climatological Series. Department of the Environment, Atmospheric Environment Service.

41 - 42   SOILS

43 - 44   SOIL CLIMATE

CLAYTON, J.S., EHRLICH, W.A., CANN, D.B., DAY, J.H. and MARSHALL, I.B. Forthcoming. *Soils of Canada.* 2 vols. Ottawa: Department of Agriculture, The Canada Soil Survey Committee and The Soil Research Institute.

45 - 46   VEGETATION REGIONS

BRITISH COLUMBIA NATURAL RESOURCES CONFERENCE. 1956. *British Columbia Atlas of Resources.* Edited by J.D. Chapman and D.B. Turner. Vancouver.

CANADA, Department of Forestry, Forest Research Branch. 1961. *Forest Classification of the Maritime Provinces.* Ottawa.

DEAN, W.G. 1952. *Albany River Cover Types.* Map. Ottawa: Department of Mines and Technical Surveys.

DEPARTMENT OF GEOGRAPHY, UNIVERSITY OF SASKATCHEWAN. 1969. *Atlas of Saskatchewan.* Edited by J.H. Richards and K.I. Fung. Saskatoon: University of Saskatchewan.

GILL, C.B. 1969. *The Forests of Manitoba.* Forest Inventory Report no. 10. Winnipeg: Department of Mines and Natural Resources, Forest Service.

GOVERNMENT OF ALBERTA and UNIVERSITY OF ALBERTA. 1969. *Atlas of Alberta.* Edmonton and Toronto: University of Alberta Press in association with the University of Toronto Press.

GRANDTNER, M. 1966. *La Végétation forestière du Québec méridionale.* Québec: Les Presses de l'Université Laval.

HARE, F.K. 1959. *A Photo-Reconnaissance Survey of Labrador - Ungava.* Geographical Branch Memoir no. 6. Ottawa: Department of Mines and Technical Surveys.

KRAJINA, V.J. 1964. *Revision of Bioclimatic Regions and Zones in British Columbia.* Appendix H. Ecology of the Forests of the Pacific Northwest. Vancouver: University of British Columbia.

MACKAY, J.R. 1963. *The Mackenzie Delta Area, N.W.T.* Geographical Branch Memoir no. 8. Ottawa: Department of Mines and Technical Surveys.

MANITOBA, Department of Industry and Commerce. 1960. *Economic Atlas of Manitoba.* Edited by T.R. Weir. Winnipeg.

NEWFOUNDLAND, Royal Commission on Forestry. 1955. *Report.* St. John's.

PORSILD, A.E. 1958. Geographical Distribution of Some Elements in the Flora of Canada. *Geographical Bulletin* 11: 57-77.

RITCHIE, J.C. 1960. The Vegetation of Northern Manitoba, V - Establishing of the Major Zonation. *Arctic* 13: 210-229.

————. 1962. *A Geobotanical Survey of Northern Manitoba.* Technical Paper no. 9. Montréal, New York, Washington: The Arctic Institute of North America.

ROWE, J.S. 1959. *Forest Regions of Canada.* Bulletin no. 123. Ottawa: Department of Northern Affairs and Natural Resources, Forestry Branch.

SJORS, H. 1958. Bogs and Fens in the Hudson Bay Lowlands. *Arctic* 12: 3-19.

TISDALE, E.W. 1947. The Grasslands of the Southern Interior of British Columbia. *Ecology* 28: 346-382.

WATTS, F.B. 1960. The Natural Vegetation of the Southern Great Plains of Canada. *Geographical Bulletin* 14: 25-43.

WILTON, W.C. 1964. *The Forests of Labrador.* Ottawa: Department of Forestry, Forest Research Branch.

Personal Communication:

GAGNON, H. University of Ottawa, Department of Geography. Ottawa.

47   WEATHER STATIONS

CANADA, Department of Transport, Meteorological Branch. 1968. *Climatic Normals/Normales climatiques.* Vol. 1, Temperature/Température. Vol. 2, Precipitation/Précipitation. Toronto.

48   AVERAGE ANNUAL PRECIPITATION

CANADA, Department of Transport, Meteorological Branch. 1967-70. Mean Annual Amount of Precipitation. Map in *Atlas of Climatic Maps/Atlas de cartes climatiques.* Series 1-10. Toronto.

49   AVERAGE ANNUAL POTENTIAL EVAPOTRANSPIRATION

CHAPMAN, L.J. and BROWN, D.M. 1966. Potential Evapotranspiration. Map in *The Climates of Canada for Agriculture.* Canada Land Inventory report no. 3. Ottawa: Department of Forestry and Rural Development.

————. 1966. Average Annual Water Deficit. Map in *The Climates of Canada for Agriculture.* Canada Land Inventory report no. 3. Ottawa: Department of Forestry and Rural Development.

50   DEGREE DAYS IN THE GROWING SEASON

CHAPMAN, L.J. and BROWN, D.M. 1966. Degree Days above 42°F. Map in *The Climates of Canada for Agriculture.* Canada Land Inventory report no. 3. Ottawa: Department of Forestry and Rural Development.

51   LENGTH OF THE GROWING SEASON

BOUGHNER, C.C. 1964. *The Distribution of Growing Degree Days in Canada.* Canadian Meteorological Memoir no. 17. Toronto: Department of Transport.

CANADA, Department of Transport. 1968. *Climatic Normals/Normales climatiques.* Vol. 1, Temperature/Température. Toronto.

51   START OF THE GROWING SEASON

52   END OF THE GROWING SEASON

**   FROST FREE PERIOD**

53   LAST FROST IN SPRING

**   FIRST FROST IN AUTUMN**

CHAPMAN, L.J. and BROWN, D.M. 1966. Start of the Growing Season. End of the Growing Season. Mean Frost Free Period. Mean Spring Frost Date. Mean Fall Frost Date. Maps in *The Climates of Canada for Agriculture.* Canada Land Inventory report no. 3. Ottawa: Department of Forestry and Rural Development.

54 - 56   SNOW COVER

POTTER, J.G. 1966. Median Depth (inches) of Snow Cover. Maps in *Snow Cover. Climatological Studies* no. 3. Toronto: Department of Transport, Meteorological Branch.

57   NUMBER OF DAYS WITH PRECIPITATION

CANADA, Department of Mines and Technical Surveys, Geographical Branch. 1958. Mean Annual Number of Days with Measurable Precipitation. Map in *Atlas of Canada, 1957*. Ottawa.

58   PRECIPITATION REGIONS

CANADA, Department of Transport, Meteorological Branch. 1968. *Climatic Normals/Normales climatiques*. Vol. 2, Precipitation/Précipitation. Toronto.

59 - 60   AVERAGE MONTHLY PRECIPITATION

CANADA, Department of Transport, Meteorological Branch. 1967-70. Mean Monthly Amount of Precipitation April through September. Maps in *Atlas of Climatic Maps/Atlas de cartes climatologiques*. Series 1-10. Toronto.

61 - 62   AVERAGE PRECIPITATION

CANADA, Department of Transport, Meteorological Branch. 1968. *Climatic Normals/Normales climatiques*. Vol. 2, Precipitation/Précipitation. Toronto.

63 - 70   AVERAGE DAILY MINIMUM AND AVERAGE DAILY MAXIMUM TEMPERATURES

CANADA, Department of Transport, Meteorological Branch. 1967-70. Mean Daily Minimum Temperatures °F, and Mean Daily Maximum Temperatures °F. Maps in *Atlas of Climatic Maps/Atlas de cartes climatologiques*. Series 1-10. Toronto.

71 - 72   INDEX OF EXPLORERS

Chambers's Encyclopaedia. 1966. Oxford, London, Edinburgh, New York, Toronto, Paris, Brunswick, Sydney, Wellington, Tokyo: Pergamon Press.

Dictionary of Canadian Biography/Dictionnaire biographique du Canada. 1966-72. Toronto: University of Toronto Press. Québec: Les Presses de l'Université Laval.

Encyclopaedia Britannica. 1970. Chicago, London, Toronto, Geneva, Sydney, Tokyo, Manila: Encyclopaedia Britannica Inc.

Encyclopedia Canadiana. 1963. Ottawa: The Canadiana Company Limited.

The Dictionary of National Biography. 1961. The Concise Dictionary, Parts 1 and 2. London. Oxford University Press.

THOMPSON, D. 1966-69. *Men and Meridians*. 3 vols. Ottawa: Queen's Printer.

73   EXPLORATION OF EASTERN AND CENTRAL NORTH AMERICA, 1524 TO 1912

BUTTERFIELD, CONSUL WILLSHIRE. 1898. *History of Brulé's Discoveries and Explorations, 1610-1626*. Cleveland: The Helman-Taylor Company.

CHAMPAGNE, ANTOINE. 1968. *Les La Vérendrye et le poste de l'Ouest*. Les Cahiers de l'institut d'Histoire no. 12. Québec: Les Presses de l'Université Laval.

DAVIES, K.G., ed. 1963. *Northern Quebec and Labrador Journals and Correspondence, 1819-1835*. London: The Hudson's Bay Record Society.

Dictionary of Canadian Biography/Dictionnaire biographique du Canada. 1966-72. Toronto: University of Toronto Press. Québec: Les Presses de l'Université Laval.

FLAHERTY, ROBERT J. 1918. Two Traverses across Ungava Peninsula, Labrador. *Geographical Review* 6: 116-132.

OTTAWA. Public Archives of Canada. Archives des Colonies - Paris. MG 1 C11E, 16: 31-45.

PRICHARD, H.H. 1911. *Through Trackless Labrador*. New York: Sturgis and Walton.

Rapports sur les missions du diocèse de Québec. 1859-74. 21 vols. Québec: L'Association de la Propagation de la Foi.

VIGNERAS, L.A. 1957. El Viaje de Esteban Gomez a Norte America. *Revista de Indias*. Vol. 68. Madrid.

WHITE, JAMES. c.1924. *Exploration in Labrador Peninsula*. Map. Ottawa.

WROTH, LAWRENCE C. 1970. *The Voyages of Giovanni da Verrazzano, 1524-1528*. New Haven, Connecticut: Yale University Press.

74   EXPLORATION OF HUDSON BAY AND THE WESTERN INTERIOR, 1610 TO 1904

BAKER, J.N.L. 1967. *History of Geographical Discovery and Exploration*. New York: Cooper Square Publishers Inc.

BELL, C.N. 1928. *The Journal of Henry Kelsey*. Winnipeg: The Historical and Scientific Society of Manitoba.

BLANCHET, GUY. 1949. "Thelewey - aza - yeth". *The Beaver* September: 8-11.

BODILY, R.B. 1928. *The Voyage of Captain Thomas James for the discovery of the Northwest Passage*. London: J.M. Dent.

BURPEE, L., ed. 1907. York Factory to the Blackfeet Country. *Transactions of the Royal Society of Canada/Mémoires de la Société royale du Canada*. Series 3, vol. 1, section 2: 307-359.

CAMSELL, CHARLES. 1916. *An Exploration of the Tazin and Taltson Rivers*. Memoir no. 84. Ottawa: Geological Survey of Canada.

CANADA, Department of the Interior. 1916. *The Yukon Territory: its History and Resources*. Ottawa.

CHRISTY, MILLER. 1894. *The Voyages of Captain Luke Foxe and Captain Thomas James in search of a Northwest Passage*. London: Hakluyt Society.

DAVIDSON, G. 1918. *The Northwest Company*. Reprint 1967. New York: Russell and Russell.

74 (cont'd.)

DAVIES, K.G., ed. 1963. *Northern Quebec and Labrador Journals and Correspondence, 1819-1835*. London: The Hudson's Bay Record Society.

DOBBS, A. 1744. *An Account of the Countries Adjoining to Hudson's Bay in the North West part of America*. London: J. Robinson.

DOUGHTY, A. and MARTIN, C., eds. 1929. *The Kelsey Papers*. Ottawa: King's Printer.

GATES, C.M. 1933. *Five Fur Traders of the Northwest*. Minneapolis: University of Minnesota Press.

GLOVER, R., ed. 1958. *A Journey from Prince of Wales Fort in Hudson's Bay to the Northern Ocean in 1769-72* by Samuel Hearne. Toronto: Macmillan of Canada.

GOSCH, C.A. 1897. *Danish Arctic Expeditions*. London: Hakluyt Society.

INNIS, H.A. 1928. Peter Pond and the Influence of Captain Cook on Exploration. *Transactions of the Royal Society of Canada/Mémoires de la Société royale du Canada*. Series 3, vol. 22, section 2: 131-143.

————. 1930. *Peter Pond, Fur Trader and Adventurer*. Toronto: Irwin and Gordon.

ISBISTER, A.K. 1845. Some Account of Peel River, North America. *Journal of the Royal Geographical Society* 15: 332-345.

KIRK, J.P. and PARNELL, C. 1942. Campbell of the Yukon. *The Beaver* December: 23-27.

LAMB, W.KAYE. 1960. *The Letters and Journals of Simon Fraser, 1806-1808*. Toronto: Macmillan of Canada.

LENT, D. GENEVA. 1963. *West of the Mountains*. Seattle: University of Washington Press.

LEVESON-GOWER, R.H. 1934. William Tomison. *The Beaver* March: 24.

MACFARLANE, R. 1891. On an Expedition down the Begh-ula or Anderson River. *Canadian Record of Science*. Vol. 4, no. 1: 28-53.

MACGREGOR, J.G. 1954. *Behold the Shining Mountains*. Edmonton: Applied Arts Products.

MACKAY, DOUGLAS. 1936. *The Honourable Company*. Indianapolis: Bobbs-Merrill Company.

MACKENZIE, ALEXANDER. 1801. *Voyages from Montreal through the continent of North America to the Frozen and Pacific Oceans, in 1789 and 1793*. London: R. Noble.

MORICE, ADRIEN GABRIEL. 1897. *Au pays de l'ours noir: chez les sauvages de la Colombie-Britannique*. Paris: Delhomme et Briguet.

————. 1904. Du lac Stuart à l'océan Pacifique. *Bulletin de la Société Neuchâteloise de Géographie* 25: 32-80.

————. 1912. Exploration de la rivière Bulkley. *Bulletin de la Société Neuchâteloise de Géographie* 21: 101-126.

MORTON, A.S. 1939. *A History of the Canadian West to 1870-71*. Toronto: Thomas Nelson and Sons.

————. 1944. *Sir George Simpson*. Toronto: J.M. Dent and Sons.

PARNELL, C. 1942. Campbell of the Yukon. *The Beaver* June: 4-6 and December: 16-18.

PETITOT, ÉMILE. 1875. Géographie de l'Athabaskaw-Mackenzie. *Bulletin de la Société de géographie*. Series 6, vol. 10, July - December: 5.

————. 1887. *Les Grands Esquimaux*. Paris: E. Plon, Nourrit et Cie.

————. 1889. *Quinze ans sous le cercle polaire*. Paris: Librairie de la Société des gens de lettres.

————. 1891. *Autour du Grand lac des Esclaves*. Paris: Nouvelle Librairie parisienne.

————. 1893. *Exploration de la région du Grand lac des Ours*. Paris: Téqui, Librairie-Éditeur.

RICH, E.E. 1958-59. *The History of the Hudson's Bay Company, 1670-1870*. 2 vols. London: The Hudson's Bay Record Society.

RUGGLES, R.I. 1958. *The Historical Geography and Cartography of the Canadian West 1670-1795*. Ph.D. thesis. University of London, England.

SHEPPE, W., ed. 1962. *First Man West*. Berkeley: University of California Press.

TYRRELL, J.B., ed. 1911. *A Journey from Prince of Wales Fort in Hudson's Bay to the Northern Ocean in 1769-72* by Samuel Hearne. Toronto: The Champlain Society.

————. 1917. Early Exploration of the Churchill River. *Geographical Review* 3: 375-381.

WALLACE, J.N. 1929. *The Wintering Partners on Peace River*. Ottawa: Thorburn and Abbot.

WILLIAMS, GLYNDWR. 1963. Captain Coats and Exploration along the East Main. *The Beaver* Winter: 4-13.

WILSON, J.T. 1949. New Light on Hearne. *The Beaver* June: 14-18.

75   EXPLORATION OF THE PACIFIC COAST, 1741 TO 1794

BANCROFT, H.H. 1887. *History of British Columbia*. San Francisco: The History Company.

BOLTON, H.E. 1927. *Fray Juan Crespi*. Berkeley: University of California Press.

COOK, JAMES. 1784. *A voyage to the Pacific Ocean, undertaken by the command of His Majesty, for making Discoveries in the Northern Hemisphere 1776-1780*. London: W.A. Strahan.

ESPINOSA Y TELLO, JOSÉ DE, ed. 1802. *Relacion del viaje hecho por las goletas Sutil y Mexicana en el año de 1792 para reconocer el estrecho de Fuca*. 2 vols. Madrid: la imprenta real.

GALAUP DE LA PÉROUSE, J.-F. DE. 1799. *A Voyage Round the World performed in the years 1785-1788 by the Boussole and Astrolabe*. London: G.G. and J. Robinson.

GOLDER, F.A. 1925. *Bering's Voyages*. New York: American Geographical Society.

MOURELLE, F.A. 1781. Journal of a Voyage in 1775 to Explore the Coast of America. In Daines Barrington's *Miscellanies*. London: J. Nichols.

75 (cont'd.)

VANCOUVER, GEORGE. 1798. *A Voyage of Discovery to the North Pacific Ocean and Round the World 1790-95.* London: G.G. and J. Robinson and J. Edwards.

WAGNER, H.R. 1937. *The Cartography of the Northwest Coast of America to 1800.* Berkeley: University of California Press.

75 - 76   THE SEARCH FOR A NORTHWEST PASSAGE, 1576 TO 1944

AMUNDSEN, R. 1908. *The North West Passage, being the record of a voyage of exploration of the ship "Gjoa" 1903-7.* London: Archibald Constable and Company Ltd.

ARMSTRONG, A. 1857. *A Personal Narrative of the Discovery of the Northwest Passage.* London: Hurst and Blacklett.

COLLINSON, R. 1857. *The Three Voyages of Martin Frobisher.* London: Hakluyt Society.

FRANKLIN, JOHN. 1823. *Narrative of a Journey to the Shores of the Polar Sea 1819-1822.* London: John Murray.

————. 1828. *Narrative of a Second Expedition to the Shores of the Polar Sea 1825-27.* London: John Murray.

LARSEN, H.A. 1947. The Conquest of the North West Passage: The Arctic Voyages of the "St. Roch" 1940-44. *Geographical Journal* 110: 1-16.

MARKHAM, A.H. 1853. *The Voyages and Works of John Davis the Navigator.* London: Hakluyt Society.

MARKHAM, C.R. 1881. *The Voyages of William Baffin 1612-1622.* London: Hakluyt Society.

M'CLINTOCK, F.L. 1859. *The Voyage of the Fox in the Arctic Sea: a Narrative of the Discovery of the Fate of Sir John Franklin and his Companions.* London: John Murray.

OSBORN, S. 1857. *The Discovery of the Northwest Passage by HMS Investigator, Captain M'Clure, 1850-54.* London: William Blackwood and Sons.

PARRY, W.E. 1821. *Journal of a Voyage for the Discovery of a Northwest Passage from the Atlantic to the Pacific 1819-20.* London: John Murray.

————. 1824. *Journal of a Second Voyage for the Discovery of a Northwest Passage from the Atlantic to the Pacific, 1821-23.* London: John Murray.

RAE, JOHN. 1850. *Narrative of an Expedition to the Shores of the Arctic Sea 1846-47.* London: T. and W. Boone.

RASMUSSEN, KNUD. 1927. *Across Arctic America.* London: G. Putnam's Sons.

ROSS, JOHN. 1819. *A Voyage of Discovery under the Admiralty in His Majesty's ships Isabella and Alexander for the purpose of exploring Baffin's Bay.* London: Longman, Hurst, Rees, Orme and Brown.

ROSS, SIR JOHN. 1835. *Narrative of a Second voyage in search of a northwest passage and of a residence in the Arctic regions during the years 1829-1833.* London: A.W. Webster.

SIMPSON, T. and DEASE, P. 1838, 1839, 1840. An Account of Recent Arctic Discoveries. *Journal of the Royal Geographical Society* 8: 213-226, 9: 325-331, 10: 268-275.

SWITHINBANK, C. 1960. *Ice Atlas of Arctic Canada.* Ottawa: Defence Research Board.

75 - 76   THE SEARCH FOR FRANKLIN, 1847 TO 1879

ANDERSON, JAMES. 1940, 1941. Chief Factor James Anderson's Back River Journal of 1855. *Canadian Field Naturalist* 54: 63, 55: 9.

BELCHER, SIR EDWARD. 1855. *The Last of the Arctic Voyages.* London: L. Reeve.

COLLINSON, R. 1855. An Account of the Proceedings of HMS Enterprise from Bering Strait to Cambridge Bay. *Journal of the Royal Geographical Society* 25: 194-206.

CYRIAX, R.J. 1942. Sir James Clark Ross and the Franklin Expedition. *Polar Record.* Vol. 3, no. 24: 528-541.

Discoveries in the Arctic Sea between Baffin Bay and Melville Island. Map. London: John Arrowsmith. 1852.

GILDER, W.H. 1881. *Schwatka's Search.* New York: Charles Scribner's and Sons.

HALL, C.F. 1879. *Narrative of the Second Arctic Expedition.* Edited by J. Nourse. Washington: Government Printing Office.

KENNEDY, W. 1853. Report on the Return of Lady Franklin's Vessel the Prince Albert under the command of Mr. William Kennedy, from the Arctic Regions. *Journal of the Royal Geographical Society* 23: 122-129.

M'CLINTOCK, F.L. 1859. *The Voyage of the Fox in the Arctic Sea: a Narrative of the Discovery of the Fate of Sir John Franklin and his Companions.* London: John Murray.

MCDOUGALL, G.F. 1857. *The Eventfull Voyage of HM discovery ship Resolute to the Arctic Regions 1852, 1853, 1854.* London: Longman, Brown, Green, Longmans and Roberts.

RAE, JOHN. 1852. Journey from Great Bear Lake to Wollaston Land and Recent Explorations along the South and East Coast of Victoria Land. *Journal of the Royal Geographical Society* 22: 73-97.

————. 1855. Arctic Exploration with Information Respecting Sir John Franklin's Missing Party. *Journal of the Royal Geographical Society* 25: 246-256.

RICHARDSON, JOHN. 1851. *Arctic Searching Expedition: a journal of a boat voyage through Rupert's Land and the Arctic Sea in search of the discovery ships under the command of Sir John Franklin.* London: Longman, Brown, Green and Longmans.

SEEMANN, B. 1853. *Narrative of the Voyage of HMS Herald during the years 1845-51.* London: Reeve and Company.

SUTHERLAND, P. 1852. *Journal of a Voyage in Baffin's Bay and Barrow Straits in the years 1850-51.* London: Longman, Brown, Green and Longmans.

77   EXPLORATION OF THE ARCTIC, 1587 TO 1941

Additions to Captain Comer's Map of Southampton Island. *Bulletin of the American Geographical Society* 45: 516-518.

77 (cont'd.)

BERNIER, J.E. 1910. *Report on the Dominion of Canada Government Expedition to the Arctic Islands and Hudson Strait on board the D.G.S. "Arctic".* Ottawa: Department of Marine and Fisheries.

————. 1939. *Master Mariner and Arctic Explorer: A Narrative of Sixty Years at Sea from the Logs and Yarns of Captain J.E. Bernier, FRGS, FRES.* Ottawa: Le Droit.

BOAS, FRANZ. 1884. A Journey in Cumberland Sound and on the West Shore of Davis Strait in 1883 and 1884. *Journal of the American Geographical Society* 16: 241-272.

BRAY, REYNOLD and ROWLEY, GRAHAM. 1938. The Canadian Arctic: A winter in Foxe Basin. *The Times* 16 May: 15. London.

CANADA, Department of Marine and Fisheries. 1898. *Report of the Expedition to Hudson Bay and Cumberland Gulf in the steamship "Diana" under the command of William Wakeham.* Ottawa.

————. (n.d.) *Report on the Dominion Government Expedition to the Northern Waters and Arctic Archipelago of the D.G.S. "Arctic" in 1910.* Ottawa.

COMER, GEORGE. 1910. A Geographical Description of Southampton Island and notes upon the Eskimo. *Bulletin of the American Geographical Society* 42: 84-90.

DAVIS, C.H. 1876. *Narrative of the North Polar Expedition, U.S. Ship "Polaris", Captain Charles Francis Hall commanding.* Washington: Government Printing Office.

FAIRLEY, T.C. 1959. *Sverdrup's Arctic Adventures.* London: Longmans, Green and Company.

FLINT, M.S. 1949. *Operation Canon: Turner of the Arctic.* London: The Bible Churchmen's Missionary Society.

GREELY, ADOLPHUS W. 1886. *Three Years of Arctic service: an Account of the Lady Franklin Bay Expedition of 1881-84, and the Attainment of the Farthest North.* New York: Charles Scribner's and Sons.

————. 1888. *International Polar Expedition: Report of the Proceedings of the United States Expedition to Lady Franklin Bay, Grinnell Land.* Vols. 1, 2. Washington: Government Printing Office.

————. 1906. *A Handbook of Polar Discoveries.* Boston: Little, Brown and Co.

HAKLUYT, RICHARD. 1589. *The principall navigations voiages and discoveries of the English nations, made by sea or over land to the most remote and farthest distant quarters of the earth at any time within the compasse of these 1500 yeares: devided into those several parts.* Reprint 1965. 2 vols. Cambridge: Hakluyt Society.

HAYES, I.I. 1867. *The Open Polar Sea: A Narrative of a Voyage of Discovery towards the North Pole in the schooner "United States".* New York: Hurd and Houghton.

HOBBS, WILLIAM H. 1937. *Peary.* New York: Macmillan and Company.

INGLEFIELD, E.A. 1853. *A Summer Search for Sir John Franklin, with a peep into the Polar Basin.* London: Thomas Harrison.

KANE, E.K. 1856. *Arctic Explorations: The Second Grinnell Expedition in Search of Sir John Franklin, 1853, 1854, 1855.* Vol. 2. Philadelphia: Childs and Peterson.

————. 1894. *Arctic Explorations: in search of Sir John Franklin.* London: Thomas Nelson and Sons.

LOW, A.P. 1906. *Report on the Dominion Government Expedition to Hudson Bay and the Arctic Islands on board the DGS "Neptune" 1903-1904.* Ottawa: Government Printing Bureau.

MACMILLAN, DONALD B. 1918. *Four Years in the White North.* New York: Harper and Brothers Publishers.

MANNING, T.H. 1943. The Foxe Basin Coasts of Baffin Island. *Geographical Journal* 101: 225-251.

MARKHAM, A.H. 1878. *The Great Frozen Sea: A Personal Narrative of the Voyage of the Alert during the Arctic Expedition of 1875-6.* London: Daldy, Isbister and Company.

————. 1880. *The Voyages and Works of John Davis the Navigator.* London: Hakluyt Society.

MARKHAM, C.R. 1881. *The Voyages of William Baffin 1612-1622.* London: Hakluyt Society.

————. 1889. *A Life of John Davis, the Navigator.* London: George Philip and Son.

MATHIASSEN, THERKEL. 1945. *Report on the Fifth Thule Expedition, 1921-24.* Vol. 1. Copenhagen: Gyldendalske Boghandel, Nordisk Forlag.

MILLWARD, A.E. 1930. *Southern Baffin Island.* Ottawa: Department of the Interior.

MUNN, H.T. 1919. Southampton Island. *Geographical Journal* 54: 52-55.

NARES, G.S. 1878. *Narrative of a Voyage to the Polar Sea during 1875-6 in H.M. Ships "Alert" and "Discovery".* London: Sampson Low, Marston, Searle and Rivington.

PARRY, W.E. 1828. *Narrative of an Attempt to Reach the North Pole in boats fitted for the purpose and attached to His Majesty's ship "Hecla" in the year MDCCCXXVII, under the command of Captain William Edward Parry.* London: John Murray.

PEARY, R.E. 1910. *The North Pole, its discovery in 1909 under the auspices of the Peary Arctic Club.* New York: Frederick A. Stokes Company.

SOPER, J.D. 1928. *A Faunal Investigation of Southern Baffin Island.* Ottawa: King's Printer.

————. 1930. Explorations in Foxe Peninsula and along the West Coast of Baffin Island. *Geographical Review* 20: 397-424.

STEFANSSON, V. 1921. *The Friendly Arctic.* New York: Macmillan and Company.

TREMBLAY, ALFRED. 1921. *Cruise of the Minnie Maud.* Québec: The Arctic Exchange and Publishing Ltd.

TURNER, CANON JOHN H. *Diaries.* Microfilm M120, reels 1 and 2. Anglican Church of Canada, General Synod Archives, Toronto.

BAIN, J.W. 1958. Surveys of a Water Route between Lake Ontario and the Ottawa River by the Royal Engineers, 1819-27. *Ontario History*. Vol. 50, no. 1:15-28.

BLAKE, W. 1868. *Stikine River, 1863*. In Executive document 177, part 2, 40th Cong., 2nd sess. Washington.

BRITISH COLUMBIA, Department of Lands and Works. 1871. *British Columbia*. Map. ("Trutch" map).

CANADA, Department of the Interior. 1892, 1897, 1898, 1900. *Annual Reports*. Ottawa.

CANADA, Geological Survey of Canada. *Annual Reports*. Ottawa.

—————. *Reports of Progress*. Montréal, Ottawa.

CANADA, Royal Commission on the Canadian Pacific Railway. 1882. *Report*. Vol. 3. Ottawa: S. Stephenson.

DAWSON, G.M. 1898. Narrative of an Exploration made in 1887 in the Yukon District. In *The Yukon Territory*. London: Downey and Company.

DAWSON, S.J. 1859. *Report of the Exploration of the Country between Lake Superior and the Red River Settlement and between the Latter Place and the Assiniboine and the Saskatchewan*. Toronto: John Lovell.

FLEMING, SANDFORD. 1874. *Report of Progress on the Explorations and Surveys on the Canadian Pacific Railway up to January, 1874*. Ottawa: McLean, Roger and Company.

—————. 1877. *Report on the Surveys and Explorations on the Canadian Pacific Railway up to January 1877*. Ottawa: McLean, Roger and Company.

GANONG, W. 1897. A Monograph of the Cartography of the Province of New Brunswick. *Transactions of the Royal Society of Canada/Mémoires de la Société royale du Canada*. Series 1, vol. 3, section 2: 313-427.

—————. 1906. Additions and Corrections to Monographs on the Place-nomenclature, Cartography, Historic Sites, Boundaries and Settlements of the Province of New Brunswick. *Transactions of the Royal Society of Canada/Mémoires de la Société royale du Canada*. Series 2, vol. 12, section 2: 3-158.

GLOVER, R., ed. 1962. *David Thompson's Narrative 1784-1812*. Toronto: The Champlain Society.

GUILLET, EDWIN. 1957. *The Valley of the Trent*. Toronto: The Champlain Society.

HANBURY, D.T. 1900. A Journey from Chesterfield Inlet to Great Slave Lake, 1898-1899. *Geographical Journal* 16: 63-77.

—————. 1903. Through the Barren Ground of Northeastern Canada to the Arctic Coast. *Geographical Journal* 22: 178-190.

HARVEY, D.C., ed. 1935. *Holland's Description of Cape Breton Island and other Documents*. Halifax: Public Archives of Nova Scotia.

HIND, H.Y. 1860. *Narrative of the Canadian Red River Exploring Expedition of 1857 and the Assiniboine and Saskatchewan Exploring Expedition of 1858*. 2 vols. London: Longman, Green, Longman and Roberts.

HORETZKY, CHARLES. 1874. *Canada on the Pacific*. Montréal: Dawson Brothers.

HOWAY, F.W. 1971. (Reprint). The Royal Engineers in British Columbia. *The Canadian Surveyor* March: 62-67.

JUKES, J.B. 1842. *Excursions in Newfoundland*. 2 vols. London: John Murray.

LEGGET, R. 1955. *Rideau Waterway*. Toronto: University of Toronto Press.

MACGREGOR, J.G. 1966. *Peter Fidler, Canada's Forgotten Surveyor*. Toronto: McLelland and Stewart.

MACKAY, CORDAY. 1946. The Collins Overland Telegraph. *British Columbia Historical Quarterly* 10: 187-215.

MURRAY, FLORENCE, ed. 1963. *Muskoka and Haliburton 1615-1875*. Toronto: The Champlain Society.

PALLISER, JOHN. 1863. *The Journals, Detailed Reports and Observations relative to the Exploration by Captain Palliser of North America during the years 1857, 1858, 1859 and 1860*. 2 vols. London: Eyre and Spottiswoode.

PALMER, HOWARD. 1918. Early Explorations in British Columbia for the Canadian Pacific Railway. *Bulletin of the Geographical Society of Philadelphia 16: 75-91*.

PALMER, H.S. 1859. *A Report on a Portion of British Columbia*. (to Colonel Moody, R.E.). Mimeographed. New Westminster.

PEMBERTON, J.D. 1860. *Facts and Figures relating to Vancouver Island and British Columbia*. London: Longman, Green, Longman and Roberts.

RAYMOND, W.O. 1910. *The River Saint John*. Saint John: John A. Bowes.

ROBINSON, NOEL. c.1915. *Blazing the Trail through the Rockies*. Vancouver.

SCHWATKA, LIEUT. F.G. 1884. The Alaska Military Reconnaissance of 1883. *Science* 3: 220; 246.

TAYLOR, D. 1839. Journal in *Report of the Commissioners on the Survey of the Ottawa River*. 13th Parl. of Upper Canada, 4th sess. Toronto.

THOMPSON, D. 1966- 69. *Men and Meridians*. 3 vols. Ottawa: Queen's Printer.

TYRRELL, J.B., ed. 1934. *The Journals of Samuel Hearne and Philip Turnor*. Toronto: The Champlain Society.

VICTORIA, British Columbia Archives. Sketch Map showing the Proposed Route of the Western Union Telegraph between Fort Fraser and Stikeen River, British Columbia. Manuscript map. 1874.

VICTORIA, British Columbia Archives. Explorations by the party under the command of Major F.L. Pope, Ass't Engineer. Manuscript map. (n.d.)

79 - 80   POSTS OF THE CANADIAN FUR TRADE, 1600 TO 1870

BAIN, J., ed. 1901. *Travels and Adventures in Canada and the Indian Territories between the years 1760 and 1776, by Alexander Henry, Fur Trader*. Toronto: G.N. Morang.

BEGG, A. 1894. *History of British Columbia*. Toronto: W. Briggs.

BIGGAR, H.P., ed. 1922-36. *The Works of Samuel de Champlain*. 6 vols. Toronto: The Champlain Society.

79 - 80 (cont'd.)

BIGGAR, H.P., ed. 1965. (Reprint) *The Early Trading Companies of New France*. New York: Argonaut Press Ltd.

BOURINOT, J.G. 1883. Some old forts by the Sea. *Transactions of the Royal Society of Canada/Mémoires de la Société royale du Canada*. Series 1, vol. 1, section 2: 71-80.

CARON, I. 1918. *Journal de l'expédition du Chevalier de Troyes à la baie d'Hudson en 1686*. Beauceville: La Compagnie de l'Éclaireur.

DAVIES, K.G., ed. 1963. *Northern Quebec and Labrador Journals and Correspondence 1819-1935*. London: The Hudson's Bay Record Society.

DELANGLEY, JEAN. 1948. *Life and Voyages of Louis Jolliet, 1645-1700*. Chicago: Institute of Jesuit History.

DESBRISAY, MATHEW BYLES. 1895. *History of the County of Lunenburg*. Toronto: M. Briggs.

Dictionary of Canadian Biography/Dictionnaire biographique du Canada. 1966-72. Toronto: University of Toronto Press. Québec: Les Presses de l'Université Laval.

FOLWELL, W.W. 1921-30. *A History of Minnesota*. Saint Paul: Minnesota Historical Society.

GALBRAITH, JOHN S. 1949. The Hudson's Bay Company under Fire. *Canadian Historical Review* December: 322-335.

GANONG, WILLIAM F. 1899. A Monograph of Historic Sites in the Province of New Brunswick. *Transactions of the Royal Society of Canada/Mémoires de la Société royale du Canada*. Series 2, vol. 5, section 2: 213-357.

—————. 1902. Dochet (St. Croix) Island - A Monograph. *Transactions of the Royal Society of Canada/Mémoires de la Société royale du Canada*. Series 2, vol. 8, section 2: 127-231.

—————. 1906. The History of Miscou. *Acadiensis*. Vol. 6, no. 2: 79-94.

—————. ed. 1908. *The description and natural history of the coasts of North America by Nicolas Denys*. Toronto: The Champlain Society.

GIROUARD, DÉSIRÉ. 1893. *Lake St. Louis, old and new, illustrated, and Cavalier de La Salle*. Montréal: Poirier, Bessette and Company.

GOSSELIN, AUGUSTE. 1894. Le Fondateur de la Présentation (Ogdensburg): L'abbé Picquet (1734-1760). *Transactions of the Royal Society of Canada/Mémoires de la Société royale du Canada*. Series 1, vol. 12, section 1: 3-28.

GRAHAM, CLARA. 1945. *Fur and Gold in the Kootenays*. Vancouver: Wrigley Printing Company.

GREAT BRITAIN, Privy Council, Judicial Committee. 1927. *In the matter of the boundary between the Dominion of Canada and the colony of Newfoundland in the Labrador Peninsula, between the Dominion of Canada of the one part and the colony of Newfoundland of the other part*. Vol. 7 of the Joint Appendix, part 19. London: W. Clowes and Sons.

HANNAY, JAMES. 1879. *The History of Acadia from its first discovery to its surrender to England by the Treaty of Paris*. Saint John: J. and A. McMillan.

HULBURT, ARCHER BUTLER. 1903. *Portage Paths, the Keys of the Continent*. Cleveland: The Authur H. Clark Company.

KELLOGG, L.P. 1935. *The British Regime in Wisconsin and the Northwest*. Madison: State Historical Society of Wisconsin.

—————. 1968. (Reprint) *The French Regime in Wisconsin and the Northwest*. New York: Cooper Square Publishers Inc.

MACFARLANE, R.O. 1935. Indian Trade in Nova Scotia to 1764. *Canadian Historical Association, Annual Report 1934*. Toronto: University of Toronto Press.

MAINE HISTORICAL SOCIETY. 1890-99. *Collections and Proceedings*. Series 2. 10 vols. Portland.

MALCHELOSSE, GÉRARD. 1957. La Salle et le fort Saint-Joseph des Miamis. *Cahiers des Dix* 22: 83-103.

MASSON, LOUIS FRANÇOIS RODRIGUE, ed. 1889-90. *Les Bourgeois de la Compagnie du Nord-Ouest: récits de voyages, lettres et rapports inédits relatifs au Nord-Ouest canadien*. 2 vols. Québec: A. Coté et Compagnie.

MORICE, A.G. 1904. *The History of the Northern Interior of British Columbia formerly New Caledonia, 1660-1880*. Toronto: William Briggs.

MURPHY, EDMUND R. 1941. *Henry de Tonty: Fur Trader of the Mississippi*. Baltimore: Johns Hopkins Press.

NUTE, GRACE LEE. c.1944. *Lake Superior*. Indianapolis: Bobbs-Merrill Company.

ORMSBY, MARGARET A. 1958. *British Columbia: A History*. Toronto: Macmillan of Canada.

OTTAWA. Public Archives of Canada. Archives des Colonies - Paris. MG1 C11A, vols 4-10.

OTTAWA. Public Archives of Canada. Archives des Colonies - Paris. MG1 C11E, vol. 13.

OTTAWA. Public Archives of Canada. Hudson's Bay Company Archives. Microfilm. (By permission of the Hudson's Bay Company).

OTTAWA. Public Archives of Canada. Public Record Office - London: Colonial Office Papers. MG 11 C.O. 42, vol. 105.

OTTAWA. Public Archives of Canada. Public Record Office - London: Colonial Office Papers. MG 11 "Q" series, part 1.

OTTAWA. Public Archives of Canada. War Office - London. MG 12, vol. 14.

PARKMAN, FRANCIS. 1965. (Reprint). *Pioneers of France in the New World*. Vol. 1 of series *France and England in North America*. New York: Frederick Ungar Publishing Company.

PHILLIPS, P.C. 1926. *The Fur Trade in the Maumee-Wabush Country*. Bloomington: Indiana University.

PRESTON, RICHARD A. 1958. *Royal Fort Frontenac*. Toronto: The Champlain Society.

QUAIFE, MILO MILTON. 1913. *Chicago and the Old Northwest, 1673-1835: a study in the evolution of the northwestern frontier together with a history of Fort Dearborn*. Chicago: The University of Chicago Press.

79 - 80 (cont'd.)

RICH, E.E. 1941-44. *The Letters of John McLoughlin from Fort Vancouver to the Governor and Committee, 1825-1846.* 3 vols. London: The Hudson's Bay Record Society.

————. 1954. *Moose Fort Journals, 1783-85.* London: The Hudson's Bay Record Society.

————.1958-59.*The History of the Hudson's Bay Company, 1670-1870.* 2 vols. London: The Hudson's Bay Record Society.

ROBINSON, PERCY J. 1933. *Toronto During the French Regime.* Toronto: Ryerson Press.

RUSSELL, NELSON V. 1939. *The British Regime in Michigan and the Old Northwest, 1760-1796.* Northfield, Minn.:Carleton College.

SEVERANCE, F.H. 1917. *An old frontier of France: the Niagara region and adjacent lakes under French control.* New York: Dodd, Mead and Company.

SEWALL, JOHN. 1907. *The Story of the Penobscot.* Detroit: Simon J. Murphy.

SMYTHE, T. 1968. *Thematic Study of the Fur Trade in the Canadian West, 1670-1870.* Unpublished. Ottawa: Historic Sites and Monuments Board of Canada.

STEVENS, WAYNE E. c.1928. The Northwest fur trade. *University of Illinois Studies in the Social Sciences.* Vol. 14, no. 3: 307-610.

STORY, NORAH. 1967. *The Oxford Companion to Canadian History and Literature.* Toronto, London, New York: Oxford University Press.

SULTE, B. 1870. *Histoire de la ville des Trois-Rivières et de ses environs.* Montréal: Eusèbe Sénécal.

THWAITES, REUBEN GOLD, ed. 1896-1901. *The Jesuit Relations and Allied Documents.* 73 vols. Cleveland: Burrows Bros. Company.

VOLWILER, A.T. 1926. *George Groghan and the Westward Movement, 1741-1782.* Cleveland: The Arthur H. Clark Company.

VOORHIS, ERNEST. 1930. *Historic Forts and Trading Posts of the French Regime and the English Fur Trading Companies.* Unpublished. Ottawa: Department of the Interior.

WHITE, JAMES. 1926. *In the Privy Council: In the matter of the Boundary between the Dominion of Canada and the Colony of Newfoundland in the Labrador Peninsula... Forts and Trading Posts in Labrador Peninsula and Adjoining Territory.* Ottawa: King's Printer.

WILLIAMSON, WILLIAM D. 1832. *The History of the State of Maine: from its first discovery, A.D. 1602, to The Separation, A.D. 1820, Inclusive.* 2 vols. Hallowell: Glazier, Masters and Company.

WOOD, EDWIN ORIN. 1918. *Historic Mackinac: the historical, picturesque and legendary features of the Mackinac country.* New York: The Macmillan Company.

Personal Communication:

ANICK, NORMAN. Department of Indian Affairs and Northern Development, National Historic Sites Service. Ottawa.

81 - 82   TOPOGRAPHIC MAP COVERAGE

See maps, pages 81-82.

83 - 86   TERRITORIAL EVOLUTION OF CANADA

CANADA, Department of Mines and Technical Surveys, Geographical Branch. 1958. Political Evolution. Maps in *Atlas of Canada,* 1957. Ottawa: Queen's Printer.

HEAD, IVAN L. 1965. *Canadian Claims to Territorial Sovereignty in the Arctic Regions.* In *International Law.* Edited by J.G. Castel. Toronto: University of Toronto Press.

NICHOLSON, N.L. 1954. *The Boundaries of Canada, Its Provinces and Territories.* Geographical Branch Memoir no. 2. Ottawa: Department of Mines and Technical Surveys.

THORNDIKE, JOSEPH J., ed. 1966. *Atlas of United States History.* New York: American Heritage Publishing Company Inc.

TRUDEL, MARCEL. 1961. *Atlas historique du Canada français.* Québec: Les Presses de l'Université Laval.

87 - 88   NORTHERN SETTLEMENTS

ADAMS, J.Q. 1941. Settlements of the Northeastern Canadian Arctic. *Geographical Review* 31: 112-126.

INNIS, HAROLD A. 1956.(Revised edition). *The Fur Trade in Canada.* Toronto: University of Toronto Press.

JENNESS, D. *Eskimo Administration: II Canada.* Technical Paper no. 14. Montréal, New York, Washington: The Arctic Institute of North America.

MARSH, D.B. 1959. *A Century at Fort Simpson, 1858-1958.* Toronto: The Canadian Church Historical Society.

POTTER, J.G. 1965. *A Catalogue of Climatological Stations in the Yukon and Northwest Territories.* Mimeographed. Toronto: Department of Transport.

ROBINSON, J.L. 1944. Eskimo Population in the Canadian Eastern Arctic. *Canadian Geographical Journal* 29: 128-142.

ROBINSON, M.J. and J.L. 1946. Exploration and Settlement of the Mackenzie District, N.W.T. *Canadian Geographical Journal* 32: 246-255, 33: 42-49.

SMYTHE, T. 1968. *Thematic Study of the Fur Trade in the Canadian West, 1670-1870.* Unpublished. Ottawa: Historic Sites and Monuments Board of Canada.

STAGER, JOHN K. 1962. *Historical Geography of the Mackenzie River Valley, 1750-1850.* Ph. D. thesis. University of Edinburgh, Scotland.

USHER, PETER J. 1971. *Fur Trade Posts of the Northwest Territories, 1870-1970.* Ottawa: Department of Indian Affairs and Northern Development, Northern Science Research Group.

WOODALL, ROBERT G. 1964. *The Postal History of the Yukon Territory, Canada.* Dorset: Robert G. Woodall.

87 - 88 (cont'd.)

Information supplied by:

Anglican Church of Canada, Diocese of the Arctic, Toronto; Canada, Department of National Defence, Chief of the Defence Staff Branch; Canada, Department of the Solicitor General, Royal Canadian Mounted Police, Liaison Branch; Canada, Department of Transport, Meteorological Branch; Canada, Post Office Department, Information and Public Relations Branch; Deschâtelets Archives, Missionary Oblates of Mary Immaculate, Ottawa; Hudson's Bay Company, Office of the Canadian Committee, Hudson's Bay House, Winnipeg.

89 - 90   SOUTHERN SETTLEMENTS

ABRAMS, GARY WILLIAM DAVID. 1966. *Prince Albert: The First Century, 1866-1966.* Saskatoon: Modern Press.

ADAMS, C. 1929. *Thetford Mines.* Thetford Mines. Le Mégantic.

ALBERT, THOMAS. 1920. *Histoire du Madawaska.* Québec: Imprimerie franciscaine missionnaire.

Aperçu historique de la cité de Salaberry-de-Valleyfield. (n.d.) Mimeographed. Salaberry-de-Valleyfield. (n.p.)

ARCHER, JOHN H. 1947. *Historic Saskatoon.* (Mimeographed extract).

Aspects de la vie quotidienne dans nos cantons de 1815 à 1965. Édition spéciale à l'occasion des fêtes du 150e anniversaire. Drummondville: La Parole. 1965.

ATKINSON, R.N. 1967. *Penticton Pioneers in Story and Picture.* Penticton: The Okanagan Historical Society, Penticton Branch.

AUCLAIR, E.J. 1934. *Saint-Jérôme de Terrebonne.* St-Jérôme: J.-H.-A. Labelle.

BAIRD, FRANK. 1948. *The Story of Fredericton 1848-1948.* Commissioned by the Fredericton City Council. Fredericton: T.A. Wilson.

BALF, MARY. 1969. *Kamloops: A History of the District up to 1914.* Kamloops: Clow Printing Ltd.

BEAULIEU, ANDRÉ and MORLEY, WILLIAM F.E. 1971. *La Province de Québec.* Toronto: University of Toronto Press.

BEAUREGARD, LUDGER. 1968. *Toponymie de la région métropolitaine de Montréal.* Québec: Ministère des Terres et Forêts.

BERTRAND, J.P. 1959. *Highway of Destiny.* New York: Vantage Press.

BLADEN, M.L. 1935. Construction of Railways in Canada to the year 1885. Construction of Railways in Canada from 1885 to 1931. *Contributions to Canadian Economics,* vol. 5. University of Toronto Studies - History and Economics. Toronto: University of Toronto Press.

BRAULT, LUCIEN. 1948. *Histoire de la Pointe-Gatineau.* Montréal: École industrielle des sourds-muets.

————. 1950. *Hull, 1800-1950.* Ottawa: Les Éditions de l'Université d'Ottawa.

BROUSSEAU, Jean-Dominique. 1937. *Saint-Jean-de-Québec (origine et développements).* Saint-Jean: Les Éditions du Richelieu Ltée.

BURKHOLDER, M. 1938. *The Story of Hamilton.* Hamilton: David-Lisson Ltd.

CADEN, JOSÉ. 1961. *L'an 1 de Shawinigan.* Trois-Rivières: Éditions du Bien Public.

CALLBECK, L.C. 1964. *The Cradle of Confederation.* Fredericton: Brunswick Press.

CARON, IVANHOË. 1927. *La colonisation de la province de Québec: les Cantons de l'Est, 1791-1815.* Vol. 2. Québec: L'Action sociale.

CHOQUETTE, C.P. 1930. *Histoire de la ville de St-Hyacinthe.* St - Hyacinthe: Richer et fils.

CLARK, A.H. 1959. *Three Centuries and the Island.* Toronto: University of Toronto Press.

————. 1968. *Acadia: The Geography of Early Nova Scotia to 1760.* Madison: University of Wisconsin Press.

CLARK, R. 1966. *A glimpse of the Past, centennial history of Brantford and Brant County.* Brantford: Brant Historical Society.

CLUBB, SALLY P. 1966. *Saskatoon - The Serenity and the Surge.* Saskatoon: The City of Saskatoon.

COMMISSION DU CENTENAIRE DE JOLIETTE. 1964. *Joliette, 1864-1964.* Joliette.

Corner Brook, Newfoundland. Pamphlet. 1969. (n.p.)

COUILLARD-DESPRÉS, A. 1926. *Histoire de Sorel.* Montréal: Imprimerie des sourds-muets.

COUTTS, M.E. 1958. *Dawson Creek, Past and Present.* Edmonton: Hamly Press Ltd.

DAWE, W. (n.d.) *History of Red Deer, Alberta.* Red Deer: Kiwanis Club of Red Deer.

DEANE, J.G. and KAVANAGH, E. (n.d.) *State of the Madawaska and Aroostook Settlements in 1831.* New Brunswick Historical Society. (n.p.)

DEMERS, LOUIS-PHILIPPE. 1969. *Sherbrooke.* Sherbrooke: Gavin et Frère Ltée.

DESBIENS, L. 1933. *Au coeur de la Mauricie.* Trois-Rivières: Éditions du Bien Public.

Dictionary of Canadian Biography/Dictionnaire biographique du Canada. 1966-72. Toronto: University of Toronto Press. Québec: Les Presses de l'Université Laval.

DORIAN, CHARLES. (n.d.) *The First 75 years, a headline history of Sudbury.* Ilfracombe, England: A.H. Stockwell Ltd.

DORMAN, R. 1938. *A Statutory History of the Steam and Electric Railways of Canada 1836-1937.* Ottawa: Department of Transport.

DRAKE, EARL. 1955. *Regina, the Queen City.* Toronto: McClelland and Stewart.

Encyclopedia Canadiana. 1963. Ottawa: The Canadiana Company Ltd.

FERGUSSON, C. BRUCE. 1967. *Place Names and Places of Nova Scotia.* Halifax: Public Archives of Nova Scotia.

GANONG, W.F. 1899. A Monograph of Historic Sites in the Province of New Brunswick. *Transactions of the Royal Society of Canada/Mémoires de la Société royale du Canada.* Series 2, vol. 5, section 2: 213-357.

GRAY, ART. 1968. *Kelowna, Tales of Bygone Days*. Kelowna: Kelowna Printing Company Ltd.

GUAY, CHARLES. 1873. *Chronique de Rimouski*. Québec: Delisle Imprimeur.

GUILLET, EDWIN C. 1933. *Pioneer Settlements in Upper Canada*. Toronto: University of Toronto Press.

—————. 1948. *Cobourg, 1798-1948*. Oshawa: Goodfellow Printing.

—————. 1957. *The Valley of the Trent*. Toronto: The Champlain Society.

HARKNESS, J.G. 1946. *Stormont, Dundas and Glengarry: a History, 1784-1945*. Oshawa: Mundy - Goodfellow Printing.

HARRIS, RICHARD COLEBROOK. 1968. *The Seigneurial System in Early Canada: A Geographical Study*. Madison, Milwaukee, London: The University of Wisconsin Press.

History of Beaconsfield. Mimeographed. Beaconsfield, Quebec. 1967 (n.p.)

HOOD, M.M. 1968. *Oshawa, Crossing between the waters*. Oshawa: McLaughlin Public Library Board.

HUNTER, A.F. 1948. *A History of Simcoe County*. Historical Committee of Simcoe County. (n.p.)

Illustrated Atlas of the Dominion of Canada - Lambton Supplement. Toronto: H. Belden Company. 1880.

JACK, D.R. 1883. *Centennial Prize Essay on the History of the city and county of St. John*. Saint John: J. and A. McMillan.

JOHNSON, P.M. 1958. *Nanaimo, British Columbia*. Nanaimo: City of Nanaimo, British Columbia Centennial Committee.

JOHNSTON, W.S. and JOHNSTON, H.J.M. 1967. *History of Perth County to 1967*. Stratford: Municipal Corporation of County of Perth.

LAJEUNESSE, E.J. 1960. *The Windsor Border Region: Canada's Southernmost Frontier*. Toronto: The Champlain Society.

LARGE, R.G. 1960. *Prince Rupert, a Gateway to Alaska*. Vancouver: Mitchell Press.

LARRACEY, W.W. 1970. *The First Hundred*. Moncton: Moncton Publishing Company Ltd.

LAURISTON, V. 1924. *Chatham, Ontario, Official Programme of the Old Boys Reunion*. Old Boys Reunion Committee. (n.p.)

LAVALLÉE, J. 1969. *Granby: centre industriel*. Montréal: Holt Rinehart Winston.

LECLAIRE, A. 1906. *Historical, Legendary and Topographical Guide along the St. Lawrence*. Montréal: Sir Joshua Reynolds Art Publishing Company.

LIZOTTE, LOUIS-PHILIPPE. 1967. *La Vieille Rivière-du-Loup: ses vieilles gens, ses vieilles choses (1673-1916)*. Québec: Éditions Garneau.

LYONS, C.P. 1958. *Milestones on Vancouver Island*. Nanaimo: Evergreen Press Ltd.

MACGREGOR, J.G. 1967. *Edmonton: A History*. Edmonton: M.G. Hurtig.

MAILHOT, CHARLES-ÉDOUARD. 1968-69. *Les Bois-France*. Édition révisée et complétée par Alcide Fleury et Roger Luissier. 2 vols. L'Imprimerie d'Arthabaska Inc.

MANITOBA, Department of Industry and Commerce. 1958. *An Economic Survey of Brandon, 1958*. Midwest Research Institute. Winnipeg.

MARSH, E.L. 1931. *A History of the County of Grey*. Owen Sound: Fleming Publishing Ltd.

MCINTOSH, C.I., ed. 1955. *Skyline … The Panoramic Pattern of a City, North Battleford's Golden Jubilee Story*. North Battleford: McIntosh Publishing.

MCKENZIE, R. 1967. *Leeds and Grenville*. Toronto: McClelland and Stewart.

MIKA, N. and MIKA, H. 1967. *Trenton, past and present*. Belleville: Mika Silk Screening Ltd.

MORLEY, ALAN. 1961. *Vancouver, From Milltown to Metropolis*. Vancouver: Mitchell Press.

MORTON, A.S. 1939. *A History of the Canadian West to 1870-71*. Toronto: Thomas Nelson and Sons.

OKANAGAN HISTORICAL SOCIETY AND BOARD OF MUSEUM AND ARCHIVES. Vernon Branch. (n.d.) *An Illustrated History of Vernon and District*. (n.p.)

ONTARIO, Department of Planning and Development. 1955. *Moira Valley Conservation Report, 1955*. Toronto: Queen's Printer.

—————. 1956. *Credit Valley Conservation Report, 1956*. Toronto: Queen's Printer.

PARADIS, A. 1951. *Commercial and Industrial Story of Magog*. (n.p.)

PEMBROKE CENTENARY COMMITTEE. 1928. *Official Program and Pictorial Souvenir of Pembroke Centenary and Old Home Week*. Pembroke.

PETHICK, DAVID. 1968. *Victoria: The Fort*. Vancouver: Mitchell Press.

PHILLIPS, T.G. *Cornwall and its Environs, 1784-1850*. B.A. thesis. University of Toronto.

PRESTON, RICHARD A. and LAMONTAGNE, LEOPOLD. 1958. *Royal Fort Frontenac*. Toronto: The Champlain Society.

PRESTON, RICHARD A. 1959. *Kingston Before the War of 1812*. Toronto: The Champlain Society.

RADDALL, T.H. 1948. *Halifax: Warden of the North*. Toronto: McClelland and Stewart.

RAYMOND, W.O. 1910. *The River Saint John*. Saint John: John A. Bowes.

ROBINSON, PERCY J. 1933. *Toronto During the French Regime*. Toronto: Ryerson Press.

ROY, J.-E. 1897-1904. *Histoire de la seigneurie de Lauzon*. 5 vols. Lévis. (n.p.)

RUNNALS, F.E. 1946. *A History of Prince George*. Vancouver: City of Prince George.

SANTERRE, LOUIS-ANGE. 1964. *Sept-Îles, terre promise*. Sept-Îles: Édition Abitation "Vieux fort".

SCOTT, H.A. 1919. *Deuxième centenaire de Notre-Dame de Foy au Canada*. Québec: L'Action sociale Ltée.

SEVIGNY, J.P., ed. (n.d.) *10th anniversary of incorporation, City of Val-d'Or, 1937-1947*. (n.p.)

SHEA, PHILIP. 1965. *History of Eastview*. Mimeographed. National Capital Commission. Ottawa.

SMYTHE, T. 1968. *Thematic Study of the Fur Trade in the Canadian West, 1670-1870*. Unpublished. Ottawa: Historic Sites and Monuments Board of Canada.

STANISLAS, F. 1950. *Historique de Ville La Salle, le vieux Lachine*. Montréal: Laurent Morin, V.G.

STORY, NORAH. 1967. *The Oxford Companion to Canadian History and Literature*. Toronto, London, New York: Oxford University Press.

SULTE, B. 1870. *Histoire de la ville des Trois-Rivières et de ses environs*. Montréal: Eusèbe Sénécal.

—————. 1882-84. *Histoire des Canadiens-Français 1608-1880*. 8 vols. Montréal: Wilson et Compagnie.

SWIFT CURRENT JUBILEE ASSOCIATION. 1964. *Swift Current Golden Jubilee, 1914-1964*. Swift Current.

TESSIER, THÉODORE (Fabien, Frère). 1964. *Asbestos: son site, son industrie, ses activités*. Asbestos: Société Saint-Jean-Baptiste.

The History of the County of Welland, Ontario: its past and present. Welland: Welland Tribune Printing House. 1887.

TRAIL GOLDEN JUBILEE SOCIETY. 1951. *Trail, B.C. A Half Century, 1901-1951*. Trail.

TREMBLAY, V. 1967. *Alma au lac Saint-Jean*. Édition du Centenaire, La Société historique du Saguenay. No.18. Alma, Quebec: Antonio Girard Ltée.

TRUDEL, MARCEL. 1961. *Atlas historique du Canada français des origines à 1867*. Québec: Les Presses de l'Université Laval.

UTTLEY, W.V. 1937. *A History of Kitchener*. Kitchener: Chronicle Press.

Visitors Guide, 1971: Rat Portage (Kenora) and Lake of the Woods. Kenora: Kenora Miner and News Limited.

WARKENTIN, JOHN and RUGGLES, RICHARD. 1970. *Historical Atlas of Manitoba*. Winnipeg: The Historical and Scientific Society of Manitoba.

WEBSTER, J.C. 1938. *An Historical Guide to New Brunswick*. New Brunswick Government Bureau of Information and Tourist Travel. Fredericton.

WINTER, BRIAN. 1967. *A Town Called Whitby*. Whitby: Raymond Huff Productions.

WOOD, F. 1964. Guelph, its founding and its growth. *Canadian Geographical Journal* 68: 122-131.

91 - 93   DISTRIBUTION OF POPULATION, 1851, 1871, 1901, 1921, 1941

CANADA, Department of Mines and Technical Surveys, Geographical Branch. 1958. Distribution of Population 1851-1941. Maps in *Atlas of Canada*, 1957. Ottawa: Queen's Printer.

CANADA, DBS. *Census/Rencensement*. 1870-71, 1901, 1911, 1921, 1931, 1941. Ottawa.

—————. *Canada Year Book, 1956*. Ottawa.

—————. —————, *1967*. Ottawa.

URQUHART, M.C. and BUCKLEY, K.A., eds. 1965. *Historical Statistics of Canada*. Toronto: Macmillan of Canada.

94   URBAN AND RURAL POPULATION CHANGES, 1871-1961

CANADA, DBS. *Census/Recensement, 1951*. Vol. 1, Vol. 10. Ottawa.

—————. —————, *1961*. 1: 1, cat. 92-536. Ottawa.

URQUHART, M.C. and BUCKLEY, K.A., eds 1965. *Historical Statistics of Canada*. Toronto: Macmillan of Canada.

95 - 96   DISTRIBUTION OF POPULATION, 1961

CANADA, DBS. *Census/Recensement, 1961*. 1: 1, cat. 92-531, 92-534 to 92-536. Ottawa.

—————. —————. SP series, cat. 92-528. Ottawa.

—————. —————. Census Urbanized Areas - Part 2. Unpublished. Ottawa.

—————. —————. Population of Enumeration Areas. Unpublished. Ottawa

STONE, LEROY O. 1967. *Urban Development in Canada*. 1961 Census Monograph, cat. 99-542. Ottawa: Dominion Bureau of Statistics.

97 - 102   DISTRIBUTION OF POPULATION, 1961

CANADA, DBS. *Census/Recensement, 1961*. 1: 1, cat. 92-531 to 92-535. 1: 2, cat. 92-517. Ottawa.

—————. —————. SP series, cat. 92-528. Ottawa.

—————. —————. Population of Enumeration Areas. Unpublished. Ottawa.

—————. —————. Population of Unincorporated Places, less than 50 persons. Unpublished. Ottawa.

DEPARTMENT OF GEOGRAPHY, UNIVERSITY OF ALBERTA. 1965. *Alberta, Population Distribution, 1961*. Map. Edmonton: Department of Highways, Surveys Branch.

DEPARTMENT OF GEOGRAPHY, UNIVERSITY OF BRITISH COLUMBIA. (n.d.) *British Columbia, Population Distribution, 1961*. Map. (n.p.)

INSTITUT DE GÉOGRAPHIE, UNIVERSITÉ LAVAL. (n.d.) *Québec, Répartition de la population, 1961*. Map. Québec: Conseil d'orientation économique du Québec.

103 - 104   POPULATION CHANGES

CANADA, DBS. *Census/Recensement, 1931, 1941, 1951, 1961, 1966*. Ottawa.

105 - 108   DENSITY OF POPULATION, 1961

CANADA, DBS. *Census/Recensement, 1961*. Native Indian and Eskimo Population for the Northwest Territories. Unpublished. Ottawa.

105 - 108 (cont'd.)

CANADA, DBS. *Census/Recensement, 1961*. Population of Unincorporated Places, less than 50 persons. Unpublished, Ottawa.

————. ————. Population of Enumeration Areas, 1961. Unpublished. Ottawa.

————. ————. Official Groupings of Enumeration Areas. Unpublished. Ottawa.

CANADA, DBS. Census Division, Geography Section. Manuscript maps of population density, 1961. Ottawa.

109 - 110 RELIGIONS

CANADA, DBS. *Census/Recensement 1961*. 1: 2, cat. 92-546. Ottawa.

111 AGE, SEX AND MARITAL STATUS, 1961

CANADA, DBS. *Population Estimates (Age and Sex)/Estimations de la population (âge et sexe), 1952-1960*. Cat. 91-506. Ottawa.

112 IMMIGRATION AND VITAL STATISTICS

CANADA, Department of Manpower and Immigration. 1970. *Country of Birth of Post-War Immigrants, 1946-69*. Ottawa.

CANADA, DBS. *Canada Year Book*, 1943 to 1972. Ottawa.

————. *Vital Statistics/La statistique de l'état civil, 1965*. Cat. 84-201, 84-202. Ottawa.

113 - 114 EDUCATION

CANADA, DBS. *Census/Recensement, 1961*. 1: 2, cat. 92-550. 1: 3, cat. 92-557. Ottawa.

115 UNSCHOOLED POPULATION, 1961

CANADA, DBS. *Census/Recensement*, 1891, 1901, 1911, 1921, 1931, 1941, 1951. Ottawa.

————. ————, *1961*. 1: 2, cat. 92-550. 1: 3, cat. 92-557. Ottawa.

116 NUMERICAL CHANGES IN THE POPULATION SPEAKING THE OFFICIAL LANGUAGES, 1921-1961

CANADA, DBS. *Census/Recensement, 1921*, 1931, 1941, 1951. Ottawa.

————. ————. *1961*. 1: 2, cat. 92-549. Ottawa.

117 - 118 MOTHER TONGUES

CANADA, DBS. *Census/Recensement, 1961*. 1: 2, cat. 92-549. Ottawa.

119 - 120 INDIAN LANDS AND LANGUAGES

121 - 122 INDIAN AND ESKIMO POPULATION

CANADA, Department of Citizenship and Immigration. *Schedule of Indian Reserves and Settlements*. 1964. Part 1, revised to January 31. Unpublished. Ottawa.

CANADA, Department of Indian Affairs and Northern Development. *Indian Population by Provinces and Territories, 1924-1967*. Unpublished. Ottawa.

————. *Schedule of Indian Reserves and Settlements*. 1966. Part II, British Columbia, revised to April 30. Unpublished. Ottawa.

————. Indian Affairs Branch. *Indian Agencies, Reserves, and Bands - Alberta, Manitoba, Ontario, Quebec, Saskatchewan, 1964; New Brunswick, Nova Scotia, Prince Edward Island, 1965; British Columbia, 1967*. Unpublished. Ottawa.

————. ————. 1965. *Indian Bands with Linguistic Affiliations*. Map. Ottawa.

————. ————. 1966. *The Canadian Indian: A reference paper*. Ottawa.

————. ————. 1966. *Indians of Ontario: An historical review*. Ottawa.

————. ————. 1967. *Indians of British Columbia: An historical review*. Ottawa.

————. ————. 1967. *Indians of the Prairie Provinces: An historical review*. Ottawa.

————. ————. 1967. *Indians of Quebec and the Maritime Provinces: An historical review*. Ottawa.

————. ————. 1967. *Indians of Yukon and Northwest Territories: An historical review*. Ottawa.

————. ————. 1967. *Linguistic and Cultural Affiliations of Canadian Indian Bands*. Ottawa.

————. ————. 1968. *Les Indiens du Canada: Document de consultation*. Ottawa.

————. ————. 1970. *Linguistic and Cultural Affiliations of Canadian Indian Bands*. Ottawa.

————. Indian-Eskimo Development Branch, Land Title Section. *Indian Reserve and Land Registry, 1968*. Unpublished. Ottawa.

————. Statistical Information Centre, Departmental Statistics Division. *Residential Distribution of Indians by Provinces, 1959-1969*. Unpublished. Ottawa.

————. *Registered Indian Population by Age, Sex, Residence*, 1966, 1969, 1970. Unpublished. Ottawa.

CANADA, DBS. *Census/Recensement, 1961*. 1: 2, cat. 92-545. Ottawa.

————. ————. SP series, cat. 92-526. Ottawa.

————. ————. Native Indian and Eskimo Population by Sex ..., 1961. Unpublished. Ottawa.

————. ————. 1961. Official Groupings of Enumeration Areas. Unpublished. Ottawa.

121 - 122 (cont'd.)

CANADA, DBS. *Census/Recensement, 1961*. Population of Enumeration Areas. Unpublished. Ottawa.

123 - 124 STANDARD INDUSTRIAL CLASSIFICATION, 1961

CANADA, DBS. *Census/Recensement, 1961*. 3: 2, cat. 94-518. Ottawa.

————. *National Accounts Income and Expenditure, 1967*. Cat. 13-201. Ottawa.

————. *Standard Industrial Classification Manual, 1961*. Cat. 12-501. Ottawa.

125 - 126 NATIONAL ACCOUNTS

CANADA, DBS. *National Accounts Income and Expenditure, 1971*. (Preprint). Cat. 13-201. Ottawa.

UNITED NATIONS. 1972. *Yearbook of National Accounts Statistics 1970*. New York.

127 - 128 INTERNATIONAL TRADE

CANADA, DBS. *Trade of Canada/Commerce du Canada, 1969*. Cat. 65-002, 65-004, 65-005, 65-007, 65-201. Ottawa.

UNITED NATIONS. 1970. *Annual Statistics, 1968*. 21st ed. New York.

URQUHART, M.C. and BUCKLEY, K.A., eds. 1965. *Historical Statistics of Canada*. Toronto: Macmillan of Canada.

129 - 130 PERSONAL INCOME

CANADA, DBS. *Census/Recensement, 1961*. 3: 1, cat. 94-505, 94-509. Ottawa.

PODOLUK, J.R. 1968. *Incomes of Canadians*. 1961 Census Monograph, Dominion Bureau of Statistics, cat. 99-544. Ottawa.

131 - 132 LABOUR FORCE

CANADA, DBS. *Census/Recensement, 1961*. 3: 2, cat. 94-522. Ottawa.

133 LABOUR FORCE

CANADA, DBS. *Census/Recensement, 1961*. 3: 1, cat. 94-503. 3: 2, cat. 94-531. Ottawa.

————. ————. Labour Force by Enumeration Areas. Unpublished. Ottawa.

134 OCCUPATIONAL STRUCTURE OF THE LABOUR FORCE

CANADA, DBS. *Classification of Occupations - Ninth Census of Canada, 1951*. Ottawa.

————. *Census/Recensement, 1951*. Vol. 4. Ottawa.

————. ————, *1961*. 3: 1, cat. 94-501 to 94-517. Ottawa.

135 - 136 AGRICULTURE; DIVERSITY OF AGRICULTURE

CANADA, DBS. *Census/Recensement, 1961*. 5: 1, 2, 3, cat. 96-530 to 96-540. Ottawa.

137 - 138 TYPES OF FARMING

CANADA, Department of the Environment, Lands Directorate, Land Evaluation and Mapping Branch. Unpublished land use maps. Ottawa.

CANADA, Department of Mines and Technical Surveys, Geographical Branch. 1958. Agricultural Regions. Map in *Atlas of Canada*, 1957. Ottawa: Queen's Printer.

CANADA, DBS. *Census/Recensement, 1961*. 5: 1, 2, 3, cat. 96-530 to 96-540. Ottawa.

DEPARTMENT OF GEOGRAPHY, UNIVERSITY OF TORONTO. 1969. *Economic Atlas of Ontario/Atlas économique de l'Ontario*. Edited by W.G. Dean. Toronto: University of Toronto Press.

139 AGRICULTURE - SELECTED CHARACTERISTICS

CANADA, DBS. *Dairy Statistics, 1956-1967*. Cat. 23-201. Ottawa.

————. *Greenhouse Industry/L'industrie des cultures de serre, 1956-1967*. Cat. 22-202. Ottawa.

————. *Handbook of Agricultural Characteristics*. Cat. 21-507, 21-508, 21-512. Ottawa.

————. *Leaf Tobacco Acreage, Production and Value/Superficie cultivée, production et valeur du tabac en feuille, 1956-1967*. Cat. 22-205. Ottawa.

————. *Livestock and Animal Products Statistics/Statistique du bétail et des produits animaux, 1956-1967*. Cat. 23-203. Ottawa.

————. *Production of Poultry and Eggs/Production de volaille et oeufs, 1956-1967*. Cat. 23-202. Ottawa.

————. *Production and Value of Maple Products*. Cat. 22-204. Ottawa.

140 PRECIPITATION

CANADA, Department of Transport, Meteorological Branch. 1962. *Monthly Record, Meteorological Observations in Canada, April through September 1960*. Toronto.

141 TOTAL VALUE OF FARM SALES

CANADA, DBS. *Census/Recensement, 1961*. 5: 1, 2, 3, cat. 96-530 to 96-540. Ottawa.

142 POTENTIAL AGRICULTURAL AREAS - NORTHWEST CANADA

DAY, J.H. *Potential Agriculture Areas*. Manuscript maps. Ottawa: Department of Agriculture, Soil Research Institute.

142 (cont'd.)

HUTTON, F.V. 1945. *Report on Agricultural Investigations in the Mackenzie River Basin.* Monograph. Ottawa: Department of Agriculture.

NOWOSAD, F.S. 1959. *Agriculture in the North.* Paper presented at British Columbia Natural Resources Conference, 18-20 November, 1959, at Harrison Hot Springs, British Columbia.

143   **WHEAT**

144   **CASH GRAINS; OATS**

145   **BARLEY; RYE**

146   **CORN; MIXED GRAINS**

147   **PIGS; POULTRY**

148   **EGGS; DAIRY PRODUCTS**

149   **HAY AND FODDER**

150   **PASTURE; CATTLE**

151   **HORSES; SHEEP**

152   **TOBACCO AND OTHER FIELD CROPS; POTATOES**

153   **TOBACCO; SUGAR BEETS**

154   **OILSEEDS; SOYBEANS**

155   **FLAXSEED; FRUITS AND VEGETABLES**

156   **ORCHARDS; MISCELLANEOUS PRODUCTS**

157   **FOREST PRODUCTS; OTHER RECEIPTS**

158   **FARM CAPITAL**

CANADA, DBS. *Census/Recensement, 1961.* 5: 1, 2, 3, cat. 96-530 to 96-540. Ottawa.

159 - 160   FORESTRY AND LOGGING - SELECTED CHARACTERISTICS

CANADA, DBS. *Canada Year Book, 1961.* Ottawa.

—————. *Canadian Forestry Statistics, 1961.* Cat. 25-202. Ottawa.

—————. *Logging/Abattage, 1961.* Cat. 25-201. Ottawa.

—————. *Census/recensement, 1961.* 3: 1, cat. 94-501. Ottawa.

URQUHART, M.C. and BUCKLEY, K.A., eds. 1965. *Historical Statistics of Canada.* Toronto: Macmillan of Canada.

161 - 162   FOREST INVENTORY

CANADA, DBS. *Canada Year Book, 1962.* Ottawa.

—————. *Canadian Forestry Statistics, 1962.* Cat. 25-202. Ottawa.

LACHANCE, PAUL E. 1954. A Study of the Pulp and Paper Industry of the Province of Quebec in Relation to its Present and Future Wood Supplies. *Pulp and Paper Magazine of Canada.* Convention Issue.

Information on inventory supplied by:

Alberta, Department of Lands and Forests; British Columbia, Forest Service; Canada, Department of Forestry; Canada, Department of Industry, Trade and Commerce, Lumber, Plywood and Panel Products Division; Manitoba, Department of Mines and Natural Resources, Forest Service; New Brunswick, Department of Lands and Mines; Newfoundland, Department of Mines, Agriculture and Resources; Nova Scotia, Department of Lands and Forests; Ontario, Department of Lands and Forests, Timber Branch; Quebec, Ministère des Terres et Fôrets, Bureau de l'économie forestière; Saskatchewan, Department of Natural Resources, Forestry Branch.

163 - 164   PULP AND PAPER MILLS

Pulp and Paper Mills in the United States and Canada (n.d.) Map. San Francisco: Miller Freeman Publications, Inc.

Personal Communication:

NEALE, R.J. Department of Industry, Trade and Commerce, Wood Products Branch. Ottawa.

165 - 166   SAWMILLS, 1966

Personal Communication:

CHARLTON, C.A. Department of Industry, Trade and Commerce, Wood Products Branch. Ottawa.

167   FUR

CANADA, DBS. *Canada Year Book, 1921, 1939, 1956.* Ottawa.

—————. *Fur Production: Season 1967-68/Production de fourrures, Saison 1967-68.* Cat. 23-207. Ottawa.

—————. *Report on Fur Farms/Rapport sur les fermes à fourrure, 1967.* Cat. 23-208. Ottawa.

168   RANGES OF SELECTED MAMMALS

YOUNGMAN, P.M. National Museum of Natural Sciences, Zoology Division. Manuscript maps. Ottawa.

169   FISHERIES - SELECTED CHARACTERISTICS

CANADA, DBS. *Apparent Per Capita Domestic Disappearance of Food in Canada, 1961 - 1971.* Cat 32-226. Ottawa.

—————. *Canada Year Book, 1961-1971.* Ottawa.

—————. *Fish Products Industry/L'industrie du poisson, 1961-1971.* Cat. 32-216. Ottawa.

—————. *Fisheries Statistics of Canada Summary/La statistique des pêches du Canada: Sommaire, 1961-1971.* Cat 24-201. Ottawa.

169 (cont'd.)

HOEK, W. Fisheries Research Board. Manuscript map. Ste-Anne-de-Bellevue, Quebec.

URQUHART, M.C. and BUCKLEY, K.A., eds. 1965. *Historical Statistics of Canada.* Toronto: Macmillan of Canada.

Personal Communication:

MANSFIELD, A.W. Fisheries Research Board. Ste-Anne-de-Bellevue, Quebec.

MCLAREN, I.A. Dalhousie University, Department of Biology. Halifax, Nova Scotia.

170   PACIFIC FISHERIES

CANADA, DBS. *Fisheries Statistics : British Columbia/La statistique des pêches: Colombie-Britannique, 1959-1963.* Cat 24-208. Ottawa.

CANADA, Fisheries Research Board, Pacific Biological Station. Manuscript maps. Nanaimo, British Columbia.

171 - 172   ATLANTIC FISHERIES

CANADA, DBS. *Fisheries Statistics: New Brunswick/La statistique des pêches: Nouveau-Brunswick, 1959-1963.* Cat. 24-204. Ottawa.

—————. *Fisheries Statistics: Newfoundland/La statistique des pêches: Terre-Neuve, 1959-1963.* Cat. 24-202. Ottawa.

—————. *Fisheries Statistics: Nova Scotia/La statistique des pêches: Nouvelle-Écosse, 1959-1963.* Cat. 24-205. Ottawa.

—————. *Fisheries Statistics: Prince Edward Island/La statistique des pêches: Île-du-Prince-Édouard, 1959-1963.* Cat 24-203. Ottawa.

—————. *Fisheries Statistics: Quebec/La statistique des pêches: Québec, 1959-1963.* Cat. 24-206. Ottawa.

CANADA, Fisheries Research Board, Atlantic Biological Station. Manuscript maps. St. Andrews, New Brunswick.

173 - 174   INLAND FISHERIES

CANADA, Department of Fisheries, Economic Service. *Fish Processing Plants.* Unpublished. Ottawa.

CANADA, DBS. *Fisheries Statistics: Alberta and Northwest Territories/La statistique des pêches: Alberta et Territoires du Nord-Ouest, 1959-1963.* Cat. 24-212. Ottawa.

—————. *Fisheries Statistics: Manitoba/ La statistique des pêches: Manitoba, 1959-1963.* Cat. 24-210. Ottawa.

—————. *Fisheries Statistics: New Brunswick/La statistique des pêches: Nouveau-Brunswick, 1959-1963.* Cat. 24-204. Ottawa.

—————. *Fisheries Statistics: Ontario/ La statistique des pêches: Ontario, 1959-1963.* Cat. 24-209. Ottawa.

—————. *Fisheries Statistics:Quebec/La statistique des pêches:Québec,1959-1963.* Cat. 24-206. Ottawa.

—————. *Fisheries Statistics : Saskatchewan/ La statistique des pêches: Saskatchewan, 1959-1963.* Cat. 24-211. Ottawa.

Information on lakes and rivers licensed for commercial fishing supplied by:

Alberta, Department of Lands and Forests, Fish and Wildlife Division; Canada, Department of Fisheries, Regional Director of Fisheries, Halifax, Nova Scotia; Canada, Department of Fisheries, Regional Director of Fisheries, St. John's, Newfoundland; Canada, Department of Fisheries, Regional Director of Fisheries, Vancouver, British Columbia; Manitoba, Department of Mines and Natural Resources, Fisheries Branch; Ontario, Department of Lands and Forests, Fish and Wildlife Service; Quebec, Ministère de Tourisme, de la Chasse, et de la Pêche, Service de la Faune; Saskatchewan, Department of Natural Resources, Fisheries Branch.

175 - 176   RANGES OF PRINCIPAL COMMERCIAL FRESHWATER FISH

SCOTT, W.B. Royal Ontario Museum, Ichthyology and Herpetology Department, Manuscript maps. Toronto.

177 - 180   FOSSIL FUELS AND PIPELINES

BERKOWITZ, N. 1969. Coal Research and Development in Canada. *Bulletin of the Canadian Institute of Mining and Metallurgy* 62: 980-985.

BUCK, W.K. 1970. *Factors Influencing the Mineral Economy of Canada, Past, Present and Future.* Ottawa: Department of Energy, Mines and Resources, Mineral Resources Branch.

CANADA, Department of Energy, Mines and Resources, Geological Survey of Canada. 1970. *Geology and Economic Minerals of Canada.* Economic Geology Report no. 1. Ottawa.

—————. (n.d.) *Oil and Gas Pools of Western Canada as of March 31, 1970.* Maps no. 1316A, 1317A, 1318A. Ottawa.

CANADA, Department of Energy, Mines and Resources, Mineral Resources Branch. (n.d.) *Principal Gas Pipelines in Canada as of December 31, 1969.* Map. Ottawa.

—————. (n.d.) *Principal Oil and Products Pipelines in Canada as of December 31, 1969.* Map. Ottawa.

—————. *Coal Mines in Canada, 1971.* Operators list no. 4. Ottawa.

—————. *Natural Gas Processing Plants in Canada, January 1971.* Operators list no. 7. Ottawa.

—————. *Petroleum Refineries in Canada, January 1971.* Operators list no. 5. Ottawa.

—————. 1971. *The Canadian Mineral Industry in 1970.* Bulletin MR 114. Ottawa.

—————. 1972. *Canadian Minerals Yearbook 1970.* Ottawa.

—————. 1972. *Mineral Reviews.* (Preprints) *Canadian Minerals Yearbook 1971.* Ottawa.

—————. 1972. *The Canadian Mineral Industry in 1971.* Bulletin MR 122. Ottawa.

CANADA, DBS. *Canadian Mineral Statistics, 1886-1956.* Reference Paper no. 68, cat. 26-501. Ottawa.

177 - 180 (cont'd.)

CANADA, Statistics Canada. *General Review of the Mineral Industries/Revue générale sur les industries minérales, 1970.* Cat. 26-201. Ottawa.

—————. *Crude Petroleum and Natural Gas Production, December 1970/ Production de pétrole brut et de gaz naturel, décembre 1970.* Cat. 26-006. Ottawa.

—————. *Mineral Statistics: Principal Statistics/Industries minérales: statistiques principales, 1970.* Cat. 26-204. Ottawa.

—————. *Coal Mines/Mines de charbon, 1970.* Cat. 26-206. Ottawa.

—————. *Gas Pipe Line Transport, 1970.* Cat. 55-202. Ottawa.

—————. *Canada's Mineral Production: Preliminary Estimates/Production minérale du Canada: calcul préliminaire, 1971.* Cat. 26-202. Ottawa.

—————. *Energy Statistics, 1972.* Cat. 57-002. Ottawa.

—————. *Oil Pipe Line Transport/ Transport du pétrole par pipe-line, 1970.* Cat. 55-201. Ottawa.

CANADIAN PETROLEUM ASSOCIATION. 1971. *Statistical Year Book 1970.* Calgary.

FRASER, J.W. and LUGG, W.G. 1970. *Petroleum and Natural Gas Industry in Canada, 1963-68.* Bulletin MR 104. Ottawa: Department of Energy, Mines and Resources, Mineral Resources Branch.

LATOUR, B.A. 1960. *Coal Resources of Canada.* Topical Report no. 17, prepared for the Royal Commission on Coal. Ottawa: Geological Survey of Canada.

————— and CHRISTMAS, L.P. 1970. *Preliminary Estimate of Measured Coal Resources Including Reassessment of Indicated and Inferred Resources in Western Canada.* Paper no. 70-58. Ottawa: Geological Survey of Canada.

MCKAY, B.R. 1947. *Coal Resources of Canada.* Ottawa: Geological Survey of Canada.

MERLIN, H.B. 1969. Energy Consumption - Its Growth and Pattern. *Bulletin of the Canadian Institute of Mining and Metallurgy* 62: 599-608.

ONTARIO, Department of Energy and Resources Management. 1970. *Gas and Oil Fields, Pipelines, Compressor Stations and Refineries, Toronto - Windsor Area.* Map no. 69-1. Ottawa.

Proceedings of the Twenty-first Canadian Conference on Coal. 1969. Calgary.

Proceedings of the Twenty-second Canadian Conference on Coal. 1970. Vancouver.

SIMPSON, R. and CHRISTMAS, L.P. 1970. Coal. *Canadian Mining Journal* 90: 133-136.

URQUHART, M.C. and BUCKLEY, K.A., eds. 1965. *Historical Statistics of Canada.* Toronto: Macmillan of Canada.

Personal Comunication:

POOLE, W.H. Department of Energy, Mines and Resources, Geological Survey of Canada. Ottawa.

Sources common to MINERAL MAPS, pages **181-190**

CANADA, Department of Energy, Mines and Resources, Geological Survey of Canada. 1970. *Geology and Economic Minerals of Canada.* Economic Geology Report no. 1. Ottawa.

CANADA, Department of Energy, Mines and Resources, Mineral Resources Branch. *Metal and Industrial Mineral Mines and Processing Plants in Canada 1969 to 1970.* Operators list no. 2. Ottawa.

—————. 1972. *Canadian Minerals Yearbook 1970.* Ottawa.

—————. 1972. *Mineral Reviews.* (Preprints) *Canadian Minerals Yearbook 1971.* Ottawa.

CANADA, Statistics Canada. *Canada's Mineral Production: Preliminary Estimates/Production minérale du Canada: calcul préliminaire, 1970.* Cat. 26-202. Ottawa.

THE FINANCIAL POST. 1972. *1972 Survey of Mines.* 46th ann. ed. Toronto: MacLean-Hunter.

THE NORTHERN MINER. 1972. *Canadian Mines Handbook 1972-73.* Toronto: Northern Miner Press.

181-182   PRIMARY IRON AND STEEL

AMERICAN METAL MARKET COMPANY. 1971. *Metal Statistics 1971.* New York.

CANADA, Department of Energy, Mines and Resources, Mineral Resources Branch. *Primary Iron and Steel, January 1971.* Operators list no. 1 part 1. Ottawa.

————— and Geological Survey of Canada. 1971. *Principal Mineral Areas of Canada.* Map no. 900A., 21st ed. Ottawa.

CANADA, DBS. *Canadian Mineral Statistics, 1886-1956.* Reference Paper no. 68. Cat. 26-501. Ottawa.

—————. *Preliminary Report of Mineral Production, 1970.* Cat. 26-503. Ottawa.

—————. *Iron Mines/Mines de fer, 1970.* Cat. 26-210. Ottawa.

—————. *Iron Ore, December 1970/Minerai de fer, décembre 1970.* Cat. 26-005. Ottawa.

—————. *Primary Iron and Steel, December 1970/Fer et acier primaire, décembre 1970.* Cat. 41-001. Ottawa.

CANADA, Statistics Canada. *Iron and Steel Mills/Sidérurgie, 1972.* Cat. 41-203. Ottawa.

GROSS, G.A. 1967. *Appraisal of Iron Ore Resources in Canada.* United Nations Iron Ore Resources Survey. New York.

—————. *Appraisal of Iron Ore Resources in Canada, 1972.* Unpublished. Ottawa: Geological Survey of Canada.

JANES, T.H. and LAFLEUR, P. 1970. *The Canadian Iron Ore Industry, Its Position and Outlook.* Bulletin MR 112. Ottawa: Department of Energy, Mines and Resources, Mineral Resources Branch.

LAFLEUR, PAUL. 1971. *Canadian Iron Ore Industry in 1970.* Bulletin MR 120. Ottawa: Department of Energy, Mines and Resources, Mineral Resources Branch.

181-182 (cont'd.)

LAFLEUR, PAUL. 1972. Iron Ore. in *The Canadian Mineral Industry in 1971.* Bulletin MR 122. Ottawa: Department of Energy, Mines and Resources, Mineral Resources Branch.

SCHNEIDER, V.B. 1971. *Canadian Primary Iron and Steel Statistics to 1969.* Bulletin MR 113. Ottawa: Department of Energy, Mines and Resources, Mineral Resources Branch.

URQUHART, M.C. and BUCKLEY, K.A., eds. 1965. *Historical Statistics of Canada.* Toronto: Macmillan of Canada.

WITTUR, G.E. 1968. *Primary Iron and Steel in Canada.* Bulletin MR 92. Ottawa: Department of Energy, Mines and Resources, Mineral Resources Branch.

183 - 186   NON-FERROUS METALS

AMERICAN METAL MARKET COMPANY. 1971. *Metal Statistics 1971.* New York.

BRITISH COLUMBIA, Department of Mines and Petroleum Resources. 1971. *Geology, Exploration and Mining in British Columbia, 1970.* Victoria.

CANADA, Department of Energy, Mines and Resources, Geological Survey of Canada. 1970. *Nickel in Canada.* Map no. 1258A. Ottawa.

CANADA, Department of Energy, Mines and Resources, Mineral Resources Branch. *Nonferrous and Precious Metals, January 1971.* Operators list no. 1 part 2. Ottawa.

—————. 1972. *The Canadian Mineral Industry in 1971.* (Preliminary) Bulletin MR 122. Ottawa.

————— and Geological Survey of Canada. 1971. *Principal Mineral Areas of Canada.* Map no. 900A., 21st ed. Ottawa.

CANADA, DBS. *Aluminum rolling, casting and extruding/Laminage, moulage et extrusion de l'aluminium, 1970.* Cat. 41-204. Ottawa.

—————. *Copper and Nickel Production, December 1970/Production de cuivre et nickel, décembre 1970.* Cat. 26-003. Ottawa.

—————. *Gold Production, December 1970/Production d'or, décembre 1970.* Cat. 26-004. Ottawa.

—————. *Nickel-Copper Mines/Mines de nickel-cuivre, 1970.* Cat. 26-211. Ottawa.

—————. *Mineral Industries: Principal Statistics/Industries minérales: statistiques principales, 1970.* Cat. 26-204. Ottawa.

—————. *Production of Canada's Leading Minerals, December 1970/Production de principaux minéraux du Canada, décembre 1970.* Cat. 26-007. Ottawa.

—————. *Silver, Lead and Zinc Production, December 1970/Production d'argent, de plomb et de zinc, décembre 1970.* Cat. 26-008. Ottawa.

—————. *Smelting and Refining/Fonte et affinage, 1970.* Cat. 41-214. Ottawa.

FERGUSON, STEWART A. 1971. *Columbium (Niobium) Deposits of Ontario.* Mineral Resources Circular no. 14. Toronto: Ontario Department of Mines and Northern Affairs.

ONTARIO, Department of Mines. *Ontario Mineral Map, 1968.* Map no. 2148. Toronto.

ONTARIO, Department of Mines and Northern Affairs. 1971. *Review 1970.* Toronto.

187 - 190   INDUSTRIAL MINERALS

CANADA, Department of Energy, Mines and Resources, Mineral Resources Branch. 1972. *The Canadian Mineral Industry in 1971.* (Preliminary) Bulletin MR 122. Ottawa.

CANADA, DBS. *Canadian Mineral Statistics, 1886-1956.* Reference Paper no. 68, cat. 26-501. Ottawa.

—————. *Asbestos, December 1970/Amiante, décembre 1970.* Cat. 26-001. Ottawa.

—————. *Asbestos Mines/Mines d'amiante, 1970.* Cat. 26-205. Ottawa.

—————. *Cement/Ciment, 1970.* Cat. 44-001. Ottawa.

—————. *Feldspar and Quartz Mines/Mines de feldspar et de quartz, 1970.* Cat. 26-208. Ottawa.

—————. *Gypsum Mines/Mines de gypse, 1970.* Cat. 26-221. Ottawa.

—————. *Mineral Industries: Principal Statistics/Industries minérales: statistiques principales, 1970.* Cat. 26-204. Ottawa.

—————. *Salt, December 1970/Sel, décembre 1970.* Cat. 26-009. Ottawa.

—————. *Salt Mines/Mines de sel, 1970.* Cat. 26-214. Ottawa.

—————. *Sand and Gravel Pits/Sablières et gravières, 1970.* Cat. 26-215. Ottawa.

—————. *Stone Quarries/Carrières, 1970.* Cat. 26-217. Ottawa.

—————. *Soapstone and Talc Mines/Mines de stéalite et de talc, 1970.* Cat. 26-218. Ottawa.

URQUHART, M.C. and BUCKLEY, K.A., eds. 1965. *Historical Statistics of Canada.* Toronto: Macmillan of Canada.

191 - 192   CONSTRUCTION, 1945-1965

CANADA, DBS. *Canada Year Book,* 1947 to 1967. Ottawa.

Information supplied by:

Aluminum Company of Canada; Bow River Pipe Lines Ltd.; British Columbia Department of Highways; British Columbia Hydro and Power Authority; British Newfoundland Corporation Ltd.; Calgary Power Ltd.; Canada, Canadian Corporation for the 1967 World Exhibition; Canada, Department of Agriculture, Prairie Farm Rehabilitation Administration; Canada, Department of Energy, Mines and Resources, Mineral Resources Branch; Canada, Department of National Defence, Finance Division; Canada, Department of Transport, Airports and Construction Services, Budget and Financial Services Branch, Railway Branch, Highway Branch and St. Lawrence Seaway Authority; Canada, Dominion Bureau of Statistics, Financial Statistics Branch and Manufacturing and Primary Industries Branch; Canada, National Energy Board; Canadian Industrial Gas and Oil

191 - 192 (cont'd.)

Company Ltd.; Canadian - Montana Pipe Line Company; Canadian National Telecommunications; Canadian Pacific Telecommunications Department; Canadian - Western Natural Gas Company Ltd.; Churchill River Power Company Ltd.; Cold Lake Transmission Ltd.; Cominco Ltd.; Gas Trunk Line of British Columbia Ltd.; Gaz Métropolitain Inc.; Gibson Petroleum Company Ltd.; Greater Winnipeg Gas Company; Gulf Oil Canada Ltd.; Home Oil Company Ltd.; Husky Oil Ltd.; Hydro-Québec; Inland Natural Gas Company Ltd.; Inter-City Gas Ltd.; Manicouagan Power Company; Manitoba, Department of Agriculture and Conservation, Water Control and Conservation Branch; Manitoba Hydro; Mitsue Pipeline Ltd.; Montreal Metropolitan Corporation; Montreal Transportation Commission; Municipality of Metropolitan Toronto; North Canadian Oils Ltd.; Northland Utilities Ltd.; Northwest Utilities Ltd.; Nova Scotia, Department of Highways; Nova Scotia Light and Power Company Ltd.; Ontario Northland Communication; Pacific Great Eastern Railway; Pacific Petroleum Ltd.; Saskatchewan Power Corporation; Sun-Canadian Pipe Line Company Ltd.; The Hydro-Electric Power Commission of Ontario; The New Brunswick Electric Power Commission; Union Gas Company of Canada Ltd.; Winnipeg Pipe Line Company Ltd.

193 - 194 LABOUR FORCE IN MANUFACTURING

CANADA, DBS. *Census/Recensement, 1961.* 3: 2, cat. 94-518 to 94-522. Ottawa.

————. ————. *Population of Enumeration Areas.* Unpublished. Ottawa.

————. ————. *Official Groupings of Enumeration Areas.* Unpublished. Ottawa.

195 - 196 MANUFACTURING CENTRES

CANADA, DBS. *Census/Recensement, 1961.* 3: 2, cat. 94-519 to 94-521. Ottawa.

————. ————. *Official Groupings of Enumeration Areas.* Unpublished. Ottawa.

197 - 202 MANUFACTURING, 1961

CAMU, P., WEEKS, E.P. and SAMETZ, Z.W. 1964. *Economic Geography of Canada.* Toronto: Macmillan of Canada.

CANADA, DBS. *General Review of the Manufacturing Industries of Canada, 1961.* Cat. 31-201. Ottawa.

Sources common to both RAILWAYS AND CANALS MAPS, Pages **203-206**

BLADEN, M.L. 1935. Construction of Railways in Canada to the Year 1885. Construction of Railways in Canada from 1885 to 1931. *Contributions to Canadian Economics*, vol. 5. University of Toronto Studies - History and Economics. Toronto: University of Toronto Press.

CANADA, Canadian Transport Commission, Railway Transport Committee. Various dates. *Orders, Decisions.* Ottawa.

CANADA, Department of the Interior. 1906. Railways. Maps in *Atlas of Canada.* Toronto: Lithographing Company Ltd.

————. 1915. Railways. Maps in *Atlas of Canada.* Ottawa. (n.p.)

CANADA, Department of Mines and Technical Surveys, Geographical Branch. 1958. Railways. Map in *Atlas of Canada, 1957.* Ottawa: Queen's Printer.

CANADIAN FREIGHT ASSOCIATION. (Series) *Official List of Freight Stations and Ports of Call in Canada - Armstrong, Thunder Bay and West Thereof.* Tariff 209. Winnipeg.

————. (Series) *Official List of Freight Stations and Ports of Call in Canada - Thunder Bay and East Thereof.* Tariff 28. Montréal.

DORMAN, R. 1938. *A Statutory History of the Steam and Electric Railways of Canada 1836-1937.* Ottawa: Department of Transport.

INTERNATIONAL RAILWAY PUBLISHING COMPANY. 1971. *Canadian Guide.* Montréal.

NATIONAL RAILWAY PUBLICATION COMPANY. 1972. *The Official Guide of the Railways.* New York.

RAND, MCNALLY and COMPANY. 1955. *Handy Railroad Atlas of the United States.* Chicago.

Maps supplied by:

Canadian Freight Association; Canadian National Railways; CP Rail; Soo Line Railroad.

Personal Comunication:

CHURCHER, C.J. Ministry of Transport, Canadian Surface Transportation Administration, Railway Branch. Ottawa.

LAVALLÉE, OMER. Canadian Pacific Ltd. Montréal.

203 - 204 RAILWAYS AND CANALS 1971 - EASTERN CANADA

CUMMING, ROSS, ed. 1970. *Illustrated Atlas of the County of Bruce.* 1880. Offset edition. Port Elgin, Ontario.

————. 1970. *Illustrated Atlas of the County of Simcoe, Ontario.* 1881. Offset edition. Port Elgin, Ontario.

————. 1971. *Guide Book and Atlas of Muskoka and Parry Sound Districts.* 1879. Offset edition. Port Elgin, Ontario.

————. 1971. *Illustrated Atlas of the County of Grey.* 1880. Offset edition. Port Elgin, Ontario.

————. 1971. *Illustrated Historical Atlas of the County of Carleton, Ontario.* 1879. Offset edition. Port Elgin, Ontario.

————. 1971. *Illustrated Historical Atlas of the County of Peel, Ontario.* 1877. Offset edition. Port Elgin, Ontario.

————. 1972. *Illustrated Atlas of Lanark County and Illustrated Atlas of Renfrew County.* 1880. Offset edition. Port Elgin, Ontario.

Illustrated Historical Atlas of the County of Elgin, Ontario. 1877. Toronto: H.R. Page.

Illustrated Historical Atlas of the County of Halton, Ontario. 1877. Toronto: Walker and Miles.

203 - 204 (cont'd.)

Illustrated Historical Atlas of the County of Northumberland and Durham, Ontario. 1878. Toronto: H. Belden and Company.

Illustrated Historical Atlas of the County of Wentworth, Ontario. 1875. Toronto: Page and Smith.

Illustrated Historical Atlas of the County of York, Ontario. 1878. Toronto: Miles and Company.

LAVALLÉE, OMER. 1972. *Narrow Gauge Railways of Canada.* Montréal: Railfare Enterprises Ltd.

PHELPS, EDWARD, ed. 1972. *Illustrated Historical Atlas of the County of Middlesex, Ontario.* 1878. Offset edition. Sarnia, Ontario.

Topographical and Historical Atlas of the County of Oxford, Ontario. 1876. Toronto: Walker and Miles.

Topographical and Historical Atlas of the County of Wellington. 1877. Toronto: Walker and Miles.

Maps supplied by:

Commandant Properties, Montebello; Quebec Cartier Mining Company; Quebec North Shore and Labrador Railway.

205 - 206 RAILWAYS AND CANALS 1971 - WESTERN CANADA

ALBERTA RESOURCES RAILWAY. *Canadian Rail.* January 1967. 184: 16-17.

JONES, CLINTON JR. 1971. Over High Trestles, into Ocean Mists. *Trains* 31: 25-28.

Maps supplied by:

British Columbia Hydro and Power Authority; Pacific Great Eastern Railway.

207 RAILWAYS

BLADEN, M.L. 1935. Construction of Railways in Canada to the year 1885. Construction of Railways in Canada from 1885 to 1931. *Contributions to Canadian Economics*, vol. 5. University of Toronto Studies - History and Economics. Toronto: University of Toronto Press.

CUMMING, ROSS., ed. 1970. *Illustrated Atlas of the County of Bruce.* 1880. Offset edition. Port Elgin, Ontario.

————. 1970. *Illustrated Atlas of the County of Simcoe, Ontario.* 1881. Offset edition. Port Elgin, Ontario.

————. 1971. *Guide Book and Atlas of Muskoka and Parry Sound Districts.* 1879. Offset edition. Port Elgin, Ontario.

————. 1971. *Illustrated Atlas of the County of Grey.* 1880. Offset edition. Port Elgin, Ontario.

————. 1971. *Illustrated Historical Atlas of the County of Carleton, Ontario.* 1879. Offset edition. Port Elgin, Ontario.

————. 1971. *Illustrated Historical Atlas of the County of Peel, Ontario.* 1877. Offset edition. Port Elgin, Ontario.

————. 1972. *Illustrated Atlas of Lanark County and Illustrated Atlas of Renfrew County.* 1880. Offset edition. Port Elgin, Ontario.

DORMAN, R.A. 1938. *A Statutory History of the Steam and Electric Railways of Canada 1836-1937.* Ottawa: Department of Transport.

Illustrated Historical Atlas of the County of Elgin, Ontario. 1877. Toronto: H.R. Page.

Illustrated Historical Atlas of the County of Halton, Ontario. 1877. Toronto: Walker and Miles.

Illustrated Historical Atlas of the County of Northumberland and Durham, Ontario. 1878. Toronto: H. Belden and Company.

Illustrated Historical Atlas of the County of Wentworth, Ontario. 1875. Toronto: Page and Smith.

Illustrated Historical Atlas of the County of York, Ontario. 1878. Toronto: Miles and Company.

PHELPS, EDWARD, ed. 1972. *Illustrated Historical Atlas of the County of Middlesex, Ontario.* 1878. Offset edition. Sarnia, Ontario.

Topographical and Historical Atlas of the County of Oxford, Ontario. 1876. Toronto: Walker and Miles.

Topographical and Historical Atlas of the County of Wellington. 1877. Toronto: Walker and Miles.

208 RAILWAYS - SELECTED CHARACTERISTICS

CANADA. DBS. *Railway freight traffic/Traffic marchandise ferroviaire.* Selected years. Cat. 52-205. Ottawa.

————. *Railway transport/Transport ferroviaire.* Selected years. Cat. 52-209, 52-210. Ottawa.

209 - 210 PORTS AND HARBOURS, 1968

CANADA, Department of Energy, Mines and Resources, Marine Sciences Branch, Canadian Hydrographic Service. 1967. *Great Lakes Pilot.* Vol. 1, 6th ed. Ottawa.

————. 1968. *Great Lakes Pilot.* Vol. 2, 3rd ed. Ottawa.

————. 1968. *Great Lakes Pilot.* 6th ed. supplement no. 1. Ottawa.

————. 1968. *Great Slave Lake and Mackenzie River Pilot.* 2nd ed. Ottawa.

————. 1968. *Gulf of St. Lawrence Pilot.* 6th ed. Ottawa.

————. 1968. *Pilot of Arctic Canada.* Vol. 2, 2nd ed. Ottawa.

————. 1968. *Pilot of Arctic Canada.* Vol. 3, 2nd ed. Ottawa.

CANADA, Department of Mines and Technical Surveys, Canadian Hydrographic Service. 1959. *Pilot of Arctic Canada.* Vol. 1, 1st ed. Ottawa.

————. 1961. *British Columbia Pilot (Canadian Edition).* Vol. 2, 4th ed. Ottawa.

————. 1963. *Pilot of Arctic Canada.* 1st ed., supplement no. 3. Ottawa.

————. 1965. *British Columbia Pilot.* Vol. 1, 7th ed. Ottawa.

————. 1965. *Labrador and Hudson Bay Pilot.* 2nd ed. Ottawa.

————. 1965. *Saint John River Pilot.* 2nd ed. Ottawa.

209 - 210 (cont'd.)

CANADA, Department of Mines and Technical Surveys, Canadian Hydrographic Service. 1966. *Newfoundland Pilot*. 3rd ed. Ottawa.

——————. 1966. *Nova Scotia (South East Coast) and Bay of Fundy Pilot*. 4th ed. Ottawa.

——————. 1966. *St. Lawrence River Pilot*. 1st ed. Ottawa.

——————. 1967. *British Columbia Pilot*. 4th ed., supplement no. 5. Ottawa.

——————. 1968. *British Columbia Pilot*. 7th ed., supplement no. 2. Ottawa.

——————. 1968. *Labrador and Hudson Bay Pilot*. 3rd ed., supplement no. 1. Ottawa.

——————. 1968. *Newfoundland Pilot*. 3rd ed., supplement no. 2. Ottawa.

——————. 1968. *Nova Scotia (South East Coast) and Bay of Fundy Pilot*. 4th ed., supplement no. 2. Ottawa.

——————. 1968. *Saint John River Pilot*. 2nd ed., supplement no. 1. Ottawa.

——————. 1968. *St. Lawrence River Pilot*. 1st ed., supplement no. 2. Ottawa.

CANADA, Department of Transport. 1966. *Public Harbours in Canada Proclaimed and Administered by the Department of Transport under Part X of the Canada Shipping Act*. Mimeographed. Ottawa.

NATIONAL BUSINESS PUBLICATIONS LTD. 1964. *Canadian Ports and Shipping Directory*. 20th ed., revised. Gardenvale, Quebec.

UNITED STATES, Department of the Navy, Oceanographic Office. 1963. *World Port Index*. Publication 150 (formerly 950). Washington.

211   SEABORNE EXPORTS AND IMPORTS

CANADA, DBS. *Canada Year Book, 1967*. Ottawa.

CANADA, DBS. *Trade of Canada/Commerce du Canada, 1964*. Cat. 65-202, 65-203. Ottawa.

212 - 214   SHIPPING

CANADA, DBS. *Shipping Report/Transport maritime, 1964*. Cat. 54-203, 54-204. Ottawa.

215 - 216   EXPORTS BY MODE OF TRANSPORT, 1966
EXPORTS AND IMPORTS THROUGH CUSTOMS PORTS, 1966

CANADA, DBS. *Exports by Mode of Transport, 1966*. Cat. 65-206. Ottawa.

——————. *Trade of Canada/Commerce du Canada, 1966*. Cat. 65-201. Ottawa.

217 - 219   DENSITY OF ROADS

See map, page 220.

220   MAJOR HIGHWAYS, 1967

CANADA, Canadian Government Travel Bureau. 1967. *Canada and Northern United States*. Map. Ottawa.

221 - 222   GRAIN ELEVATORS IN OPERATION, 1972-73

CANADA, Department of Agriculture, Canadian Grain Commission. 1972. *Grain Elevators in Canada for Crop Year 1972-73*, (as at August 1972). Ottawa.

Personal Communication :

MCDONOUGH, J.M. Department of Agriculture, Canadian Livestock Feed Board. Ottawa.

223 - 224   SELECTED AIR SERVICES, DECEMBER 1967

CANADA, Canadian Transport Commission, Air Transport Committee. 1967. *Directory of Canadian Commercial Air Services*. Ottawa.

CANADA, Department of Energy, Mines and Resources, Surveys and Mapping Branch, under the authority of the Minister of Transport. 1967. *Canadian Aerodrome Directory*. Ottawa.

225 - 226   AIRPORTS, AERODROMES AND TIME ZONES

ALBERTA AVIATION COUNCIL. 1966. *Alberta Air Facilities*. Map. (n.p.)

BRITISH COLUMBIA AVIATION COUNCIL. 1967. *Air Facilities of British Columbia*. Map. (n.p.)

CANADA, Department of Energy, Mines and Resources, Observatory Branch. 1967. *Time Zones of Canada*. Map. Ottawa.

CANADA, Department of Energy, Mines and Resources, Surveys and Mapping Branch, under the authority of the Minister of Transport. 1967. *Canadian Aerodrome Directory*. Ottawa.

227 - 230   COMMUNICATIONS

CANADA, DBS. *Canada Year Book, 1968*. Ottawa.

Maps supplied by:

Alberta Government Telephones; Bell Canada; British Columbia Telephone Company; Canada, Department of Communications, International Telecommunications Branch; Canada, Department of Transport, Telecommunications and Electronics Branch; Canadian National and Canadian Pacific Telecommunications, Joint Office; Manitoba Telephone System; Maritime Telegraph and Telephone Company Ltd.; Northern Telephone Ltd.; Okanagan Telephone Company; Ontario Northland Communications; Pacific Great Eastern Railway; Quebec North Shore and Labrador Railway; Québec Téléphone; Saskatchewan Government Telephones; The Avalon Telephone Company Ltd.; The New Brunswick Telephone Ltd.

231 - 232   RADIO; TELEVISION

CANADA, Canadian Radio - Television Commission. *Broadcasting Stations in Canada, by Provinces*. Maps. Ottawa.

CANADA, Department of Communications, Telecommunications Regulation Branch. Manuscript maps. Ottawa.

231 - 232 (cont'd.)

CANADIAN BROADCASTING CORPORATION. *Broadcasting stations (studios) by provinces, 1967*. Ottawa.

——————. *Low power relay transmitters, 1967*. Unpublished list. Ottawa.

233 - 236   ELECTRICITY

ALBERTA POWER COMMISSION, Office of the Director of Surveys. 1966. *Transmission Lines, Power Plants, Service Areas*. Maps. Edmonton.

CANADA, Department of Energy, Mines and Resources, Inland Waters Branch. 1969. *Electric Power in Canada, 1968*. Ottawa.

——————. 1969. Map supplement to *Electric Power in Canada, 1968*. Ottawa.

CANADA. DBS. *Electric and Gas Meter Registrations, 1968*. Cat. 57-201. Ottawa.

——————. *Electric Power Statistics, 1968*. Cat. 57-202. Ottawa.

——————. *Electric Power Survey of Capability and Load, 1968*. Cat. 57-204. Ottawa.

——————. *Inventory of Prime Mover and Electric Generating Equipment as at December 31, 1961*. Cat. 57-202. Ottawa.

——————. Energy Statistics Section. *Electric Power Generating Stations - capacity and production, 1964*; capacity, 1968. Unpublished. Ottawa.

CANADA, National Energy Board. *Major Canadian Electric Utilities with Interprovincial and International Connections*. Manuscript map, no. 1095-E. Ottawa.

——————. 1969. *Principal High Voltage Transmission Lines and Generating Plants in Canada, as of December 31, 1968*. Map. Ottawa.

237 - 238   RETAIL TRADE; WHOLESALE TRADE

CANADA, DBS. *Census/Recensement, 1961*. 3: 2, cat. 94-518. 6: 1, cat. 97-502, 97-512. Ottawa.

239 - 240   FINANCE, DEFENCE AND PUBLIC ADMINISTRATION;
SERVICE INDUSTRIES

CANADA, DBS. *Census/Recensement, 1961*. 3: 2, cat. 94-518. Ottawa.

241 - 250   ECONOMIC REGIONS

CAMU, P., WEEKS, E.P. and SAMETZ, Z.W. 1964. *Economic Geography of Canada*. Toronto: Macmillan of Canada.

251 - 254   CENSUS DIVISIONS AND SUBDIVISIONS, 1961

CANADA, DBS. *Census/Recensement, 1961*. 1: 1, cat. 92-537, 92-538. Ottawa.

Date Due

BJJJ

Orbiting far above the earth, a satellite produced these images of Canada . . .

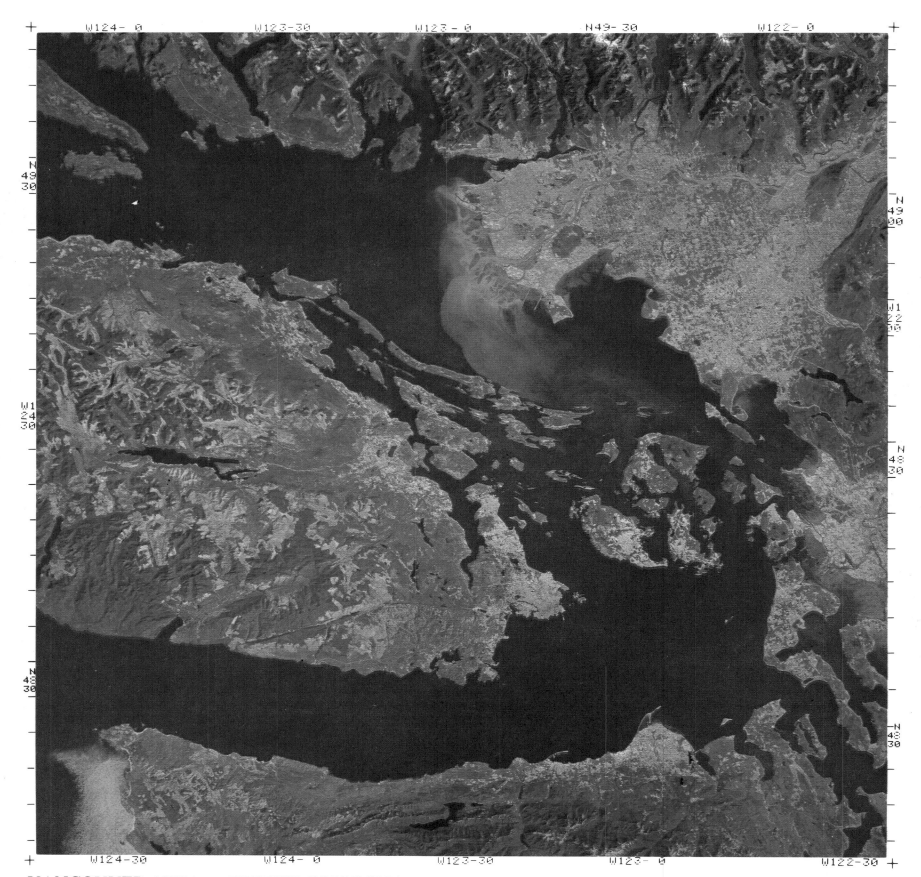

VANCOUVER AREA — BRITISH COLUMBIA
E−1385−18365
August 12, 1973

Part of the snow-capped Coast Mountains of British Columbia occupy the upper part of this image.

To the right of centre is the Fraser River, its delta, and the urbanized area of Greater Vancouver merging with the agricultural grid pattern inland. At the edge of the delta, turbid water of the Fraser River mixes with clearer water in the Strait of Georgia. Causeways leading to the Tsawwassen Ferry terminal and the new port of Roberts Bank can be seen jutting out into the Strait.

On Vancouver Island, to the left of centre, settlement is concentrated on the east and south-east coasts but the interior has also been drastically altered by man. Recently logged areas cover many of the mountain slopes and appear in marked contrast with the dark red forest.